Teaching Reading to Every Child

Teaching Reading to Every Child

Fourth Edition

Diane Lapp
San Diego State University

James Flood
San Diego State University

Cynthia Brock
University of Nevada, Reno

Douglas Fisher
San Diego State University

LEA LAWRENCE ERLBAUM ASSOCIATES, PUBLISHERS
2007 Mahwah, New Jersey   London

KH

Senior Acquisitions Editor: Naomi Silverman
Assistant Editor: Erica Kica
Cover Design: Tomai Maridou
Full-Service Compositor: MidAtlantic Books & Journals

This book was typeset in 10 pt. Cheltenham Roman, Bold and Italic. The heads were typeset in Cheltenham Roman, Bold and Italic.

Lawrence Erlbaum Associates, Inc., Publishers
10 Industrial Avenue
Mahwah, New Jersey 07430
www.erlbaum.com

CIP information for this volume can be obtained from the Library of Congress.

ISBN   0-8058-4006-0 (paper)

Books published by Lawrence Erlbaum Associates are printed on acid-free paper, and their bindings are chosen for strength and durability.

Printed in the United States of America

10 9 8 7 6 5 4 3

11/3/06

Brief Table of Contents

Table of Contents

Chapter 12   **Technology and Media in the Literacy Classroom**   345

Chapter 13   **Teaching Reading to Students Who Are Learning English**   367

Preface

The gift of teaching a child to read is the most precious gift a teacher can give. Reading is the key to unlocking vast worlds of information and pleasure. Every child, regardless of what he or she brings to school, needs quality instruction in understanding all of the nuances and complexities of reading. Children need to be taught to appreciate reading for its power and its beauty as fully as you understand this phenomenon. In this book, we emphasize the importance of teaching EVERY child to become as competent as you are in reading. As you read this book, we want you to think about all of the experiences that you have had with reading throughout your lifetime; your experiences will serve you well as you learn to teach reading. As you see your students progressing in reading, you will be delighted at their vocabulary growth, their acquisition of new information, and their thirst for more and more knowledge. As you see them starting on the road to becoming life-long readers, you can be proud that you were instrumental in helping them unlock the beautiful world of books.

PURPOSE OF THE BOOK

The purpose of this book is to introduce you to the most current theories and methods for teaching reading to children in elementary schools. The methods included in this book are based on scientific findings that have been tested in many classrooms. As you begin to read this book, we encourage you to activate all of your previous experiences with reading and teaching. We have included a feature throughout the text entitled "Your Turn" where we invite you to think about your views on the thoughts we are presenting to you. We ask that you talk to your colleagues and teachers about "your best ways" of learning this new information. As you involve yourself in reflecting on the material and talking with others, you'll be joining teachers all over the globe who discuss "best methods" every day with one another. As you discuss your ideas with one another and as you write about your impressions, you'll find that you're expanding and refining your knowledge in the most positive ways.

ORGANIZATION OF THE BOOK

The book consists of 15 chapters, one for each week of the semester. In addition to state-of-the-art information on all aspects of teaching reading, the book contains many "teacher stories." We tell these stories as models of the thoughtfulness of teachers and as models of very successful teaching. Each teacher's story is really a conversation between you and her or him. His or her thoughts and questions are for you just as your thoughts and questions are for him or her and all of your professional colleagues. We hope that you'll realize the incredible support that you can gain from your fellow teachers as you read this book. The book also contains goals, questions, chapter summaries, the most recent bibliographic references, lesson plans, assessments, lists of children's literature books, and much more.

The book is divided into two main parts: "The Wonderful World of Literacy: Getting to Know Your Students, Classrooms, and Your Instructional Style" and "Developing Literacy Performance and Preferences." Part I is further divided into three chapters that introduce you to the effective teaching of reading. In chapter 1, we introduce you to two teachers who tell you what they think teaching is all about; they share their triumphs and agonies. As you meet them, we will constantly ask you to think about your future students. In this chapter, we also present ideas that you can use to get to know your students as individuals, as learners, and as literacy learners.

Chapter 2 is Ms. Cunningham's story. We invite you on a virtual tour of her classroom and her mind. In this chapter, Ms. Cunningham reveals her secrets. The untrained eye would miss the magnificence of her organizational structure. Her classroom runs so smoothly that you would hardly know that there were any rules. She explains to you that she spent her life preparing for this classroom; she tells you that there are indeed rules, routines, and guidelines that make the room flow in harmony. The smiles on her children's faces tell even the most casual observer that they are happy here. We can add that they are also learning and learning. Ms. Cunningham takes you on a tour of the ways in which she designed her room so that all of her children will learn to their fullest capacity. She explains how she assesses her children, forms her groups, and matches each child with the "perfect-fitting" book. You'll be dazzled by her story.

Chapter 3 deals with the complex issue of assessment. In this chapter you'll learn how teachers work with children who come to them with a variety of skills. You all know that the first days of many kindergarten classes bring with them the reality that some of the children don't yet know the letters of the alphabet and the reality that some are already reading chapter books. All teachers need to know their children's strengths and needs if they are to teach them in a way that they deserve. This chapter explores the role of assessment in the classroom as well the ways in which effective assessment can be conducted.

In Part II of the book, "Developing Literacy Performance and Preferences," we have included 12 chapters on "best practices" to ensure that every child will become a life-long reader.

Chapter 4 introduces the very important issue of oral language development. As you know some of your children will listen well, others will speak well, and still others will be just beginning to practice their skills in English and in other languages. In this chapter we introduce you to the ways in which children acquire and develop their language skills, and we share their ideas with you for planning an effective oral language program in your classroom.

Chapter 5 welcomes you to the world of "Word Identification Strategies." In this chapter we discuss the ways in which children learn to read words, and we recommend a series of instructional strategies for helping children with their word identification skills. The strategies that we recommend are tied to the phases of word level development because we believe in a developmental approach to learning how to decode.

Chapter 6, "Vocabulary Development," carefully explains the relationships between vocabulary development and reading comprehension skills. We explain ways for choosing the vocabulary words that you will teach to help children learn new words on a regular basis. Deep, explicit, robust vocabulary instruction will help every child to progress in word knowledge.

We believe that chapter 7, "Comprehension Instruction," is the "heart" of the matter. When children don't understand what they are reading, they are not really reading. In this chapter we take a tour of a fifth grade classroom to see how a remarkable teacher designs his program for maximum comprehension growth for each student. The strategies that we recommend are divided into three parts: before reading, during reading, and after reading. In chapter 8 we extend our discussion of reading practices to the content areas. We use examples from social studies, science, mathematics, art, and music to demonstrate how reading strategies and content area learning strategies can be integrated into one seamless lesson. As discussed earlier, we believe comprehension is what matters most in any reading methods course. For this reason, Chapter 9 explores the psychological, linguistic, and sociocultural factors that play such an important role in meaning-making.

Chapter 10 will introduce you to the world of writing. In this chapter, we point out the differences in writing instruction for primary students and intermediate grade students, and we include ideas for developing a writing workshop model that you may use in your classroom. In chapter 11 you'll journey into the wondrous world of children's literature where you'll realize the importance of selecting "perfectly fitting" literature for each and every child. As we begin to talk about ways to teach literature to children we stress the point that choice is a critical feature of every effective children's program. In our "How Should Literature Be Taught?" section, we present models of three effective literature strategies: read alouds, shared reading, and independent reading.

In chapter 12, "Technology and Media in Reading," we discuss the critical role of technology in the classroom. As you know children in today's world are greatly affected by technology in its many forms, and they are quite comfortable using it. In this chapter, we suggest effective ways of integrating technology into all of our lessons. In chapter Thirteen, "Teaching Reading to Students Who Are Learning English," we discuss ways to work with students who are just learning English as well as ways to work with children who are fully bilingual. In this chapter we present the important foundations for helping all children develop their language skills. Chapter 14 deals with students with special needs. In addition to providing classroom guidelines that address federal laws, we also include suggestions for effective instruction that will meet each child's individual needs. We offer ideas for students with cognitive disabilities, physical disabilities, and emotional or behavioral disabilities.

In chapter 15, we tie all of the ideas from the book together by presenting a chapter on the history of reading. You'll notice how reading instruction has evolved over the years to a point where we are providing effective instruction for every child. In this chapter we invite you to define what good reading instruction means to you. We know that you will design wonderful programs for all of your students that will showcase your individual philosophies of teaching reading.

Let the journey begin.

NEW CONTENT AND FEATURES IN THE FOURTH EDITION

We've added a new chapter on technology with state-of-the-art applications and a more comprehensive chapter on the stages of reading development from the pre-alphabetic to the full alphabetic stage. Responding to the national renewed interest in vocabulary instruction, we have included a chapter on the most up-to-date information on how vocabulary is learned and on how it is best taught. We've provided broader coverage of writing instruction and a new section on reader's/writer's workshop. Our chapter on teaching reading to students who are learning English is more comprehensive than in the third edition; it includes extensive information on assessment and evaluation.

ACKNOWLEDGMENTS

We are thankful for all of the people who have provided us with feedback, guidance, and comments on previous editions of this text. Although too numerous to list, their assistance has made this edition the best yet. We owe a special acknowledgment to all of our students who have taught us so much throughout the years.

We also thank Dr. Linda Lungren for her expert assistance with so many aspects of this book and Dr. Helen Foster James for her assistance in obtaining permissions for the beautiful book covers we were able to incorporate into this book. We also gratefully acknowledge the guidance and assistance of Naomi Silverman, Senior Editor at Lawrence Erlbaum Associates.

We would also like to thank the following reviewers who provided feedback on this edition: David A. Monti, Central Connecticut State University, Kelly Moore, San Diego, CA, Unified School District, and Julie L. Pennington, University of Nevada, Reno.

Teaching Reading
to Every Child

The Wonderful World of Literacy: Getting to Know Your Students, Classrooms, and Your Instructional Style

1

Getting to Know Your Students as Literacy Learners

---CHAPTER GOALS---

To help the reader

- explore ways to get to know students as individuals.
- explore ways to get to know students as learners.
- explore ways to get to know students as literacy learners.

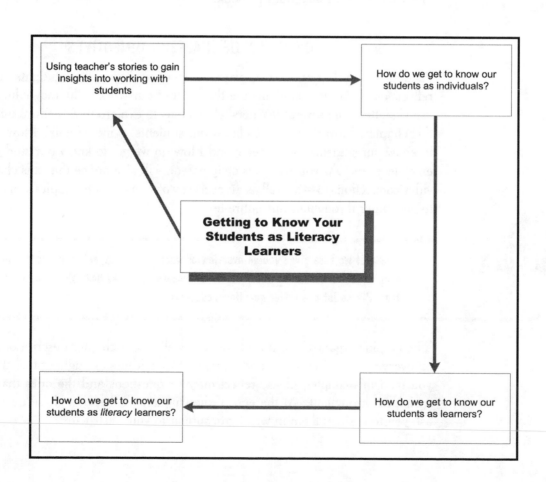

"… What could be clearer; what could be more simple? How could we have lost sight so easily of the solution to our school problems? What our educators need is a camaraderie. A commitment to public education, an independence from bureaucracy, an involvement of parents and a belief in students. But … to think that's all that's needed would be a serious miscalculation. What else is needed is something the teachers themselves are reluctant to talk about openly. And it is our respect for them. It is what's missing in America, and it is what's been too long withheld from a profession as important to our national well-being as doctors or captains of industry or TV commentators. From sunup to sundown, the school teacher works harder than you do—no matter what you do. No calling in our society is more demanding than teaching; no calling in our society is more central to the vitality of a democracy than teaching."

Roger Mudd on Learning in America, PBS

CONGRATULATIONS to you! As Roger Mudd notes, you have chosen to be a member of society's most important profession. As a teacher your knowledge base must be continually growing if you are going to make a positive difference in the lives of your students.

This text is one of the many tools that you can use in your ongoing journey as you gain insights that will help you teach students to explore and develop their multiple literacies. We're glad to be traveling on your learning journey with you. One of our personal goals is to make this text informative and engaging. Consequently, we'll be asking you to write, think, and talk with others about the ideas and issues that we present throughout this book.

OVERVIEW OF CHAPTER 1 OBJECTIVES

As depicted in the graphic organizer, the focus of chapter 1 is students. This focus reflects our belief that students are the heart of our work as literacy educators. We use vignettes from several teachers' classrooms to explore three central questions in this chapter: How do we get to know our students as individuals? How do we get to know our students as learners? and How do we get to know our students as literacy learners? As you read this chapter, you will also notice that this chapter provides connections to—as well as an overview of—many of the topics you can expect to encounter throughout this entire text.

Now that we have given you an overview of what you can expect to encounter in this chapter, we're wondering what questions/concerns you may have about the chapter content. Please jot down your questions/concerns.

The graphic organizer for this chapter, as well as our chapter description, provides an overview of the questions and issues that we address throughout this chapter. As you read this chapter, please reflect on your questions and the ones that we have sprinkled throughout. At the end of the chapter, we'll review these questions and ask you to address them in writing to submit to your instructor.

TEACHERS' STORIES: GAINING INSIGHTS ABOUT STUDENTS

When we ask classroom teachers about the most important advice they would give to a new teacher, they always say: Get to know your students so that you can meet their literacy learning needs. It so important that new teachers know 1) how their students learn, 2) how their students should be assessed, and 3) how their students will bring different backgrounds to their classrooms—such as English language proficiency, musical talents, and athletic accomplishments as well as some special needs.

There is a large repertoire of instructional strategies that teachers can draw upon as they strive to meet student's literacy learning needs. This wide variety of topics and issues will be addressed throughout this text. Our conversation in this chapter, however, focuses on ways to get to know students as individuals and learners. We begin our conversation with the stories of two of our teacher friends, Ashley and Larry. Both stories offer insights about getting to know students and about working with them as individuals.

Ashley: Wondering About Grouping for Literacy Instruction

Ashley, a first grade teacher, described her biggest dilemma: "I never felt like I had my reading groups right. How could I when my students were so varied in performance? Shortly after the beginning of the year, some of my students were still learning the alphabet, and others were reading at the third grade level. I remember thinking that everyone's performance would become more similar as the year progressed, but I was wrong. Throughout the year, everyone gained knowledge so I had to keep changing my groups. I had so many questions about grouping my students effectively for literacy instruction." Everyone with whom Ashley was speaking, regardless of grade level or years of teaching experience, agreed that the issue of determining which students comprise a reading group is a never-ending question that needs to be continually addressed as we strive to assess and teach all students.

Ashley's dilemma is common. Some might interpret her concern as simply the fact that she doesn't understand grouping, but grouping children is really a complex situation for all teachers. One of Ashley's colleagues, a fourth grade teacher, explained that he struggled with similar issues even though he was a veteran teacher. He explained that after completing initial assessments of his students, he placed five students, Marcus, Karina, Alan, DeAngelo, and Lajuana, in one group. Karena's family decided to enroll her in an after-school program. Additionally, they started spending considerable time reading with her in the evenings at home. After many months of this intensive work outside the classroom as well as her in-class work, Karena showed significant growth and progress. Karena's teacher felt that she would need to become a member of a new group. From this experience, Ashley learned that the structure of her reading groups must remain flexible. The specific children in particular groups should change to meet the evolving needs of the children in a classroom.

Another colleague noted that at the beginning of the year in her second grade classroom, she had become very successful at introducing stories and modeling the use of reading strategies through Shared Reading with the whole class. However, by November, she noticed that some students didn't seem challenged enough during Shared Reading time, and others seemed bored by the repetitious activities. She knew that she needed to group her students in new ways to make sure that they were motivated and receiving appropriate reading instruction each day.

Each of these stories illustrates how difficult it is to establish effective reading groups that serve all students. These stories show us that learning to read and write occurs differently for different individuals. Students are unique; they grow and change in different ways at different rates. Consequently, grouping for literacy instruction is a complex undertaking that should vary across time and contexts. Decisions about grouping for instruction should always be based on the assessment of student's strengths and instructional needs.

Your own students will also have a great deal of variance in their literacy needs, even though they may be quite young. For example, in her research with young students, Patricia Cunningham (2000) found that prior to kindergarten students from middle-class homes may spend up to a thousand hours or more listening to their parents read bedtime stories to them. Clearly, students with this extensive exposure to print have background knowledge about early literacy skills such as concepts of print and the nature and function of written language and story structure that students without exposure to written texts do not.

Fortunately, as teachers, we are capable of complex decision making on an ongoing basis throughout the school year. Your role as an effective teacher will be to learn about your students as individuals as well as literacy learners, and you will need to find appropriate methods, materials, and grouping approaches to develop each student's literacy learning. Making time to learn about your students and then thinking about and planning how to meet their literacy learning needs is a must. Effective teachers allow many hours for instructional planning each week.

Just as students have individual traits so do their teachers. The search for one best method for teaching reading has a long and unsuccessful history (Duffy,

DID YOU NOTICE . . .
Did you notice that all of the teachers with whom Ashley was speaking grouped their children for literacy instruction? Reading groups must be flexible, and children should be grouped for literacy instruction across all of the grade levels not just in the early elementary grades.

1999). There are many ways to teach reading. Consider for a moment what you would do if you felt seriously ill. You'd go to a doctor, right? Then you'd probably try to explain to the doctor what seemed wrong. Now, assume that your doctor said, regardless of what might be wrong with his patients, he always engages in the same set of procedures to try to restore their health. We're guessing that you'd probably go to a different doctor. You'd undoubtedly want a doctor who diagnosed your specific ailments and worked to correct the specific problem. Although we realize that teaching students to read and write is different from the work of doctors, good teachers, like good doctors, don't employ a one-size-fits-all approach in their work. Just as good doctors carefully assess the specific needs of their patients, good teachers get to know their students and carefully assess their specific literacy strengths and needs. Also, good teachers use instructional methods, materials, and strategies that facilitate the learning of each individual in their classrooms.

Although the ideas we have just presented are important, we realize that you need more. We invite you to read on. The important question that we raised—How can assessment and instruction be ongoing and designed to meet the needs of individual students?—is addressed briefly in the following vignette about Larry and again in more depth in chapter 2.

Larry: Working with Individuals in a Whole-Class Setting

Many teachers find it difficult to focus on students as individuals when they first begin teaching. New teachers are often so concerned about their own behaviors, schedules, and activities, that they don't pause to carefully examine their students' attributes and abilities. Larry's story shows how a teacher can accomplish this important goal. He is a fifth grade teacher who is known for promoting exceptional growth in his students.

Larry is always highly involved with the subject matter of the curriculum, but he also knows each and every one of his students in a variety of ways. For example, he makes it a point to get to know his student's interests, concerns, hopes, and fears. He gets to know their families and the roles that his students play in their families. In addition to getting to know his students as individuals, Larry gets to know them as readers and writers. Here are examples of some of the many different ways that Larry begins to accomplish his goals at the very beginning of the school year.

Before the year begins, Larry gets a list of the names and addresses of his students. He has an introductory form letter (see Table 1–1) on his computer that he personally addresses to each of his students. As you can see, the letter welcomes the students to fifth grade and alerts them to one of his first class assignments—an autobiography. In the letter Larry explains what an autobiography is and suggests that students speak with their families about events to include in their autobiographies. Additionally, he suggests that students bring family pictures and other artifacts to school to include in their autobiographies. Larry begins the school year with this assignment because he is interested in hearing the voices of his students as they describe how their literacies have been constructed. As he gains insights about the formation of each student's literacy identity, he makes decisions about the best instructional practices to support each student's personal and shared literacy growth.

This initial letter, which is sent to each student's home, also includes two brief questionnaires—one for the students to complete and one for their family members

TABLE 1–1
Letter to New Students

DATE_____

Dear (Student's Name),

Welcome to grade 5. I am really looking forward to being your teacher. For me to be able to be the best 5th grade teacher you will ever have, I need to get to know you real well. I need your help to do so.

I'm excited to know a little bit about you and your life. You can share this information through pictures of you with friends and family, through stories about your experiences, through interviews of family members and friends, and by telling about your hobbies, interests, favorite books, movies, videos, games, and music.

Please start to collect these artifacts (objects that help to tell who you are and who you want to become) and also to jot down a few notes about yourself that tells: Who you are?, Where and when you were born?, What a day in your life is like?, Why it will be fun to spend a year with you?, and also other things that you'd like to share.

I'm also interested in knowing what you're excited about learning this year. So, thanks for also thinking about this. I've started to plan a few terrific field trips for all of us. I'll start putting our classroom together the week before school begins so if you're in the neighborhood please stop by to say hello.

Once we meet on the first day of school we'll each start putting our information together into an autobiography which is the story of someone's life as told by them. I'll also be working on my autobiography so that you can get to know me too.

I'm really looking forward to meeting you and your family and to sharing a year of our lives together. Have a wonderful remainder of your vacation and happy collecting.

Best regards,

Mr. Cunningham
Your 5th Grade Teacher

DID YOU NOTICE . . .
Did you notice that Larry is realistic about the many different kinds of parents with whom he will work. Not all parents behave as teachers believe that they should. Rather than assuming an attitude of blaming parents for not acting as he believes they should, Larry decides to focus upon that which he has control over providing the highest quality literacy instruction possible for the children in his classroom.

to complete. The questionnaires ask about the student's interests and strengths. They also ask the students and their parent/guardian(s) to provide insights about who they perceive the students to be as readers and writers as well as information about the student's attitudes toward reading and writing, The questionnaires also ask about current reading and writing practices and past reading and writing experiences at home and school.

Larry never receives all of the completed surveys from the parents or students. He believes this lack of response also gives him some initial information about how involved the parents will be in their student's education. Larry believes that the primary responsibility for teaching the fifth grade curriculum is his so he does not rely too heavily on parent involvement. He realizes that although many parents will be very involved, some have limited time, knowledge, and interest in day-to-day school activities. This does not suggest to him that these parents love their students any less but just that parents, like students, are very different.

Before meeting his class, Larry examines and takes brief notes on the cumulative record files of each of his students. The cumulative folders in Larry's school district contain selected work samples, such as portfolio writing samples as well as standardized test scores across each student's school history. The folders also provide information about his student's medical histories, any special education services or English as a Second Language (ESL) services they may have received in the past. The contents of each student's cumulative record folder serve as one of the many different tools that Larry uses to begin to get a picture of each student's strengths and needs.

During the first week of class, Larry reads autobiographies to his students such as Carmen Lomas Garza's book Family Pictures. He uses his own autobiography as a model to teach his students how to write one. As his students write and revise drafts of their autobiographies, Larry gets an initial picture of who his students are as writers and as individuals.

Additionally, Larry begins to assess each student's reading by administering several informal whole group comprehension assessment measures such as having children complete written retellings after Larry reads a story aloud to the class. (We will tell you more about written retellings and other assessment measures in chapter 3.) Larry also spends time during recess talking informally with each student. By compiling his notes from these many sources, Larry becomes acquainted with his students as individuals and as literacy learners. He uses this information to design literacy activities for individuals or small groups of students who have similar strengths or needs. By spending considerable time thoughtfully observing, assessing, and interacting with his students, Larry learns that no matter how similar they may be in outward characteristics, they are very different from one another in many subtle ways (Clay, 1998). A key to successful literacy education lies in finding out how to address differences while helping students reach goals that are established according to their grade levels.

Larry's story provides you with some initial ideas for getting to know your students. In the next few sections of this chapter, we present additional ideas that Larry, and educators like him, use to get to know their students in a variety of ways. We think that you'll find these ideas useful as you think about getting to know your own students.

HOW DO WE GET TO KNOW STUDENTS AS INDIVIDUALS?

Individuals who are good at making friends and getting along with others know that it is important to listen to and respect other people. This type of respectful interaction is also important in a school setting. Teachers who make a habit of really getting to know their students—not just reading through the cumulative record folders—have an easier time gaining cooperation and reaching academic goals with their students.

Thoughtful Conversations and Careful Observations

Dialogue ... is about a shared inquiry, a way of thinking and reflecting together. It is not something you do to another person. It is something you do *with* people. Indeed, a large part of learning this has to do with learning to shift attitudes about relationships with others, so that we gradually give up the effort to make them understand us, and come to a greater understanding of ourselves and each other. (Isaacs, 1999, p. 9, emphasis in original)

Polite inquiries about any good books that you've read lately can prompt discussions about books as well as newly born siblings, favorite songs, games, pets, television shows, trips taken over the weekend, visits to the doctor scheduled for that day, and many other pieces of information that can be filed away in your memory or in notes for future reference. Informal conversations with your students can also help you see the many positive attributes of each student. You might learn about students' daily activities such as the fifth grader who cooks dinner for his family or the second grader who made a present for her grandmother. Larry, the teacher we mentioned earlier, spent time engaging in informal conversations with each of the students in his class-room, and, as a result, he came to know and care about them as individuals. He used this information not as judgments about their lives but rather as personal infor-mation that would help him to plan better individualized literacy instruction. Fostering an atmosphere of mutual respect and concern helps students take risks in their learning, and it positively impacts student's behavior in the classroom. We will talk more about this issue in chapter 15.

Larry also realized that one of the best places to gain insights into a student's strengths is on the playground. The school yard context allows a youngster to interact with you, avoiding awkward feelings that might arise from similar conversations held in the classroom. You can gain valuable incidental information about students from such encounters. You can also learn about your students by making home visits to meet their families. Attending community or neighborhood functions can also give you deeper insights into your students and their backgrounds and experiences. Getting to know your students and their families is a central part of responsive and responsible teaching. However, we offer some cautions about making judgments of others as we are getting to know them. Families are all different. You will not find one exactly like yours. It's important to remember that your purpose for trying to learn about the fam-ilies of your students is so that you can plan appropriate instruction.

Getting to Know Others: Some Cautions for Interpreting Other People's Behaviors

We will begin this section with a brief interaction between two people. Read the sce-nario and then write your interpretation of the situation. Plan to compare your inter-pretation with the interpretations of several of your peers.

Scenario: A young student went into a very small grocery store and carefully picked out several types of candies. After making her selections, she shyly placed her candies on the counter in front of the clerk. The clerk, a young man in his early twenties, asked her if she was ready for him to ring up her purchases. She raised her eyebrows but remained silent. He asked a second time. Again, she raised her eyebrows but remained silent. Feeling somewhat confused about the student's lack of response, the clerk rang up the purchases anyway. After the student paid for the candies, the clerk placed them in a small bag and handed them to the student. The student quietly turned around and left the store.

Please jot down your interpretation of the preceding scenario. What was going on? How would you interpret the situation? Why?

Now, compare your interpretation with that of several others in your class. How did they interpret the scenario? Was your interpretation similar to theirs? Explain.

Next, we provide you with a bit more information about the context of the sce-nario. See if the additional contextual information alters your initial interpretation.

The scenario took place in a remote Eskimo village in Alaska. The student was an Inupiat Eskimo. The young man in the scenario, Nick Jans, a recent college graduate from Maine, had arrived in the student's village several days prior to the described incident because he had taken a job as a shopkeeper in the tiny village store. Does this additional contextual information alter your initial interpretations in any way? Explain.

The following is Nick Jans' description of the same scenario (1993, pp. 24-25):

A patter of footsteps announced my first customer—a skinny little girl, maybe four years old, with long black hair and a runny nose. She regarded the strange *nalu-aqmiu* before her with alarm. When I smiled, she steadied herself and solemnly laid a grubby handful of change on the counter, still eyeing me warily. In my best store-keeper's voice, I asked her what she needed today.

Silence.

"Candy?" I prompted.

She didn't answer, but her eyes widened at the array behind the counter—cases of Milky Ways, Twizzlers, Drax Snax, LifeSavers, Garbage Can-dy—at least twenty varieties.

"Which one?"

More wide-eyed silence.

"This one?"

The student seemed to be on the verge of glaucoma.

"What about this one?"

Finally in exasperation I laid a Drax Snax and some Twizzlers on the count-er and sorted out her change. With an expression of complete ecstasy the pretty little girl opened her mouth, exposing a row of blackened stumps. I'd just met my first candy junkie.

It took me a couple of weeks to figure out that she'd been talking to me all along. The Inupiat are subtle, quiet people, and much of their communication hinges on nonverbal cues. Raising the eyebrows or widening the eyes means yes; a wrinkled nose is a negative. The poor girl had been shouting at me, 'Yes! Yes! YES!' All these years later, I still recall that first simple failure to understand; it reminds me of all my failures since then and of the distance that remains.

So, what's the point of this scenario? Why would we introduce such a scenario at this particular point in the chapter? We wish to make two points. First, getting to know someone—really getting to know someone—is a complex undertaking. Moreover, our interpretations and observations of others and their actions and interactions are heavily value laden and based on our own background experiences and beliefs. Although a context such as an Eskimo village in remote Alaska is far removed from contexts that many of us may have experienced, as teachers, we must be critically aware that the students we serve in our classrooms come from social and cultural backgrounds that may vary significantly (Au, 1993).

As teachers, we must thoughtfully and carefully critique our own perspec-tives—the lenses through which we talk with and observe our students. Otherwise, as was the case with Nick Jans, our interpretations of our conversations and obser-vations may be misguided or simply wrong. As teachers, we must be acutely aware that our beliefs, values, and norms for engaging in interactions are just that—ours (Gee, 1996). The students in our classrooms may have cultural or social back-grounds that are very different from ours. Our second point is that the scenario illustrates how contexts and knowledge about contexts can inform and impact our observations, interpretations, and interactions with others. We briefly address each of these two key points in the next section. These issues will be addressed in greater detail later in the text.

Understanding Contexts and Monitoring Our Actions
and Interpretations

At the beginning of the 21st century, we can look back at several decades of research in which educators (e.g., Cazden, 2001; Mehan, 1979) have examined the ways in which specific characteristics of interactions in classroom contexts have affected student's learning. Thus, these educators have found that the ways in which individuals think are determined by the kinds of talk in which they engage and that talk is influenced by interactions (past and present) in social and cultural contexts. Thus, speakers' backgrounds as well as the organization of conversational contexts tremendously impact the quality and nature of learning that occurs within a classroom.

As you visit your students' homes you will find differences existing among them. An individual's approach to living and learning is linked to economics, values, and beliefs that are nurtured within the home and the broader cultural community. For example, students whose parents grew up in conditions in which a long day at school was followed by a long night of homework may expect their students to do similar things. Sometimes the values and behaviors of the school and home are not the same. Sometimes students who are exposed to adult patterns of speaking and interacting in the home may or may not find the patterns to be similar in the school environment. Long-term studies by educators such as Shirley Brice Heath (1983) have provided intimate looks at the contrasting kinds of talk that occur in the homes of family and friends of different cultural and economic groups. Heath's work shows that these different kinds of social and cultural interactions at home have tremendous implications for students as they learn at school.

Just as the ambiance of a restaurant can affect the interactions within, so can the qualities of a classroom and its contents affect the learning that occurs within its walls. From the windows (or lack of them) to the carpet (or lack of it), from the soft couch in the library (or lack of it) to the stacks of books on the shelves (or lack of them), the physical attributes of the classroom can affect students' classroom behaviors and interactions. For example, in careful analyses of the classroom interactions of young students, observers have noticed how materials, furnishings, and arrangement affect the ways in which students interact with reading materials and how they affect the ways that students acquire and retain knowledge. Further details about environments will be discussed later in the text. In the meantime, as a practicing teacher or someone about to become a teacher, you will want to notice the classroom arrangement choices made by effective teachers as you observe their teaching.

The classroom context is, of course, shaped and affected by the classroom teacher. Teachers speak and act in many ways during a day. Tape recordings of teachers at various grade levels have shown that sixth grade teachers speak differently than kindergarten teachers when they speak to their students (Sadker & Sadker, 1994). Also, teachers tend to speak differently to boys than they do to girls and use different tones of voice and body language when they address different students in different classroom contexts.

The classroom context is also shaped by the students. For example, some students are highly sensitive to their environments and to other individuals; others are less affected by what goes on around them. One individual's set of beliefs may predispose him or her to think positively about a circumstance; another may think the opposite. Students from different cultures may be socialized to act and interact in different ways (Gee, 1996). For example, students in some Asian cultures may not speak to an adult unless they are spoken to first (Walker-Moffat, 1995). Just remember, that despite the complexity presented by their differences, 25 to 30 students can have a positive experience in a supportive classroom environment in which the teacher strives to understand and design lessons that are sensitive to the different social and cultural backgrounds of all students.

HOW CAN WE GET TO KNOW OUR STUDENTS AS LEARNERS?

Teachers, especially new teachers, frequently think about the act of teaching more than the impact of teaching on student learning (Florio-Ruane, 1999). Thinking about student learning first, rather than the act of teaching, increases our teacher effectiveness. You want to make sure that you not only learn ways to promote effective learning, but also acquire skill at developing your class as a community of learners. You certainly want to be a good learner yourself. Think about yourself as you read this section of chapter 1. This book is designed to be a learning tool for you, and because we are also teachers, not just authors, we believe that it is important to "spiral" information throughout the chapters in ever-increasing layers of detail and depth to promote effective learning for you. We would not be doing our job if we thought that we could introduce a concept only once. Instead, we will spiral ideas and examples throughout various chapters to challenge you to deepen your knowledge. Here is your first encounter with concepts related to human learning. We will be back with more.

A crucial first step in striving to understand student learning is realizing the importance of exploring student learning in the first place. However, as you probably already know, explanations of human learning are complex. There is an entire academic field—educational psychology—devoted to studying, exploring, and describing human learning. Moreover, and this probably doesn't surprise you either, different scholars have different ideas about the "best" explanations for how people learn. We'll give you a brief overview of some ideas that we consider most important for you to know. We believe that these ideas will serve as a foundation for you when you make decisions about how to teach students to read and write.

We'll start where we think any good teacher should start; let's explore what you already know as you think about the question we're posing in this section. To be in a class such as the one in which you're using this text, you have to have been a learner for a long time in many different contexts. Additionally, you may have had experience "teaching" people in a host of possible different contexts. For example, you may have taught students in a summer camp, as a coach, a school volunteer, or a baby sitter or you may have already had a number of practicums in your previous education classes. Given your years as a learner and the different experiences you've undoubtedly had as a teacher, you have background knowledge to draw upon as you articulate your own ideas about how students learn. We'll pose a few questions to get you started and then ask you to jot down your own ideas about how students learn.

Think back to your own life as a student and a learner across the years. Take a few minutes to think carefully about your many different learning experiences. Identify one of the most powerful learning experiences you've had in your past. You don't have to limit your thinking to formal classroom contexts. You may have had many very powerful learning experiences in other contexts. Describe in detail the context you are pondering. For example, you may consider contexts as diverse as learning algebra, learning to jump rope, learning tennis, learning a second or third language, exploring the meaning of a poem, and so forth. When did this learning occur? What were you doing? What were others in the context doing? Why do you think that this was one of your most powerful learning experiences? What, specifically, did you learn as a result of this experience? How, specifically, did your learning occur?

Now that you've thought about and written your own ideas about how students learn, contact someone in your class either by phone or e-mail, or you could meet in person. Discuss your ideas and your peer's ideas. What are the similarities and differences in your respective responses to the questions you addressed about your own powerful past learning experiences?

Exploring How Students Learn from a Sociocultural Perspective

In this section we present a brief overview of some current ideas about how students learn. As you read this section, think about the ideas that you just wrote down as well as your peer's ideas about learning. We suspect that you'll see some interesting overlap between your respective ideas and the work of scholars.

Most learning theorists (e.g., Dewey, 1938/1997; Piaget, 1969/2000; Vygotsky, 1978) believe that our capacity to learn is influenced by both our genetic or biological "hardwiring" and our interactions with others in different social contexts across our lives. Although we agree that both biological and social factors are important to consider in discussions of learning, we focus on the social factors that influence learning in our discussion because the social factors are the ones that we have the most direct influence over as teachers. Some important recent work in connectionist theory, however, reveals that social interactions may impact biological development and the capacity of the human brain (Harré & Gillett, 1996).

Learning theorists (e.g., Vygotsky, 1978; Wertsch, 1985, 1991, 1998) maintain that learning, or the development of the human mind, originates first through effective interactions with others. Consequently, complex processes such as learning to read and write develop first through directed interactions with others. Over time with the appropriate guidance, we, as individuals, begin to "learn" to assume control over the complex processes of reading and writing. Throughout this text we will share ideas and information with you to help you develop effective interactions around reading and writing in your classroom.

The gist of what we are saying here is that learning does not originate in our individual minds; rather, the origin of our individual learning is our social interactions with others. Let's explore a concrete example to further clarify this point. Remember the example we gave you earlier in the chapter about Ashley? A troubling dilemma that Ashley faced her first year of teaching was grouping. She wanted to get her reading groups "right." Recall, however, that other teachers, even veteran teachers, were trying to sort through the same dilemma. Quality literacy instruction requires us to realize the importance of grouping students effectively for reading instruction and then further understanding that reading groups must be flexible and adjusted across the year to meet different student's varying learning needs. Ashley was a first year teacher. Where do you think that she developed such a sophisticated understanding of this particular aspect of literacy instruction? We'll talk through her learning about grouping students for literacy instruction by situating our discussion within a sociocultural perspective of human learning.

A great deal of research on teaching illustrates that teachers tend to teach the way they were taught unless they are enrolled in strong teacher preparation programs that challenge their unexamined assumptions and beliefs about teaching and learning and provide strong models for alternative ways to teach (e.g., Shulman, 1986; Wilson, 1990). When Ashley was in elementary school, many of her teachers used basal texts in whole-class instruction. Ashley was a strong student in elementary school, so she was able to do her classroom reading work and read her grade level basal texts with little problem. However, because there was only one group (i.e., the whole class) in many of Ashley's elementary grades, many students "fell through the cracks." That is, the grade-level basal text was too hard for some of Ashley's classmates and too easy for others. When Ashley entered her teacher preparation program, her initial image of what literacy instruction looked like was whole-class instruction using a basal text because her own personal experiences were all that she knew about literacy instruction. In time, she realized that multiple texts including leveled readers were needed to meet the developing literacies of all of her students. She also realized that basal texts had changed to accommodate this literacy reality.

At the beginning of her teacher preparation program, when her professors asked Ashley to explain her conception of quality literacy instruction, not surprisingly, she told them about whole-class instruction. However, throughout her teacher preparation program, as she interacted with teachers, professors, peers, and students, and as she read, wrote, spoke about, saw, and practiced alternative models of literacy instruction, Ashley's conception of grouping for literacy instruction changed. Through her many social interactions with others in her teacher preparation program, Ashley changed her original ideas about literacy instruction. For example, she developed a much more sophisticated understanding of grouping to better meet the ongoing and changing needs of individual students. She also realized that she needed reading materials at several different difficulty levels that could be used with a wide range of readers and that basal texts had changed to accommodate a range of reading differences. When she grouped her students for instruction during her student teaching placement, it became clear to her cooperating teacher as well as her university supervisor that she had developed a much more sophisticated understanding of grouping students for literacy instruction.

So, why does all of this matter? We're guessing that you can see the implications of a sociocultural notion of learning for us as teachers. The very nature of the interactions we structure in our classrooms determines the opportunities our students have for literacy development. Moreover, our beliefs drive our actions and the instructional decisions that we make in our classrooms. In Ashley's case, without

DID YOU NOTICE . . .
Do you realize that this will be true for you, too? Your ideas about literacy instruction are shaped by your past experiences as well as your current experiences. As you sort through your own literacy background, it is a good idea to ask yourself which experiences were most useful to promote your learning and which may have been problematic. As you make instructional decisions in your own classroom, it is important to ask yourself why you re doing what you re doing. Are your instructional decisions forged out of habit or because you are carefully sorting out what is best for your children s learning?

carefully examining her beliefs about grouping for literacy instruction and without having had the opportunity to learn alternative models, she would have grouped her students for instruction in ways similar to the ways in which she was grouped for instruction as an elementary school student.

Clearly, we have a profound responsibility to think carefully about how we organize and manage interactions in our classroom contexts. However, another important aspect of a sociocultural perspective on learning is that learning is shaped and influenced by more than just immediate interactions in any one context. Our learning is also shaped and influenced by our individual histories as well as our cultural backgrounds. At first glance, this tenet of sociocultural theory may not seem like a "big deal." It turns out that it really is. We'll draw on the example of Ashley again to illustrate another point.

When Ashley entered her teacher preparation program, her teachers knew that she had powerful beliefs about literacy instruction and learning based on her previous experiences in various teaching and learning encounters. They surmised that some of her beliefs were consistent with our current understandings about best practices to promote the literacy learning of all students. They also suspected that some of her beliefs were inconsistent with current notions of best practices in literacy. Her professors knew that to help Ashley become the best beginning teacher of literacy that she could be, they needed to learn what Ashley already knew and believed, and they also needed to help her figure out and explore her incoming as well as developing beliefs about quality literacy instruction.

Without taking the time to understand and explore our students' personal histories as learners, we run the risk of not meeting their needs. We may be teaching above or below their instructional needs and levels. But, there could also be a different problem. What we're teaching may differ greatly from our students' cultural and linguistic beliefs, understandings, and experiences. We may be operating from two such different frames of reference that we may not be reaching our students at all. This lack of learning can occur when the cultural and linguistic backgrounds of the students and teachers are vastly different. We devote chapter 13 and parts of other chapters to the important issue of working effectively with cultural and linguistic differences among students.

HOW DO WE GET TO KNOW STUDENTS AS LITERACY LEARNERS?

So far in this chapter we have emphasized getting to know students as individuals and learners. Now we will talk about how to use and build upon this valuable background information to get to know students as literacy learners. Here's something that is crucial for teachers to understand: all students have unique life experiences as literacy learners.

Let's start with you and your own classmates to begin to illustrate this point. Briefly describe highlights of your own personal literacy journey. Talk with your classmates. Are there similarities and differences across stories? Reflect on these similarities and differences.

In the section that follows, we introduce two literacy learners, Cara and Patrick, who, like you and your classmates, have unique literacy learning biographies. Both came from homes in which reading and writing were valued and practiced. Their early lives were very privileged. As adults, they like to read for both pleasure and information, but they acquired their literacy through different paths. In the remainder of this chapter we draw on the literacy life stories of Cara and Patrick, as well as your own literacy life stories, to explore possible ways that we can get to know students as literacy learners. Your students will come from varied home environments and have many different literacy biographies. Your role as a teacher is to value and expand the literacies of all of your students.

Patrick's Story: The "Red Carpet" of Reading

Growing up in a home where bedtime meant a time to share a book or a story with Mom or Dad meant that Patrick was engaged with some sort of literature for 25 minutes a day. Starting when he was only 8 months old, his family observed their bedtime ritual, meaning, that by the time Patrick turned 5 years old in August and went off to kindergarten, he had experienced 39,200 minutes of shared literacy activities. Patrick also attended a local preschool for 2 years, enjoying a minimum of 20 minutes of reading activities a day for 5 days a week. Thus, he experienced an additional 4,000 minutes, adding up to a total of 720 hours. Educators such as James Trelease (1995) and Nancy Atwell (1998) sometimes called these hours of literacy learning "lap time" because the student is often participating in reading by sitting in the caregiver's lap.

Given that many other literacy activities occurred during his preschool day, Patrick was well-prepared for reading as he entered school. He was not yet a reader of unfamiliar text, but he read many words on his own whenever he saw those words in their familiar contexts (e.g., he knew the McDonald's sign when he saw it). Family travels in his community meant that he learned to decode environmental print—words from local stores, restaurants, and traffic signs, such as sale, gas, taco, and stop. No one was surprised when he began really reading during December of kindergarten. Patrick is an example of a student who, according to Stanovich (1986), is not only "rich" in literacy capabilities, but he will get even "richer" because of the many experiences and vocabulary words to which he can attach new meanings. Patrick's school friend David, on the other hand, came from a family in which the adults were too busy to be engaged with books and stories. Compared to Patrick's 720 hours of exposure to literacy events, David had less than 30 hours of incidental experiences. Clearly, when David and Patrick started school, they started from vastly different places, and they needed very different kinds of literacy instruction from their teachers. Stanovich (1986) gave a name to this literacy dichotomy. He coined the term "Matthew Effects" because of the verse from the Bible describing the phenomenon of the rich getting richer and the poor getting poorer.

Cara's Story: Paying Attention/Not Paying Attention

Cara's mom wishes she had a quarter for every time a teacher wished that Cara would pay attention. She insists that she would be a wealthy woman today. Nevertheless, she is the proud mother of a girl who is in her senior year of high school and will attend college next year. She was identified as a student with attention deficit hyperactive disorder (ADHD) during her kindergarten year and began taking medication during first grade. By first grade she was able to sit down and sit relatively still.

According to her cumulative grade point average, Cara is an average student. She does very well in some situations and quite poorly in others. If the subject is science or a computer lab she is at the top of her class. When a topic or a course appeals to her, she is able to learn quickly and go beyond basic expectations to engage in a subject. If she doesn't find a class interesting she is sure to be at the bottom of the group. In English and history classes, she has established a record of relying exclusively upon the textbook that she reads instead of listening in class. One thing is for sure, however: Cara loves to read. She reads constantly, both in and out of school, and she remembers what she reads. If she chooses to read, she remembers the material.

When Cara was a toddler, her family read a great deal with her and around her. Reading for 1 hour a day or more was typical. She loved and reread all of Dr. Seuss, and she read all of Shel Silverstein's poems. She confirmed her love of fantasy and read such works as The Hobbit (Tolkien, 1976) during middle school. Reading books and talking about books was ongoing and pleasurable for Cara all her life. Then, as a freshman in high school, she couldn't resist Harry Potter although she discovered that none of her friends shared her interest in what they considered "a little kids' book." She is considering the possibilities for reading texts online for the first time, not to supplant her passion for reading but to enhance it.

DID YOU NOTICE . . .
Did you notice that teachers must be aware that children s backgrounds, life experiences, and literacy experiences may be vastly different from their own. Teachers sometimes assume that children s experiences are similar to theirs. This is dangerous, of course, because it may prompt teachers to plan instruction for their students that is not appropriate.

At this point, you have thought about your own life experiences as a literacy learner. You have also read about the literacy learning stories of Patrick and Cara. What similarities and differences do you see between your life story and the stories of Patrick and Cara? This question is significant because learning to become aware of the nuances of each student's literacy learning background is crucial because good teachers draw upon their student's backgrounds and experiences to craft instruction to meet their unique needs.

In the previous section we discussed the importance of the social interactions in which we engage in shaping our learning opportunities. Of course, we also mentioned that the capacity for learning is influenced by genetic and/or biological factors. Clearly, Cara's diagnosis of ADHD had an impact on her learning. While acknowledging the role of biological/genetic factors in shaping students' capacities to learn, we cannot underscore strongly enough the central role that effective social interactions play in facilitating student's learning. The ways that Cara and Patrick (and you) were socialized to engage with literacy impacted who they (and you) became as literacy learners. Understanding the significance of orchestrating effective social interactions in our classrooms is crucial for teachers. There is much that we can do to promote our student's literacy learning in our classrooms by carefully structuring the nature of the interactions and activities in our classrooms regardless of the very different literacy learning backgrounds that each student will have in our classrooms.

Let's turn now to explore some issues that might help or hinder the literacy success of your students. There is much that each of us can learn about getting to know students as literacy learners and designing a classroom context to promote the learning of each of our students. We begin with some fundamental ideas here including (a) attending to student's physical, social, and emotional needs, (b) matching students with books, and (c) exploring some more and less formal ways to assess student's reading and writing. The initial ideas we present here will serve as an introduction for ideas presented in more detail throughout the text.

First Things First: Student's Physical Needs and Social/Emotional Well-Being

No student with vision problems can find easy success with literacy. If the letters dance on the page or if they look like blurry squiggles, the distinctions that must be made by young eyes for reading and writing tasks are impossible. If the teacher's words or the lyrics to a song on the tape player cannot be heard, appropriate communication won't be accomplished, and further tuning out is quite probable. The student who is in discomfort because of hunger or allergies or is sitting on a chair of inappropriate proportions may be inattentive. Students, like adults, are able to compensate for many physical ills and inadequacies and the existence of difficulties may be hidden for a long time. As teachers we need to monitor student's physical needs and well-being to make sure that unattended physical needs do not impede their literacy learning opportunities.

Just as parents sometimes fall into the trap of seeing what their students have NOT yet accomplished, teachers can miss many of their students' positive traits if they focus on what students can't do rather than what they CAN do. Spending time regretting what the student's parent or last teacher did NOT do can create a negative mindset that is hard to undo. We can shift our thinking from negative to positive by using interviews with students and their parents to inform ourselves about the student's prior experiences. This knowledge can help us to establish a positive foundation on which to build each student's literacy learning. It is important to realize that you may not recognize some qualities that have laid important foundations for literacy growth. For example, a student who knows several songs can learn several poems. A student who loves to talk and tell stories can become an excellent storyteller.

Matching Students with Books: Determining Topics That Appeal to Students

Students and adolescents find books interesting if they already find the topics covered in the books to be interesting. Ongoing conversations with your students can provide a great deal of individualized information that can help you guide students in their library selections and help you to recommend books that will appeal to your students. Some books and materials have very good track records with young people.

When topics appeal to students, you will notice that they are much more interested in listening to or reading stories; they are much less likely to be reluctant readers. Remembering that all students are not alike, you will want to find strategies that work to determine each student's true interests. To add to your assessment repertoire, you will find examples of three interest inventories in chapter 2. They may be used as is, but more than likely, you will eventually want to design similar instruments that target the ages and contexts of the students with whom you work (see Figures 1.1, 1.2, and 1.3). You may even want to ask your students to work with you to develop interest inventories that can be used across time periods in your classroom.

Whereas students will have unique interests in certain topics, you may find that there are some topics that most students like. One study revealed that when elementary students designed and wrote their own word problems for others to solve, their most favorite real-life situations involved food (Rubenstein & Shirley, 1995). Also, students often enjoy stories and factual accounts about pets. Over and over, students tell us that some other favorite topics are famous people (as in sports and television stars), unusual people and events (as in *Guinness World Records*), sports (as in the sport that they play), and pastimes (such as collecting dolls and baseball cards).

Figure 1–1   Reading attitude inventory.

Name _____ Grade _____ Teacher _____

1. How do you feel when your teacher reads a story out loud?

2. How do you feel about reading books for fun at home?

3. How do you feel when you are asked to read out loud to your group?

4. How do you feel about how well you can read?

5. How do you think your friends feel when you read out loud?

6. How do you think you'll feel about reading when you're bigger?

Reprinted by permission of Paul Campbell.

Yes	No	
_____	_____	1. I visit the library to find books I might enjoy reading.
_____	_____	2. I would like to read a magazine in my free time.
_____	_____	3. I enjoy reading extra books about topics we study in school.
_____	_____	4. I would like to read newspaper articles about my favorite hobbies or interests.
_____	_____	5. My best friend would tell you that I enjoy reading very much.
_____	_____	6. I would enjoy spending some time during my summer vacation reading to children in a summer library program.
_____	_____	7. Reading is a very important part of my life. Every day I read many types of materials.
_____	_____	8. My friends would tell you that I'd much rather watch TV than read.
_____	_____	9. Sometimes the book that I'm reading will remind me of ideas from another book I've read.
_____	_____	10. I never do extra reading outside of schoolwork because reading is so dull.
_____	_____	11. Before I make up my mind about something, I try to read more than one writer's ideas.
_____	_____	12. When I read, I sometimes understand myself a little better.
_____	_____	13. Some characters I have read about help me to better understand people I know.
_____	_____	14. Reading is a very important part of my life. I read nearly every day in books or newspapers and I enjoy doing so.
_____	_____	15. I would feel disappointed if I could not find a book that I was very interested in reading.

From "Critical Factors in the Development of Attitudes Toward Reading as Defined by Individual Perceptions of Students, Their Teachers and Parents" (pp. 17–21) by M. Ransbury, 1971. Unpublished doctoral dissertation, Indiana University School of Education, Bloomington. Reprinted by permission of the author and Indiana University School of Education.

Matching Students with Books: Choosing Good Books

Our experiences with students in many different types of elementary and middle school settings tell us that some kinds of books are immediately selected; over the years students choose them from libraries and bookstores without being coaxed. As you become a more experienced teacher, you will gain a sense of what might be typical in certain types of classrooms. For example, many young students enjoy books about dinosaurs and other stories about animals. Favorite books for young students also often include stories such as *Where the Wild Things Are* (Sendak, 1963), *Alexander and the Terrible, Horrible, No Good, Very Bad Day* (Viorst, 1972) *The*

Figure 1–3   Survey of students' reading interests.

Name _____ Age _____
Date _____

1. What other cities or states have you visited or lived in?
2. Do you ever read a book after you have seen the television or movie version?
3. What movies have you seen that you really liked?
4. What are your favorite TV programs?
5. How much TV do you watch each day?
6. Circle the kinds of books and stories you like; cross out the ones you don't like:

Adventure	Mystery	Magazines
Animal stories	Motorcycles	Comic books
Hobby stories	Love and romance	Ghost stories
Biography	Science fiction	Family stories
Autobiography	Car magazines	Riddles and jokes
Science	Fables and myths	Horse stories
Western stories	Sports	Humor
Art and music	Religion	Fantasy
Fairy tales	History	People of other lands
Poetry	Newspapers	Geography

7. On a sunny day I like to _____
_____
8. The best thing I ever read was _____
9. My hobbies are _____
10. I get really mad when _____
_____
11. When I grow up I'd like to be _____
because _____
12. Right now I'd like to _____
13. What is it that you do well? _____
14. The most fun I ever had was when _____
_____
15. The person I would most like to meet is _____
because _____

Story of Ruby Bridges (Coles, 1995), and *Chato's Kitchen* (Soto, 1995). Students in intermediate grades often like to read books that involve mystery, sports, or adventures. Favorites for intermediate grade students include *Where the Red Fern Grows* (Rawls, 1961), *Tuck Everlasting* (Babbitt, 1975), *The Cay* (Taylor, 1969), *Island of the Blue Dolphins* (O'Dell, 1960), *Across Five Aprils* (Hunt, 1964), *Roll of Thunder, Hear My Cry* (Taylor, 1976), *Baseball in April and Other Stories* (Soto, 1990), and *A Little Princess* (Burnett, 1972). Some favorite series that are enjoyed by children in a range of ages include *Goosebumps* (Stine, 1995), *The Adventures of Captain Underpants: An Epic Novel* (Pilkey, 1997), *Magic Treehouse Bundle* (Osborne, 1999), and Harry Potter (e.g., *Harry Potter and the Sorcerer's Stone*, Rowling, 1997) as well as books by Judy Bloom. We will be introducing you to many titles that students love in chapter 11.

Older students are often captivated by stories of survival and overcoming injustice such as *To Kill a Mockingbird* (Lee, 1960/1997) and *Hatchet* (Paulsen, 1999) They may be intrigued by characters who enter into emotional relationships and cope with social issues. Both boys and girls often like scary stories. All of the books by Shel Silverstein (e.g., *Where the Sidewalk Ends*, 1974) have a magnetic attraction for students at every grade. His humorous ways of dealing with daily life, outrageous situations, and plain old bad manners gain admirers year after year.

Popularity sells. The Harry Potter books are captivating in and of themselves to many students, but the "halo effect" of being so sought after by so many young readers may make these thick volumes even more attractive to large numbers of students. When movies are being shown in theaters or certain cartoon characters are in vogue, books about them are often well read. Library copies of novels by authors such as Judy Blume (e.g., *Tales of a Fourth Grade Nothing*, 1976) and Judith Viorst are also always well-worn. Reading materials that depict students' daily lives, including their visits to fast food restaurants and local attractions also hold interest. More information on students and young adult literature will be found in chapter 11.

Informal and Formal Assessment Strategies and Tools

If watching and listening were easy to do, we would not have so many complaints from people like "You never notice! You never listen!" Real attentiveness is not easy to accomplish. Working with students in a variety of contexts using a variety of

instructional and assessment approaches may be the surest way to get to know their capacities. A variety of techniques can help you to learn about students' interests; it will also take multiple types of assessment to determine what they can do in the areas of reading, writing, speaking, and listening. For young students, these capabilities overlap a great deal in how you investigate literacy proficiency. For older students, you will want to establish many avenues for assessment. A detailed treatment of assessment will follow in the next chapter. Briefly, however, we encourage you to assess your students' literacy-related skills and practices using both formal and informal assessment tools. Informal assessment involves careful "kid watching" (Goodman, 1978). That is, good "kid watchers" notice the reading and writing behaviors that their students exhibit, and they use this knowledge to help them to plan for instruction. Formal assessments include, but are not limited to, studying student's past performance records, including their scores on standardized tests as well as various reading and writing inventories. Of course, we will have much more to say about both formal and informal assessments in the next chapter.

CHAPTER SUMMARY

The focus of chapter 1 was students. We chose this focus because we believe that students are "the heart of the matter" for literacy teachers. We divided this chapter

Hatchet by Gary Paulsen. Used with permission from Simon & Schuster Children's Publishing.

into four major sections. The first section dealt with teachers' stories about getting to know students as individuals. Recall that Ashley, a first grade teacher, learned a great deal about ongoing flexible grouping to meet the changing needs of her students as literacy learners. Larry, a fifth grade teacher, did an exceptional job of getting to know his students as individuals. He drew upon what he learned about his students to design quality literacy instruction for and with them. After introducing Ashley and Larry, we talked about how teachers such as Ashley, Larry, and you can get to know your students as individuals. Thus, the second section focused on ways to get to know our students as individuals. We explored different conceptions of learning in the third section and getting to know students as learners. Finally, in the fourth section we explored some initial ideas for ways to begin to get to know your students as literacy learners. As you read the rest of this book and learn more about students, quality student's literature, assessment, and quality instructional approaches, keep in mind that, as literacy teachers, our central goal is to inspire each student who we teach to become a lifelong reader. Throughout the remainder of this book we will help you to understand how teachers such as Larry and Ashley inspire their students to become avid lifelong readers, and we will provide you with the tools so that you, too, can help your students to become avid lifelong readers.

At the beginning of this chapter we asked you to jot down questions you may have about how to get to know your students as literacy learners. Please list and address the questions you were wondering about as you began to read this chapter. Did new questions emerge as you read? If so, how would you address them?

QUESTIONS

Please answer the questions below that we posed at the beginning of this chapter.

1. How can you get to know your students as individuals?
2. Why do some teachers believe that the more they know about a student the better able they are to teach the student?
3. How can you get to know your students as literacy learners?
4. If a colleague said, "I think that visiting a student's home is intrusive" what would you say?
5. What are your beliefs about the significance of parental involvement in a student's learning? If your views differ from those of the parents of your students, how will you accommodate these differences?

REFERENCES

Atwell, N. (1998). *In the middle: New understandings about writing, reading, and learning* (2nd ed.). Portsmouth, NH: Heinemann.

Au, K. H. (1993). *Literacy instruction in multicultural settings*. Fort Worth, TX: Harcourt Brace College Publishers.

Cazden, C. B. (2001). *Classroom discourse: The language if teaching and learning* (2nd ed.). Portsmouth, NH: Heinemann.

Clay, M. M. (1998). *By different paths to common outcomes*. York, ME: Stenhouse.

Cunningham, P. M. (2000). *Phonics they use: Words for reading and writing*. New York: Longman.

Dewey, J. (1997). *Experience and education*. New York: Peter Smith. (Original work published 1938)

Duffy, G. G. (1999). In pursuit of an illusion: The flawed search for a perfect method. *The Reading Teacher, 53*, 10–16.

Florio-Ruane, S. F. (1999). Revisiting fieldwork in preservice teachers' language: Creating your own case studies. In M. A. Lundeberg, B. B. Levin, & H. L. Harrington (Eds.), *Who learns what from cases and how?* Mahwah, NJ: Lawrence Erlbaum Associates.

Gee, J. P. (1996). *Social linguistics and literacies: Ideology in discourses* (2nd ed.). Philadelphia, PA: Falmer Press.

Goodman, Y, M. (1978). Kid watching: An alternative to testing. *National Elementary Principal, 57*, 41–45.

Harré, R., & Gillett, G. (1994). *The discursive mind*. Thousand Oaks, CA: Sage.

Heath, S. B. (1983). *Ways with words: Language, life, and work in communities and classrooms*. New York: Cambridge University Press.

Isaacs, W. (1999). *Dialogue and the art of thinking together*. New York: Currency.

Jans, N. (1993). *The last light breaking: Living among Alaska's Inupiat Eskimos*. Alaska Northwest Books.

Mehan, H. (1979). *Learning lessons: Social organization in the classroom*. Cambridge, MA: Harvard University Press.

Piaget, J. (2000). *The psychology of the child*. New York: Basic Books. (Original work published 1969)

Rubenstein, D., & Shirley, B. (1995). *Topics selected for word problems written by students*. Paper delivered at The International Reading Association Conference, Anaheim, CA.

Sadker, M., & Sadker, D. (1994). *Failing at fairness: How America's schools cheat girls*. New York: Scribner.

Shulman, L. S. (1986). Paradigms and research programs in the study of teaching: A contemporary perspective. In M. C. Wittrock. *Handbook of research on teaching* (3rd ed., pp. 3–36). New York: Macmillan.

Stanovich, K. E. (1986). Matthew effects in reading: Some consequences of individual differences in the acquisition of literacy. *Reading Research Quarterly, 21*, 360–407.

Trelease, J. (1995). *The read-aloud handbook* (4th ed.). New York: Penguin Books.

Vygotsky, L. S. (1978). *Mind in society: The development of higher psychological processes*. Cambridge, MA: Harvard University Press.

Walker-Moffat, W. (1995). *The other side of the Asian American success story*. San Francisco, CA: Jossey-Bass.

Wertsch, J. V. (1985). *Vygotsky and the social formation of mind*. Cambridge, MA: Harvard University Press.

Wertsch, J. V. (1991). *Voices of the mind: A sociocultural approach to mediated action*. Cambridge, MA: Harvard University Press.

Wertsch, J. V. (1998). *Mind as action*. Cambridge, MA: Harvard University Press.

Wilson, S. M. (1990). The secret garden of teacher education. *Phi Delta Kappan, 72*, 204–209.

CHILDREN'S LITERATURE

Babbitt, N. (1975). *Tuck everlasting*. New York: Farrar.

Blume, J. (1976). *Tales of a fourth grade nothing*. New York: Bantam Doubleday Dell.

Burnett, F. H. (1972). *A little princess*. New York: HarperCollins.

Coles, R. (1995). *The story of Ruby Bridges*. New York: Scholastic.

Garza, C, L. (1993). *Family pictures*. San Francisco, CA: Children's Book Press.

Hunt, I. (1964). *Across five Aprils*. New York: Berkley Books.

Lee, H. (1997). *To kill a mockingbird*. Evanson, IL: McDougal Littell. (Original work published 1960)

O'Dell, S. (1960). *Island of the blue dolphins*. New York: Houghton.

Osborne, M. P. (1999). *Magic treehouse bundle*. New York: Random House.

Pilkey, D. (1997). *The adventures of captain underpants: An epic novel*. New York: Scholastic.

Paulsen, G. (1999). *Hatchet*. New York: Aladdin.

Rawls, W. (1961). *Where the red fern grows*. New York: Doubleday.

Rowling, J. K. (1997). *Harry Potter and the sorcerer's stone*. New York: Scholastic.

Sendak, M. (1963). *Where the wild things are*. New York: Harper Collins.

Silverstein, S. (1974). *Where the sidewalk ends*. San Francisco: Harper & Row.

Soto, G. (1990). *Baseball in April and other stories*. Orlando, FL: Harcourt.

Soto, G. (1995). *Chato's kitchen*. New York: Putnam.

Stine, R. L. (1995). *Goosebumps*. New York: Scholastic.

Taylor, M. D. (1976). *Roll of thunder, hear my cry*. New York: Viking Penguin.

Taylor, T. (1969). *The cay*. Nnew York: Doubleday.

Tolkien, J. R. R. (1976). *The hobbit*. Boston: Houghton Mifflin.

Viorst, J. (1972). *Alexander and the terrible, horrible, no good, very bad day*. New York: Atheneum.

2

Looking Inside Classrooms: Organizing Instruction

──────────── CHAPTER GOALS ────────────

To help the reader

- recognize the factors contributing to effective classroom operation.
- learn how to develop and implement thematic teaching.
- learn successful grouping techniques.
- recognize learning objectives as an essential instructional tool.
- sample a variety of instructional methods and materials.
- recognize the importance of continuous evaluation.

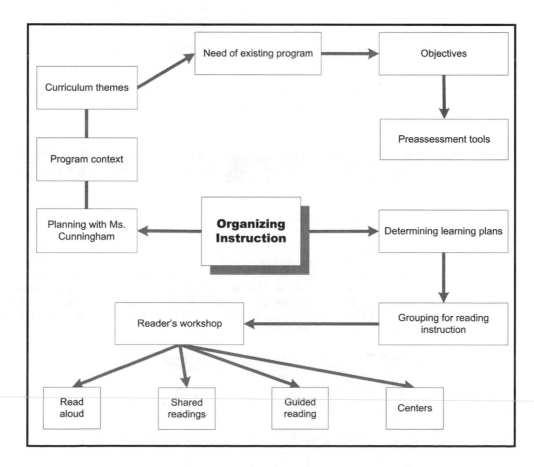

Throughout this book we will introduce you to many teachers and share vignettes of the classroom management styles they use. Although there will be differences, one common factor is that each classroom is child centered, and each teacher implements the use of flexible groups to accommodate a wide range of student differences.

Think back to your elementary school experiences. What procedures did your teachers use to operate their classrooms? How was time used? What was your favorite part of the school day? Why? Did you work alone, in groups, or in other configurations? How did your teacher decide which group was "a best fit" for you?

PLANNING ALONGSIDE MS. CUNNINGHAM

In this chapter, we visit a second grade classroom and observe a teacher, Ms. Cunningham, to learn how she assesses student and program strengths and needs, develops curriculum units of study, and plans and implements instruction for her diverse learners.

Early in the school year, Mr. and Mrs. Jensen received a note from their child's teacher (see Figure 2–1) which relayed the teacher's (Ms. Cunningham) joy at meeting their daughter Shannon, explained Shannon's literacy development, and then invited them to visit the classroom.

During their visit to Shannon's classroom, they realized that the way it was managed contributed greatly to the success of the learning program. Ms. Cunningham explained that she believed learning environments should include provisions for

1. motivating children through engaging lessons to develop a love of language, literacy, and learning.
2. encouraging student participation in determining procedural and discipline plans.
3. supporting students as they worked alone, in pairs, and in a variety of flexible groups with peers and/or the teacher.

Figure 2–1   Letter to Shannon's parents.

Dear Mr. and Mrs. Jensen,

I have had the opportunity to spend some time during the past week with your daughter, Shannon, and have observed her literacy development. Shannon is a strong reader with interests in fantasy and sports. This year we will be expanding the types of material she'll be reading and also working on her writing as she learns to produce longer and more descriptive pieces of writing. I hope you'll come by the classroom to visit. Room 302 is a wonderful place, and I'm so pleased that Shannon is a part of it!

Sincerely,

Ms. Cunningham

Ms. Cunningham explained further that these beliefs were best accomplished because she viewed herself as a classroom facilitator. In this role she works with children alone and in flexible groups. She continually assesses their developing literacy growth through observations and, subsequently, plans the next steps in their instruction. In chapter 3 we share specific details about the classroom assessments that she and other teachers often use in their child-centered classrooms in which meeting the individual needs of children is the primary goal.

UNDERSTANDING PROGRAM CONTEXT

As you plan a child-centered program of this type, consideration must be given to the existing structures that directly affect what happens in your classroom. Although the operation of your classroom may be governed by your philosophy of education and your beliefs about how children learn, other factors such as school budget allocations, curricular requirements, and time schedules may be outside your range of authority and may have been established before you joined the faculty.

You need to be familiar with these structures and the extent of your decision-making power regarding each. You may gain initial insights through social and professional interactions with colleagues and administrators. A review of existing school policies and curriculum guides will also offer you some insights into the structure of the existing curriculum. As you begin to collect information about existing structures, remember to ask the following questions:

1. How is the day divided?
2. Is the time schedule predetermined? By whom?
3. Is your classroom self-contained? If so, this means that you teach all of the subjects.
4. What special teachers (e.g., music or art) or special services (e.g., gym or theater) are provided?
5. Is there an organized curriculum committee for your grade level? If so, how can you join?
6. What funds are available to you?
7. How are text materials adopted?
8. Are there state or local curriculum standards you must follow?
9. What types of assessments are mandated? Which assessments do your grade level colleagues use?
10. Are resource specialists, peer coaches, team leaders, or mentors available to answer your questions?

Questions such as these may also be asked during an early interview. Always attempt to compare the answers you receive with your philosophy of teaching. Is there compatibility? If so, you will avoid conflict later on. If not, can alterations (compromises) be made by you?

The development of your classroom curriculum must successfully adhere to larger working units, the school, and the community. To establish compatibility among all elements, it is important that you become aware of program context. To do so you'll need to consider questions such as the following:

Administration

1. Is there a philosophy of decentralization or local control meaning that individual schools have decision-making authority?
2. What are the line-staff relationships (line of command) within this school or district?
3. What appear to be the major objectives of the administration?
4. How are these objectives related to education?
5. How is the administration's apparent philosophy similar to or different from mine?
6. What role do teachers have in decision making?
7. What decisions are made by whom?

Colleagues

1. Who are my colleagues?
2. Do any major educational beliefs appear to be shared by the majority of this faculty?
3. What are the faculty's initial impressions of me?
4. What will be my role as a member of this educational community?
5. What decision-making responsibilities are mine? My colleagues?
6. What types of decision making responsibilities do my colleagues want?

Parents

1. Who are the parents of my children?
2. What are their values with regard to the education of their children?
3. Are they heavily involved with the decision-making processes of this school? Do they want to be?
4. How do they view the existing faculty and administration?

Community

1. Is the surrounding community well represented (economically, socially) by the family makeup of the students in my classroom?
2. What segment of the community controls school-board decision making?
3. What are the apparent and less apparent feelings of the school board with regard to the administration, faculty, and education?
4. Is there an interest in restructuring the school to better meet the needs of the students?
5. If so, what dimensions of the school community are being given the greatest restructuring attention?

Students

1. Who are my students? What are their cultures?

2. What have been their life exposures thus far?

3. What may be their projected life goals?

4. Are their life exposures similar or dissimilar to mine?

5. What will be their projected view of me?

Self

1. What will be my function in this educational community?

2. Do I harbor any prejudices or fears with regard to the people in the community?

3. Are there any barriers that may interfere with my effective functioning as a teacher?

4. If so, how is it possible to eliminate these barriers?

5. What do I need to learn to better teach these children?

DID YOU NOTICE . . .
Did you notice that a big part of education is reflection? Ask questions, wonder out loud, and reflect on as much as you can. Developing as a professional includes questioning the process of teaching and learning. Don t be afraid to ask about whatever s on your mind!

As a veteran or as a beginning teacher, you must continually pursue answers to these questions. When Ms. Cunningham made these inquiries, she found that the children in Shannon's class were like students in most primary grades: multiethnic and culturally diverse, with various languages and dialects, levels of cognitive development, levels of sensory and perceptual readiness, degrees of physical health, degrees of social and emotional development, various interests and attitudes about learning, and a range of oral and silent reading proficiencies.

Ms. Cunningham realized that to attempt to meet the learning needs of each of her 26 second graders she would have to acquaint herself with the existing program structures in her school.

Your Turn

Visit your state Department of Education Web site and search for the curriculum or content standards. You will also notice specific themes in social studies, language arts, science, mathematics, and visual and performing arts that you can use to plan instruction.

CURRICULUM THEMES

After Ms. Cunningham had gained a general understanding of the existing structures and individuals in her educational community as well as their decision-making effects on the management of her classroom, she began planning her classroom curriculum. Naturally, she used the state content standards as her guide. Importantly, she also thought about her students' interests, strengths, and needs. Ms. Cunningham explained to the Jensens that her role was to prepare lessons, to teach, to facilitate learning, to continuously assess the effectiveness of all dimensions of the learning plan, and to replan based on these continuous evaluations (Eby, Herrell, & Hicks, 2001; Johnston, 1997). Meeting the needs of each child through a flexibly grouped classroom was her central focus. She attempted to accomplish this through thematic instruction.

What Is Thematic Instruction?

Teaching language arts and content area skills through themes or topics that are currently of interest to your students is often referred to as thematic teaching (Jacobs,

1997). Thematic teaching has been developed from an earlier teaching strategy referred to as unit teaching. Unit teaching stressed the importance of teaching children to read in one specific content area, such as science. Thematic teaching, however, broadens the base of reading in the content areas by integrating many content areas, reading, and language arts skills. Books and children's strengths and needs are often the integrating thread. Thematic teaching is based on a natural phenomenon: reading, talking about, and writing about a particular theme. For example, a teacher may introduce a lesson on train transportation in Boston by reading *The Polar Express* by Chris Van Allsburg, *Trains* by Donald Crews, or *The Little Engine That Could* by Watty Piper. In addition to introducing a theme through a book, you may wish to discuss with your students their prior experiences with train transportation. Encourage them to discuss experiences lived, read, or heard about.

For example, throughout the study of transportation, the students in Ms. Cunningham's class engaged in oral and written discussion about the use of trains in Boston, experiences with trains, and train use throughout Massachusetts and the country (language arts and social studies). Students also constructed cardboard trains (measurement, mathematics) while verbally listing and copying all the new vocabulary words associated with train transportation (language arts). They also had a discussion about train construction and the mechanics of building an engine (science). As a concluding activity related to this theme, the students drew pictures of trains and paired these pictures with poems that they had written. The whole class then had an opportunity to perform their poems and share their art.

At this point, let's brainstorm to determine some general themes you may plan to share with your students. Many of these themes will be provided through the state and local curriculum standards or by the materials you are using. For example:

Life cycles (biological, emotional, social)

Making choices (family, school, friends)

Exploring your environment (geographically, culturally, emotionally)

Life in the American past (family, environment, economic structures)

Building a nation (the U.S. Constitution, interstate and international relations)

Examples of some of the standards that could be addressed through these are noted in Figure 2–2.

As you add to this list of themes, remember that many veteran teachers spend many hours developing thematic units, so don't be discouraged if you find that you are not able to accomplish this development immediately. Your intent in creating any theme will be to convey the basic skills of communication, as well as the skills and areas of information that eventually will result in the development of independent learners. It may be helpful to select themes that facilitate the incorporation of literature, the arts, science, math, and social studies lessons. If your topic isn't broad enough, it's fine to just integrate one content area (i.e., science, social studies, or mathematics) with the language arts of reading, writing, oral language, listening, and viewing. You can also easily add music and art experiences to most themes. The important point as you begin is to develop thematic instruction that you are able to manage.

To create an independent learner, remember that your task is to introduce the joy of language through communication and study strategies in a practical, useful,

DID YOU NOTICE . . .
Did you notice that organizing your classroom around themes is manageable for you and makes sense for your students? What themes seem interesting to you? What themes seem to match the content standards that you are expected to cover?

Figure 2–2   Themes and related objectives.

Theme	General Objectives
Life cycles	1. Define a life cycle. 2. Develop an understanding of the life cycle of plants. 3. Develop an understanding of the biological life cycle of animals. 4. Promote an awareness of emotional and psychological cycles in humans. 5. Establish an appreciation for each stage of life from birth to death. 6. Develop a personal awareness of one's own physical and emotional place in the cycle. 7. Evaluate personal and societal feelings about life and death.
Exploring your environment	1. Develop an awareness of self. 2. Identify significant others. 3. Identify geographic boundaries. 4. Identify cultural boundaries. 5. Compare the strengths and weaknesses of boundary limitations. 6. Evaluate a social change you can effect.

synthesized, and interesting manner. That's some task! But who ever told you that the effective teacher's job was easy? Through the selection of topical themes, you have begun the process of thematic teaching, which includes integrating content area learning, literature, language arts processes, and study strategies into a manageable, practical, interesting learning endeavor.

When you are working with classroom teachers who are attempting to implement an integrated thematic curriculum, one initial problem seems to exist for all: the teaching of specific skills. Teachers initially ask, "How can I have an integrated program and still teach the skills that pertain to my grade level? How can I teach thematically and still address individual student needs through flexible grouping patterns?" The answer to this question is, teach skills through the delineated theme. For example, in a kindergarten program, after student assessment you may wish to work on the following skills or processes:

Language Arts

1. Expand language skills
2. Expand listening skills
3. Letter identification
4. Emerging writing skills
   a. Letters
   b. Names
   c. Labels
5. Read names and classroom labels

Mathematics

1. Count from 1 to 50
2. Develop a basic understanding of number sequence

Social Studies

1. Expand positive self-concept
2. Develop awareness of self and others in one's community

Science

1. Understand the concept of time (second, minute, hour, day, week, month, year)
2. Develop an awareness of weather (seasons, temperature)

General

1. Recognition of colors
2. Development of motor skills
3. Identification of left and right

Many of these skills can be accomplished through the lessons discussed earlier that pertained to train transportation in Boston by simply showing a picture of a modern train and discussing the following:

1. Who can name the different parts of the train? (Language arts skills 1, 2, 5)
2. How many parts have we named? (Language arts skills 1, 2; Mathematics skills, 1, 2)
3. How close is the nearest train station to our school? (Social studies skills 1, 2; Language arts skills 1, 2; Mathematics skill 2)

Now present a picture of an older train and ask:

4. How do these trains differ? (Science skill 1; Language arts skills 1, 2)
5. Let's draw a picture of a train we would like to ride on. (General skill 2; Language arts skill 4)
6. After you have finished drawing your picture, let's each tell a story about it. (Language arts skills 1, 2)

The skills you wish to include are often general enough to be integrated and developed through any theme. It is important to begin planning by specifying the skills to be created. Once they have been specified, you will feel more at ease when you attempt to integrate your thematic program. The theme offers the context through which to teach the skills and strategies.

Now that we understand the possibility of addressing standards, skills, and individual needs through thematic instruction, let's focus more specifically on the individual.

If you are working in a classroom as a student teacher, interview the guide teacher and find out how he or she collects assessment information about students to plan instruction. Share these ideas with the members of your class. If you are reading this to help you more effectively plan instruction in your classroom, pause to think about why you have chosen the specific classroom assessments you use and how they inform your instruction.

STUDENT PREASSESSMENT

In a study on teacher decision making regarding reading instruction, Borko, Shavelson, and Stem (1981) asked, "Do teachers use all of the available information about students to form reading groups?" (p. 452). The short answer is "No," teachers tend to base these decisions largely on information about reading ability, rather than on any other aspect of the child or situation. Although grouping by reading ability all day long was popular in the past, it is now regarded as tracking and many teachers realize that children's literacy is more effectively developed when they implement flexible grouping patterns that also address the child's interests, attitudes, and emotional needs. A portfolio or compilation of information that provides a comprehensive understanding of the student is a better basis for making decisions. Many materials that illustrate a child's performance, including samples of students' writing, papers students believe show their best work, teachers' comments during conferences, parents' responses to work taken home or seen when visiting classrooms, daily journals, and books read, should be considered as teachers plan "the next steps" in instruction.

As we will discuss in chapter 3, we never finish assessing student learning. The student and the teacher continually add information that tells the story of the student. Ms. Cunningham uses many informal measures, including student work, observation scales, teacher-made checklists, interest inventories, running records, and textbook placement exams, to assess each student's interests, ability to work alone

DID YOU NOTICE...
Did you notice that you can use assessment information to plan for individual, small-group and whole-group lessons? It is also a good idea to collect assessment information on your students in these different settings. Sometimes students exhibit different literacy behaviors depending on their group configurations.

Book and Author	Read Alone	Shared with Others	Developed Written Responses	Recommend	
				Yes	No
Grandfather Twilight by Barbara Berger		X		X	
It Wasn't My Fault by Helen Lester	X		X	X	
East of the Sun and West of the Moon by Mercer Mayer	X	X		X	
Ride a Purple Pelican by Jack Prelutsky		X		X	

and with peers, language, listening, and writing abilities, and sensory, perceptual, emotional, and social developmental needs. In addition, assessments should provide you with knowledge of students' oral reading fluency and any reasons that they are not developing their fluency. For example, are they spending too much time trying to figure out sight words? Do they not have adequate knowledge of vowel configurations, consonant elements, and structural patterns? If so, this will slow down their reading and interfere with their comprehension, which you can also assess through retells after oral or silent reading. More specific information about comprehension skills and instruction is discussed in chapters 7, 8, and 9.

Collecting Student Information

Like Ms. Cunningham, effective teachers need to develop a plan that can be easily managed for continuous assessment of factors that affect reading achievement. Collected information can be compiled and used to plan individual, small-group, and whole-class instruction. As shown in Figures 2–3 and 2–4, students can be actively involved in collecting and analyzing information about their literacy behaviors and preferences. Their responses will aid your instructional decision making.

When developing your own forms, be simple in the design and specific about the information you wish to collect. For example you may want your students to keep track of the books they have read, shared, or discussed with others, responded to through writing, and would recommend to others. If so, Figure 2–3 would be appropriate.

Primary grade students may need to develop charts that are less detailed than those compiled by older students. Figure 2–4, which is for older students, is more detailed in terms of the types of data students are asked to collect and the types of responses they are asked to make. The data collected in Figure 2–4 illustrate the student's reading level, interest, and personal responses to the literary figure, as well as a personal comparison of himself or herself to the character. The Nonfiction Interest Survey (Moss, 2003) found in Figure 2–5 is another form that, when completed, enables the teacher to better understand a student's interest in nonfiction books.

If you and your students complete charts and checklists such as these, you will be able to observe the patterns of change and growth in your students as well as

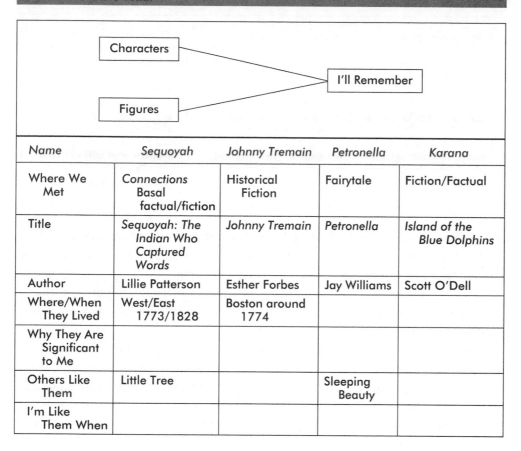

Name	Sequoyah	Johnny Tremain	Petronella	Karana
Where We Met	Connections Basal factual/fiction	Historical Fiction	Fairytale	Fiction/Factual
Title	Sequoyah: The Indian Who Captured Words	Johnny Tremain	Petronella	Island of the Blue Dolphins
Author	Lillie Patterson	Esther Forbes	Jay Williams	Scott O'Dell
Where/When They Lived	West/East 1773/1828	Boston around 1774		
Why They Are Significant to Me				
Others Like Them	Little Tree		Sleeping Beauty	
I'm Like Them When				

Nonfiction Interest Survey

DIRECTIONS: Please write the answer to each question on the line provided.

I'd like to learn about _____ and _____ during this year.

One famous person I'd like to read about is _____.

Magazines I like to read include _____.

One sport I'd like to read about is _____.

One science topic I'm interested in is _____.

One social studies topic I'm interested in is _____.

My favorite hobby is _____.

My favorite subject in school is _____.

A nonfiction book I've read before and liked was _____.

When I'm not in school, I like to _____.

Figure 2–6 "How Am I Doing?", a chart for student self-evaluation.

Things I can do well	Things I am working on	Things I plan to learn
I can ask questions in conferences.	I am learning how to piggyback comments on other students' comments.	I want to compare books to other books by the same author.
I can read riddle books.	I am reading articles in sports magazines.	I want to read a biography of a hockey player.
I can find root words.	I am learning the meanings of suffixes and prefixes.	I want to learn lots of prefixes and suffixes and use tons of them in one humorous poem.

their knowledge about books, knowledge and use of reading and writing skills, personal views of themselves as readers and writers, and general reading behaviors. This knowledge can assist in your instructional planning.

Lapp, Fisher, Flood, and Cabello (2001) promoted the development of charts for students that encourage self-evaluation. Many evaluative insights may come as a result of student-teacher conferences when a form such as "How Am I Doing?" (see Figure 2–6) is discussed while being completed. Another form that we think provides insights about student performance is shown in Figure 2–7. Forms can be completed in segments or as a whole when working with or observing students. Information collected through these charts, plus student work, interests, conversations, informal assessments, and daily observations will help you understand the multiple dimensions of each of your students.

Your Turn

What types of individual assessments are used in the classrooms in which you teach or observe?

DIFFERENTIATING INSTRUCTION THROUGH FLEXIBLE GROUPING

Planning Groups

Students often engage in learning activities in a variety of group settings. Most classrooms are composed of three to six groups of students with similar needs for the guided reading portion of the day (Fountas & Pinnell, 2001). Unfortunately, once the groups have been formed, they often remain permanent, therefore limiting a middle- or low-group student's chances of ever joining the upper or advanced groups. Flexibility of group composition encourages greater opportunities for student growth (Tomlinson, 2001).

Realizing these inadequacies, many teachers are expanding instructional arrangements to include whole-class, partners, and cooperative peer work groups (Putnam, 1998). They are also becoming more sensitive to meeting the needs of individual students and are therefore no longer planning groups according to the single factor of ability levels.

Figure 2–7 Transitional literacy development checklist. (Adapted from Bailey, J., et al. (1988) "Problem solving our way to alternative procedures." Language Arts, pp. 364–373. National Council of Teachers of English. Reprinted with permission.)

Observations and Student Behavior

Student _____ Teacher

_____

Observations About...	Date	Contextual Notes

I. Interest in Books
demonstrates interest in books
samples different genres
uses library
engages in spontaneous book talk
brings additional books to class

II. Book Knowledge and Library Skills
external organization—narrative
external organization—expository
demonstrates use of...
    glossary
    encyclopedia
    dictionary
    card catalog
    alphabetical ordering
can choose appropriate books

III. Reading Comprehension
adequate retelling of story or major events
demonstrates understanding of...
    plot
    main idea
    characters
    setting
    climax
can interpret figurative language
differentiates fact and opinion
when questioned, can make comparison
show cause and effect
    predict outcomes
    begin to make inferences
can identify mood and tone
reads familiar material fluently with suitable intonations and phrasing
can use text to support statements
makes connections to own experiences
views reading as a predictive process
knowledge of story structure
uses prior knowledge

IV. Reading Strategies
self-corrects when meaning is lost
when encountering unfamiliar words...
    returns to beginning of sentence/phrase
    uses pictures and other support clues
    makes use of reference tools
makes integrated use of semantic and syntactic cueing systems
makes use of graphophonic cueing
increases sight word vocabulary
adjusts speed of reading to material
declining use of voice or finger as fluency increases
observes punctuation to obtain meaning

(continued)

Figure 2—7   (Continued)

knows how to skim material
previews text for general content
reads silently with greater ease
reads familiar material fluently
uses organization of text to read content material
substitutes word(s) making syntactic or semantic sense for unknown word(s)
will skip a word and read on
views self as an effective reader
takes risks in...
    predicting
    pronunciation
    discussion
uses prior knowledge

V. Writing Strategies
takes risk in spelling
    sharing own writing
    length of text
generates topics and writing ideas
willingly shares writing
willingness to edit (makes contextual changes)
develops revising skills (editing)
    proofreading skills
makes conventional use of...
    capitals
    question marks
    possessives
    contractions
    apostrophes
    paragraphing
attempts spelling generalizations
begins to use dialogue
makes use of descriptive language
is developing awareness of audience
demonstrates development of topic
uses forms appropriate to purpose
views self as effective writer
uses prior knowledge

DID YOU NOTICE . . .
Did you notice that groups should be flexible and ever changing? If you decide to publicly post your different groups on the board or a pocket chart, do not laminate the paper. This will help you remember that these groups are not static and will send the message to students that their progress is continuously changing, just like the different groups in your classroom.

Groups should be modified as a student's knowledge and literacy develops and changes. This is a reality because all students do not progress at the same speed. If the objective has been met or if it is determined to be unrealistic, the group may be dissolved. Based on student performance, objectives may then be formed for different purposes and with different groups of children.

For grouping to be effective, not only do specific instructional objectives need to be defined, but also constant evaluation of students' progress is necessary to maintain the validity of the group. Never forget that the groups are composed of individuals who are constantly changing.

The fact that children's abilities constantly develop as a result of instruction emphasizes the need for continual evaluation, regrouping, and elimination of some groups and formation of new ones. Groups should be viewed as temporary and changing. At the same time, note that not all students need to be included in groups all the time. This is especially true of students capable of working independently. Ms. Cunningham changes group membership every 3 to 5 weeks based on student performance and development.

How do you perform in group situations? Do you learn more after interacting with others during class discussions and activities? What type of assignments would you prefer to do as a group and which would you prefer to complete alone?

In effective classrooms, teachers do not adhere to only one grouping plan. Instead, they use many grouping arrangements, selecting at a given time the one that best enables the students to learn. Realizing this, you may be interested in developing an understanding of the advantages of several different instructional arrangements.

Grouping for Reading Instruction

Effective grouping is the hallmark of quality literacy instruction when the group configurations and instruction within each group are based on continuous assessment of students' strengths and needs.

Such grouping practices are a reality in Ms. Cunningham's classroom because effective, explicit reading instruction occurs within flexible groups that have been composed as a result of continuous assessment to instruction practices. Students in this classroom work in a variety of group configurations including whole-group participation in an interactive read aloud or engaging in shared reading instruction or working independently as the teacher confers with individuals, in small heterogeneous groups at centers, or in small homogeneously guided reading groups in which students are explicitly taught the skills and strategies they need to comprehend texts.

Ms. Cunningham's classroom organizational plan combines a reader's workshop plan for instruction and a Center Activity Rotation System for grouping. Let's look closer to get a better understanding of the specifics of this classroom organization and instructional plan.

What Is Reader's Workshop?

The reader's workshop is a plan for implementing instructional routines and child-centered lessons. It involves instruction through interactive read alouds, shared reading, independent reading, guided reading, and work at learning centers. During these times, teachers introduce and model literacy concepts as students work in whole-group, small-group, and independent configurations with their peers and their teacher.

Interactive Read Aloud

An interactive read aloud involves the teacher presenting a book that has been selected to expand children's experiences, knowledge, and love of reading. To conduct an interactive read aloud, follow these guidelines, which are based on the work of Hoffman, Roser, and Battle (1993):

1. Allot 10 to 15 minutes of uninterrupted time.
2. Select a lively text that will keep students interested.
3. Preread the text.
4. Seat the children so that they can see, hear, and respond.

5. Introduce the book topic to activate background and to promote the sharing of personal experiences.

6. Read expressively.

7. Stop throughout the reading to ask open-ended questions.

8. Encourage lively thought-provoking conversations.

9. Encourage all students to respond.

10. Invite students to make connections to other books read by the same author or similar books by other authors.

Interview four different teachers about whole-class instruction. When do they use whole-group instruction? What are the factors they suggest to make whole-class instruction effective? What do you need to be sure to do to manage a large group of students?

Shared Reading

Working with the entire class is also effective when you want to do a shared reading, introduce a story, topic, or project, or conduct a mini-lesson to emphasize a skill or other information that all students need to learn, practice, or appreciate together as one self-contained body. Some of the advantages of whole-class shared reading instruction include the following:

1. Allowing time for modeled mini-lessons of a targeted concept or strategy

2. Allowing a longer lesson to be presented

3. Allowing students to use each other and the teacher as resources

4. Needing fewer sets of materials

5. Providing individual teacher help to be given, because all students will be doing silent work at the same time

Shared reading of a text that can be seen by everyone provides teachers with a perfect opportunity to model fluent reading and also to teach concepts of print (author, title, directionality).

To conduct a share reading, follow these guidelines:

1. Select a book, song, rap, poem, or chant that is engaging and through which you can provide a targeted mini-lesson.

2. Preread the book and plan by determining your teaching points, storyline, use of pictures and illustrations, notable language patterns, or other features that will enhance literacy development. Mark your stopping times and identify the open-ended questions you'll ask. These will be expanded once the conversation begins.

3. Be sure everyone can see the text. If you aren't using a big book, you may need to use an overhead projector.

4. Introduce the book through exploration. Look at the front and back covers while asking, "What do you see?" Allow enough time for talk.

5. Peruse the cover further, talking about the title, author, and illustrator.

6. Take a picture walk-through and invite children to predict what they think will happen. Be sure to ask them "Why?."

7. Read the book, pausing where appropriate to check the predictions. If there are repeated or predictable parts, invite children to join in with the reading.

8. When you are finished reading, invite responses, question children about their favorite parts, and discuss books by the same authors or similar books by other authors.

9. The book may be reread on other days, inviting more student participation of the reading.

10. After a second reading, conduct a targeted mini-lesson to study a print feature such as sight words, a repeated letter (e.g., all words that start with "t"), a spelling pattern, or a repeated phrase. Words or phrases to be studied may be covered by a post-it note or tape in advance and uncovered as the children and the teacher make the discovery. When the children return to their seats, they can read books at their independent levels and then engage in word work that corresponds to what was presented in the mini-lesson during shared reading. For example, they can put a post-it note everywhere they see the. When finished reading, they can copy the word the on a card, cut it into individual letters, and then put it back together by writing it on a whiteboard or a second note card. While they are busy with these independent activities, the teacher can move among them offering help as needed. This is often referred to as teacher conferring time.

Guided Reading Groups

As the children continue to work independently or at centers that are heterogeneously grouped, the teacher can begin to work with small groups of children who have similar strengths and needs. These groups are often referred to as guided reading groups.

This practice of purposeful grouping allows individualization of instruction and provides for economy of teacher effort and increased student participation. It is more efficient for a teacher to instruct a group of children with similar needs, interests, and purposes than it is to work with a total classroom of separate individuals all day long. When you attempt to use purposeful guided reading groups, you are ensuring individual literacy growth and classroom flexibility. The advantages of same need, homogeneous guided reading include the following:

1. Instruction is better matched to need.
2. The attention of a smaller group of students is easier to ensure.
3. Shy students are less inhibited in sharing with a smaller group.
4. Conversation is not controlled by students with greater knowledge about the topic.
5. Students within the group can be given attention and instruction that is better correlated with their learning needs.
6. Oral reading for all students becomes more realistic.

The meaning of homogeneous groups is often misunderstood and needs clarification. The research showing poor results from homogeneous grouping, which began in 1926 and has continued until recently, is based on attempts at interclass homogeneous grouping, or what today we call tracking. However, most studies of homogeneous grouping that involve differentiated instruction within the reader's workshop classroom have produced favorable results when the groups are flexible. These are often referred to as guided reading groups (Fountas & Pinnell, 2001).

Guided reading groups allow materials to be matched to the learner more effectively than would be possible if instruction were geared to a class. Grouping according to individual performance assessment is beneficial to the learner because the instruction is matched with the learner's interests, needs, purposes, and skills.

Successful grouping practices are contingent on what is to be taught and learned. Groups should be flexibly designed to meet the needs of all students. Continuous assessment will help you keep apprised of such needs. By evaluating students' progress through their behavior and work, informal tests, and teacher checklists, children's literacy can be assessed with the intent of moving them to independent activities. Groups should be flexible and redesigned to support student growth.

With these parameters in mind, Ms. Cunningham began her program by creating the grouping patterns shown in Figure 2–8. Although there are six guided reading groups with different reading needs in this classroom at this time, this fact should not be taken to indicate that there may be six groups within any given class or that there must be at least six groups.

Because grouping is intended to increase students' participation, materials used for instruction are not necessarily uniform for all groups. For instance, the practice of grouping elementary school readers into "red," "blue," and "yellow" birds has often been the extent of grouping. Having each group use the same materials, purposes, and teaching methods, but at differing rates, is highly questionable because purposes, teaching methods, and materials should be modified, changed, and geared to meet the needs and interests of the learners in a specific group in accordance with the various themes being pursued. This can be accomplished by using books at various levels of difficulty. There are many ways to level books, but most teachers refer to the levels provided by Fountas and Pinnell (2001).

Learning Goals and Groups

Like Ms. Cunningham, once you have determined the groups' composition and needs, you will have to plan your instruction. Determining learning goals will help you with individual and group planning.

Goals can be shared with groups of students because they help to communicate the behaviors and anticipated outcomes of the teacher and students. Such communication helps students understand what they are expected to learn and enables them to allocate study time and monitor personal progress.

There are many instances in which a general goal is contrived and then formulated into a specific learning goal. For example, a classroom goal may be to introduce children to the theme of community helpers. The following example is a learning goal derived from such a broad goal:

> After discussing and reading about community helpers, the child will be able to name at least one such community helper and describe his or her role in the community with complete competence.

Figure 2–8   Guided reading groups.

No. of Students	Needs	Grouping Plans
4	Have very positive attitudes about reading but have difficulty with fluent reading because of inability to automatically recognize sight vocabulary. This also interferes with comprehension.	Group A: Utilize child's interests to employ language experience activities to further conceptual development, as well as to introduce and reinforce basic beginning reading, word-recognition, and comprehension skills. Expose students to stories containing patterned language. Develop sight word automaticity through writing and reading the words individually and in many contexts.
4	Able to sound out all of the words and understand what is read but needs to gain confidence to read more fluently.	Group B: Use the neurological impress method (NIM*) to improve fluency.
5	Have become fluent oral readers. Have difficulty with sequential retells and identifying the main idea.	Group C: Model through a think along how to retell what is read, incorporating the main idea. Also model summarizing because this will help identify main idea.
5	Reads at grade level in basal and other texts. Needs to read more widely and for longer periods of time.	Group D: Reinforce basic oral and silent reading skills while extending fluency and mastery of study skills. Encourage wide reading of magazines, trade books, fiction, newspapers, etc. Model partner talk that emphasizes supporting personal responses.
4	Reads independently above grade level. Needs to become more proficient in reading non-narrative texts.	Group E: Develop study skills and aid students in transferring and applying them to content area situations. Expose students to non-narrative books, magazines, and newspapers.
4	Very fluent readers across many genres. Need to develop better summarizing and paraphrasing strategies.	Group F: Model note taking, summarizing, and paraphrasing strategies.

*As Heckelman (1966) noted, NIM is a fairly simple instructional strategy. The steps include the following:
• The teacher selects a text at the student's reading level.
• The teacher sits at the student's desk so that he or she can speak into the student's ear.
• The student's finger rests on top of teacher's finger as they read.
• The teacher moves his or her finger under each word as it is spoken.
• The teacher reads aloud slightly faster than the student reads aloud and models good fluency (chunking phrases and stopping where punctuation dictates).
• The teacher gives the "lead" to the student as the student becomes comfortable with the text.
• The student retells the text to the teacher at the completion of the NIM intervention.

DID YOU NOTICE . . .
Did you notice that the
needs of the students
should dictate what
happens in your class-
room? A student-cen-
tered classroom is one in
which the strengths and
needs of the students
are always taken into
account when the
teacher plans a lesson.

Why is a goal of this type needed or used by the teacher? When asked to state in specific learning terms what one wants to accomplish with a specific lesson, the teacher will be able to determine the following:

1. If the student has accomplished the goal:
   a. If there are related goals within the theme that are to be designed and utilized at this time.
   b. Methods of instruction and performance level needed for implementation of related goals.
2. If the student has not accomplished the goal:
   a. Whether it can be accomplished by the student at this time.
   b. Whether the performance level of the objective was too difficult.
   c. What new methods of instruction are needed to better enable the student to accomplish the goal?

Continuous evaluation depends on a clear explanation of the learning that you are attempting to measure. Although teachers may choose from a variety of evaluative models, you must be careful not to base your total evaluation on a few specified behaviors that have previously been outlined. We should never be so naive as to believe that measured behaviors of learning are the only positive occurrences within the classroom. Teachers must be so aware of their students and their programs that they can intelligently estimate growth that has not yet been planned and/or measured objectively. Effective student learning should dictate what happens in your classroom.

Once Ms. Cunningham determined the guided reading group compositions, which were based on students' needs, she had to determine the methods of instruction for each group. Although she reinforced reading and language arts strategies whenever she taught content-specific subjects, she had also decided to allot 90 minutes each morning for reader's workshop. The schedule for her literacy program includes the following:

Activity	Number of Minutes
Interactive read aloud	10
Shared reading and mini-lesson	15
Independent practice of mini-lesson skill	15
Centers/guided reading groups	50
Total	90

Ms. Cunningham realized that while she was working with children in guided reading groups she would need to ensure that the other children were engaged in experiences that would also enhance their literacy growth. To answer the questions, "What are the other children doing while I'm working with guided reading groups?" Ms. Cunningham used a Center Activity Rotation System (CARS) to support purposeful instruction for the other children. She would manage the entire program, but she would not be involved verbally with the direct instructional input of each activity.

Figure 2–9 Think along: Wilfrid Gordon McDonald Partridge by Mem Fox.

Comprehension Strategy	Teacher says:
Previewing	As I look through this text, I see pictures of a little boy and old people. The little boy looks like he is playing with shells, puppets, and animals. He looks very happy. Some of the adults look happy, too. Some of them look sad though.
Building background	I wonder why the boy is collecting all of those things and putting them in the basket? The title says Wilfrid Gordon McDonald Partridge. I wonder if that is the boy's name. That sure is a long name.
Setting purpose	I wonder why he is playing with all the old people in the story. I am going to read this story to find out why a little kid would play with old people. That doesn't seem like that much fun.
Checking understanding	As I start to read I learn that this little kid, Wilfrid Gordon McDonald Partridge, lives next to an old folks home. That must be why he hangs out with old people.
Monitoring comprehension	After a few pages I learn that he wants to find out what a "memory" is since Miss Nancy at the old folks home has lost her memory. That's like when my grandma forgot my birthday. I guess that's what happens when people get older. So Wilfrid asks all the people in the old folks home to show him what a "memory" is. Ms. Jordon says it's something warm. Mr. Tippett says it's something that makes you cry.
Integrating old information with new information	Oh yeah, I remember one time my mom and dad went to Hawaii for the weekend. I was so sad it made me cry. That's a sad memory. And here it says Miss Mitchell says a "memory" is something that makes you laugh.
Visualizing	I imagine Wilfrid laughing so hard at Miss Nancy's jokes that he rolls on the ground until his tummy aches.
Predicting	And on this page, I read that Mr. Drysdale said a memory is as precious as gold. That reminds me of what I saw as I looked through the book before I read it. I think Wilfrid is going to collect shells, puppets, and animals and give it to Miss Nancy.
Checking prediction	Yep! Now that I have finished the book I learned that Wilfrid was collecting happy, sad, warm, and golden memories so he could show them to Miss Nancy. I think he was trying to find her memory. I guess it worked. She seems happy.
Making connections	This text reminds me of how I feel when I visit my grandpa in Ohio. He is getting old and sometimes he forgets things. But I always try to cheer him up and play games with him. Maybe I will start collecting memories like Wilfrid did so he won't be sad when I leave.
Summarizing	After I read this book I know why a little kid would be playing with old people. Wilfrid really enjoyed being around these people. And he was trying to help them too!"

The small-group instruction occurring at the centers and in the guided reading groups was preceded by a whole-group shared reading during which Ms. Cunningham modeled, through a think along (see Figure 2–9), the comprehension strategies she uses when reading one of their favorite books, Wilfrid Gordon McDonald Partridge by Mem Fox.

Wilfrid Gordon McDonald Partridge by Mem Fox © Kane Miller Book Publishers. Used by permission of Kane Miller Book Publishers, San Diego.

Wilfrid Gordon McDonald Partridge
Written by Mem Fox   Illustrated by Julie Vivas

She chose a book they had previously read because she wanted to review strategies they had previously discussed while focusing on a comprehension strategy that she thought would further enhance comprehension for everyone and also help them with their descriptive writing. After she and the students discussed the story and the strategies she used (see Figure 2–9), she focused on the strategy of visualizing. After attempting this in the target book, she asked them to return to their seats and to use post-it notes to record author passages they could clearly visualize while reading books at their independent level. While they were doing so, Ms. Cunningham circulated among them, conferring with them individually about the author language that helped them to clearly visualize. She also offered other help as needed.

Once she was comfortable that they had begun to efficiently use this strategy as a means to further their reading comprehension (refer to chapter 7) she asked them to move to their center rotations (CARS), which involved working in heterogeneous center groups and also with her in homogeneous groups at the teacher center. Ms. Cunningham continuously observed and assessed the needs of all students throughout all of these literacy activities. As their reading competencies change, so do the groups.

How Does CARS Support Flexible Grouping in a Child-Centered Classroom?

The classroom arrangement facilitated the development of individual needs and accommodated short-term grouping situations. Grouping arrangements were altered as students' skills developed and changed. Grouping patterns (see Figure 2–10) also varied according to the content area being studied at any given time, as well as the changing interests of the students.

CARS: A Model for Organizing and Managing Groups

CARS is a rotation plan designed to help children work independently in small heterogeneous groups while the teacher meets with small guided (homogeneous) groups. The following center activities that occurred in Ms. Cunningham's classroom span a wide range of reading competencies and were designed to engage students in discussion and to offer assistance to each other.

Center 1—Computer Station. At Center 1, which is the computer station, four children can be involved in comprehension and word study activities as they explore Reader Rabbit. They can also practice making words that contain the phonograms being studied. Although Ms. Cunningham creates and implements many integrated thematic units, she chooses words for word study because of the developmental needs of the children rather than those that would be dictated by the theme.

Center 2—Content Area Connections. Center 2 is currently the volcano center. This center changes to accommodate whichever content area topic is being studied. Four children who are reading a range of leveled expository texts as they answer "who, what, when, where, why, and how" questions that have been identified earlier by the class as a part of a KWL exploration can be accommodated at this center. Some of the leveled texts that the children are exploring and discussing are I Can Read About Earthquakes and Volcanoes by Deborah Merrians, Shake, Rattle and Roll: The World's Most Amazing Volcanoes, Earthquakes and Other Forces by Spencer Christian, Volcanoes and Other Natural Disasters by Harriet Griffey, and The Magic School Bus Blows Its Top: A Book About Volcanoes by Joanna Cole.

Center 3—Word Study Adventures. Four children at Center 3 are studying real and nonreal words as they practice writing and spelling them on whiteboards. Dictionaries are available if the children have questions about the meaning or authenticity of a word. Ms. Cunningham analyzes patterns of errors in students' writing assignments to plan developmentally appropriate word study activities. The children were introduced to words that have a one-to-one sound letter correspondence during initial word study activities. Once the children were able to read and spell these words, Ms. Cunningham planned additional word study activities with more complex sound symbol correspondences. Children were also taught sight words for them to feel confident reading sentences and developmentally appropriate texts.

Center 4—Library Explorations. The library serves as Center 4. Here, five children engage in buddy reading and discuss I Like Me by Nancy Carlson. Ms. Cunningham has all the books in the library leveled. She encourages children to read at their independent level when they are in the library. Although these books may be at all three children's independent levels, their instructional levels may not be the same because they are heterogeneously grouped at the centers.

Center 5—Listening and Sharing. Five children at Center 5, the listening center, are listening and reading along with a tape of Alexander and the Wind Up Mouse by Leo Lioni. Ms. Cunningham believes their fluency is increasing by doing this activity. When the children finish their reading they are asked to share their responses to the text and make text connections as they discuss story elements such as characters, setting, and plot.

Center 6—Authors at Work. At Center 6, four children are writing letters to friends to share memories of their weekend experiences. These children are encouraged to think about their experience and to first share it orally with a partner. The partner asks them "who, what, where, when, and how" questions in an attempt to

Figure 2–10   Center activity rotation system (CARS).

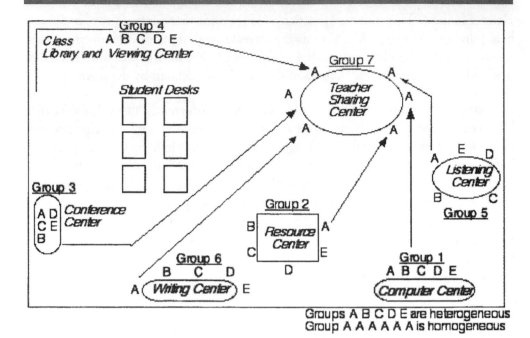

Groups A B C D E are heterogeneous
Group A A A A A A is homogeneous

help them expand what they plan to share in writing. The first draft is always an oral draft. After conferencing with their partner, the children write the second draft. Once finished they again share and discuss their letters. Children are then encouraged to work together to peer edit their letters.

As the children worked at the centers, Ms. Cunningham called children with similar strengths and needs (see Figure 2–8) to work with her at the teacher center where she meets with a group of children who have been homogeneously grouped on the basis of their literacy needs. Depending on students' needs, they may be called to work with Ms. Cunningham in more than one homogeneous group instructional activity. In addition to working with children in groups, Ms. Cunningham also meets with the children individually when they have a need that cannot be addressed in a group.

Note that students are divided into heterogeneous cooperative groups for center rotations. The major feature of each center is that the work being done is further developing each student's literacy. In addition to these heterogeneous center groups Ms. Cunningham works at a teacher center with small, homogeneous groups on a specific skill or information that needs direct, explicit attention. On Friday students work at the centers they missed while they were at the teacher center. Ms. Cunningham doesn't convene the groups at the teacher center but instead works with children at the other centers.

How Much Time Should Children Spend at Centers?

Time at learning centers depends on how much time you have set aside for reader's workshop and whether you are using part of the workshop for an interactive read aloud or a shared reading. Depending on these decisions, time at centers in a 90-

Figure 2–11   Center rotation plan.

Student Name	Centers						Student Name	Centers					
Ashley	6	5	4	3	2	1	Trent	6	5	4	3	2	1
Billy	5	4	3	2	1	6	Trevor	5	4	3	2	1	6
Lajuana	4	3	2	1	6	5	Stacy	4	3	2	1	6	5
Anthony	3	2	1	6	5	4	Jimmy	3	2	1	6	5	4
Angul	2	1	6	5	4	3	Sarah	2	1	6	5	4	3
Malik	1	6	5	4	3	2	Elisabeth	1	6	5	4	3	2
Unique	6	5	4	3	2	1	Ryan	6	5	4	3	2	1
Devin	5	4	3	2	1	6	Alissa	5	4	3	2	1	6
Mike	4	3	2	1	6	5	Andrew	4	3	2	1	6	5
Megan	3	2	1	6	5	4	Dhru	3	2	1	6	5	4
Luke	2	1	6	5	4	3	Mayanka	2	1	6	5	4	3
Nicholas	1	6	5	4	3	2	Precious	1	6	5	4	3	2
							Jacob	6	5	4	3	2	1
							Shannon	5	4	3	2	1	6

minute workshop can range from 15 to 90 minutes. If your workshop time is longer, you can expand the time spent at centers. Work at centers must be purposeful and well planned. It can focus on many areas that support literacy development including decoding, spelling, word work, handwriting, reading along and listening to previously recorded books, paired and buddy reading and writing, writing process, content area study, computer work, and independent library reading.

"How does everyone know what to do?" Shannon's parents asked Ms. Cunningham. She explained that she lists all of the children's names on a chart as seen in Figure 2–11 and beside their names she lists their rotation plan. This approach enables students to take responsibility for their work tasks. While observing Shannon's class, her parents realized that children were grouped by strengths, needs, and interests. The program was very manageable. Ms. Cunningham had designed a program that she was able to manage. Having a plan that you are able to manage is the key factor for success that you will need to remember when you design your program. Shannon's parents asked about the time constraints of this management plan.

Ms. Cunningham explained that, as a new teacher, she had initially been overwhelmed by the evaluation component of many of her colleagues' management plans. Therefore, she had decided to make her program succeed by devising a manageable plan for evaluating everyone's learning. She knew that although she was a dedicated teacher, she also had many personal responsibilities and was, therefore, unable to devote entire evenings or weekends to school work.

She explained that continuous evaluation was an essential part of this program because succeeding assignments were based on the competencies and needs of all the children as they completed their tasks. She decided to have the types of centers remain constant but to change the activities weekly. Children also read independently if they had completed the assigned daily center activities. Ms. Cunningham explained that during the day she made minor assessments whenever time permitted. Immediately after school, she continued the process of assessing and evaluating students' work. Assessments not completed during the day were finished during the evening or the next morning before school.

When developing, evaluating, and replanning a child's personalized program, Ms. Cunningham asked herself the following questions:

1. What are the literacy strengths and needs of this student?
2. Is the student completing the learning tasks successfully?
3. How can I continue to teach and motivate this student?
4. Does the student work better at long or short assignments?
5. How can I best reinforce each student's learning successes?
6. What types of materials are most meaningful and interesting to this student?
7. How can I encourage the student to take more responsibility for his or her learning?
8. How can I best teach this student to transfer what has been learned in one subject area to other areas?
9. How can I best encourage the student to synthesize and generalize the information being learned?
10. How can I best encourage the student to make evaluative decisions about the validity of the information being learned?

By answering these questions, Ms. Cunningham was able to continually assess what had been mastered and to plan the next step for each student. You may also want to pursue these questions if you are interested in implementing Ms. Cunningham's program strategies.

An additional type of grouping that is used by many teachers, especially those in the intermediate grades, is called cooperative grouping.

How Does Cooperative Grouping Work?

Do you remember the last time you were at a party and played Trivial Pursuit? All the members of the team pooled their knowledge to answer the questions. As a team member, you were less threatened when you didn't know an answer than you would have been if you were alone. It was fun, and you learned a lot.

Think for a minute about other group situations in which you've been a member of a team working toward a common goal. For many of us, these have been some of our most intellectually rewarding experiences. As part of a group, we realize that we must all contribute and work together for the success of the group.

Although there are several ways to implement an individualized instructional program—small-group presentations, tutorials, differentiated curriculum—there is one current instructional strategy that seems to be quite successful in helping students learn content area material. It is a strategy that encourages student involvement and accommodates student differences. It has been called cooperative problem solving and collaborative problem solving.

Researchers have demonstrated that groups consisting of high and low achievers, males and females, and students of different ages, races, and social, economic, and ethnic backgrounds can work together effectively and experience significant increases in reading and learning (e.g., Sharan, 1999). Although many educators have found cooperative grouping to be successful, it is still infrequently used as an instructional tool in many classrooms.

Implementing Cooperative Problem Solving in Your Classroom

As you begin to think about implementing cooperative problem solving in your classroom, you will need to consider these three questions:

1. Are your students learning as well as you would like? Think about your students. Are they all interested and learning? If the answer is "no" or "not totally," it is time to make some changes. A well-designed assessment can be translated into statements that will allow you to discuss effectively your ideas about changes with your supervisor or principal.

2. Do I really want to change my current instructional practice? Ask yourself questions such as these: "What are the goals of my program?" "Do I believe that there is a need to alter my program?" "What type of curriculum can I imagine?" "How can I design effective instruction for such diverse groups?" After you answer these questions, think about possible instructional changes that you are able to manage realistically.

3. Do I thoroughly understand the rationale and procedures for implementing cooperative problem-solving?

Once you have answered these questions and decided that you need to change your instruction, you will need to read and think about alternative strategies. As you attempt to evaluate and alter your instructional practices, make changes slowly. It is important for you to be able to manage each change. It is critical to the success of these changes that comprehensive planning occur before actual implementation.

What Are the Procedures for Implementing Cooperative Problem Solving?

The use of cooperative learning tasks that organize students into groups who work together toward a common goal enhance the participation of all members of the group and promote a positive learning environment (Stahl, 1994). You will be able to implement cooperative grouping successfully in your content area by following these seven steps:

1. Identify lesson objectives based on student performance and curriculum standards.
2. Orient students to the management routines.
3. Design cooperative teams.
4. Explain team tasks to each group.
5. Monitor and facilitate group interaction and progress.
6. Prepare students for learning from their textbooks.
7. Evaluate group and individual success.

Let's consider each of these steps in turn.

1. Identifying objectives. Before you formalize your groups, it is important that you specify the academic objectives of the topic being presented. Once you have identified the academic objectives, you will be ready to

DID YOU NOTICE . . .
Did you notice that some of your cooperative groups will work best when not confined to their desks? Allow students to work on the rug, on the floor, while standing up, on the playground, in the hallway, etc. Some of your learning tasks will need a lot of room and working at desks may cause confusion and management problems.

think about potential group size, composition, materials, and room arrangements.

2. Orienting students. As you begin to use cooperative grouping, students need to be oriented to the rationale, procedures, and expected outcomes of this instructional activity. They need to be told that cooperation is the key to successful learning in this model and that their willingness to work toward a common goal as team members will enhance their comprehension of and appreciation for the material that is to be learned.

3. Designing teams.
    a. Team size. How many teams should there be? How big should each team be? When you begin to use grouping practices in your classroom, it is important to keep the groups small so that students can learn to work as group members. Groups of three to six afford opportunities for everyone to engage in discussion as they accomplish the team's objectives. Teams with more than six members often have many problems; some students find it difficult to participate fully because they are afraid of speaking to so many people.
    b. Team composition. Groups should reflect real-life situations. Each team should consist of socially, racially, ethnically, and intellectually diverse groups of boys and girls. If students do not select effective group situations, you may have to design optional combinations to make sure that the group membership is diverse. You should alter group composition only when high-quality, rich, involved learning is not occurring. Sometimes there is a student who simply cannot function in a group. If this is the case, permit the student to work independently.
    c. Materials. Before distributing group tasks, be sure that the materials each group needs are available in your classroom or school library. If the same materials are needed by more than one group, you may need to design a schedule for using them.
    d. Room arrangement. Within the classroom, groups should be arranged so that all members can see each other and can see the assigned task to engage in quiet discussion. Students do not necessarily need to be seated at desks. The room arrangement must emphasize the need to share and work together.

4. Explaining team tasks.
    a. Team member roles. Within each team, students are given responsibilities that must be fulfilled if the team is to function effectively and accomplish the academic objective. Group member roles might include all or some of the following:

    Initiator—a student who explains the objective (what is to be accomplished)

    Summarizer—a student who makes sure that everyone understands what is being learned

    Searcher—a student who finds the materials needed by the group

    Recorder—a student who keeps track of what is being learned

Monitor—a student who makes sure that everyone stays involved

Communicator—a student who shares information with the whole class or the teacher

Students can serve in one or more roles. If roles are assigned, all members of the group realize that they have a significant role to play in determining the group's success.

    b. Team tasks. Each team should be assigned a task that provides information for the whole class. Students will need to know that there are topical objectives that can be met only if the task of the team is accomplished.

5. Monitoring and facilitating group interaction. After students have begun to work on their group assignments, it is important for you to spend time observing each group to determine the problems the members may encounter while working with one another. You may wish to design an observation sheet that can help you record the names of students who talk in each group, students who appear cooperative, students who manage time well, students who are helpful to other team members, and students who accomplish their tasks. If you see that a team is experiencing difficulty, you may wish to intervene and offer new strategies for more effective team functioning.

Knowing when and how to intervene is important, Once you have intervened and provided the needed input, be sure to allow the group to assume responsibility for fulfilling its task. It is important to encourage students to take responsibility for solving each task.

6. Preparing students for learning from their textbooks. Students will need to know how and when to use their textbooks. Before you begin the group tasks, make sure that students are familiar with the book's various parts (table of contents, glossaries, indices, summaries, charts, and diagrams), as well as with the author's approach to the topic. As students within the group use their textbooks, it is important that they comprehend the content adequately. If necessary, you may want to supply a group with copies of various materials that may help them solve their problem (e.g., reference works, journals, periodicals, newspapers, and magazines).

7. Evaluating group and individual success. Cooperative learning is successful only if every member of the team is involved. To be sure that this occurs, you will need to assess each team member's performance. You can accomplish this through observation and frequent assessments including tests, questions asked randomly of individuals within a group, and evaluations of each other's work by team members. You may wish to establish criteria for the group and for the individual. For example, the group task may be to develop a written or oral report, whereas an individual might be asked to write a summary of the report or answer a set of questions about the topic.

Efficient and effective learning can become a reality through cooperative problem solving. To begin implementing this approach in your classroom, you will have to think about the needs of your present instructional plan. If you decide that you want to change your plan, begin by reading about alternatives; then think them through thoroughly and proceed with caution.

It has been suggested that practice makes perfect. Our experience suggests that "planning makes perfect." Without solid instructional plans, thoughtfully assembled materials, grouping arrangements in place, and a management system, reading instruction is less than effective.

QUESTIONS

1. What considerations must be evaluated when you develop a classroom management system?
2. Explain the process and value of interrelating your curriculum through thematic teaching.
3. On what basis should groups be formed, and how should they be used?
4. Of what value are learning objectives in a reading program?
5. Discuss the range of materials and equipment available for instructional purposes.
6. How is individualized instruction facilitated by continuous evaluation?

REFERENCES

Borko, H., Shavelson, R. J., & Stern, P. (1981). Teachers' decisions in the planning of reading instruction. *Reading Research Quarterly, 16,* 449–466.

Eby, J. W., Herrell, A., & Hicks, J. (2001). *Reflective planning, teaching and evaluation: K–12* (3rd ed.). Upper Saddle River, NJ: Merrill Prentice Hall.

Fountas, I., & Pinnell, G. S. (2001). *Guiding readers and writers (grades 3–6): Teaching comprehension, genre, and content literacy.* Portsmouth, NH: Heinemann.

Heckelman, R. G. (1986). N.I.M. revisited. *Academic Therapy, 21,* 411–420.

Hoffman, J. V., Roser, N. L., & Battle, J. (1993). Reading aloud in classrooms: From the modal to a "model." *The Reading Teacher, 46,* 496–503.

Jacobs, H. D. (1997). *Mapping the big picture: Integrating curriculum & assessment K–12.* Alexandria, VA: Association for Supervision and Curriculum Development.

Johnston, P. H. (1997). *Knowing literacy: Constructive literacy assessment.* York, ME: Stenhouse.

Lapp, D., Fisher, D., Flood, J., & Cabello, A. (2001). An integrated approach to the teaching and assessment of language arts. In S. R. Hurley & J. V. Tinajero (Eds.), *Literacy assessment of second language learners* (pp. 1–26). Boston: Allyn & Bacon.

Moss, B. (2003). *25 strategies for guiding readers through informational texts.* San Diego, CA: Academic Professional Development.

Putnam, J. (1998). *Cooperative learning and strategies for inclusion: Celebrating diversity in the classroom* (2nd ed.). Baltimore: Brookes.

Sharan, S. (1999). *Handbook of cooperative learning methods.* New York: Praeger Publishers.

Stahl, R. J. (1994). *Cooperative learning in language arts: A handbook for teachers.* Upper Saddle River, NJ: Pearson.

Tomlinson, C. A. (2001). *How to differentiate instruction in mixed-ability classrooms.* Alexandria, VA: Association for Supervision and Curriculum Development.

3

Assessing Reading Achievement

────────────── CHAPTER GOALS ──────────────

To help the reader

- understand the potential array of reading performances in the classroom.
- recognize the importance of assessment in the instructional process.
- learn formal and informal assessment measures.
- understand how to match readers to texts.

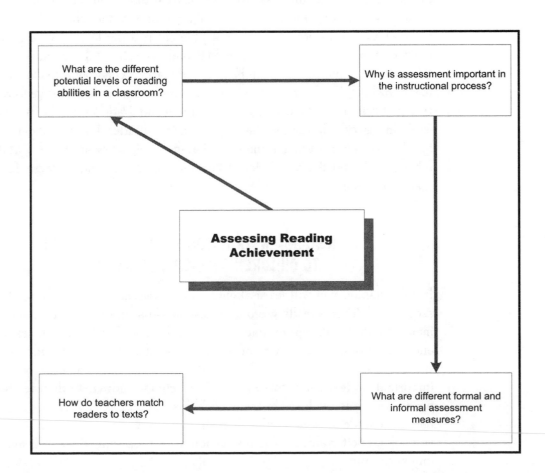

Assessment is a continuous process that you will use constantly as you set goals, identify students' needs, and plan instruction. In this chapter, we will provide information about assessment and instruction that you can use to make decisions about reading instruction for each student in your classroom.

Let's begin this chapter by finding out what you already know about literacy assessment. Identify the literacy-related assessments that you are familiar with and have used in the past. Also, write about how you would use these assessments in your own classroom.

We'll begin here with background information about why initial and ongoing assessment in your classroom is so important. Then, we'll share vignettes from Kelly's first grade classroom and Larry's fifth grade classroom to give you a sense of how two experienced teachers use assessment in their classrooms. In the remainder of this chapter we provide you with important background information that Kelly and Larry know—and that you should know—so that you can make appropriate instructional decisions in your classroom.

If you have ever worked in a classroom, you will know that not all children in the same grade are reading with the same proficiency. Although this fact is common knowledge, due largely to media interest in public school reading achievement, the actual range of reading proficiency found among students within a single classroom can be astonishing. According to Goodlad (1966) the "broad spread from high to low achiever steadily increases with the upward movement of heterogeneous classes (relatively homogeneous in chronological age) through the school" (p. 34). Thus, in the past as well as now, the range of different reading levels increases as children move up through the grades in school (Kamil, Mosenthal, Pearson, & Barr, 2000). We'll draw on information from Kelly's and Larry's classrooms to illustrate what we mean. In Kelly's first grade classroom, children's reading levels range from emergent readers to children who can read at the mid-second grade level. The range of reading levels in Larry's fifth grade classroom is much broader, however. Some children in his classroom are reading at the second grade level, a few are reading at the middle school level, and the remainder of his children reflect reading levels for all of the grades between.

READING INSTRUCTION NEEDS TO BE GEARED TO CHILDREN'S READING PERFORMANCE

In this chapter, you will learn about various assessment tools that can help you to ascertain children's reading proficiencies and—based on this information—how to match children with appropriate texts for guided and independent reading experiences. Although it is important to be prepared to help your students by understanding the range of reading levels that may exist within any classroom, it is more important, indeed vital, to your role in teaching reading, to discover the reading needs of each individual. To accomplish this complex task, your first step is to evaluate your students to determine their strengths and needs. Through this evaluation, you will be better able to plan instruction to develop individual skills and strategies for every child.

To begin meaningful assessment, you need to consider the following points:

1. The strengths and needs of the students.
2. The role of evaluation in your classroom.
3. The knowledge brought by the students to a specific topic.
4. The skills and background knowledge needed to pursue different topics of study.

In thinking about these areas, you are already evaluating the competencies of your students. Let's take a look at how Kelly and Larry draw on these ideas and use assessment to make decisions to help them craft appropriate literacy instruction for their children. We'll begin by visiting Kelly's first grade classroom.

Vignette 1: Kelly's First Grade Classroom

Kelly Moore is a first grade teacher in California. Assessment in Kelly's classroom is continuous and begins before she personally meets each child. Like many states, kindergarten isn't mandatory in California, but because most children attend, Kelly studies the folders of those who have attended kindergarten at her school to gain an understanding of their early literacy experiences. As she reads the folders, she jots notes on an individual profile she has designed for each child (see Table 3–1). She wants to know

1. The primary language spoken in the home.
2. Each child's proficiency in speaking English
3. The child's performance on early literacy tasks (phonemic awareness, alphabet recognition, concept of print, sound/letter correspondences, word recognition, reading, and writing).

After looking through the folders that the kindergarten teachers have sent to her, Kelly has a better picture of what her incoming students' reading behaviors are like. But she continues her daily assessments as she meets and gets to know her students.

On the First Day of School. Kelly starts to build community in the classroom from the first day. She doesn't do any formal assessments because she wants the students to feel comfortable and to get to know one another. She does, however, do lots of "kid watching." The first day of school is devoted to sharing feelings and past experiences, building relationships, and understanding the unique characteristics of

TABLE 3–1
Initial Student Literacy Information

Child's Name	Language Spoken in the Home	Phonemic Awareness Knowledge	Can Identify Letters— Which Letters?	Analysis of Reading Sample

each child. During the first day she asks questions and encourages responses to the whole group or to a partner. During this time, she makes mental notes (that later get written down) about each child's oral language. She asks herself questions like "Did José feel comfortable speaking in front of a whole group?" "To a partner?" "Does Maria speak in complete sentences?" "How does Yesenia's first language of Spanish impact her English syntax?" "Who is dominating the conversations?" "How many languages are spoken in this classroom?" She also pays close attention to the children on the playground to see how their "playground talk" does or does not come back into the classroom after recess. Teachers need to acknowledge this playground talk and use it to teach the academic language of school. This talk is not seen as a deficit but is useful to teachers to understand students' prior knowledge and experiences with language and to plan subsequent instruction.

During the First Week of School. Kelly groups the entire class of 20 into 4 groups randomly as she introduces literacy centers. Because she does not know the exact reading levels and capabilities of all of her students, the literacy activities are designed so that each student can feel successful. The idea is to get the students into cooperative groups quickly so that she can begin more thorough individualized assessments. Here are some examples of the centers Kelly uses.

Listening center: Students listen to a story on tape or CD while following along in the text. As Kelly observes them she becomes aware of their knowledge of concepts of print and word.

Library: The students explore books, and at the end of the day they are asked to select their favorite book. Kelly notes the titles of these texts so that she can understand the interests of her students. This information helps her plan instruction based on the motivation and interests of her students.

Writing: Students use different colored paper, markers, colored pencils, stickers, crayons, etc., to express how they feel about the first week of school. Kelly encourages them to write words and draw pictures. This gives her an idea of the writing behaviors of each student.

Computers: Because she is not sure of her students' proficiency with technology, she assigns them to work on KidPix. This program allows students to use the mouse and keyboard to draw pictures, write letters and words, identify symbols, etc. By glancing over to the computer center during her one-on-one assessment time, she can see what students know about computers.

Initial Assessment. Because Kelly has each child's folder from kindergarten, she has a place to start instruction. However, with new students, for whom she has no data, she must collect all of the information needed to design appropriate instruction for each of them. The following is an example of how Kelly would assess Anthony, a child who came to her classroom with no kindergarten records.

DID YOU NOTICE . . .
Did you notice how Kelly is assessing students literacy behaviors during this center time? She can note students word and print knowledge, book selection, writing proficiency, and technology knowledge and proficiency informally as students work independently at these literacy centers.

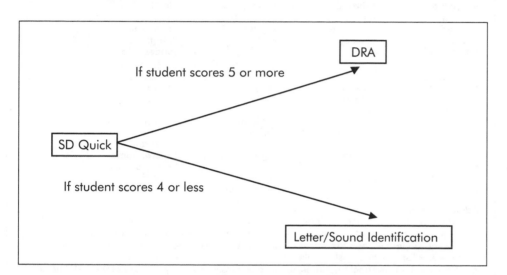

The graphic organizer shows how Kelly starts assessing students using the San Diego Quick (SD Quick) Assessment. If students score 5 words or more, she will use Developmental Reading Assessment (DRA) passages according to the score on the SD Quick. If the student scores 4 or less, Kelly moves to the Letter/Sound Identification. More assessments may follow each of these assessments if necessary.

1. First, Kelly would administer the SD Quick, so that she could understand a child's approximate reading level. Kelly wants to determine Anthony's reading level on words out of context so she knows approximately where to begin when assessing Anthony's ability to read narrative and non-narrative reading passages. Administering this assessment gives the teacher a starting point. A sample of the SD Quick is included in Figure 3–1.

Although the words on the San Diego Quick are out of context, they do tell Kelly a bit about a child's sight word vocabulary and knowledge about sound/letter correspondence. This is important so sight word and word study instruction can be planned based on student needs.

2. If Anthony is unable to read 5 or more of the words on the preprimer list, Kelly would ask Anthony to identify the letters of the alphabet and to complete a

Figure 3–1 San Diego Quick Assessment.

Preprimer	Primer	1	2	3
see	you	road	our	city
play	come	live	please	middle
me	not	thank	myself	moment
at	with	when	town	frightened
run	jump	bigger	early	exclaimed
go	help	how	send	several
and	is	always	wide	lonely
look	work	night	believe	drew
can	are	spring	quietly	since
here	this	today	carefully	straight

4	5	6	7	
decided	scanty	bridge	amber	
served	business	commercial	dominion	
amazed	develop	abolish	sundry	
silent	considered	trucker	capillary	
wrecked	discussed	apparatus	impetuous	
improved	behaved	elementary	blight	
certainly	splendid	comment	wrest	
entered	acquainted	necessity	enumerate	
realized	escaped	gallery	daunted	
interrupted	grim	relativity	condescend	

8	9	10	11	
capacious	conscientious	zany	galore	
limitation	isolation	jerkin	rotunda	
pretext	molecule	nausea	capitalism	
intrigue	ritual	gratuitous	prevaricate	
delusion	momentous	linear	risible	
immaculate	vulnerable	inept	exonerate	
ascent	kinship	legality	superannuate	
acrid	conservatism	aspen	luxuriate	
binocular	jaunty	amnesty	piebald	
embankment	inventive	barometer	crunch	

Administration
1. Type out each list of 10 words on index cards.
2. Begin with a card that is at least 2 years below the student's grade-level assignment.
3. Ask the student to read the words aloud to you. If he or she misreads any on the list, drop to easier lists until he or she makes no errors. This indicates the base level.
4. Write down all incorrect responses, or use diacritical marks on your copy of the test. For example, *lonely* might be read and recorded as *lovely*. *Apparatus* might be recorded as *a per' a tus*.
5. Encourage the student to read words he or she does not know so that you can identify the techniques he or she uses for word identification.
6. Have the student read from increasingly difficult lists until he or she misses at least 3 words.

Analysis
1. The list in which a student misses no more than 1 of the 10 words is the level at which he or she can read independently. Two errors indicate the instructional level. Three or more errors identify the level at which reading material will be too difficult for him or her.
2. An analysis of a student's errors is useful. Among those that occur with greatest frequency are the following:

Error	*Example*
reversal	*ton* for *not*
consonant	*now* for *how*
consonant clusters	*state* for *straight*
short vowel	*cane* for *can*
long vowel	*wid* for *wide*
prefix	*inproved* for *improved*
suffix	*improve* for *improved*
miscellaneous	(accent, omission of)

3. As with other reading tasks, teacher observation of student behavior is essential. Things such as posture, facial expression, and voice quality may signal restlessness, lack of assurance, or frustration while reading.

[From: LaPray, Margaret, and Ross, Ramon. The graded word list: Quick reading ability. *Journal of Reading*, Vol. 12 (January 1969): 305–307. (Used with permission of the authors and the International Reading Association.)]

Figure 3–2   Letter/sound assessment. Used with permission.

sound/letter identification assessment. She would ask Anthony to identify the letter, the sound, and a word that begins with each letter of the alphabet. A sample of the Letter/Sound Assessment is included in Figure 3–2.

This assessment tells Kelly what letters and sounds the child knows. This is important so that Kelly can plan subsequent phonics instruction and pick texts that include words with familiar and unfamiliar sound/letter correspondence.

3. If Anthony is able to read 5 or more of the words on the preprimer list of the SD Quick, she would continue until she found an approximate reading level. To follow up, she would administer the DRA. Kelly administers the DRA individually to each student. Each student reads a passage to Kelly and retells the story. Kelly records errors, fluency rate, and comprehension. A sample of the DRA is included in Figure 3–3.

The purpose of administering the DRA is to determine an instructional reading level for each student. This will be helpful when Kelly groups students homogeneously for explicit small group instruction.

Kelly does not spend more than 20 minutes formally assessing each child during the first week. However, she gains additional information through observing

Page 1

DRA Reading Worksheet *Trouble at the Beaver Pond* Level 38

Name _____ Grade ____ Teacher _____ Date _____

INTRODUCTION TO THE TEXT: PREVIEWING AND PREDICTING

T: "This wilderness story tells about a beaver family and how the mother saves her kits. Please read the first page aloud." **Show the student where to stop reading.**

RUNNING RECORD	Take a running record as the student reads. Use the notations provided to assure standardization across classrooms, schools, and contexts.

Accurate Reading: √   Repetition: √√√¹R or √√√R   Omission: - / mess   Appeal/You Try It: A / Y

Substitution: Aunt - student / Aunty - text   Self-Correction: now | SC / all   Insertion: help / -   Teacher Told: - / all | T

	E	SC	E M S V	SC M S V
The mother beaver rested by the log dam for a moment and watched her young son and daughter playing on the shore of the beaver pond. She was uneasy about their being on land. They belonged in the water, where they could move quickly and surely. They could dive deep, and they could swim underwater like two big brown fish. The mother beaver climbed out of the water and began packing mud into the dam. Her broad, hairless tail lay flat on the dam behind her, supporting her while she worked. Her strong front paws looked like little hands as they packed the mud into place. Again and again the mother beaver stopped working to watch her kits. Their father was far upstream, cutting down more trees for the dam.				
Total				

Direct the student to read the rest of the book independently.

T: "Now you read the whole book by yourself. When you have finished, please come to me so we can have a conversation about the story. I've already read the book, and I think we'll have a good talk."

Circle accuracy rate: (word count = 130)

%	100	99	98	97	96	95	94	93	92	91	90
Miscues	0	1	2–3	4	5–6	7	8–9	10	11–12	13	14

Circle self-correction rate:

Self-correction formula: E+SC / SC	Excellent 1:2–1:3	Good 1:4–1:6	Needs Improvement 1:7+

each child at the centers and during all of the whole-group, small-group, partner, and individual learning times. Kelly is careful not to frustrate her children by giving them too many formal assessments. The information she has gathered during the first week is enough to get started. She will learn a lot more about the students once she has them grouped homogeneously for small-group explicit instruction. She can usually assess all students within the first week of school and be ready for small group instruction beginning week 2.

Ongoing Assessments. After the first week of school Kelly begins to assess during small-group instruction. She feels that she can learn about her students' concepts of print, phonemic awareness, fluency, and comprehension through observa-

Figure 3–3 (Continued)

READING STRATEGIES USED   Page 2

At difficulty the student problem-solved using:
_____ pictures _____ rereading _____ letter/sound _____ letter/sound clusters _____ syllables
_____ multiple attempts _____ meaning _____ syntax _____ appeals for help _____ pausing
_____ no observable behaviors

Analysis of miscues:
Number of tolds given by the teacher_____ Number of miscues that interfered with meaning
Number of self-corrections or attempts to self-correct using: meaning _____ syntax _____
visual information _____

FLUENCY AND EXPRESSION   The student read this passage with:

Fluency	all word by word with some long pauses between words	mostly word by word with some short phrases	a mixture of short and long phrases	generally in longer, meaningful phrases with a few word-by-word slow downs for problem solving
Expression	little/no change in intonation; little awareness of punctuation	mostly monotone with some expression	some expression and attention to punctuation	effective expression throughout with attention to punctuation and syntax

COMPREHENSION AND RESPONSE
When the student has completed the book use the essential questions and any combination, variation, or sequence of the additional prompts and extenders to promote a conversation. The book should be available to the student during the conversation.

Essential Questions:	Some Additional Prompts:	Conversation Extenders:
• Summarize the story in your own words. Include important characters, events, and details. (literal) • What do you think is one of the author's most important messages/ideas in this story? Tell why. (interpretive)	• What were some of the problems that the characters experienced in this story, and how were they resolved? (literal) • What do the characters learn in this story? (literal or interpretive) • How do the characters change in this story and why? (interpretive) • What do you think is the most important event in the story? Tell why. (reflective)	• Tell me more about what you're thinking. • Could you say more about why you think that happened? • Talk about what else happened. • What happens in the story that makes you think that? • Keep going. • I'm confused. Can you show me where it says that? • Would you like to add anything?

RECORD OF CONVERSATION   Record the child's responses (i.e., key phrases):

tions and questioning during her interactions with them in daily literacy instruction. If she feels the need to assess the students in a more formal way, she may administer other assessments.

Table 3–2 shows what information Kelly has gathered about a student's reading ability throughout the year. This one-page form is helpful to get a snapshot picture of each student's reading progress. It is helpful to show parents and administrators as well. More detailed assessment information (running records, comprehension tests, phonemic awareness, oral language, and writing assessments) can be kept in a child's assessment folder.

Table 3–3 shows how students can be grouped according to needs and instructional levels. After initial assessments are made in September, the students in this

TABLE 3–2
Student Individual Profile

Student: _____ Teacher: _____ School: _____

D.O.B.: _____ Grade: _____

Instructional Reading Level:

Preprimer	*DRA–8 (Kindergarten)*	*DRA–16 (First)*
September	*February*	*June*

	September	February	June
Letter/Sound Assessment	Knows most consonant letters and sounds; confuses short vowel sounds		
SD Quick	Knows "at, go, can"; did not attempt initial sounds on most words; said "my" for "me"		
DRA		Can decode most passages at level 8; comprehension good; needs a lot of prompting at level 10	Level 16—fluent reading, decoding well, retell is accurate including main idea and details
Other (CORE, Observation Survey, SOLOM, etc.)	Knows book handling skills, some phonemic awareness— limited ability to rhyme		

DID YOU NOTICE . . .
What did you notice about the reading strengths and needs of this student? What might you recommend as appropriate instruction for this student? What materials could you use? Is there anything you do not know about the literacy proficiencies of this child by looking at this running record?

class are grouped into five small homogeneous groups. Continuous assessment ensures that groups are ever changing and meeting the needs of the students.

Throughout the first half of the year, Kelly also conducts a running record on each child weekly during small group instruction. Figure 3–4 shows an example of how and why Kelly would do a running record with Anthony, the child we introduced you to earlier.

This assessment takes no more than 5 minutes and proves invaluable to her instruction with each individual learner because Kelly can determine what reading strategies a child is using. While a child is orally reading text, Kelly is able to note problems with graphophonics, semantics, and syntax. Graphophonics refers to sound-symbol relationships, semantics refers to the meaning children make with respect to their reading, and syntax refers to knowledge about the structure of the language. Kelly always asks for a retell after the child reads a passage so comprehension can be assessed. Gathering information from a running record directly affects the instructional focus of future small group lessons. Kelly can also see patterns that are emerging among her readers and can plan lessons based around similar needs.

TABLE 3-3
Student Groups Using DRA Levels

Date: September 2006

DRA Levels					
14+	Audrey	Kailey			
12	Betty	Bart			
10					
8					
6	Johanna				
4	Amir	Shannon	Devin	Jose B.	
2	David	Angela	Harrison		
1	Jim	Darrell			
A	Luis	Elizabeth			
Letters/Sounds	Juan	Michelle	Yesenia	Jose S.	

As Kelly's students gain proficiency with reading, she assesses individual students through conferencing during independent reading. Sometimes she will sit with a reader for up to 15 minutes as she notes information about their fluency, comprehension, and decoding. To get a quick picture of what her students look like as readers, Kelly uses the one-page form shown in Table 3–4. She is able to capture a little bit about each of her students' reading behaviors using this form.

For a more in-depth picture of the students' reading behaviors Kelly uses 436 index cards held together by a brass ring. She can take more detailed notes about the

Figure 3–4   Running record.

Name: _Anthony_   Date: _10/5_   Teacher: _Williams_

PP		Primer		1		2	
see	✓	you	✓	road	*ride rid*	our	
play	✓	come	*came*	live	✓	please	
me	✓	not	✓	thank	✓	myself	
at	✓	with	✓	when	*went*	town	
run	✓	jump	✓	bigger	✓	early	
go	✓	help	*hop*	how	✓	send	
and	✓	is	✓	always	*away*	wide	
look	✓	work	✓	night	✓	believe	
can	✓	are	✓	spring	✓	quietly	
here	✓	this	✓	today	✓	carefully	

Comments: _Anthony's instructional level is primer. He accurately identifies beginning sounds but needs more instruction w/ vowels. Will begin w/ beginning of 1st grade text for running record._

TABLE 3–4
Notes About Student Reading Behaviors

Juan 9/3—Trouble decoding; retell weak	Mary 9/5—Confusing B and D; fluency slow	Anthony 9/6—Needs practice with sight words, phonemic awareness	Kaitlyn 9/3—Does well at predicting	Jose
Maria	Marco	Yesenia	Erik	Amanda
Terrence	Adrienne	Darrel	Angel	Malik
Lajuana	Doumas	Vicki	Reina	Ricky

students' reading using individual student cards. She can still note strengths, areas for improvement, text read, and plans for future instruction on each individual index card. This is a nice way to capture reading over time and will be helpful when she has conferences with parents and administrators about a student's progress.

Vignette 2: Larry's Fifth Grade Classroom

Do you remember Larry from chapter 1? If so, you may recall some of the many different ways that he spent time at the beginning of the school year getting to know his students as individuals and as literacy learners. Recall, for example, that, like Kelly, Larry sees one of his first assessment tasks as getting to know his children and their families because he knows that he can make more effective instructional decisions for his children if he knows them and their strengths, needs, interests, concerns, hopes, and fears.

7 × 9 Trouble! © by Claudia Mills. Illustrations © G. Brian Karas. Used with the permission of Farrar Straus Giroux

Recall, also, that Larry spends time at the very beginning of the school year getting to know his students as readers and writers. In chapter 1 we provided an overview of some of the many different formal and informal assessment measures that Larry uses to get to know his children as literacy learners. For example, Larry begins to get a sense of his students' strengths and needs when they complete one of their first assignments—the creation of a written autobiography. (Please note that we talk more about teaching and assessing writing in chapter 10.) Assessment doesn't just happen at the beginning of the year for Larry, however. Assessment, especially informal assessment, is an ongoing process that Larry uses daily to make instructional decisions. More formal assessments—typically in the form of standardized tests—occur, at most, only several times a year.

Like Kelly, Larry spends time at the very beginning of the year determining his children's reading levels so that he can group them appropriately for reading instruction. Because Larry teaches fifth grade and his children have been in school for some time, he can usually find information about their reading levels from the previous year in each child's cumulative record file. Larry is aware, however, that even if he receives general information about each child's reading levels and capabilities in their cumulative record files, children may lose ground in their literacy development during the summer months (Allington & McGill-Franzen, 2003). Consequently, he uses the information he learns about each child from the cumulative folders as a general guideline. He knows that the literacy assessment of his children must start at the beginning of the year and continue throughout the year.

During the First Week of School. Because Larry teaches fifth grade, the cumulative record folders that he examines for each of his children provide a profile of each child's literacy achievement across time. Larry uses this past information as well as new information that he collects about each child during the first week of school to place his children in small groups for reading instruction at their appropriate reading levels. Here's what Larry does during the first week of school, and his reasoning. First, Larry knows that he is going to want to determine each child's independent reading level (i.e, the approximate grade level at which a child can read on her or his own), instructional reading level (i.e., the approximate grade level at which a child can read with the assistance of a teacher), frustration reading level (i.e., the level at which a child cannot accurately read a text even with assistance), and listening comprehension level (i.e., the child's potential reading level). We will have much more to say about each of these reading levels later in this chapter.

Ongoing Assessment. From experience, Larry knows that the information contained in his children's cumulative record files provides enough data to give him a general sense of his children's reading levels so that he can tentatively place his children in small groups for reading instruction. Using this initial information, Larry constructs tentative reading groups before he even meets his children. Next, Larry uses several whole-group assessment measures to begin to get a sense of each child's literacy strengths and needs. For example, Larry does a whole-group written retelling with his class the first week of school. Here's how he does it. He reads a segment of a text or a short book aloud to his class. Then, he asks the students to retell the story in writing after they have heard it. As students write about the story they have just heard, they reveal information such as their listening comprehension abilities, knowledge of story structure, comprehension abilities, and writing abilities.

Larry knows that he will need to assess his students individually; however, he can't assess all of them at once and in depth, so here's how he decides which children to assess individually first and in more depth. First, Larry assesses the children enrolled in his class who are new to the district and do not yet have cumulative record files. Second, Larry assesses his lowest readers because he knows that it is going to be imperative not to place them in groups with reading materials that are too hard and frustrating for them. Last, Larry assesses the children reading at and above grade level.

You may be wondering how Larry assesses his children individually. He uses a modified version of an Informal Reading Inventory (IRI) to determine and/or check his children's reading levels. Please note that we provide much more information about IRIs later in the chapter. Typically, initial individual assessments in Larry's room take from 5 to 10 minutes per child—depending on the extent of the assessments. Larry spends more time initially assessing children for whom he has no cumulative record information and the children who are the lowest readers in his classroom.

What are the other children doing while Larry administers individual reading assessments during the first week of class? Like Kelly, Larry sets up several centers that his children work independently at and rotate through while he is assessing children individually. Here are some examples of the centers that Larry arranges.

Reading center. Children at this center select texts that they can read silently or with a partner.

Writing center(s). Recall from chapter 1 that Larry asks his children to write autobiographies the first week of school. After providing some whole-group instruction about this writing assignment, Larry develops a center where children can work on writing, revising, and illustrating their autobiographies.

Listening center(s). Larry has several listening centers at the back of his room. At these centers, children can listen to books on tape as they follow along with their own copies of the text being read.

Throughout the rest of this chapter, we provide a close-up look at a host of additional different formal and informal assessment measures that teachers like Kelly and Larry use in their classrooms. We explain the conceptual rationale behind various different formal and informal assessment measures. Additionally, we provide specific information about how to engage in the various different kinds of assessments that we discuss.

Stepping Back From the Vignettes: Kelly and Larry's Background Knowledge About Assessment

Classroom teachers like Kelly and Larry use many kinds of data to make decisions about children's instruction. Just as insights are gained from ongoing informal observations of children's performances during reading and writing, teachers' instructional decisions should also be influenced by both informal and systematic measures of assessment. For example, an informal teacher observation may occur when a kindergarten teacher notices that a child in her classroom takes a book and turns it right-side-up before pretend reading. This informal observation may indicate to the teacher that the child possesses important book-handling knowledge. More formal and systematic assessments of a child's literacy abilities would be reflected in a child's literacy scores on a standardized test. Experienced teachers like Kelly and Larry have a lot of background knowledge about assessment that they draw upon as they make instructional decisions. In the remainder of this chapter, we provide three broad categories of assessment-related background information that Kelly, Larry, and other experienced teachers draw on as they teach. The first category involves norm- and criterion-referenced measures of assessment. The second category focuses on informal classroom based assessment measures. The final category involves matching readers to texts that are appropriate for them.

NORM- AND CRITERION-REFERENCED ASSESSMENT MEASURES

Do you recall taking standardized tests when you were in school? We're guessing that you do. Most students who go through schooling in the United States recall taking yearly standardized tests in elementary and middle school, for example, SATs in high school and GREs for graduate school admission, to name a few of the common standardized tests. Although evaluation may seem to be a contemporary topic, it is not new. Early forms of school evaluation consisted of oral recitation because the major goal of most colonial educators was to train students to recite from memory. As written materials became more readily available, measures of evaluation began to include essay or problem-solving tests. Standardized testing became part of educational evaluation at the turn of the century when Alfred Binet and Therese Simon (1905) developed standardized intelligence tests in an attempt to differentiate children with "normal" intelligence from those who had special learning needs. Binet and Simon eventually broadened their studies to include the measurement of intelligence of all children.

Standardized assessment measures have become more and more prominent in U. S. schools in the last three decades. For example, "prior to 1970 no state used criterion-referenced testing [we'll explain criterion-referenced tests shortly] and today every state mandates the use of some standardized test" (Hoffman, Paris, Salas, Patterson, & Assaf, 2003, p. 619). Although standardized tests have been criticized as being unfair, narrow, and nonpredictive of school performance, "more and more states are imposing 'high-stakes' consequences for performance on their testing plans" (Hoffman et al., 2003, p. 619). For example, in some states and districts, if schools consistently score low on standardized tests, principals may be removed from their positions and reassigned. It is beyond the purview of this chapter to discuss the reasons for the increased use of and reliance on standardized tests by states and districts. For an in-depth discussion of this topic, please see Pennington (2004). Because of the importance placed upon these formal assessment measures in every state, you should understand them. It is also important for you to know that standardized tests can be useful in some situations and contexts and problematic in others. The standardized tests themselves are often not the problem; rather, it is the misuse of tests that can cause difficulties. Standardized tests can provide teachers and parents with useful information about children's knowledge, and they can be useful for teachers as they plan instruction.

Understanding and Using Norm-Referenced and Criterion-Referenced Reading Tests

Both norm-referenced and criterion-referenced tests can be useful instruments to measure a student's reading ability. The basic difference between the two types of tests lies in what the test results are referenced to (or compared with). Norm-referenced tests assess performance of a task in relation to the achievement levels of other people who have taken the same test; criterion-referenced tests assess student performance of a task but do not compare the results with those of a previously established population. Norm-referenced test results are interpreted in statistical terms including percentile rankings, stanine scores, and grade levels. Criterion-referenced tests provide information regarding placement on a performance continuum relative to a given behavior, the extreme ends being mastery and nonmastery of the task.

Norm-referenced testing became prominent in the 1930s as one dimension of the process of evaluation. It is useful to think of norm-referenced tests as survey instruments, designed to measure competency in a broad manner, rather than as diagnostic tools (Stanley & Hopkins, 1972). They are useful for measuring students' progress when administered infrequently (i.e., once a year), and nationally normed tests provide an "external basis of comparison" (Shepard, 1979, p. 29) that highlights a student's or program's relative strengths and weaknesses in the national context. State and local norms are often available, and these may provide a more useful and more accurate picture of individual and program accomplishments.

Norm- and criterion-referenced measures differ in the ways in which they are designed, as well as in the type of information conveyed through students' responses. Criterion-referenced tests can function well as diagnostic instruments due to the precise nature of the test items. Items on such a test must reflect competencies within a specified behavioral domain. For a criterion-referenced instrument to be effective, this domain of behavior must be well-defined. According to Nitko (1980), "a domain is well-defined when it is clear to both the test developer and the test user which categories of performance (or which kinds of tests) should and should not be considered as potential test items. Well-defined domains are a necessary condition for criterion referencing since the basic idea is to generalize how well an examinee can perform in a broader class of behaviors, only a few of which happen to appear on a particular test form" (p. 465). Table 3–5 provides a comparison of norm- and criterion-referenced tests.

The scoring of a criterion-referenced test should be designed to provide information about the already developed skills and strategies of students, as well as their existing needs. If behavioral objectives have been written to define the competencies to be tested within a specified domain, and if the test items accurately reflect these objectives, the problem of assessing the child's degree of proficiency is minimized. For example, a criterion-referenced test should provide descriptive information regarding an individual's degree of competence on a specified task. A criterion might be "Can Bart recite the Gettysburg Address?" The criterion is clear, and the assessment is relatively simple. Here Bart's performance is compared with an established criterion; that is, he can or cannot recite the Gettysburg Address. The test is criterion-referenced.

The criterion-referenced instrument may be designed to aid the classroom teacher in assessing individual competencies and designing alternative programs based on individual needs. The norm-referenced tests can also look at the individual's competency in relation to that of others in the group. A question that could be asked on a norm-referenced test is, "How do the various students rank on the Gettysburg Address test?" Each of these measures assesses the same behaviors,

TABLE 3–5
Comparison of Norm-Referenced and Criterion-Referenced Tests

Test Feature	Norm-Referenced	Criterion-Referenced
Test design	Design is related to subject matter information and process skills.	Design is related to specific instructional behavioral objectives.
Item preparation	Designed to determine variances among students.	Designed to measure individual competency on a given task.
Item types	Many types are used (multiple choice, true-false, completion).	Many types are used (multiple choice, true-false, completion).
Item difficulty	Moderate; designed to determine a middle range.	Wide variance, but with adequate instructional preparation, responses are generally correct.
Interpreting results	A student's accomplishments are compared with those of a norm group by computing his or her subscore or total test score.	A student's performance on a specified behavioral item is determined by comparing his or her response to the correct one.
Test availability	Consult Oscar Buros' *Mental Measurements Yearbook* to ascertain information about norm-referenced tests.	The tests, which are often designed by teachers for use in their classrooms, may now also be maintained as part of the management systems of many basal reading programs.
Test use	Used to determine a comparative score between one pupil and a normative group and to determine global student achievement.	Used to diagnose student strengths and needs and to evaluate an instructional program.

but each has a different purpose. Therefore, when you are selecting or developing an instrument for use in your classroom, it is necessary to specify your reasons for testing and the criterion being tested. Whether you use criterion- or norm-referenced evaluation, you will need to select your instrument very carefully.

Until recently, the practice has been to evaluate students against some norm group, whether their own or an arbitrarily chosen group. This has at least two disadvantages: (a) it makes the same children fall at the bottom in every situation, and (b) it encourages the development of curriculum unrelated to the needs of the students. Because of these and other disadvantages, the use of properly designed criterion-referenced tests is encouraged by educators. Two advantages of criterion referenced tests are that (a) comparison problems are minimized because students are being evaluated only against themselves, and (b) criterion-referenced tests may be designed by the classroom teacher to measure a specific behavior.

A test devised by a classroom teacher is often called an informal test. It can be either norm- or criterion-referenced. A standardized test can also be either norm- or criterion-referenced. The distinction between informal and standardized tests is that the latter has been administered to many students and standardized before being used in an actual situation. Whether you are using an informal or a standardized test, it is essential that the test be valid and reliable.

Validity

The basic question to be answered is "Does the test measure what you think it is measuring?" For example, if a college instructor announces a test and says that it will measure understanding and application and if the test actually consists of five questions related to details on a footnote on page 47, is it measuring what he or she thinks (or says) it is? Obviously not. That test would have no content validity. If, as a teacher, you want to measure problem-solving ability through story problems and you proceed to give a page of 50 long-division problems, your test will have no content validity.

Content validity must be established for achievement tests. This may be accomplished by first deciding what you intend to measure and then deciding if your test (or the standardized test) gives a representative sample of the entire field you are interested in testing. If it does, your test has content validity. Although there are other kinds of validity (e.g., predictive validity, construct validity, and concurrent validity) designers of formal or informal elementary school measures are more concerned with content validity than they are with the other types of validity. Statisticians who develop standardized tests for testing companies would be an example of some scholars who attend to the many different, and complex, forms of test validity.

Reliability

Another factor that must be determined is the stability of your test (informal or standardized). If you give a reading comprehension test on Monday and again on Friday and if the scores are not similar for each student, then the test may not be reliable. Ambiguous test items are not reliable because students are guessing at answers, for the most part, and students seldom guess twice in the same way. Long tests and very difficult tests are often unreliable because students tend to guess due to fatigue; very short tests are seldom reliable because the sample of work is so limited that you may or may not have selected the items that the student knows. A correlation coefficient indicates the reliability of a test. It represents the relationship between two specific behaviors of a group of students. The tendency of the students to have systematically similar or dissimilar relative positions in the two distributions is demonstrated by computing a correlation coefficient. A positive correlation exists between the two measures if students who are high or low in one distribution are also high or low in a second distribution. For example, if Sharon receives a high score on each of two measures and Todd receives a low score on each of the same two measures, the correlation coefficient is positive. If r/tt 5 .00 (read: The correlation equals 0), the test is completely unreliable. If r/tt 5 1.00 (read: The correlation equals 1), the test is completely reliable. Unfortunately, tests are never completely reliable, but a correlation of .75 or .99 is usually acceptable as a measure of reliability. If a test is both reliable and valid and you want to use it as a criterion-referenced test, you have no further concerns. However, if you want to use it as a norm-referenced test, you must investigate appropriate norming procedures.

Norms

Norms are as important to the teacher as they are to the doctor. If you took a child to be weighed and measured, and the doctor told you that the child was greatly overweight, you would ask, "Overweight compared with whom?" If you felt the comparison to be inappropriate, you would reject the doctor's statement. The same is true for achievement tests. The score that the child receives may be accurate, depending on the validity and the reliability of the test, but the comparisons you make may be totally inappropriate. Students should be compared only with their own group; for example, a 10-year-old urban child should be compared with other 10-year-old children in similar urban environments. To make wrong comparisons is totally misleading and provides no helpful information. In fact, the information may be considered destructive if students are labeled intellectually inferior because of their scores on measures for which they have had no preparation. In addition to examining reliability, validity, and norming samples when choosing a test, you should also consider the following:

1. Original publication date and/or most recent test revision. Remember that words and concepts change with each generation. Many students today have never heard of an outhouse or an icebox.

2. Individual or group test.

3. Scoring. If the test is scored by the testing company, remember to request that the student answer sheets be returned. You can plan instruction if you know the consistency of errors made by the students. An IQ score of 103 or a reading score of 6.2 tells you nothing that will aid your planning.

4. Availability of test forms. If you plan to retest after instruction, you will need twice as many forms.

5. Administration time. Be careful to measure desired behavior rather than rate.

6. Cost.

7. Availability of subtests. It is often unnecessary to administer the entire test to measure the desired behavior. Sometimes one subtest is so highly correlated with all the other subtests in a specific test that you need only give one subtest to ascertain reading achievement information for a student. To determine if you can use one subtest as a valid predictor of overall achievement, you should consult the statistics provided in the manual for each standardized test.

8. Legibility. The tables, maps, and graphs included in the test should be legible.

9. Clarity of directions. Lack of clarity in directions often measures one's ability to interpret directions, as well as, or instead of, the previously desired behavior. The directions should be written in vocabulary appropriate to your grade level. Would it invalidate the test if you explained the directions to your students?

Some of this information can be found in the testing manual you will use as a teacher. However, keep in mind that the manual is written by an author or a publisher, whose major intent is to sell the tests. A less biased review of most tests can be found in the Mental Measurements Yearbook (Spies, R. et al., 2005). This reference should be consulted before you invest time and money in a testing program.

As a teacher, you will already know a great deal about the abilities of your students. Use testing to fill in the gaps and tell you what you don't know. There is little point in overtesting your students. It is important that you know your reasons for testing: "What do I want to know about this student?" "How will this knowledge help me in planning better activities for him or her?" After answering these questions, select your instrument, using the previously stated criteria. After scoring, diagnose and plan your curriculum accordingly.

Diagnostic Tests

DID YOU NOTICE . . .
Did you notice that it is never a good idea to make instructional decisions based on one assessment measure? You will need to administer many different assessments so you can have an entire photo album of data rather than just one snapshot.

As you attempt to analyze student assessment further, you may want to use a diagnostic test, which provides a more thorough analysis of individual skill competencies. For example, a standard reading survey test will provide you with general information regarding students' abilities in vocabulary, comprehension, and rate, whereas a diagnostic instrument provides scores in knowledge of consonant sounds, blending, syllabication, morphemes, several aspects of comprehension, study skills, and reading rate. A more thorough analysis of information is provided by the diagnostic test. Diagnostic tests are often individually administered and require administrative and scoring skills because interpretation may be a complex task. Whichever type of test you use, if it is computer scored, remember to remind the publishing company to return the individual answer sheets so that continuing diagnosis can take place.

Standardized achievement test results, which can be used to diagnose and plan instructional needs, can be correlated with informal test results to acquire a more valid understanding of individual students' skills. Correlation of standardized and informal tests, if used correctly, can provide a reliable and accurate assessment of student growth.

Informal measures, teacher checklists, textbook tests, and interest and attitude inventories are easily constructed if teachers are aware of the behavior they want to measure. We discuss these informal measures in the next section of this chapter. The behavior to be measured must be stated clearly so that appropriate materials can be prepared to measure it. Too often, teachers' tests are not correlated with material that has been taught. The need for accurate measurement cannot be overemphasized because student growth is the single most frequently used basis for evaluating teaching methods, teacher effectiveness, curriculum, instructional procedures, and grouping practices.

Assessing the growth of the student is essential for making decisions related to individualization. Student evaluation must be continuous so that program changes can be made in accordance with the progress of the student. Correct use of test results helps the teacher in planning for both group and individual instruction. The process of diagnosing the strengths and needs of your students forms your instructional base. Whether your measure has been standardized or designed informally, your instruction should center on facilitating comprehension of what is read. (Learning to use relevant test instruments effectively requires practice and critical evaluation as to the best application purposes.) In the area of testing, it is imperative to never rely on a single measurement instrument to provide the necessary diagnostic information about a student. Test results should serve as a reference point from which to begin diagnostic-prescriptive instruction, never as an end in itself.

Contemporary Statewide and National Assessments

Most states continually develop new assessment instruments that are designed to assess reading skills more comprehensively. The developers of these tests argue that there are regular paradigmatic shifts in the ways reading is viewed and that these changes in philosophy should be reflected in current state testing practices. You should be aware that each state in the United States requires standards based testing in some form. Moreover, school districts within states may have unique testing practices. You will need to familiarize yourself with the tests and testing practices in your local and state school districts.

PERFORMANCE MEASURES

In an effective reading program, you need as much information as possible about your students to ensure their learning. In addition to standardized tests, you will find that informal assessments also provide you with valuable information regarding the reading competencies of your students. Informal instruments differ from standardized measures because they do not involve formal procedures for constructing, administering, and scoring. The quality of the informal measures used in your classroom will depend on your ability to design, implement, and evaluate them. There are many informal measures that will be useful to you as a reading teacher. We discuss several of the informal assessment measures that Kelly and Larry draw upon in their teaching.

Let's see what you already know about informal literacy assessment measures. Describe the different informal assessment measures you are familiar with and tell how/when/why you would use them with children.

Past Performance Records

Children's cumulative record folders contain various different kinds of information about their past performance and learning. For example, the results of yearly standardized achievement tests are usually included in children's permanent folders. Although the nature of standardized tests can vary from state to state and district to district, standardized tests can give you a sense of how each child's scores in subjects, such as reading and math, compare with other children of similar age levels for whom the tests were normed.

Some districts also include work samples and writing samples in children's cumulative record files in addition to information about children's reading levels. Samples of children's work may be more formal such as selections from children's writing portfolios from different points across each school year. The samples may be less formal; teachers may merely choose a few work samples from subjects such as math, writing, social studies, or science to include in the cumulative folder. Individual districts determine the contents of cumulative record folders.

Larry and Kelly read the cumulative record file for each of their children each year. Before they even meet their children, they can study their records and files and

DID YOU NOTICE . . .
Did you notice that there is a lot you will not learn from a student s parent or previous teacher or from the school secretary? It is always a good idea to gather as much information, both social and academic, about the child as possible. You will continually be learning about the student as the school year progresses. Always be ready to add new information to a student s portfolio and to your mental file cabinet.

begin to get a general sense of their children's literacy-related strengths and needs. As we already mentioned, Larry starts the school year using IRIs with his children. (We describe IRIs in detail in the next subsection.) IRIs contain many different levels of tests. By studying his children's cumulative record files, Larry begins to develop a sense of which tests he should begin administering to his children to assess their incoming literacy knowledge.

We wish to make two additional points about cumulative record files. First, although both Kelly and Larry use them to get a general sense of their students' strengths and needs, they also exercise caution while interpreting their children's past records. They want to make sure that they base their instructional decisions on their impressions of their children once they have met them and begun to work with them. Second, cumulative files can provide other valuable information about children in addition to information about their academic progress. For example, one year as Larry was going through the cumulative records for his class, he noticed that one of his children was severely allergic to bee stings. Neither the child's parents nor the office secretary had mentioned this to Larry. He was glad that he knew about his student's medical condition.

Informal Reading Inventory

There are a variety of different IRIs that can be used to assess children's reading abilities. IRIs give children and their teachers a sense of children's strengths and needs as readers. IRIs are primarily used to guide a teacher in making instructional decisions. IRIs typically consist of the following components: (a) a discussion between the teacher and student to determine the child's background knowledge about the topic to be read, (b) oral reading by the child so that the teacher can assess the child's oral reading proficiency, (c) an assessment of the child's comprehension during oral reading through questioning or retellings, (d) silent reading of a portion of a passage of text and assessment of comprehension during silent reading through questioning or retellings, and, possibly, (e) an assessment of the child's listening comprehension whereby the teacher reads aloud to the child and assesses the child's comprehension by questions or retellings.

IRIs contain passages from material at a variety of grade levels. Questions on content and vocabulary pertaining to each passage help assess the comprehension level of the student. IRIs are useful in determining a student's independent reading level, instructional reading level, and frustration level. The independent reading level is believed to be the one at which the student can read successfully with little or no aid because the child can actually read most of the words in the passage and she or he understands the gist of the passage. The instructional level is the one at which teacher assistance is required. At this level, the students' comprehension skills are not as well developed as when they read at the independent level. The frustrational level signals an area of difficulty to be avoided by the student. The level of the book at the student's frustration level is too difficult. When teachers administer IRIs to their children, they ask them to read graded passages aloud. Then, the teacher ascertains the child's reading level (i.e., independent, instructional, or frustrational) for the graded passage. Additionally, IRIs help the teacher to determine specific reading strengths and needs for each child. There are many published IRIs you can choose from as a teacher. Different school districts may use different IRIs. Larry uses the IRI of Burns and Roe (1999). If you want detailed information regarding the development of IRIs, we refer you to Stieglitz Informal Reading Inventory: Assessing Reading Behaviors from Emergent to Advanced Levels 3/E (2002), Allyn and Bacon.

Interpreting Oral Reading Tests

The number and types of errors made in oral reading provide clues to a student's reading level and may help in diagnosing special reading needs. Stieglitz (2002) maintained that children are reading at their independent reading level if they score 99% to 100% (one error) in their oral reading word analysis skills in a 100-word passage. If children average two to five errors, or 95% to 98%, they are reading at their instructional reading level. Children have reached their frustrational reading level when they cannot master at least 94% of the text.

Administering an Oral Reading Test

The procedure for administering an oral reading test is as follows:

1. Select a 100-word passage from the material you wish the student to read.
2. Ask the student to read the passage orally.
3. Record the types of errors listed in Table 3–6. The test administrator may record the reading and score the student afterward.

Recording Errors. Figure 3–5 is an example of correction procedures in an oral reading test. The teacher notes student errors directly on a copy of the text.

Administering a Silent Reading Test

The procedure for administering a silent reading test is as follows:

1. Prepare questions that determine the student's ability to use various parts of the text (index, glossary, etc.).
   a. On what pages will you find information about prehistoric humans?
   b. How does the author define prehistoric?
2. Prepare questions that measure both the vocabulary and comprehension of what has been read.
   a. Where did prehistoric humans originate?
   b. Define the word skeletal used in the following sentence.

TABLE 3–6
Types of Errors in Oral Reading Tests and Corrective Procedures

Types of Errors	Correction Procedures
Mispronunciation	Record the incorrect response above the word missed.
Substitution	Record the substituted word above the one missed.
Omission	Circle the omitted word or words.
Insertion	Caret in the extra word.
Hesitations	Supply the needed word and write (H in a circle) if the student pauses for longer than 5 seconds.
Repetitions	Draw a wavy line under repeated words.

Figure 3–5   Correction procedures.

Name: __Anthony__ Age: _5_ Date: _10/5_ Teacher: __Williams__
Title: __Baby Bear Goes Fishing__   Level: __7__

# of words	# of errors	Error rate	# of self corrections	Self correction rate
112	9	1:12	4	1:3

Accuracy rate and reading level: __92% instructional__
Comments:
__Anthony is mostly reading word by word. Attempts__
__unfamiliar words with initial sounds.__

ANALYSIS OF
CUES USED
M = meaning
S = structure
V = visual

Page #	# of errors	# of self corrections	Text	Errors	Self corrections
3		1	I am /sc ✓✓ I'm	M S V	✓
			✓ ✓ ✓ ✓ ✓ ✓		
	1		✓ brown ✓ baby	M S V	✓
	1		✓ wish ✓ ✓ ✓ will	M S V	✓
	1		✓ h··· ✓ help	V	
5	1		✓ ✓ ✓ l··· /T little		
			✓ ✓ ✓ ✓ ✓ ✓		
		1	✓ ✓ no /sc ✓✓ not	V	M S V
			✓ ✓ ✓ ✓ ✓		
7	1		✓ ✓ ✓ — ✓ baby		
	1		walked ✓ ✓ ✓ ✓ went	M S V	✓
			✓ ✓ ✓ ✓ /R		
			✓ ✓ ✓		
8+9			✓ ✓ ✓ ✓ ✓ ✓ ✓ ✓ ✓		
11			✓ ✓ ✓ ✓ ✓		
13	1		L··· ✓ ✓ ✓ Look	✓	

3. When preparing these questions, you must be careful to provide items that assess the many operations of comprehension skills. Please refer to chapter 9 for practice in developing the complex range of questions necessary to assess the comprehension competencies of your students.

4. Direct the students to read the selection.

5. Time the students if you are interested in measuring their reading rates.

Record Keeping

You may want to devise a chart such as the one in Figure 3–6, that will help you to determine students' needs at a quick glance.

Interpreting Silent Reading Tests

On the silent reading test, students are believed to be reading at their independent reading level if they are able to answer 90% to 100% of the questions correctly. If 70% to 90% of the questions are answered correctly, they are believed to be reading at their instructional level. Their instructional plans can now be developed.

Careful planning of instructional procedures will eliminate any areas of weakness that were evidenced at this level. The frustrational level has been reached if the student cannot answer at least 70% of the questions.

The IRI standards for oral reading and comprehension are summarized in Table 3–7. These criteria are presented to guide you in determining students' reading levels. Be flexible in using them. Remember, all instruments are designed to facilitate your decision making about students' needs and competencies. The final decision is yours; therefore, we encourage you to judge wisely and flexibly, always remembering that you are the trained teacher.

Figure 3–6   IRI standards for oral reading and comprehension.

Name	Parts of Books	Vocabulary	Recall	Main Ideas	Recognition	Translation	Inference	Evaluation	Details
Betsy									
Sunny									
Denny									
Michael									
Sophie									
Sadie									
Audrey									
Gertrude									
Marilyn									
Juan									
Armin									
Kyle									

TABLE 3–7
Informal Reading Inventory Standards

Level	Oral Reading	Comprehension
Independent	99%–100%	90%–100%
Instructional	95%–98%	70%–90%
Frustrational	Below 94%	Below 70%

Consider the precautions when using IRIs:

1. The type of error may be more important than the number of errors.
2. Inventory accuracy may be hampered by teacher inexperience in construction, administration, and scoring.

Using a Variety of Writing Types in IRIs

Many educators have been urging teachers to use a variety of writing types within their IRIs to better ascertain students' abilities. Caldwell (1985) asserted: "Most IRIs ignore the global divisions of narrative versus expository prose" (p. 170). IRIs should include both expository and narrative passages.

According to Stieglitz (2002), "Expository selections should be of interest to students and contain content unfamiliar to the reader. The comprehension questions asked after the initial reading are more likely to be passage dependent if the content is unfamiliar. Obviously, questions that can be answered correctly without reading the selection are not valid indicators of how much the student learned from reading the material. Narrative passages should also be unfamiliar to the students and must have clear episodic structures, i.e., problem, setting, resolution" (p. 6). Two of Stieglitz's passages for third and fourth graders, one narrative and one expository, are presented in the following, with appropriate questions.

Narrative Passage: The Story of an Old Attic

Late one rainy November afternoon, Mary Dillon lay on her stomach, in the musty attic of the old farmhouse. She was absorbed in the story of a haunted house found in one of the old yellowed magazines stacked there. Finishing the story, she closed her eyes for a short rest.

When she awoke, it was pitch dark. The rain was still falling with a steady patter on the roof. The attic was a pleasant place in the daytime, but after dark, and after one had been reading a ghost story, it was definitely otherwise. As she sat up uneasily, Mary heard something move in front of her. She quickly grabbed a flashlight resting at her side, fumbled with the switch, and pointed the beam of light in the direction of the sound. Suddenly, Mary encountered a pair of glowing eyes staring back at her out of the darkness. Ghosts had eyes just like that! She felt her red hair rising on end. The eyes slowly approached her, and Mary was fascinated, frozen with fear. She tried to cry out, but no sound came from her throat.

"Meow," said Dusty, the family cat, whose throat was in perfectly good order, and whose eyes were as bright as cat's eyes should be. Snatching Dusty in her arms, Mary hurried downstairs.

Sample Questions: The Story of an Old Attic

- Mary Dillon was reading a story in a magazine. What was this story about? (A haunted house) (Ghosts)
- How did Mary feel at the end of this story? (Relieved) (Happy)
- Could this story have happened? What makes you think so? (The events sound real.) (It could have happened.)

(This material was adapted from D. H. De Witt [1914], "The Old Attic." St. Nicholas: An Illustrated Magazine for Young Folks, 41, 474.)

Expository Passage: Hide and Seek

Many children like to play hide and seek. Hide and seek did not begin as a game. It started many years ago in a faraway land.

Hide and seek was something grown-ups did each year when winter was over. People were tired of the cold and the long nights. They wanted to know if spring was on the way.

Grown-ups would leave their village and go into the woods. They tried to find or "seek out" birds and flowers. It was important to return with a bird or flower. If one did, this was a sign that spring had really started.

Sample Questions: Hide and Seek

- During what time of the year did grown-ups do hide and seek? (After winter) (At the beginning of spring) (Springtime)
- Hide and seek was something grown-ups did each year. Why was it so important for them to do hide and seek? (It was used to find out when spring had really started.) (It was an important custom.)
- Hide and seek is different today. Why is this so? (It is no longer a ritual or custom.) (It's just a game.) (We have better ways of determining the start of spring.)

RETELLINGS

Asking students to retell a story or text can be a useful assessment technique. As students retell the story, you can obtain valuable information about their sense of story structure, comprehension abilities, and oral language proficiency. Retellings provide different kinds of information than simple questioning. They provide information about the students' memory, attention to detail, and organizing abilities.

Procedure for Assessing Retellings

The procedure for assessing retellings is as follows:

1. Select a story to be read or listened to and identify the most important aspects of the story (e.g., beginning, middle, turning point, resolution, theme(s), setting(s), etc.)
2. Have the student practice and then read the story. Ask the student to tape-record a retelling. Use Figure 3–7 to record performance.

DID YOU NOTICE . . .
Did you notice that retellings provide a lot of information about the student's reading proficiency? You may need to prompt your student with questions if the student is unable to retell a passage. Sometimes students just need a little push to get them going when retelling what they have read. You should note whether the retell was prompted or unprompted in your notes.

Figure 3–7 Mitchell and Irwin's retelling profile.

Directions: Indicate with a checkmark the extent to which the reader's retelling includes or provides evidence of the following information.

	none	low degree	moderate degree	high degree
1. Retelling includes information directly stated in text.				
2. Retelling includes information inferred directly or indirectly from text.				
3. Retelling includes what is important to remember from the text.				
4. Retelling provides relevant content and concepts.				
5. Retelling indicates reader's attempt to connect background knowledge to text information.				
6. Retelling indicates reader's attempt to make summary statements or generalizations based on text that can be applied to the real world.				
7. Retelling indicates highly individualistic and creative impressions of or reactions to the text.				
8. Retelling indicates the reader's affective involvement with the text.				
9. Retelling demonstrates appropriate use of language (vocabulary, sentence structure, language conventions).				
10. Retelling indicates reader's ability to organize or compose the retelling.				
11. Retelling demonstrates the reader's sense of audience or purpose.				
12. Retelling indicates the reader's control of the mechanics of speaking or writing.				

Interpretation. Items 1–4 indicate the reader's comprehension of textual information; items 5–8 indicate metacognitive awareness, strategy use, and involvement with text; items 9–12 indicate facility with language and language development.

From *The Reader Retelling Profile: Using Retellings to Make Instructional Decisions* by J. N. Mitchell and P. A. Irwin, Copyright © 1990. Submitted to Reading Teacher.

3. Analyze the retelling by examining whether the student was able to recall the units of the story. Also, check for details and appropriate sequencing.

COMPREHENSIVE ASSESSMENT

There has been substantial interest in various forms of comprehensive assessment over the past decade, in which teachers and students develop portfolios or folders to demonstrate multiple aspects of a child's skills and abilities, thus providing a broader, more holistic look at each student.

Before we begin discussing how you can develop a comprehensive assessment system for each of your students, let's address some frequently asked questions.

1. What is comprehensive assessment?

   Comprehensive assessment is

   • a form of process evaluation that consists of a multidimensional profile of student progress. It is designed and collected by students, teachers, and parents to gather information about students' efforts toward self-monitoring, as well as students' growth and achievement in literacy endeavors.

2. Why compile a portfolio of comprehensive assessment?

   Comprehensive assessment informs teachers, students, and parents about

   • the capacity and depth of each student's overall performance.

   • the breadth of each student's performance.

   • the development/growth of each student.

   • the willingness/attitude of each student.

   • the collaborative stance of each student (social aspects of literacy).

   • the knowledge of the literacy process and the evaluative process that each student possesses: declarative (what), procedural (how), and conditional (why).

   • the ownership for learning of each student.

   • the multidimensionality of the whole child.

3. Who does comprehensive assessment inform?

   Comprehensive assessment informs at least seven potential audiences:

   • students

   • current teachers

   • future teachers

4. How is comprehensive assessment different from traditional assessment?

   Comprehensive assessment includes

   • a wide array of literacy endeavors, whereas traditional assessments examine limited sets of objectives and texts.

   • student involvement in the process, whereas traditional assessments rarely include the child as scorer, informant, or decision maker (about what will be tested and what will be done with the results).

   • a variety of tasks, whereas traditional assessment is limited to a single task.

   • appropriate instruction as a primary goal, whereas traditional assessment rarely includes instructional improvement as a goal.

   • collaborative partnership among students, whereas traditional assessment is noncollaborative.

5. What does comprehensive assessment look like?

   Portfolios or folders of comprehensive assessments should be self-designed to deal with issues of

   • individual preferences (aesthetic, functional)

   • space constraints.

- budget constraints.
- multiple copies for various audiences
- flexibility (ongoing change, choice, cleaning out)

6. What should a comprehensive assessment folder contain?

- Portfolios or folders of comprehensive assessments should contain a variety of information that is selected by students, teachers, and parents. The contents of the portfolio will change regularly, depending on the specific focus of the assessment (evaluative or instructional). One possible way of creating a portfolio for assessment has been proposed by Flood and Lapp (1989). They suggest that students (and their teachers) collect information from six different sources: norm-referenced and criterion-referenced scores, informal measures, writing samples, voluntary reading program reports, self-assessments, and sample materials used in school projects.

Standardized Tests

If collected as part of the comprehensive assessment folder, norm-referenced and criterion-referenced test scores should be presented in as clear and comprehensible a way as possible to explain the ways in which scores can be interpreted.

Informal Assessments

Farr, Tulley, and Pritchard (1989) explained that informal measures are extremely useful because they help students and parents understand information about specific, ongoing classroom instruction. They stated that informal measures are advantageous because "they take place in the natural context of the classroom and they provide the type of information teachers need for making daily instructional decisions" (p. 8). Scores at various intervals can be used to show growth.

For example, you may want to use an informal comprehension measure at the beginning, middle, and end of the year to show how the student has progressed. Many different forms can be developed by the teacher to show student growth. One example can be found in Figure 3–8. Periodic assessment can show how the student's comprehension of a single text grows over time. In this example, the student has progressed from a score of 30% to 50% to 90% when reading the same Level 1 text.

The inclusion of these kinds of graphs in the comprehensive assessment folders helps explain growth. School districts often develop their own formal and informal reporting measures that they require their teachers to use in assessing and reporting student progress. There are many informal measures that can be used; these are but a few. (For more information on an array of informal measures, please see Farr & Carey, 1986; Fisher, Lapp, & Flood, 2005; Damico, 2005.)

Writing Samples

Two samples from the student's writing might be included to show how the writing changes over time. In the early grades, growth is usually immediately apparent due to the sheer number of words the student has written. Teachers' comments should explain in what ways the writing has changed.

For example, comments could be made about the student's growing understanding of audience and voice, organizational skills, thinking processes (e.g., proving a point by presenting logical arguments with persuasive details), command of the lan-

Figure 3–8   Example of informal comprehension measures.

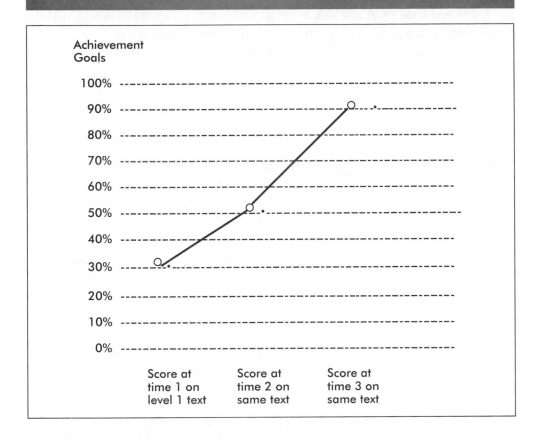

Achievement
Goals

100%	
90%	
80%	
70%	
60%	
50%	
40%	
30%	
20%	
10%	
0%	

Score at
time 1 on
level 1 text

Score at
time 2 on
same text

Score at
time 3 on
same text

guage (vocabulary and mechanics of grammar), or handwriting (Anderson & Lapp, 1988; Flood & Salus, 1984). A brief checklist may be used to show the differences between then and now.

By seeing the sample, growth is usually quite obvious. The two examples in Figure 3–9 demonstrate this phenomenon; it is taken from the journal of Johanna, a first grader.

Figure 3–9   Two samples from a first grader's journal showing growth in writing.

Today is wednesdy,
September 16, 1987.
it is a sunny day.

April 27, 1988 A rainbow
is colorful, beutiful too.
I can see different
colors. the colors I see
are purple, red,
blue, pink, orange,
yellow, green, peach, yellow,
green, yellow-orange,
too. when you come
to the end of the
rainbow you find a pot
of gold. but if you get
there to late you will
not get the gold
some one else will.

Voluntary Reading Program Reports

A study conducted by Anderson, Wilson, and Fielding (1988) demonstrated the relationship between leisure-time reading and reading achievement. The message was clear: Children need to spend time reading to become better readers. Morrow and Weinstein (1986) maintained that voluntary reading programs in classrooms where students select their own reading materials enhance reading development.

Voluntary reading programs are a must in every classroom, and a report of the results should be included in a portfolio, with a clear explanation about the importance of out-of-school reading to a student's overall reading success (Greaney, 1980; Dearman & Alber, 2005).

The number of books that students read or the number of minutes that they spend doing voluntary reading or writing can be plotted over time to show how a student's reading increases. Sometimes external tokens such as certificates or coupons can be used to motivate students to read and write. If you use such incentives, samples of them may be included in the portfolio.

In Figure 3–10, a student's voluntary reading growth is demonstrated. Notice how the lines of the graph differ. If one were to look only at the bottom line, it would seem that the student's progress was inconsistent, moving up and down by month. However, the top line shows the accumulated growth; this line goes in one direction: up.

The amount of time (minutes or hours) that the student spends in voluntary reading in and outside of the classroom or in sustained silent reading could be plotted in a similar way.

Figure 3–10 Chart representing cumulative growth and books per month of voluntary reading by a student.

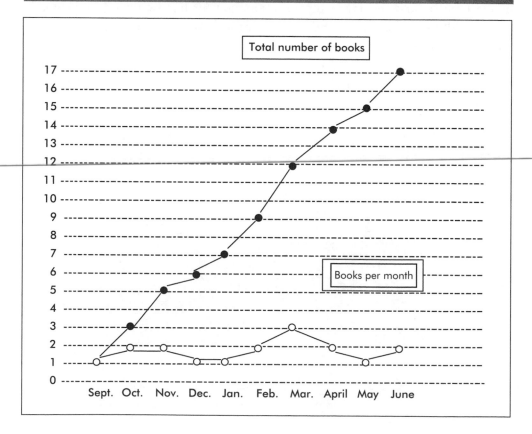

Self-Assessments and Interest Inventories

Wixson, Bosky, Yochum, and Alvermann (1984) found self-assessments of students' progress to be an effective way to gather information. These self-assessments can also be included in the portfolio. They add a personal statement from the student that enhances both the teacher's and the parent's understanding of the student's progress.

The instrument can be a written report by the student describing strengths and weaknesses, or a scoring system, or a series of answers to questions. For example, questions like the following might be used:

1. How well do you think you do in reading?
2. What do you do when you try to read a hard word?
3. How do you select your own reading material?

We provide an example of a student self-assessment survey in Figure 3–11.

Parents can also provide invaluable information about children's strengths, needs, and interests. The sample survey in Figure 3–12 illustrates a survey that you may ask parents to complete. Be aware that if the families of your children don't

Figure 3–11   Survey of students' reading interests.

Survey 1: Survey of students' reading interests

Name: _____

Age: _____   Date: _____

1. What other cities or states have you visited or lived in?
2. Do you ever read a book after you have seen the television or movie version?
3. What movies have you seen that you really liked?
4. What are your favorite TV programs?
5. How much TV do you watch each day?
6. Circle the kinds of books and stories you like; cross out the ones you don't like:

Adventure	Animal stories	Hobby stories
Biography	Autobiography	Science
Western stories	Art and music	Fairy tales
Poetry	Mystery	Motorcycles
Love and romance	Science fiction	Car magazines
Fables and myths	Sports	Religion
History	Newspapers	Magazines
Comic books	Ghost stories	Family stories
Riddles and jokes	Horse stories	Humor
Fantasy	People of other lands	Geography

7. On a sunny day I like to_____.
8. The best thing I ever read was_____.
9. My hobbies are_____.
10. I get really mad when_____.
11. When I grow up I'd like to be_____ because_____.
12. Right now I'd like to_____.
13. What is it that you do well?
14. The most fun I ever had was when _____.
15. The person I would most like to meet is_____ because_____.

Figure 3–12   Parent survey about child's interests.

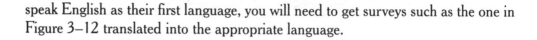

Survey 2: Parent Survey about Child's Interests

Thank you for completing this survey which will help me to know your child better. The better I know _____ the better I can plan instruction that will help_____ learn.

1. What are some of the things that your child enjoys doing at home and at school?
2. What are the types of things your child likes to read and learn?
3. Is your child a good reader and writer?
4. How would you describe your child?
5. What are some things your family likes to do together?
6. Does your child have any health issues?
7. What are you hoping I'll accomplish with your child this year?
8. How much time does your child have available each evening to spend doing homework?
9. What do you think is the best type of homework for your child to do?
10. Are there any extra types of help your child needs?

speak English as their first language, you will need to get surveys such as the one in Figure 3–12 translated into the appropriate language.

What additional things would you ask parents to better understand their child in the classroom? How would you use this information in your instructional day?

School Work Samples

Students and parents are often unaware of the complexity of the material that is being read. Sometimes it is enlightening to show samples of materials that students read at the beginning of the year and compare them with materials read at the end of the year.

For example, photocopied samples for a first-grade reader's portfolio might include a page from a book read early in the year, with few and repetitive words (such as Hop on Pop by Dr. Seuss) and one from a book read at a later date, with a varied text (such as Peter Rabbit by Beatrix Potter).

MATCHING READERS AND TEXTS

A central component of effective reading instruction is matching readers to texts. To match readers to texts, you need information about readers and texts. In the previous subsections we presented many examples of ways you can gather information about your children's reading strengths and needs. In this subsection, we shift our focus to texts. Children learn most effectively when they receive appropriate instruction, which includes reading texts at the appropriate level of difficulty. When children read texts on their own, the texts should be at their independent reading level. The texts you use for your children's reading instruction should be at their independent or instructional level—depending on the nature of the activities you're doing with them. In this subsection, we teach you how to determine the level of a text. This information can assist you when you're matching children to texts.

During the past 70 years, researchers developed instruments that they believed would help determine how difficult a text is to comprehend. Vocabulary difficulty and sentence length are the two factors most commonly used to determine text readability in readability formulas. The incorporation of polysyllabic, difficult words in complex sentences often indicates an advanced readability level. Several readability formulas exist; they include those by Gray and Leary (1935), Lorge (1944), Flesch (1943), Dale and Chall (1948), Spache (1953), Fry (1968), and Aukerman (1972). These researchers have attempted to design and measure the factors that cause children to have difficulty with reading materials. The use of these formulas, based on these factors, aids the classroom teacher in estimating the appropriateness of certain material for a particular student.

You should remember that readability levels are only approximations of text difficulty because it is not possible to hold constant all of the factors that are related to comprehension (e.g. text organization, conceptual difficulty, semantics, syntax, reader interest, and background knowledge).

Computation: The Fry Readability Graph

Edward Fry developed a readability formula that has been used extensively for the past several decades. Because it is computed quickly and easily, it is presented here to assist you in determining the approximate readability of materials that might be appropriate for your students (see Figures 3–13, 3–14, and 3–15).

Cautions

Although it is easy to use readability formulas, it is equally easy to misuse them. We must point out that it is virtually impossible to arrive at an absolute level for any text for several reasons; two of these reasons are sampling methods and the unevenness of textbooks. The sampling methods used in most formulas are usually limited to counting the syllables within a word and the sentences within a passage. If only these two variables are considered, it is possible that a score might not accurately reflect the actual difficulty of a text. A second reason why readability formulas cannot accurately assess a textbook is the unevenness of textbooks. Frequently, the introductory chapters of a text are the most difficult. Content area materials are often used inconsistently throughout a book; for example, literary devices such as metaphorical and poetic language, tone, mood, and style are not constant. As a result of this inconsistency, there may be varying degrees of reading difficulty within one textbook, which, in turn, makes a readability score serve only as an approximation of difficulty.

Other factors, outside of the actual text structure, may also contribute to the real readability level, as opposed to the level obtained by the formula used. Chief among these factors are the experiential background and interest of the reader. This problem is illustrated in the following example. Two passages that appear to be equally difficult are presented:

Passage 1

Christmas always meant going to Grandma's house. On Christmas Eve the entire family tramped out to the woods. Dad was in charge of bringing back the

Figure 3–13 Assessing reading achievement. [From: Fry, Edward B. (1968, April). A readability formula that saves time. *Journal of Reading* 11(7), 513–516.]

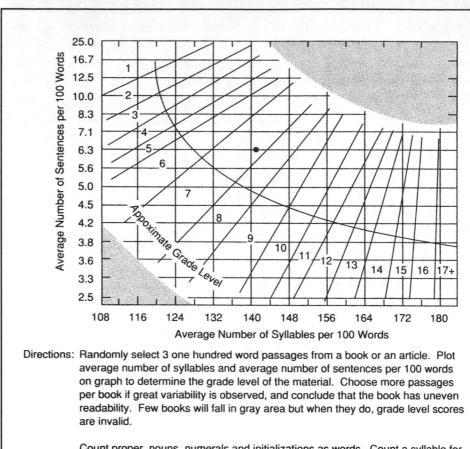

Directions: Randomly select 3 one hundred word passages from a book or an article. Plot average number of syllables and average number of sentences per 100 words on graph to determine the grade level of the material. Choose more passages per book if great variability is observed, and conclude that the book has uneven readability. Few books will fall in gray area but when they do, grade level scores are invalid.

Count proper nouns, numerals and initializations as words. Count a syllable for each symbol. For example, "1945" is 1 word and 4 syllables and "IRA" is 1 word and 3 syllables.

Example:	Syllables	Sentences
1st hundred words	124	6.6
2nd hundred words	141	5.5
3rd hundred words	158	6.8
Average	141	6.3

Readability 7th grade (see dot plotted on graph)

tree, and the rest of us cut fir branches for house decorations. That evening Grandma would distribute the homemade ornaments. We hung up a cookie universe: suns, stars, moons, and unearthly men with raisin eyes. Mom arranged candles in silvery paper on the branches. With dignity and care, Grandpa chained the tree with yards of cranberries and popcorn. We decorated the tree the way Grandma had when she was young; we were learning tradition.

Passage 2

One of the oldest drinks known to man is milk. Man requires liquids as well as solids to remain healthy because he is a mammal, a warm-blooded being. Prehis-

---

A SHORT PASSAGE READABILITY FORMULA

Rules

1. Use on a passage that is at least three sentences and 40 words long.
2. Select at least three key words that are necessary for understanding the passage. You may have more key words.
3. Look up the grade level of each key word in *Living Word Vocabulary: A National Vocabulary Inventory* by E. Dale and J. O'Rourke (Chicago: World Book/Child Craft International, 1981).
4. Average the three hardest key words. This gives you the Word Difficulty.
5. Count the number of words in each sentence and give each sentence a grade level using the Sentence Length Chart.
6. Average the grade level of all sentences. This gives you the sentence difficulty.
7. Finally, average the sentence difficulty (step 6) and the word difficulty (step 4). This gives you the readability estimate of the short passage.

$$\text{Readability} = \frac{\text{word difficulty} + \text{sentence difficulty}}{2}$$

Cautions

A. This method should be used only when a long passage is not available. For any passage of 300 words or longer, use the regular readability graph.
B. This method was developed for use with passages at least three sentences and 40 words long. For anything shorter than that, use the method at your own risk. It may be better than nothing, but it certainly has less reliability.
C. When looking up the grade level of the key words, make sure that you get the grade level for the same meaning as the meaning of that key word as it is used in the passage.
D. The range of scores is 4.0 to 12.0. In reporting any score of 4.0 or below, call it "4th grade or below"; in reporting any score above 12.0, call it "12th grade or above".

---

toric man did not consume as much liquid as modern man. He devoured fruit from the trees he inhabited. However, man had to change his habits to exist on the arid plains. No longer a fruit eater, he soon began to hunt plains animals. This new activity required much energy; man perspired and needed to drink liquids directly. To this day, man needs liquids such as milk to be able to exist.

Did you find one passage more difficult than the other? If so, ask yourself, "What factors within the passage created the difficulty?" Both passages, according to readability formulas, are identical. The statistics on each passage are presented in Table 3–8.

This table demonstrates some of the pitfalls of relying exclusively on readability formulas to determine passage difficulty. If one passage was easier for you, it may have been so because you found that passage more interesting than the other. This may have been related to your experience; you may have celebrated Christmas in the same way as the people in the passage. On the other hand, you may have found it more difficult than the other passage because you have had no experience with Christmas.

A SAMPLE PASSAGE

These record-smashing *feats* were accomplished at the 39th annual *convention* of the International *Jugglers Association*, held in San Jose, California. In that *contest*, Anthony competed against the world's best jugglers. Many were more than twice his age, but there was no doubt who was best.

Sentence			Key Words
Length	Grade		(3 hardest only)
21	8.5		6 (feats)
10	3		6 (convention)
15	6		8 (contest)

$3\overline{)17.5}$ $\qquad\qquad$ $3\overline{)20}$

5.8 Average sentence difficulty $\qquad$ 6.7 Average key word difficulty

5.8 sentence difficulty
6.7 key word difficulty

$2\overline{)12.5}$

6.3 readability score (in grade level)

Notes:

The word *jugglers* was suggested as a possible key word, but that word is not in the list in *Living Word Vocabulary: A National Vocabulary Inventory* by E. Dale and J. O'Rourke (Chicago: World Book/Child Craft International, 1981). For this reason, it was not included.

Four other words were looked up. One word, *association*, (Level 6) was not used because the formula rules state that only the three hardest words must be used in obtaining the average key word difficulty.

The word *convention* has three different meanings, with a different grade level for each meaning. This passage used "convention = meeting Level 6", not "convention = custom Level 10" or "convention = diplomatic agreement Level 12."

TABLE 3–8
Readability Analysis of Passages 1 and 2

	Passage 1	*Passage 2*
Number of words	100	100
Number of sentences	8	8
Average sentence length	12.5	12.5
Number of syllables	146	146

Assessing the Difficulty of Textbooks

Singer (1986) developed an informal scale for assessing whole textbooks. An adaptation of his scale, "Criteria for Selecting Friendly Texts," is included in Figure 3–16. This scale assesses the "friendliness" of textbooks in terms of their organization, explanations, style, and instructional devices. The questions in Figure 3–16 are asked about textbooks to determine how helpful they may be for students.

Figure 3–16   Selecting friendly texts.

Text Evaluation Checklist

Directions: Enter the intended grade level of the text. Compute an estimate of text readability using the Raygor Readability Estimate. Complete the 19-item checklist to determine the acceptability of the text for your students.

Title of textbook: _____

Author(s): _____

Publisher: _____

Copyright date: _____

Cost: _____

Evaluated by: _____

A. Readability

____ 1. Intended grade level of text: _____. Readability estimate: _____. Is the computed reading level realistic for the students who will be using the text?

B. Format

____ 2. The book is recently copyrighted and the contents genuinely up-to-date.

____ 3. The text is suitable for achieving the stated course objectives.

____ 4. The text contains a table of contents, an index, and a glossary.

____ 5. The table of contents indicates a logical development of the subject matter.

____ 6. When the text refers to a graph, table, or diagram, that aid is on the same page as the textual reference.

____ 7. Captions under graphs, tables, and diagrams are clearly written.

____ 8. Pictures are in color and are contemporary, not dated by dress unless author's intention is to portray a certain period.

____ 9. Various ethnic groups and male and female characters are depicted authentically in the text.

____ 10. The text suggests out-of-class readings and projects to stimulate additional student interest.

C. Organization

____ 11. The main idea(s) or purpose(s) for reading a chapter are stated at the beginning.

____ 12. Difficult new vocabulary words are highlighted, italicized, or underlined.

____ 13. Context clues and synonyms for difficult vocabulary words are used in the text.

____ 14. The writing is coherent in that ideas are clearly developed and related to each other, within and across sentence and paragraph boundaries.

____ 15. New concepts are introduced by relating them to previously learned concepts so that the volume of new information doesn't frustrate students.

____ 16. The text refers to practical, real-life situations and multicultural contexts in which students can relate and have an interest.

____ 17. The text includes references to, and quotations from, other sources and authorities to support its statements.

____ 18. The authors include a summary at the end of each chapter.

____ 19. When there are questions and activities at the end of a chapter, they elicit different levels of thinking, ranging from text-explicit to experience-based, problem-solving tasks.

Decision ____ **Appropriate** ____ **Marginally Appropriate** ____ **Unacceptable**

QUESTIONS

1. Why is it useful to determine the range of reading levels in your classroom, and how is it done?

2. What end does assessment serve in the instructional process?

3. Explain the differences between norm- and non-norm-referenced tests and their respective uses.

4. Describe portfolio assessment and tell when, why, and how you'd use it.

5. Explain the issues involved in assessing readability.

REFERENCES

Allington, R. L., & McGill-Franzen, A. (2003). The impact of summer reading setback on the reading achievement gap. *Phi Delta Kappan, 83*(1), p. 8.

Anderson, P., & Lapp, D. (1988). *Language skills in elementary education* (4th ed.). New York: Macmillan.

Anderson, R., Wilson, P., & Fielding, L. (1988). Growth in reading and how children spend their time outside of school. *Reading Research Quarterly, 23,* 285–303.

Aukerman, R. C. (1972). *Reading in the secondary school classroom.* New York: McGraw-Hill.

Binet, A., & Simon, T. (1905). *The development of intelligence in children.* Baltimore: Williams & Wilkins.

Burns, P. C., & Roe, B. D. (1999). *Informal reading inventory: Preprimer to twelfth grade.* New York: Houghton Mifflin.

Caldwell, E. (1985). Dangers of PSI. *Teaching of Psychology, 12,* 9–12.

Dale E., & Chall, J. (1948). A formula for predicting readability. *Educational Research Bulletin, 27,* 11–20.

Damico, J. (2005, April). Multiple dimensions of literacy and conceptions of readers: Toward a more expansive view of accountability. *The Reading Teacher, 58*(7), 644–652.

Dearman, C., & Alber, S. (2005, April). The changing face of education: Teachers cope with challenges through collaboration and reflective study. *The Reading Teacher, 58*(7), 634–640.

De Witt, D. H. (1914). The Old Attic. *St. Nicholas: An Illustrated Magazine for Young Folks, 41,* 474.

Farr, R., & Carey, R. F. (1986). *Reading: What can be measured?* (2nd ed.). Newark, DE: International Reading Association.

Farr, R., Tulley, M., & Pritchard, R. (1989). Assessment instruments and techniques used by the content area teacher. In D. Lapp, J. Flood, & N. Farnan (Eds.), *Content area reading and learning: Instructional strategies* (pp. 85–97). Englewood Cliffs, NJ: Prentice-Hall.

Fisher, D., Lapp, D., & Flood, J. (2005). Consensus scoring and peer planning: Meeting literacy accountability demands one school at a time. *The Reading Teacher, 58*(7), 656–666.

Flesch, R. F. (1943). *Marks of readable style: A study of adult education.* New York: Bureau of Publications, Teachers College Press, Columbia University.

Flood, J., & Lapp, D. (1989). Reporting reading progress: A comparison portfolio for parents. *The Reading Teacher, 42,* 508–514.

Flood, J., & Salus, P. (1984). *Language and the language arts.* Englewood Cliffs, NJ: Prentice-Hall.

Fry, E. (1968). Readability formula that saves time. *Journal of Reading, 11,* 513–516, 575–578.

Goodlad, J. I. (1966). *School, curriculum and the individual.* Walthom, MA: Blaisedell.

Gray, W. S., & Leary, B. E. (1935). *What makes a book readable?* Chicago: University of Chicago Press.

Greaney, V. (1980). Factors related to the amount and type of leisure reading. *Reading Research Quarterly, 15,* 337–357.

Hoffman, J. V., Paris, S. G., Patterson, E., Salas, R., & Assaf, L. (2003). High-stakes assessment in the language arts: The piper plays, the players dance, but who pays the price? in Flood, J., Lapp, D., Squire, R., & Jensen, J. (Eds.), *Handbook of Research on Teaching the English Language Arts* (2nd ed., pp. 619–630). Newark, DE: International Reading Association.

Kamil, M. L., Mosenthal, P. B., Pearson, P. D., & Barr, R. (2000). (Eds.) *Handbook of reading research* (Vol. III). Mahwah, NJ: Lawrence Erlbaum Associates.

Lorge, I. (1944). Predicting readability. *Teachers College Record, 45*, 404–419.

Morrow, L. M., & Weinstein. C. S. (1986). Encouraging voluntary reading: The impact of a literature program on children's use of library centers. *Reading Research Quarterly, 21*, 530–546.

Nitko, A. J. (1980). Distinguishing the many varieties of criterion-referenced tests. *Review of Educational Research, 3*, 461–485.

Pennington, J. (2004). Teaching interrupted: The effects of high-stakes testing on literacy instruction in a Texas elementary school. In F. Boyd, C. Brock, with M. Rozendal (Eds.), *Multicultural and multilingual literacy and language: Contexts and practices*. New York: Guilford.

Shepard, L. (1979). Norm-referenced vs. criterion-referenced tests. *Educational Horizons, 1*, 26–32.

Singer, H. (1986). Friendly texts: Description and criteria. In E. K. Dishner and others (Ed.), *Reading in the content areas: Improving classroom instruction* (2nd ed., pp. 175–187). Dubuque, IA: Kendall Hunt.

Spache, G. (1953). A new readability formula for primary grade reading materials. *Elementary School Journal, 53*, 410–413.

Stanley, J. C., & Hopkins, K. D. (1972). *Educational and psychological measurement and evaluation*. Englewood Cliffs, NJ: Prentice-Hall.

Stieglitz, E. (2002). Steiglitz Informal Reading Inventory: Assessing Reading Behavior from Emergent to Advanced Levels. 3/E. Boston: Allyn and Bacon.

Wilson, P., Martens, P., & Arya, P. (2005, April). Accountability for reading and readers: What the numbers don't tell. *The Reading Teacher, 58*(7), 622–631.

Wixson, K. K., Bosky, A. B., Yochum, M. N., & Alvermann, D. E. (1984). An interview for assessing students' perceptions of classroom reading tasks. *The Reading Teacher, 37*, 346–552.

Two

Developing Literacy
Performance and Preferences

■　■　■　■　■

4

The Importance of Oral Language in Developing Literacy

--- CHAPTER GOALS ---

To help the reader

- support oral language development in the classroom.
- define the components of language.
- understand how language develops.
- plan instruction to enhance speaking and listening skills.
- evaluate speaking and listening performance.

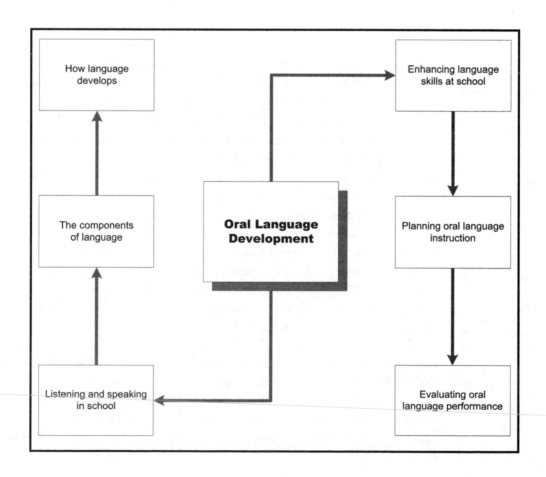

On a recent talk show, people were asked to describe their greatest fear. Not surprising, the number one fear was public speaking. Do you have similar feelings about public speaking? Don't worry, students of all ages are overwhelmingly reticent to volunteer to speak in class and are quite anxious when the teacher calls on them.

Have you ever wondered about your ability to speak? Are there times that you are more or less comfortable speaking? How will you ensure that your students become proficient, confident speakers? Take a minute and write down your thoughts about the relationship between oral language development and literacy—how are these ideas connected?

At a recent inservice, we shared the information about the talk show survey. One teacher, Ms. Jimenez, noted, "It's different when you're talking with kids, they're much more forgiving! I don't want my students to have this fear. I want them to learn to speak well and overcome any fears they might have about speaking publicly." We believe that Ms. Jimenez's thoughts reflect those of most teachers. In this chapter, we provide an overview of oral language development. Let's look inside Ms. Jimenez's classroom as she implements oral language development activities with her third graders.

VIGNETTE: LISTENING AND SPEAKING IN SCHOOL

As they arrive one cold day in November, the students in Ms. Jimenez's third grade class can't wait to tell their teacher about the sounds they heard during the first snow of the year. They have been waiting for this opportunity for weeks! Ms. Jimenez asks her students to begin the conversation by recording their thoughts in journals. When they have had a few minutes to write, Ms. Jimenez asks each student to turn to a partner and share their observations of the first snow. The room becomes a buzz with students excitedly talking with one another. Ms. Jimenez knows that these short partner conversations are one way that she can ensure that every student has the opportunity to talk and to listen in her classroom. After a few minutes, Ms. Jimenez puts her hand in the air, fingers extended, and starts to silently count down on her fingers, 5–4–3–2 and then 1. When she is left holding 1 finger in the air, every student has stopped talking, turned to face her and is seated quietly. They learned this procedure during the first few weeks of the school year. Ms. Jimenez asks a few students to share their conversation with the whole class as she and the other students use the chart found in Table 4–1 to provide students' feedback on their public speaking (an alternative format for large group presentations can be found in Table 4–2).

Ms. Jimenez then transitions to her read aloud. She has been saving the book *Stranger in the Woods: A Photographic Fantasy* by Carl Sams II and Jean Stoick (2000) for this day. This particular book is an informational text with real photographs of animals in the snow. In 2001 it won a Children's Book Award from the International Reading Association in the Younger Reader Category. Ms. Jimenez uses interactive read alouds to convey content and model fluent reading for her students. In addi-

DID YOU NOTICE . . .
Did you notice that this is a think, write, pair, share activity? It ensures the participation of every child in all of the language arts while eliminating the fear of public speaking.

DID YOU NOTICE . . .
Did you notice that classroom management technique eliminates teacher shouting and makes every child personally responsible for his or her behavior?

DID YOU NOTICE . . .
Did you notice that the use of this chart helps Ms. Jimenez plan the next steps in her instruction while providing speaking criteria the children can internalize?

DID YOU NOTICE . . .
Did you notice that Ms. Jimenez uses read aloud selections that are usually above the independent reading level of the students? This provides them with motivation and language and topical knowledge expansion.

TABLE 4–1
Sample Speaking Checklist

Name: _____

When _____ speaks in a group, he/she:

	Sept.	Dec.	Mar.	June
sticks to the topic.				
builds support for the subject.				
speaks clearly.				
takes turns and waits to talk.				
talks so others in the group can hear.				
speaks smoothly.				
uses courteous language.				
presents in an organized and interesting way.				
supports the topical thesis.				
answers questions effectively.				
is comfortable speaking publicly.				
maintains listeners' interest.				
volunteers to answer in class.				

A = always, S = sometimes, N = never.

TABLE 4–2
Public Speaking Assessment

Components	3—well done	2—average	1—poor
Presentation content			
Opened with a statement that caught the interest of the listeners			
Clearly stated the main idea			
Supported the main idea			
Provided clear examples			
Presented ideas that followed from one to the next			
Maintained the interest of the audience			
Concluded by drawing all ideas together			
Presentation skills			
Uses a clear voice			
Keeps head up and makes eye contact with audience			
Maintains stance and posture, including use of hands			
Is self-assured			
Use of language			
Paused appropriately			
Maintained subject and verb agreement			
Used appropriate descriptive words			
Incorporated previously studied vocabulary			

Stranger in the Woods: A Photographic Fantasy © **Carl R. Sams II and Jean Stoick**

DID YOU NOTICE ...
Did you notice that
Ms. Jimenez s class-
room is set up as a
reader s workshop (see
chapter 10)?

DID YOU NOTICE
Did you notice that this
allows Ms. Jimenez to
meet individual needs
even when children are
in a group?

DID YOU NOTICE
Did you notice that
classroom book clubs
invite students to share
their responses to a wide
array of genres? Doing
so promotes ownership
of ideas, expands
insights, and encour-
ages language and lis-
tening development.

tion, she knows that interactive read alouds provide her students with an excellent opportunity to expand their language and listening skills. She pauses periodically during her reading to ask questions of her students. For example, after the first few pages, she asks "Who do you think the stranger in the woods will be?" Later, she asks students to retell various parts of the text to check their comprehension and ability to summarize information they have heard.

Following the read aloud, students transition to their heterogeneously grouped learning centers while Ms. Jimenez meets with small homogeneous groups of students to further develop their reading and comprehension skills. More specific details on these centers and grouping activities can be found in chapter 2. The interesting thing to note here is the variety of learning centers that Ms. Jimenez uses to ensure that her students develop oral literacy skills. For example, Ms. Jimenez likes to have four to six students at a time use the listening center. At the listening center, several students listen on headphones to a tape recording. Although she knows that she can buy books recorded on tapes, she prefers to record her own books so that she can speak directly to her students about the book she is reading. She also adds comments during her recordings asking listeners to write down vocabulary words, pay attention to graphics, or notice something specific about the text.

At another center, Ms. Jimenez asks students to create Reader's Theater scripts from the books they are reading in class. Together, small groups of students at this center re-read texts at their independent reading level and transform them into a Reader's Theater script that they can perform later in the day. Ms. Jimenez knows that re-reading is important for comprehension and she likes the fact that the Reader's Theater allows students to speak publicly.

At a third center, a group of students are meeting to discuss a book they have all read. These book club discussions are an important way for students to share their thinking about books and to listen to and consider the perspectives of others. Ideas for whole-class, small-group, and center activities will be explored further in a section of this book. Before that, however, we'd like to explore further the reason that Ms. Jimenez and teachers like her focus instructional time on speaking and listening activities.

SUPPORTING ORAL LANGUAGE DEVELOPMENT IN THE CLASSROOM

As students listen, they may be interacting with the speaker by mentally formulating opinions or questions, but they are often shy about voicing their thoughts because they think they may be "wrong" or may hold an opinion different from those of their peers. Their silence may not be due to their lack of involvement but instead a fear of exposure because they realize that they are being judged by what they say and how they say it. As you consider this, think about the judgments you make about public speakers within the first 10 seconds of listening to them, whether the contact is via the phone, television, lecture hall, or classroom. James Chesebro, past president of the National Communication Association, has encouraged us to teach our children strategies that will help them become effective communicators because he contends that the "lack of oral communication skills is one our most critical national problems."

Observe three different public speakers—a TV talk show host, a radio personality, and a teacher. Observe each of these people for 30 seconds. Use the criteria in Table 4–1 or 4–2 to evaluate their speaking ability. What influenced your perceptions? Discuss your reactions with a peer. Did you both have similar insights?

Students need instruction in public speaking. Instruction should help them realize that the ideas they are sharing orally must be crafted so that the *contents* as well as the *mechanics* are appropriate to the audience and the situation. Instruction should also allow for time to practice many types of public speaking (e.g., conversations, debates, interviews, and speeches), sharing first with one person and then expanding the group size as students become more comfortable. In addition, instruction should provide modeling that helps students realize that the many contexts in which they speak (e.g., home, playground, classroom, and eventually workplace) require adjustments to the *information* they present as well as the *style* of their presentations (e.g., speech, conversation, or reading). When teachers implement an oral literacy curriculum, students understand that the context determines the ways in which the audience should be treated and that the familiarity the audience has with the speaker and the topic influences the speaker's selection of tone, vocabulary, grammar, and amount of information (detail) conveyed.

Oral literacy involves communication through speech and is considered the foundation for the development of reading and writing. Effective oral exchanges encourage students to develop oral literacy, to expand their vocabulary, to participate in and contribute to group discussions, to resolve conflicts, and to communicate

DID YOU NOTICE . . .
Did you notice that speaking skills are developed when teachers devote classroom instructional time to this literacy skill?

DID YOU NOTICE . . .
Did you notice that language is the basis for all other learning?

ideas, feelings, and experiences. These exchanges need to be based in authentic literacy tasks as Vygotsky (1978) explained: children develop their literacies (listening, speaking, reading, writing, and viewing) while engaging in purposeful, meaning-centered literacy activities.

Teachers need to model effective oral communication because students learn best when they work with competent adults to initiate and complete daily oral language activities including solving problems, discussing issues, investigating a hypothesis, planning a performance, sharing a debate, reflecting in a book talk, and reading, writing, reviewing, or discussing a play.

Through literacy interchanges during which teachers model a wide range of strategies and children participate as partners, they internalize the interactive format as well as the information that is being learned. Over time students become very capable of performing these tasks independently. Literacy experiences in all areas of the language arts exist in most classrooms. Unfortunately, if children continually struggle to perform literacy tasks that are too difficult for them, their confidence often deteriorates (Schunk & Zimmerman, 1997).

Literacy activities that encourage positive student growth include (a) the teacher modeling literacy strategies, (b) the teacher providing explicit instruction as needed; and (c) peers providing support for each other's efforts. Before we turn to a discussion about the ways in which teachers can facilitate the development of oral language skills, we will provide some background information about language, language development, and the role of listening and speaking in the language arts curriculum.

What Is Language?

Language is an arbitrary set of symbols, systematic in nature, agreed upon by a community of users, which are designed to explain experiences and thoughts. Communi-

"You don't say 'he taked my chair' . . . it's 'my chair was tooken.' "

© Bill Keane, Inc. Reprinted with special permission of King Features Syndicate.

cation, on the other hand, refers to the ways that people interact to construct meanings. Speech is one method of representing language as a vehicle for communicating. The primary purpose of language is communication. By the time children enter kindergarten, they have learned the basic structures of their home language, although their syntax grows increasingly complex throughout the years. By the time they begin elementary school, they have developed extensive speaking vocabularies, consisting of approximately 2,500 words (Salus & Flood, 2002).

Linguistics, the study of language, views language in several parts. The first is *phonology* or the smallest units of sound. The sounds of English are typically broken down into consonants and vowels. These sounds, or phonemes, carry no meaning but are the building blocks of language. *Morphology*, however, is the study of the smallest units of meaning. Smallest implies that they cannot be divided without changing the meaning. The word *sisters*, for example, has two morphemes (sister and -s). The system we use to combine words into sentences is called syntax. A list of syntactic rules is called grammar. Our *syntax* system tells us, for example, that the sentence "cat away the ran" is not acceptable. *Semantics* is concerned with the meaning of language or how sentences fit together. The last field of linguistic study is called pragmatics. *Pragmatics* is a relatively new field that is concerned with the social role of language.

How Does Language Develop?

There are many theories about how language is acquired. Behaviorists, such as Skinner, believe that language is an interactive process wherein the child learns from the model of adult language. Positive reinforcement has a beneficial effect on language acquisition by encouraging children to continue experimenting and imitating the language model presented to them. Nativists, such as Chomsky, Lennenberg, and others, describe an innate ability to acquire language that needs no real interaction as it involves an internalization of grammatical rules. Part of the rationale for this theory is that all infants will acquire speech and there are stages through which all children pass in their language development. The schedule for almost all children looks like this:

Age	Vocalization
At birth	Crying
1–2 months	Cooing and crying
2–6 months	Babbling, cooing, and crying
9–14 months	First words
18–24 months	First sentences
3–4 years	Almost all basic syntactic structures
4–8 years	Almost all speech sounds correctly articulated
9–11 years	Semantic distinctions established

A more detailed description of language development can be found in Table 4–3 and in Salus and Flood (2002). Athough this development schedule holds true for most children, many researchers have noted that both first and second language acquisition is an active, individual process wherein children construct and create language through their own dialogues, which are often replete with errors. In fact, oral language is part of almost every activity a child does—from a baby in a crib babbling to stuffed animals to a preschooler detailing every stroke of the paintbrush. The sounds themselves (or the way the words are strung together) represent the child's attempts to further his or her communication skills.

The individuality of the language acquisition process and the fact that making errors is a way of learning what is correct are two crucial elements to keep in mind when one teaches young children, especially those who are English language learners. The willingness to accept children at their own stage of language development needs to be extended from early childhood to the first school years. The emphasis should be on the child, not the curriculum. In terms of general goals, however, Table 4–4 provides a sample list of listening and speaking skills by grade level for the Long Beach Unified School District in California. Most districts and states have goals similar to those identified by the Long Beach Unified School District.

Ask a parent or other family member what they remember about your language development years. If this isn't possible, think about a child you have observed learning language. Refer to Table 4–1 to associate his or her behavior with the described developmental stages. After thinking about this, share the information with a partner. How similar were your experiences?

WHAT IS THE ROLE OF LISTENING IN THE LANGUAGE ARTS CURRICULUM?

Some say that owls are wise

Because they keep so quiet.

Could most of us fare better

On an expert listening diet? (Quoted in Lundsteen, 1979, p. 1280)

TABLE 4–3
Speech and Language Development

ZERO TO 1 MONTH
- Startled to loud, sudden noises
- Stops activity when approached by sound
- Frequent crying
- Vowel-like sounds similar to "e" and "a"

1 TO 2 MONTHS
- Will give direct attention to other voices
- Appears to listen to speaker
- Has special cry for hunger
- Vocal signs of pleasure
- May repeat the same syllable while cooing or babbling

2 TO 3 MONTHS
- Looks directly at speaker's face
- Localizes speaker with eyes
- Watches lips and mouth of speaker
- Vocalizes with two or more different syllables
- Occasionally responds to sound with vocalizations

3 TO 4 MONTHS
- Turns head to source of voice
- Looks in search of speaker
- Disturbed by angry voices
- Laughs during play with objects
- Babbles (regularly repeats series of same sounds)
- Often uses sounds like "p," "b," and "m"

4 TO 5 MONTHS
- Regularly localizes source of voice
- Responds to own name
- If known adult talks softly to the child he or she will usually stop crying
- Uses vowel-like sounds similar to "o" and "u"
- Expresses anger by vocal patterns other than crying
- Usually stops babbling in response to vocal stimulation

5 TO 6 MONTHS
- Appears to distinguish general meanings of warning, anger, or friendly voice
- Appears to recognize words like daddy, bye-bye, mama, etc.
- Stops or withdraws in response to "no" at least 50% of time
- Takes initiative in vocalizing with others
- Occasionally vocalizes with four or more different syllables
- Plays at making sounds and noises while alone

6 TO 7 MONTHS
- Appears to recognize names of family members in speech
- Responds with appropriate gestures to words such as *up*, *come*, *high*, and *bye-bye*
- Gives some attention to music
- Begins some two-syllable babbling
- Responds with vocalizations when called 50% of time

7 TO 8 MONTHS
- Frequently appears to listen to whole conversations
- Regularly stops activity when name is called
- Appears to recognize the names of some common objects
- Occasionally vocalizes in sentence-like utterances without using true words
- Plays speech-gestures games like pat-a-cake or peek-a-boo
- Occasionally sings along with some familiar song or music without using true words

(continued)

TABLE 4–3 (Continued)

8 TO 9 MONTHS

- Appears to understand some simple verbal requests
- Regularly stops activity in response to "no"
- Will sustain interest for up to a full minute in picture naming
- Uses some gesture language (i.e., shaking head appropriately)
- Mimics the sounds and number of syllables used by others
- Now includes more consonants in utterances

9 TO 10 MONTHS

- Appears to enjoy listening to new words
- Generally able to listen to speech without being distracted by other sounds
- Often gives toys or objects to parent upon verbal request
- Uses some exclamations like "oh-oh"
- May attempt first words ("da-da," "ma-ma," etc.)

10 TO 11 MONTHS

- Occasionally follows simple commands ("put it down")
- Appears to understand simple questions
- Responds to rhythmic music with body or hand movements
- Usually vocalizes in varied jargon while playing alone
- Occasionally tries to imitate new words

11 TO 12 MONTHS

- Responds with appropriate gestures to several kinds of verbal requests
- Increased attention to speech—longer periods of time
- Some appropriate verbal responses to requests ("say bye-bye")
- Uses three or more words with consistency
- Talks to toys or people with longer verbal patterns
- Frequently responds to songs by vocalizing

12 TO 14 MONTHS

- Appears to understand new words each week
- Seems to understand some psychological feelings of speakers
- Interest in picture naming is 2 or more minutes
- Uses five or more true words with consistency
- Attempts to obtain desired objects by using voice and pointing
- Uses some true words in jargon utterances

14 TO 16 MONTHS

- Responds to verbal request to get familiar object from room
- Identifies many objects and pictures of objects when named
- Recognizes names of various body parts
- Consistently uses seven or more true words
- Uses such as "t," "d," "w," "n," and "h" more frequently
- Communicates mostly with true words and gestures

16 TO 18 MONTHS

- Carries out two consecutive directions with an object
- Remembers and associates new words by category (food, clothing, animal, etc.)
- Identifies two or more familiar objects from a group
- Begins to use words rather than gestures for wants and needs
- Begins repeating words overheard in conversation
- Gradually increases speaking vocabulary

18 TO 20 MONTHS

- With verbal request, points to several body parts
- Understands specific action words (verb form) such as "sit down," "come here," "stop that"
- Understands personal pronouns (her, me, him, etc.)

(continued)

TABLE 4—3 (Continued)

- Imitates some two- and three-word sentences
- Imitates environmental sounds (motors, animals, etc.)
- Has speaking vocabulary of 20 words

20 TO 22 MONTHS

- Follows a series of two or three simple, related commands
- Recognizes new words daily
- Recognizes most common objects
- Begins combining words into simple sentences ("go bye-bye," "daddy come")
- Speaks more words daily
- Attempts to tell of experiences using jargon and true words

22 TO 24 MONTHS

- Will select an item from a group of five
- Appears to listen to meaning and reason, not just words
- Understands more complex sentences ("When I go to the store, I'll buy ice cream.")
- Occasionally uses three-word sentences ("There it is." "Play with me.")
- Refers to self with own name
- Begins using some pronouns but makes errors in syntax

24 TO 27 MONTHS

- Demonstrates understanding of action words (verb form)
- Understands smaller parts of the body (elbow, chin, etc.)
- Identifies general family name categories (grandma, mom)
- Usually uses two- or three-word sentences
- Often uses personal pronouns correctly ("I," "you," "he," "it," "me")
- Asks for help with some personal needs (hand washing, using the toilet)

27 TO 30 MONTHS

- Understands word association through functional identification (What do you eat with? What do you wear?)
- Understands size differences
- Recognizes the names and pictures of most common objects
- Names at least one color correctly
- Refers to self by using a pronoun rather than proper name
- Repeats two or more numbers correctly

30 TO 33 MONTHS

- Demonstrates understanding of all common verbs
- Understands longer and more complex sentences
- Demonstrates an understanding of common adjectives
- Tells gender when asked
- Names and talks about what he or she has drawn when asked
- Gives both first and last name when asked

33 TO 36 MONTHS

- Shows interest in explanations of why and how things work
- Carries out three verbal commands given in one long utterance
- Demonstrates an understanding on prepositions ("in," "on," "under")
- Regularly relates experiences from the recent past
- Uses several verb forms correctly
- Uses some plural forms correctly

LATER LANGUAGE DEVELOPMENT

- Regular plural (-s) (33 months)
- Possessives ("mommy's hat") (40 months)
- Irregular past tense ("fell," "broke") (46 months)
- Articles ("a," "the") (46 months)
- Regular past tense (-ed) (48 months)

TABLE 4–4
Goals for Speaking and Listening by Grade Levels

Kindergarten Through Second Grade

Students listen critically and respond appropriately to oral communication.

Students will:
- Determine the purpose or purposes of listening (e.g., to obtain information, to solve problems, for enjoyment).
- Ask for clarification and explanation of stories and ideas.
- Paraphrase information that has been shared orally by others.
- Give and follow three- and four-step oral directions.
- Speak clearly and at an appropriate pace for the type of communication (e.g., informal discussion, report to class).

Students deliver brief recitations and oral presentations about familiar experiences or interests.

Students will:
- Describe story elements (e.g., characters, plot, setting).
- Report on a topic with facts and details, drawing from several sources of information.

Third Through Fifth Grade

Students deliver focused, coherent presentations that convey ideas clearly and relate to the background and interests of the audience.

Students will:
- Ask questions that seek information not already discussed.
- Interpret a speaker's verbal and nonverbal messages, purposes, and perspectives.
- Make inferences or draw conclusions based on an oral report.
- Retell, paraphrase, and explain what has been said by the speaker typically listened to for recreational, informational, or functional purposes.
- Select a focus, organizational structure, and point of view for an oral presentation.
- Clarify and support spoken ideas with evidence and examples.
- Analyze media sources for information, entertainment, persuasion, interpretation of events, and transmission of culture.

Students will deliver well-organized, formal presentations employing traditional rhetorical strategies (e.g., narration, exposition, persuasion, and description).

Students will:
- Deliver narrative presentations that establish a situation, plot, point of view, and setting with descriptive words and phrases and show, rather than tell, the listener what happens.
- Deliver informative presentations about an important idea, issue, or event by framing questions to direct the investigation, establishing a controlling idea or topic, and developing the topic with simple facts, details, examples, and explanations.
- Deliver oral responses to literature that summarize significant events and details, articulate an understanding of several ideas or images communicated by the literary work, and use examples or textual evidence from the work to support conclusions.

Sixth Through Eighth Grade

Students will formulate adroit judgments about oral communication. They deliver focused and coherent presentations that convey clear and distinct perspectives and demonstrate solid reasoning. They use gestures, tone, and vocabulary tailored to the audience and purpose.

(continued)

TABLE 4–4 (Continued)

Students will:

- Paraphrase a speaker's purpose and point of view; and ask relevant questions concerning the speaker's content, delivery, and purpose.
- Deliver a focused, coherent speech based on organized information which generally includes: an introduction, transitions, preview and summaries, a logical body, and an effective conclusion.
- Evaluate the credibility of a speaker and evaluate the various ways in which visual image makers communicate information and affect impressions and opinions.
- Demonstrate appropriate group discussion behavior by listening attentively, collaborating equitably, and asking questions and extending discussions.

Students deliver polished formal and extemporaneous presentations that combine traditional rhetorical strategies of narration, exposition, persuasion, and description. Student speaking demonstrates a command of standard American English and the organizational and delivery strategies outlined in the Listening and Speaking Standard.

Students will:

- Deliver narrative presentations that relate a coherent incident, event, or situation and elegantly express the significance of and the subject's attitude about, the incident, event, or situation.
- Deliver oral responses to literature that interpret a reading and provide insight through textual references. Judgments are supported and discussed using text connections (text-to-self, text-to-text, and text-to-world).
- Deliver research presentations that define a thesis, express important ideas using direct quotations from significant sources, and utilize visuals (charts, maps, and graphs) as a tool for presenting important information.
- Deliver persuasive presentations that use supportive arguments with detailed evidence, examples, and reasoning, and anticipates and answers listener concerns and counter arguments effectively.
- Recite poems, sections of speeches, or dramatic soliloquies, using voice modulation, tone, and gestures expressively to enhance the meaning.

Source: Published by the Office Curriculum, Instruction, and Professional Development, Long Beach Unified School District. Reprinted with permission (2005).

Peek into classrooms and you will frequently find that listening occupies a major portion of the time children spend there. In addition to classroom time spent listening, in today's complex world a child also watches and listens to television, radio shows, CDs, and DVDs and listens and talks on the telephone. Too often, parents and teachers have assumed that quiet children are listening children. But are they? The obvious answer is: "Not necessarily." Students need to develop listening skills that will enable them to function well in a complex society. Teachers can facilitate this process by teaching listening skills and by fostering an environment in which these skills can be acquired easily.

Children are exposed to sounds from the earliest moments of life. Brown (1954) referred to this listening/language process as *auding*.

> Auding is to the ears what reading is to the eyes. If reading is the gross process of looking, recognizing, and interpreting written symbols, auding may be defined as the gross process of listening to, recognizing, and interpreting spoken symbols. (p. 86)

In other words auding means listening with comprehension and understanding. Given this definition, a major difference between hearing and listening is an individual's focus of attention; attention is certainly a necessary element in the process of comprehending auditory cues whether these cues are presented as directions by

DID YOU NOTICE...
Did you notice that teachers can learn the most from observing the performance of their students?

the teacher, last-minute parental admonitions before the child leaves for school, or plans for after-school playtime shouted across the schoolyard.

Part of your job as a classroom teacher will be to identify children with hearing disabilities rather than poor listening skills because children with disabilities should be referred to a specialist. Most students who have hearing-related disabilities are identified by their teacher. Detecting these problems is not always an easy task. However, through observation you may notice that a student

1. is abnormally inattentive.
2. relies on gestures when speech would be more effective.
3. is slow in speech development.
4. strains to hear what is being said.
5. gives inappropriate answers to your questions.
6. ignores a speaker with whom he or she does not have direct eye contact.
7. has difficulty relating sequences to the one presented.
8. may be unable to reproduce consonant phonemes.
9. has difficulty repeating long, detailed sentences.
10. evidences voice production (pitch, stress, or rhythm) difficulties.

In addition, you need to be particularly alert to any student who may exhibit one or more of these signs when you are aware that the child has any of the following medical complaints: (a) frequent colds or ear infections; (b) allergies; or (c) measles, mumps, or rubella. If you detect possible hearing difficulties, refer the student to a speech and hearing specialist or to the school doctor or nurse.

In your diagnostic efforts, be careful not to confuse linguistic variations in speech patterns with hearing impairment. You may observe omissions, additions, distortions, and substitutions in the speech patterns of your children that are an outgrowth of dialect rather than a function of hearing difficulty. For example, a speaker of Black English (African American Vernacular English [AAVE]) will sound different from a speaker of Standard English. If you are working with students who have dialects other than your own, be careful not to diagnose their listening/language needs incorrectly or as a disability. If you do not have an understanding of their language pattern, it's very important for you to consult with another adult who does. Be careful to not make judgments about the appropriate instructional needs of your students until you have acquired a thorough understanding of the home language and cultures.

WHAT CAN TEACHERS DO TO ENHANCE LISTENING SKILLS?

As you attempt to integrate all language processes throughout your curriculum, it is important to be aware of the following dimensions of both students and the environment.

Planning Your Classroom Environment

Increasing your students' receptiveness to what they hear may be possible by organizing your classroom environment in the following way:

1. Develop a classroom environment (seating arrangements or bulletin boards) that can help to focus attention on the speaker. Ms. Jimenez has the desk arranged in the center of the room facing her presentation area so that when she talks or other students perform, everyone in the room can see and hear. She has other areas of the room devoted to other activities such as the classroom library that has bookshelves and beanbag chairs around to absorb sound and create a quieter area.

2. Speak clearly and loudly enough to be heard. Don't "talk to the chalkboard." Whenever possible, be animated. Ms. Jimenez models her "presentation voice" when she reads to students. She also refrains from writing on the board while she speaks; instead she prepares the board in advance of her discussion and uses an overhead so that she can speak directly to her students.

3. Emphasize concrete, not abstract, ideas (for example, say "Rosa Parks Elementary School," not "school"). Ms. Jimenez knows that this is especially helpful for her English language learners as it increases their understanding of her presentations.

4. Use vocal variety when you are speaking to keep shifting the students' attention so that they continue listening to you.

In addition to planning an environment that ensures productive listening, be sure to plan situations that encourage positive listening attitudes and habits.

Developing Positive Listening Attitudes

The development of a positive attitude toward listening is accomplished by

1. discussing the importance of listening with your children. Ms. Jimenez reminds her students of this very important skill on a regular basis through her questioning and prediction activities.

2. beginning each lesson by establishing a specific purpose. For example, Ms. Jimenez might say, "Listen and raise your hand when you hear two words that rhyme."

3. encouraging children to listen and share ideas. For example, students may be prompted before a book club discussion with "listen for your partner's major idea and write that one down. Then ask your partner what his or her idea was and discuss it."

4. reinforcing good listening habits. Ms. Jimenez lets her students know when she catches them listening well. She might say something like, "Jessica, you listened so well to that story that you even remembered the name of the cat!"

5. being a good listener yourself. When students speak, try not to grade papers, talk with another adult, or the like. Ms. Jimenez models the listening skills she expects from her students and encourages them to ask her questions about the presentations as well.

Listening and Sharing the Sounds of the World

You can learn a great deal about your students by having them share the sounds of their personal worlds. Ask your students to share a number of sounds they hear, including sounds they hear on the way to school, sounds of things they enjoy the

DID YOU NOTICE...
Did you notice that you can expose students to language and many new concepts through read alouds and shared reading?

most, sounds of a quiet, relaxed time, sounds of someone they love, or sounds that remind them of school. Remember that Ms. Jimenez gave the assignment to listen for the sounds of the first snow and she gave that assignment in October. Her students were listening and ready when the first snow finally came in November!

Often these conversations about sounds in the world can be followed with a big book read aloud or shared reading. For example, you may discuss telephone conversations with your students and then share the book *Ring! Yo?* (Raschka, 2000) because the book models a telephone call with very few words. Alternatively, you may discuss the difference between loud and soft sounds and share the book *Too Much Noise* (McGovern, 1967) as this book notes these differences.

Sometimes Ms. Jimenez starts class with an interesting question for her students to discuss. These questions often focus on something that the students listened to during the previous day. She may ask her students to share what they liked or disliked about the music class the day before. Another day, she may ask her students to talk with a partner about all the sounds dogs make and what those sounds may mean (scared, happy, angry, hurt, etc.). Her purpose in these exercises is to encourage her students to develop their listening comprehension and conversational skills. She often relates these conversations to class books. For example, the class conversation about dogs was used as an introduction to the book *How to Talk to Your Dog* (George, 2000), a humorous look at pet companions.

Creating Sounds

Students of all ages enjoy producing sounds from objects such as metal lids, water taps, paper, and other materials that are easy to collect. One student used a round oatmeal container with 1 cup of rice to create a shaker. Another taped the ends of a paper towel roll closed after placing 10 popcorn seeds inside. Provide a large cardboard box where sound makers may be stored. Each time students devise new sounds, encourage them to share the sounds with others. Keep your curriculum flexible enough to accommodate new developments.

Ms. Jimenez loves creating sounds. She knows that her students will naturally tap and shake things to hear new sounds. She has incorporated this natural interest into her curriculum. Students know that they can try some "noise-makers" out during specific periods of time, whereas other times are reserved for quiet.

Listening for a Definite Purpose

Listening involves both hearing and inferring meaning from what is heard. Ideas for the development of comprehensive listening lessons include the following:

1. *Illustrated Sequencing* (numbers, letters, directions). Ms. Jimenez likes to provide oral instructions for students to write. One day she might give oral instructions about drawing something (e.g., start with a straight line across your paper. Put a circle above the line, etc.). Other days, she lists letters that spell words. She asks students to "see the pattern in their minds" and say the word. For example, she asked students to listen to the following letters (not writing them down) D I N O S A U R. When she finished, she asked Lajuana what the word was.

2. *Anticipate What's Next.* Ms. Jimenez uses this activity to encourage students to listen and anticipate what may follow. For example, she reads stories and poems to her students and omits some obvious words. She encourages the children to listen for context clues that will help them to supply missing information. During a recent read aloud of the book The Class Artist (Karas, 2001), a charming book about a boy who thinks he can't draw anything, she omitted the words in the following passage:

"I'll show you how. Let's make Pilgrims. First you __(draw)__ a circle, and then you ___(draw)___ their hair." Fred caught on quickly. "See I told you that was _(easy)_," said Martha. "It is _(easy)_!" said Fred.

3. *Drawing Inferences.* This activity encourages students to infer meaning from what they have heard by reading short paragraphs or stories. Ms. Jimenez follows her listening activities with questions such as

—Why do you think …?

—How would you feel …? Why?

—What would you do …? Why?

—How do you know …?

4. *Questioning the Text.* This activity provides students an opportunity to answer questions that are based on a text they have read. For example, one afternoon Ms. Jimenez read the following passage:

Devin and Heather were spending the summer with Grandmother. Devin awakened early one morning and tiptoed into Grandmother's kitchen. As he crept around the corner of the pantry feeling for the cookie jar, he jumped with fright. A shadow! Someone else was in the kitchen. He momentarily forgot about the cookie jar and groped for the light. There was Heather also inching her way toward the cookie jar.

After reading the passage, she asked her students:

—At what time do you think the story occurred?

—How did Devin know Heather was in the kitchen?

—How did he feel when he realized the "shadow" was Heather?

—What were the kids doing in the kitchen?

—Has anything similar ever happened to you?

It is important to ask a wide range of questions because answering them encourages the students to engage in various thinking activities. Be careful, however, not to dominate the discussion with teacher-directed questions. Open-ended questions tend to generate the most elaborate responses, especially if the teacher encourages elaboration by saying things like "Tell me more" and "Why do you say that?" The point is that anticipated questions can underscore students' attention to listening, but too many teacher-centered questions can make for a boring, less effective classroom.

TABLE 4–5
Listening Checklist

Name: _____

When _____ listens, he/she:

	Sept.	Dec.	Mar.	June
directs attention to the speaker.				
takes turns and waits to talk.				
determines the validity of statements made by the speaker.				
listens for the organizational style of the speaker.				
thinks carefully about the message being sent.				
listens until the speaker has completed the statement.				
thinks of appropriate responses.				
weighs the value of a response.				

A = always, S = sometimes, N = never

Evaluating Listening Competencies

Assessments are an important part of classroom instruction. Teachers such as Ms. Jimenez use assessments to plan their instruction. As noted in the opening, Ms. Jimenez uses a speaking checklist to evaluate her students' public speaking skills. She also uses a listening checklist. She is especially interested in teaching her students to evaluate their own strengths as listeners. Table 4–5 contains the listening checklist.

During one of your interactions with a classmate, evaluate your listening competencies using the listening checklist from Table 4–5. What do you notice about yourself as a listener? If you pay too much attention to the criteria, what will happen to your conversation?

WHAT IS THE ROLE OF SPEAKING IN THE LANGUAGE ARTS CURRICULUM?

Most children come to school with language and the desire to communicate. Given this potential, why is there so often a communication breakdown in the classroom? Perhaps it is because we insist on correct language (i.e., school talk), and we fail to understand differences and discrepancies in the child's pronunciation, phrasing, lexicon, and construction. In fact, the tension between correct language (the language of the school and teacher) and effective language (the language of the child) can lead to student failure. Although the basics of language are learned long before a child enters your classroom, you can continue to encourage a positive language experience and a variety of language expressions in the classroom.

Language is a means of expressing the self. The language of self-expression is seldom neutral because it conveys our ideas, love, humor, hate, anger, excuses, and other human sensations. Classroom teachers have the opportunity as well as the responsibility to encourage the use of language as self-expression by fostering a climate of acceptance. Students will interpret rejection of their language as a rejection of themselves. This has been well documented for the thousands of children who speak Black English (AAVE) and who were told by well-meaning adults that their language was unacceptable. Today, we understand that AAVE is unique and that students can maintain this language and its structure while also adding a register of standard English. Because an important process of life is the continual identification of self in a constantly changing environment, it is paramount that teachers accept a child's language and then provide a safe classroom environment with many opportunities for language expansion.

An important factor in the development of self-expressive speech is time. We must first try sharing a small amount of information, weigh the results and consequences of sharing bits of ourselves through language, and perhaps, finally, if the consequences are not too harsh, try again. If these early attempts at self-expression are rejected, students will be wary of taking such a risk again. They may even alter their own ideas to express those that will receive the teacher's acceptance.

You will notice that the language of young children is often egocentric and focuses on themselves and their world as they know it (e.g., I go or I want a cookie). As they engage in group situations, use of this egocentric language lessens. As they become involved in sender-receiver exchanges, their language becomes more expository and descriptive, which ultimately enables them to receive and convey an even wider variety of messages (Jacobson, Lapp, & Mendez, 2003).

In addition to self-expression and conversation, language is a means of acquiring information. Alone, people are often unable to fully understand the world around them. However, through language interchanges, people continually experience larger segments of the universe. Many of these interchanges are verbal: "How do I get to City Hall?" "What are your views regarding …?" "Have you read …?" Such interchanges supply us with topics of discussion as well as bits of valuable information. A person's ability to use language is heavily dependent on an ever-increasing vocabulary and security in self-expression.

Other tasks and activities that can give your students an opportunity to expand their oral language skills include small-group discussions, interviews, Readers' Theater, storytelling, formal and informal speeches, role playing, choral speaking, puppetry, and creative dramatics. These activities are not only valuable tools for building oral language skills, but they are also fun for the teacher and students.

What Can Teachers Do to Enhance Speaking Skills?

The question for classroom teachers is how to channel a child's natural affinity for talk into practice for effective oral communication. Formal oral language training must exist in classrooms. Language arts programs should begin to provide more ways for students to participate in oral communication.

One way to incorporate speaking into the curriculum is to structure classroom activities around a presentational mode. The following activities can be adapted for use at both primary and intermediate levels.

Illustration

Ms. Jimenez asks each student to create a colorful illustration for a vocabulary word. On the back of the illustration, students write the selected word and a complete sentence that contains the word. Shannon selected the word *create* and illustrated this by showing a pair of hands kneading bread. Her sentence was, "I can create art with my hands." She volunteered to share her illustration with the class. The other students in the class looked over the vocabulary words and Tommy said, "That picture is creative because you are showing how to make something." Shannon then shared the sentence she had written and called on the next presenter. In addition to providing oral practice, students are practicing their sentence-writing skills (you may direct students to write a simple sentence, a sentence beginning with a prepositional phrase, a compound sentence, etc.), and you will have their colorful artwork to display in your room.

Dramatization

Role playing and dramatics can take on many forms and are universally fun for students from primary to secondary grades. During the early years, students can dramatize or role play their stories, perhaps with different groups being responsible for different stories so that all children have a chance to participate. Even very shy members of a group will usually feel comfortable beginning their dramatic "careers" as a stately tree or a door that must open and close. Similarly, in later years, students can dramatize a crucial scene from a piece of literature or write their own script and recreate a hypothetical scene such as being pioneers around a campfire. During center activity time, one group of students in Ms. Jimenez's class chose to dramatize the book *Aunt Chip and the Great Triple Creek Dam Affair* (Polacco, 1996) because she wanted her students to understand the importance of books in society. As in the story, they used books for all kinds of things besides reading—they were doormats, picture holders, and even chairs! During their dramatization, they retold the story of how books were rediscovered by the people in town and how people reopened the library.

Making Puppets Do the Talking

Puppets provide another vehicle for dramatizations. Simple puppets can be created by drawing a face on a sock or paper bag and using it as a hand puppet, drawing construction paper figures and gluing them to sticks, and decorating paper towel or toilet paper rolls. Staging can also be simple as students enact through their puppets their language experience stories or stories they have read in class. Many students who are inhibited by face-to-face contact with others feel much freer to express themselves orally through their puppet creations. Ms. Jimenez has a bucket full of puppets she has purchased or her students have made. She often observes her students interacting with one another or talking about books through these puppets.

Let's Act It Out

Dramatizations do not always have to be accompanied by words. Pantomime exercises develop an awareness of the importance of body movements and gestures that accompany spoken language. Like Ms. Jimenez, you may want to include pantomiming concepts related to vocabulary words or everyday scenes and situations with which children may be familiar (e.g., a flower rising toward the sun, a scene from a movie, a favorite book or story title, a classroom routine, or how their pet gets their attention). Students who are presenting quickly lose much of their stage fright when they realize the enthusiasm they are generating in their classmates. As another suggestion, these dramatizations can be performed at "Back-to-School Nights" or for children in different grade levels.

Choral Reading

The dramatic presentation of a poem, story, or dialogue by groups of children is called a choral reading. Nursery rhymes and songs are appropriate choral readings for younger children, as are classic poems such as "Casey at the Bat" by Ernest Lawrence Thayer or "The Raven" by Edger A. Poe and modern poems by Shel Silverstein, Paul Fleishman, and Langston Hughes.

Choral readings can be orchestrated in a variety of ways. A leader can begin with the group chiming in on the refrain, small groups can each be assigned a line or stanza to read, a narrator's part can be read by one group while another group reads the dialogue, or one group can begin, with an additional group contributing with each successive line or stanza, until all are reading together at the end in a crescendo effect.

Ms. Jimenez wanted her students to experience the famous poem by Lewis Carroll, "Jabberwocky" (see Table 4–6). However, she knew that she could not assign

TABLE 4–6
"Jabberwocky" by Lewis Carroll

'Twas brillig, and the slithy toves
    Did gyre and gimble in the wabe:
All mimsy were the borogoves,
    And the mome raths outgrabe.

"Beware the Jabberwock, my son!
    The jaws that bite, the claws that catch!
Beware the Jubjub bird, and shun
    The frumious Bandersnatch!"

He took his vorpal sword in hand:
    Long time the manxome foe he sought—
So rested he by the Tumtum tree,
    And stood awhile in thought.

And, as in uffish thought he stood,
    The Jabberwock, with eyes of flame,
Came whiffling through the tulgey wood,
    And burbled as it came!

One, two! One, two! And through and through
    The vorpal blade went snicker-snack!
He left it dead, and with its head
    He went galumphing back.

"And, has thou slain the Jabberwock?
    Come to my arms, my beamish boy!
O frabjous day! Callooh! Callay!"
    He chortled in his joy.

'Twas brillig, and the slithy toves
    Did gyre and gimble in the wabe;
All mimsy were the borogoves,
    And the mome raths outgrabe.

Source: Through the Looking-Glass and What Alice Found There, 1872.

---

this poem as independent reading because it contained a number of nonsense words and difficult concepts. Instead, she decided to chorally read the poem. Her approach was to read it once aloud to students. She then shared the text of the poem with her students by placing the text on the overhead. They then read aloud with her. Finally, she assigned different stanzas to different groups and gave them 3 minutes to practice the words. Remember that her students had heard the pronunciations twice before they had to read aloud as a small group. Only after they had read the poem together a number of times did she begin to ask them questions about the poem, such as "Where did this poem take place?" "Who are the characters?" "Was someone or something killed?" "What nouns can you find in this poem?" "How do you know?"

Oral Reports

Although the term *oral report* is a tortuous sound for many students, it actually can encompass many types of presentations, from show-and-tell and sharing to biographical sketches.

The term *show-and-tell* is probably best used at the primary levels, but the concept of sharing is appropriate for students of all ages. Times of sharing can involve reporting news items, sharing a favorite belonging, reporting on a favorite food, sharing the events of a special trip, and reporting on a job accomplished. The possibilities are limitless. During these times, it is important that the teacher not dominate the talk, but that students be allowed to develop their own styles of sharing as a first step in a progression toward public speaking. Ms. Jimenez uses a variation of this with her students. While studying different social studies concepts, students are encouraged to bring related items to class and share them with their peers. These items, or *realia*, help everyone understand difficult concepts. Some of the items are photos whereas others are manipulatives. During her westward expansion unit, students shared wagon wheels, miniature covered wagons, gold nuggets, and fool's gold, among other things. Because she realizes that many children are shy, she always provides time for the oral presentation to first be shared with one child or to a small group before the presenter is asked to share it with the whole class.

Biographical Sketch

Another vehicle for sharing information is the biographical sketch. This is particularly effective at the beginning of the school year when students may not know one another well. Students develop a series of questions and interview a classmate; this information is then presented to the class. Typically, students are less shy when talking about someone else than when talking about themselves because attention seems to be focused on the person interviewed rather than on the interviewer.

Classified Ads

Ms. Jimenez invites her students to keep classified ads and to keep these updated. Students submit items for two columns—help wanted and help offered. Given that everyone participates, Ms. Jimenez doesn't worry that students will be teased for acknowledging their need for help. Justin advertised for help with math by writing, "The numbers are crazy to me. Can you help me? I need someone during afterschool to help with the math homework—please! Justin." She is also pleased when her students consult the ads for help offered. She observed Kisha looking through the ads one afternoon and finding Tonja's help-offered ad, "Miss Mary Mack, Double Dutch, and all. If you want to learn to jump that rope, give me a call." Ms. Jimenez was thrilled to see the two girls discussing jump rope skills after writing and reading the classified ads.

Discussion

Classroom discussions range from whole-class discussions to informal, small-group activities to formal panel discussions and debates. Whole-class discussions in which all students are encouraged to participate are a powerful, and often overlooked, way to give students the opportunity to try out their oral skills in a group setting. Small groups can be given problem-solving tasks in which everyone in the group participates in the brainstorming and synthesis of ideas. In these groups, students can rotate high-profile roles such as leader, reporter/presenter, recorder, and so on. Although the entire group may not be in front of an audience, members get a chance to participate orally with their peers in a classroom situation.

Ms. Jimenez uses a number of small-group instructional strategies and encourages her students to talk with members of the group before they share with the whole class. This allows everyone in the group to practice speaking, even though only one or two members may share with the whole class. In addition, Ms. Jimenez provides her students with multiple opportunities to partner talk before sharing with the whole class. She knows that this allows her students to check out their answers with another person and increases the likelihood that all students will participate in whole-class activities.

Panel Presentations

Panel discussions involve researching a topic and presenting information to the audience. Because panel members are together in the presentations, they are more likely to participate enthusiastically than if they are alone. After the presentation, the panel's leader can field questions from the audience. This type of presentation lends itself well to chapter reviews or reports on geography, culture, and history, and audience members can be prepared with questions they have written before hand. It is productive for the teacher to work with students as they write their questions so that various levels of questions from concrete to abstract are asked.

Ms. Jimenez often closes an instructional unit with panel discussions. For example, after researching different U.S. presidents, each group shared interesting information about their selected leader. These were brief reviews so that everyone in class had some information about these leaders. It also signified the end of the unit for students and allowed them to gain closure.

Oral Practice

Because of the many potential differences between an individual's private and public language, Standard English may simply "sound wrong" to students. Therefore, just as the ear of a musician can be trained to hear the right sounds, language arts teachers can train the ears of their students so that standard forms of English begin to "sound correct" for use in most public situations. The following ideas for oral practice can be adapted to all grade levels and for a multitude of usage experiences.

1. The best way to expand usage habits is by illustrating private and public language constructions. For example, it's not uncommon to hear children say "I seen...." When this occurs in Ms. Jimenez's class, she tells them that "I saw" is the public form, and to practice, students in the class will share what they saw on the way to school. First, the teacher will begin; then all students can share, one at a time, what they saw.

    Teacher: I saw a hawk sitting on a fence.
    Child 1:   I saw a big yellow car.
    Child 2:   I saw the ice cream truck go by.

2. The more students can participate in oral practice, the more adept they will be as effective communicators. A way to increase this participation is to allow them to be teachers as well as students. For example, to alter the usage pattern of "I ain't," choose one student to ask a question that begins "Are you ..." and then call on another student to respond, continuing until all students have participated. The response must begin "I am" or "I'm not."

Student 1 calls on Student 2:	Are you 10 years old?
Student 2:	I'm not 10 years old. I am 9½ years old.
Student 2 calls on Student 3:	Are you wearing tennis shoes?
Student 3:	I am wearing tennis shoes.

Make sure that students ask their questions and provide answers in complete sentences. Also, the pace of this practice must be quick to keep students interested in the activity.

3. Students' ears can become attuned to hearing speech patterns appropriate for a given situation. Brainstorm 25 to 30 words that begin with the target sound. S is an initial sound that children often need to practice. List common words on the board that begin with S:

sand   soap   saddle   sick   sofa   sock

Give each student a moment to choose a word and form a clue to its identity. Then allow one student to present his or her clue and pick another student to respond to the clue by saying one of the words on the board.

Student 1:	I always try to wash my hands with this.
Student 2:	Soap.

Book Clubs

Students communicate orally throughout the day in both formal and informal situations. Teachers frequently use literature circles and book clubs to encourage students to express their understandings, reactions, and responses to ideas they have read (Roser & Martinez, 1995). In one book club in Ms. Jimenez's class, the students were reading *In the Year of the Boar and Jackie Robinson* (Lord, 1984), an interesting book about an immigrant family set in the times of Jackie Robinson, the first black baseball player on an integrated professional team. Jessica leaned over to Dominique and said, "Now I understand why you like baseball so much, but I think the book is more about a person coming to this country and not knowing how everything works." Dominique responded, "I got into the book because I wanted to read about baseball. But I've learned a lot more than that. Remember when Shirley couldn't find her way home? I wonder if that is what happened to my parents when they moved here."

Book clubs build children's confidence, which in turn permits them to orally participate in class. Ms. Jimenez uses the following guidelines for organizing her book clubs:

- After reading the selection, write a journal response (2 to 4 minutes; individually). This ensures that students will have something to say about the selection to be discussed.

- Review journal entries and revisit the text by scanning (1 to 2 minutes; individually). Ask students to silently read what they have written and underline or highlight a word or phrase they want to share and/or to write a brief entry, a reflection about their written response, or a new thought/question based upon their review of the text.

- Share responses with a partner (2 to 4 minutes; pairs). Pair students off and ask them to share thoughts based upon their reading/writing and discussion of text with their partner. This begins the oral exchange and because it only involves a pair the chances of intimidation are lessened.

- Model how to lead a discussion with the group (1 to 15 minutes; group). Allow students to volunteer and share the discussion they had with their partners. Encourage students to become discussion leaders. When they are ready to do so, a book club discussion group of five or six is very effective. Have content-specific questions ready to focus the discussion if it strays too far afield or becomes bogged down on a point that seems to be unresolvable.

- When the discussion seems to have run its course, ask students to write a response to a pointed question (4 minutes; individuals). For example, What surprised you most when you read the text? What caused you to say "Wow"? What questions do you have about the text or discussion at this point? What's still puzzling you? What word or phrase caught your attention enough for you to have savored it? Why do you think it was so memorable?

- Again have students share their responses with a partner (4 minutes; pairs) before returning to a discussion with their group (10 minutes; group).

- Have students write their reflections about the text, the discussion, and their growth in their interpretation and participation (2 to 4 minutes; individuals). These reflections may be shared within the individual groups or as an entire class.

- Each group may summarize their reflections to be shared with the entire class through conversation, a performance, a book talk, a poster, a billboard, or other appropriate form of expression (10 to 30 minutes; group).

HOW CAN TEACHERS ASSESS ORAL LANGUAGE SKILLS?

Although most teachers include conversations in their classrooms in ways similar to those we have described, the development of oral literacy for some "will remain an unimportant subject in the schools as long as it goes unevaluated" (Buckley, 1992, p. 626). Continuous assessment and instruction should be tightly integrated in classrooms in which student performance is valued. When assessing oral literacy, teachers use retelling inventories and speaking checklists (Lapp, Flood, Fisher, & Cabello, 2001). These tools are often informal checklists that are used to assess students' comprehension, sentence structure knowledge, and vocabulary development. The inventories and checklists can be used continuously throughout the year to demonstrate a child's reading progress as well as his or her oral fluency (see Table 4–1). Teachers such as Ms. Jimenez use these tools to check student knowledge of mechanics, syntax, and oral language patterns. Teachers can also use this information (or the version in Table 4.2) to assess students' knowledge of story comprehension and plot development, including things uch as roles played by various characters. Once this information is collected, teachers can plan appropriate learning experiences that provide opportunities for students to expand their oral literacy.

In addition to this type of speaking checklist, the Student Oral Language Observation Matrix (SOLOM) has been used to describe oral language development for English language learners. This informal assessment tool should be administered several times in different situations before a score is reported (see Table 4–7). The infor-

TABLE 4–7
Student Oral Language Observation Matrix (SOLOM)

Student Name: _____   **Grade:** _____   **Age:** _____   **Language:** _____

	1	2	3	4	5	Scores
Comprehension	Cannot be said to understand even simple conversation.	Has great difficulty following what is said. Comprehends only social conversation spoken slowly with frequent repetitions.	Understands most of what is said at slower-than-normal speed with repetitions.	Understands nearly everything at normal speed, although occasional repetition may be necessary.	Understands everyday conversations and normal classroom discussions without difficulty.	
Fluency	Speech is so halting and fragmentary as to make conversation virtually impossible.	Usually hesitant; often forced into silence by language limitations.	Speech in everyday conversation somewhat limited because of inadequate vocabulary.	Speech in everyday conversation and classroom discussion is generally fluent, with occasional lapses while student searches for the correct manner of expression.	Speech in everyday conversation and classroom discussion is fluent and effortless, approximating that of a native speaker.	
Vocabulary	Vocabulary limitations so extreme as to make conversation virtually impossible.	Misuse of words and very limited vocabulary make comprehension quite difficult.	Frequently uses the wrong words; conversation somewhat limited because of inadequate vocabulary.	Occasionally uses inappropriate terms and/or must rephrase ideas because of lexical inadequacies.	Use of vocabulary and idioms approximates that of a native speaker.	
Pronunciation	Pronunciation problems so severe as to make speech virtually unintelligible.	Very hard to understand because of pronunciation problems. Must frequently repeat to be understood.	Pronunciation problems necessitate concentration on the part of the listener and occasionally leads to misunderstanding.	Always intelligible, although one is conscious of a definite accent and occasional inappropriate intonation patterns.	Pronunciation and intonation approximate those of a native speaker.	
Grammar	Errors in grammar and word order so severe as to make speech virtually unintelligible.	Grammar and word errors make comprehension difficult. Must often rephrase and/or restrict self to basic patterns.	Makes frequent grammar and word order errors that occasionally obscure meaning.	Occasionally makes grammatical and/or word order errors that do not obscure meaning.	Grammatical usage and word order approximate those of a native speaker.	
Stages of language development	Preproduction Score: 20%	Early Production Score: 24–40%	Speech Emergence Score: 44–60%	Intermediate Score: 64%–80%	Advanced Native-like Fluency Score: 84%–100%	TOTAL ____ × 4 = ____ %

(Developed under the leadership of the California Department of Education, Bilingual Education Office.)

mation gained from the SOLOM can also be used in planning instruction in grammar, fluency, vocabulary, pronunciation, and grammar.

CONCLUSIONS

"Words, words, words … I'm so sick of words." Unlike Eliza Doolittle in *My Fair Lady*, teachers never seem to tire of their students' words. Meaningful conversations do not just happen. Teachers must continue to develop ways to foster and assess oral literacy experiences that will provide the foundation for effective language participation throughout one's life.

Using the speaking checklist, the listening checklist, and the SOLOM from the appendices, find one child to assess. Focus the assessment on the student's listening and speaking processes. From these assessment tools, determine the student's strengths and needs. From those, develop three lessons that can be implemented to improve this student's oral language development. Be sure that at least one of the lessons is a whole-class lesson and at least one is an individual lesson.

QUESTIONS

1. Why should you encourage communication among students?
2. How are the language arts related?
3. Select one instructional strategy for developing speaking skills and describe how you will use it in your classroom to expand the language registers of children who speak AAVE.
4. Select one instructional strategy for developing listening skills, and describe how you will use it in your classroom.
5. How will you link speaking and listening assessments with your instruction?

REFERENCES

Brown, D. (1954). *Auding as the primary language ability*. Unpublished doctoral dissertation, Stanford University, Palo Alto, CA.

Buckley, M. H. (1992). Focus on research: We listen a book a day; we speak a book a week: Learning from Walter Lobin. *Language Arts, 69*, 622–626.

George, J. C. (2000). *How to talk to your dog*. New York: HarperCollins.

Jacobson, J., Lapp, D., & Mendez, D. (2003) *Accommodating differences in English language learners: 75 literacy lessons*. San Diego, CA: Academic Professional Development.

Karas, G. B. (2001). *The class artist*. New York: Greenwillow.

Lapp, D., Fisher, D., Flood, J., & Cabello, A. (2001). An integrated approach to the teaching and assessment of language arts. In S. R. Hurley & J. V. Tinajero (Eds.), *Literacy assessment of second language learners* (pp. 1–26). Boston: Allyn & Bacon.

Lord, B. B. (1984). *In the year of the boar and Jackie Robinson*. New York: HarperCollins.

Lundsteen, S. W. (1979). *Listening: Its impact on reading and the other language arts*. NCTE/ERIC Clearinghouse on Reading and Communication Skills. Urbana, IL: National Council of Teachers of English.

McGovern, A. (1967). *Too much noise*. Chicago: Scott Foresman.

Polacco, P. (1996). *Aunt Chip and the great Triple Creek Dam affair*. New York: Philomel.

Raschka, C. (2000). *Ring! Yo?* New York: Dorling Kindersley.

Roser, N. L., & Martinez, M. G. (1995). *Book talk and beyond: Children and teachers respond to literature*. Newark, DE: International Reading Association.

Salus, P., & Flood, J. (2002). *Language: A user's guide*. San Diego: Academic Professional Development.

Sams, C. R., II, & Stoick, J. (2000). *Stranger in the woods: A photographic fantasy*. Milford, MI: Carl R. Sams II Photography.

Schunk, D. H., & Zimmerman, B. J. (1997). Developing self-efficacious readers and writers: The role of social and self-regulatory processes. In J. T. Guthrie & A. Wigfield (Eds.), *Reading engagement: Motivating readers through integrated instruction* (pp. 34–50). Newark, DE: International Reading Association.

Vygotsky, L. S. (1978). *Mind in Society: The development of higher psychological processes*. Cambridge, MA: Harvard University Press.

5

Word Identification Strategies: Pathways to Comprehension

──────────────── CHAPTER GOALS ────────────────

To help the reader

- explore phonics and why it is significant.
- explore whether there is more to the study of words than phonics.
- explore the phases of development as children learn to read words.
- explore how phonics should be taught during the developmental phases.

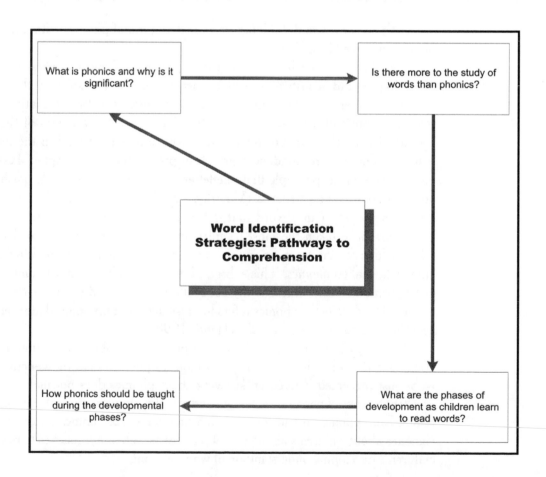

John Donne said that "No man is an island"; neither is any child, nor is word identification or phonics instruction. Although the philosophical implications of Donne's statement reach far beyond the classroom, it is helpful to put children and their efforts to decode written language into a larger context. No one influence has shaped the child, and no one instructional method will develop all necessary academic skills for a child. Most people have an immediate reaction to the word *phonics*. Reactions range from rapturous advocacy to near nausea, depending partly on the positive or negative impact of the person's childhood phonics experiences. Teachers are not immune to this reaction and consequently may avoid teaching phonics at all costs or, alternatively, may use it to the exclusion of all else. Whether or not to teach phonics is not the question. To read, one must be able to automatically identify sound-letter relationships and that, basically, defines phonics (Archer, Gleason, & Vachon, 2003; Beck & Juel, 1995; Stahl, Duffy-Hester, Dougherty, 1998). The questions to be addressed are to what degree phonics is needed by each reader and how to present phonics instruction in the most meaningful ways.

WHAT IS PHONICS AND WHY IS PHONICS SIGNIFICANT?

Please write your answer to the question that frames this section. That is, what is your current definition of phonics and why do you think that phonics is significant?

Let's see how you did. Compare your definition of phonics with a definition of phonics that we like as follows.

The study of speech sounds is called *phonetics*. The *phonetician* studies the physiological and acoustical aspects of speech sounds. The study of the sound system of a language is called *phonology*. The *phonologist* seeks information about the relevant sounds of a language. Educators have used the analysis of the relevant sounds of English to set up *sound-letter* correspondences to aid in the teaching of reading. These correspondences are fairly predictable but complex. Rather than being based on the principle that one letter equates to one sound, English depends on letter-combination patterns (Venezky, 1970). Thus, it is partly the way letters are strung together in a word that determines the sound the letter will produce. Educators have taken the most useful parts of this knowledge about letter-sound relationships for the teaching of reading and have attempted to develop a body of knowledge called *phonics*. This subset, phonics, includes the most common sounds of English and the most frequently used letters or strings of letters that record those sounds. Put succinctly, phonics refers to "instruction in the sound-letter relationship used in reading and writing" (Strickland, 1998, p. 5).

This definition is important because it provides valuable background information about phonics; there is, however, much more to phonics than the general definition we've just presented. Moreover, knowing about phonics does not make someone an excellent teacher of phonics. In the remainder of this chapter, you will learn more about phonics and phonics instruction. This information will be contextualized in classroom vignettes about children's knowledge of phonics as well as approaches to best facilitate children's developing understanding of word learning.

Opinion regarding the significance of phonics as a major component of the reading process is seldom constant. In the early 1980s, for example, Fulwiler and Groff noted that intensive phonics programs were in favor. With the climate of emergent literacy (Morrow, 1989), in the mid to late 1980s, phonics instruction appeared to change focus from intensively focused programs devoted primarily to phonics to a broader application within an integrated developmental reading program. Most recently, the significance of phonics instruction has again found favor with many educators as well as the general public (Cunningham & Stanovich, 1998; Ehri & McCormick, 1998; Gunn, Biglan, Smolkowski, & Ary, 2000). Regardless of the most current climate and of whether the mention of phonics conjures up the vision of a tropical paradise or a desert nightmare, we believe that to be able to read fluently one must have automaticity with sound-letter associations. There are many ways that phonics instruction can be integrated meaningfully and effectively into your overall literacy program.

As we have just mentioned, the merits of phonics have been—and are—debated in academic settings as well as in the general public. What may be missing from phonics debates—especially political debates involving the general public—is actual information about phonics and its importance in learning to read. Of course, to make effective instructional decisions about phonics in your own classroom, you need to know about phonics so that you can design effective instructional reading practices that include phonics. However, you also need to know how phonics relates to other aspects of literacy instruction and learning. We turn briefly to this issue now.

Is There More to the Study of Words Than Phonics?

As usual, let's start with what you think. Do you think that there is more to the study of words than phonics (which we've defined briefly as sound-letter relationships)? If not, why not? If so, what do you think constitutes the "more"?

Now that you've jotted down what you think, we'll tell you what we think. As emphasized in earlier chapters, the development of reading is an emergent behavior, with many factors contributing to it and many influences working that are not fully seen until the child emerges as a reader. Earlier we mentioned Donne's island metaphor with respect to phonics and phonics instruction. To change metaphors from islands to butterflies, we can compare the forces at work on a burgeoning reader to those that work on a caterpillar in the cocoon. Forces are at work inside the cocoon that are not visible until the butterfly emerges, completely changed from a creature bound to the land into one that soars in the air. The forces working on children from before birth until the time they sit in a classroom may be just as unseen (or perhaps seen, but not carefully observed) as those that go on inside a cocoon, but these early influences are the power source that will launch a child into the world of reading.

Among the powerful influences working to bring a child to literacy is vocabulary acquisition (Cunningham & Stanovich, 1998). Educators have argued that children have a spoken as well as a listening, writing, and reading vocabulary. It should be noted that knowledge of the language of one of these vocabularies does not necessarily ensure transfer to knowledge of any other vocabularies. The first vocabulary that a child acquires is a listening vocabulary, followed closely by a spoken vocabulary. Individuals' expressive capabilities generally exceed their expressive vocabulary. Most individuals comprehend a far greater range of language patterns auditorily than they use in their spoken text. Their listening vocabulary also exceeds their early writing and reading vocabularies. Most native English-speaking children have acquired a basic understanding of the syntax, or structure, of the English language by the age of 4. By the time children begin formal instruction in reading, they have also acquired substantial listening and speaking vocabularies, and they can discriminate among most of the sounds of the English language.

You may be wondering why this information about children's vocabulary acquisition and understanding of syntax, or language structure, matters. By using the abilities that children have acquired in informal family contexts, the transition from the listening and speaking vocabularies to the reading and writing vocabulary can be made. Thus, the teaching of reading involves the specialized task of helping children decode the written, symbolic representation of a language they already know. They can say and hear, with understanding, words that they have never seen written down. When faced with their own language in this written "code," many children fail to understand that they already know what is on the page. The children will only "already know what is on the page," however, if the classroom teacher is careful to base his or her instruction on the children's own language. In your own classroom, you will find that what children know about language and the written code will vary a great deal. That's why you need to know specific information about your individual children and their word knowledge as well as the developmental process that children move through as they acquire word knowledge. Knowledge in all of these areas will help you provide effective instruction for your children. In the following section, we present a vignette of a first grade teacher and some of her children who have different backgrounds and developmental needs. We draw on the work of current scholars in literacy to discuss how the teacher might best design instruction to facilitate her children's learning about words.

WHAT ARE THE PHASES OF DEVELOPMENT AS CHILDREN LEARN TO READ WORDS AND HOW SHOULD PHONICS BE TAUGHT DURING THESE DEVELOPMENTAL PHASES?

Mrs. McKay teaches a combination first and second grade class in Houston, Texas. After implementing various formal and informal assessments during the first week of school, Mrs. McKay has come to realize that her children's word knowledge spans a wide variety of developmental levels. Based on her 6 years of teaching experience at the first and second grade levels, she couldn't say that she was surprised. This was her first experience teaching a combination class, however, and she was beginning to realize that she would have to provide some vastly different instructional experiences for her children. She knew that her planning would be complex, but she still felt that she made the right decision to teach a combination class. She had had about half of the children in her class as first graders, so she already knew a lot about their backgrounds and knowledge of literacy. In fact, her principal had been the one to suggest that Mrs. McKay consider a combination class. Mrs. McKay loved first grade and didn't want to move up to second grade with her entire class, but she had made such significant progress with some of her children that her principal wanted her to continue to work with them.

Throughout this section, we present various profiles of children in Mrs. McKay's class and her plans for meeting their instructional needs. These profiles will give you a sense of the various levels of her children's word knowledge as well as some of Mrs. McKay's instructional plans for the different children in her classroom. We begin by profiling two children, Anthony and Kayla, about whom Mrs. McKay worried the most. Neither Anthony nor Kayla knew all of the names of the letters in the alphabet. They also lacked awareness of individual letter sounds and the sounds of letters in words. Because Mrs. McKay had studied extensively about emergent literacy, she understood the general phases of development that children move through as they acquire word knowledge. She knew that Anthony and Kayla were in the beginning phase of word knowledge acquisition.

According to literacy scholars Linnea Ehri and Sandra McCormick (1998), children move through five general phases of development as they acquire word knowledge. These phases include the *Pre-Alphabetic Phase*, the *Partial-Alphabetic Phase*, the *Full-Alphabetic Phase*, the *Consolidated-Alphabetic Phase*, and the *Automatic Phase*. Mrs. McKay also knows that these phases are general heuristics, not stringent stages. That is, whereas "each phase highlights a characteristic of word learning that becomes prominent," the phases may—and often do—overlap (p. 140). Moreover, complete mastery of one phase may or may not be a prerequisite for movement to the next phase. Thus, Mrs. McKay uses her knowledge of these developmental phases in a flexible way as general guidelines to assess her children and plan instruction. Mrs. McKay judged that Anthony and Kayla were in the Pre-Alphabetic Phase of word knowledge because they both lacked general knowledge of letter-sound relations (Ehri & McCormick, 1998). Mrs. McKay was particularly worried about Anthony and Kayla because she knew that this phase was typical for children in preschool and early kindergarten. She also knew that she and Anthony and Kayla would have to work hard that year to make up for lost time. Of course, Mrs. McKay would also enlist the help of Anthony's and Kayla's parents and family members in this endeavor.

E is for Enchantment: A New Mexico Alphabet. Used with permission from Sleeping Bear Press.

The Pre-Alphabetic Phase: Anthony's and Kayla's Instructional Needs

Mrs. McKay knew that she needed to help Anthony and Kayla acquire letter knowledge—including knowledge of both upper and lower case letters and phonemic awareness. She knew that she needed to provide Anthony and Kayla many opportunities to engage in various literacy activities that would strengthen their knowledge in these two areas. We'll explain a bit about what Mrs. McKay meant by letter knowledge and phonemic awareness. Then, we'll share some of the literacy-related activities that Mrs. McKay might choose to use with Anthony and Kayla.

Letter Knowledge: Letter Discrimination and Knowledge of Letter Names

Even though most children can visually discriminate between objects by 4 years of age, discriminating between words and letters in words is a complex undertaking for children. For example, note the following letter pairs:

mn   bd   oc   qg   and   QO   JT   EH   RP

The differences between the letters in these pairs are very subtle. It is therefore easy to understand why children may not always see these differences. Difficulty with visual discrimination of letters becomes even more obvious when one reads the following sentences quickly:

Sam sat in the sand in front of the band.

The band man said to Sam, "Sit on the land, not the sand."

Sam's son ran on the land and landed in the sand by the band.

Did Sam and his son land by the band man on the sand?

Did you have any difficulty in discriminating between letters as you read sentences? Surely, you didn't; however, young children just learning to read don't have the skills of competent adult readers. Gibson and Levin (1975) researched the ways in which children identify abstract visual symbols, and they suggested that they use a set of distinctive features to discriminate between these symbols. The four distinctive features that children attend to are the following:

1. *Straight-line segments:* In the Roman alphabet there are several letters that are made up of this type of visual symbol: E F H I L T.

2. *Curved segments:* In the Roman alphabet the following letters are examples of curved segmental visual symbols: C O.

3. *Symmetries:* The following alphabetic letters constitute examples of symmetries: M W X.

4. *Discontinuities:* Several alphabetic letters are examples of discontinuities: K B G J.

Children process these features to discern letters. For example, one child might look at the letter *J* and see straight-line segments and curved segments. A second child may see only the top part of the letter *J*, which looks like *T*, and may fail to perceive the curved line segments and attend to both stimuli. To avoid initial difficulties, teachers can instruct children in letter discrimination using a developmental plan similar to the one described here:

Step 1: Ask children to look at single letters that appear in the words they are chanting, writing, and reading.

1. a d
2. d b
3. b a
4. b b

Step 2: Ask children if the letters are the same or different.

Step 3: Ask children to look at sets of letters and to determine whether the sets are the same or different.

ad   ba   dbad

Step 4: Ask children to examine sets of words and determine whether they are the same or different.

pat mat   sat rat   cat bat

After children have completed this assignment, it is important to explain to them that a word can be written in different forms.

Step 5: Ask children to examine the following set of words and to determine if they are the same or different.

MAT mat   LAB lab

The importance of letter-name knowledge in the acquisition of reading skills has long been a subject of interest and study for teachers and researchers. Over a quarter of a century ago, Durkin (1974) argued convincingly that knowledge of letter names is helpful in carrying out initial reading instruction. Murphy and Durrell (1972) used a letter-naming system for initial phonics instruction (see Table 5–1).

Since the creation of *Sesame Street*, most children arrive in kindergarten knowing the names of the letters of the English alphabet. The child who begins first grade knowing the letter names is more likely to succeed in learning to read than is the child who has not acquired this knowledge. This is correlation, not causality.

TABLE 5–1
Letter Naming System

d	Initial	Medial	Final
	dean	au_dience	la_d
	de_cent	come_dian	spee_d
	de_cide	ra_dio	plai_d

Several studies have shown that teaching the letter names in isolation does not have much effect on later success in reading (Jenkins, Bausel, & Jenkins, 1972; Silberberg, Silberberg, & Iverson, 1972). Thus, Mrs. McKay knew that she would work to help Anthony and Kayla learn the letter names using meaningful words and activities. Knowledge of letter names is an important indicator of a child's phase of word knowledge development. Letter names are relatively easy to learn, and the experience may help children (through general transfer) with the more difficult task of making letter-sound associations in words.

Developing Phonemic Awareness: Where to Begin

'Twas brillig, and the slithy toves
    Did gyre and gimble in the wabe:
All mimsy were the borogroves,
    And the mome raths outgrabe.

Lewis Carroll, "Jabberwocky," 1865

Phonemic awareness is the ability to manipulate sounds and to recognize that words are made up of a discrete set of sounds (Ehri & McCormick, 1998). To be able to identify words, children must have phonemic awareness. Phonemic awareness develops from the general to the more specific. That is, first children learn that language is made up of words, then they learn that words are made up of letters and syllables that are related to the sounds of their spoken language. They are learning that these letters and syllables are made up of phonemes—the individual speech sounds in words (Cunningham, 2000; Fountas & Pinnell, 1996). As with everything else we present to children, we must help children develop phonemic awareness by building on what they already know. If we began word work with the language in Lewis Carroll's "Jabberwocky," it is doubtful that the children would see any usefulness in absorbing and applying the skills taught. "Brillig," "slithy toves," and "mome raths" may certainly call up vivid images when read aloud with feeling, but to begin reading instruction with nonsense words out of context is in itself nonsense. Although there is evidence that children who are instructed in phonics as part of their introduction to reading fare well in reading (Adams, 1990; Chall, Conrad, & Harris-Sharples, 1983; Moats, 2001; Manzo & Manzo, 2005; Williams, 1985), phonics skills are useful only if they are applied to words that are already in the student's oral language vocabulary (Cunningham, Moore, Cunningham, & Moore, 1989; Ehri, Nunes, Stahl, & Willows, 2001). It is not useful to force children to tediously sound out *mimsy*, only to produce a word with no meaning to them. When phonics instruction originated in the 1890s, children were drilled endlessly on letter sounds. The emphasis was on sounds in isolation, moving to phonograms (word families such as *mat, cat, rat, sat, bat,* and *hat*) and then to phrases (Pollard, 1989). Children would recite phonics drills such as *da ra pa sa la na ma di re pi si li ne me.*

This noncontextual sound calling is a feature of the "popcorn" school of phonics, so named because children pop out these sounds at random, never pulling them together into a meaningful whole. Popcorn-style phonics lessons are neither applied nor useful.

Rather than sitting children down for a "phonics lesson" that involves isolated drills, more recent philosophies advocate using "teachable moments" to develop children's phonemic awareness (Cunningham, 2000; Durkin, 1987). Moreover, the focus of phonemic awareness activities should be to help children understand the sounds of language. For example, if the classroom is filled with children whose names start with J, create a lesson using their names. You could stretch out the *J* sound and ask all children whose names begin with *J* to step forward (Cunningham, 2000). Reciting nursery rhymes or singing songs with rhymes are important ways to help children develop phonemic awareness. If the school is presenting a puppet show to the students, work on the letter P, pulling from the pupils possible p-phrases such as "The principal presents pretty puppets playing pranks on precious pets. The price: a penny."

What did Mrs. McKay need to know to help her children at this and the remaining phases of development? We present some of the background knowledge that Mrs. McKay possessed and drew upon in her instruction. Mrs. McKay's background knowledge includes knowledge of syllables, consonants, vowels, digraphs, consonant blends, and diphthongs. We draw upon Durkin's (1964) ideas to present this information in a format that will give you the opportunity to check on your current level of understanding of these various concepts related to phonics. We wish to emphasize, however, that Mrs. McKay was mindful of the fact that there is little or no value in having children memorize phonics rules for which they have no understanding. That is, Mrs. McKay's instructional goal was not to have her children memorize the phonics rules that she knows as a professional educator; rather, she sought to draw upon her professional knowledge about phonics and phonics rules to help her children develop meaningful word identification skills. Mrs. McKay was well aware of the fact that there are plenty of teachers who know phonics rules but aren't effective teachers of phonics. You'll see that we refer to this phonics information in our discussions throughout the remainder of this chapter.

Syllables

A syllable gives a vowel context. Just as reciting letter sounds out of context has no particular meaning, teaching vowels in isolation does nothing to etch them into the minds of beginning readers. The teaching of syllabication as a tool for decoding written words is one of the many controversial areas in reading instruction. However, research does indicate that as a context for vowels in polysyllabic words, syllabic units have a strong place in phonics instruction.

Formal rules of syllabication have been taught to beginning readers for decades. As with most memorized data, we tend to retain what we use and forget the part that is less useful. Although readers do break apart words when decoding them, they may not necessarily do so by separating them into formal syllables. As Groff

(1971) pointed out in his discussion of the syllable, English is "stress-timed language"; therefore, it is easy to identify the number of syllables in a given word, but it is very difficult to determine syllable boundaries. The syllable presents a problem similar to that of a cartographer trying to decide exactly how much of the valley between the two hills belongs to each hill.

We include some generalizations about syllabication in the following chart. It is important to remember that the following generalizations are subject to scrutiny and exception, however. Fill out the chart as directed; then check your answers.

Please break the words below into syllables.	Your explanation of the rules you used to divide the words into syllables:
1. catnip	
2. sale	
3. odor	
4. trundle	

Answer key:
1. cat/nip: All syllables have a vowel sound.
2. sale: When a final e appears as a vowel in a word, it usually does not add another sound.
3. o/dor: When a consonant exists between two vowels, a division occurs between the first vowel and the consonant.
4. trun/dle: When a word ends in le, and it is preceded by a consonant, the consonant and le, make up a new syllable.

Consonants

It is important to understand the difference between sounds and letters and the correspondence (or lack of correspondence) between them. Several consonant letters have only one sound in English; others have a variety of sounds. We briefly introduce you to several examples that represent rules that govern the pronunciation of consonants. See what you can discern about the examples we present.

What do you notice about the following examples? Which consonants from this chart are missing? Why?

b—baby	n—not	j—juice	t—took
d—doll	p—pipe	k—kit	v—very
f—fan	r—ran	l—lady	w—was
h—home	s—saw	m—me	z—zoo

The beginning sounds of the words in the chart represent the 16 most common consonant sounds. Each of these 16 letters usually has only one sound in the initial position in English words (especially in common words). As you may have noticed, words beginning with the consonants c, g, q, and x were not included in the list. C and g were not included because they have two different sounds: hard and soft sounds. Q and x do not represent sounds of their own. We briefly discuss each of these letters below.

The *hard sound of c* is heard in words such as *cat, candy, cape, coat, cuff, cough, calf, fabric,* and *picnic*. The hard sound of c is heard as /k/. The *soft sound of c* is heard in words such as *city, cell, cent, cigar,* and *cyst*. The soft sound of c is heard as /s/. When the consonant c is followed by a, o, or u, the sound of /k/ is often heard. When c is followed by e, i, or y, the sound of /s/ is often heard.

The *hard sound of g* is heard in words such as *game, give, gate, goat, good, gulp,* and *guest* and in the final position in words such as *bag* and *gag*. The hard sound of g is heard as /g/. In many words when g is followed by a, o, or u, the hard or /g/ sound is heard. The *soft sound of g* is heard in words such as *gym, gentle, gender,* and *gent* and in the final position in *badge* and *rage*. The soft sound of g is heard as /j/. When the consonant g is followed by e, i, or y, the sound of /j/ is heard. The principles regarding the pronunciation of g are not as reliable in their application to g as they are in their application to c.

The consonant q most always appears with the vowel u. When it does not, it is usually in a proper noun (i.e., Qantas Airlines). Together they represent the following sounds: *qu* as the /k/ sound in *antique* and *queue*, and *qu* as the /kw/ sound in *quack* and *quail*.

The letter x, like the letters c and g, represents no sound of its own and is used to represent the following sounds: x as the /z/ sound in *xylophone* and *Xavier*, x as the /ks/ sound in *sox* and *taxi*, and x as the /gz/ sound in *exist* and *exotic*.

The letters w and y are unique because they can function as both consonants and vowels. These letters function as consonants only when they appear as the initial letter in a syllable. For example, the y in *yard* and the y in *canyon* both function as consonants because they appear as the initial letter in a syllable. Similar examples for w are in the words *paw* and *powwow* when the w becomes part of a vowel digraph.

Vowels: Long and Short

Very often, vowels record what are generally called *long* sounds and *short* sounds. Let's check your knowledge of both long and short sounds below.

In each of the rows of words listed below, underline the word that begins with a long vowel sound. After underlining the appropriate words, check your answers. Discuss your reasons for your answers with others in class.

1. apple	able	4. odd	open
2. eat	Ed	5. use	under
3. ignite	ice		

In each of the rows of words listed below, underline the word that begins with a short vowel sound. After underlining the appropriate words, check your answers. Discuss your reasons for your answers with others in class.

1. ate	antique	4. October	over
2. eagle	end	5. undone	use
3. ice	inside		

Answer key (long): 1) able, 2) eat, 3) ice, 4) open, 5) use
Answer key (short): 1) antique 2) end, 3) inside, 4) October, 5) undone

The vowel sounds of English are often complex for children who are learning to read because each vowel letter may represent several sounds. Please note the following generalized vowel rules. You should refamiliarize yourself with this information so that you can draw upon it in your reading instruction.

Generalized Vowel Rules

1. When a single vowel in a syllable is followed by the letter *r*, the vowel is affected or influenced by it (e.g., *chart, cart; dollar, her; fir, first; for, fort; work, curl*).

2. When the letter *a* is followed by a *ll* or *lk* in a syllable, the *a* represents the sound of *ou* or *au* as in the word *awful* (e.g., *all, ball, enthrall, chalk, walk*).

3. When the letter combinations *gn, bh, ght, ld,* or *nd* follow the single letter *i* in a syllable, the *i* represents a long vowel sound (e.g., *sign, sigh; tight, light; mild, mind*).

4. When the letter combination *ld* follows the single letter *o* in a syllable, the letter *o* generally represents a long vowel sound (e.g., *cold, told, fold, old, mold, behold*).

5. When the letter combination *re* follows a single vowel in a syllable, you generally hear an *r* sound (e.g., *core, here, tire, tore, bore, cure, lure*).

6. *E*'s at the end of a monosyllabic word usually make the first vowel a long sound. This is sometimes called the *magic E rule* (e.g., *cape, time, dote, vane, note, hate, wine, cube, Pete, code*).

Consonant Digraphs

Some combinations of consonants are called digraphs. The exercises below will help you to check your knowledge of digraphs.

A. What is a consonant digraph?

B. In the words listed randomly below, find the words that contain a consonant digraph. In each of these words, underline the two letters that make up the digraph.

ran	ring	butter
chair	believe	rich
happy	top	red
them	yellow	book

Answer key: When two consonants appear together in a word and form one sound, they are referred to as a consonant digraph. The following words contain examples of consonant digraphs: <u>ch</u>air, <u>th</u>em, ri<u>ng</u>, and ri<u>ch</u>.

Table 5–2 presents examples of consonant digraphs in the initial and final positions. Note that there is a difference between the /th/ sound that is voiced and the voiceless /th/ sound.

Consonant Blends

Certain combinations of consonants are called consonant blends. Check your knowledge of consonant blends here.

TABLE 5–2
Consonant Digraphs in the Initial and Final Position

Consonant Digraphs in the Initial Position

ch	sh	th (voiced)	th (voiceless)	wh
chin	ship	this	thin	whip
chip	shall	those	thank	whistle
chop	shop	that	thick	whale
chuck	shell	there	thump	whisper
chill	shut	them	thorn	whack
chest	shot	these	thumb	wheel
chair	shout	the	thing	white
chick	shed	than	thunder	when
chain	shoe	their	thud	where
cherries	shine		thermometer	why

Consonant Digraphs in the Final Position

ch	sh	th (voiceless)	ng
much	wish	tooth	bang
rich	mash	both	sang
lunch	dash	health	sing
such	dish	math	ring
crunch	crush	with	song
march	flash	breath	strong
branch	fresh	wealth	rung
ranch	fish	myth	hung
bunch	wash	bath	gang
pinch	rash	path	wing

A. What is a consonant blend?
B. Find the words that contain a consonant blend. Circle the letters that make up the blend.

free	skate	sad
smile	blind	train
golden	gone	caper
dwarf	toast	came

When two or more consonants appear in succession in a word and are both pronounced or are blended when pronouncing the word, they are referred to as consonant blends. Table 5–3 presents examples of consonant blends in the initial and final positions. Look at Table 5–3 to identify the consonant blends in the chart in section B that you just completed.

Diphthongs

Certain combinations of vowels are called diphthongs. At times, the consonants *y* and *w* function as vowels; consequently some diphthongs are a combination of a vowel with *y* or a combination of a vowel with *w*. Knowledge of diphthongs is evaluated here.

TABLE 5–3
Consonant Blends in the Initial and Final Positions

Consonant Blends in the Initial Position

bloom	flee	prize	screw
bright	free	scout	straight
clown	glad	skate	stop
cradle	grape	sled	sweep
draw	kraut	smile	train
dwarf	plum	snap	twinkle

Consonant Blends in the Final Position

-st	-sk	-sp	-nt	-nd
must	ask	crisp	went	bend
fast	desk	grasp	spent	send
rest	brisk	clasp	want	sand
coast	task	wisp	ant	hand
most	dusk	rasp	bent	wind
last	risk		elephant	hind
best	mask			blind
toast	tusk			
chest	flask			

-mp	-ft	-lm	-nk	-lt
limp	left	calm	bunk	felt
skimp	lift	balm	sunk	melt
lamp	loft		brink	belt
clamp	graft		sink	salt
lump	raft		honk	bolt
dump			spunk	silt
bump				pelt

-lp	-ld
help	held
gulp	hold
kelp	old
scalp	mold
	told
	cold

Your Turn

A. What is a diphthong?

B. In the words listed randomly below, find the four words that contain a diphthong. In each of these four words, underline the two letters that make up the diphthong.

soil	float
see	howl
bat	they
toy	pout

Answer key: A diphthong consists of two vowel letters in one syllable, both of which are sounded, but the sound is not like either of the vowels. (Please note that y and w function as vowels.) A diphthong is a king of sound that, in the process of being made, requires a change in the mouth position. For this reason vowel combinations such as au (auto) and oo (look) are not diphthongs. Also, a diphthong is a particular sound, not just a particular combination of letters. This is why ou is considered a diphthong in couch but not in four. 1) soil, 2) howl, 3) pout, 4) toy.

So, how did you do? How much do you know about phonics? If you did not get all of the answers correct, you may be wondering, "How can I read effectively if I don't know some of this foundational knowledge about phonics? It turns out that you do not need to have all of this background information about phonics memorized to read. This has important implications for your own phonics instruction with your children. You don't need to have your children memorize the information you were just quizzed on. We do think, however, that YOU need to know this information about phonics to be an effective reading teacher. Why? Because knowing how to read and teaching someone else how to read are *not* the same things. As a teacher of reading you need to have a great deal of explicit background knowledge about issues pertaining to reading so that you can make effective instructional decisions (Strickland, 1998). Clearly, knowing the information you just read is not sufficient, however. Our challenge as teachers of literacy is to use our knowledge to design effective instructional plans for our children. We will talk further about effective instructional plans as we continue with our discussion of Ehri and McCormick's (1998) developmental phases of word learning.

The Partial-Alphabetic Phase: Most of Mrs. McKay's First Graders

Most of Mrs. McKay's first graders were at the partial-alphabetic phase of word understanding at the beginning of the school year. This phase is typical of children in kindergarten as well as novice first grade readers; however, older children with reading difficulties may also be at this phase (Ehri & McCormick, 1998). Here's what Mrs. McKay noticed about her children at this phase. First, she noticed that these children could read some words by sight. In addition, they were beginning to detect some letters in words, match some letters in words to sounds, and use analogy to detect simple words. For example, they could recognize that the names of three of their classmates started with an *M* (*Mike, Matt,* and *Melissa*), and they knew what an *M* sounded like. Knowing the word *cat* enabled them to sound out by analogy the word *bat* because they recognized the *at* ending and knew the sounds of *c* and *b*. However, because these readers had limited alphabetic knowledge, they often misread words with similar letters (e.g., *thin* and *than*), read similar words backwards (e.g., *pot* and *top*), and overlooked the sounds in some words—especially in the medial position of words. That is, these children tended to attend to the initial and final sounds in words. Finally, these children knew the sounds of many consonants but did not effectively use decoding strategies for unfamiliar words (Ehri & McCormick, 1998).

Drawing on ideas suggested by Ehri and McCormick (1998), Shafer, Campbell, and Rakes (2000), and Cunningham (2000), here are some of the ways that Mrs. McKay planned to work with these children. First, because these children were only attending to some of the sounds in words, Mrs. McKay knew that she wanted to direct their attention to the sounds that they were overlooking in words. For example, as she worked with Drevaun one day she noticed that he read the word *fled* as *fed*. She acknowledged that he pronounced beginning and ending of the word correctly, and then she drew his attention to the letter *l* in *fled* and helped him to blend all of the sounds in the word by moving her finger under the word and pronouncing all of the sounds in the word correctly. [Cunningham (2000) calls this process stretching out the sounds in words.] Mrs. McKay asked Drevaun to engage in this word-stretching

DID YOU NOTICE . . .
Did you notice how Mrs. McKay learns a great deal about Drevaun s reading strengths and needs based on his writing progress? Remember, continuous assessment of all of the related language arts (reading, writing, speaking, listening, viewing) will help teachers plan more effective instruction for each child.

TABLE 5–4
Consonant Correspondences

Phoneme	Grapheme	Phoneme in Initial Position	Phoneme in Medial Position	Phoneme in Final Position
/n/	n	nest	diner	pin
	nn		thinner	
	gn	gnat		
	kn	knight		
	pn	pneumonia		
	mn	mnemonic		
/ŋ/	ng		stinger	song
	n		think	
/p/	p	point	viper	hip
/r/	r	rat	boring	tear
	rr		merry	
	wr	write		
	rh	rhyme	hemorrhage	
/š/	sh	shadow	crashing	dish
	s	sure		
	ci		precious	
	ce		ocean	
	ss		obsession	
			pressure	
			assure	
	ch	chic	machine	
		chevron		
/t/	ti		motion	
	t	test	water	cat
	tt		letter	putt
	pt			receipt
	bt		debtor	debt

(continued)

process with the word *fled* after she showed him how to do it (Ehri & McCormick, 1998). Mrs. McKay also knew that it is important to ask children to write during this phase of development because writing can draw children's attention to the letters in words. She was aware that her children would use invented spellings in their creative writing. She used what she noticed about the ways that her children were spelling words to determine where she should intervene in their instruction. For example, when Drevaun was writing about a trip that he took to his cousin's farm, he wrote the word *farm* as *fam*. Although she knew that she wouldn't focus on each of Drevaun's invented spellings, Mrs. McKay decided she would draw his attention to this word because it was a central word in his story. She modeled the same stretching out process described earlier with the word *farm* for Drevaun. Then she asked him to practice the stretching out process with the word *farm*.

As a teacher, your task is to assist the child to recognize the correspondence between letters and sounds. The child has language—phonology, syntax, and vocabulary—and can discriminate visually between many different symbols. Once the child knows the names of the letters of the alphabet and can discriminate

TABLE 5-4 (Continued)

Phoneme	Grapheme	Phoneme in Initial Position	Phoneme in Medial Position	Phoneme in Final Position
/θ/	th	thin	either lethal	wreath
/ʒ/	th	then	either	bathe
/v/	v	violet	hover	dove
/w/	w ui	will	throwing sanguine	how
/ks/	x cc		toxic accent	
/y/	y	yarn	lawyer	day
/z/	z s	zipper	razor visit	blaze
	zz x	xanthippe xylophone xanadu	amuser drizzle	fizz
/ž/	z su si ss g	genre	azure treasure allusion fissure	decoupage
/gz/	x gs	xeroxes	exhibit exert exact	digs
/θ/	th	think, thin	mythology	bath
/ʒ/	th	thy, this	bother	bathe, lathe

between them, all that the child needs now is the knowledge of the code, the link between letters and sounds.

Letter-Sound (Grapheme-Phoneme) Correspondence

Tables 5–4 and 5–5, containing consonant and vowel correspondences in various positions within a word can be extremely useful in teaching students how to analyze words that appear in the stories they are reading. The lists represent most of the sounds of the English language. If a child is able to read all these correspondences within meaningful contexts, he or she can probably be considered a competent decoder. The phonemes in these lists, written between slash marks (e.g.,/t/), are symbols for the sounds of English. Each symbol stands for one sound.

Discriminating Between Words

A Chinese woman studying in the United States for the first time quipped, "All words in English look alike." Most first graders who are beginning to read might

TABLE 5–5
Vowel Correspondences

Sound Label	Vowel	Letter Label	Example
Unglided or short	/æ/	a	an
		au	laugh
Glided or long	/ey/	a.e*	pain, bake
		ai	rain
		ea	steak
		ei	feign
		ay	tray
		ey	obey
		ua	guard
Unglided or short	/e/	e	pen
		ea	lead
		eo	jeopardy
		ei	heifer
		ai	stair
		ie	friendly
Glided or long	/iy/	e.e*	mete
		e	he
		ea	heat
		ee	tree
		ei	conceive
		ie	believe
Unglided or short	/i/	i	hit
		ui	guild
		y	gym
		u	business
Glided or long	/ay/	i.e*	write
		uy	buyers
		ie	tries
		ai	aisle
		ia	trial
		y	spy

(continued)

agree with her. As a competent adult reader of English, you might reply that all words in Chinese look the same to you. If you were beginning to learn to read in Chinese, you would probably see sentences like those in Figure 5–1.

Do the words in each of these sentences look alike to you? This is what happens to the young child when he or she first sees written words in English. We have to be extremely patient to make sure that the child can distinguish each separate word. In English the two Chinese sentences mean

Every day the moon is bright.

At the end of autumn, the villager gathers wood in the forest.

We have no difficulty in distinguishing each word in the English translation. This proficiency is the result of a great deal of exercise, practice, and experience. Most children in first grade are able to distinguish the letters of the English alpha-

TABLE 5–5 (Continued)

Sound label	Vowel	Letter Label	Example
Glided or long		i	find
		ei	height
		igh	night
Unglided or short	/a/	oo	not
Glided or long	/ow/	o.e*	shone
		oa	goat
		ow	snow
		o	no
		ew	sewing
		ough	dough, through
		oo	floor
		eau	beau, bureau
		oe	hoe, doe
Unglided or short	/∂/	u	nut
		oo	flood
		ou	enough, curious, pretentious
		ough	rough
		o	hover, cover, come
Glided or long	/yuw/	u.e*	yule
		eau	beauty
		ew	dew
Unglided or short	/u/	oo	good
		u	put
Unglided or short	/o/	a	walk
		au	maul
		o	frog
		aw	saw
Unglided or diphthong	/aw/	ow	down
		ou	cloud
Glided or diphthong	/y/	oy	boy
		oi	loin

*The dot stands for an omitted letter.

Figure 5–1   Chinese symbols.

日日有明月

秋季末森林内村人採木材

TABLE 5–6
"Little" Words

inn	on	and	are
ache	ate	ace	atom
to	too	toe	tow
it	in	if	is
of	off	oft	often
for	from	form	foam
each	eat	ear	earn
here	her	hear	heart

bet in a relatively short period of time and with little practice, but it is not uncommon to hear a young child say, "I have trouble reading the little words." This might mean that young children have difficulty in quickly identifying "little" words such as *in, and, on, an, or, for, from, form,* and *foam*. Test yourself again by quickly reading the little words in Table 5–6 aloud.

Undoubtedly, you read these words quickly and easily. For young children just developing alphabetic knowledge, however, reading the words like the ones you just read can be a difficult undertaking.

The Full-Alphabetic Phase: Some of Mrs. McKay's First Graders

Mrs. McKay knows that this phase of development is characterized by children who "acquire and use orderly relationships for associating sounds to the letters they see in words" (Ehri & McCormick, 1998, p. 149). She also knows that mastery of this phase of development is crucial for her children's reading success in the following phases. Here's what Mrs. McKay noticed about her children when they were in this phase of development (Ehri & McCormick, 1998). First, children in this phase of development can decode unfamiliar words because they have developed phonemic awareness and they understand major letter (including consonants and vowels-sound relationships. Second, decoding is cumbersome at this phase of development. The extent to which reading is laborious for children at this phase depends partly on the texts they are reading, however. If children read texts at their independent reading levels, their reading is less cumbersome. Recall that a student is reading at his or her independent reading level if text reading accuracy is more than 95% and he or she is sufficiently comprehending the text. (See chapter 3 for a reminder about reading levels.) Third, because children are actually reading more at this phase of development, their sight vocabularies improve. Fourth, readers begin to use decoding by analogy at this phase of development (Cunningham, 2000). That is, for example, a child may be able to read the word *hall* by analogy because she knows the word *ball*.

So, what does Mrs. McKay do to facilitate her children's learning at this phase of development? First, she knows that she wants her children to engage in a lot of practice reading of texts that are at their independent reading levels. She also knows that it is a good idea for her children to re-read the texts she has read to them. Consequently, she does several read-alouds every day and makes those texts available for her children to read. (See chapter 11 for a discussion of read-alouds.) Mrs. McKay

DID YOU NOTICE . . .
Did you notice that as students become more proficient at reading they have a larger repertoire of known onsets and rimes? Remember, an onset of a word is the initial consonant sound. A rime in a word (not rhyme) is made up of the vowel and any consonants that follow within a given syllable. For example, the onset in the word *book* is *b* and the rime is *ook*.

has had to work hard to try to find appropriate texts for her children in this phase of development. Here's what we mean. The texts she wants her children to read must contain words that are simple enough that they aren't too challenging for children's beginning sight vocabularies, and the words must not pose too much challenge to beginning decoders. (See chapter 11 for a list of books that Mrs. McKay would recommend for beginning readers.) One of the major instructional approaches Mrs. McKay emphasizes at this phase of development is decoding by analogy (Cunningham, 2000). She works with her children to help them to divide words into syllables to decode (Treiman, 1985). In particular, she helps her children discern onset and rime in monosyllabic words. Here's how it works. Onset "is a part of a syllable that comes before a vowel (e.g., the *h* in *hall*), whereas the rime is the rest of the syllable (i.e., the *all* in *hall*)" (Ehri & McCormick, 1998). In particular, Mrs. McKay focuses on helping her children to discern words using rimes because she knows that children—especially at the beginning of this phase of development—find it easier to attend to the ends of words as they're using analogy to decode words (Goswami & Bryant, 1990). When Mrs. McKay observes her children reading at this developmental level, she looks to see that they are using their sight word memories for familiar words, using decoding strategies—including decoding by analogy—for words that are new to them, and using prediction to confirm or disconfirm the effectiveness of their decoding. That is, if her children are saying words that don't make any sense in the context of their reading and not self-correcting, Mrs. McKay knows that they aren't attending to comprehension as they read. If this happens, she makes sure to emphasize the importance of making sense of the text that one is reading.

The Consolidated-Alphabetic Phase

One of the most significant distinctions between the full-alphabetic phase and the consolidated-alphabetic phase is that readers become more astute at focusing on spelling patterns in this phase in addition to grapheme-phoneme relations. That is, readers pull together—or consolidate—their developing understandings of spelling patterns as they process text. What spelling patterns are we referring to, and what does the ability to focus on spelling patterns buy readers? Readers at this phase of development can discern larger chunks of words including root words, prefixes and suffixes (i.e., affixes), onsets, rimes, and syllables (Ehri & McCormick, 1998). As you might guess, facility with these spelling patterns buys readers a lot. When readers can attend to these chunks of words in their reading, they can read faster and more accurately. "For example, the word *interesting* contains 10 graphophonic units (including *ng*, symbolizing on phoneme), but only 4 graphosyllabic units" (Ehri & McCormick, 1998, p. 154). Clearly, it would be easier for you to read the word *interesting* if you recognized 4 graphosyllabic units that make up the word rather than laboring through the 10 graphophonic units that make up the word. Another important characteristic of this phase of development is that readers' sight word vocabularies increase substantially. This is due, in large part, to the fact that readers can more clearly see parts of words (i.e., spelling patterns) and how these spelling patterns are connected or related to one another and other words.

Average readers show signs consistent with this stage of development around the second grade, and they continue to develop their facility with spelling patterns through middle school and beyond (Juel, 1989). A few of the children in Mrs. McKay's first grade classroom (i.e., Tyler and Jasmine) demonstrated signs of reading at this phase of development. Mrs. McKay worked with the decoding by analogy approach with these children just as she did with her children who read at the full-alphabetic phase. Mrs. McKay's instructional emphasis with these children was slightly different, however. Mrs. McKay spent considerable time providing prompts to help her readers in the full-alphabetic phase decode by analogy. Mrs. McKay worked with Tyler and Jasmine to develop metacognitive awareness of decoding by analogy so that they could identify their own prompts during decoding. For example, when Tyler was reading and came to the word *invent*, rather than pointing out that he knew the word *tent* and could use his knowledge of that word to say *invent*, Mrs. McKay asked Tyler what words he knew that rhymed with *vent*. Tyler identified the word *tent* that was similar to *vent* and easily said the word *invent*. Mrs. McKay worked hard with Tyler and Jasmine to help them appropriate the decoding by analogy strategy so that they could use it independently in their own reading.

Mrs. McKay also worked with Tyler and Jasmine to help them develop implicit understandings of syllabication (Ehri and McCormick, 1998). Here's what we mean. Mrs. McKay knew that it was not useful to ask Jasmine and Tyler to memorize syllabication rules in isolated contexts. She knew that when students memorized isolated rules, they can rarely apply them in the context of real reading. However, Mrs. McKay knew that if she pointed out regularities about syllables in the context of real reading, children can often then use this information in their own reading. For example, when Jasmine was trying to read the word *butterfly*, Mrs. McKay pointed out that Jasmine had recently learned to read the word *flutter*. Jasmine replied that she read the word in two syllables *flut-ter*. Mrs. McKay asked Jasmine what the words *flutter* and *butterfly* had in common. Jasmine noted that they both had double consonants that were dividing lines between syllables. Jasmine then sounded out *but-ter-fly*.

Mrs. McKay also knew that building fluency was important for children reading at this—and all—phases of development. Fluency refers to reading rate and accuracy, but it also refers to automaticity, phrasing, and use of expression during reading. Thus, fluent readers can read smoothly, vary reading rates depending on the nature/meaning of the passage they are reading, read words automatically, and use expression in their reading (Worthy, Broaddus, and Ivey, 2001). One of the most important ways to increase fluency is to encourage lots of purposeful reading practice in texts that children can read independently. Both Jasmine and Tyler had younger brothers and sisters. Mrs. McKay worked with Jasmine and Tyler's parents to encourage Jasmine and Tyler to read easy (for them) books to their younger brothers and sisters several nights a week. Of course, Jasmine and Tyler practiced over and over reading the texts they would read to their siblings in the evenings. Also, Mrs. McKay coached them to read the books with meaningful rates, voice tones, and expression.

Mrs. McKay's Level of Word Knowledge: The Automatic Phase

Mature, proficient readers—like Mrs. McKay and you—read words at the automatic phase. At this phase, competent readers read words with both speed and automaticity; moreover, most of the words readers encounter are a part of their sight vocabularies (Ehri & McCormick, 1998). However, if a competent reader does encounter an unfamiliar word, he or she is able to identify it quickly and efficiently. Typically, readers at the automatic phase flexibly use a range of strategies including *decoding, analogy, sight,* and *prediction.* Decoding "involves identifying the sounds of individual letters, holding then in mind, and blending them into pronunciations that are recognized as real words" (Ehri & McCormick, 1998, p. 137). As we have mentioned previously, analogy involves recognizing a pattern in an unfamiliar word that can be used to identify it (Cunningham, 2000). For example, reading *bench,* a reader may apply by analogy the "ench" ending to the new word *stench.* Prediction involves using context cues such as pictures, other words surrounding the unfamiliar word, and/or specific letters in a word to identify the unfamiliar word. Finally, reading words by sight "involves using memory to read words that have been read before. Sight of the word immediately activates its spelling, pronunciation, and meaning in memory" (Ehri & McCormick, 1998, p. 137). Of course, the huge advantage of word knowledge at the automatic phase is that readers can shift most of their attention from identifying the words they are reading to concentrating on constructing meanings of the text they are reading.

PHONICS INSTRUCTION:
SOME ADDITIONAL CONSIDERATIONS

It is one thing to understand the principles behind phonics instruction and quite another to know how to use phonics strategies to help children develop meaningful decoding skills. Answers to questions such as these may help you to design your phonics program: "How do I begin phonics instruction?", "Is there a proper sequence for instruction?", "How should I incorporate phonics into a language-based reading program?", and "Do I teach a formal program of phonics to children who already understand and use most of the phonics strategy rules?" Of course, every teaching situation is unique, based totally on the teacher and the students involved. You, as the instructor, must be knowledgeable about and comfortable with phonics strategies to generate enthusiasm and comprehension in your students. Flexibility to seize "teachable moments" will make phonics instruction a natural part of your academic day. We hope to answer some instructional questions that teachers of reading often ask, reemphasizing the fact that every situation is different. The instructional answers that are provided here are only guidelines for you as a teacher. You will have to implement the teaching of phonics in your own manner to meet the specific needs of your students.

The following information provides some specific information on generally accepted tenets of phonics instruction (Durkin, 1987; Mason & Au, 1986). In a field as controversial as phonics instruction, there are always other ways of doing things and other sides to arguments. In the suggestions presented after these tenets, we offer alternatives and enhancements to the generally accepted ways of introducing phonics.

Suggestions for Teaching Phonics

1. Begin phonics instruction with auditory-discrimination (i.e., phonemic awareness) activities. Children must be able to hear the differences between

sounds of their language if they are to distinguish which letter represents that sound in a word. These exercises must be done in context. It is inefficient and meaningless to conduct auditory discrimination instruction using non–print-related material. Although it might be useful for music appreciation to identify which notes are the same when played on a piano, it does little to help distinguish which letters make which sound. These exercises should be done in context and with words.

2. Consonants are more consistent in letter–sound correspondence and are less influenced by dialectic differences. Consonants have therefore been presented first in traditional published phonics programs. Suggestions for sequencing consonants are the following:

   • Start with those that are distinct in shape and sound (*f, s, m, v, p,* and *t*). Teach the first consonants by using the /f/, /s/, /v/, and /m/ sounds in words. Coleman (1967) maintained that children find continuants, consonants that are produced by the constant release of air (e.g., /s/), easier to blend with other sounds than consonants that are formed by stopping the air flow (e.g., /t/). He suggested that the continuants are easily learned and should be among the first consonants that are taught to the beginning reader. Continuants include the following: /s/ *sat,* /f/ *fat,* and /v/ *vat.*

   • Do not teach easily confused letters one after the other (*b, d, p, m,* and *n*). Do not present visually contrastive pairs (*d* and *b*) together or in close sequence. In the past, teachers have been encouraged not to introduce simultaneously two letters that are easily confused with one another, such as *d* and *b.* However, another opinion is that the introduction of contrastive pairs *d* and *b, q* and *p, m,* and *n* has instructional value because the child has to focus on the distinctive features of each of the letters within a specific context (e.g., *dog* and *bog*). Some may argue that this initial struggle will reduce later confusion for the child. We believe that it may increase confusion and should therefore be avoided.

   • Save letters without clear letter–sound correspondence for last (*c, g, h,* and *w*).

3. Begin with initial consonant sounds. Introduce children to variations in letter–sound correspondence. One criticism of the linguistic method of reading instruction, which is described in detail in chapter 15, is that children begin to expect one-to-one letter–sound correspondence (e.g., *pan, man,* and *can*), and they find it difficult to transfer their phonics strategies to new words that do not fit the pattern. These findings suggest that children should be introduced to variations in letter–sound correspondence, such as *tap* and *tape,* from the very beginning to prepare them for later reading.

4. Teach single consonants before consonant digraphs. (Consonant digraphs are two letters together that make a combined sound different from that of the two parts, e.g., *sh, ch, th,* and *ph*).

5. Introduce vowels simultaneously so that words can be formed (e.g., *mat, pat, sat, Pam, tam,* and *tap*). Offer vowel instruction early in the program. Many teachers delay teaching vowels because they believe that all the con-

sonants need to be taught first, based on the reasons stated in the prior tenets. This view fails to consider the high correlation between the letter–sound correspondences of many vowels and the importance of the ability to decode vowels to read independently without adult guidance. Most children can clearly articulate vowels by the ages of 4 or 5, and most children have had some experience in decoding vowels, such as when they memorize certain sign words such as *stop* or *happy birthday*. The early introduction of vowels will help children to become involved independently in the reading process from the very beginning of instruction. Again, phonics instruction should be presented through meaningful language experiences. A logical question follows: Which vowel sounds should be introduced in the early stages of instruction? Fairbank's work may provide us with some meaningful answers. Fairbank suggests that teachers should present vowels to children based on their decibel ratings because children can more easily discriminate the vowel sounds with the highest decibel ratings. Thus, this natural phenomenon should dictate the sequence of instruction. During shared readings with children they identify words and patterns containing these vowel sequences. Fairbank found that the vowels in the following words shown in Table 5–7 have different decibel levels.

6. Present sight words so that newly learned words can become contextualized in a sentence. For example, if you were teaching *a, the,* and *on,* you could introduce the sentence "Pam sat on the mat" or "Tap the mat, Pat." You could also ask children to draw a picture of the sentence.

7. Teach digraphs (i.e., two consonants that appear together in words and form one sound, such as the *gh* in *cough*) before blends (combinations of letters wherein each sound is voiced but the whole is blended together, e.g., *bl, fr, str,* and *sl*). Marchbanks and Levin (1965) maintained that it is also important to note that children use definite order strategies when decoding. First, they look at the initial letter(s), then the final letter(s), then the middle letter(s), and finally, the configuration of the word. This phenomenon underlies the need for children to learn independent phonics strategies so that they will be able to cope with new and unfamiliar words.

8. Introduce children to word families through phonograms. Teachers often use word families to teach phonics. These word families are sometimes

TABLE 5–7
Decibel Ratings

Word	Vowel Sound	Decibel Rating
cap	/ce/	4.5
talk	/a/	3.8
shop	/a/	3.7
choke	/ow/	3.0
check	/e/	2.2
coop	/yu/	1.9
cup	/a/	1.1
cheek	/iy/	1.0
cook	/u/	0.3
pit	/i/	0.0

called phonogram lists. Teachers can use these lists to create games or activities for children. Brainstorming as a group is another way of establishing the concept of phonograms. Write *an* on the board and have the students tell you as many words as they can that have this sound. Then change *an* to *ane* and ask them again to give you words that have the same ending as *ane*. Begin with the phonograms that appear in the reading materials you and your children are sharing.

"Vocabulary of Rhymes," in Webster's Collegiate Dictionary, is a very useful list of phonograms that may help you in developing students' early reading vocabularies. Examples from that list are as follows:

ace	brace, face, grace, lace, place, race, space
eal	deal, heal, meal real seal, veal
ig	big, dig, fig, jig, pig, rig, wig
oat	boat, coat float, goat, throat

9. Practice new words by verbalizing. Kibby (1979) found that words learned by the phonics method were retained best when practiced in the production mode or by verbalization. Using the concept of phonograms in oral games or using the tape recorder may facilitate retention of words learned phonetically. Oral reading practice provides many "teachable moments" for phonics instruction. As with any oral reading lesson, a silent reading preview for comprehension is important so that the reader will have a better understanding of what will be presented orally. It is helpful to select material that is familiar and somewhat easy for the students, as this facilitates expressive oral reading. Asking other students to keep their books closed when someone else is reading will minimize corrections for miscues that do not change the meaning and allow the reader to be more successful. Children should be encouraged to be attentive, polite, interactive listeners.

10. Combine writing practice with phonics. Because elementary students are initially more interested in learning to write than in learning to read, use writing time to foster phonics awareness (Durkin, 1987). As children learn to write the letters of the alphabet, emphasize letter–sound correspondences and the fact that children can write words that they use.

Questions and Answers About a Sequential, Effective Phonics Program

Based on these suggestions, the following questions and answers will help you to develop a sequential, effective phonics teaching program. Try answering each question on your own before you read our answers.

1. Q. Should consonants or vowels be introduced first?
   A. They should be introduced simultaneously in patterned language contexts.
2. Q. Should short vowels or long vowels be introduced first?
   A. Short vowels should be introduced in the order presented in the decibel rating chart. Long vowel sounds should be introduced as contrasts to

short vowel sounds, using words that have become part of the child's sight vocabulary, such as *cap* and *cape*. When introducing graphemes and graphemic patterns, you should tell the children that graphemes represent sounds not that graphemes make phonemes. All vowels should be presented in natural language contexts.

3. Q. Should vowel correspondence be reinforced by teaching vowels within words, such as *cat*, *bat*, and *rat*?
   A. Definitely. Children should be introduced to the concept of syllable and word meaning from the beginning of their reading programs.

4. Q. Should the sound of initial consonants within the word be emphasized?
   A. Yes. Consonants should be within consonant-vowel-consonant words (e.g., *pan*, *bat*, and *sun*). Do not stress the sounds; instead, emphasize each sound within the context of the word. These consonants can be effectively presented through patterned language phrases that appear in reading materials. (*Rooster and rabbit ran and ran through the rain.*)

5. Q. Should dialect variations in children's pronunciation be considered in evaluating phonics acquisition?
   A. Dialect variation will result in different sounds for letter–sound correspondences. However, this should not concern you because your students will develop letter-sound equivalents that reflect their own dialect.

Sample Lessons for Teaching Phonics Strategies

Keeping in mind the suggestions and answers to the questions offered in the previous section, we offer the following lesson plan to illustrate one way of presenting an introductory lesson on the topic of letter–sound correspondence of the grapheme *m* that may provide you with a framework on which to build your phonics lessons. The letter to be presented should be part of the big book selection.

Lesson Plan

Goal: To introduce the grapheme *m* and its corresponding phoneme /m/.

Grade Level: Primary

Procedures:

1. Read a big book selection that contains patterned language illustrating the oral and written phoneme /m/.

2. After reading and talking about the story, write *m* on the board. Ask students to listen again for all of the words they hear that begin with the sound of *m* that they hear in *mouse*.

3. List on the board the words that students have named:

   mother   monkey   mouse   Mike   moose   music

4. To reinforce this skill, divide an oak-tag board into four sections. In section 1, draw a picture of a man; in section 2, a mit; in section 3, a mouse; and in section 4, a mask. Ask students to name the picture; then write the words *man, mit, mouse,* and *mask* under each of the pictures. Have the students copy the same pictures and words on their own papers. When the

students seem to have grasped the idea, have them present their pictures and help them write their own words under each picture.

Evaluation: Write another *m* on the board and ask students to draw pictures and write words under each picture. They may want to write a story about their picture.

This lesson can be followed by a lesson on *n*. Point out the similarities of these two letters to the students and ask them to explain the differences.

Instructional Activities

In the next few pages, we present several activities that you might find useful for your reading program. Although we have isolated them for presentation and discussion, each of these activities should be only one of many experiences during a language-based reading lesson. You can select from these activities once you have a sense of your children's developmental word knowledge. You will find that different activities can be used to meet students' instructional needs across the range of developmental levels we described previously. When choosing instructional activities for your children, you will need to draw on your professional judgment regarding your specific children to decide which activities may make the most sense to use with different children and groups of children.

1. All Around the Room

Goal: Letter discrimination

Grade Level: K-6

Construction: Label as many items around the room as possible, making sure that there is at least one label for each student in the class. (The higher the grade level, the more difficult the labels should be.) Prepare a stack of cards containing the letters representing the initial sounds of these items. Be sure to make enough cards for all the labels. You will also need a stopwatch or a clock with a second hand.

Utilization: Divide the students into teams. Deploying one team at a time, on the "go" signal, have the students find the labeled item that matches the card they have been given. Time how long it takes until the entire team is standing next to its labeled item. Record the time on the board. Check to make sure that all the letters match. Deduct time for any that do not. Do the same for the rest of the teams. The team with the fastest time wins. This can also be done with pairs of students, with the one arriving at his or her label first being the winner.

Variations: This game can be played with other phonics elements, including long and short vowel sounds, ending letters, number of syllables, and so on. For each variation a different set of cards is necessary.

2. Space Shuttle Voyage

Goal: Letter recognition

Grade Level: K-1

Construction: Make large flash cards showing frequently confused letters such as *b*, *d*, *g*, *p*, and *q* (one letter per card).

Utilization: Have the students sit in a circle on the floor. One student begins by standing behind the person on his or her right. Hold up a flash card (in the shape of a star) while both students attempt to name the correct letter. Whoever is first (or correct) gets to continue around the circle. (The other student sits down.) The student who beats everyone wins by going into orbit and back to earth.

3. Bug-Eyed Monster

Goal: Visual discrimination of beginning or ending letters

Grade Level: K-2

Construction: Make a deck of 25 cards containing 12 pairs of various words that begin or end with the same letter. Write one of the 12 words on each card. Also, design one card for the Bug-Eyed Monster, which is a word that cannot be paired with any of the other cards.

Utilization: Have all the cards dealt out, and have each student take a turn drawing a card from the person on his or her left. If the student gets a pair, he or she puts it down on the table, saying the two words and stating whether they end or begin with the same letter. The game ends when all the cards are paired and someone is left with the Bug-Eyed Monster.

4. Letter Bingo

Goal: Recognition of frequently confused letters

Grade Level: K-1

Construction: Make a Bingo board with the lower case and upper case letters.

Utilization: Play this game with the regular Bingo rules. The caller names a letter (e.g., "capital B," "small b"), and the players have to cover the correct letter.

5. Roll Your Word

Goal: Discriminating between letters and their use in spelling words

Grade Level: K-2

Construction: Construct two piles of index cards representing each letter of the alphabet. One pile contains the vowels; the other pile contains the consonants. Make at least five cards for each vowel.

Utilization: Each student rolls the dice and is allowed to pick up the number of cards he or she has rolled on the dice. He or she is allowed to select from either the consonant or the vowel pile. The student receives one point for each letter of the word he or she has created. The object of the game is to collect points.

6. Phonics Challenge

Goal: Discriminating vowel sounds

Grade Level: K-2

Construction: Whiteboard and markers

Utilization: Divide the classroom into two teams. Choose a vowel sound (e.g., short *a*). Taking turns, the teams call out a word with the sound and an aide (or the teacher) writes it on the board. The first team that makes a mistake or is unable to think of a word is out, and the other team wins the round. Continue with other vowel sounds until one team has won five rounds.

Variations: Use initial consonants, blends, digraphs, two- or three-syllable words, and so on.

7. Phonics Concentration

Goal: Discriminating vowel sounds

Grade Level: K-2

Construction: Choose or draw pictures that represent long (and short) vowel sounds, and paste (or draw) them on one side of a card with the word written below it, one to each card. You must make or find pairs of pictures, at least two pairs for each vowel sound (more for older students). On the other side of the card, write the vowel sound the picture represents.

Utilization: Mix up the cards and place them picture side down. Each player in turn flips over two cards with the same vowel sound, hoping to find a pair or match. If they don't match, the cards are turned back over and the next player has a turn. When the cards are matched, they are removed from the game. The player with the most pairs at the end wins. (Players must be able to say the word indicated by the pictures in order to take the pair.)

Variations: Any sound you wish to teach may be represented. The more sounds and more pairs, the more complex the game is.

8. Welcome to the Short Vowel Hotel

Goal: Discriminating short vowel sounds

Grade Level: K-2

Construction: Construct a large chart. The chart should be large enough to be subdivided into five columns. At the top of the first column write an *a*. At the top of columns 2 through 5, continue with the rest of the vowels *e, i, o,* and *u,* one letter at the top of each column. Draw several rectangles in each column. Design 40 to 50 rectangular cards. On each card, write one word containing a short vowel sound.

Utilization: Word cards are placed in a deck. The first student selects a card and pronounces the word without exposing it to the other players. The student beside him identifies the column containing the correct vowel sound heard in the word. If the student is correct, he or she places the card in the correct column (the proper "floor") and scores one point. The game continues until all the cards have been placed on the proper floor.

9. Ship of Vowels

Goal: Distinguishing long and short vowel sounds

Grade Level: K-2

Construction: Design cards as in activity 8, but include words with the long vowel sound as well. On a blackline master, draw two ocean liners with several smokestacks. Label one "USS Long Vowel" and the other "USS Short Vowel." Make a copy for each student.

Utilization: The game is played in the same way as "Welcome to the Short Vowel Hotel" (activity 8), except that in this game, the student must write the word behind the correct engine.

10. Spin the Word Family

Goal: Instruction in phonograms and initial consonants

Grade Level: K-2

Construction: Make a wheel out of cardboard and write various phonograms at different points on the wheel. Attach the wheel to another piece of cardboard and write four initial consonants that form words with the phonograms at four sides of the cardboard. (Examples of phonograms are *ack, ag, ay, ug, at, ell, an, ent,* and *ank.* Initial consonants to go with these are *s, b, t,* and *r.*)

Utilization: Have each student spin the wheel and try to form a word from the phonogram and initial consonant. Award a point for each word formed correctly. The student with the most points wins.

QUESTIONS

1. Define phonics.
2. Why is phonics significant to you as a teacher?
3. Is there more to the study of words than phonics? Explain.
4. What are the phases of development as children learn to read words and what are some distinguishing behaviors of children in each phase of development?
5. How should phonics be taught during these developmental phases?

REFERENCES

Adams, M. J. (1990). *Beginning to read: Thinking and learning about print.* Cambridge, MA: MIT Press.

Archer, A. L., Gleason, M. M., & Vachon, V. L. (2003). Decoding and fluency: Foundation skills for struggling older readers. *Learning Disabilities Quarterly, 26,* 89–101.

Beck, I. L., & Juel, C. (1995, Summer). The role of decoding in learning how to read. *American Educator,* 8–42.

Carroll, L. (pseudonym Charles L. Dodgson). (1963). *Alice's Adventures in Wonderland.* New York: Macmillan.

Chall, J. S., Conrad, S. S., & Harris-Sharples, S. H. (1983). Textbooks and challenges: An inquiry into textbook difficulty, reading achievement, and knowledge acquisition. *Final Report to the Spencer Foundation.* Chicago: Spencer Foundation.

Coleman, E. (1967). *Collecting a data base for an educational technology* (Parts I and III). El Paso, TX: University of Texas Press.

Cunningham, P. M. (2000). *Phonics they use: Words for reading and writing.* New York: Longman.

Cunningham, A. E., & Stanovich, K. E. (1998, Spring/Summer). What reading does for the mind. *American Educator,* 8–15.

Cunningham, P. M., Moore, S. A., Cunningham, J. W., & Moore, D. W. (1989). *Reading in the elementary classrooms: Strategies and observations* (2nd. ed.). Boston: Allyn & Bacon.

Durkin, D. (1964). *Phonics test for teachers.* New York: Teachers College Press.

Durkin, D. (1974). *Teaching them to read*. Boston: Allyn & Bacon.

Durkin, D. (1987). *Teaching young children to read* (4th ed.). Boston: Allyn & Bacon.

Ehri, L. C., & McCormick, S. (1998). Phases of word learning: Implications for instruction with delayed and disabled readers. *Reading & Writing Quarterly: Overcoming Learning Difficulties, 14*, 135–163.

Ehri, L. C., Nunes, S. R., Stahl, S. A., & Willows, D. M. (2001). Systematic phonics instruction helps students learn to read: Evidence from the national reading panel's meta-analysis. *Review of Educational Research, 71*, 393–447.

Fairbanks, G. (1966). *Experimental phonics: Selected articles*. Urbana: University of Illinois Press.

Fountas, I. C., & Pinnell, G. S. (1996). *Guided Reading: Good first teaching for all children*. Portsmouth, NH: Heinemann.

Fulwiler, G., & Groff, P. (1980, Fall). The effectiveness of intensive phonics. *Reading Horizons, 21*, 50–54.

Gibson, E., & Levin, H. (1975). *The psychology of reading*. Cambridge, MA: MIT Press.

Goswami, U., & Bryant, P. (1990). *Phonological skills & learning to read*. Hillsdale, NJ: Lawrence Erlbaum.

Groff, P. (1971). *The syllable: Its nature and pedagogical usefulness*. Portland, OR: Northwest Regional Educational Laboratory.

Gunn, B., Biglan, A., Smolkowski, K., & Ary, D. (2000). The efficacy of supplemental instruction in decoding skills for Hispanic and non-Hispanic students of elementary school. *The Journal of Special Education, 34*, 91–103.

Jenkins, J., Bausel, R., & Jenkins, L. (1972, February). Comparison of letter name and letter sound training as transfer variables. *American Educational Research Journal, 9*, 75–86.

Juel, C. (1989, Spring). Comparison of word identifying strategies with varying contexts word type, and reader skill. *Reading Research Quarterly, 15*, 358–376.

Kibby, M. W. (1979, January). The effects of certain instructional conditions and response modes on initial word learning. *Reading Research Quarterly, 32*, 147–171.

Marchbanks, B., & Levin, H. (1965, September). Cues by which children recognize words. *Journal of Educational Psychology, 56*, 57–61.

Manzo, A. V., & Manzo, U. L. (2005). 'bdp' syndrome: Problem and solution for a nagging academic language learning dilemma in literacy and content area reading. *California Reader, 38*(2), 14–23.

Mason, J. M., & Au, K. H. (1986). *Reading instruction for today*. Glenview, IL: Scott, Foresman.

Moats, L. C. (2001). When older students can't read. *Educational Leadership, 58*, 36–40.

Morrow, L. M. (1989). *Literacy development in the early years: Helping children read and write*. Englewood Cliffs, NJ: Prentice-Hall.

Murphy, H., & Durrell, D. (1972). *Speech to print phonics*. New York: Harcourt Brace Jovanovich.

Pinnell, G. S., & Fountas, I. (1998). *Word matters: Teaching phonics & spelling in the reading/writing classroom*. Portsmouth, NH: Heinemann.

Pollard, R. S. (1989). *Pollard's synthetic method*. Chicago: Western.

Shafer, G. L., Campbell, P., & Rakes, S. (2000). Investigating the status and perceived importance of explicit phonics instruction in the elementary classroom. *Reading Improvement, 37*, 110–118.

Silberberg, N., Silverberg, M., & Iverson, I. (1972, March). The effects of kindergarten instruction in alphabet and numbers on first grade reading. *Journal of Learning Disabilities, 5*, 254–261.

Stahl, S. A., Duffy-Hester, A. M., & Dougherty, K. A. (1998). Everything you wanted to know about phonics (but were afraid to ask). *Reading Research Quarterly, 33*, 338–355.

Strickland, D. S. (1998). *Teaching phonics today: A primer for educators*. Newark, DE: International Reading Association.

Venezky, R. L. (1970). *The structure of English orthography*. The Hague, Netherlands: Mouton.

Williams, J. P. (1985). The case for explicit decoding instruction. In J. Osborn, P. T. Wisonson, & R. C. Anderson (Eds.), *Reading education: Foundations for a literate America*. Lexington, MA: Heath, Lexington Books.

Worthy, J., Broaddus, K., & Ivey, G. (2001). *Pathways to independence: Reading, writing, and learning in grades 3–8*. New York: Guilford Press.

6

Vocabulary Development

———————— CHAPTER GOALS ————————

To help the reader

- understand the importance of vocabulary development.
- understand the distinction between meaningful, rich vocabulary development and shallow vocabulary knowledge.
- choose words for vocabulary instruction.
- use vocabulary instructional strategies involving structural analysis.
- use vocabulary instructional strategies involving contextual analysis.
- understand how the dictionary fits into vocabulary instruction.

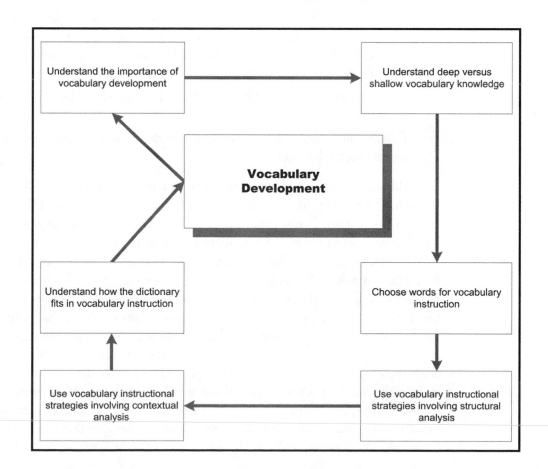

. . . Words are the instruments that authors and poets use to enchant us, delight us, sadden us, amaze us. (Beck, McKeown, and Kucan, 2002, p. ix)

Emily recently graduated from a teacher preparation program and was hired by Clarke County School District to teach third grade. Her elementary school is situated in a huge school district in the midst of a very large city. In a recent conversation with her principal, she found out that 28 students are currently listed on her class roster. She has several weeks to prepare for the beginning of the school year. She knows she has important decisions to make about how she wants to structure literacy instruction in her classroom. On this particular day, she is planning how she will structure vocabulary instruction in her classroom. She starts thinking about how most of her teachers taught vocabulary to her when she was in school.

Your Turn

Think back to the vocabulary instructional practices you recall best from your own school experiences. What are your most vivid memories about how your teachers structured your vocabulary instruction?

In general, Emily's memories of her own vocabulary instruction are not fond ones. We suspect that this might be true for you, too. Typical vocabulary instruction for Emily went something like this:

Her teachers introduced a list of vocabulary words on Monday. (She was never quite sure where the words came from.)

Over the next few days she wrote a dictionary definition for each word and turned this list in to her teacher. (She recalls that it was sometimes difficult to choose which definition to write on her list since so many words have a host of possible definitions.)

Then she used each word in a sentence and turned this list of sentences in to her teacher.

Finally, on Fridays, she had to write the definitions of each word during the weekly vocabulary quiz.

Although most of Emily's vocabulary instruction proceeded in that "typical" manner, she recalled one teacher who did things differently—her 6th grade Language Arts teacher. Rather than giving the students the words they were to learn, Mr. Hansen asked the students to identify five words from their own reading each week that they wanted to learn. Rather than making up a sentence for the words, Mr. Hansen asked the students to write the sentence from the book where they encountered the word. They still looked up the dictionary definition of each word, but Emily found this easier to do because she could jot down the word meaning that made the most sense based on the context of the story in which she found the word. Emily's class also talked about some of the vocabulary words they identified from their reading each week. For example, Mr. Hansen devoted some class time during the week to a discussion of the words that the students found the most unusual, appealing, or problematic. During these discussions Emily found that she came to understand her own words better. She also noticed that she learned words from the lists of other students. To this day, Emily still recalls some of the words

Buttermilk Hill © 2004 by Ruth White. Used with the permission of Farrar Straus Giroux.

that she learned in Mr. Hansen's class. She also recalls that this was the first time she ever really got excited about and interested in words.

Emily knew that she wanted vocabulary instruction in her third grade classroom to be meaningful, exciting, and interesting—much like Mr. Hansen had made it for her. She also knew that she learned a lot about how to teach vocabulary in her teacher preparation program that would help her to make decisions about how she wanted to structure vocabulary instruction in her own classroom. In fact, some of the background knowledge about vocabulary instruction that Emily learned in her teacher preparation program helped her to understand why Mr. Hansen's instructional practices seemed to work better for her than most vocabulary instruction she received throughout her schooling. She also learned how she could further improve upon the instructional practices she recalled from Mr. Hansen's room. Emily pulled out her books and notes from some of her college literacy methods classes. She thought she'd revisit some of the ideas she learned about quality vocabulary instruction. Then she would finalize her plans for structuring her own vocabulary instruction in her third grade classroom.

MEANINGFUL VOCABULARY INSTRUCTION: WHAT EMILY LEARNED IN HER TEACHER PREPARATION PROGRAM AND WHAT YOU NEED TO KNOW

One of the many things that Emily learned in her teacher preparation program was that meaningful vocabulary instruction was much more important than she had ever realized. Here are some reasons why. First, children's socioeconomic status (SES) plays an important role in their vocabulary development (Beck, McKeown, & Kucan, 2002). Children from higher SES backgrounds across the grade levels may know from two to four times more words than children from low SES backgrounds (Graves & Slater, 2006). Second, some studies (e.g., Nagy & Anderson, 1984; Nagy, 1988) have shown that children acquire a great deal of vocabulary from wide reading; however, some of the children in greatest need for vocabulary development are struggling readers who do not, or cannot, read widely. You're probably coming

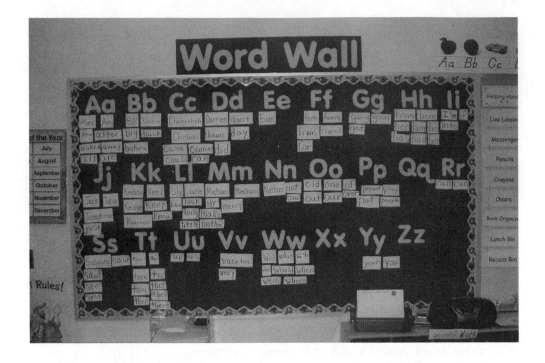

to the same conclusion as Emily: Meaningful vocabulary instruction is a serious professional responsibility—especially for struggling readers and children from low SES backgrounds. As Emily continued to study about vocabulary instruction, she realized that meaningful vocabulary instruction is important for all children—even children who are wide readers—for a third important reason. Vocabulary, or word knowledge, is linked inextricably to reading comprehension in many complex ways (Davis, 1944, 1968; Nagy, 1988; Singer, 1965; Thurstone, 1946). We will share just a few of the complex connections between vocabulary and reading comprehension that have been identified.

Research, as well as intuition, tells us that vocabulary knowledge and reading comprehension are related. Anderson and Freebody (1981) present three views of vocabulary's relationship to reading comprehension. One, the instrumentalist position, suggests that if students understand the words in a passage, then they will be able to understand the passage itself. A second view, the aptitude position, posits the existence of a general verbal talent. The point here is that students with this talent have a facility for understanding words as well as passages. The assumption might be that students who are more skilled in word-recognition strategies may be better comprehenders. Finally, the third view, referred to as general knowledge, contends that the richer students' background knowledge and experience, the more able they are to understand words, their concepts, and the passages in which they are found. In truth, these are not three separate positions but rather three interrelated ways of approaching vocabulary instruction. Each suggests that it is difficult to understand a passage in which many words are unknown. The question that these different views raise, however, is just how comprehension and vocabulary are related. In other words, which came first? Are readers good comprehenders because they know a lot of words, or do they know a lot of words because they are good comprehenders?

The research on vocabulary instruction doesn't give a clear answer to this question. In some cases, when students are given direct instruction in words in isolation, they learn words to the point of being able to pass objective tests on definitions and their reading comprehension did improve (Beck, McCaslin, & McKeown, 1980; Draper & Moeller, 1971; Kameenui, Carnine, & Freschi, 1982; Konopak, 1988; Stahl & Fairbandk, 1986). Other studies call into question the theory of whether direct vocabulary instruction precedes improvement in reading comprehension (Harris & Jacobson, 1973; Jenkins, Pany, & Schreck, 1978; Tuinman & Brady, 1974). These studies suggest that comprehension instruction may have a positive impact on vocabulary development. However, whether the egg comes before the chicken, or vice versa, virtually all vocabulary instruction studies succeeded in increasing vocabulary knowledge (Cunningham, 1988; Draper & Moeller, 1971; Haggard, 1982; Jenkins, Pany, & Schreck, 1978; Kameenui, Carnine, & Freschi, 1982; White, Sowell, & Yanagihara, 1989). Moreover, most scholars agree that vocabulary and comprehension are related (e.g., see Nagy, 1988). Additionally, vocabulary instruction can improve students' writing in areas related to the words taught (Duin, 1983, 1986; Duin & Graves, 1986), and vocabulary used in speech and writing influences readers' perceptions of what is written, as well as their judgments about the speaker and the writer (Bradac, Bowers, & Courtright, 1982; Neilson & Piche, 1981). Thus, our opinion and that of Beck, McKeown, and Kucan (2002), Smith (1988), Cunningham (1987), Graves (1984), Calfee (1981), and Stotsky (1976) is that students at all grade levels need to be engaged in systematic programs of vocabulary development and expansion in an effort to enhance their overall reading comprehension. Now, a question you may be asking as you read along—and one that Emily asked at this point in her studies once she realized the importance of vocabulary instruction—is: "Just what is meaningful vocabulary instruction?" It turns out, of course, that there aren't easy answers to this question either. We'll spend the rest of the chapter sharing information about this important question and telling you about ways that you can plan for meaningful vocabulary instruction in your own current or future classroom.

What Do We Mean by Meaningful Vocabulary Instruction?

Meaningful vocabulary instruction is complex. It involves teaching students to recognize and become familiar with words, but it is much more. Words are merely labels for concepts, and each concept is more than the simple definition of a word. A concept may require 100 or 1,000 words to describe it.

From infancy we begin building concepts through our ever-expanding world experiences. Our experiences may include going to the beach, the zoo, and school, engaging in reading and writing for school-related activities or pleasure, and/or living on a farm or in the midst of a large city. Whatever our experiences, they contribute to our knowledge about the world. As our knowledge grows, so does the number of concepts that we understand. This makes sense and may sound more trite than profound, but the idea of ever-expanding repertoires of conceptual knowledge is crucial to the view of vocabulary instruction as concept development. Concepts can be envisioned as the way we structure our knowledge. After all, if we tried to understand everything in our world separately, on its own merits and dissociated from any other information, our heads would be spinning with minutiae, with unrelated bits of information. Nothing would be more important than anything else;

there would be no significance, no differences and no relationships. Here the word relationship is significant. To make sense of our world, we form relationships among events. We form associations; we organize information into hierarchies of superordinates and subordinates. For example, children learn that not all four-legged animals are cats, like their own playful kitten. Depending upon their personal experiences, they will become familiar with the superordinate concept of animals and will place four-legged creatures that are encountered, such as cows, dogs, and cats within subordinate classes. As children become even more educated and gain experience with scientific concepts, they may begin to develop concepts with even finer distinctions. For example, they may conceptualize cats as belonging to the class Felidae, which includes not only cats, but also lions, tigers, and jaguars.

Thus, it's possible to say that all words that convey meaning are labels for concepts, and it is these concepts that we wish to help children to understand to increase their proficiency with words and enhance their reading comprehension. Beck and her colleagues (2002) make an important distinction between shallow and deeper word knowledge. Shallow word knowledge is like much of the vocabulary instruction that many of us may have experienced in school. It refers to memorizing definitions of words without understanding, at a deeper level, the concepts that the words represent. If students have deep word knowledge, they understand the concept(s) the word represents, and they can use the word flexibly in a variety of contexts.

Your Turn

Please complete the following chart (chart based on Beck et al., 2002, p. 12). This exercise helps to illustrate the multifaceted nature of word knowledge. That is, it helps to clarify the shallow/deeper levels of knowledge that we may have about words. It also illustrates the fact that the shallow/deeper distinction is probably best characterized as a continuum from more to less. After completing the chart yourself, compare your responses to the responses of some of your peers in your class.

Word	I own this word. I can use it when I write and speak.	I know this word when I read or hear it, but I never say it.	I may have heard or seen the word, but I'm not comfortable with its meaning.	I don't know this word.
morphology				
affixes				
suffixes				
prefixes				
compound words				

As your answers and your peers' answers in the chart probably illustrate, we don't necessarily have only shallow or deep knowledge of a word; rather, we may have shallower or deeper knowledge of a word—depending upon our experiences with and understandings of the word. Emily's goal for vocabulary instruction in her classroom (and yours, too, we'd suspect) is to help her children to develop deeper, more meaningful, understandings of the concepts that important words represent so that her children can explain the words and use them flexibly across a variety of contexts. What is her plan for doing this? First, she has to make decisions about which words she should teach; then she has to decide how she will teach them. We begin with the former issue and move to the latter.

One of Emily's First Instructional Questions: What Words Should I Teach?

"The number of languages used in the world today comes close to three thousand. Our English tongue is only one out of that number.... It is also the language that has more words in its vocabulary than any other."

—E. Lambert, 1955, p. 11

Okay, you probably can tell from the previous quote that it is no small feat to decide which vocabulary words you will teach your children! According to Nagy and Anderson (1984), students in grades 3 through 9 encounter in print approximately 88,500 different word families (groups of words consisting of a root with all of its compounds and derivatives, e.g., vest, invest, investments, divest, divestiture). However, not all of these word families have high utility for readers. In fact, Nagy and Anderson estimate that approximately half of them are used so rarely that a reader may encounter them only once in a lifetime. Given the variety of words used and the overwhelming number of words in classroom materials, it's not surprising that many teachers wonder which words to choose for explicit instruction.

The good news is that vocabulary scholars have some excellent guidelines for helping us make these decisions. Beck and her colleagues (2002) suggest that it's useful to consider three different tiers of words found in a mature, literate individual's vocabulary. The first tier consists of basic words such as school, hot, red, mother, cat, and hospital. These words are in the spoken vocabulary of most students but may not be in their reading vocabulary when they first enter school. Most educators would agree that little, if any, time need be spent teaching the meanings of these words. However, to become fluent readers, students need these words in their sight-word repertoire. Recall that we discussed helping children to develop their sight-word repertoires in chapter 5.

The second vocabulary tier consists of general utility words such as convenient, general, moral, and compromise. Students may encounter these words in a variety of contexts. Consequently, these are the words for which teachers, as we will discuss later, will want to provide "rich instruction" (Beck, McKeown, & Omanson, 1984) in meaning and usage.

Finally, the third tier of vocabulary consists of specialized words that tend to be used in specific domains. Examples include words such as hemp, fistula, nucleotides, and marsupial. These words are best taught when they are necessary for passage comprehension, as in discussing fibula in a lesson on the skeletal system. On the other hand, a specialized word, such as mauve, might be mentioned incidentally in a story as part of the snapshot description of the many colors observed by a pitcher standing poised on the pitcher's mound, glancing into the crowd. In this case, if the meaning of the word is not crucial to understanding the passage, the teacher probably would not want to spend time incorporating it into direct instruction. The following example illustrates the high-utility (tier 2) and technical words (tier 3) that might be found in a unit on volcanoes. Examples for teaching the high-utility words are provided. We also explain how we decided which words are tier 2 words and which words are tier 3 words.

Why Mount St. Helens Blew Its Top (topic being studied)

High-Utility Words (Tier 2 Words)	Technical Words (Tier 3 Words)
geologist	tectonic plates
pressure	magma
expand	mantle
erupt	lava
prediction	

Instructional Example 1

Tier 2 Word: geologist

Definition: a scientist who studies the structure of the earth's crust, its layers, and its rock formations

Strategy: present positive and negative examples and discuss and rehearse the contextual definition

The teacher displays the word and its definition and says:

Teacher: Some scientists have studied the layers of rock in the Grand Canyon to see when they were formed. Are these scientists geologists? Why?

Teacher: Some scientists have studied the animals that live in the ocean. Are these scientists geologists? Why?

Teacher: Some scientists study plants that grow on the earth's surface. Are these scientists geologists? Why?

Teacher: Some scientists study how the earth's continents have moved over many years. Are these scientists geologists? Why?

Instructional Example 2

Tier 2 Word: expand

Definition: to increase in size

Strategy: present example and contextual definition; students elicit and expand meaning

The teacher displays the word and the following paragraph:

As I blew up the balloon, it began to expand. As it grew in size, I was afraid that it was going to pop.

Teacher: What do you think expand means?

Student: To get bigger.

Teacher: What other things can you think of that can expand?

Student: Rubber bands and bread dough.

Teacher: Think of a sentence using the word expand that illustrates the meaning of the word expand. Turn to your neighbor and tell the sentence to her or him.

DID YOU NOTICE...
Did you notice that vocabulary instruction should include words from three different tiers? Depending on your students spoken vocabulary and cultural backgrounds, you may need to spend more or less time discussing the meaning of tier one words. Also, the unit/theme being studied or text being read will determine how many tier two or three words need to be examined. The bottom line, the choice of vocabulary words to teach, will vary depending on students needs and the topic being studied.

(The teacher then asks several pairs of children to share their sentences with the whole group.)

Instructional Example 3

Tier 2 Word: prediction
Definition: a guess about the future
Strategy: provide definition and contextual use

The teacher writes the following sentence on the board:

Prediction: a guess about the future

The weatherman made a prediction that _____.

Teacher: What is the definition of prediction?

Student: A guess about the future.

Teacher: Read the incomplete sentence. How could we complete it?

Student: The weatherman made a prediction that it would rain tomorrow.

Teacher: What other predictions can you think of?

Student: Fortune tellers make predictions about your future. People make predictions about who will win football, soccer, baseball, or basketball games.

Teacher: Now, think of another sentence where you can use the word prediction. Turn to your partner. Share your sentence with your partner.

(After students have shared sentences with partners, ask several students to share their sentences with the whole class.)

Teacher: Let's add this word to our classroom word wall. (see page 164)

You may be thinking at this point in your reading: "Okay, you've identified the different tiers of words pertaining to a possible lesson on why Mount St. Helen's erupted, and you've suggested some ways to introduce vocabulary words to my students. However, you haven't addressed ways to help me identify tier 2 (i.e., high-utility) words for my vocabulary instruction when I'm sorting through completely unfamiliar reading materials and trying to make decisions about which words to emphasize in my explicit vocabulary instruction." This is crucial. As teachers, we must constantly make decisions about which words we should teach—of all the many possible words we might teach.

Focusing on the practical decisions that we, as teachers, must make concerning which words to teach, Graves and Slater (2006) suggested the following two steps, which can help in this decision-making process.

1. Determine which words students are likely to know. This can be accomplished by
    a. asking students which words they know
    b. giving pretests to determine which words in a selection the students do not know
    c. assessing students' knowledge and performance through informal classroom discussions
    d. using The Living Word Vocabulary found in Vocabulary Building: A Process Approach (Dale & O'Rourke, 1986). This book reports the

results of testing approximately 30,000 words. It presents the words tested, the meaning given, the grade level at which 67% to 84% of the students knew the word, and the percentage of students who knew the word at that grade level. With this information, teachers can make general predictions concerning which words their students will be most likely to know or not know.

2. Use the following four questions to help set criteria for selecting words to be taught.

   a. Is an understanding of the word necessary for the student to understand the passage in which it is found?

   b. Can students determine the meaning of the word themselves through structural and/or contextual clues?

   c. Can learning the word help reinforce a skill that students will need later? (For example, understanding the word unicycle would help students who had not mastered the prefix uni.)

   d. Is this word useful? (That is, is the word a tier 2 word that the students will probaby encounter often?)

Although these questions are not mutually exclusive, we can make some generalizations about them. If the answers to questions 2a and 2b are "No" and "Yes," respectively, then it is probably not necessary to spend time on explicit vocabulary instruction. However, if the answers to questions 2c and 2d are "Yes," then you will want to consider using strategies that will make the word part of students' productive vocabulary. In question 2d, it's important to clarify the words useful and often. They refer to the frequency of a word's use. To answer this question, one suggestion is to use the 2-year test. Ask the question: "How much will students need the word in 2 years?" Another suggestion is to consult the American Heritage Word Frequency Book (Carroll, Davies, & Richman, 1971), which lists the frequency of approximately 86,000 words found in materials for school-age children.

Once you have developed some strategies that help you decide what words to teach, you can address in more depth two other issues: how and when to teach vocabulary. We will address these issues in the remainder of this chapter as we examine two major approaches to vocabulary instruction—structural analysis and contextual analysis (Nagy, 1988). Additionally, we will share the limitations of each of these approaches to vocabulary instruction. Many, but not necessarily all, words can be taught by looking within the word (i.e., at its structure) or at the text around the word (i.e., at the context in which the word is embedded). Words that can be comprehended through analysis of their parts are best taught through structural analysis. Words that students can comprehend through clues presented in the reading passage itself are best taught through contextual analysis.

WHAT IS STRUCTURAL ANALYSIS, AND HOW MIGHT IT BE USED AS AN INSTRUCTIONAL APPROACH?

As Emily sorted through her college books and notes, thinking about ways to structure the vocabulary instruction in her classroom, she found some notes from a practicum experience in her teacher preparation program. For this particular experience, she had been in Mrs. Garcia's fourth grade classroom. She had jotted down some observations about how Mrs. Garcia taught vocabulary to her children. One day, Mrs. Garcia was focusing on John R. Gardiner's book Stone Fox. In the story, Little Willy is worried about being disqualified from a dog sled race. Mrs. Garcia discussed with the class what it meant to qualify for an event like a race. Because dis as a prefix means apart from or not, students could see that Willy is worried about being qualified, literally, apart from everyone else. In other words, he would no longer be a part of the race that he so desperately needed to win. By drawing her students' attention to this—and other—structural analysis strategies, Mrs. Garcia helped to make this an increasingly automatic part of the reading process for her children.

Through her readings for her literacy methods classes, as well as practicum observations such as the ones in Mrs. Garcia's room, Emily learned that parts of the words themselves can provide clues to the concepts that the words represent. Structural analysis, which consists of breaking words into their smallest parts, is a useful decoding skill when the word is not in the student's sight vocabulary. Finding meaning in parts of words may not only help in decoding them, but it may also help in understanding their meanings. For example, a student who knows that in = not and able = capable can unravel a word such as indefinable and arrive at the meaning "not capable of being defined." Background knowledge about some of the rules of morphology helped Emily to make decisions about the structural analysis portion of her vocabulary instruction program. We think that you, too, will find this background information useful as you make decisions about how to plan for vocabulary instruction in your own classroom.

Morphology. The smallest unit of meaning in any language is a morpheme. A morpheme is not necessarily a word, as a word may have a single morpheme (e.g., venture) or several morphemes (e.g., ad-venture-some). Free morphemes can stand alone as a word (e.g., mix); bound morphemes cannot stand alone (e.g., -ing as in mixing). Free morphemes are often found as root words, whereas bound morphemes are usually affixes (prefixes and suffixes). For example, in the word previewing, pre and ing are bound morphemes because they cannot stand alone as words, whereas view is a free morpheme because it can stand alone as a word.

Affixes. Knowledge of how words are constructed is an important step in knowing how to unlock word meanings. To do so, students must be introduced to English affixes. Affixes are bound morphemes (i.e., they cannot stand alone as words); they include prefixes and suffixes. Affixes can be found in four major classes of words: nouns, verbs, adjectives, and adverbs. Examples are histor*ian*, *en*liven, ador*able*, and sweet*ly*. A prefix is an affix at the beginning of a word that changes its meaning. Many common English prefixes will be valuable for your students to learn (see Table 6–1).

Examples:

inter	(between): interstate
pre	(before): preview
sub	(under): submarine

TABLE 6–1
Strategies for Vocabulary Development: Key to 100,000 Words

Prefixes	Other Spellings	Meaning	Master Words	Root	Other Spelling	Meaning
1. de		down or away	detain	tain	ten, tin	to have, to hold
2. inter		between	intermittent	mitt	miss, mit, mis	to send
3. pre		before	precept	cept	cap, capt, ceive, ceit, cit	to take or seize
4. ob	oc, of, op	to, toward, against	offer	for	lat, lay	to carry, bear
5. in	il, im, ir	into or not	insist	sist	stat, sta, stan	to stand, endure, or persist
6. mono		one or alone	monograph	graph	gram	to write
7. epi		over, upon, beside	epilogue	log	logy	speech or science
8. ad	op, a, ab, ac, af, ag, al, am, an, ap, ar, as, at	act to or toward	aspect	spect	spec, spi, spy	to look
9. com, up	co, col, con, cor	with or together	uncomplicated	plic	play, plex, ploy, ply	to fold, twist, or intervene
10. non, ex	o or of	not out, formally	nonextended	tend	tens, tent	to stretch
11. re, pro		again or back forward or in favor of	reproduction	duct	due, dult	to lead, make, or fashion
12. dis	di or dif	apart from	indisposed	pos	pon, post, pound	to place or put
13. over, sub	suc, suf, sug, sup, sur, sus	above, under, supporting	oversufficient	fic	fac, fact, fash, feat	to make or do
14. mis, tran	tra, tran	wrong, or wrongly, across, beyond	mistranscribe	scribe	crip, criv	to write

Source: "Fourteen Words That Make All the Difference" by L. A. Stevens, Coronet, August 1956, 40, pp. 80–82. Copyright 1982 by Coronet. Reprinted by permission.

The meaning of a word can also be modified by a new ending, a suffix that is also an affix. Thorndike (1932) listed the five most common English suffixes:

-er	as in	long*er*
-ion	as in	educat*ion*
-ity	as in	pur*ity*
-ness	as in	salt*iness*
-y	as in	rain*y*

These five common English suffixes are undoubtedly important to point out to your students in the context of their reading; however, there are also many other suffixes you can help your students learn and recognize.

It's important to realize that teaching lists of affixes in isolation will not automatically transfer to passages in which students will need to analyze word structure. Teach students about affixes as they encounter them in the texts they read. You can model the process of discerning the meaning of words using their structure as you look with students at the words they might analyze in their reading. Recall, for example, the way that Emily's practicum teacher, Mrs. Garcia, helped her children to learn the word disqualified by recalling the meaning of the prefix dis and talking through the meaning of disqualified—a word that came from the children's reading of the text Stone Fox.

Compound Words. Most students are able to identify and define compound words quickly and easily because they are familiar with the words that combine to form compound words. Gleason (1969) conducted a study of children's definitions of compound words and discovered that the children had the following definitions for the words airplane, breakfast, and Friday.

> They knew what the words referred to and how to use them, but their ideas about the words were rather amusing. One little boy said that an airplane is called an airplane because it is a plain thing that goes in the air. Another child said that breakfast is called breakfast because you have to eat it fast to get to school on time. Several subjects thought that Friday is called Friday because it is the day you eat fried fish. (p. 12)

During beginning reading programs, students may be taught to identify many compound words as sight words (e.g., stepchildren and grandmother). Because many of these words are part of the students' spoken vocabularies, they can be used as a base for forming generalizations about other compound words. Some examples of other common compound words frequently found in basal readers are airplane, cowboy, sidewalk, and birthday.

Using and Teaching Structural Analysis Skills

Emily knew that an understanding of structural analysis would help her students deal with many new words they would encounter in their reading. Thus, structural analysis skills give students one additional tool to help them recognize and understand words. Emily was aware, however, that structural analysis is useful only as a contextually presented aid to learning; no strategy is itself the objective of the word-learning process, the objective being, of course, reading success. Recall, again, how the teacher Emily observed, Mrs. Garcia, taught her children the prefix dis in the

DID YOU NOTICE . . .
Did you notice that Mrs. Garcia modeled the process for discussing meanings of words? A great way to do this could be a think aloud in which teachers can speak out loud the thought processes going on in their heads. Modeling think alouds for vocabulary development can be done during shared reading when all students have access to the text.

context of their actual reading. Also, Emily was aware that she must be a discerning teacher as she decides which words to address in the structural analysis component of her vocabulary instruction program. Knowing the definitions of affixes does not always help readers to understand a word. For example, "knowing that abs means 'away from' and tract means 'to draw, pull' is not likely to help a student encountering the word abstract for the first time" (Nagy, 1988, p. 38). By understanding the many ideas we have presented about structural analysis, you can use this information to make thoughtful decisions about how and when to teach your children to use structural analysis skills in the context of their actual reading.

Emily plans to use the following general suggestions to help her to implement the structural analysis component of her vocabulary program. You, too, may find them useful.

1. Encourage students to analyze affixes of words with which they are already familiar, for example, re-view-ing. These analyses can be done in the context of readings from literature, basal readers, and content area textbooks.

2. Encourage students to guess the pronunciation of a new word by looking at the parts of the word that are familiar to them. Lists of affixes and base words can be placed beside one another, and students can have fun creating new or known words by matching items from both lists.

3. Encourage students to make their own "new" compound words. They can do this by matching words from paired lists that you have provided. In addition to being fun, this will help them to better understand how compound words are formed.

Exercises to Reinforce Structural Analysis Skills

The following vocabulary exercises are provided as aids for reinforcing students' structural analysis skills.

1. **Attractions**

   Goal: Forming compound words

   Grade Level: 3–6

   Construction: Write parts of compound words on two pieces of masking tape and affix each to a paper clip. A horseshoe magnet is also needed.

   Utilization: Children pick up two words with a horseshoe magnet that, when joined together, form a compound word. They write the word and try to form as many different words as possible. Children then write the definition they think the word has and then with a friend check the dictionary to see if they are correct.

2. **Connection Puzzles**

   Goal: Matching appropriate suffixes with a root word

   Grade Level: K–3

   Construction: Design pairs of puzzle pieces out of heavy cardboard. On some pieces write root words, and on connecting pieces write appropriate suffixes (there may be more than one suffix for each root word).

Utilization: The student connects word pieces to appropriate suffix pieces to make new words. If the suffix is incorrect, the child will not be able to connect them.

3. **Affix Relay**

    Goal: Making new words by adding a suffix

    Grade Level: All grades

    Construction: Only a chalkboard and chalk are needed.

    Utilization: Divide the class into two teams. Write on the board two words to which endings can be added to make new words. The difficulty of the word will depend on the age and abilities of the students. The first member of each team goes to the board and writes a new word, using the derivative. This student runs back and gives the chalk to the next team member, who must then add a new ending. Whichever team writes the most words in 1 minute wins. Examples:

tire	note
tires	notes
tired	noted
tiring	noting
tiresome	notation

    This game can be modified to stress prefixes or both prefixes and suffixes.

4. **Wordy Spider**

    Goal: Adding prefixes and suffixes to root words

    Grade Level: 3–5

    Construction: Draw a spider on a bulletin board, chalkboard, or overhead transparency. The body of the spider should contain a root word. On the arms of the spider, write various prefixes and suffixes.

    Utilization: Each student writes as many different word combinations as possible. Whoever makes the most words wins.

5. **Can of Words**

    Goal: Adding prefixes and suffixes to root words

    Grade Level: 3–6

    Construction: Take three coffee cans and label them "Prefixes," "Root Words," and "Suffixes." Construct several 3 × 5 inch cardboard-backed cards. On each card write a prefix, suffix, or root word.

    Utilization: The student draws a card from each can and attempts to make a word using all three pieces. Examples:

    pre   tend   ing

If the prefix or suffix does not apply, only one need be used. The student tries to make as many different words as possible.

WHAT IS CONTEXTUAL ANALYSIS, AND HOW MIGHT IT BE USED AS AN INSTRUCTIONAL APPROACH?

DID YOU NOTICE . . .
Did you notice that there are many ways to teach students to use contextual clues? You will find yourself using most of these clues in grade 2 and beyond. However, emerging readers in kindergarten and first grade can use pictures and metacognition to help understand the meanings of unfamiliar words.

The second vocabulary instructional strategy that Emily plans to use in her overall vocabulary instructional program consists of analyzing words surrounding an unknown word to determine its meaning. Emily understands that most of the time, words are not very useful when they are presented as isolated elements. They are most functional when they appear in a meaningful context, and, in fact, a word's meaning often depends on the context in which it is used. For this reason, skill in utilizing clues in the surrounding text to arrive at word meaning is an essential skill for all readers. In addition, context may sometimes facilitate the identification of words with difficult letter-sound patterns. Emily plans to expose students to all of the available clues for understanding unknown words by instructing them to examine not only the unknown word, but also any contextual clues that may be provided.

Emily is aware, however, that, as with structural analysis strategies, contextual analysis strategies also have limitations. Recall that a central goal of vocabulary instruction should be to help children to understand the concepts that words represent. This is a much deeper level of understanding than merely memorizing definitions of words. "A good context might help a student figure out the meaning of a less familiar form of a known word, but a single context is in general not adequate for teaching a new concept" (Nagy, 1988, p. 8). Also, the contexts in which words are embedded may be misleading or provide incomplete clues for understanding a word. Consider, for example, the following sentence: "Although Mary was very thin, her sister was obese" (Nagy, 1988, p. 7). If a student doesn't already know the meaning of obese, a number of definitions might make sense in this context. For example, the sentence suggests that Mary is very thin. It is feasible that obese might just mean "thin" as compared with "very thin." It is also conceivable that obese might mean "normal." Clearly, the sentence is setting up some kind of contrast; however, there is no way for the reader to ascertain the nature of the contrast from the sentence. Nothing about the structure of the sentence gives the reader the clue that the contrast is extreme. That is, the extreme opposite of "very thin" is "very heavy" (the definition of obese). We're not suggesting here that it is not useful and important to teach your children to use context clues to ascertain the general meaning of words. We are suggesting that it is important for you and your students to be aware of the potential limitations of this tool. As with all of the tools we are providing in this chapter and throughout the book, they must be used thoughtfully and carefully by teachers and students to be most useful in helping children to learn to read effectively.

Some of the more common contextual clues students may encounter are these: definition statements, synonyms, antonyms, summaries, examples, similes, appositions, and groupings. Let's see what you already know about these words. We will examine each of these clues in greater detail in the following section.

Please complete the following chart with respect to key contextual clues you will want to know and help your students to use.

Word	I have ideas about how I might use the underlying concepts pertaining to this word (these words) to help my children discern the meanings of the text they are reading.	I own this word (these words). I can use it (them) when I write and speak.	I know this word (these words) when I read or hear it (them), but I never say it (them).	I may have heard or seen the word (words) but I'm not comfortable with its (their) meaning(s).	I don't know this word (these words).
Definition statements					
Synonyms					
Antonyms					
Summary					
Examples					
Simile					
Apposition					
Groupings					

Okay, let's see how you did. Please check your answers on the chart with our comments below about the words we presented above. We'll present the words along with an example of what the word (words) mean with respect to instruction.

- Definition Statements
  Authors monitor the introduction of new words in beginning readers' text-books. One common way of presenting a new word is to introduce and define it in the same sentence: "The cornea is the transparent outer coating of the eyeball."

- Synonym
  Students can often infer the meaning of a new word by relating it to an already known word: "Brett yearned to visit Ireland; it was his greatest desire."

- Antonym
  Sometimes the meaning of a word is made clear through an antonym, a word with an opposite meaning: "The harbor was usually so placid that it was a shock to see the raging waves."

- Summary

  A summary in the form of a brief listing of the qualities or characteristics of a word can clarify a new word for the reader: "This report contains many redundant words and ideas. The extra words are not needed, and you state the same idea over and over again."

- Examples

  Using examples is a clear and useful method for illustrating the meaning of a new word: "Circus clowns are jocular. They wear funny clothes and tell jokes to make people laugh."

- Simile

  A simile is a figure of speech that uses like or as to make a comparison: "The diamond glistened like a bright star"; "The young ballplayer was as tenacious as his idol, Willie Mays."

- Apposition

  An apposition is a word or phrase that is equivalent to the subject. It is usually adjacent to the subject and may or may not be set off by commas: "The Statue of Liberty, a famous New York City landmark, was awe-inspiring."

- Groupings

  When an unfamiliar word is grouped in context with other words to depict similarities, the meaning of the word is more readily recognized by the reader: "The balloons were yellow, blue, red, orange, and magenta."

Several other types of contextual clues can be beneficial to readers: italics, capitalization, quotation marks, boldface type, parenthetical statements, and footnotes. In addition, you can instruct your students how to use picture clues, lexical (word and sentence meaning) clues, relational (word-order) clues, and interpretation clues.

Contextual analysis is a tool to help students unlock word meanings and develop reading comprehension. As you encourage your students to pay attention to the context of a passage, the following suggestions will help you assist your students to develop their skills in contextual analysis.

1. When students are stumped by an unfamiliar word, tell them to ask themselves the following questions:

   a. Are there clues to the meaning of this word in the surrounding words?

   b. Will I understand this word if I continue to the end of the sentence?

   c. Are there pictures that will provide clues to the meaning?

2. Discuss with children what they do when they encounter a word they do not know. Through these discussions, students will walk through a metacognitive process while making predictions and testing their hypotheses about meaning. They become aware of their own strategies as well as the variety of language clues, while at the same time realizing the importance of making sense of what they read.

3. Highlight the role of context in word meanings by discussing with students words that have multiple meanings. For example: The farmer bent down to

DID YOU NOTICE . . .
Did you remember that dictionaries can help students with spelling, pronunciation, usage, and derivation? Teachers must explicitly teach students how to use dictionaries to understand all the important features of this resource. Understanding what accent marks, italics, parentheses, and abbreviations mean can be confusing for students.

plant his corn in a long, straight row. The children wanted to row the boat across the lake.

Exercises to Reinforce Contextual Analysis Skills

The following vocabulary exercises are provided as aids for reinforcing students' contextual analysis skills.

1. **Crosswords**

    Goal: Utilizing contextual definitions

    Grade Level: 3–6

    Construction: Design a crossword puzzle in which students have to choose a word from a list to complete a sentence. The selected word is to be defined within the context of the sentence.

    Utilization: The student completes each sentence and then writes the correct letters in the appropriate puzzle boxes.

2. **Don't Do What I Do**

    Goal: Utilizing contextual antonyms

    Grade Level: 1–3

    Construction: Make up descriptive sentences that contain antonyms.

    Utilization: Read a sentence containing antonyms and have members of the class act out the sentence at the same time, showing opposite actions—for example: "She laughed so hard she cried." One student should pantomime laughter and another student should pantomime crying.

3. **Scrambled Synonyms**

    Goal: Utilizing contextual synonyms

    Grade Level: 3–6

    Construction: Design sentences that use synonyms to introduce or define unfamiliar words. Do not include the new word in the sentence. Instead, construct a chart consisting of missing words and deceptive letters mixed vertically, horizontally, diagonally, forward, and backward.

    Utilization: Each student is given a dittoed copy of the sentences and word chart. The student reads the sentence and then looks to the chart and selects the missing synonym. The student circles the synonym and writes it in the sentence.

4. **For Example**

    Goal: Utilizing contextual examples

    Grade Level: 4–6

    Construction: Prepare a list of introductory sentences. One sentence should appear at the top of a blank sheet of paper.

    Utilization: One piece of paper, with an introductory sentence, is given to the first person in each row or at a learning center. The paper is passed throughout the group or row, and each student adds an example that clarifies the introductory statement. When all groups have finished, the statements are read, and one point is given for each acceptable example. The team receiving the most points wins. Examples:

Carol is an ambitious girl.

Carol has red hair.

Carol does all her homework.

Carol has read two books today.

5. Drawing Similes

Goal: Utilizing contextual similes

Grade Level: 2–5

Construction: Divide large pieces of drawing paper into sections. Design a series of sentences using similes with one word omitted. Example:

His voice sounded like the roar of a _____.

Utilization: A student selects a sentence and mentally fills in the blank. She then illustrates the sentence on a piece of drawing paper and labels the picture with the completed sentence.

So far, we've discussed a major facet of vocabulary instruction in the form of two vocabulary instructional strategies. These include providing our students (a) with structural and (b) context analysis skills that will serve as lifelong tools to help them find clues to word meanings on their own.

HOW DOES THE DICTIONARY FIT INTO VOCABULARY INSTRUCTION?

Before we end this chapter, we need to discuss a subject that has been conspicuous by its absence: use of the dictionary in vocabulary instruction. The intent here is not merely to present dictionary work as a postscript to vocabulary instruction skills. However, historically, the dictionary has been the forefront of vocabulary teaching. The "look up and write a definition" cycle has been perpetuated in classrooms across the nation but has done little to improve overall vocabulary proficiency. The problem with this strategy is twofold. Words listed in dictionaries are separated from any meaningful context or experience that students can relate to, and the multiple meanings listed for words may confuse a student who is depending on the dictionary to provide a clear definition.

One way teachers can help eliminate these problems is to remove the dictionary from the core of their vocabulary programs and guide students in the use of the dictionary as a reference tool. As such, it has utility when students' vocabulary instructional strategies have not helped them discover the meaning of a word that is significant to their reading. Teachers then can guide students through the process of looking up a word that may be blocking meaningful comprehension of a passage. In this process, it's crucial that teachers consistently direct students back to the context of what they are reading so that they can determine which meaning (if, in fact, there are multiple meanings) best fits the passage.

Furthermore, it's important that students understand the value of this reference tool in assisting them in areas other than definitions, such as spelling, pronunciation, usage, and derivation. Varied and consistent practice in these areas will help students view the dictionary as a useful tool both in school and in other areas of life.

QUESTIONS

1. Describe how you would decide which words to teach in a chapter in a science textbook.

2. A layperson tells you that it is important for a child to know the meaning of every word in a passage to comprehend it. How would you respond to this statement? Defend your answer.

3. You have a class of beginning readers. How would you structure their vocabulary program? Include your philosophy behind the program and some strategies you would use.

4. You are being interviewed for a teaching position in third grade. One of the questions you are asked is "What is your idea of the ideal vocabulary program?" How would you answer?

5. A new teacher at your school asks you why you don't just have students look up words in the dictionary and write the definitions. She asks why you don't think this is enough vocabulary instruction. Explain your goals for a vocabulary program and describe some ideas that show how you achieve them.

REFERENCES

Anderson, R. C., & Freebody, P. (1981). Vocabulary knowledge. In J. T. Guthrie (Ed.), *Comprehension and teaching: Research reviews* (pp. 77–117). Newark, DE: International Reading Association.

Beck, I. L., McKeown, M. G., & Omanson, R. C. (1984). The effects and uses of diverse vocabulary instructional techniques. In M. G. McKeown & M. E. Curtis (Eds.), *The nature of vocabulary acquisition* (pp. 14–25). Hillsdale, NJ: Lawrence Erlbaum Associates.

Beck, I. L., McKeown, M. G., & Kucan, L. (2002). *Bringing words to life: Robust vocabulary instruction.* New York: Guilford Press.

Beck, I. L., McCaslin, E. S., & McKeown, M. G. (1980). *The rationale and design of a program to teach vocabulary to fourth-grade students.* Pittsburgh, PA: Learning Research and Development Center, University of Pittsburgh.

Bradac, J. J., Bowers, J. W., & Courtright, J. A. (1982). Lexical variations in intensity, immediacy, and diversity: An axiomatic theory and causal model. In R. N. St. Clair and H. Giles (Eds.), *The social and psychological context of language* (pp. 85–97). Hillsdale, NJ: Erlbaum.

Calfee, R. C. (1981). *The book: Components of reading instruction.* Unpublished paper, Stanford University, Stanford, CA.

Carroll, J. B., Davies, P., & Richman, B. (1971). *Word frequency book.* New York: American Heritage.

Cunningham, P. (1987, September). Polysyllabic word strategies for content-area reading. *Clearing House, 61,* 42–45.

Cunningham, P. (1988, April). When all else fails .... *Reading Teacher, 41*(8), 800–805.

Dale, E., & O'Rourke, J. (1986). *Vocabulary building: A process approach.* Columbus, OH: Zaner-Bloser.

Davis, F. B. (1944, June). Fundamental factors of comprehension in reading. *Psychometrika, 9*, 185–197.

Davis, F. B. (1968, Summer). Research in comprehension in reading. *Reading Research Quarterly, 3*, 499–545.

Draper, A. G., & Moeller, G. H. (1971, April). We think with words (therefore, to improve thinking, teach vocabulary). *Phi Delta Kappan, 52*, 482–484.

Duin, A. H. (1983). *The effects of intensive vocabulary instruction on a specific writing task.* Paper for Master of Arts, University of Minnesota, Minneapolis. (ERIC Document Reproduction Service No. ED 239 222).

Duin, A. H. (1986). *The effects of intensive vocabulary instruction of expository writing.* Unpublished doctoral dissertation, University of Minnesota, Minneapolis.

Duin, A. H., & Graves, M. F. (1986, Fall). Effects of vocabulary instruction used as a prewriting technique. *Journal of Research and Development in Education, 20*, 7–13.

Gleason, J. B. (1969). Language development in early childhood. In J. Walden (Ed.), *Oral language and reading* (pp. 35–42). Urbana, IL: National Council of Teachers of English.

Graves, M. F. (1984). Selecting vocabulary to teach in the intermediate and secondary grades. In J. Flood (Ed.), *Promoting reading comprehension* (pp. 245–260). Newark, DE: International Reading Association.

Graves, M. F., & Slater, W. H. (2006). Vocabulary instruction in the content areas. In D. Lapp, J. Flood, & N. Farnan (Eds.), *Content area reading and learning: Instructional strategies* 2nd ed. (pp. 214–224). Mahwah, NJ: Erlbaum.

Haggard, M. R. (1982, December). The vocabulary self-collection strategy: An active approach to word learning. *Journal of Reading, 26*, 203–207.

Harris, A., & Jacobson, M. (1973, January). Basic vocabulary for beginning reading. *Reading Teacher, 26*, 392–295.

Jenkins, J. R., Pany, D., & Schreck, J. (1978). *Vocabulary and reading comprehension: Instructional effects.* Technical Report 100. Urbana, IL: University of Illinois, Center for the Study of Reading.

Kameenui, E. J., Canine, D. W., & Freschi, R. (1982). Effects of text construction and instructional procedures for teaching word meanings on comprehension and recall. *Reading Research Quarterly, 17*, 367–388.

Konopak, B. C. (1988, January). Using contextual information for word learning. *Journal of Reading, 31*, 334–339.

Lambert, E. (1955). *Our language: The story of the words we use.* New York: Lothrop, Lee & Shepard.

Nagy, W. E. (1988). *Teaching vocabulary to improve reading comprehension.* Newark, DE.: International Reading Association.

Nagy, W. E., & Anderson, R. C. (1984, Spring). How many words are there in printed school English? *Reading Research Quarterly, 19*, 304–330.

Neilson, L., & Piche, G. (1981, February). The influence of headed nominal complexity and lexical choice on teachers' evaluation of writing. *Research in the Teaching of English, 15*, 65–73.

Singer, H. A. (1965, Fall). A developmental model of speed of reading in grade 3 through 6. *Reading Research Quarterly, 1*, 29–49.

Smith, R. (1988, October). Developing higher-level comprehension with short stories. *Reading Horizons, 29*, 43–50.

Stahl, S., & Fairbandk, M. (1986, Spring). The effects of vocabulary instruction: A model-based meta-analysis. *Review of Educational Research, 56*, 72–110.

Stotsky, S. L. (1976). *Toward more systematic development of children's reading vocabulary in developmental reading programs for the middle to upper elementary grades.* Unpublished doctoral dissertation, Harvard University, Cambridge, MA.

Thorndike, E. (1932). *The teaching of English suffixes.* New York: Bureau of Publications, Teachers College, Columbia University.

Thurstone, L. A. (1946, June). A note on a reanalysis of Davis' reading tests. *Psychometrika, 11*, 18–188.

Tuinman, J. J., & Brady, M. E. (1974). How does vocabulary account for variance on reading comprehension tests?: A preliminary instructional analysis. In P. Nacke (Ed.), *Twenty-third national reading conference yearbook.* Clemson, SC: National Reading Conference.

White, T. G., Sowell, J., & Yanagihara, A. (1989, January). Teaching elementary students to use word-parts clues. *The Reading Teacher, 42*, 302–308.

7

Comprehension Instruction: Strategies at Work

―――――――――――――――― CHAPTER GOALS ――――――――――――――――

To help the reader

- understand what effective comprehension instruction includes.
- understand the nature of reading comprehension.
- learn comprehension instruction strategies and develop various instructional practices that aid students in comprehending.

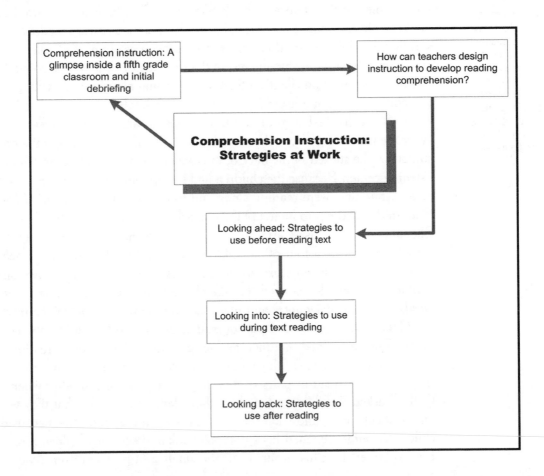

COMPREHENSION INSTRUCTION:
A GLIMPSE INSIDE A FIFTH GRADE CLASSROOM

Colleen, a fairly new third grade teacher, was talking with a small group of her colleagues at her school one Friday afternoon before the beginning of a staff meeting. She mentioned that she knew comprehension was a central goal of reading, but she wasn't certain how to provide the best instruction to foster her children's reading comprehension. Larry, the fifth grade teacher we introduced you to in chapter 1, said that he had been working hard to improve the reading comprehension of his students in his own classroom for many years. He asked Colleen if she'd like to come to his room some day during reading to observe how he organized his classroom to foster his children's comprehension. Colleen thought that was a great idea, so she asked her principal, Mrs. Chin, if she would work with her class for an hour and a half one morning the following week so that she could observe in Larry's classroom. Of course, Colleen and Larry also scheduled time after school the day of Colleen's visit so that they could discuss her observations in Larry's classroom.

The following Wednesday, Mrs. Chin arrived to work with Colleen's students while Colleen observed in Larry's classroom. Larry and his students had just begun reading when Colleen arrived at his classroom. Because Colleen knew that she would be discussing her observations with Larry later that day, she decided to take some notes about what she saw during her visit.

The first thing Colleen noticed was that Larry was sitting on the floor at the front of the room working with a group of five students. All of the students had with them copies of the children's book *Shades of Grey* as well as spiral-bound notebooks. Colleen thought that the spiral-bound notebooks were reading logs of some sort that the children could use to write about their reading. As Colleen scanned the classroom, she noticed that the rest of the students in class were also reading. Some children were reading silently, others were reading aloud quietly with partners, and two children were at a listening center at the back table.

Colleen decided to walk around the classroom to get a closer look at what everyone was doing before she settled in to watch Larry work with the group of five students. She started in the back of the room near the two children who were at the listening center. Because the children had headphones on and were actively turning pages while they were reading along and listening to the text *Behind Rebel Lines*, Colleen decided not to interrupt them to ask questions about what they were doing. She made a note to ask Larry later why these two children were at the listening center. She noticed that four other children were reading the same text, *Behind Rebel Lines*. These children were sitting in pairs reading aloud in low tones to one another. Colleen also noticed that the children occasionally stopped reading to jot words down on sticky notes and place the notes in the text they were reading.

Colleen stopped by one pair of readers and asked the children what they were doing. They explained that their teacher gave them the option of reading silently or in pairs. Because some of the words in the text were a bit difficult for them at times, they decided to read in pairs so that they could help one another when necessary. Colleen asked the children how long they planned to read, what they were writing on the sticky notes, and what they would do when they were finished reading. One child, Alexander, opened his spiral notebook and showed Colleen a reading plan. He explained that his group (i.e., the small group of children reading the text

Behind Rebel Lines) had established a reading plan when they started reading their book. Their plan included the number of pages they were to read each day. Alexander said that the children were jotting down questions on the sticky notes about the story that they found confusing or that they wanted to discuss later with their teacher and peers. He further explained that once he and his partner finished reading and jotting down questions on sticky notes, they would each write a bit about their questions in their reading logs. Colleen asked what they would write about. Alexander explained that they would each look over the questions they had noted on their sticky notes and write why they had those questions, the pages in the text that prompted their questions, and tentative answers to their questions. Finally, they would look to see if they could group their questions in categories of similar questions. Colleen made a note to ask Larry how the children learned to use this approach of identifying questions to bring to their small-group teacher-led discussions.

Before heading to the front of the room to watch Larry work with the group of five children, Colleen quickly scanned the rest of the classroom. Four children were silently reading the text *Across Five Aprils*, and four children were silently reading the text *Who Comes with Cannons?* One pair of children was reading *Who Comes with Cannons?* quietly to one another. Colleen suspected that the children reading these additional texts also had reading plans they were following. Additionally, she guessed that they would also be writing in reading logs once they finished their reading for the day. Meanwhile, Colleen began to watch and listen in on the lesson that was in progress with Larry.

As Colleen approached the front of the classroom, she noticed that the books of the children reading *Shades of Grey* also contained yellow sticky notes. Colleen wondered what was up with the yellow sticky notes in Larry's room. Larry and the children appeared to be using the sticky notes to construct a large chart

Text-to-Self	Text-to-Text	Text-to-World

together. The chart, standing next to Larry, had three columns, one labeled "Text-to-Self Connections," another labeled "Text-to-Text Connections," and a third column labeled "Text-to-World Connections." The children were discussing the text and their sticky notes as a group. As they talked, they removed the notes from their texts and placed them in various locations on the large chart. As Colleen edged closer to the chart she noticed that each sticky note contained a child's name, the previous day's date, a page number from the text, and a sentence that began with some version of the phrase "This reminds me of ..." She heard the following conversation.

Larry: I noticed that you removed a sticky note from your text to share with the group Drevaun. What did you write on your note?

Drevaun: On my sticky note I explained that the situation Will is facing reminds me of something I read in an informational text while I was working with my friends on our Civil War report that we completed before we started the book Shades of Grey. Earlier we learned that sometimes some family members were on the side of the North and other members from the same family were on the side of the South. This is exactly the situation Will was in. Will and his family were Rebels, and Will's Uncle Jessie and his family lived in the North and were Yankees.

Larry: Where do you think you want to place your sticky note on the chart, Drevaun?

Drevaun: I think I should place it in the section labeled "Text-to-Text" because I remembered reading in an informational text about families sometimes being split apart and fighting for opposite sides during the Civil War. In this case, I was comparing what I read in an earlier text to Will's experience in the text Shades of Grey.

As Colleen continued to listen in on Larry's lesson, she noticed the following pattern. Children read or restated the ideas they had written on their sticky notes, Larry invited them to consider where they would place their sticky notes on the larger chart, the children explained where they were going to place their

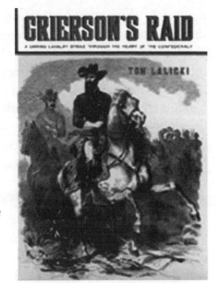

Grierson's Raid: A Daring Cavalry Strike through the Heart of the Confederacy. © by Tom Lalicki. Used with the permission of Farrar Straus Giroux.

notes, and then the children offered a justification for the locations they chose. Colleen noticed that on several occasions, children suggested a location on the chart, but either Larry of one of the other children disagreed. When this happened the group negotiated where the sticky note should be placed and why.

After about 15 minutes of talking through connections that the children were making between *Shades of Grey* and other texts and experiences, Larry mentioned that the children would next be reading a part of the text that they may find confusing. He reminded the children that they had already learned to note questions about the story as they were reading. He suggested that they may want to jot down any questions they had on sticky notes as they read the next section of their text. The children collected their things and headed back to their seats. They immediately began to read from their texts once they got to their desks.

As the *Shades of Grey* group left, Larry called for the *Across Five Aprils* group. Four children quickly collected their texts and writing notebooks and moved toward the front of the classroom. Larry asked the children to summarize briefly the section of text that they had read that morning. As the children spoke, some of them mentioned the difficulty that they were having trying to understand what was going on in the story. Larry said that the difficulty the children were experiencing was quite normal. He asked them if they could identify the source of their difficulty. One student, LeShaun, said that the words the characters were using were confusing. Larry asked LeShaun to explain further. LeShaun opened her book and read a brief excerpt from her text and said that she had never heard anyone talk like that before. Larry praised LeShaun for identifying a source of confusion regarding this text. He further explained that the author, Irene Hunt, used authentic dialogue between characters throughout the text. Because the dialogue was similar to the ways that folks from rural areas in the United States spoke in the late 1800s, however, it could be a source of confusion for readers. Larry said that he would introduce a strategy called PQR (parsing, questioning, and rephrasing) to the children that they may find helpful to use from time to time as they were reading this text (Flood, Lapp, & Fisher, 2002). Larry explained that the PQR strategy contained three steps. First, the children should identify a troubling segment of text that they thought contained one or more important ideas and note the subject, verb, and object/descriptor in this segment of text. Next, they should use their own words for the subject, verb, and object/descriptor. Finally, they should rephrase the segment of text in their own words. Drawing upon the confusing part of the text that LeShaun had already identified, Larry worked through an example of the PQR strategy with the children.

At this point, the 15-minute small group lesson time was over. While the group had worked together through an example of applying the PQR strategy, Larry mentioned that this strategy was somewhat complex and he wasn't sure that the children could complete it on their own yet. Consequently, he asked them to work in pairs when they returned to their seats to identify at least one additional segment of the text that they found confusing and to apply the PQR strategy with their partner. He asked the children to record their work in their journals and reminded them that they would be discussing their work from today, as well as their additional reading of the next segment of text tomorrow when they met the next day.

Colleen noticed that Larry called the group reading *Behind Rebel Lines* to the front next. Colleen recalled that earlier the children from this group had been noting questions on yellow sticky notes during their reading. Larry worked with the children in this group, discussing the questions they had raised on their yellow sticky notes as they read their assigned reading for the day. Larry worked with the children to categorize the kinds of questions that they listed as they read. Larry used chart paper and guided the children to place questions under categories that the group created through their discussion. It soon became apparent that many of the children's questions centered around the main character Emma. Larry wasn't surprised here. Because the main character was a spy for the North, she dressed up in many different costumes and assumed many identities. The children were finding it difficult to keep track of her many different identities in the story. Larry decided that for the next lesson with the children, they would begin to develop a character chart (see chart on p. 186) that they could post in the room and add to as the story evolved.

After 15 minutes all but two of the children left the group. Colleen noticed that these two children were the ones who had been sitting at the listening center at the back table earlier in the reading lesson. Colleen noticed that Larry worked with these two children for 15 minutes using a much simpler text than *Behind Rebel Lines*. In fact, the children seemed to read their books aloud with few difficulties. Colleen noted that she wanted to talk with Larry later about these two children and what he was doing with them.

For the last 20 to 25 minutes of their reading time, Larry brought the students together as a whole group. He asked the students to describe key events from each of their stories. Larry recorded key events for each story on large sheets of butcher paper. He asked the children to describe what the term *theme* meant. As the class talked, Larry and the children used examples of themes from books they had read earlier that year. He reminded the children to think about possible themes the authors of their current stories were developing throughout the books. The class also talked about the strategies the children were using as they read their books. The class talked about using strategies in meaningful ways when they were needed in the context of their reading.

At this point, it was time for Colleen to return to her own classroom. She looked forward to talking more with Larry after school that day to talk about the questions she had as she watched him teach that day.

If you were Colleen, what questions would you have for Larry about his reading lessons for the day? Please list them. (If some of your questions are different from the ones that Colleen asks at the end of the chapter, please raise your questions with your professor in your own class.)

Comprehension Instruction in a
Fifth Grade Classroom: Initial Debriefing

Once school was over later that afternoon, Colleen headed to Larry's room to discuss his reading lessons with him. Larry and Colleen settled in at a large table at the back of his classroom. Colleen said, "Larry, I have a whole list of questions to ask you about your lesson today." Larry replied, "Fire away." Then he added, "You may want to choose some of your overarching questions first, then perhaps we can discuss the particular details of the lesson once we have addressed some of your main questions about comprehension instruction." Colleen looked across her list of questions. She started with this question, "Larry, I know that there are lots of strategies to teach during comprehension lessons. How do you begin to decide what it is that your children need to know about comprehension and how to best teach that?"

Colleen's question was a complicated one. Larry suspected that their talk would extend over several afternoons rather than just this afternoon. Larry replied, "You know, Colleen, I'm impressed with your question. Quality comprehension instruction involves much more than just choosing a list of strategies to teach. One important aspect or comprehension instruction emphasizes the importance of *the reader* (characteristics such as age, ability, background knowledge, and experiences) in the comprehension process. Although this might appear to be a simple notion, classroom instruction in comprehension has not always acknowledged and capitalized on the role of the reader. Then there's the role of *the text* itself. It does play a role, but its role is not dictated simply by its physical presence; rather, it is shaped by the ways we, the reader, interact with it and its characteristics such as whether it is a fantasy, realistic fiction, informational text, and so forth. Additionally, there is also the role of *the context* (for example, environment, social grouping, and purpose). Comprehension occurs in a certain time and place, that is, in a context. Finally, comprehension instruction is also dependent on another crucial variable: the characteristics of *the teacher* (such as knowledge, experience, attitude, and use of instructional approaches)."

In the remainder of this chapter, we present an overview of key strategies that Larry draws upon in his comprehension instruction. As we discuss these strategies, we will refer to various aspects of Larry's reading lessons that you read about at the beginning of this chapter. We begin by exploring briefly conceptions of reading comprehension and meaning making. (We address reading comprehension in much more detail in chapter 9.) We'll begin with you where Larry began with Colleen when they spoke. That is, we'll talk about what reading comprehension is.

Let's start with your current ideas about reading comprehension. Undoubtedly you know how to read well or you wouldn't be in a class such as the one in which you're using this text. Please write your definition of reading comprehension. What does it mean to comprehend what you read? How do you know when you have/have not comprehended? What do you do when you have not comprehended? Once we have sorted out what comprehension is, then we will talk more about how to best teach it.

Reading comprehension is constructing meanings from transactions with printed materials. That is, reading is a transaction between the reader and the text (Rosenblatt, 1994). Reading is about comprehension—making sense of written text. If comprehension has not taken place, then reading has not occurred. Although researchers are not positive about every aspect of reading comprehension, they are certain that the child who comprehends a text is the child who is actively involved in interpreting written material. Reading is not a passive process; successful reading demands active participation. More than 70 years ago, Thorndike (1917) discussed the importance of recognizing reading as an active, participatory process when he wrote:

> Understanding a paragraph is like solving a problem in mathematics. It consists in selecting the right elements of the situation and putting them together in the right relations, and also with the right amount of weight or influence or force for each. The mind is assailed as it were by every word in the paragraph. It must select, repress, soften, emphasize, correlate and organize, all under the influence of the right mental set of purposes or demands. (p. 329)

HOW CAN TEACHERS DESIGN INSTRUCTION TO DEVELOP READING COMPREHENSION?

We have just given you a brief overview of reading comprehension. Now we'll talk about various families of strategies that you can use as a teacher to help your students learn to construct meaningful interpretations of the texts they read. We alert you to the fact that comprehension strategy instruction is only effective, however, if teachers (a) understand what comprehension is in the first place, (b) understand how texts are structured and use that knowledge to foster children's engagement with different kinds of texts, and (c) teach children to use strategies effectively while they are actually in the process of reading.

The key question that we explore in this chapter is: "What can I do to help children develop their abilities to comprehend texts?" First, we suggest that you analyze students' texts for difficulties they may encounter. Ask yourself, "Is the text written clearly? Does it make sense?" If there are severe problems, you can (a) abandon the text and select an alternative text that is more clearly written or (b) target difficult passages for additional discussion and/or instruction. Second, ask yourself what you will actually have your children do during their reading instruction time. Take a few seconds to read the following passage. As you're reading, see how you'd compare this passage to the information about reading instruction from Larry's room that we presented at the beginning of this chapter.

In one classroom a third-grade boy had been working diligently for about 50 minutes during reading time, answering main idea and detail questions related to preprinted passages on a reading skills worksheet titled "Comprehension Skills." Finally, he was ready to have his paper checked, so he got out of his seat and stood in line behind two other children who were there for the same reason. This boy, who we'll call Tommy, was the last student in the class to give his paper to the teacher.

Tommy's turn came; he stepped up to the teacher and put his paper on the desk in front of her. She matched the answer key to his paper and quickly scanned through his answers, making check marks on the paper as she went. As she looked up, Tommy asked, "Can I read one of those books now?" (His teacher had several books displayed in the front of her room, and students were allowed to choose one to read if they finished their work—at an appropriate level of correctness—before the end of the reading period.)

The teacher answered, "Tommy you can't read now. You've missed far too many of these answers. Go back to your seat, read more carefully, and bring the worksheet back to me. Hopefully, next time you'll do better." Crestfallen, Tommy returned to his seat to work on his "reading skills."

"Tommy" is a fictitious name, but the story is true, and it is not a story out of the 1950s but from 1990s. Based on what you have read so far in this chapter, what would you say is wrong with this picture of comprehension instruction?

Actually, we could spend a lot of time analyzing the problems implied in this situation, not the least of which is that it appears, from the format of the activity, that this teacher subscribes to an approach that values isolated skill-based activities over reading itself. We might infer that this young boy has received two distinct messages from this student-teacher interaction: One message is that he is clearly not trying and, if he will just work harder, he will eventually get it right; the other is that answering worksheet questions about canned, and probably very dull, passages is much more important than the reading that Tommy wants to do—real reading in a real text.

The point here is not to criticize the explicit teaching of comprehension, for we have known for some time that explicit instruction does result in increased understanding of text (Flood & Lapp, 1990). The question is, What should quality comprehension instruction look like? We suggest that comprehension instruction should look more like what you read about in Larry's room. Effective teachers of reading comprehension do not simply function as evaluators of right versus wrong answers like Tommy's teacher did. Instead, like Larry, they function as facilitators, providing models that tell and/or demonstrate how comprehension occurs. Teachers help students set purposes for reading and establish occasions for guided practice in which students attempt to follow the model presented by the teacher, who then provides timely feedback and conferences. Effective teachers of comprehension give students myriad opportunities to practice reading comprehension strategies independently when they are reading real texts. Finally, effective teachers understand that

DID YOU NOTICE . . .
Did you notice that teachers who provide timely feedback and conferences will provide more effective comprehension instruction than those who do not? Because some classrooms have more than 30 students, grouping students with similar needs for comprehension instruction will help teachers meet the needs of all students when individual conferencing is not possible each day.

the goal of comprehension strategy instruction is not to focus on making sure that children memorize strategies. Rather, the end goal is to help children learn to use strategies effectively in their reading of real texts so that they can construct deeper and richer interpretations of the texts that they read.

Effective reading comprehension strategies have one major element in common: They acknowledge the student's central position as meaning maker in the reading act. Instructional scaffolding has become the most appropriate metaphor for reading instruction, replacing the medical metaphor of diagnosis and prescription. Teachers, as facilitators, provide support and direction where and when necessary. However, in this process-centered approach, teachers never lose sight of the fact that students are ultimately responsible for making their own meaning; teachers and students are collaborators, working together to ensure that students internalize the strategies necessary for constructing meaning from text. In short, we advocate the types of classroom instruction that Larry provides as discussed at the beginning of this chapter. We're certain that you can see important differences between the kind of classroom learning environment that Larry creates in his room and the kind of classroom learning environment that Tommy's teacher creates in her room.

The following portion of this chapter will discuss what you can do to help students develop their reading comprehension. We focus our discussion around nine different types of strategies that can aid children in their reading comprehension (Harvey & Goudvis, 2000; Keene & Zimmerman, 1997; Pearson & Gallagher, 1983; Raphael & Hiebert, 1996). For the purposes of discussion, we group these types of strategies into three main categories that correspond to the process of reading. Please note that in the process of actual reading, these strategies are intertwined. For the purposes of discussion, however, we discuss them separately. Table 7–1 provides an overview of these categories of strategies.

We call the first category "Looking Ahead." Before children actually start reading, the teacher can help them *look ahead* to what they will encounter in the text. Strategies in this first category include (a) building background knowledge and (b) activating prior knowledge. Once children start reading the text, there are strategies that they can use to *look into* the text more deeply. The strategies in the second category "Looking Into" include (a) making connections, (b) questioning, (c) drawing inferences, and (d) evoking sensory images. As students have sampled or read portions of text, there are strategies that they can use to step back and think about what they have read. These strategies are in the category called "Looking Back" because students can *look back* at the portions of text they have read to sort out their interpretations of it. The strategies in this third column include (a) using fix-up strategies to repair comprehension when it breaks down, (b) prioritizing informa-

TABLE 7–1
Categories of Reading Comprehension Strategies

Looking Ahead	Looking Into	Looking Back
Building background knowledge	Making connections	Prioritizing information
Activating prior knowledge	Questioning	Fix-up strategies
Frontloading vocabulary	Drawing inferences	Retelling/synthesis strategies
	Evoking sensory images	

tion (i.e., deciding the big ideas relative to the text), and (c) using retelling or synthesizing strategies. As you are reading through these discussions of various categories of strategy lessons that teachers can use with their children, try to identify the ones that Larry used in our discussion of his classroom at the beginning of this chapter. We will help you out a bit by explicitly pointing out some of these connections to Larry's room. After we present samples of strategies in the various categories of strategies, we will return to a final discussion/debriefing of more of Larry's thinking behind his instructional decisions in his classroom.

Looking Ahead: Strategies to Use Before Reading Text

You can help your children interpret text if you help them to think about the ideas they will encounter in the text before they actually read it. In this section, we discuss two categories of strategies: *building background knowledge* and *activating prior knowledge*.

Strategies That Address Building Background Knowledge

Think back to our discussion of Larry's classroom at the beginning of this chapter. Do you recall that Larry had asked his class to do reports on the Civil War before they actually started reading narrative texts pertaining to the Civil War? Larry's decision to build his children's background knowledge about the Civil War before he asked them to read narrative texts about it was purposeful. He knew that his children would understand their texts much better if they understood the historical context in which their stories were couched. He also knows that it is wise to integrate social studies and literacy whenever possible. Such integration can enhance children's understandings in both subject areas.

Drawing on ideas from Raphael and Hiebert (1996), Larry modeled the development of his Civil War Unit on the classroom of fifth grade teacher Laura Pardo. Like Laura, Larry had his children identify questions they wanted to know about the Civil War. Then, his children worked in small interest-related groups to explore answers to their questions about the Civil War. Larry worked closely with his school librarian to acquire a cart of books that the children could use right in his classroom to explore answers to their questions. Larry knew that he would have to carefully model the research process to his children or they would simply copy information out of resource books to write their reports rather than engaging in a meaningful research process. Thus, he taught his students to use note cards to take notes from reference books. Then, he taught his children to group their reference card notes into categories that would later become the major sections of their reports. Larry's children also engaged in process writing in their classroom, so teaching his children to write expository text was part of his broader classroom literacy plan. For more information about helping children to write expository text, see chapter 10. A thorough discussion of guiding children to do meaningful research projects is beyond the purview of this chapter. We refer you to the excellent work of Levstik and Barton (2001) for a thorough discussion of how you can help your students to engage in meaningful research.

Strategies That Address Activating Prior Knowledge

Another group of strategies that Larry drew from in his strategy instruction included strategies that help to activate children's prior knowledge. Larry knows that children sometimes have background knowledge that they can draw upon to make sense of text; however, Larry also knows that he often needs to help children connect what they already know to ideas that they will encounter in their reading. For example, one of Larry's read alouds during Black History Month was *The Story of Ruby Bridges*. Before reading the text, Larry asked his children if they had ever heard of Ruby Bridges. No one had. Then he asked his children what they knew about Martin Luther King, Jr. and the Civil Rights Movement. Hands flew in the air; the children knew a lot about these topics. Larry and his children discussed the considerable knowledge they had about these topics. Then Larry told the children how *The Story of Ruby Bridges* fit within this context. This discussion before Larry's reading of the text helped his children to have a much deeper understanding of the actual text as he read it to them. In the remainder of this subsection, we introduce three additional pre-reading strategies that Larry draws upon in his comprehension instruction. These include the Pre-Reading Plan Strategy, the Previewing Strategies, and use of Anticipation Guides.

Activating Prior Knowledge Pre-Reading Plan. We have already discussed the important role of prior knowledge in comprehension. Students may lack prior knowledge, or they may have sufficient background for what they read but have difficulty linking their prior knowledge with the text. A strategy devised by Langer (1982, 1984) called a Pre-Reading Plan (PReP) can be effective in enhancing students' background knowledge and in letting the teacher know when insufficient knowledge might be a hindrance to learning. This plan prepares students for reading by taking them through three steps:

1. The teacher asks students to brainstorm ideas and associations related to an important concept in the text. For example, if the class is studying the Civil War, the teacher may ask, "What comes to mind when I say the word 'slavery'?"

2. Students then reflect on their associations, discussing why they came up with them and how they relate to the target concept. For example, the teacher can ask questions such as, "What made you think of that idea?"

3. Students discuss any new ideas that have come up as a result of their discussion. During this portion of the activity, they expand and revise their knowledge through social interaction with their peers. The teacher may ask, "What new insights and information have you gained from our discussion about slavery?"

Langer found that average readers benefitted most from this activity. She surmised that perhaps highly skilled readers engaged in this process automatically, whereas poorer readers needed more direct instruction in the concept being discussed.

Previewing.   Graves, Penn, and Cooke (1985) tested a strategy in which students participated in a comprehensive preview of an assigned text. The purpose of the session, which was prepared by the teachers, was to motivate students using the following format:

1. Through discussion, the teacher activates prior knowledge, eliciting personal experiences that relate to the text.

2. The teacher provides any other information deemed necessary to ensure that students have a sufficient range of background knowledge to comprehend the major concepts presented in the text.

3. Finally, an organizational framework is developed for the text that matches the framework the author(s) uses to present the information.

Graves et al. (1985) found that students who took part in these previewing sessions did significantly better on several comprehension measures than students who did not have such a pre-reading activity.

Another previewing activity that Larry frequently used involves simply discussing the overall subject of a story, book, or text passage in terms of two questions: (a) "What information/ideas do you think you will read about?" and (b) "What questions would you like to have answered as you read?" Students can answer these questions based on input from looking at book covers, title, pictures, and headings. In relation to the first question, students will not only refer to their prior knowledge, bringing it into the open for discussion and idea sharing with their peers, they will also predict what they might encounter in the text. In response to the second question, they will again call on their prior knowledge to anticipate questions they would like to have answered and will, additionally, set purposes for their reading. A similar but more extensive learning/questioning strategy, the K-W-L Guide, designed by Ogle (1986), addresses *what* the student currently knows, *wants* to learn, and *learns*.

DID YOU NOTICE . . .
Did you notice that these class discussions can precede more formal student-led debates? It is also a great time to introduce persuasive writing as students try to persuade the reader to favor one side of the argument over the other.

Anticipation Guides.   Larry used Anticipation Guides when he wanted his students to predict what they would be reading in the text (Herber, 1978). Then, as they read, Larry's students compared their predictions to what they actually encountered in the text.

The following Anticipation Guide was based on a passage about the pony express (*The Cornerstone Anthology*, 1986, New York: Globe):

Directions: The following sentences are about the pony express. Read each one and put an X beside those you agree with.

_____ The pony express can be compared to a relay race.

_____ Pony express riders would race across the country, covering about 500 miles in 1 day.

_____ Mail carried by the pony express rider cost $5.00 a letter.

_____ Pony express riders could travel twice as fast as a stagecoach.

_____ Pony express riders could only travel with their cargo of mail when weather permitted.

When developing Anticipation Guides, Larry first identifies major concepts he wants his students to learn. Then, with his students in mind, he looks for information that will either support or challenge their beliefs about the concept, in this case the pony express. For these guides to be effective, students must have some prior knowledge about the topic but not so much as to be totally familiar with it.

In presenting a guide to your class, you may put it either on an overhead, a whiteboard, or a copied worksheet. In any case, you will want to go over the directions and the statements in the guide. Then, individually, in pairs, or in small groups, students can respond to the statements and be prepared to defend their responses. Class discussion can begin by asking students how many agree and disagree with each statement. In short discussions, ask students to present ideas from both sides of the argument. Students will be actively involved in thinking about their own and their peers' responses as they hear diverse opinions from others in their class.

Through this activity, students are engaged in an active form of processing that can enhance their comprehension. These guides are designed to stimulate students' curiosity about the text, thus piquing their interest and providing motivation for the reading. They can be used at any grade level and with virtually any medium that presents information, including films and lectures. They help students focus on accurate prior knowledge and, at the same time, bring out any misconceptions. From this point of view, these guides can be informative for the teacher who is attempting to discern the scope of knowledge that students bring to the text.

Looking Into: Strategies to Use During Text Reading

As we begin this subsection, you may find it helpful to think back to our discussion of Larry's classroom at the beginning of this chapter. Recall that Larry worked with his students in small groups and that they were making connections between the texts they were reading and their own life experiences. Recall also that they were noting questions and confusions they had as they encountered different ideas in their reading. In both of these cases, Larry was teaching his children to use strategies to engage more deeply and meaningfully with texts. In this subsection, we explore four different kinds of strategies (i.e., making connections, asking questions, drawing inferences, and evoking sensory images) that Larry teaches his children as he works with them to help them develop deeper understandings of the texts that they read.

Strategies That Address Making Connections

In his own studying about reading comprehension, Larry read Doug Hartman's important ideas about intertextuality (Hartman, 1995). In brief, intertextuality refers to connections that readers make across a variety of different texts and textual experiences. Intertextuality refers to the idea that the books we read are situated in a complex contextual web of potential connections in the world, between other books and within our own lives. Stephanie Harvey and Anne Goudvis (2000) categorized these important intertextual connections as text-to-world connections, text-to-text connections, and text-to-self connections.

Larry draws on these ideas in his work with his children. Recall the small group of children reading *Shades of Gray*. As they read, they used small yellow sticky notes to identify text-to-text, text-to-self, and text-to-world connections. They placed these notes on the appropriate pages in their books where the connections were evoked. When they came to the front of the room to work with Larry, he helped them to discuss these important connections they were making during their reading. Remember that he had a large chart labeled "Text-to-Text," "Text-to-Self," and "Text-to-World" that he was using in his discussion with his children. When the children worked together with Larry, they placed their sticky notes from their individual reading on the chart. (They had each written their own names and dates on their individual sticky notes so that they could keep track of which children were making which connections.) This small group discussion helped the children to develop a deeper understanding of the story they were reading because they were able to connect events and ideas from the story with their own lives, other books they had read, and events in the world. In addition to this making connections activity that Larry borrowed from Harvey and Goudvis (2000), Larry used other ideas to help his children make connections while reading.

Reader Response Prompts. Reader response is an approach to text rather than a specific strategy. It represents a way of devising questions and thinking about text that incorporates but moves students beyond literal elements and actively engages their prior knowledge and experiences as they relate to a reading. As students think about text from a reader response perspective, they begin to apply critical thinking skills of analysis and generalization as they construct meaning by combining what they already know with what they perceive in a text (Farnan & Kelly, 1989). Although this approach has been used primarily with narrative text, it has also been successfully applied to expository materials (Brozo, 1988).

Specific prompts or questions that allow a reader response approach can be used to guide classroom discussion. Probst (1988, pp. 35–36) has suggested prompts similar to the following as possibilities:

1. What was your first reaction or response to the text?
2. What feelings did you have about what you read?
3. What did you see happening in the text?

DID YOU NOTICE . . .
Did you notice that this strategy can be used with students in all grades? Primary grade students can simply write T-T (text to text), T-S (text to self), or T-W (text to world) and place the sticky note in the appropriate place in the small book, big book, or charted poem. In addition to writing T-T, T-S, or T-W, intermediate grade students can jot down a few thoughts on the sticky note to support the connection they are making.

4. What image was called to mind by what you read?

5. What does the text remind you of in your own life—what people, places, events, sights, smells?

6. What word (or image, phrase, or idea) did you think was most important in the text?

7. What was the most important word (phrase or aspect) in the text?

8. What was the most difficult word (or part) in the text?

9. What sort of person do you think the author of this text would be?

10. Did you like what you read?

11. Did this text make you think of anything else you have read? (If so, what was the connection?)

12. If you were asked to write about this text, what would you focus on?

13. Was your reading of the text different from (that of) other members of the class (your discussion partner, etc.)? In what ways were they different? Alike?

14. How did your feelings about what you read change as you read further or talked about what you read?

As you can see, a reader response approach not only allows an interactive view of reading, it encourages student-student and student-teacher discussions about what was read. Remember that these prompts represent points of departure for discussion, not forums for short-answer responses that are heard and then dropped. Students should be encouraged to elaborate on their responses. You will find that your students' involvement with what they have read will include the following: retelling parts of the reading, paraphrasing, describing, and supporting their opinions and interpretations.

Here's how Larry used these reader response prompt questions with his students. First, he typed these questions on a sheet and each student stapled the sheet in the front of her or his writing response log. Larry also wrote these questions on large chart paper and displayed them at the front of the classroom. Second, when the teacher or children came up with additional prompt questions, they added them to the chart in the front of the room as well as to their personal lists. Larry wanted his children to learn that they, too, could make decisions about important topics and issues to write and talk about with respect to the texts they read. Finally—and this is very important—Larry explicitly modeled how to write and talk about books using these prompts. While teaching about and using these prompts with his children, Larry sometimes directs his children to the prompts he wants them to address. Other times he invites his children to choose from a selection of prompts he has taught them.

Questioning Strategies

One of the most frequently used classroom techniques is questioning. There is an extensive body of research literature that demonstrates the importance of directing and focusing students' reading through teachers' questions. It is critical for you to understand that a question is a useful tool, a stimulant for learning.

Too often in the past, teachers have fallen into the trap of thinking that a question automatically produces a certain type of thinking (a specific mental operation). The operation is done by readers in their thinking processes, not by the question; the question is merely a device that may or may not stimulate the type of thinking that is desired by the teacher. We have spent a great deal of time and effort labeling questions as literal, inferential, creative, and critical (evaluative). (We talk about these categories of questions in depth in chapter 9.) Much of this time and effort has been futile; we should turn our attention to examining the processes and operations involved in reading, remembering that questions merely serve as stimulants to thinking, not as substitutes for it.

Because questions are sources for thinking, it seems obvious that we should ask our students many different types of questions to stimulate many different mental operations. It seems equally obvious that students interpret questions in many different ways; it is possible that a question a test maker or textbook publisher intended to elicit recall of explicitly stated information may not serve the purpose for some students. Finally, one of our instructional goals with respect to questions should be to teach children to ask and address meaningful questions in the process of their own reading. We begin our discussion of questioning strategies with this last point.

Recall from the beginning of this chapter that the children in Larry's small instructional group reading *Behind Rebel Lines* were using sticky notes to list questions that they had about the story and characters as they read. Larry drew on ideas from Harvey and Goudvis (2000) to teach his children to monitor their engagement with text as they noted questions involving confusions and curiosities about the story they were reading. When this group of children came to the front of the room to work with Larry, they collectively sorted out answers to the questions they posed during their reading. By exploring the children's questions about the text, Larry was able to see what aspects of the text that the children found confusing. This allowed him to provide instruction to help the children sort through their confusions. Another important thing happened during this type of instruction. By using this strategy with his children, Larry was teaching them to assume control over their own reading. Rather than passively answering the questions that others posed for them (either the teacher or the textbook publisher), the children were learning to address the real questions that they had as they read. In addition to this strategy, Larry used a variety of other important strategies with his children.

Question–Answer Relationships. Raphael (1984, 1986) sought to discover an effective way to teach children about various sources of information available to them in relation to a text. Thus, she developed four types of question–answer relationships (QARs). These included the following:

1. Text-explicit QARs in which answers to questions are explicitly stated in the text
2. Text-based QARs in which the student has to think and look in more than one place in the text to find the answer
3. Knowledge-based QARs in which the student is conscious of being on his or her own, a situation in which the student has to read the text to formulate the answer, which is not in the text

DID YOU NOTICE . . .
Did you notice that effective instruction involves a gradual release of responsibility? This is when teachers first assume a high level of responsibility in discerning content and modeling their thought process. Slowly, with guided support, teachers begin to release the responsibility to the students. Finally, students assume full responsibility for the task and learning during independent practice. It s like riding a bike. First children ride with their parents, next with training wheels, and finally they ride on their own.

4. Knowledge-based QARs that do not require the student to read the text to formulate an answer.

Raphael and her colleagues found that, particularly in grades 4 through 8, teaching students to answer and create different types of questions sensitized them to the demands of certain questions and improved the quality of their answers. Also, students who were trained in the QAR activity demonstrated significant gains in comprehension.

To provide appropriate scaffolding for students and ensure that they will internalize and be able to use the QAR strategy as independent learners, Larry knew that it was important at the beginning that he accept total responsibility for modeling this activity. Initially, he assigned the text, generated the questions, provided the answers, identified the QAR being targeted, and clearly explained the rationale supporting the QAR. Gradually, he released control to his students, ultimately allowing them to generate the questions, identify the QAR, and explain it.

ReQuest.   Another useful technique for helping children understand texts is called ReQuest. The technique involves teacher-student question-and-answer sessions. It begins with both the teacher and the student silently reading the first sentence of a passage. The teacher reads the entire passage, but the student does not; then the student asks as many questions as he or she desires. The teacher answers the questions as completely as possible. After the student has asked as many questions as desired, the teacher begins to ask questions and the student has to answer. Through this procedure, the student gains insight into the questioning process as both a participant and an observer of the teacher who acts as a role model. The procedure continues until the student is capable of answering, for example, the question, "What do you think is going to happen in the rest of the selection?" This procedure results in the development and retrieval of one's schemata and concepts.

To illustrate the ReQuest technique, we turn to the topic of spiders. To begin, encourage the student to ask the teacher as many questions as possible about the first line. The student may ask, "Why do many people think that spiders are insects?" The teacher responds with appropriate answers. At this point, it would also be useful to indicate the types of mental processes involved in answering the questions. This could demonstrate the process of schema formation and information retrieval (i.e., the use of prior knowledge to answer questions). The teacher could follow the student's questions with a question such as "Do you think that spiders are insects?" This procedure could be repeated with each succeeding passage until the student feels comfortable.

Strategies That Help Children Draw Inferences

Inferencing is one of the most important aspects of comprehension. Raphael's (1986) knowledge-based QARs that we just described relate to inferencing. In the case of knowledge-based QARs, Raphael asks the reader to draw on his or her own experiences and knowledge as well as the text to interpret the text. In other words, the answer to a question is not explicitly provided by the text; rather, the reader must infer an answer to a question (i.e., read between the lines) based on information presented in the text. We will refer to our earlier discussion of

Larry's work with a small group of children reading *Behind Rebel Lines* to illustrate one of the ways that Larry helps his children to draw inferences from their reading.

Recall that in our earlier discussion of Larry's work with the *Behind Rebel Lines* group the children used sticky notes to identify their questions about the story. When the children moved to the front of the room to work with Larry, he asked them to put their initials on each sticky note. Then, the group proceeded to sort through the children's questions. As they sorted the children's questions, Larry discovered that many of the children were having trouble following the story line because they were confused by the many identities of Emma, the main character. In the story, Emma was a spy for the North during the Civil War. She assumed many different identities and forayed into Rebel territory many times in her quest to gain sensitive information for the Yankees. As Larry looked closely at the children's questions about the story, he noticed that many of them were inference-related questions. Answers to the children's questions would require a reader to "read between the lines" to interpret story events. For example, Emma assumed the identity of a man among her Union colleagues at the army base in the North where she was stationed. Some of Larry's children were confused as to why she couldn't just tell her superiors that she was a woman. Larry had to explain that times were very different in the 1860s. Emma would not have been allowed to be a spy for the Union army if her superiors had known that she was a woman. In fact, as a woman she wouldn't have been allowed in the army.

One of the things that Larry noticed over the years as he worked with children was that the more background knowledge they had about the stories they were reading, the easier it was for his students to draw inferences while reading. Consequently, he spent considerable time helping his children build background knowledge and/or access their background knowledge prior to reading stories. Even though his class had done research on the Civil War before they started reading their texts, there was still important background knowledge that they lacked about the war and the time period to comprehend their texts. In addition to helping his children acquire the background information they needed to make inferences while reading, Larry also provided explicit instruction to help his children learn to draw inferences while reading. We share another approach he uses with his children in the following.

Guided Learning Plans.   Like traditional study guides, Guided Learning Plans (GLPs) guide or direct the reader purposefully to the text. They differ from most traditional guides in two specific ways: (a) They actively involve students through open-ended questions that ask them to infer, to make applications to new situations, and to evaluate; and (b) they prompt students to respond personally to information in the text, thereby integrating new information with their prior knowledge. GLPs should begin with questions that ask for explicit information so that students will have a knowledge base for comprehending the text's information. Also, it is important to let students know that their use of the guide will help them understand and remember what they read. Let them know that completing the guide will make their learning more meaningful and more complete. Typical directions for a GLP follow with a sample shown in Table 7–2.

TABLE 7–2
King Tut Guided Learning Plan.

Directions: As you read the text, complete the following guided learning plan. Read each section, then fill in the guide.

Name

TREASURE OF THE BOY KING TUT: Video study sheet 1
1. What is an obelisk?
2. What is the capital city of Egypt? What is the capital city of California?
3. Is the capital of Egypt a small rural city or a crowded modern city? How does this city compare to the capital city of California?
4. In the capital city of Egypt, do people sell most of their goods in shops or on the street? How do these merchants compare to San Diego merchants you buy from?
5. What is the primary river of Egypt? What are the major rivers of the United States? What makes a river a primary river?
6. What is the land like around the primary river in Egypt, and what is this land used for?
7. What is land like away from this river?
8. Why did the ancient Egyptians bury their pharaohs in pyramids?
9. What were some of the objects that were buried in the tombs?
10. What would you have done if you had found some of these objects? Why?

The GLP in Table 7–2 was developed to accompany a video about King Tut. Notice that it begins with explicit questions and that interspersed with questions about King Tut are questions about California, the state in which this GLP was used, and the United States. By mixing questions related to the video with questions related to elements students are more familiar with (e.g., the capital of California and major rivers of the United States), the teacher, in essence, is causing students to apply actively what they already know to the new information. Also, notice that question 10 is an open-ended question that elicits students' personal responses based on their prior knowledge and experiences. Students are also asked to apply what they have learned to new situations, as in question 5, where they are asked to apply their knowledge to the importance of rivers. In addition, many questions ask students to compare and contrast ideas presented in the text.

GLPs are especially useful study guides because they address the complex processes associated with successful reading. They guide students not only to look for specific information but also to link their prior knowledge with the text and to think critically about ideas presented (e.g., applying, comparing, contrasting, and evaluating).

Strategies That Help Children Visualize During Reading

Visualizing—or creating pictures in your mind—during reading is an important strategy that good readers use to help them interpret texts (Harvey & Goudvis, 2000). Larry uses several ways to help his students learn to visualize as they read. First, when Larry reads aloud to his students, he tells them the way he visualizes various characters, settings, and scenes in stories. He also encourages his students to visualize while he is reading aloud to them from books like *Maniac Magee* and *Turn Homeward, Hannelee*. So, for example, when he has just read a particularly poignant segment of text, he often stops reading momentarily and asks his students to close their eyes and create a mental picture of what he has just read. Then, he takes a few moments to ask several students to share their visual images. On occasion, whether he has read aloud to his students or whether his students are reading one of their assigned texts, Larry may ask his students to draw a picture or series of pictures to represent the visual images they are imagining from their reading.

Finally, Larry also draws his students' attention to compelling visual images in the picture books he regularly reads to his class. For example, when he started the Civil War unit with this class, he read Patricia Polacco's moving picture book *Pink and Say* to his class. While he showed most of the pictures from the text to his class, he spent time discussing the symbolism of the provocative image at the end of the text whereby the main characters—Pink (an African-American boy in his teens fighting for the Union) and Say (a European-American boy in his teens also fighting for the Union)—tried to hold onto one another's hands while they were being pulled apart by Confederate soldiers to hang Pink and place Say in Andersonville prison. Larry believes that sharing and discussing powerful visual images from the texts that he reads to his class can help his children learn to create their own visual images from the texts they read.

Looking Back: Strategies to Use After Reading

There are three major categories of strategies that readers can use after reading texts or excerpts of texts. These categories include strategies that help readers prioritize information, fix-up strategies that readers can use to repair their comprehension of texts, and retelling/synthesis strategies that readers can use to help make sense of texts or portions of texts. We describe each of these categories of strategies in this subsection.

Strategies That Address Prioritizing Information or Deciding the Big Ideas

Reciprocal Teaching. Questions that are part of a structured format can be effective for developing students' process-oriented comprehension abilities after they have read sections of text or entire texts—depending on the length of the texts. Reciprocal Teaching (Palincsar, 1984; Palincsar & Brown, 1985) is an instructional framework in which students and teachers take turns assuming the teacher's role through a structured dialogue. The teacher first models four comprehension strategies and then gives students an opportunity to practice them.

The following steps can be used to help students use Reciprocal Teaching as they read and comprehend text:

1. Select a short passage either to read to students or for them to read on their own.
2. Summarize the passage in one or two short sentences.
3. Generate a question about the passage to ask one of the students.
4. Ask someone in the class to clarify (or resolve) something in the text that may have been unclear.
5. Finally, ask a student(s) to make a prediction about what might happen next in the text.

After conducting this process several times with you, the teacher, modeling the steps, gradually turns over control of the activity to the students. Beginning with step 2, allow students to start taking responsibility for the activity by summarizing what was read, generating a question or questions, making clarifying statements, and predicting what will happen next. Ultimately, students can engage in Reciprocal Teaching in small groups or in pairs, guiding themselves through the reading process. Strategies like this can help students, as we discussed earlier, become aware of when they might not have understood and when they have, in fact, been successful comprehenders.

Don't forget to explain at each step a rationale for that portion of the activity. For example, (a) when students summarize a text, let them know that they are consciously rethinking what they have read and organizing the ideas before restating them. Therefore, if they have not understood the text, they will find summarizing a difficult task. This will be a strong clue that they must use a corrective strategy like rereading, reading further for clarification, or seeking help to comprehend the passage. Also, let them know that summarizing will help them internalize and remember what they have read. (b) Let students know that by generating questions about a reading, they are consciously going back to the text, thinking about it, and developing questions based on what they have understood. Therefore, if they have not understood what they read, they will know this right away. (c) Asking another student for clarification provides an opportunity to clear up any confusing points and helps the student being asked to clarify to rethink the material and see whether or not she has clearly understood the passage. (d) Finally, let students know that by predicting what will come next, they are constructively using everything they already know to set a purpose for their continued reading. However, predicting can be a very difficult process when the reader has a limited knowledge of the topic or when there is no best sequence for presentation of the topic (Lapp, Flood, & Hoffman, 1989). Through these kinds of explanations you can increase your students' awareness of their own reading skills, in addition to giving them on-the-spot strategies for correcting any problems they may have. Palincsar's (1984) results with Reciprocal Teaching highlight its effectiveness. She reported that after 20 days of instruction in this strategy, students gained 35% or more on assessments of their reading comprehension.

Retelling/Synthesis Strategies

Good readers can look back at portions of the text they just read and retell main events/ideas and synthesize key aspects of the story. Good teachers of reading know that an important aspect of comprehension is the ability to sort out and articulate "big ideas" in stories. By teaching children retelling and synthesis strategies, teachers help children learn to identify the "big ideas" in stories and synthesize main ideas. In this subsection we share the following three approaches that Larry and other reading teachers use to help their children learn to identify main events and synthesize key aspects of a story: *group retellings*, *cybernetic sessions*, and *directed reading activities* (or DRAs).

Group Retellings.   Larry typically works with four small reading groups per day for approximately 15 minutes per group. He often then engages in a whole-group culminating activity with his whole class. Because his small groups of students read at different reading levels, the groups read different books. However, Larry is careful to choose books for the groups to read that deal with common themes. Then, students can be assigned to heterogeneous groups of three or four in which each student has read a different portion of a different text. Larry is careful to choose class texts that cluster around central themes. Additionally, the material, though topically related, may come from varied sources and reflect multiple reading levels. In this way, Larry gives the less able students in the class shorter and easier books to read. When students meet with their heterogeneous retelling groups, they retell the portion of their text they read for that particular day in their own words to other group members. At any point, group members may interject with a similar fact from their reading or elaborate with information from their background knowledge.

Nature of Activity: Students work in heterogeneous groups of three and review/ share information on literature or content area subjects.

Description of Teacher's Role: Set up groups of students. Assign area in the room for each group to work. Give each student an assignment to read. The material may come from varied sources and may even reflect multiple reading levels to account for different reading abilities. Students read and study material assigned during a timed period. When the signal is given to share, students take turns retelling information in their own words to their group. Each person takes his or her turn retelling. Time must be allowed for students to ask questions of each other and interject other facts from their reading.

Cautions: To be successful each child must have material that he or she is able to read and comprehend. Monitoring, explicit directions, and modeling are also imperative for a successful activity.

Cybernetic Sessions.   In cybernetic sessions, small groups of students respond to preplanned questions within a limited period of time. In the preplanning phase, Larry puts one question on each of several poster boards or sheets of butcher paper and hangs them around the room. Carefully worded, thought-provoking questions that may elicit misconceptions are most useful here. During the response-generating phase, Larry's students are grouped (three to five students) around each poster question. When instructed by Larry, students contribute as many answers as possible while a group recorder writes them down on a separate sheet of paper. After the allotted time, the groups move to another question station and the process is repeated. Each time, a new recorder is chosen. The next phase involves data synthesizing, wherein the groups pool their responses to each question. This phase occurs after each group has had the chance to circulate around the room and answer all questions. Here Larry or an appointed student writes the classes' responses under each posted question. In the final presentation phase, posters may be placed on bulletin boards, typed as handouts, or reread later as a form of review. This technique works well using questions related to content material or questions could be designed to elicit background knowledge prior to reading a novel or story.

Nature of Activity: Small groups of no more than three to five students respond to preplanned questions within a limited time period. Use questions related to content material or to elicit background knowledge prior to reading novel or story.

Description of teacher's role:

1. Preplanning—Put one thought-provoking question on each of several sheets of poster board or butcher paper. Hang them around the room.
2. Response/Generating Phase—When instructed by the teacher, students contribute as many answers as possible while the recorder writes them down on separate piece of paper. When the time is up, students rotate to new question to repeat the process.
3. Data Synthesizing—Groups respond orally to each question and the teacher or a student writes responses under each posted question.
4. Final Presentation—Posters may be placed on bulletin board, typed as handouts, or reread later as a review.

Cautions: Teacher must model process, give explicit instructions, and monitor groups closely for activity to work effectively.

The Directed Reading Activity.   When teaching his children to synthesize and retell key ideas from their reading, Larry sometimes uses a comprehensive teaching method, the directed reading activity (DRA). We will explain a shortened version of the DRA in the following and then give an example of a DRA lesson.

1. During the first stage, encourage involvement with the subject matter by calling on your students' prior knowledge of the subject.
2. During the second stage, introduce key vocabulary terms. This stage helps students to preview key conceptual content that they will encounter during their reading.
3. During the third stage, springboard questions are used by the teacher to provide the student with a guide for searching for the key content.

The following lesson on spiders illustrates how Larry has used the DRA. The topic of *spiders* is often included in middle-grade science texts. It was a topic in Larry's current science text. The DRA can be used with narrative and informational texts, however. Rather than merely telling the students to read the lesson and answer some follow-up questions, Larry uses a DRA format that includes the following:

- *Background.* Larry involves the students in a discussion of spiders (e.g., "Why do they like spiders?"). He may bring spiders to class to let children experience spiders with other children in a controlled educational setting.
- *Vocabulary.* Larry isolates and teaches the words that will give the students problems with the reading material. For example, in the spider material, some potentially difficult words are *spinnerets*, *lasso*, and *digest*. By pre-teaching these words, Larry helps children over the rough spots before they become unduly frustrated.
- *Springboard questions.* Larry provides the students with reading guides to alert them to the important parts of each text. Some important pre-questions Larry uses include "What are spiders like?" "Where can spiders be found?" Sometimes authors use these questions as part of the text. With the DRA format, the questions also precede the actual reading.

- *Silent or oral reading.* At this point, Larry asks his children to read the text.
- *Follow-up questions.* Larry uses follow-up questions to check comprehension of text-explicit learning while stimulating interpretive thought. To check text-explicit learning, springboard questions can be repeated. To stimulate interpretive thought, Larry might ask "What would the world be like without spiders?"

Fix-up Strategies That Help Children Repair Comprehension

Think Alouds

Larry uses an approach called *think aloud* to model how his students can use fix-up strategies to make sense of text if they are experiencing difficulty understanding what they are reading (Davey, 1983). This think aloud technique helps children improve their metacognitive skills. Metacognition refers to your ability to think about your own thinking (Baker, 2002). When Larry uses the think aloud approach with his children, he asks his children to listen carefully as he verbalizes his own thoughts while he reads aloud. As an example of how Larry uses the think aloud approach, we return to Larry's work with his *Behind Rebel Lines* group. One of the things that his children did not understand was why Emma refused to go to the doctor at her own army base when she was violently ill. When Larry's *Behind Rebel Lines* group came to work with him one day, he read the excerpt of text describing this situation and thought aloud as he read. Here's what happened in a portion of the lesson with Larry's small group.

Reading aloud to his children, Larry came to the place in the text where Emma decided not to go to the doctor even though she was violently ill. Larry made the following comments to his children to illustrate how he monitored his own comprehension of the story.

> I wonder why in the world Emma wouldn't go to the doctor when she is so ill. This doesn't really make sense since Emma is at her own Union army base, and there is a doctor readily available to see her. Hmmm ... Let me think about this. What could be some possible reasons for Emma's behavior. Let me see.... What do I know about Emma? One of the most important things I know about Emma is that she is a woman spy. No one at the army base—except the base commander's wife—knows that she is a woman. Everyone else at the base thinks that she is a man. I know that she has to pretend to be a man because women weren't allowed to serve in the army during the Civil War. I bet that choosing not to go to the doctor has something to do with keeping her identity as a woman secret. If she went to the army doctor (who was a man), he would find out that she is a woman. He might then reveal her identity as a woman to the base commander who, in turn, would probably make her stop being a Union spy.

When we look at the characteristics of less able readers, we see that they tend not to activate their prior knowledge and link it to what they read. Additionally, they tend to not stop to sort out comprehension difficulties when they become confused during their reading. Larry uses the following additional ideas from Davey (1983) as he works with his children to teach them to monitor their own comprehension during reading. We suggest that you practice these ideas with people in your class.

Read the following strategy and then plan to practice this strategy with peers in class using either this text or another text. Assign someone in the group to be the teacher, and the remaining group members will be students.

1. The teacher selects a passage, either narrative or expository, that you think might contain ambiguous or otherwise difficult material and/or unknown words.

2. Give students a copy of the text and ask them to read silently as you read aloud. As you read, you can use strategies such as the following:

    a. Make predictions based on the title, pictures, headings, and so on. Say things like "I think this is going to be about ..." and "I think that next we find out about ...".

    b. Describe mental images you form as you read. Say things such as "I can see what the author is describing here. It looks like ...".

    c. Actively link what you are reading to your prior knowledge and experience: "I remember when I ..." or "That reminds me of when ...".

    d. Identify anything that might be confusing. Show what you do when you get to a confusing part of the text. "I thought this was going to say something else" and 'I'm not sure what that means, but I think ...".

    e. Demonstrate how you would solve a problem with understanding. Say things like, "I think I'll read further to see if ...", or "I need to stop and think about this for a minute ...".

3. When the teacher finishes this process, she or he should ask the students to add their thoughts to yours. What did the students think as you were reading?

Remember that when you use these ideas with children, you should conduct several modeling sessions. Then, you should let your children practice this process in pairs. Also, encourage them to practice these strategies silently and independently. When you meet with them in small groups ask them to share their independent thinking with the group.

QUESTIONS

1. What is the nature of reading comprehension?

2. What instructional strategies enhance children's abilities to activate and build background knowledge? Explain.

3. What instructional strategies enhance children's abilities to address questions pertaining to texts, infer meanings from engagement with texts, and make intertextual connections? Explain.

4. What instructional strategies enhance children's abilities to synthesize ideas and information from their reading, prioritize information, and monitor their own comprehension while reading?

5. What does effective comprehension instruction look like?

REFERENCES

Baker, L. (2002). Metacognition in comprehension instruction. In C. C. Block & M. Pressley (Eds.), *Comprehension instruction: Research based best practices* (pp. 77–95). New York: Guilford.

Brozo, W. G. (1988). Applying a reader response heuristic to expository text. *Journal of Reading, 32,* 140–145.

Davey, B. (1983, October). Think aloud: Modeling the cognitive processes of reading comprehension. *Journal of Reading, 27,* 44–47.

Farnan, N. J., & Kelly, P. R. (1989). Reader response: What kids think really counts. In M. Douglass (Ed.), *Claremont reading conference 52nd yearbook* (pp. 82–98). Claremont, CA: Claremont Reading Conference Center for Developmental Studies.

Flood, J., & Lapp, D. (1990, April). Reading comprehension instruction for at-risk students: Research based practices. *Journal of Reading, 33,* 7, 490–496.

Flood, J., Lapp, D., & Fisher, D. (2002). Parsing, questioning, and rephrasing (PQR): Building syntactic knowledge to improve reading comprehension. In C. Block, L. Gambrell, & M. Pressley (Eds.), *Improving comprehension instruction* (pp. 181–198). San Francisco: Jossey-Bass.

Graves, M. F., Penn, M. C., & Cooke, C. L. (1985, April). The coming attraction: Previewing short stories. *Journal of Reading, 28,* 594–598.

Hartman, D. K. (1995). 8 readers reading: The intertextual links of proficient readers reading multiple passages. *Reading Research Quarterly, 30,* 220–261.

Harvey, S., & Goudvis, A. (2000). *Strategies that work: Teaching comprehension to enhance understanding.* York, ME: Stenhouse Publishers.

Herber, H. L. (1978). *Teaching reading in content areas* (2nd ed.). Englewood Cliffs, NJ: Prentice-Hall.

Keene, E. L., & Zimmerman, S. (1997). *Mosaic of thought: Teaching comprehension in a reader's workshop.* Portsmouth, NH: Heinemann.

Langer, J. A. (1982). Facilitating text processing: The elaboration of prior knowledge. In J. A. Laner & M. T. Smith-Burke (Eds.), *Reader meets author/bridging the gap: A psycholinguistic and sociolinguistic perspective* (pp. 149–162). Newark, DE: International Reading Association.

Langer, J. A. (1984, Summer). Examining background knowledge and text comprehension. *Reading Research Quarterly, 19,* 468–481.

Lapp, D., Flood, J., & Hoffman, R. (1989, December). *Reciprocal teaching and its effect on comprehending science information.* Paper presented at the National Reading Conference, Tucson, AZ.

Levstik, L. S., & Barton, K. C. (2001). *Doing history: Investigating with children in elementary and middle schools.* Mahwah, NJ: Lawrence Erlbaum Publishers.

Ogle, D. (1986, February). K-W-L. A teaching model that develops active reading of expository text. *The Reading Teacher, 39,* 564–570.

Palincsar, A. S. (1984). Reciprocal teaching of comprehension fostering and comprehension monitoring activities. *Cognition and Instruction, 2,* 117–175.

Palincsar, A. S., & Brown, A. L. (1985). Reciprocal teaching activities to promote reading with your mind. In E. J. Cooper (Ed.), *Reading, thinking and concept development: Interactive strategies for the class.* New York: The College Board.

Pearson, P. D., & Gallagher, M. C. (1983). The instruction of reading comprehension. *Contemporary Educational Psychology, 8,* 317–344.

Probst, R. E. (1988, January). Dialogue with a text. *English Journal, 77,* 32–38.

Raphael, T. E. (1984, January). Teaching learners about sources of information for answering comprehension questions. *Journal of Reading, 27,* 303–311.

Raphael, T. E. (1986). Teaching question-answer relationships, revisited. *The Reading Teacher, 39,* 516–522.

Raphael, T. E., & Hiebert, E. H. (1996). *Creating an integrated approach to literacy instruction.* New York: Harcourt Brace College Publishers.

Rosenblatt, L. M. (1994). The transactional theory of reading and writing. In R. S. Ruddell, M. R. Ruddell, and H. Singer (Eds.), *Theoretical models and processes of reading* (4th ed., pp. 1057–1092). Newark, DE: International Reading Association.

Thorndike, E. L. (1917). Reading and reasoning: A study of mistakes in paragraph reading. *Journal of Educational Psychology, 8,* 323–332.

CHILDREN'S LITERATURE

Beatty, P. (1984). *Turn homeward, Hannelee.* New York: Troll Associates.

Beatty, P. (1992). *Who comes with cannons?* New York: Morrow Junior Books.

Hunt, I. (1964). *Across five Aprils.* New York: Berkley Books.

Polacco, P. (1994). *Pink and say.* New York: Philomel Books.

Reeder, C. (1989). *Shades of gray.* New York: Avon Books.

Reit, S. (1988). *Behind rebel lines.* San Diego, CA: Harcourt Brace & Company.

Spinelli, J. (1990). *Maniac Magee.* New York: Little Brown.

CHAPTER 8

Content Area Learning

───────────────── CHAPTER GOALS ─────────────────

To help the reader

- understand the role of reading in content area learning.
- understand the role of the teacher in content area reading and learning.
- understand the role of the text in content area learning.
- examine the various types of text structures common to expository text.
- learn a variety of instructional strategies to enhance content area learning in social studies, science, math, and the arts.

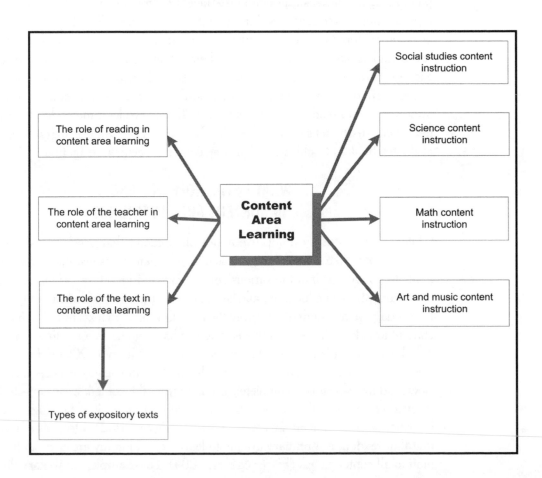

When you first opened your advanced math book and looked at the pages, what did you think? If you are like most students, you became nervous and wondered how you would ever learn anything from that book. You were fortunate, though, to have a teacher who could teach you to read the textbook and how to understand the content of the course. To understand content texts, students must understand the vocabulary and the concepts related to the topics in the text. The information about vocabulary instruction that is presented in chapter 6 can also be applied to teaching your students how to read content area textbooks. Additionally, students must understand how to self-monitor their comprehension of content information. Students should also be taught how to use their content area textbooks and how various texts are structured.

Your Turn

Why are some content texts difficult to read? If you were to pick up an advanced calculus book, a biochemistry book, or a research report on the economy, would these be difficult for you to read? Why? What could you do to increase your comprehension of these texts? What could a teacher do to help you with these texts?

Ms. Donnelly is a sixth grade teacher. She is responsible for the math, science, social studies, and English language arts instruction for her 32 students. Ms. Donnelly has a preparation period during which her students participate in physical education. Given the limited number of hours that Ms. Donnelly has to cover the standards in each of these areas, she plans some integrated instructional units. For example, during her social studies unit on Ancient Egypt, she uses information texts on the topic for her shared readings during language arts time. She also creates a number of learning centers that require students to use their language arts skills to comprehend social studies materials. Ms. Donnelly knows that students must master the content for each of these disciplines, but she also knows that her students need to continue developing their reading strategies and skills. She wants her students to have multiple opportunities to read in the content areas. Before we look more closely at Ms. Donnelly's classroom, let's explore the role of reading in content learning as well as the role of the textbook in teaching and learning content-specific information.

WHAT IS THE ROLE OF READING IN CONTENT AREA LEARNING?

Children are naturally inquisitive about phenomena that occur in their world, phenomena not unlike those we might teach in our science lessons. Every day, we ask students to go with us into the various content areas of literature, science, social studies, math, art, physical education, and music for the purposes of learning and enjoyment. Every day, we ask students to apply their reading skills to texts full of rich and exciting content area knowledge, and this is exactly what content area reading is all about.

This concept is not new. Many years ago, McMurry (1909) defined *studying* as "reading to learn" content. Unfortunately, through the years, teachers have tended to view reading as a subject completely separate from the content area subjects. However, most teachers agree that among their many jobs is the task of helping students glean information from content area texts (Vacca & Vacca, 2002). Decades of research suggest that reading is a primary avenue to learning, and many areas of reading are common to all content areas (Fisher & Frey, 2004). For example, vocabulary development and comprehension skills are keys to understanding in all disciplines (see chapters 6 and 7), and study skills are common to all areas of the curriculum.

In this chapter, information will be provided (a) to help you develop an understanding of content area reading skills and (b) to enable you to gain an understanding of the processes involved in using reading skills and strategies to understand content materials.

WHAT IS THE ROLE OF THE TEACHER IN CONTENT AREA LEARNING?

What Is Your Self-Perception as a Teacher?

"Well-written materials will not do the job alone. Teachers must instruct students in strategies for extracting and organizing critical information from text" (National Academy of Education, 1985, p. 71). This quote presents an idea that we probably all can agree with: teachers matter, and what they do in terms of instruction matters the most (e.g., Darling-Hammond, Berry, & Thoreson, 2001). Of course, teachers cannot do the learning for their students. However, knowledgeable teachers can design instruction in ways that will allow and promote a high degree of learning. Look for a moment at a question that is important for teachers to ask themselves: *What is your self-perception as a teacher*? Do you view yourself as a dispenser of information into an unfilled vessel or as a facilitator to help students acquire knowledge? Research, based on what we know about how students learn, suggests that we will be more effective teachers if our self-perceptions are aligned with the latter perspective, if we view our role as that of a primary and knowledgeable support for our students' learning rather than as a dispenser of ready made wisdom (e.g., Darling-Hammond, 1997).

Pedagogical Content Knowledge

As teachers, we plan objectives and instruction to meet the demands of content and the needs of our students (Fisher & Frey, 2001). To teach content areas well, teachers must develop their understanding of both the content and the pedagogy required to teach that content. This is referred to as *pedagogical content knowledge* or PCK (Kinach, 2002; Veal, van Driel, & Hulshof, 2001). Importantly, one without the other is insufficient. A teacher who understands science, but does not know how to teach it, will not ensure that his or her students reach high standards. Similarly, a person who has a limited understanding of history but knows a number of instructional strategies will not be terribly helpful in scaffolding student knowledge.

Teachers with strong PCK are also strategic teachers. Central to the concept of strategic teaching is a revision of the traditional definition of learning. Instead of viewing learning as a passive activity in which students simply see and somehow magically absorb information from content materials, *learning* is defined "as thinking, that is, using prior knowledge and specific strategies to understand the ideas in a text as a whole or the elements of a problem as a whole" (Jones, Palincsar, Ogle, & Carr, 1987, p. 5). In this definition, emphasis is placed on students' active construction of meaning, which incorporates elements of composition and problem solving. The principles presented in Table 8–1, divided into those that focus on the student and those that focus on the teacher, can be used as guidelines when you plan for reading in any content area lesson.

TABLE 8–1
Guidelines in Planning for Reading

Students

- Students need to have a purpose for learning. This purpose should be related to their concerns and interests.
- Students need to be motivated to learn. Involved, motivated students will learn more and remember longer. Many of the activities at the end of this chapter can be used as motivational devices.
- Students learn most effectively when they have a positive attitude. Students who have a purpose for learning and who are presented with interesting, challenging activities develop positive attitudes.
- Students comprehend by relating their school experiences to their life experiences. The teacher must determine how much a student knows about a particular topic. Instruction should then begin at the student's level of readiness.
- Students need word-recognition, comprehension, and study skills to learn through reading.
- Students learn in many ways. Some students learn best through activities that emphasize listening; others thrive on integrated reading, writing, and language activities. By offering a variety of learning activities, you will be able to meet the needs of all your students.
- Students learn at different rates. Setting a time limit can be counterproductive unless your purpose is to measure the rate of learning.
- Students need to be active participants, for learning is not a passive process. Activities that involve them in planning, as well as participating, are suggested throughout this chapter.

Teachers

- Teachers must have a thorough understanding of the content material they are teaching.
- Teachers must have a thorough knowledge of the students they are teaching.
- Teachers need to plan activities that will encourage the growth of all students (such activities are included throughout this book).
- Teachers must have a thorough understanding of the various methods designed to teach reading and language through content area subjects (see later sections in this chapter).
- Teachers should make proper adjustments for word-recognition, comprehension, and study skills application for effective teaching of reading in any content area (as discussed throughout this chapter).
- Teachers need to understand the practical application of learning theory, asking themselves, for example, How do children learn? Does their rate of learning coincide with their physical and social growth?
- Teachers should be well versed in assessment and evaluative techniques.
- Teachers must remember that content area reading and language strategies can be applied to all subject areas (as discussed throughout this chapter).

Given these guidelines, the teacher's job is to bridge the gap between learning goals and actual learning. We believe that classroom instruction, the strategies that teachers implement to cause learning to take place in their classrooms, represents this bridge (e.g., Moss, 2003). In other words, emphasis is on how we structure and present material so that students can best learn. Unfortunately, as Hamman, Berthelot, Saia, and Crowley (2000) noted, strategic teaching is not yet commonplace. These authors also noted that when strategic teaching is in place, student achievement significantly increases. Throughout this chapter, we will share vignettes of Ms. Donnelly's strategic content area teaching.

Having said that and knowing that strategic teaching is important, we want to turn our focus to the text. As noted in the discussions of PCK, teachers need more than a handful of instructional strategies. They also need to understand the content well and, most importantly, they need to understand their students. One area of confusion is often the text and the role the text can and does play in content area learning.

WHAT IS THE ROLE OF THE TEXT
IN CONTENT AREA LEARNING?

Before looking specifically at instruction, it is important to examine an element crucial to most content area instruction: the textbook. The foundation of a content area reading program is the knowledge that all of our students will need to learn from a variety of texts with a variety of organizational formats (e.g., Kaplan & Grabe, 2002). Reading from content texts is not the same as reading literature, which tends to have high interest, predictable story topics and formats, and to introduce words slowly, with the purpose of helping students learn to read. By contrast, content texts are not predictable and are conceptually dense; they contain unfamiliar words that may be defined with additional unfamiliar technical terms and topics (Bakken & Whedon, 2002). If students are successful in their basal reading, we can say that they have achieved a level of basic literacy, but we cannot say that they have learned to read all types of texts. Even for us as adults, experienced readers that we may be, some texts may be difficult. For example, the following is an excerpt from a computer manual:

> Each layer in an After Effects composition can contain one to 127 masks. You create and view masks in the Layer window, and set interactions between mask properties in the Time Layout window. You can also animate the shape of the mask by animating individual control points on a mask path. (Adobe Systems, 1998, p. 304)

Unless you are well versed in computer and software terminology, you would need thoughtful input from a knowledgeable facilitator to make this passage comprehensible.

Content materials that we present to our students are not unlike the preceding passage because they often contain new material about which students may have very little background knowledge and, perhaps, very little initial interest. Reading text material can be difficult for several reasons, even for good readers. Most of us can recall reading textbooks we considered dull and dry. Unfortunately, those perceptions cannot be attributed solely to the zany priorities of our childhood and adolescence. Researchers have demonstrated that textbooks, even the most modern and enlightened versions, contain sentences, passages, and even whole chapters that are incoherent, obscure, and conceptually dense (Anderson & Armbruster, 1984). Interestingly, the issue of textbook difficulty and coherence continues through to college-level courses (e.g., Griggs, 1999). But even more discouraging than this are two features of most content area textbooks (Schallert & Roser, 1989). One is their impersonal objectivity, a tendency to present facts and details without expressing any particular point of view of the topic. Students are asked to read about passionate topics—wars, scientific breakthroughs, medical miracles, charismatic leaders, and fiendish rulers—from an unemotional, seemingly unbiased, and tepid perspective that they, indeed, find pointless and not worthy of their engagement. A second feature that creates difficulty in content areas is that they tend to be "contentless." That is . . .

> The constraints of rigid vocabulary and readability guidelines cause authors to leave out important elaborations that are essential for comprehension. Connections are left out; details that would allow a reader to understand distinctions being presented are eliminated. (Schallert & Roser, 1989, p. 29)

Given the objections to content texts, a logical suggestion might be to discard them or at least use them as little as possible. However, textbooks offer potentially valuable resources for teachers; and we know that teachers rely on their content area texts in varying degrees. Some consider it simply as one classroom resource among many; others view it as the backbone of classroom content information. Current textbooks are aligned with state content standards and provide the teacher with pacing guides to ensure that the required course content is covered. Therefore, suggesting that we should discard all textbooks would be foolish as well as undesirable.

Instead, the solution lies in appropriate use of content area materials. It is important that we understand the nature of comprehension and how to design instructional strategies that will develop our students' comprehension of content area texts. In addition, an understanding of the text structures used in expository text is important. Understanding these types of texts will allow you to guide your students through them.

Expository or Informational Text

In contrast with narrative texts—texts with story grammars—expository texts are designed to convey information. Also called informational texts, the writing used in these texts is often descriptive. Understanding the different structure of informational texts has become quite important because educators know that expository texts are used to educate post-primary students. Educators also know that expository texts are the ones that adults use most often in their workplace (Burke, 2000). See Table 8–2 for a list of the various types of expository texts that are commonly used and what students should be able to do with these texts.

Niles (1970), a pioneer in expository structural analysis research, identified four organizational patterns of internal relationships for expository writing:

Type	Example
1. Cause and effect	In history texts, causes and effects of revolutions
2. Comparison and contrast	In science texts, a comparison of planets in our solar system
3. Chronological	In history texts, chronological description of events
4. Simple listing (taxonomy)	In mathematics texts, the steps in solving word problems

It would be a rare teacher who, when teaching students to read a story such as *Sisterhood of the Traveling Pants* (Brashares, 2001), failed to discuss and model character development and analysis. Students would also be helped to identify the problem and to make predictions about and later evaluate the conclusion. Explicit instruction of this type is also needed to teach students to read the various expository organizational styles.

In attempting to do so, Vacca and Vacca (2002) suggested that students need to be taught signal words within texts that announce to the reader or listener the type of organizational pattern used by the writer or speaker. In their scheme, the word *because* is tied to the cause-and-effect pattern, *however* to comparison and contrast, *when* to time order, and *to begin with* to simple listing.

Additionally, most texts have organizational devices that are designed to support the reader. For example, you've probably come to expect the chapter openers,

TABLE 8–2
Types of Expository Texts (and what students should be learning to do)

Text Type	Features of This Genre	Student Should Be Learning to
Descriptions	• Give details of things, events, people, and situation • May be specific (e.g., a report of a particular road accident) or general (e.g., a pamphlet on highway crashes)	• Confirm accuracy • Distinguish between general and specific descriptions • Classify and organize ideas into hierarchies • Summarize the ideas into their own words • Understand graphic presentations and symbols (e.g., maps, plans)
Explanations	• Descriptions of how things work and behave • May include details of why things behave as they do	• Retell the explanation in their own words • Summarize the content in their own words • Recognize false steps and omissions • Understand graphics
Instructions	• A sequence of directions (e.g., on how to work a device or cook a meal) • Instructions may be ordered by time (first, next, later) or logic (so that, as a result, in order)	• Understand and follow logical sequences, including sequence of instruction often found on labels • Understand the conventions in instructions (e.g., headings, numbered steps, diagrams, parts)
Tables	• Matrices in which information is presented horizontally and vertically (e.g., bus or train schedules, road distance schedule, graphs, score cards, order forms, etc.)	• Be clear about what information is needed • Cross-reference and narrow down the possibility in the table quickly to comprehend and act on the information
Forms	• Documents with blank spaces for information to be inserted (e.g., account information, job applications, permission slips, library card applications, etc.)	• Handle complex sentences, unfamiliar vocabulary, and complex layout
Arguments	• Supporting ideas presented in a sequence to justify a particular stand or viewpoint that a writer is taking	• Summarize the argument in their own words • Identify sequence of ideas • Recognize bias and emotive language • Distinguish fact from fiction • Understand graphics and symbols used

Reports	• A means of describing and classifying information
	• Reports can be straightforward recounts of events but may be more than this: some state a problem and suggest a solution;
		• See how the content of the report is divided into parts, for example
		  • opening statement, problem, or need
		  • cause and effect or consequences
		  • comparison and contrast and solution

(continued)

TABLE 8–2 (Continued)

Text Type	Features of This Genre	Student Should Be Learning to
Reports (continued)	some argue a case for or against an option and make recommendations	• recognize bias and emotive language • distinguish fact from opinion • check the accuracy of the text • understand graphics, symbols and other devices used in the text • evaluate the effectiveness of the proposed recommendations or solutions
Notices and signs	• Information, instructions, directions, and warnings, which are usually short and presented in such a way as to attract attention • Signs usually use nonverbal features	• Understand the message in signs and evaluate the effectiveness of the message • Explain how the meaning is created • Note abbreviations used and visual or graphic features • Make connections between verbal and visual signs
Catalogs and directories	• Books or lists of names, items, products, etc., usually presented alphabetically under headings • May be presented in paper form, on microfiche, or computerized onto database • Often uses specialized symbols and abbreviations	• Use alphabetical and numerical ordering with ease • Use telephone and street directories, atlases, content pages, indices, and databases • Become familiar with classification systems (e.g., the Dewey system, keyboards, species)
Letters	• Formal and informal written communication of ideas to another person or organization	• Distinguish between personal and business letters • Understand the conventions of letter writing
Diaries	• Records of appointments and things to do • Recountings of events and/or thoughts and ideas, usually sequential and nearly always private and personal (sometimes diaries of famous people become available for study)	• Discuss the style and type of writing used in diaries • Appreciate the voice and tone of the writing and explain why they are used • Understand the private nature of the writing
Advertising and propaganda	• Persuasive announcements in the media or in public places • Propaganda is usually issued by organized groups in a systematic way	• Note the different language features used to persuade the reader (e.g., vocabulary, register, metaphor) • Note other features such as repetition, music, pace, graphics, fonts, color • See the values and concerns behind the text and be able to decode bias • Distinguish fact from hype

Source: New Zealand Ministry of Education. (1997). *Reading for life: The learner as a reader.* Wellington, New Zealand: Learning Media.

"Your Turn" sections, and chapter questions in this text. Other organizational devices are shared in Table 8–3.

Bakken and Whedon (2002) argued that reading comprehension is enhanced when the reader is aware of the structure of the text being read. Students who use their knowledge of text-structure tend to comprehend and recall more than students who do not, and students can be taught to identify different top-level struc-

TABLE 8–3
Organizational Devices in Texts

Feature	Example	Teaching Strategy
Introductory: Overview; establishes purpose.	This unit will cover three parts of government: executive, judiciary, and legislature.	Explain role of overview as advance organizer.
Definitional: Defines meaning of a word.	Politics is the art of decision making.	Relate definition to observations or to concrete examples.
Description: sets the scene, provides for visualization.	The governor's mansion is on a hill overlooking the harbor.	Have students draw a picture or diagram or simply imagine the scene.
Narrative: Tells a story (character, plot, time, location, problem, or goal).	In the early 1800s, the governor tried to solve the rum problem.	Have students answer wh-questions (who, what, when, where, how, and sometimes why).
Expository or explanator: Explains or informs (steps in a process, chronology, directions, cause-effect, problem-solution, question-answer).	The soldiers were corrupt, which led them to exploit the people they controlled.	Outline the sequence of events; search for cause-effect relationships.
Summary and conclusions: Restates essential ideas; frequently introduced with the phrase *to summarize* or *in conclusion* or *thus*, *therefore*, or *to review*.	Thus, we can see that Australia is an outstanding member of the Commonwealth.	Test to determine whether the (a) summary is comprehensive and (b) conclusions follow from the evidence.
Transitional: Relates what preceded to what follows; some signaling words are *however*, *meanwhile*, *although*, *nevertheless*.	Now that we have covered the geography and history of Australia, we are reading to consider its economy.	Explain that this type of paragraph prepares the reader for what is coming next.

Source: Singer, H., & Simonson, S. (2004). Comprehension and instruction in learning from a text. In D. Lapp, J. Flood, & N. Farnan (Eds.), *Content area reading and learning: Instructional strategies* (p. 55). Mahwah, NJ: Lawrence Erlbaum Associates. Reprinted by permission.

tures. Because reading scholars have argued that knowledge of expository text structure can help children to comprehend text, we will describe four types of organizational patterns delineated by Niles (1970) and model the ways in which they may be effectively used for reading instruction. These in turn can be used in your teaching.

Cause and Effect

This pattern of text organization answers the questions "What is the cause of . . .?" and "What are the effects of . . .?" Cause-and-effect text organization is found in many content area materials.

The following selection illustrates the cause-and-effect pattern. As you are reading the passage, see if you can identify the main causes and effects discussed by the author.

Excerpt of Cause and Effect Text: From "Me" to "Us"

The last half of the 1970s has been called the "me" era, with people focusing a great deal of attention on themselves. Sociologists argue about the ultimate effect of this egocentric fascination. They are concerned with whether or not this lack of concern for greater social and political issues and disregard for traditional values, including the importance of the family, planning for the future, and so on, will have a deteriorating influence on our society. While the social scientists may disagree in many of these areas, one benefit of the "me" concentration on which they do agree is the increased awareness of the importance of physical fitness, often including fastidious attention to diet and exercise.

The American people now recognize that what they eat and what they do determine how they look. The number of calories taken into the body every day must equal the number of calories that the body burns in a day in order to maintain a certain weight. If an excessive number of calories is consumed, the body will turn these "leftovers" into fat, adding body weight. If the body burns more calories than it is fed, it will use the extra fat for energy, thus reducing body weight. There are, of course, some sources of calories that are more beneficial to the body's functions than others. The calories in protein sources such as meat, eggs, and fish provide more nutrition than the same number of calories supplied by sugar.

For people to be healthy and maintain a desirable weight, they must balance the kind and number of calories they take in with the energy they use. This is one reason so many Americans have begun regular exercise programs. Health clubs and spas that offer exercise classes and weight reduction machines have become very popular. Quite often, people find that it is easier to exercise in groups than alone. In fact, health clubs have become new places to meet people and develop friendships. Perhaps the sociologists should stop arguing and start exercising. They may find that the "me" generation has inadvertently become the "us" generation.

To introduce cause and effect texts, Ms. Donnelly printed the text on a transparency and displayed it on the overhead. Ms. Donnelly likes to teach using an overhead projector so that she can look at her students while they work. She first read the entire text through as a shared reading (see chapter 11). On her second

Your Turn

Please retrace the text to identify the primary causes and their effects that are noted. Include them in the following table.

Causes	Effects

Check your responses with the ones that the students in Ms. Donnelly's class identified.

Causes	Effects
The "me" generation	Focus on self
Become more interested in physical appearance	Learn how to improve appearance
Diet and exercise are important	Join clubs to exercise
Make new acquaintances	Become the "us" generation

reading, she paused periodically and asked her students if the statement was a cause or an effect. She wanted to ensure that all of her students participated in this whole-class activity, so she provided each student with two 3 × 5 cards. One card was yellow and had the word "cause" printed on it. The other card was green and had the word "effect" printed on it. As they worked through the text, Ms. Donnelly paused several times and provided the students with an opportunity to hold up one of their cards. She could easily assess their understanding of causes and effects with this strategy. Together the class created the preceding cause and effect "T" chart.

During their study of cause and effect text structures, Ms. Donnelly also used the social studies textbook during her guided reading groups (see chapter 11). This provided her an opportunity to ensure that students understood the text structure and the content. She also used cause-and-effect texts regularly as her shared reading material and used the response cards to continually assess her students' understanding of increasingly complex texts.

Comparison and Contrast

By identifying how things are alike and how they are different, comparison–contrast discourse goes beyond offering simple descriptions by presenting relationships between and among topics. Text patterns of this sort provide answers to the questions "How are _____ and _____ alike?", "How are _____ and _____ different?", and "How are these things related to each other or to another factor?"

The following passage presents a comparison–contrast format for a discussion of certain aspects of life in England versus life in the United States. The outline presented after the passage categorizes in a systematic way the details of the written discourse. As you are reading, jot down similarities and differences you identify between transportation modes in England and the United States.

English Feet vs. American Cars

Just because we speak the same language and have common ancestors doesn't mean we live the same life. Life in England is different from life in the United States. It is different in all the obvious ways: their money doesn't look like ours, and they use different words than we do to name various items found in daily life. Life in England is also different from life in the United States in many subtle ways. One of these ways is in the methods of transportation.

Although it is obvious that the English drive on the opposite side of the street than we do, it may not be quite so evident that there are fewer cars per capita in England and fewer women drivers. While it is almost unheard of for an American over 18 to lack a driver's license, many English people, especially middle-aged women, have never learned to drive. How do they manage to get around, you ask? They use their feet! Both for walking and for pedaling bicycles, feet are a much more useful body part in England than they are in the United States. English feet often walk or pedal the rest of the body to a bus stop, train station, or, if they are London feet, to a "tube" (subway) station. Public transportation in England is more efficient and convenient to use than most such systems in the United States. It must be remembered, however, that England is much smaller than America, and consequently, it is perhaps easier to have a more effective national train system.

DID YOU NOTICE . . .
Did you notice how holding up these cards is a nonthreatening way to assess student learning? No students are put on the spot and called on to respond in front of the whole class. Teachers can make mental notes or jot down the names of students who may not be holding up the right colored card and teach this concept to them at a later time. Using this card system is also a great way to spice up classroom discussions as students defend their thinking.

Not only do the methods of transporting oneself differ from country to country, the means of taking children from place to place differ as well. In the United States, the safety-conscious parent straps the child into a car seat (officially called an infant-restraining device) to ensure that the child does not bounce around inside the car, either from youthful exuberance or from sudden use of the brake. The fancier and more complex the car seat, the more sophisticated and expensive the car, the higher the status enjoyed by the American parent. Those English women who are using their feet to get from place to place obviously do not strap an infant-restraining device on their backs. No, they push their young loved ones in front of them, lying in or strapped into the English child's traditional mode of transport—the perambulator or pram, as it is more commonly called. When these mothers walk down to the local shops pushing their babies in front of them, one somehow knows that there will indeed always be an England.

Please identify the similarities and differences you noted in the text you just read.

To teach her students about comparison–contrast text structures, Ms. Donnelly used a simple graphic organizer with attributes that would be found in the reading listed on the left. This graphic organizer was created on chart paper hung on the wall. During her shared reading of the text passage, Ms. Donnelly paused periodically and asked students if the attribute was shared or not. She recorded their responses on the chart paper:

	Shared	Unshared
Drive on the right		x
Speak English	x	
Frequently walk		x
Frequently use car seats		x
Travel for work	x	

Following the whole-class shared reading and discussion, Ms. Donnelly provided each student with the "Different and Alike" graphic organizer and asked them to reread the text and identify as many similarities and differences that they could. The comparison–contrast outline from the students in Ms. Donnelly's class is listed as follows. Please compare your outline with theirs.

English	American
Differences	
drive on the left	drive on the right
fewer cars	more cars
fewer women drivers	more women drivers
use feet more	use feet less
more efficient public transportation	less efficient public transportation
push children in prams	strap children into car seats
Similarities	
speak English	speak English
English ancestors	English ancestors
must travel to do daily business	must travel to do daily business

Chronological Order

Very often found in history texts, this discourse pattern uses sequencing of events to organize information. The obvious questions answered by chronologies are "What happened first? Second? Third?" and "What is the consequence of these events?" Time-order relation texts are among the easiest to recognize and comprehend because of their straightforward, time line style of organization. As you are reading, note the passage of time and how the author uses signal words to indicate the chronological order of events.

They Found Her

When the Nazi's arrived, they searched the house. First downstairs and then upstairs. They looked behind furniture and under beds. As one soldier worked his way through the house, searching each nook and cranny, he noticed a small crack in the wall. He knocked. The wall sounded hollow. Using his night stick, he hit the wall. The hinges on the hidden door squeaked. The baby startled, but didn't make a sound. The soldier hit the wall again, and the door gave in. The family in hiding was discovered.

Upon their discovery, the family was taken to the ghetto. But they weren't there long. They were soon "processed" which meant that they were assigned to a transport car and sent to a concentration camp.

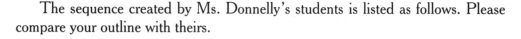

Please identify the time sequences you noted in the text you just read.

The sequence created by Ms. Donnelly's students is listed as follows. Please compare your outline with theirs.

    a. Nazi's arrive
    b. Search downstairs, then upstairs
    c. The Nazi's found the family hiding
    d. The family was taken away

To teach the chronological text structure, Ms. Donnelly asked her students to list, in order, the events detailed in the text. She then asked them to create a visual timeline and provided them pictures to put in order according to the events outlined in the text. To further reinforce the time-order relation text pattern, Ms. Donnelly asked her students to write their own chronology or draw a timeline of their own lives or the history of their school, town, or state.

Simple Listing (Taxonomy)

Description and classification of characteristics are typical of the listing style of text organization. This format provides information about a subject in a taxonomic structure, progressing from the most general aspects to the more detailed ones. Pertinent questions concerning a taxonomic pattern of discourse are "What kind of thing is _____?" "What makes it so?", and "What varieties of it are there?"

The tree or branching style of outline is useful for demonstrating the relationships among the attributes of subjects discussed in a listing format. Read the following text excerpt. See if you can create a tree diagram delineating the major ideas and their relationship after reading the excerpt.

The Piano

Of all the keyboard instruments, the piano is perhaps the most popular, both for concert and for home use. The reason for this may be its availability and versatility, which allows the player to interpret it with an unlimited range of nuance and flexibility.

The acoustic piano and the electronic piano are the two main piano categories. The acoustic piano has been around for centuries while the electronic piano was developed much later.

There are two main types of acoustic piano—the grand piano and the upright piano. The difference in their shape controls the difference in their musical action and thus in the quality of the sound they produce.

The grand piano (which comes in two versions, the baby grand and the concert grand) houses the strings in a wing-shaped body that stands parallel to the floor. The hammers hit the strings in an upward movement, coming below the strings. This is the piano seen most often in concert halls.

The upright piano, as the name suggests, is box-shaped and stands with its strings in a vertical position. The action of the hammers in an upright piano is a forward motion. This piano is found most often in homes or classrooms because it takes up less space.

In addition to the acoustic pianos, the modern era's fascination with amplification, electronics, and computers has produced a second category of piano—the electronic piano. Some have midi capabilities with computers and others are stand alone electric keyboards. These developments have resulted in a wide variety of electric keyboards that are used throughout the field of popular music.

Please create a tree-type listing of key ideas from the excerpt you just read.

The taxonomy created by Ms. Donnelly's class is listed in Diagram 8.1. Please compare your taxonomy with theirs.

Diagram 8.1   Keyboard Instruments

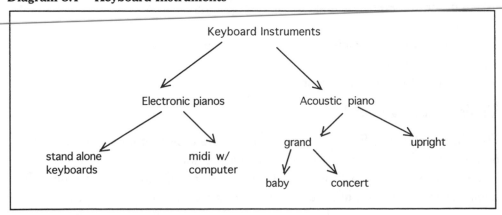

Ms. Donnelly teaches her students about this type of text structure by providing students with an incomplete outline and asking them to complete the blanks as (or after) they read. She asks students to elaborate on the simple tree diagram by providing additional information for each branch. This additional information is the response to the question "What makes it so?" In preparation for writing an original essay in the listing format, Ms. Donnelly asks students to organize information into a taxonomic diagram and discuss it with a peer before writing.

By encouraging students to become familiar with text structures, you will be providing them with valuable tools for attacking many types of content text structures that might otherwise be overwhelming because of the complexity of the information discussed. The ability to reduce the discourse to an elemental outline form may provide the key to unlocking its meaning.

DID YOU NOTICE . . .
Did you notice that encouraging students to take notes using these text structures will help students in their writing as well? Once students are comfortable using these graphic organizers as a tool for notetaking in content area reading, students can use them as a prewriting activity to organize thoughts when responding to narrative and nonnarrative texts.

HOW CAN CLASSROOM INSTRUCTION ENHANCE CONTENT AREA READING AND LEARNING?

Reading in Social Studies

Social studies draws its content from several fields, including anthropology, economics, civics, geography, sociology, and psychology. The selection in Figure 8–1, taken from an elementary social studies text, incorporates history, geography, government, sociology, and language.

It is quite common to find passages with information integrated from several disciplines in social studies texts. Social studies stresses the roles and responsibilities of the individual in society and encourages the study of the interactions of people.

To explore successfully the vast amount of knowledge included in social studies, students need to learn not only the factual content but also the skills that are needed to become independent learners of this information. In the following pages, we provide you with information about the skills related to reading in social studies and discuss the processes for implementing these skills in the classroom.

Teaching Social Studies Vocabulary

Reading a social studies text requires students to read about and comprehend concepts that may be unfamiliar to them. This problem is complicated by the different types of vocabulary the student will encounter. Because our students' experiences in social studies do not come close to those of the textbook writers, it is easy to see why vocabulary development is an important issue. It is also important to realize that you need to be selective when deciding which words to teach. Words that have high utility and are essential for comprehension are the ones that should be taught. The potential vocabulary difficulties in social studies are common to all content areas. They are (a) technical vocabulary (words unique to the content area), (b) specialized vocabulary (common words that have a specific meaning in the content area), (c) words with multiple meanings, and (d) acronyms and abbreviations. Examples of these vocabulary problems are presented in the following.

Vocabulary Problems in Social Studies

Vocabulary	Examples
1. Technical vocabulary	socialism, republic
2. Specialized vocabulary	court, Third World
3. Multiple meanings	state, cycle
4. Abbreviations and acronyms	sq mi, NATO

Figure 8–1   Example of social studies text. From *World History Journey Across Time* (2005), p. 28. Glencoe/McGraw-Hill. Reprinted with permission.

Assyrian Empire

NATIONAL GEOGRAPHIC

Using Geography Skills

The Assyrians conquered lands from Mesopotamia to Egypt.
1. What major rivers were part of the Assyrian Empire?
2. What geographical features may have kept the Assyrians from expanding their empire to the north and south?

▲ Assyrian winged bull

The Assyrians were ferocious warriors. To attack cities, they tunneled under walls or climbed over them on ladders. They loaded tree trunks onto movable platforms and used them as battering rams to knock down city gates. Once a city was captured, the Assyrians set fire to its buildings. They also carried away its people and goods.

Anyone who resisted Assyrian rule was punished. The Assyrians drove people from their lands and moved them into foreign territory. Then they brought in new settlers and forced them to pay heavy taxes.

A Well-Organized Government Assyrian kings had to be strong to rule their large empire. By about 650 B.C., the empire stretched from the **Persian Gulf** (PUHR•zhuhn) in the east to Egypt's Nile River in the west. The capital was at **Nineveh** (NIH•nuh•vuh) on the Tigris River.

Assyrian kings divided the empire into **provinces** (PRAH•vuhn•suhs), or political districts. They chose officials to govern each province. These officials collected taxes and enforced the king's laws.

Assyrian kings built roads to join all parts of their empire. Government soldiers were posted at stations along the way to protect traders from bandits. Messengers on government business used the stations to rest and change horses.

Life in Assyria The Assyrians lived much like other Mesopotamians. Their writing was based on Babylonian writing, and they worshiped many of the same gods. Their laws were similar, but lawbreakers often faced more brutal and cruel punishments in Assyria.

As builders, the Assyrians showed great skill. They erected large temples and palaces that they filled with wall carvings and statues. The Assyrians also produced and collected literature. One of the world's first libraries was in Nineveh. It held 25,000 tablets of stories and songs to the gods. Modern historians have learned much about ancient civilizations from this library.

Assyria's cruel treatment of people led to many rebellions. About 650 B.C., the Assyrians began fighting each other over who would be their next king. A group of people called the Chaldeans (kahl•DEE•uhns) seized the opportunity to rebel. They captured Nineveh in 612 B.C., and the Assyrian Empire soon crumbled.

✔ Reading Check Explain Why were the Assyrian soldiers considered brutal and cruel?

CHAPTER 1   The First Civilizations

The following list presents several suggestions to help you develop the language/reading skills necessary to master social studies vocabulary (e.g., Brassell & Flood, 2004). The specific vocabulary strategies presented in chapter 6 are also applicable here.

1. Use concrete supplementary materials (realia) such as pictures, maps, globes, models, films, recordings, and exhibits to demonstrate and reinforce vocabulary and concepts.

2. Examine new words as they appear in the text. The students can learn the meanings of such words through discussion, contextual analysis, and using the glossary or a dictionary.

3. Point out words that involve the concepts of distance, space, or time: *beyond* and *age*, for example. This provides a concrete base for abstract concepts.

4. Discuss word derivations and forms of words. For example, *democracy* comes from two Greek roots (*demos*, meaning "people," and *kratos*, meaning "rule") and has several forms: *Democrat, democratic, democratization, democratically*. Use base words that have meaning to students.

5. Introduce social slogans, figures of speech, and slang.
   a. End the Draft!
   b. Uncle Sam Wants You!
   c. It's a bummer.

6. Have the students categorize words according to historical periods, for example, *Whig, carpetbagger, pharaoh*. Be sure that students have an understanding of the period; otherwise, the words will be meaningless.

7. Develop word histories of key words to use as mnemonic devices. A mnemonic device is an aid that helps you to remember something. It is derived from Mnemon, a companion of Achilles who functioned as Achilles' memory. Encourage students to develop their own mnemonic devices.

Comprehending Pictorial Data.   Social studies facts and information are frequently supplemented or explained by maps, diagrams, pictures, charts, graphs, and time lines. Too often, teachers assume that these graphic aids are self-evident, when, in fact, they frequently require instruction for the student to be able to comprehend them. You are likely to encounter illustrations similar to those in Figures 8–2 to 8–5. Many texts present graphics but do not require students to use them or fail to explain them sufficiently so that they can be used. You should point out to your students that graphics can help them to understand concepts and facts presented in the text. To ensure that each student is able to analyze the information being presented, ask the following questions about each illustration:

1. What is being illustrated?
2. What is the purpose of the illustration?
3. What information is provided by the caption, key, symbols, and scales?
4. What do you know about this topic?
5. What do you wonder about this topic and/or illustration?

When reading social studies materials, students are required to draw heavily on several comprehension skills, such as understanding cause-and-effect relationships, making comparisons, detecting propaganda, differentiating fact from opinion, sequencing, and conceptualizing time, space, and place relationships.

Cause and Effect.   Facts, events, and interactions in social studies texts are often depicted through cause-and-effect relationships. Children need to be taught to recognize such relationships and to identify the cause(s) and the

Alphabets

Modern Characters	Ancient Phoenician	Ancient Hebrew	Ancient Greek	Early Roman
A				
B				
G				
D				
E				
F				
Z				
TH				
I				

▲ The Phoenician idea of an alphabet was passed on to the Greeks and then the Romans. It is the basis for the English alphabet today. *Which modern letter most closely resembles its Phoenician character?*

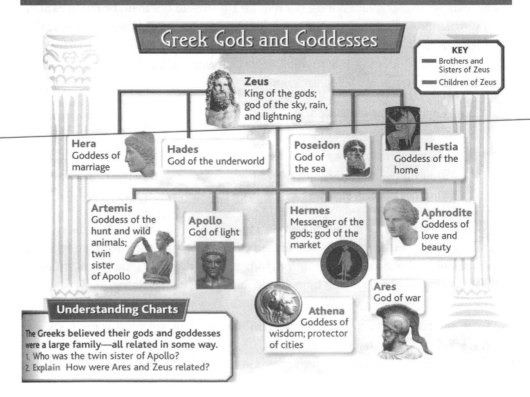

Greek Gods and Goddesses

KEY
- Brothers and Sisters of Zeus
- Children of Zeus

Zeus King of the gods; god of the sky, rain, and lightning

Hera Goddess of marriage

Hades God of the underworld

Poseidon God of the sea

Hestia Goddess of the home

Artemis Goddess of the hunt and wild animals; twin sister of Apollo

Apollo God of light

Hermes Messenger of the gods; god of the market

Aphrodite Goddess of love and beauty

Ares God of war

Athena Goddess of wisdom; protector of cities

Understanding Charts

The Greeks believed their gods and goddesses were a large family—all related in some way.
1. Who was the twin sister of Apollo?
2. Explain How were Ares and Zeus related?

Figure 8—4   Example of map with legend and symbols in social studies text. From *World History Journey Across Time* (2005), p. 293. Glencoe/McGraw-Hill. Reprinted with permission.

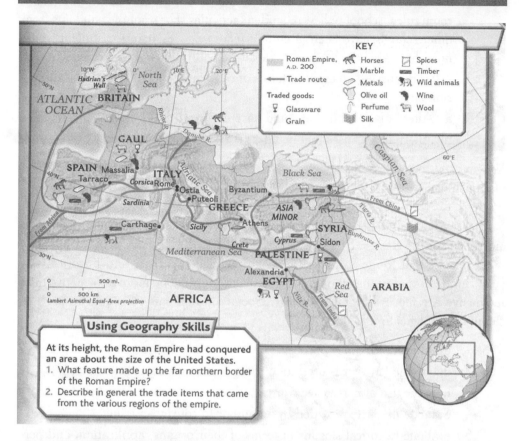

Figure 8—5   Example of timeline in social studies text. From *World History Journey Across Time* (2005), p. 568. Glencoe/McGraw-Hill. Reprinted with permission.

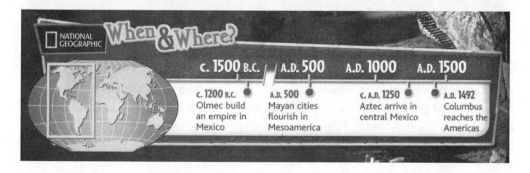

effect(s). The following suggestions and activities can help you to develop these skills in your students:

1. Have your students list causes and effects based on social studies reading.

Cause	Effects
Attack on Pearl Harbor	Destruction
	Death
	Declaration of war

2. Prepare charts for key events, listing their causes and effects.

3. Discuss current events or news items in terms of cause and effect.

4. Make discussions relevant to the students. Topics may come from classroom rules, school policy, or student activities. For example, students from other schools have been attending school dances (cause); students must now show a school ID card to be admitted to a school dance (effect).

5. After discussing an event in terms of cause and effect, have a class discussion on
   a. Alternative effects that could have occurred.
   b. Alternative causes that could have resulted in this effect.

Activity 1 at the end of this chapter is designed to help you teach cause-and-effect relationships.

Propaganda. Students are generally taught to recognize propaganda in English and social studies classes. Students must be made aware that not all propaganda is as obvious as that found in advertisements, political speeches, and historical slogans. Subtle uses of propaganda in writing that appears to be more informative than persuasive are more difficult to detect. Social studies materials can be used to encourage students to

1. examine an author's purpose.

2. determine key words used to introduce propaganda.

3. note the use of persuasive words.

4. evaluate the facts provided by an author to convey an issue.

5. evaluate historical slogans in terms of their origins, application, and persuasive appeal.

Children should be urged to look for propaganda in both written and oral forms. Activity 4 at the end of this chapter can be used as a propaganda-detection activity for your classroom.

Comparison. Social studies materials are well suited to having students learn by making comparisons. Children should be encouraged to make comparisons between governments, countries, customs, policies, land formations, languages, climates, religions, and people. Have your students look for both similarities and differences in the materials they read. Plan classroom activities that will help your students become accustomed to making comparisons. Some of these activities might include the following:

1. Have the students compare the customs, culture, and language of several different countries.

2. Have the students compare historical documents from different countries. For example, you may want them to compare the Magna Carta with the Bill of Rights.

3. Have the students compare current modes of transportation with those of a specific period from the past.

4. Have the students compare the governments of two or more countries.

Sequencing. History evolves chronologically as time passes. Students need to become aware that they are part of history and the sequencing of historical events. In addition, students must acquire an understanding of the historical eras and how these overlap with historical movements. By using activities at the end of this chapter, you can continuously encourage children to develop a chronological perspective by

1. discussing present-day occurrences while identifying historical factors.
2. developing historical time lines.
3. reviewing events that have occurred repeatedly throughout history: assassination, war, treason. What human characteristics are responsible for the continued perpetuation of these behaviors? What societal factors contribute to human nature?

Differentiating Fact From Opinion. Being able to differentiate fact from opinion is an important reading skill for students of all ages in all content areas. To develop the concept of fact versus opinion, have the students analyze each other's statements in any class discussion. Demonstrate how an opinion can be strengthened when it is supported by facts. Separating fact from opinion is an important skill that must be developed by students to enable them to become wise consumers and independent decision makers. Too often, children have the notion that, if an adult makes a statement or if something can be found in printed material, it must be true. Students should be encouraged to evaluate supporting premises. Some ways in which you can help your students to differentiate fact from opinion are the following:

1. Help students become aware that words and phrases such as *perhaps, think, in my opinion, maybe, one possibility,* or *my beliefs suggest* often indicate statements of opinion.
2. Have students use reference materials to verify the accuracy of information that may be based fully or partially on opinion or conjecture.
3. Provide paragraphs or short selections that the students can use to practice the skill of distinguishing fact from opinion.
4. Encourage students to examine the author's point of view.

Conceptualizing Relationships. To understand and appreciate social studies information, students must be able to conceptualize time, space, and place relationships. You may help your students to develop an understanding of these concepts by instituting activities such as

1. having students compare different aspects of their city today with those of their counterparts 50 or 100 years ago.
2. discussing the implications of advanced technology with respect to transportation and communication.
3. illustrating variations in life-span expectancy and world-time evolution.
4. having students compare old and ancient maps of regions with modern maps.
5. having students develop a time line showing important dates and events in their lives.

Activity 3 at the end of this chapter will assist your students in understanding time, space, and place relationships.

Teaching Social Studies

Both the activities suggested in this text and those at the end of the chapter will aid you in teaching your students to read social studies texts, evaluate the new information, and respond in oral and written forms.

In earlier chapters we discussed the directed reading teaching activity (DRTA). The following is a sample social studies DRTA about the start of Islam. A similar format can be adapted for any content area subject. The DRTA is an effective strategy to use when teaching content area material (Stauffer & Harrell, 1975).

Directed Reading Teaching Activity

I. Background and Motivation

Ask students to take 2 minutes and write words and phrases they associate with the word *religion*. At the end of the 2 minutes, have students share their ideas with peers. Then ask the pairs to combine their ideas and group them, labeling each category (e.g., according to people, ceremonies, special days, and denominations). Finally, ask the pairs to share their categories and the words associated with each. In 15 to 20 minutes you will have a wealth of information indicating your students' background knowledge of religion.

Now as you introduce new information, you can consciously link it to students' prior knowledge. You might say something such as the following: "Most of you know that there are many different religions with different beliefs. But, at least in this country, most people worship one God. There was a time when people worshiped other things. Look at this stone. [Show students a small black stone.] This is similar to a stone that people once worshiped in Arabia. A meteorite had fallen to the earth in Mecca, Arabia. The people put this stone in a temple called the Kaaba. Around the Kaaba were 360 idols (religious objects) that the people also worshiped. The people of Arabia (Arabs) came to think of Mecca as a holy place.

"Can you think of any reasons why a meteorite might have been worshiped by the Arabs?" (People didn't know what it was; it came from the sky, the "heavens." There were no other stones like it; it was unique.)

II. Vocabulary

A. *Peninsula*—"A peninsula is an area of land that is almost completely surrounded by water. Peninsula comes from two Latin words: *paene*, meaning 'almost,' and *insula*, meaning 'isle or small island.' Can you think of any areas close to us that could be called a peninsula?" (Coronado, Baja California)

B. *Meteorite*—"A meteorite is a piece of stone or metal that has fallen to earth from space. As a matter of fact, the word comes from the Greek word *meteoron*, meaning 'a thing in the air.' Most meteorites never make it to earth; they burn up or disintegrate in space before they get here. You might be interested to know that the largest meteorite ever found on earth weighs about 132,300 pounds. This meteorite is in Africa. You can be glad you weren't standing around when that one hit!"

C. *Caravan*—"A caravan is a group of people traveling together for safety, usually through the desert. You might also think of it as a convoy. (Remember the movie and/or the song *Convoy*? There were many trucks traveling together.) One

DID YOU NOTICE ...
Did you notice that bringing in realia will help your students understand difficult concepts and vocabulary? Remember, your students may come from a variety of backgrounds and some vocabulary may be too abstract and unfamiliar to comprehend. Bringing in the real thing or something close to it will help students see and understand the concept or word.

little trick to remember the word might be *car* and *van* in *caravan*. These word parts don't really mean *car* and *van*, but you know that *car* and *van* have to do with traveling. This will help you remember the meaning of the word."

D. *Idol* (on board: Britney Spears, Usher, Ricky Martin)—"An idol is something used as an object of worship. (Remember the stone we saw earlier?) It usually is a picture or an image of a religious person or object. Actually, the word *idol* means 'image' (from the Latin, *idolum*).

Today, idol doesn't always have a religious meaning. It can mean anyone or anything that many people greatly admire or adore. Look at the names on the board. Some people call them 'teenage idols' or 'rock idols.' What do you think this means?" (You may have the students add or delete names or just discuss the concept in terms of the definition generally.)

E. *Persecuted*—"Did you ever feel as if someone was picking on you or was really out to get you for something? If you did, you felt persecuted. To persecute is to harass constantly. Suppose your favorite color was red and you wore a lot of red clothes. Now suppose that I hate red. Every time you wore a red shirt, I either tried to rip it off you or color it green with my pen. I also followed you around, calling you the 'Red Menace' and laughing at you. You'd be absolutely correct if you said I was persecuting you. Being persecuted isn't much fun."

F. *Ministry* (on board: minister, administer, administration)—"You've probably all heard the word *minister*, referring to a religious person. Ministry is the job or profession of a minister. You may not know that both words come from the Latin word *minis*, meaning servant. A minister is a servant of God and a servant of the people. Ministry could then be defined as the job or profession of a person who is a religious 'servant.'" (You might also point out that someone who administers first aid is serving someone. An administration is the people who manage or serve an organization—the administration of your school.)

G. *Vision* (on board: television, (in)visible, visit—"You can see that many English words come from Greek or Latin words. For example, *vis* in Latin means 'has seen.' All these words have to do with seeing. (You see television; being visible or invisible is being able or not able to be seen; visit is to go see someone.) When a person has a vision, they see something or someone that is not really there; other people usually can't see it. Some people may think of it as a powerful dream while you're awake or hallucinating."

III. Springboard Questions

    A. Why did Mohammed start a new religion?

    B. What is the most important city to Moslems? Why?

    C. Why is the Battle of Tours important?

    D. Why is the city of Baghdad important?

IV. Silent Reading

V. Comprehension Questions

    A. What events persuaded Mohammed to start a new religion?

    B. Why is Mecca an important city to the Moslems?

C. Explain why Mohammed had to leave Mecca.

D. Why did Moslems want to follow the teachings of Islam?

E. Explain why the Battle of Tours was significant.

F. What was the name of the Frankish leader at the Battle of Tours?

G. What city did the Arabs build on the Tigris River? Why?

H. The Franks and the Moslems both conquered many people in many lands. What was different about the effects of their conquests? (Hint: Remember, the Franks were barbarians.)

I. The Kaaba is _____

J. The Koran is _____

VI. Optional Activity

This activity can be used to demonstrate how word parts can be used to form common words that the students already know. Draw a tree on the board. On the trunk of the tree, put a common root word. Students fill in the branches with words from the root word; example: *ped* from the Latin, meaning "foot" (see Figure 8–6).

Other possible root words are:

> *graph, graphy* (from the Greek), meaning write: photograph, photography, phonograph, autograph, biography, stenographer, geography, bibliography, paragraph, lithograph, telegraph
>
> *tele* (from the Greek), meaning far, distant: telegram, telegraph, telephone, telephoto, telescope, television

Through a lesson such as this you can integrate reading with social studies materials. This DRTA (a) included unusual and interesting facts relevant to the material, (b) discussed vocabulary by relating it to the students' lives, (c) offered exam-

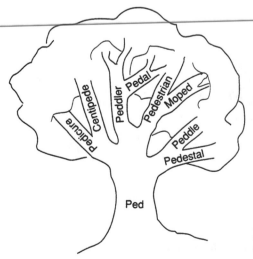

FIGURE 8–6 Tree used to teach root word derivations.

ples of structural analysis and word derivations, (d) used visual aids, and (e) included a follow-up or optional activity.

One of your primary goals as a classroom teacher should be the integration of reading and language activities into the content area curriculum. By emphasizing the various aspects of social studies texts discussed in this section, you can foster and nurture this integration of skills.

Reading in Mathematics

Mathematics is far more than basic computation. The reading and studying of mathematics requires both understanding and development of specific concepts and principles. Mathematics instruction should have two purposes:

1. To enable the child to develop an understanding of the patterns that are used to formulate concepts and principles.
2. To enable the child to solve problems.

The accomplishment of these objectives will ensure both problem mastery and conceptual understanding.

Reading in math is very different from reading in other content areas, and mastery of the language of mathematics is essential to accomplishing the preceding objectives.

> When reading a mathematics book, the student is actually reading several kinds of language: (a) the language that appears in a mathematics lesson and rarely elsewhere, such as the vocabulary words *rhombus* and *equation*; (b) words that have multiple meanings with very specific meanings in mathematics, such as *prime* and *set*; and (c) the language of symbols and numbers. (Curry, 1996, p. 229)

As in the mastery of any other language, the child hears, explores, discusses, experiments, uses, and tests words that might be part of the conceptual framework of this language.

To meet the dual objectives of understanding and problem solving, a child must have some competence in reasoning, a process that involves the ability to reorder known data in an attempt to derive new relationships. Reasoning is closely related to comprehension because both entail the ability to detect problematic clues, to hypothesize, and to evaluate conclusions. Finally, in an attempt to achieve understanding and to solve problems, the child must be able to estimate and to compute. Curry (1996) explains that a strong connection exists between reading skills, understanding of mathematics vocabulary, and problem-solving capabilities. These skills can be grouped into the following five categories:

1. Recognizing and pronouncing symbols.
2. Attaching literal meaning to math concepts.
3. Attaching literal meaning to math symbols (i.e., graphs, charts, equations, and formulas).
4. Analyzing information to solve word problems.
5. Using specialized study skills (i.e., locational skills, following directions, and test-taking skills).

TABLE 8–4
Types of Vocabulary in Mathematical Language

Vocabulary Types	Examples
1. Technical words peculiar to some area of mathematics	Geometry: arc Algebra: polynomial
2. General words with mathematical meanings	prime, radical, square
3. Words that indicate a mathematical process	times, difference, subtract
4. General words that can determine a student's comprehension	after, compare, over, each, than

Mathematical Language

Reading a mathematics text requires the interpretation of two types of language. The first involves an understanding of the printed word, through which mathematical concepts are explained. The second involves interpretation of signs and symbols. Four types of vocabulary are included in the printed language of mathematics (see Table 8–4).

It is important for students to learn to recognize and understand various mathematical terms. You can facilitate this process by

1. providing concrete and abstract illustrations.
2. defining terms.
3. discussing concepts.

This understanding of the printed word is necessary as the child encounters story or word problems. Quite often, children have difficulty solving word problems, even if they have previously exhibited competence in mathematical computations. Children should be taught to analyze word problems and should be encouraged to

- read the problem carefully and begin to conceptualize.
- reread to decide what problem is posed.
- reread to detect the clues given for solving the problem.
- determine procedures for solving the problem.
- solve the problem.
- check the results.

These steps are illustrated in the following problem:

Jessie is 2 years older than Perla. Perla is 9 years old. How old is Jessie?

1. Ages?   (Problem conceptualization)
   Perla (9 years old)
   Jessie (2 years older)
2. How old is Jessie?   (Problem posed)
3. 9 years old   (Clues)
   9 years old + 2

4. Addition   (Procedure)

5. 9 years old (Solve)
   $+2$
   11 years old
   Jessie is 11 years old.

6. $11 - 2 = 9$ (Check)

In addition to vocabulary words and story problem concepts, the student of mathematics encounters the symbols and signs $=$, $\times$, $+$, $-$, and $/$, which represent the words equal, times, plus, minus, and divide.

Reading Tables, Graphs, and Pictorial Data

The study of mathematics often requires students to read and interpret tables, graphs, and other pictorial data. Figures 8–7 through 8–11 show some examples of the types of visual representations that might be found in mathematics texts. To understand and develop representations such as these, the child must understand that formulas, equations, and symbols are forms of mathematical shorthand. When attempting to read and study these representations, children should be encouraged to

1. read descriptive phrases that tell what the table or graph represents.

2. carefully study any given numbers, letters, or words to determine what has been measured.

3. read any column of data presented to gain a clearer understanding of what is being represented.

4. analyze any pictorial representations and convert them to numbers.

5. compare and draw conclusions, if requested.

Figure 8–7   **Example of pictoral graph in mathematics text. From *McGraw-Hill Mathematics, California Edition* (2002), p. 317. Reprinted with permission.**

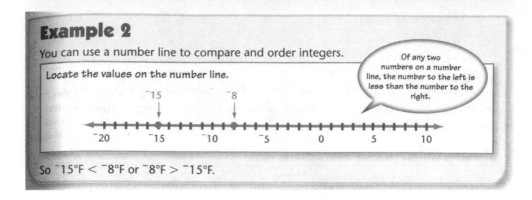

Students will have a better understanding of bar, line, circle, and picture graphs and tables and histograms if they analyze them using the five preceding steps.

Teaching Mathematics

For your students to acquire the mathematical knowledge and concepts required of them, we recommend the following teaching procedures:

1. Children need intense practice in reading, speaking, and computing the succinct language of words and symbols in mathematics.

Figure 8–9   Example of line graph in mathematics text. *From McGraw-Hill Mathematics, California Edition* (2002), p. 451. Reprinted with permission.

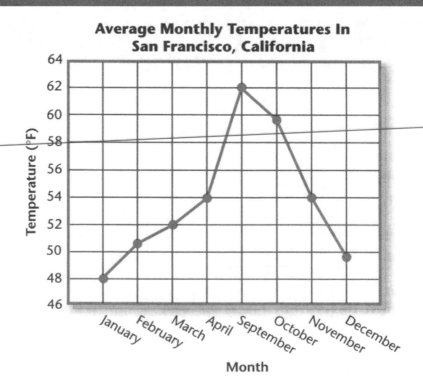

Figure 8–10 Example of Venn diagram in mathematics text. From *McGraw-Hill Mathematics, California Edition* (2002), p. 650. Reprinted with permission.

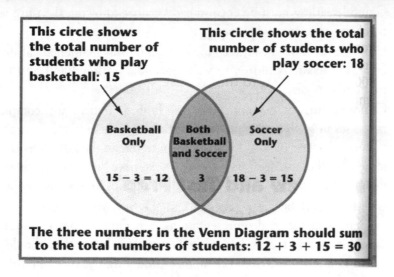

This circle shows the total number of students who play basketball: 15

This circle shows the total number of students who play soccer: 18

Basketball Only

Both Basketball and Soccer

Soccer Only

15 − 3 = 12

3

18 − 3 = 15

The three numbers in the Venn Diagram should sum to the total numbers of students: 12 + 3 + 15 = 30

Figure 8–11 Example of pie chart in mathematics text. From *McGraw-Hill Mathematics, California Edition* (2002), p. 654. Reprinted with permission.

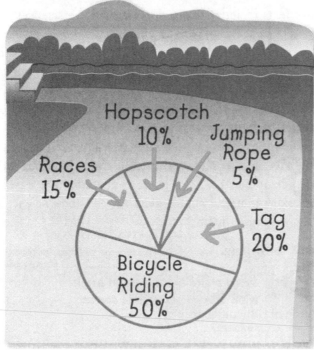

Which of these outdoor activities is your favorite?

Hopscotch 10%

Jumping Rope 5%

Races 15%

Tag 20%

Bicycle Riding 50%

2. Activities need to be designed to reinforce the technical terms, labeling processes, and symbolic representations of mathematics.

3. Children must be encouraged to read for the purpose of the problem. Careful reading must be encouraged because knowing the purpose of the problem is necessary for solving it.

4. Children must be encouraged to view symbols as mathematical shorthand. Begin by asking children to write formulas in longhand and to restate them in symbols.

5. Children must be encouraged to use both analytical and computational processes in solving story problems. Encourage them to read a problem and picture it in their minds. Then ask them to reread the last sentence to determine what they are being asked to do. Next, have them reread and determine the process, estimate an answer, and then attempt to solve the problem.

6. Children must be given practice and the opportunity to design tabular, graphic, and pictorial representations. Encourage your children to read the table or graph and determine its purpose. Next, they should analyze the columns to determine their meaning. Finally, they should read all bindings and additional notes. If they are reading a graph instead of a table, they will need help in noting the quantity or units of measurement.

7. Children must be given practice in following directions. Ask them to read or listen to the directions to gain an overview of the task. Next, have them reread each phase of the directions while thinking about the exact application. Then have them synthesize or combine all parts of the directional task and proceed.

8. Practice in reasoning, estimating, generalizing, and computing is part of a successful math program.

Reading in Science

Elementary science texts include information from all the sciences—geology, biology, ecology, physical science, botany, and chemistry. The emphasis is on involvement through observation, inquiry, and discovery. You can help your students to discover the world of science by presenting information through many types of media, including videos, pictures, observations, models, and a variety of reading materials. Whenever possible, plan activities that allow students to experience scientific phenomena through all the senses, in addition to listening, talking, and reading.

Language and reading skills are essential to a child's mastery of science materials. Students use these skills to discover scientific data, interpret factual material, and formulate generalizations. You must guide your students in developing the language and reading skills that will enable them to read their science materials. Be aware that scientific writings contain

1. a terse style of writing.
2. an extremely high readability level.
3. a density of facts and details.
4. a multitude of difficult concepts.

Many of the skills required to read science texts successfully are also common to other content areas. This makes it possible to reinforce the common reading and study skills through a variety of content material. In a science classroom specifically, your instruction should enable students to

1. understand scientific language.
2. adjust their rates of reading to match their purpose for reading.
3. utilize the various parts of their texts.
4. understand and utilize scientific formulas.
5. read graphic aids.
6. follow directions.
7. evaluate data.
8. make generalizations.
9. apply new data to solve problems.

Scientific Language

The vocabulary of science is so vast that it is sometimes overwhelming to a student. In recognition of this fact, a "hands-on" approach to science can help students develop basic concepts before they confront the technical language of science. Santa, Havens, and Harrison (1996) suggest some reasons why science readings are such a challenge for students include:

1. Most students simply lack the background knowledge to pick up a science text and learn the content. Looking back to the excerpt on page • • • from the computer manual, it is easy for us to see the importance of prior knowledge in understanding content information.

2. Often, science texts are not written clearly. Relationships between ideas are not well formulated, and concepts may not be thoroughly explained and exemplified.

3. Students have difficulty organizing the conceptually dense information in their texts. From research in the area of learning theory, we know that learning is increased if the material is internalized in some organized fashion, rather than as isolated, unrelated bits of information. However, when students read the complex material in their science texts, they tend to see much of the information as collections of facts and details and are often unaware of their association. Students are often unaware of textual organization that could help them better understand and learn the material.

It becomes the job of the teacher to build prior knowledge and to design instruction that will help students understand concepts, their relationships, and the organization of material, with the result being a more thorough understanding and learning of science content. The following excerpt illustrates the extent of the complexity in elementary science materials:

Scientists now know that atoms are made up of even smaller particles called *subatomic particles*. The **nucleus** (NOO.klee.uhs) is the very tiny center of an atom. The nucleus is made up of protons and neutrons. A **proton** (PROH.than) is a subatomic particle with a positive charge. A **neutron** (NOO.trahn) is a subatomic particle with no charge. The rest of an atom is made up of electrons, which surround the nucleus. An **electron** (ee.LEK.trahn) is a subatomic particle with a negative charge.

In 1913, Niels Bohr proposed a model of the structure of an atom. In his model, electrons circle the nucleus at fixed distances from it. The paths in which the electrons move are called *orbits*. They are also referred to as *energy levels*, because their distance from the nucleus depends on the energy of the electrons in them. Low-energy electrons orbit close to the nucleus. High-energy electrons orbit farther away.

(Excerpt from *Harcourt Science*, Grade. 5, © 2000 by Harcourt, Inc., reprinted by permission of the publisher. (p. C41)

This material might even be difficult for a competent adult reader. However, if that were the case, the reader would probably have the dictionary skills necessary to add meaning to this passage. An intermediate student may not possess the study skills necessary to interpret and comprehend this passage.

Let us examine a second excerpt:

Probably the most familiar fungi are mushrooms. Mushrooms grow in damp, dark places. You may have seen them growing on lawns after a rain, or in shaded areas such as forests. And you have probably tasted mushrooms on pizza.

Like molds, the body of a mushroom is largely mycelium, a mass of hyphae. A mushroom has parts below and above the ground. Below the ground are root-like hyphae. They obtain food in much the same way as bread mold does. That is, food is digested outside the mushroom's cells. The food is then absorbed by the hyphae.

The part of the mushroom above the ground is used for reproduction. Notice the umbrella-shaped cap at the top of the stalk. Beneath the cap are ridges called gills. Each gill contains thousands of hyphae that produce spores. In a few days a single mushroom can produce billions of spores. The spores are usually carried away by wind. If a spore lands in a favorable environment, it may grow into a new mushroom. (Jantzen & Michel, 1986, p. 103)

Although this is a relatively short selection, it contains many difficult vocabulary words (*fungi, mycelium, hyphae, gills, spores*) that may interfere with a child's comprehension. One scientific selection may introduce several new concepts. The student must learn to perceive the necessary relationships, classifications, and relevance of the material. Readers of science materials are also expected to derive information from the interpretation of pictures, maps, graphs, charts, tables, and formulas—a process that may create further difficulties for a child. You can reduce the possibility of language and conceptual difficulties by planning activities with the focus on first-hand observation. Such activities might include field trips, experiments, films, models, and pictures. Following are some additional suggestions for your classroom:

1. Discuss the scientific concept before adding the technical label.
2. Define new words with your students, giving both examples and nonexamples of the concept.
3. Have students analyze word parts, and provide them with lists or charts showing common word part meanings.

cyto	cell, hollow
logy	science, study of

hemo   blood

poly   many, much

4. Substitute common terms for technical terms. For example, *balance* may be an acceptable substitute for *equilibrium*.

5. Discuss the multiple meanings of scientific words. For example, *mass*, *core*, and *cell* all have multiple meanings.

6. Use visual aids to help students understand abstract concepts.

7. Encourage students to use context clues to help unlock the meaning of new words.

8. Develop scientific word charts that clarify and/or classify scientific terms.

Heat

radiation

conduction

convection

Or have students classify materials as liquids, solids, or gases.

Directed Reading Activity

We can also help our students understand science material if we teach them to develop a sense of control over their text. For example, you might make an overhead transparency of a portion of the textbook to demonstrate to students how they can acquire this control. This process begins with teacher demonstration and discussion, followed by guided practice, and results in students' independent application of strategies. A sample lesson might include the following:

1. Place the transparency on the overhead projector. Read it aloud, describing, as you read, how you use the writer's clues, such as introductory statements, bold face items, italics, headings, and subheadings.

2. Underline these clues as you read. This will provide visual confirmation of the many aids students have at their disposal when reading their science texts.

3. Discuss the author's organizational format, that is, how the text was developed, how paragraphs are structured, how main ideas are presented, and how details are used to provide clarifying information.

4. Evaluate the text in terms of what might cause problems for a reader. For example, the text might include poorly defined concepts, sketchy and therefore unclear information to explain a concept, and passages that are poorly written, perhaps being ambiguous or not clearly related to the point.

5. Describe what you do to understand and remember what you have read. Demonstrate some strategies your students might use. For example, you could introduce the concept of two-column notes, in which students take notes and, in essence, test themselves on the material.

6. Ask students to summarize the methods you have just demonstrated.

7. Finally, allow students to practice what you have modeled. In small groups, students can develop a classroom presentation on the strategies they used to read and comprehend a difficult passage. They can analyze the strengths and weaknesses of a chapter and/or portion of text and describe how they

thought about that text to render it more understandable. For example, they might mention that they mentally provided transitions from one idea to the next to relate pieces of information and, thus, make sense of it; they might discuss how they identified and focused on main ideas and important explanatory in formation while ignoring extraneous details.

The goal of such activities is twofold: (a) to help students become aware of their own strategies for comprehending and (b) to develop new ones, which they can actively use to gain control of their content material and the language it contains. Note that at the same time they are discussing strategies, students are working with and discussing the content to which their strategies were applied, thus gaining increased control over the science concepts.

Comprehending Scientific Language

Young children are naturally curious; therefore, many children in the primary grades are very interested in science. This interest sometimes wanes during the intermediate school years because of the difficulties students encounter in reading printed scientific material. As a classroom teacher, you may be able to lessen these difficulties by following the following suggested procedures when introducing and implementing a unit of scientific study:

A. Planning for unit implementation
   1. Begin by surveying the unit of study to identify potentially difficult vocabulary.
      a. Which words contain the stems of other words?
      b. Which words rnay cause multiple-meaning difficulty?
      c. Which words present entirely unexplained concepts?
      d. Which words can be associated with objects?
      e. Which words draw on the experiences of your students?
   2. Determine which of these words contain key bits of understanding that will be necessary for comprehension of the text.
   3. Categorize all of the remaining terms under key terms.
B. Implementing the unit
   1. List the key terms and the words categorized with them on the board or on a wall chart.
   2. Present an illustration for each word. Illustrations may be made through pictures, live specimens, and slides.
   3. Ask questions that will help youngsters to use the new words.
   4. As the unit progresses, introduce other categories of terms in the same manner.
   5. Utilize magazines, newspapers, and trade books to supplement textbook reading.
   6. Actively involve students in the unit by having them
      a. collect specimens or pictures of specimens.
      b. label specimens or picture displays.
      c. draw charts.
      d. develop models.

e. perform experiments.

f. plan field trips.

When planning an instructional unit, it is important to consider an often neglected aspect of science instruction, one that emphasizes the explanatory properties of science. Scientific information exists because, as human beings, we have attempted to understand and improve upon the world in which we live. In textbooks, scientific explanations are often buried in facts, definitions, and details. Authors create what we referred to earlier as pointless texts, which do nothing to emphasize the importance of one piece of information over another or scientific explanations over minor details. As a result, it is important to "pull out" what you most want students to glean from your unit.

Strategic planning for such a unit would include the following:

1. Decide on a question, or allow students to brainstorm potential questions related to a particular unit topic. For example, you might design a unit on plants around the question "How do plants get their food to grow?"

2. Once a question is chosen, elicit students' prior knowledge. This is an important step because students' previous conceptions, which are often misconceptions, are difficult to change and often interfere with students' learning. For example, many students believe that plants take their food directly from the soil instead of making it themselves.

3. Design classwork and discussions around strategies that can help students learn from their texts and overcome the interference of previously held conceptions. Some of these strategies include the following:

   a. Provide an advance organizer to give students an overview of what they will learn.

   b. Introduce concepts to be learned clearly and explicitly. Show how these concepts are meaningful and relevant to students' lives and to the world at large. One strategy is to introduce a topic in the form of a meaningful problem, such as how to produce nutritious crops to feed the world's starving populations.

   c. Encourage observation and discussion of the phenomena being studied.

   d. Help students understand how scientific concepts are different from their own conceptions, yet are not so different that the conflicting information cannot be comprehended.

   e. Discuss various applications of the concept to help students transfer their learning to other situations.

These are just some suggestions to help you with strategic planning of your science lessons. Several points stand out. (a) Overreliance on prior knowledge and learning of vocabulary words (labels), definitions, and details may interfere with students' learning of scientific concepts. However, it remains true that students' prior knowledge is valuable, giving you and the students a point of reference in knowing which conceptions are valid and which ones they must change. (b) Make certain that students are not merely learning terms and facts without reaching conceptual understanding of the unit topic. Be aware of the true nature of scientific inquiry, that is, exploration, and the necessity that students learn scientific concepts, not just facts, details, and definitions.

It is also important, when implementing a unit, to make certain that students have mastered the skills of locating information, interpreting formulas, and understanding graphic representations. Using these study skills, students can collect adequate data to make evaluative judgments about a topic. As you know, mastery of these skills is a key element in content area reading.

Throughout this chapter, we have attempted to help you understand clearly the application procedures necessary for implementing these integrated processes in your classroom. Mathematics, science, and social studies have been given special consideration because they are the content areas in which children seem to have the most difficulty.

As a teacher in a self-contained classroom, you may find yourself responsible for teaching art and music. Let us briefly explore the relationships between reading and the arts.

Reading and the Arts

Music and art should be a part of every classroom, even when a school is fortunate enough to have music and art specialists as part of the staff (McDonald & Fisher, 2002). Some teachers underrate the role of the humanities in a school curriculum and fail to incorporate these areas into content area subjects.

We urge you to provide both art and music activities that will foster lifetime interest, enjoyment, and pursuit of these arts in your students. The integration of reading and the arts is similar to that of other content areas. We examine each of these areas briefly.

Music

Although young children do not become involved with in-depth studies of musical theory, they do encounter new vocabulary and symbols that must be read and interpreted. Music has a technical vocabulary, as do other content area subjects, plus an array of musical symbols that have specific meanings. Music texts often contain materials similar to those in Figures 8–12 to 8–14.

Learning music is not unlike learning language. Figures 8.12 to 8.14 illustrate how music and reading include complementary skills. As you attempt to integrate music and reading, remember that children must be helped to

1. perceive the technical terms and symbols.
2. interpret and understand the symbols.
3. follow performance directions.
4. evaluate music criticisms.

Art

Elementary school children rarely have art textbooks per se; rather, they often encounter reproductions of artworks in content area texts, such as in social studies. These opportunities can be used to encourage children to compare artistic styles and trends and to show how artworks are often a reflection of their times.

Hear It Again...And Again!

Follow this map as you **listen** to *Open the Kingdom*. **Identify** the bass and other ostinatos in the piece.

CD 2–24
Open the Kingdom

by Philip Glass and David Byrne
David Byrne was one of the founding members of the rock group Talking Heads.

OPEN THE KINGDOM LISTENING MAP

Reading skills are related to art in that there is a technical vocabulary (e.g., *relief, fresco,* and *chroma*) and also because following directions is very important in art instruction. For example, students must follow directions in mixing paints or other art materials. They are also often asked to evaluate works of art. As you can see, the relationship between reading and art is very similar to that for other content area subjects.

Activities 15 through 18 at the end of this chapter will help you integrate music, art, and reading into your curriculum.

FUNCTIONAL OR COMMUNITY LITERACY

One of the primary goals of all teachers at all levels is to help students become functionally literate. As you prepare children to analyze content area materials critically, you need to include items such as job application forms, newspaper classified ads, labels on cans, tax forms, bank loan applications, insurance policies, and bank statements. Including such literacy materials in your curriculum is both desirable and legitimate because students who can use critical communication skills to meet their basic daily needs are functionally literate.

In recent years, criticism has been levied against the educational system because some adults seem unprepared to meet the challenges of daily life in a literate society. Functional literacy, therefore, has become a major emphasis in educational literature. It has also become the basis of many educational programs because students as adults often encounter difficulty when applying for schooling, housing, health care, and employment. By exploring some of these situations and materials, middle-school-aged children often become aware of the reading/language criteria needed for future success in these encounters.

The age of your students will determine what type of activities and materials are appropriate in your classroom. For example, in elementary classrooms you may have your children "play store" to learn the value of comparative shopping and handling money. A play station or new computer game manual may be of interest to intermediate-grade children, whereas older students may prefer reading drivers' educational manuals or examining job application forms.

The inclusion of functional or community literacy programs can be viewed as a first step toward building positive educational experiences for students of all ages. A well-planned literacy curriculum should provide the study of topics and skill areas that will be of value in encounters outside of school and in school-related activities. Being able to read and follow recipe directions, for example, may spark interest and competence in projects related to content area knowledge, such as the reading of graphs and measurement techniques.

Functional literacy skills should be included as an integral part of your total curriculum and should not be viewed as a separate subject. The functional literacy component should extend reading, writing, speaking, and listening skills through a well-planned unit of thematic instruction. For example, as you study "Our Community" with a group of second-graders, you may want to discuss the procedures their parents engaged in when they bought a house or rented an apartment. A question such as the following may be all that is needed to spark a lively conversation: "How did your parents find out that your home or apartment was for rent or sale?" Simulated natural language, such as interviewing a bank teller or a rental agent, may provide all the understanding needed by that age group.

You can implement a functional literacy program by making it relevant to all aspects of daily life and by integrating it into content area units of study.

ACTIVITIES THAT INTEGRATE READING AND SOCIAL STUDIES

1. The Nightly Cause-and-Effect Show

Goal: Understanding cause-and-effect relationships

Grade Level: 4–9

Construction: Have one group of students prepare a radio script or newscast to be presented to the class. The news can be of a serious or a humorous nature. Possible topics include upcoming school events, student elections, or fictional stories about students or teachers; alternatively, the news items may reflect current events. A microphone from a tape recorder or even a tin can may be used for the radio microphone.

Utilization: The audience listens to the newscast and makes a cause-and-effect chart, noting five effects of five causes. The team of newscasters determines whether they are correct.

2. Compare First, Vote Later

Goal: Making comparisons in social studies

Grade Level: 3–8

Construction: Have two or more volunteer students from the class run for political office, assuming the identities of prominent people currently campaigning for president, senator, mayor, or city councilor. The campaigning students must research their platform, using newspapers, radio, television, or the campaign headquarters.

Utilization: The class develops a record of the collected information, making a chart of each candidate's positive and negative aspects. At the end of an allotted time period, the class votes on the basis of the charted information, identifying, for example, statements of fact, opinion, and propaganda.

3. Different Perspective

Goal: Conceptualizing time, space, and place relationships

Grade Level: 4–8

Construction: Have students make a three-dimensional model of the neighborhood surrounding the school. First, if possible, have drivers take groups of students to survey the area and make general maps of it showing streets, buildings, and landmarks.

Modeling Mixture for Relief Maps

2 cups salt (500 grams)	1 cup water (250 ml)
1 cup flour (150 grams)	

Mix the ingredients until they are smooth and pliable. On a piece of plywood, draw the outline to be molded. Apply a thin layer of modeling mixture of no more than one-fourth of the thickness of plywood to the entire surface. Depress the clay where there are to be rivers and lakes, and add additional clay to form mountains. Away from a radiator or heater, the clay takes 1 week to dry. Paint with temperas and run strings to pinpoint specific locations.

Utilization: The class can then make a three-dimensional model of the area, using salt clay or regular modeling clay (see the recipe). Mark buildings, the students' homes, and the school with small flags, using toothpicks and construction paper. If desired, the students can also make charts stating the number of miles or blocks between two points and how long it takes to travel between the points by walking and by car.

4. Such a Deal!

Goal: Detecting propaganda

Grade Level: 3–9

Construction: A student chooses a topic or item to persuade other students. After a selection has been made, an oral presentation is given to the class.

Utilization: The class then discusses what motions, words, and propaganda devices the student used. They can vote on which devices were most convincing.

ACTIVITIES THAT INTEGRATE READING AND MATHEMATICS

5. Student Tycoons

Goal: Interpreting information portrayed through graphs

Grade Level: 4–8

Construction: Assist students in choosing a particular kind of stock and aid them in keeping track of its losses and gains by reading the newspaper.

Utilization: Students can graph the daily fluctuations by putting the date on the *x*-axis and the losses or gains on the *y*-axis. The class might also want to have a bake sale or car wash and buy a few shares of stock for their own.

6. Getting There Prepared and on Time

Goal: Reading representational information and organizing schedules

Grade Level: 4–9

Construction and Utilization: Make arrangements for the class to go on a field trip. The class is responsible for arranging the transportation, reservations, meals, supplies, and equipment. A different group could be responsible for each aspect of the preparation. This would involve reading bus or train schedules, lists, and tables of the hours museums are open. Another activity that would involve using tables is figuring the expenses involved.

7. Treasure Clues

Goal: Following directions in mathematics

Grade Level: 3–8

Construction: Hide a small "treasure" somewhere in the room. Plant clues around the room that describe tasks to be completed to find the object. The clues could say "Measure 82.5 meters from the desk" or "Multiply 6 × 6 and walk that number of centimeters." Make a different set of clues for each player.

Utilization: The first person to find the object using his or her clues wins.

8. Our Community

Goal: Understanding picture graphs

Grade Level: 5–8

Construction: Assist students in collecting data about the areas surrounding their homes or school. From the library, chamber of commerce, weather station, or state house, they can find amount of rainfall in the different areas, the location of natural resources, or the elevations, for example.

Utilization: From the information gathered, students should choose a color code representing various levels, amounts of rainfall, and so on. Using the color code, they can design a picture map showing the different elevations or the amounts of rainfall in the selected geographical areas.

ACTIVITIES THAT INTEGRATE READING AND SCIENCE

9. Matched Pairs

Goal: Understanding science vocabulary

Grade Level: 3–S

Construction: Make paired sheets of index cards, so that one card is a science vocabulary word and the other is a short definition of that word.

Utilization: Cards are scrambled and placed face down in rows. Each player, in turn, turns over two cards. If the word and the definition match, the player retains them and takes another turn. If they do not match, the cards are turned over again and another player takes his turn. Whoever has the most pairs when all the cards have been matched wins the game.

10. Scrambled, But Not Eggs

Goal: Understanding science vocabulary

Grade Level: 1–2

Construction: Divide a sheet of laminated paper in half. Label one side "Carnivores" and the other "Herbivores." Under each heading, write the names of appropriate animals, but scramble the letters. Underneath each word, draw small boxes in which students can write the unscrambled words.

Utilization: The students should first try to think of animals that are plant or meat eaters, and then they should try to unscramble the names. The headings can be changed to reinforce any vocabulary words: reptiles and amphibians, conductors and nonconductors of electricity, and so on.

11. Meaning, Meaning

Goal: Developing science vocabulary

Grade Level: 1–8

Construction: On a large piece of cardboard or oak tag, draw circles with scientific vocabulary written in each. Examples: mass, energy, work, heat, standard, substance, power.

Utilization: The board is placed on a table, and players sit about 1 meter away. Using small plastic or cardboard disks, the players aim for any word. For whatever word the disk lands on, they must give both the technical and nontechnical meanings. A student judge decides if the definitions are acceptable.

The players receive 5 points for each acceptable definition—5 points if they know only one meaning; 10 points if they know both. The game ends when each word has been given both a technical and a nontechnical definition. No word can receive more than one technical and one nontechnical definition.

12. Moon Landing

Goal: Interpreting scientific formulas

Grade Level: 4–8

Construction: Make a large board game with a path of squares to follow. The beginning square should be labeled "Blast Off," and the ending square should contain a picture of the moon. The remaining squares should be blank or labeled with "Draw a card" "Lose a turn," "Go back three spaces, and so on. For "Draw a card," construct small oak-tag cards, each stating a scientific formula. One die or two dice should be secured for the player.

Utilization: Each player is given four playing pieces. The object of the game is to land all four pieces on the moon. Each player rolls one die, moves one of the four playing pieces the specified number of squares, and then follows the instruction on the square. If a player lands on a space that says "Draw a card," he or she must draw a card and interpret the formula correctly or lose a turn. The first person to land all four playing pieces on the moon wins the game.

13. Science Between Grades

Goal: Developing location skills involving the glossary

Grade Level: 5–8

Construction and Utilization: Have each student write a short article concerning any area in science for someone in a lower grade. At the end of the story, the student author should provide a glossary of the more difficult terms. Perhaps after the younger student has read the article, he or she can discuss it with the student author, reviewing the terms in the glossary.

14. Domino Demons

Goal: Analyzing word derivations

Grade Level: 5–8

Construction: Make a domino game using derivatives of scientific words. Cut rectangle dominoes measuring 5 by 8 cm from stiff cardboard. On one domino, write two derivatives of the same word on both ends. This double derivative is to be used as the starting domino. For the rest, write two words with different derivatives on each domino.

Utilization: Play begins by turning all the dominoes face down, with each player drawing five dominoes. Whoever has the double domino puts it out. If no one has the double domino, all the dominoes are returned face down to the middle, and players draw again. In turn, each player tries to match one end of the domino to an open end of another domino already played. The player who cannot make a match draws up to five dominoes from those remaining; if a match is still impossible, the player loses the turn. The game ends when one player has used up all his or her dominoes or no one can play. In this case, the player with the fewest number of dominoes is the winner. Examples:

mitotic	analyze	hydrolysis	evaporate
mitosis	analysis	hydrate	vaporize
osmosis	analytic	dehydrate	vaporous
osmotic			

ACTIVITIES THAT INTEGRATE READING, ART, AND MUSIC

15. Socks Talk

Goal: Incorporating reading and art activities

Grade Level: 5–8

Construction: Students choose a play they want to perform with puppets. If they cannot decide on a particular play, assist them in rewriting a favorite story in dialogue form. Make puppets out of old socks, with buttons and other pieces of material sewn on for facial features. If desired, paper bags can be used instead of socks. Decorate with yarn and construction paper.

Utilization: Students present the puppet show to the class, reading from the prepared script during practice. If possible, the students should be encouraged to memorize the lines for the final production.

16. Singing Syllables

Goal: Developing reading skills through singing

Grade Level: K–3

Construction and Utilization: Simply learning a song is an excellent way to practice rote memorization, rhythm, proper inflection, accenting, and syllabication. For syllabication, in particular, have a group walk and clap the beat of a song, separating the words into correct syllables. Next, have them sing part of the song, leaving out certain syllables, words, or phrases to develop an ear for the proper separation of words.

17. Secret Word

Goal: Applying the skills needed to read music textbooks

Grade Level: 2–6

Construction: Instruct students in the basics of music reading—in particular, how to tell if a note is a C, B, or G, for example, by the line the note is standing on. Prepare laminated music sheets, placing notes in such a position that, when interpreted as letters, they will spell out a word or message.

Utilization: Students write the correct letter next to the note and read the secret word or message.

18. The Greatest Show on Earth

Goal: Combining reading, art, and music skills

Grade Level: 3–8

Construction and Utilization: Assist the class in planning a small-scale musical. First, they must select a play or write their own show about the people at their school. After the script has been chosen, parts should be assigned, including those of actors, stage crew, scenery painters, prop collectors, and costume makers. Next, the music for the show should be selected from contemporary songs on radio or TV or songs that everyone knows. Everyone should have a chance to help paint the scenery, practice the parts, and perform for other classes.

QUESTIONS

1. Imagine that you are in a meeting with your fellow teachers to discuss your school's science curriculum. Defend the following position: Your curriculum committee should consider designing science units around the concept of science as exploration. Provide them with at least one example so that they can see the usefulness of the concept.

2. One of your fellow teachers, who has specialized in teaching a block of science and math, complains to you that her students are not doing as well as she would like. You suggest that she might try some content reading strategies. However, she counters that she is not a reading teacher. How would you respond? Explain your point of view thoroughly.

3. In the teachers' lounge you overhear one teacher, Sarah, tell another teacher that she has always been a successful first grade teacher, but that she feels like a failure this year with fourth graders. She says that the textbooks seem to be too hard for students and that she doesn't know what to do to help them. As you enter the conversation, explain to Sarah why she may be experiencing frustration and provide her with a few suggestions that might help her feel more successful.

4. Discuss the role of prior knowledge in content area learning. Include in your discussion an explanation of how prior knowledge can both aid and hinder comprehension.

5. It is generally accepted that vocabulary development and concept development are synonymous. Explain what it means and how it this relates to conetent area reading and learning.

REFERENCES

Adobe Systems. (1998). *Adobe after effects 4.0.* San Jose, CA: Author.

Anderson, T. H., & Armbruster, B. B. (1984). Content area textbooks. In R. C. Anderson, J. Osborn, & R. J. Tierney (Eds.), *Learning to read in American schools: Basal readers and content texts* (pp. 193–226). Hillsdale, NJ: Lawrence Erlbaum Associates.

Bakken, J. P., & Whedon, C. K. (2002). Teaching text structure to improve reading comprehension. *Intervention in School and Clinic, 37,* 229–233.

Brashares, A. (2001). *Sisterhood of the traveling pants.* New York: Delacorte.

Brassell, D., & Flood, J. (2004). *Vocabulary strategies every teacher needs to know.* San Diego, CA: APD Press.

Burke, J. (2000). *Reading reminders: Tools, tips, and techniques.* Portland, ME: Boynton/Cook.

Curry, J. F. (1996). The role of reading and writing instruction in mathematics. In D. Lapp, J. Flood, & N. Farnan (Eds.), *Content area reading and learning: Instructional strategies* (2nd ed.) (pp. 227–243). Boston: Allyn & Bacon.

Darling-Hammond, L. (1997). *The right to learn: A blueprint for for creating schools that work*. San Francisco: Jossey-Bass.

Darling-Hammond, L., Berry, B., & Thoreson, A. (2001). Does teacher certification matter? Evaluating the evidence. *Educational Evaluation and Policy Analysis, 23*, 57–77.

Fisher, D., & Frey, N. (2001). *Responsive curriculum design in secondary schools: Meeting the diverse needs of students*. Lanham, MD: Scarecrow Education.

Fisher, D., & Frey, N. (2004). *Improving adolescent literacy: Strategies at work*. Upper Saddle River, NJ: Merrill Prentice Hall.

Griggs, R. A. (1999). Introductory psychology textbooks: Assessing levels of difficulty. *Teaching of Psychology, 26*, 248–253.

Hamman, D., Berthelot, J., Saia, J., & Crowley, E. (2000). Teachers' coaching of learning and its relation to students' strategic learning. *Journal of Educational Psychology, 92*, 342–348.

Jantzen, P. G., & Michel, J. L. (1986). *Life science* (grades 6–8). New York: Macmillan.

Jones, B. F., Palincsar, A. S., Ogle, D. S., & Carr, E. G. (Eds.). (1987). *Strategic teaching and learning: Cognitive instruction in the content areas*. Alexandria, VA: Association for Supervision and Curriclum Development.

Kaplan, R. B., & Grabe, W. (2002). A modern history of written discourse analysis. *Journal of Second Language Writing, 11*, 191–223.

Kinach, B. M. (2002). A cognitive strategy for developing pedagogical content knowledge in the secondary mathematics methods course: Toward a model of effective practice. *Teaching and Teacher Education, 18*, 51–71.

McDonald, N., & Fisher, D. (2002). *Developing arts-loving readers. Top 10 questions teachers are asking about integrated arts education*. Lanham, MD: Scarecrow Education.

McMurry, P. M. (1909). *Reading comprehension*. Palo Alto, CA: Scott Foresman.

Moss, B. (2003). *25 strategies for guiding readers through informational texts*. San Diego, CA: APD Press.

National Academy of Education, Commission on Reading. (1985). *Becoming a nation of readers*. Washington, DC: National Institute of Education.

Niles, O. (1970). *School programs: The necessary conditions in reading: Process and program*. Urbana, IL: National Council of Teachers of English.

Santa, C., Havens, L., & Harrison, S. (1996). Teaching secondary science through reading, writing, studying, and problem solving. In D. Lapp, J. Flood, & N. Farnan (Eds.), *Content area reading and learning: Instructional strategies* (2nd ed.) (pp. 165–179). Boston: Allyn & Bacon.

Schallert, D. L., & Roser, N. L. (1989). The role of reading in content area instruction. In D. Lapp, J. Flood, & N. Farnan (Eds.), *Content area reading and learning: Instructional strategies* (pp. 25–33). New York: Prentice Hall.

Stauffer, R. G., & Harrell, M. M. (1975). Individualized reading-thinking activities. *The Reading Teacher, 28*, 765–769.

Vacca, R. T., & Vacca, J. L. (2002). *Content area reading: Literacy and learning across the curriculum* (7th ed.). Boston: Allyn & Bacon.

Veal, W. R., van Driel, J., & Hulshof, H. (2001). PCK: How teachers transform subject matter knowledge. *International Journal of Leadership in Education, 4*, 285–291.

9

What the Teacher Needs to Know to Enable Students' Text Comprehension

──────── CHAPTER GOALS ────────

To help the reader

- understand the nature of reading comprehension.
- understand the role of the reader in reading comprehension.
- understand the role of the text in reading comprehension.
- understand the role of language and context in reading comprehension.

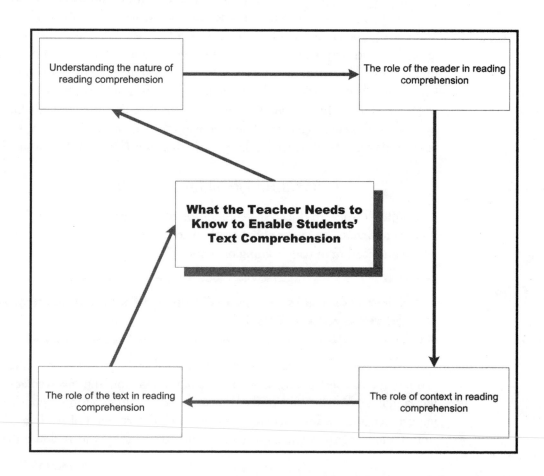

Understanding the nature of reading comprehension

The role of the reader in reading comprehension

What the Teacher Needs to Know to Enable Students' Text Comprehension

The role of the text in reading comprehension

The role of context in reading comprehension

A stop sign can be large or small, metal or wood, on a post or hanging from a wire, but none of those physical details is of great significance since the sign does not physically stop us. Rather, we stop ourselves because we treat the object as sign and respond accordingly. As physical object, it is inert and powerless; only as sign does it have any strength, and it becomes a sign only when it enters the mind of a reader.

—Probst, 1988, pp. 21–22

Based on the title of this chapter, you have undoubtedly already made some predictions about what you will read, and those predictions most likely had nothing to do with stop signs, despite Probst's focus on them in the opening quotation. However, your predictions may have been confirmed when you read the last two lines of the quotation: "It becomes a sign only when it enters the mind of a reader." Now perhaps we're on firmer ground because your expectation was probably that we would talk about readers and how they understand what they read. In fact, that is exactly what Probst is talking about. If you reread his quotation, you can see that he addresses three crucial aspects of comprehension.

One aspect emphasizes the importance of *the reader* (characteristics such as age, language fluency, background knowledge, and experiences) in the comprehension process. Although this might appear to be a simple notion, a foregone conclusion, classroom instruction in comprehension has not always acknowledged and capitalized on the role of the reader. Probst also talks about the role of *the text* itself. It does play a role, but its role is not dictated simply by its physical presence; rather, it is shaped by the way we, the readers, interact with it and its characteristics (such as language, genre, type, features, and considerateness). Finally, Probst touches on another significant aspect of reading: *the context* (for example, environment, social grouping, and purpose). Comprehension occurs in a certain time and place, that is, in a context. For example, the message of a stop sign changes if it is displayed as a trophy on a bedroom wall rather than posted on an iron bar at the corner of a three-way intersection. In this chapter, first we explore conceptions of reading comprehension and meaning making, then we will touch in various ways on how *readers*, *texts*, and *contexts* influence reading comprehension (Ruddell & Unrau, 1995).

REVISITING READING COMPREHENSION

In chapter 7 we introduced a definition of reading comprehension. We promised that we'd have more to say about reading comprehension in this chapter. Let's see what you recall from your reading of chapter 7.

Quickly jot down the key ideas you recall about the definition of reading comprehension that were suggested in chapter 7.

Let's review. Reading comprehension involves the process of "simultaneously extracting and constructing meaning through interaction and involvement with written language. We use the words *extracting* and *constructing* to emphasize both the importance and the insufficiency of the text as a determinant of reading comprehension. Comprehension entails three elements: the reader who is doing the comprehending, the text that is to be comprehended, and the activity in which comprehension is a part" (The Rand Report, 2002, p. 11). The *reader, text,* and activity of reading occur in particular *contexts* that shape and influence reading comprehension. Much of this chapter is devoted to a discussion of these dimensions of reading comprehension: the reader, the text, and the context. We also discuss the significant ways that educators have characterized comprehension before addressing these important dimensions of comprehension. Many practices in the teaching of comprehension are based on the idea that there are *different types of comprehension*. These types of comprehension are often divided into four categories: *literal* or text explicit comprehension, *inferential* or text implicit comprehension, *critical* comprehension, and *creative* or aesthetic comprehension. These types of comprehension undoubtedly sound familiar to you from chapter 7. For example, when we discussed question–answer relationships (QARs), we emphasized "in the book" types of responses or answers. These, of course, refer to literal comprehension—information that can be found explicitly in the text. "Text and me" answers, on the other hand, refer to inferential comprehension—ideas that can be deduced from the text, but that are not explicitly stated in the text. We draw on a picture book, *The Rainbow Fish*, to illustrate further the distinction between these categories.

The main character in the book is Rainbow Fish, the most magnificently beautiful fish in the ocean. Rainbow Fish is covered with an array of pretty multicolored scales—some of which are dazzling luminescent silver scales. In addition to being beautiful, however, Rainbow Fish is also haughty and selfish. One day, perplexed about why he had no friends when he was such a gorgeous fish, Rainbow Fish poured out his heart to a starfish. Being unsure how to help Rainbow Fish with his problems, the starfish suggested that Rainbow Fish talk with the wise octopus. Rainbow Fish embarked on a long journey to find the deep, dark cave of the wise octopus. When he found the octopus the following conversation ensued:

> "I have been waiting for you," said the octopus with a deep voice. "The waves have told me your story. This is my advice. Give a glittering scale to each of the other fish. You will no longer be the most beautiful fish in the sea, but you will discover how to be happy." (Pfister, 1992, p. 13)

From *The Rainbow Fish by Marcus Pfister,* © 1992 by Nord-Süd Verlag AG, Gossau Zürich Switzerland. Used by Permission of North-South Books, Inc., New York

Rainbow Fish decided to take the advice of the octopus. He began to be nice to the other fish. He also gave many of his scales to the other fish. After following the octopus' advice, Rainbow Fish soon had many friends.

Literal comprehension refers to questions pertaining to a text that are explicit in the text. For example, questions such as "How did Rainbow Fish make friends?" (sharing his scales) and "To whom did Rainbow Fish first turn for help regarding his problem?" (the starfish) are text explicit because the answers to these questions are literal—they are stated specifically in the text.

Inferential comprehension refers to questions pertaining to a text that are implicit to the text. That is, the answers to inferential questions are not "in" the text, per se, but they are implied based on textual information. Take, for example, a question such as "Why do you think that Rainbow Fish did not have friends at the beginning of the story"? A reasonable answer to this question is that Rainbow Fish did not initially have friends because he wasn't very nice to the other fish; he was haughty and selfish. While the text doesn't state explicitly that Rainbow Fish did not have friends because he was haughty and selfish, most readers would probably agree that the text implies this. Consequently, inferential comprehension refers to ideas that are not stated explicitly in the text, but are implied in the text and can be inferred by the reader.

Critical comprehension refers to the practice of critiquing the ideas presented in the text. For example, the reason for Rainbow Fish's lack of friends probably seems quite obvious. A reader may ask why it is that Rainbow Fish couldn't ascertain in the first place why other fish didn't want to be friends with him. Moreover, why couldn't the starfish help Rainbow Fish determine the source of his problem? A reader might even question some of the advice that the octopus gave to Rainbow Fish. Is it only, or primarily, by giving things to others that they will become our friends? What might have happened if Rainbow Fish had solely changed the ways in which he interacted with the other fish by treating them in a kinder manner? Would that have been enough to make friends, or was it also necessary to give his silver scales away? Conversely, what might have been the implication of giving his scales away and not changing his behavior toward his friends? You get the idea. Even with a picture book, it is possible to critically explore textual ideas.

Creative or aesthetic comprehension refers to affective and artistic dimensions of reading and interpreting text. For example, how does the story about Rainbow Fish make you feel as a reader? Perhaps you felt frustrated as a reader by the fact that Rainbow Fish couldn't understand that if you treat people badly they will not want to be friends. You may have felt relief at the end of the story when Rainbow Fish actually made friends and was much happier. Perhaps you were intrigued by the notion that the waves told the octopus about Rainbow Fish's story before Rainbow Fish even met the octopus. You may have even speculated about how/why this could have occurred.

This four-part distinction has been useful because it divides the world of comprehension into manageable categories. Unfortunately, many problems have arisen from this classification because educators may think linearly about these categories, assuming that they represent four distinct *levels* of difficulty. Some educators, for example, may see these categories as being ordered hierarchically and that literal or text-explicit comprehension is easier than inferential or text-implicit comprehension, which in turn is easier than critical or creative comprehension. In the following section we briefly articulate some cautions when using this four-part classification scheme. Moreover, some educators may not realize that the categories are not always discrete and distinct. In reality, they often overlap and intertwine.

Cautions When Using a Four-Part Linear Classification Scheme

Because the four-part division of explicit/literal comprehension, implicit/inferential comprehension, world knowledge/critical comprehension, and creative/aesthetic comprehension is used by many publishers of reading comprehension tests and reading texts, it may be useful for you to think of this categorization scheme as an attempt to divide the sources of reading comprehension into several important components:

1. Literal comprehension—extracted from text-explicit information.
2. Inferential comprehension—extracted from text-implicit information.
3. Critical comprehension—extracted from world knowledge and experiences.
4. Creative/aesthetic comprehension—extracted from our feelings regarding lived experiences.

It is important to be cautious about using this classification scheme in a linear fashion for two reasons:

Objection 1: It implies that there is a linear progression of difficulty in these four categories of comprehension, and it is assumed that tasks that measure comprehension can be labeled correctly as literal, inferential, critical, or creative/aesthetic with little or no overlap.

Objection 2: It primarily takes the *source* of comprehension into consideration. It does not take into account the dynamic, active process of comprehension in which the reader participates. The operations in which the learner engages during the reading process are ignored as are the social, cultural, and historical backgrounds of readers and texts.

The first objection, the assumption that questions in these categories of comprehension exist in a linear progression and can be labeled literal, inferential, critical, or creative stems from certain current discoveries. Please read the following passage. After you read the passage, we'll ask you to categorize questions about the passage.

(1) Zoe and Zeke, two talented masons, were building an internal fireplace for a cantankerous architect. (2) The architect was inflexible with his prints, insisting that the measurements had to be absolutely perfect despite his annoying habit of altering the plans every 20 minutes. (3) After 3 hours of utter frustration, Zoe and Zeke thought they understood the plans. (4) As they started to lay the foundation, the architect decided that he wanted an external fireplace and announced, "I think your work is unprofessional. You're fired." (5) Zoe and Zeke, flabbergasted, said, "Sir, you are a poor excuse for an architect and the bane of all craftsmen. Your sense of professionalism is a sham."

Please label the following questions literal, inferential, critical, or creative.
1. How many times did the architect alter the plans while Zoe and Zeke were working?
2. Why did the architect tell the masons that they were unprofessional?
3. What was the masons' reaction to being fired?
4. When did the masons understand that the architect was troublesome?

The entire passage is straightforward and comprehensible. The details of the story are explicit, and the characterizations of the architect and the masons are direct and thorough (for interpreting the author's point of view). However, the four questions, while easily answered, are quite difficult to label as literal, inferential, critical, or creative. The source of the answer to each question is in the text, thereby making the question appear to be a test of literal comprehension, but the exact answer is not in the text. For example:

Question: How many times did the architect alter the plans while Zoe and Zeke were working?

Text source: The architect was inflexible with his prints, insisting that the measurements had to be absolutely perfect despite his annoying habit of altering the plans every 20 minutes. After 3 hours of utter frustration, Zoe and Zeke thought they understood the plans.

Operation: Convert 3 hours into 180 minutes. Divide 20 minutes into 180 minutes to arrive at the answer: nine times.

The answer is not stated explicitly in the text; the reader is called on to perform certain arithmetic operations beyond the text. Therefore, you may be tempted to label the question inferential. However, it is clear that the reader has to operationalize previous knowledge (arithmetic computation) to answer the question. Does this straying from the text qualify the question for the label *critical comprehension*?

The difficulty of assigning the correct label to a question is real. We have carefully explained the entire process of answering the question without giving the question a label. This strongly suggests that we should be investigating the processes involved in answering the question (in comprehending) and that too much time arguing about the appropriateness of labels may not be time well spent.

The second objection to the four-level classification scheme proposed is that it only takes the source of comprehension into consideration. This is a reasonable objection because this scheme does not account for the many different mental operations the reader uses when he or she reads the text. Let us illustrate this point by analyzing several operations that are involved in answering these seemingly simple questions:

Question: What did Zoe and Zeke do for a living?

Text source: Two talented masons

Operations:

    a.   The reader has to understand *apposition:* "Zoe and Zeke, two talented masons" means that Zoe and Zeke *are* two talented masons.

    b.   The reader has to process *synonym:* step 1, "do for a living" = occupation/job; step 2, occupation/job = masons.

Although the question is easily answered, the sophistication and complexity of the operations suggest that a facile label such as *literal comprehension* is an inadequate descriptor for the entire process of comprehension. Rather than primarily labeling particular kinds of comprehension, it seems important to examine characteristics of good readers, the different kinds of texts that readers read, and the ways in which the broader reading context influences how and what the reader comprehends during reading. We now turn to these issues.

DID YOU NOTICE . . .
Did you notice that although reading comprehension is often characterized as literal, inferential, critical, and creative, comprehension is more accurately depicted as a process in which readers engage that involves the reader, the text, and the reading context?

ENGAGING IN THE PROCESS OF TEXT COMPREHENSION: THE READER, THE TEXT, AND THE CONTEXT

The proficient reader makes sense of text by performing many operations while reading. This process, a transaction between the reader's background information and the text within a specific context, is an indivisible whole, as illustrated in Figure 9–1.

Refer to Figure 9–1. In this figure, Devin is reading a text about tops. Take a few minutes to notice carefully what you think Devin is doing as he reads. Jot your ideas down. Please note that the kind of thinking we're asking you to do here is important. To teach children how to read, we, as teachers, must have a sense of what it is that readers do. That is, we must understand how readers comprehend as they engage in the process of reading.

Figure 9–1 Exploring Devin's Comprehension about Tops.

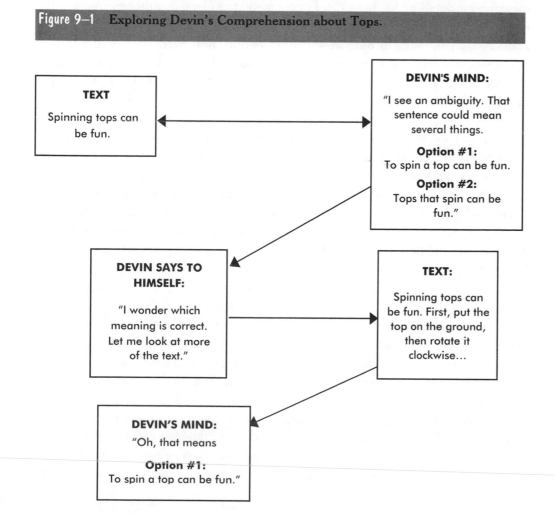

All of the information you see in Figure 9–1 happens in Devin's mind in a moment. The time that it takes may not be the critical element in the reading process; the critical element may be the active participation of the reader.

Okay, let's see where there is overlap between your ideas and our ideas regarding Devin's reading as depicted in Figure 9–1. First, Devin is actively engaged in sampling textual cues from the page. Consequently, he clearly knows a great deal about *graphophonics* (sound–symbol relationships), *syntax* (the grammar of the language), and *semantics* (the meaning of the language) because he is able to decode the words on the page and construct two plausible hypotheses about what the text may mean. He knows to check his hypotheses to see which one makes the most sense by attending to the broader context of the text (i.e., reading ahead). After sampling more textual information, he is able to figure out that one of his hypotheses makes the most sense. Thus, he is able to reflect on his own thinking (i.e., engage in *metacognition*). He maintains the most plausible interpretation of the text and dismisses the option that doesn't "work" as well. Now he is ready to read on by looking at more text and engaging in the whole process again.

THE ROLE OF READER IN READING COMPREHENSION

One of the most important observations we can make about excellent comprehenders, like Devin, is that they are self-regulated readers. They do not construct meaning randomly or haphazardly. For competent readers, comprehension is not a serendipitous event. They control their comprehension from the time before they actually start to read, through the reading period, and even after reading. You might say that they create plans for reading, plans that vary from one reading to the next and from one individual to another. We can generalize, however, that commonalities exist among competent readers and among less able readers.

First of all, competent readers set purposes for reading. They are aware of whether they are reading for information, for recreation, to understand more about a character, to confirm or negate predictions, or for a variety of reasons. They may also preview the text, looking at the title, pictures, and print, to get an overview of the content and how it is structured. Competent readers not only have access to pertinent background knowledge, but they also consciously apply it to what they are reading. They actively use their prior knowledge and therefore have specific expectations; not only of the content but also of the way language is used in the text. Their knowledge of language centers on (a) letter–sound correspondence, (b) words and their various forms, (c) syntax, i.e., grammatical structures, and (d) semantic relationships, i.e., meaning as it is encompassed in texts. In addition, these readers structure their attention so that significant information is separated from trivial facts and details. During reading, competent readers are able to maintain their attention and check their understanding. They monitor their comprehension often and apply strategies to improve it when they don't understand. And finally, after reading, they rethink what they have read. They ask themselves whether they have met their goals for reading. They may perhaps summarize content and review main points. When readers are unable to retell what they have read or are unable to answer about what they have read they are not reading with competency. When this occurs in your classroom what should you do? To answer this question, think about the informa-

DID YOU NOTICE . . .
Did you notice that affect matters in reading? Reading is NOT just a cognitive process. It also involves feeling. Teachers must attend to affect as they design reading instruction for children.

tion presented in the previous chapters. Remember that after you assess that the text is at the student's appropriate reading level and that he or she is decoding fluently you need to provide instruction that is similar to the example in Table 9–1.

Specific instruction similar to this is important for all students but especially for less competent readers because they tend not to set purposes and not to think about the content before reading. Even if they have prior knowledge, they tend not to activate it consciously. During reading, they do not monitor their comprehension and, consequently, do not apply corrective strategies. Instead, they tend to read simply to get from the first word on the first page to the last word on the last page, although they may not remember or understand what they read.

Reading is a thinking activity (Rumelhart, 1984) made up of a series of complex processes, some of which we have already described in our discussion of the prior knowledge and characteristics of competent readers. It is important to remember that throughout these processes, competent readers activate prior knowledge, are aware of the role of text, make inferences, make predictions about what the author is trying to communicate, and employ metacognitive (self-monitoring) strategies. This is the process that you analyzed and we discussed pertaining to Figure 9–1 earlier.

Among other things, this means that your more able readers will realize that when they have failed to understand a passage, it is necessary to reread, seek help, or continue reading for clarification. The point is that they are aware that a problem exists and that they have the ability to try a variety of ways to solve it.

Knowing that many students will not have internalized the skills of mature, competent readers, we can teach them to realize when they are in trouble; give them a broad repertoire of strategies to use; and show them how to tell when they are succeeding. We can make instruction more successful if we are careful always to let students know how to use a strategy and why it works. If they understand the why as well as the how, students will begin to apply metacognition, or self-monitoring strategies, to their own reading, and will begin increasingly to resemble more mature and competent readers.

Up to this point, we have been discussing reading comprehension as a thinking activity. Although this is so, one aspect that is often overlooked is the idea that reading is also a feeling activity. How you feel during reading is as influential as what you do. An important component of reading comprehension is affect. We can help students become more strategic, effective readers through a variety of instructional techniques; but if we ignore the importance of affect—readers' interests, attitudes, and feelings—we are ignoring a crucial aspect of comprehension.

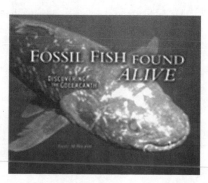

Walker, S. M. (2002). *Fossil Fish Found Alive: Discovering the Coelacanth*. Minneapolis, MN: Carolrhoda Books, Inc.

TABLE 9–1
Modeling the Processes Engaged in by a Competent Reader

Model what competent readers do before they begin to read.

1. Model for students how to preview the text by looking at the title, the pictures, the print, and format to evoke relevant thoughts and memories about the topic.

2. Discuss how you gain appropriate background when you are reading about an unfamiliar topic. Model for them how to select a less difficult book on the same topic—a book with pictures and diagrams that will help to build mental images. Encourage them to search the Internet or to talk with others to gain background. Explain to them that you also build background through self-questioning about what you already know about the topic (or story), the vocabulary, and the form in which the topic (or story) is presented. Model for them the use of a dictionary, glossary, or the context as sources to help you gain an understanding of unfamiliar words.

3. Explain how you think about the topic or the story title and set a purpose for reading by asking questions about what you want to learn (know) while reading. Explain that this helps you to be sure that you are understanding what you are reading and that when you are not understanding you stop and get help.

Model what competent readers do while reading.

4. Through example model how you monitor your understanding while you're reading by using context clues to determine the meaning of unknown words and by imaging, imagining, drawing inferences, and predicting. Model reading a selected passage, discussing how you think about the main ideas being presented by the author. If you're reading about a character such as *Maniac Magee* explain that when you read the Before The Story section of the book you picture the dump where the author Jerry Spinelli tells you Maniac was born. Explain that even though the author doesn't say, you were sure it must have had maggots and have been real stinky. You think that you're glad you were born in a clean hospital and later as you read on you're relieved to learn that Maniac was really born in a house. Do similar thinking aloud when reading a non-narrative text such as *Fossil Fish Found Alive*.

   Share how the author Sally M. Walker's selection of language "Deep in a leafy forest, a tiny, shrewlike mammal leaps at a flower and snaps at a nectar butterfly." (p. 4) helps you to visualize by making a picture in your mind of what the Earth looked like 70 million years ago.

5. Illustrate how you check your understanding of the text by paraphrasing the author's words. Discuss how you do this more often when you're reading a text that is difficult for you because it is about an unfamiliar topic, or it has many words and phrases that you don't recognize, or it's written in a format that you don't read often (charts, graphs, etc.). Encourage students to identify parts of the text that aren't making sense to them. Explain that this is how you can begin to get appropriate support.

6. Throughout your reading be sure to emphasize how you integrate new concepts with existing knowledge while continually revising the purposes for reading.

Model what competent readers do after reading

7. Model how you check your understanding by summarizing and retelling the plot of the story or the main ideas of the text you've been reading.

(continued)

TABLE 9–1 (Continued)

Show them how you use frames to help you with your summarizing. For example, if you've just read a section in a social studies basal text about the great state of Ohio you could model building the following frame to support your summary.

Ohio: The 17th state
Became a state in 1803
State bird is a cardinal
State flower is a carnation
Columbus is the capital
Motto: In God all things are possible
Interesting Facts: 7 Presidents; 16-year-old boy wrote the motto;
tomato juice is state drink because...,Wright Brothers

Or if you've just finished reading about the American Revolution your frame might look like this.

American Revolution

What was it? _____

Who was involved? _____

Important facts about it. _____

When did this occur? _____

Why did it happen? _____

What were the consequences? _____

Other facts worth remembering _____

Explain that frames are also helpful to summarize a story. A story frame might look like the following.

Title

Settings	Characters	Plot

	Name	Problem

	Traits	Complications
	1.	1.
	2.	2.
	3.	3.

Conclusion

(continued)

TABLE 9–1 (Continued)

8. Encourage students to evaluate the ideas contained in the text. Model for them how when reading a cartoon you try to target the main ideas the author presented both positively and negatively. Do the same with advertisements for merchandise that is of interest to them. Also analyze editorials to detect author bias. Once they are familiar with this process, model how you use the same strategies to evaluate character motive, intent and story development.

9. Model for the students how you apply the ideas in the text to unique situations, extending the ideas to broader perspectives. For example when you read in a newspaper that skateboarders may be required to wear helmets, you wonder whether this law should also be applied to kids who are roller skating because they too could get injured from a fall.

Affect and Reading Comprehension

We know that students' interests, attitudes, and feelings attract them to certain materials and not others. This makes sense when we think about our own adult preferences for certain books and types of reading and avoidance of others. We certainly do not want to develop students who are able comprehenders but who never choose to read, for in the final analysis, there may be little difference between individuals who cannot read and those who will not read because in both cases children in these two categories don't read.

When talking about the relationship between cognitive and affective domains, Piaget (1986) said that "while these two aspects cannot be reduced to a single aspect, they are nevertheless inseparable and complementary" (p. 21). Effective instruction and positive attitudes about reading are intertwined. Students who are successful readers, who feel a sense of competence and efficacy when they read, are more likely to have positive attitudes toward reading; good instruction and classroom practices have the power to change students' attitudes about reading.

When are you motivated to read? Why do you read? Jot your ideas down and share them with a partner. How can this relate to your teaching?

Teachers need to be as concerned about developing positive, productive attitudes as they are about developing cognitive skills. In the primary grades, teachers should read frequently to students and involve them extensively in oral language activities. Children should listen to recordings of stories on tapes and records; they should be encouraged to share their own stories orally with their peers; stories they create can be written down for them to read and share with other students and with the teacher. Because reading and writing are closely linked language skills, developing positive attitudes about writing will complement your goals to develop positive attitudes about reading (see chapter 10).

Ask students why they read. Take your own survey; compile your results. You may be surprised at what you find. Do your students say that they read because they have to? Do they say that they read for information? Or do they say that one of the reasons they read is for enjoyment?

During the primary years, teachers tend to focus more on making reading and learning enjoyable. There seems to be an almost intuitive sense among these teachers that affective and cognitive development are, indeed, inextricably linked. However, as students move into the intermediate grades, this focus on affect seems to decline (Tunnell and Jacobs, 2002). There are several possible reasons for this phenomenon. One is that teachers begin to place more emphasis on instructional goals. This emphasis includes a focus on conceptual development and on making students more knowledgeable and strategic readers. There also may be an assumption that the groundwork for reading enjoyment has already been laid by the primary teacher and, therefore, does not require as much attention. Also, the shift from narrative to the use of more expository materials in the classroom might contribute to a de-emphasis on interest and enjoyment.

Although these changes in reading instruction are positive and necessary, they do not have to mean that teachers no longer have affective development as one of their goals. As students grow in their cognitive skills, they can also grow in motivation and interest by experiencing feelings of excitement, curiosity, and competence related to their reading. Scholars (e.g., Helmstetter, 1987; Tunnell & Jacobs, 2002) suggest ways to help students to become engaged readers by emphasizing the following aspects of a reading program:

1. *Discuss with students their reading attitudes and interests.* You can do this only if you have some idea about their interests and attitudes. An informal assessment process consists of asking students to bring in their favorite book, magazine, cartoon, and so on. They can share their materials with the class and discuss elements that made these their favorites. You can record what they shared and what comments they made about each item. Students' responses to this assignment should be placed in an assessment portfolio file for future reference, for they will provide you with valuable input concerning their attitudes toward reading. Several examples of checklists are found in chapter 3.

An important component of attitude assessment includes sharing results with the class. Let the class know the variety of responses that occurred. Elicit input from your students as you attempt to answer the question "How can we make sure that reading is interesting and enjoyable for everyone in the room?"

Another suggestion for sharing reading interests with the class and fostering positive attitudes toward reading is to create a class list of favorite books. Each student in class lists favorite books next to her or her name. Encourage children to include a variety of different kinds of favorite books including narrative texts, expository texts, picture books, and books from many different genres. You, as the teacher, also list some of your favorite children's books. Then you can photocopy the list for everyone in class. That list of "favorites" can spark lots of interest as students scamper to the library to check out one another's favorite books. This activity can be done several times throughout the year as children read new books and acquire new favorites.

2. *Make sure that students feel a sense of competence when reading.* To feel competent, children must read texts that they can handle. That is, if texts are too hard for children, they will often become discouraged. As mentioned in chapters 1 and 3, it is important for teachers to help children find texts that are at their appropriate reading levels and that relate to their interests as readers.

3. *Frequently share literature through oral reading.* Cullinan (1987) said that "literature informs the imagination and feeds the desire to read" (p. 6). Oral readings that are accompanied by discussions in which students are encouraged to predict what will happen next will emphasize the importance of understanding while reading. After the teacher reads a story, the group can read in unison, with each student feeling like a successful part of the reading process. As children get older, they can share readings with the class and small groups. Children enjoy taping their readings on either audio- or videotapes. As their skill and confidence grow, they may even exchange their recordings with other classes. Oral readings, in person or on tape, shared by a student from an upper grade with a lower-grade class can also increase reading enjoyment for students at both grade levels.

Thus far, we have discussed *characteristics of readers*. We have also shared ideas about affect and readers. It is important to realize, however, that the nature of the text being read and a reader's familiarity with the nature of the text impact a reader's comprehension. In the next portion of this chapter, we will examine the role of the text structure on comprehension.

DID YOU NOTICE . . .
Did you notice that the process of reading is active, not passive? Devin was actively engaged in the process of making sense of the text he was reading. He made decisions about plausible meanings of the text as he read.

THE ROLE OF THE TEXT IN READING COMPREHENSION

"Of all the needs a book has the chief need is that it be readable."

—Anthony Trollope (1978, p. 15)

From reading research that has focused on text structure and comprehension, investigators have been able to describe how text structures influence comprehension. Central to this work is the idea of relationships—among words, sentences, and larger portions of text. Most textual structure research begins with the assumption that there are two major structural categories for prose: narration and exposition. Narrative text refers to stories. As discussed in chapter 8, expository, or informational text, refers to texts such as this one and others including social studies and science texts. Clearly, not all texts fall nicely into these two discrete categories and, in the field of literacy, there is debate about the utility of discrete categories. These categories are, however, used extensively in the field of literacy. Consequently, they serve as useful background for understanding reading and reading comprehension.

Narrative Text

A large body of research has focused on the analyses of the structures of narrative texts, called *story grammars* or *story structures*. Rumelhart (1984) defined story grammars as "internalized story structures," and other scholars (e.g., Guthrie, 1977; Trabasso & Bouchard, 2002) have identified the elements of story grammars or story structures that are common to particular sets of narratives. We suspect that these terms will look familiar to you. They include characters, setting, theme, plot (including the problem(s) encountered by the character(s) in the story), and resolution.

As an example of what we mean by story grammar, we'll share and discuss a story with you. Mem Fox's story *Tough Boris* (1994) is a picture book about a rough, tough pirate. Of course, his name is Tough Boris. The narrator of Fox's story is a young boy. As the story opens and progresses, the young narrator reveals information about the character of Boris; like all pirates, he is tough, mean, and scary. One day, however, Tough Boris's parrot dies, and he "cries and cries." When this problem happens in the story, we see a very different side of Tough Boris. He gently places the body of his beloved parrot in a violin case and buries the parrot at sea. At the end of the story the young narrator says, "All pirates cry, and so do I," thus revealing that even tough pirates and young boys have something in common—they share the common human emotions of sadness and pain when they lose someone they love. Table 9–2 shows a narrative Thinksheet (adapted from Englert & Raphael, 1990) that depicts the story grammar of *Tough Boris*.

Stein and Feldman (1977) classified stories as simple and multiple episodic narratives. For Stein, simple stories consist of setting and episodic structure, and multiple-episode stories consist of sequential, causal, or simultaneous happenings. The story, *Tough Boris*, is an example of simple episodic narrative. More complex stories, such as, for example, Nobel Prize winner Toni Morrison's novel *Beloved*, is an example of a complex story that is a multiple episodic narrative.

Although many scholars have focused on the what of narrative structure, others have examined how story structures are encoded by readers. Scholars (e.g., Stein & Feldman, 1977; Trabasso & Bouchard, 2002) maintain that most people acquire "internalized story structures" through the telling and retelling of stories that contain such structures. As a result of familiarity with these structures, the reader uses information for hypothesis formation and testing. Flood and Lapp (1981) argued that "children and adults expect specified types of information to be explained in a fixed order within the framework of the story" (p. 36).

Because readers seem to have certain expectations for stories, students tend to have less recall of story information and to be confused by stories when those expectations

TABLE 9–2
Story Map Thinksheet for *Tough Boris*

CHARACTERS: Who are the main characters?

The main character in the story is Tough Boris. The entire story focuses on him, and the book is even named after him.

SETTING: Where and when does the story take place?
The story takes place on a huge ship in the middle of the ocean. Based on the pictures in the text, it appears to have taken place several hundred years ago. The pirates' clothes look old fashioned, and the ship looks like the kind of ships from several hundred years ago.

PLOT: What are the major events in the story? (This includes the major problem and the turning point in the story as well as the resolution to the story.)

Mem Fox begins the story by developing the rough, tough, mean, and scary character of Tough Boris. Then his parrot dies. This is the main problem in the story. It is also the turning point of the story. After this event, we see that even Tough Boris has a softer side. He is so upset about losing the parrot that he loves that he cries in front of his whole crew. The resolution of the story occurs when Tough Boris places his parrot's body in a violin case and buries it at sea.

THEME: What is the central idea the author may have wished to convey in the story

The young narrator of the story sees a change in the character of Tough Boris. Even though he is a tough pirate, Tough Boris, too, has a softer side. He cried when he lost someone he loved. Thus, the young narrator and Tough Boris share the common human emotion of sadness. Moreover, readers learn that it is normal to have, and express, emotions—for young boys as well as full-grown men who are tough pirates.

are not met. It appears that well-formed, familiar stories facilitate comprehension. Therefore, stories with varied structures, such as flashbacks and embedded episodes, tend to interfere with comprehension. The implication, then, is that stories that deviate from the expected need more instruction than simple, predictable stories such as *Tough Boris*. Through questioning and guided discussions, confusions that arise can be discussed and eliminated. Although some have argued that explicit instruction in story structure is unnecessary because students will naturally internalize this information through hearing and viewing (Moffett, 1983), others (e.g., Buss, Ratliff, & Irion, 1985; Englert & Raphael, 1990; Raphael, Englert, & Kirschner, 1989) found that children's comprehension can be improved when they receive explicit instruction in story structure.

THE ROLE OF CONTEXT IN READING COMPREHENSION

Historically, views about the nature of comprehension have shifted significantly. Prior to the mid-1900s, comprehension was not specifically discussed in the literature about reading (Smith, 1963). Presumably, this was because comprehension was thought to follow, as a by-product, from learning to decode. The assumption was that if students could "say" words, then comprehension would result. As experienced readers, however, we know that being able to "say" words, either aloud or in our heads, does not necessarily mean that we know what we're reading. Perhaps the following activity will illustrate this point for you. Read the following paragraph. What do you think that the author is saying?

DID YOU NOTICE . . .
Did you notice that explicit instruction in story structure can improve reading comprehension?

For Bakhtin, the unity of an act and its account, a deed and its meaning, if you will, is something that is never a priori, but which must always and everywhere be *achieved*. The act is a deed, and not a mere happening (as in "one damned thing after another"), only if the subject of such a *postupok*, from within his own radical uniqueness, weaves a relation to it in his accounting *for* it. Responsibility, then, is the ground of moral action, the way in which we overcome the guilt of the gap between our words and deeds, even though we do not have an alibi in existence— in fact, *because* we lack such an alibi: "It is only my non-alibi in being that transforms an empty possibility into an actual answerable act or deed ...." (Holquist, p. xii, cited in Bakhtin, 1993, p. 113 of original, p. 42 of translation).

So, what did you think? We'd surmise that the preceding paragraph did not make a lot of sense for most of our readers. Why do you think that this is the case? Take a few minutes to speculate.

First, even though the excerpt is an entire paragraph, it is isolated from the other paragraphs in the book. You may have found more context helpful as a reader trying to interpret this paragraph. More context may not even have been enough, however, for you to really make sense of what the author is saying. We suspect that you could "say" most of the words in the paragraph—except perhaps for the Russian word *postupok*. Clearly, comprehension involves more than merely saying words. It also involves more than merely adding more context (in terms of more sentences) and understanding what the individual words in a passage mean. Background knowledge about what the writer is discussing as well as knowledge about how writers construct arguments in various disciplines is also crucial. For example, if you knew that Bakhtin was a Russian literary theorist and if you had read some of Bakhtin's work, you might be better prepared to interpret the paragraph he wrote. Moreover, if you were familiar with Bakhtin's work, you'd undoubtedly know that Michael Holquist has translated much of it to English from the original Russian. The manner in which Holquist and Bakhtin are cited (e.g., p. xii, cited in Bakhtin) may even alert you to the fact that the paragraph comes from an introduction to one of Bakhtin's original works entitled, "Toward a Philosophy of the Act." In his overall introduction to Bakhtin's work, Holquist is informing the reader that Bakhtin is drawing on literary theory and philosophy to construct an argument to refute Kant's ethical imperative.

So, what's the central point of this activity, and how does it relate to you as a reader and a teacher of reading comprehension? Being able to sound out words and knowing the definitions of individual words in sentences is crucial, but it is not enough to ensure comprehension. Readers also need to have some background information regarding the topics about which they are reading. Additionally, readers need to know something about the broader contexts and disciplines in which they are reading and the ways in which texts are constructed in those disciplines.

As a quick recap of what we have been saying, we know that reading is a collection of processes involving an individual's underlying cognitive and linguistic skills, which often occur concurrently, including recognizing words (see chapter 6), phrases, clauses, sentences, paragraphs, and whole texts; drawing inferences and

DID YOU NOTICE . . .
Did you notice that the context of reading shapes a reader's ability to comprehend? For example, background knowledge about topics, genres, and memberships in particular discourse communities shapes readers' abilities to comprehend. As another example, have you ever with no prior experience or background picked up a text by Shakespeare and tried to read and understand it? If you had the guidance and instruction of an excellent English teacher, however, you probably not only came to understand Shakespeare, but you may have also grown to appreciate the beauty and complexity of his work.

developing meaningful concepts based on information contained in print; relating print concepts to prior knowledge and concepts already embedded in memory; and monitoring understanding throughout. Not only do these processes take place, but many of them also take place concurrently. Comprehension, then, results from an interaction among several factors: our knowledge of the world; our knowledge of words and of how they are linked to create ideas; our understanding of the purposes and strategies associated with successful reading; and our affective involvement or interest in what we are reading. Most recently, however, scholars of reading have alerted us to the fact that reading is also a social process (Gee, 1996; Green, 1992). That is, not only do readers draw on background knowledge and use various processes during reading, but readers also act and interact in various communities whereby community members use language (oral and written) in varieties of ways.

The Bakhtin example can help to illustrate this point. Texts are written and interpreted in social and cultural milieus that shape both the writing and the reading of them. Readers privy to norms of particular social and cultural milieus will have the background knowledge and expertise to interpret the texts that other readers will not have. The social contexts of which we are a part shape the ways in which we read, write, use, and interpret oral and written language (Bloome, 1986; Gee, 1996; The Rand Report, 2002).

This social nature of language use has, of course, serious implications for us as reading teachers. First, we, as teachers need to attend carefully to the ways in which we structure our classroom communities because our classroom community norms influence what children learn about reading and writing. Second, ways of using oral and written language—our norms for language use in various social and cultural milieus—are often invisible and taken for granted. A mismatch between the ways in which teachers and students use language may have a negative impact on children's literacy learning opportunities if teachers don't realize that there are alternative ways of using oral and written language (Brock, Boyd, & Moore, 2002; Heath, 1983).

QUESTIONS

1. Define reading comprehension. Make sure to include the important dimensions of comprehension we discussed in chapter 9.
2. Explain what competent readers do before, during, and after reading.
3. Describe the role of affect in reading comprehension.
4. How does knowledge of text structure influence reading comprehension?
5. What role does context play in reading comprehension?

REFERENCES

Bakhtin, M. M. (1995). *Forward a philosophy of the act.* Austin, TX: University of Texas Press.

Bloome, D. (1986). Building literacy and the classroom community. *Theory into Practice, 25,* 1–6.

Brock, C. H., Boyd, F. & Moore, J. (2003). Variation in language and the use of language across contexts: Implications for literacy learning. In D. Lapp, J. Flood, & J. Jensen (Eds.), *Handbook of research in the English Language arts.* Matwah, NJ: Lawrence Erlbaum Associates.

Buss, R. R., Ratliff, J. L., & Irion, J. C. (1985). Effects of instruction on the use of storystarters in composition of narrative discourse. In J. A. Niles & R. V. Lalik (Eds.), *Issues in literacy: A research perspective* (pp. 55–58). Rochester, NY: National Reading Conference.

Cullinan, B. E. (1987). Inviting readers to literature. In B. E. Cullinan (Ed.), *Children's literature in the reading program* (pp. 35–51). Newark, DE: International Reading Association.

Englert, C. S., & Raphael, T. E. (1990). Developing successful writers through cognitive strategy instruction. In J. E. Brophy (Ed.), *Advances in research on teaching (Vol. 1): Teaching for meaningful understanding and self-regulated learning* (pp. 105–151). Greenwich, CT: JAI Press.

Flood, J., & Lapp, D. (1981). *Language/reading instruction for the young child.* New York: Macmillan.

Gee, J. P. (1996). (2nd ed.). *Social linguistics and literacies: Ideology in discourses.* Philadelphia, PA: Falmer Press.

Green, J. L. (1992). Multiple perspectives: Issues and directions. In R. Beach, J. L. Green, M. L. Kamil, and T. Shanahan (Eds.), *Multidisciplinary perspectives on literacy research* (pp. 19–34). Urbana, IL: National Conference on Research in English and National Council of Teachers of English.

Guthrie, J. (1977). Research views: Story comprehension. *The Reading Teacher, 30,* 575–577.

Heath, S. B. (1983). *Ways with words: Language, life, and work in communities and classrooms.* New York: Cambridge University Press.

Helmstetter, A. (1987). Year-long motivation in the 8th grade "reluctant" class. *Journal of Reading, 31,* 244–247.

Moffett, J. (1983). Reading as meditation. *Language Arts, 60,* 315–322.

New directions in reading instruction (1988). Newark, DE: International Reading Association.

Piaget, F. (1986). Piaget's theory of director development. *Child Care Information Exchange, 50,* 10–13.

Probst, R. E. (1988). Readers and literary texts. In F. Nelms (Ed.), *Literature in the classroom: Readers, texts, and contexts* (pp. 21–22). Urbana, IL: National Council of Teachers of English.

Raphael, T. E., Englert, C. S., and Kirschner, B. W. (1989). Students' metacognitive knowledge about writing. *Research in the Teaching of English, 23,* 343–379.

Ruddell, R. & Unrau, N. (1994). Reading as a meaning-construction process: The reader, the text, and the teacher. In R. Ruddell, M. Ruddell, & H. Singer (Eds.), *Theoretical models and processes of reading* (Vol. 4, pp. 996–1056). Newark, DE: International Reading Association.

Rumelhart, D. (1984). Understanding understanding. In J. Flood (Ed.), *Understanding reading comprehension.* Newark, DE: International Reading Association.

Smith, N. B. (1963). *Reading instruction for today's children.* Englewood Cliffs, NJ: Prentice Hall.

Stein, N. L., & Feldman, S. S. (1977). The effects of different modes of verbalization on the recognition of object detail in pictures. *Child Development, 48,* 1544–1551.

Trollope, A. (1978). *An autobiography.* Berkeley, CA: University of California Press.

Trabasso, T., & Bouchard, E. (2002). Teaching readers how to comprehend text strategically. In C. Collins Block & M. Pressley (Eds.), *Comprehension instruction: Research-based best practices* (pp. 176–200). New York: Guilford.

Tunnell, M. O., & Jacobs, J. S. (2002). *Children's literature, briefly.* Upper Saddle River, NJ: Prentice Hall.

Walker, S. M. (2002). Fossil Fish Found Alive: Discovering the Coelacanth. Minneapolis, MN: Carolrhoda Books, Inc.

CHILDREN'S LITERATURE

Fox, M. (1994). *Tough Boris.* New York: Scholastic.

Morrison, T. (1998). *Beloved.* New York: Plume.

Pfister, M. (1992). *The rainbow fish.* New York. North South Books.

Spinelli, J. (1990). *Maniac Magee.* New York: Little Brown.

Walker, S. M. (2002). *Fossil fish found alive.* Minneapolis, MN: Carolrhoda Books.

10

Teaching Children to Write

CHAPTER GOALS

To help the reader

- understand the processes writers use.
- understand how writing can be taught in a workshop model.
- understand the developmental nature of writing skills.
- understand the types of writing instruction that are useful for students.
- understand how writing allows teachers' to understand students' thinking.
- understand the use of technology in writing instruction.

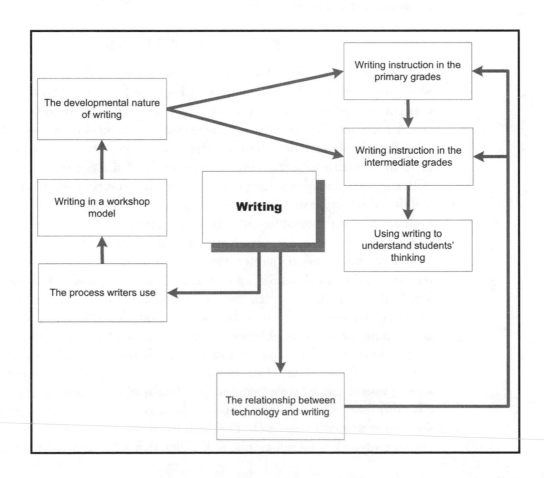

Write a complete sentence. How do you know it is complete? Share your sentence with a peer from class. How are your sentences alike, and how are they different? Who taught you to write?

Writing, like speaking, provides students with an outlet for the expression of ideas. Writing is the process of using language to bring meaning to our experiences. Written expression may be conveyed through many different forms, including compositions, letters, poems, reports, e-mails, and short stories. Writing involves inventing, selecting, eliminating, and arranging one's ideas. In addition, proofreading, editing, and revising are laborious but critical tasks in writing.

Many educators distinguish between *creative* and *practical* writing experiences by referring to stories and poems as creative writing and to letters, reports, e-mails, and essays as practical writing. Although we understand their rationale, we believe that any time a person conveys his or her thoughts through written language, regardless of the form, that person has engaged in an act of creativity. Throughout this chapter, we avoid making a distinction between creative and practical writing.

Far too often, teaching writing is a matter of (a) the teacher assigning a topic, (b) the student agonizing over the assignment, (c) the student turning in the completed assignment, and (d) the teacher making comments and corrections, assigning a grade, and returning it to the student. In this approach, the teacher is constantly in control of students' writing.

THE PROCESSES WRITERS USE

Over the past several decades, educators have examined the ways in which writers write (e.g., Calkins, 1994; Emig, 1971; Fearn & Farnan, 2001; Graves, 1983). Current theories of writing instruction emphasize writing as process rather than as product. Current theories also emphasize that there is no one process that works for all writers. Within this framework, writers are not only concerned with correctness of form, but also with learning, generating, and discovering through writing. Although we emphasize writing in this chapter, it seems prudent to remind you that theories of writing instruction as well as practical teaching recommendations have been included throughout the entire book. For instance, one of the examples focused on teaching students to write summaries from their texts, videos, and lectures. In the reading comprehension chapter, you were introduced to the concept of reader response and types of instruction that help students respond to texts through writing. In the vocabulary chapter, many of the examples that were used to teach children to create new words are, in fact, writing strategies. It is our belief that reading and writing are mutually enhancing activities and that it is dangerous to separate them. However, we are equally aware of the importance of focusing on writing instruction. Thus, in this chapter, you'll meet two teachers who provide excellent writing instruction for their students. Ms. Jacobson is a second grade teacher and Ms. Yarr teaches a fourth/fifth grade combination class. Despite the differences in the ages of students they teach, they both teach students about the ways in which writers write. They do not ascribe to the idea that all writers write using the same

Figure 10-1 Information from a writing development poster.

1. Developing the assignment
   - Establish the purpose of the writing
   - Identify the intended audience
2. Discussing and planning for writing (prewriting)
   - Brainstorm, concept map, or outline
   - Discuss ideas with others
   - Find resources (as needed) for the topic
3. Writing
4 Sharing/responding
5. Reread
   - Invite another person to read and comment
6. Editing and revising
   - Consider the goal in the writing
   - Focus on topic, support for the topic, and mechanics
7. Rewriting

process. They each teach students about writing development using the information in Figure 10–1. Ms. Yarr has this on a poster in her classroom highlighting important components of writing processes, and she knows that students will modify the components as they identify processes that work for them.

These two teachers know that any particular writing assignment may extend over several days. Additionally, they suggest that children be provided a particular and specific time each day for writing. This writing can be in a journal or can be any other form of writing the student chooses. Students often do not become enthusiastic about their work because it has no consequences. This is an important point, for real-world writing always has consequences. We write letters of complaint, expecting a response; a book review may put a book on the best-seller list or relegate it to a lonely life on a bookstore shelf; a report on dolphin communication may change the way animal research is conducted. The point is that real writing has real consequences. It is purposeful, with content and context meaningful for the writer. Unfortunately, some school-based writing assignments are merely training exercises, in which dutifulness (rather than inventiveness, uniqueness, or any form of risk-taking) is the supreme virtue.

Above all, Ms. Jacobson and Ms. Yarr know that writing tasks must be significant for the writer. For example, Ms. Yarr found a writing assignment on the Internet that asked students to compare and contrast early colonial life to life today. Concerned that this prompt was merely a "training exercise," she changed the prompt and asked student to write information for a book chapter. Thus, each student could contribute an entry to the book and everyone in the class could read the book and learn more about colonial life. Her students could choose to focus their papers based not on what they thought that their teacher wanted, but instead on what they thought would be most interesting to their audience (other students in the class).

Ultimately, the writings were shared and the points of view of the respective student authors discussed. As students progressed, their papers were copied and compiled into a comprehensive class book to be read by all students. Ms. Yarr's modified assignment supplies content and context while also addressing a rhetorical style,

DID YOU NOTICE . . .
Did you notice that writing should have a purpose? Authentic writing will help students connect more with their writing (and reading), as it will have intent and purpose. Think about the writing you have done as you have read this textbook. What is the purpose? What is it teaching you? How has it been meaningful and connected to real life?

thus providing students with an opportunity to invest their writing energies in a situation that has an outcome with meaning and significance.

Of course, writing must be assessed. Ms. Johnson and Ms. Yarr do not grade every piece of writing their students produce. Instead, they select pieces and invite their students to select pieces for closer scrutiny. We agree with these teachers that assessing student writing based on specific writing traits is helpful. As we discussed in the chapter on assessment, students must know the criteria on which they are being judged. For this reason, we share the writing trait rubrics with students, invite students to evaluate their own writing against these rubrics, and use these rubrics when providing students feedback. (See the sample rubrics in the Appendix at the end of the chapter.) In general the writing traits we are concerned with (Flood, Lapp, & Fisher, 2004; Spandel, 2001) are:

- Ideas: Good writing contains ideas—it conveys a message. These ideas matter to the reader and capture the reader's interests.
- *Organization:* Good writing has organization—this means that the writing has a logical structure, transitions that help the reader, and a flow that matches the genre of writing.
- *Voice:* Good writing has its own voice—a personal tone and flavor chosen by the writer. When writing is flat or dry, the problem is usually in the voice.
- *Word choice:* Good writing shows a thoughtful approach to word choice—the writer uses the right vocabulary to get the message across. The writer also knows how to use word variations and play with words with the reader.
- *Sentence fluency:* Good writing has sentence fluency—there is a rhythm and flow to the writing that helps it convey the message. In addition, not all of the sentences are the same length or style.
- *Conventions:* Good writing shows correct use of the conventions of written English, including grammar, spelling, punctuation, capitalization, and usage.
- *Presentation:* Good writing looks good on the page. Good presentation means that it is ready to read! If people can't read it, the message won't get through!

TEACHING WRITING IN THE WRITER'S AND READER'S WORKSHOP

Similar to the reader's workshop, there are a number of common components of the writer's workshop. For a comparison of the two, see Table 10–1. In general, the writer's workshop begins with a whole class lesson in which the teacher provides instruction. Some call this the *minilesson* whereas others call it a *focus lesson* (e.g., Frey & Fisher, 2005) or a *maxilesson* (e.g., Fearn & Farnan, 2001). For example, during one whole-class lesson, Ms. Yarr may model the use of dialogue in narrative writing. She may specifically focus on where the quotation marks should be made, and the words that can be used instead of *said*. While doing so she is thinking out loud about *how she is constructing* her piece of writing.

Her *write aloud* provides explicit modeling of the actual thinking she does as she writes. While doing so she charts the information so that her students can listen to and read what is being written. As she writes the sentence, *"Come in to see the surprise, exclaimed Linda"* she might say to the class, "I want the reader to hear the excitement in Carol's voice so I think I'll go back and add the word excitedly

TABLE 10-1
Comparing the Reader's and Writer's Workshop

Writer's Workshop Component	Reader's Workshop Component	Group Size
Minilesson or maxilesson	Read aloud and shared reading	Whole class
Guided practice, including peer editing	Guided reading	Small groups
Independent writing with conferring, publishing of work, and author chairs	Independent reading and conferring	Individuals

and also an exclamation mark." As Ms. Yarr edits the sentence she rereads it aloud, "*Come in to see the surprise, excitedly exclaimed Linda!*" and then adds, "Now my sentence really let's the reader know how exited Linda is to share her surprise." The write aloud lets the students in on what really happens as a writer constructs. Write alouds are effective at any grade level.

Following the whole class *focusing lesson*, students typically work in groups. Similar to the reader's workshop, during this guided practice students must be engaged in small-group learning activities so that the teacher can work with a group on a specific lesson. Using Ms. Yarr's classroom as the example again, she has her young writers work in groups of four or five students. Some groups use the computers to search for information or to type their papers. Other groups use the skills they have developed in editing to review each other's papers. Still other groups are illustrating their writing or reading aloud to the group for content feedback. During this time, Ms. Yarr meets with small groups of students to discuss topics, writing conventions, or thesis development.

The final component of the writer's workshop is independent writing. During this time, students work individually on their papers. Ms. Yarr meets with individual students to review their final drafts before they publish. In addition to the traditional, typed papers, Ms. Yarr also invites students to publish their papers on the Internet, in bound classroom books, and in anthologies that groups of students have created on specific topics. Each week, Ms. Yarr also sets aside time for the author's chair, a time in which students sit in the specially decorated chair and read aloud the texts that they have written. These published pieces and the shared writing during author's chair are the goal of the workshop—independent writing.

The following sections provide more specific suggestions and activities for your student writers at each grade level. Before we take a closer look at writing instruction, let's examine how writing develops.

THE DEVELOPMENTAL NATURE OF WRITING: TYPES OF WRITING SYSTEMS USED BY CHILDREN

Your Turn

Think back to your earliest writing stages. Can you remember the first time you tried to write something? Can you remember the first word you wrote? What were your earliest experiences as a writer?

Ms. Jacobson, like most primary grade teachers, knows that children come to school with a wide range of experience and competence in writing. Children typically

Drawing

FIGURE 10–2   Drawing.

Scribbles

FIGURE 10–3   Scribbles.

DID YOU NOTICE . . .
Did you notice one of the systems of writing is copying environmental print? Because you may have students at this stage in your classroom and because it can stimulate thought, creating a print-rich classroom is essential. You will want to have a room full of charts, word walls, student work, banners, and books to make your environment come alive with words.

progress in a series of stages in their writing development. We'll review each of these stages using figures from Teale (1987).

Random marks. The beginning of writing is often a series of random marks that children make when given a writing instrument. As many new parents learn, these random marks are often made on walls, furniture, toys, and other nontraditional writing surfaces.

Drawing. Figure 10–2 contains an example of a drawing that was made by an emerging writer who wanted to share part of a story. At this stage, children have learned that they can convey meaning with writing instruments.

Scribbles. Scribbles are an important developmental stage in writing. Scribbles like the ones in Figure 10–3 demonstrate that children know that writing (in English)

Copying Environmental Print

FIGURE 10–4   Copying environmental print.

Random Letters

FIGURE 10–5   Random letters.

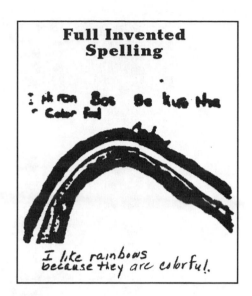

Early Invented Spelling	**Full Invented Spelling**

FIGURE 10–6   Early invented or transitional spelling.

FIGURE 10–7   Full invented or transition spelling.

moves across a line and has returns. At this stage, children can often "read" their scribbles and will use pictures to remember what the scribbles say.

Copying environmental print. Along the lines of scribbles and before they learn to write consistent letters, children will copy environment print. If given time and writing instruments, children at this stage will often select different samples from around the room to write. Additionally, as seen in Figure 10–4, children often add drawings from the environment or from their imagination to their copied print.

Random letters. As the letters from the environment become part of children's memories, they often write random letters as they play or draw as evidenced in Figure 10–5. These random letters often do not connect with specific examples from the environment, and children often cannot "read" their writing. However, this stage is important as children are committing letters to memory.

Early invented or transitional spelling. Following the use of random letters, children attempt to record words or thoughts in writing. These early attempts often have a consonant from the word as it is traditionally spelled, but the other letters are random or invented as seen in Figure 10–6.

Full invented or transitional spelling. At this stage, most teachers can read the writing of children despite the number of spelling irregularities. Children are now making educated guesses in their writing and have mastered some of the rules for the language as noted in Figure 10–7.

THE PRIMARY YEARS

The primary grade teacher has an opportunity to capitalize on children's enthusiasm for language, and the most effective way to do this is by structuring natural language activities through the language experience approach (LEA). Several LEA activities have already been described. They include prompting students with cues to encourage their oral responses. For example, a teacher might ask students to describe the best part of their day yesterday. As children share ideas, the teacher

can transcribe the words for students to read and share (second and third graders could talk into a cassette recorder and then transcribe their own words). Once the words have been transcribed by the teacher, students can be given a piece of paper on which to copy the transcription. Transcriptions can also be illustrated. Students will enjoy reading and rereading their work and sharing it with their classmates. They will also enjoy seeing it displayed in the room.

"I'm 5 and I know how to write my name!"

If all students have been encouraged to talk about a particular theme or set of experiences, these writings can be bound into a classroom book for all students to read. Students will also love sharing these books with parents on special occasions such as school open house sessions. Parent organizations, such as PTSA (Parent Teacher Student Association), also enjoy seeing such works presented at their meetings, and students can be a part of the presentations. Such experiences not only communicate to the school district the progress of students, but also provide opportunities for students to garner esteem-building accolades for their work beyond their teacher's comments.

Kindergarten classes can create books by using their own names and two other words, such as *will* and *run*. For example, a child could write and illustrate "Tina will run" or "Will David run?" LEA activities allow students to function both as readers and as writers, helping them to begin understanding the roles of both. They begin to see the interconnection between the skills of composition and comprehension.

Interactive Writing

You will find that children love to listen to and create stories. When encouraged, young children will engage freely in storytelling. If you capitalize on these situations by recording their stories, your students can listen to their own stories and tales while creating illustrations for them. One especially useful way that Ms. Jacobson teaches writing to younger students is called *interactive writing* (e.g., McCarrier, Pinnell, & Fountas, 2000). Interactive writing serves as the basis of her entire writing curriculum. Ms. Jacobson takes her time with daily interactive writing because she knows the value of teaching students the conventions of English as well as the importance of teaching them to love writing.

Interactive writing starts with a whole-class or small-group conversation. Recently Ms. Jacobson asked the students in her class about their upcoming field trip to the zoo. Each student excitedly talked with a partner about the upcoming trip. After 2 minutes, Ms. Jacobson asked the class for some sentences that described their thinking. After a few minutes, the class had agreed on the first sentence, "We plan to visit the zoo on Friday, and we hope to see snakes and lions."

Using her dry erase board, Ms. Jacobson invites the first student to walk up and write the first word on the board. Tammy volunteers. Based on her assessment information, Ms. Jacobson knows that Tammy often forgets to capitalize letters. While Tammy is walking to the front of the room, Ms. Jacobson asks the class, "What do we need to remember to do when we start a new sentence?" In unison, they respond, "make it a capital!" Tammy correctly writes "We" on the board. Then Ms. Jacobson invites the class to say the whole sentence aloud.

The next student to volunteer is Alvin. He writes the second word for their sentence as plan. Ms. Jacobson asks him to stay at the board for a minute. At another place on the dry erase board, she asks the class for words that rhyme with plan. They give her the words *Dan*, *span*, *fan*, *toucan*, and *pan*. As she writes these words on the board, Alvin looks back to his word and corrects the spelling. Then the whole class repeats the sentence, including the words that have been written and those that have yet to be written. Ms. Jacobson also adds appropriate words to the class word wall so that students can use these new words in their independent writing.

DID YOU NOTICE ...
Did you notice that Ms. Jacobson is calling on students who are volunteering? Because she is aware of her students writing strengths and needs she is able to call on students and support them while up in front of the class. Interactive writing engages students in a comfortable, nonthreatening way with which all students can feel successful as writers.

Ms. Jacobson continues this level of instruction until the sentence has been completed. Each time a student approaches the board, Ms. Jacobson provides spelling, grammar, or punctuation instruction to the whole class. When they have finished writing their shared sentence, the students copy the sentence into their writer's notebooks and add a few sentences of their own that are on the same topic as the shared sentence.

As you can see, Ms. Jacobson knows that she has a profound influence on her students' attitudes toward writing. She is flexible with her assignments, remembering that there are many ways in which to complete any task. Through discussions, she is able to encourage students to believe that they have many things to write about. Correct style, form, and spelling receive secondary attention during these early writing attempts. Please note that Ms. Jacobson does not ignore style, form, or spelling, but she knows that there is a natural progression of development and that students must take risks with language, matching sounds and letters to communicate. As discussed in the chapter on vocabulary, children's spelling is developmental and improves with instruction and practice (e.g., Bear, Invernizzi, Templeton, & Johnston, 2003).

Can you think of other topics that could be shared as a group writing experience such as the one described in the interactive writing process? Jot those three or four topics down and share with other members of the class.

Other Motivational Devices

In addition to her interactive writing instruction, Ms. Jacobson uses any motivational device that encourages children to talk and eventually turns that talk into writing. The story in Figure 10–8, written by Shannon, a second grade student, is an example of turning one's talk and experiences to writing.

At this early age, narratives are frequently a reflection of the student's experiences. It is not necessary to correct every error in these early writing attempts. This may discourage the child. Note that Shannon's spelling errors are phonetic representations of the words she chose to use. Through experience, she will realize that not all words are spelled phonetically. This is a valuable part of the writing experience for a young child.

Although many students see editing as an arduous task, Ms. Jacobson points out to her students that it is a necessary task in which all writers engage. Too often the editing process is not explained to students. The student thus incorrectly assumes that a successful writer produces a finished piece after only one attempt. When student writers are not able to do the same, they view themselves as being punished when they engage in the editing process. Because they feel that they have failed when they are asked to edit, many students view themselves as poor writers and consequently never explore the idea of themselves as writers. Many of Ms. Jacobson's students want to have a friend help them with the editing of their work before Ms. Jacobson reads it.

As another component of her writing instruction, Ms. Jacobson invites her students to share their written products aloud (with illustrations) with other students.

Figure 10–8   Shannon's writing (second grade).

My Dog Had A Cold

Once upon a Time There was a dog named
Muffen he was so cute one day we went
outside. he began To sneeze then. I ran
down To the docter's. he said that Muffen
had the flu. Muffen was very scared so I said Muffen
your lucky. I broke my finger. you better hurry and get
better so you can come to my Birthday Monday.
all have the docter give you a shot. arrr said Muffen
you have to have a shot its the only way to get
better for my Birthday Monday. The next morning was
a desaster. I took Muffen to the docter and then
the stuff began Muffen bit the docter's leg
bit my hand and he didn't get a shot he
got a Spanken instead.

The
End

by
Shannon
(age: 8)

Teacher comment:

> Shannon,
>   I hope Muffin was able to come
> to your party because I know that
> would have been your favorite present.

They may also share their work with their families by writing a note or a letter to accompany it. Activities such as these integrate the language arts (listening, speaking, reading, and writing) and make writing real for students.

Ms. Jacobson has learned that the best stories are often shared accounts of detailed perceptions. Thus, it is very important to plan activities that will heighten students' sensory awareness. The following activities can serve to encourage students' awareness of their world while extending language development:

- Ask children to describe the face of someone they love.
- Have the children close their eyes and listen to a variety of sounds. Then have them describe the sounds.
- Let the students try to identify objects by touch. A variety of objects can be placed in paper bags.
- Ask the students to describe pleasant or frightening odors.

Figure 10—9   Eric's writing (fifth grade).

Missy Maetian's Mission

One day a very, very small spaceship came out of the sky. It looked like a beer can. It even opened like one. I know that because I saw it.

A little person came out and said," La ba." I said, "Ha ha". She said, "Oh, that's the lauguage you speak." "Yes, it is," I said. "I have been taught to speak all langues on the planet Earth.

"What planet do you come from?" "Ram Bam," she said. "Will you say T.V. in your language," I said . "Boob tube, by the way, what is T.V.?" "It's a picture that flashes on a box." "Oh, then what does picture, flash, and box mean?" "Never mind."

"What is your name?" "Missy! What is yours?" "Charles." "My mission is to bring back a human being. Will you come?" "How long will it be?" "Only about a magratriairn." "How long will that be in my time?" "Oh, only

T.C.
I like the way you created new words.

Given one of these prompts, Ms. Jacobson begins by recording (by writing and/or on tape) student responses. Over time, students can begin generating their own writings. When appropriate, students can also begin copying/writing their responses from recorded models. It is important to keep in mind the need, even in the primary years, to assign writing activities that students will view as purposeful and meaningful. For example, along with the four activities listed, Ms. Jacobson prompts students by saying that they should write their descriptions so vividly that their classmates will be able to guess what the subject is without actually knowing.

THE INTERMEDIATE YEARS

During the intermediate school years, opportunities abound for engaging students in writing. Ms. Yarr knows that it is important to emphasize writing in her language arts curriculum because writing activities (a) provide students with an opportunity for self-expression, (b) provide a channel for extending language development, and (c) arouse students' interest in literary materials.

Figure 10–9 *(Continued).*

about ten minutes." "Ok, I'll go." Caboom and we were there. "What was that, double light speed?" We came down out of the sky and landed on a landing pad. I was taken for test.

"Hey, that's a needle!" "We are going to test your blood." "Ouch!" "Hey, your blood is red, ours is green! We're ready to take you back." Caboom and we were home. We said goodbye to each other and then of to Ram Bam she flew again.

by Eric (age: 11)

Mere Can

**T.C.

Eric,
your pictures
add a lot to
your story!

**T.C. = TEACHER COMMENTS

**T.C. Eric,
your story is very good and very creative.

The story in Figure 10–9 was written by Eric, a fifth grade student. Note the wry humor and imagination it displays. The contents of this story exemplify how children are influenced by their experiences. Eric willingly shared his fascination with *Star Wars*, *Star Trek*, and other space and adventure films. Because Ms. Yarr encourages conversation, writing, and editing, Eric gladly shared his ideas through a fictional piece.

You may encounter students who are not anxiously awaiting an opportunity to participate in a writing activity. For the reluctant writer or the student who has difficulty with writing, you may need to provide

- "starter" packets (possible topics, locales, characters, themes, etc.).
- basic language activities.
- word lists.
- alternative assignments.
- areas of interest that can be integrated into writing activities.

One excellent activity that you may want to use in your writing curriculum is sentence combining.

Teaching Sentence Combining

Several researchers in the field of written composition have reported success having students manipulate sentences to expand their ability to organize. This device of manipulating sentences organizationally is called *combining*. These sentences can be drawn from students' writing, books that the class is reading, or ideas that the teacher has to teach a specific language construct.

Although Mellon (1969) and O'Hare (1973) were among the first to create sentence combining activities for children, this practice has been successful in improving syntactic fluency for many years. The following examples illustrate sentence combining:

One day a dog came into our yard.

The dog was little and brown.

Combined—One day a little brown dog came into our yard.

Elaine is tall.

Elaine is slender.

Elaine is pretty.

Combined—Elaine is tall, slender, and pretty.

Depending on the age and abilities of your students, the sentences may be more complex.

The old woman stood silently on the street corner.

She was watching a burning apartment building.

She was wearing a tattered coat.

A solitary tear trickled down her cheek.

Combined—An old woman in a tattered coat stood silently on the street corner watching a burning apartment building while a solitary tear trickled down her cheek.

Explain to your students that they may change the words or the order of the words as long as they do not change the meaning.

Sentence combining will help students with most types of writing and can be especially valuable in editing compositions. It is important, however, that students be aware that sentence combining may not be appropriate for all forms of writing. Poetry, tall tales, or musical creations are examples of writing activities that may not lend themselves well to sentence combining.

Write your own set of sentences that can be used in a sentence combining exercise: two sentences; three sentences; four sentences; five sentences. Share them with your classmates.

Alexander and the Terrible, Horrible, No Good, Very Bad Day by Judith Viorst. Used with permission from Simon & Schuster Children's Publishing.

Teaching Narrative Story Structures

When students first come to school, they are well versed in the narrative structure of writing. They have been told stories, they have been read to, and they have watched cartoons and movies. Each of these activities embodies narration, which is basically storytelling. However, Ms. Yarr knows that being familiar with story structure does not ensure that students will be able to generate good stories. She helps her students create their own stories through a discussion of story elements. For example, Ms. Yarr helps students understand characterization by discussing their impressions of characters, what they are like, and how they change throughout the book.

After reading and discussing parts of the story, the students in Ms. Yarr's class wrote questions that required further analysis of the parts discussed. For example, from the story *Alexander and the Terrible, Horrible, No Good, Very Bad Day* by Judith Viorst (1972), the students generated the following questions:

Who was Alexander?

Where did the story take place?

Why was he having a bad day?

What did he do when he felt bad?

How is Alexander like/unlike me?

Did any part of the story sound like something that has happened to you?

Before writing their own stories, children can work in another way with story parts that have been prefabricated. While Ms. Yarr uses the technical terms such as *characterization*, *setting*, *plot*, *conflict*, and *resolution*, other teachers use terms like

DID YOU NOTICE . . .
Did you notice that most student writing can be a form of assessment? Collecting student writing often throughout the school year will be helpful when planning instruction and assigning grades for report cards. It is especially helpful when conferencing with students and parents about student progress. Oftentimes, teachers, students, and parents may forget just how much progress is being made. Collecting student work for portfolios reminds us of the huge leaps children make throughout a given school year.

who, *what*, *where*, and *when* especially when they are teaching younger students or students who are not familiar with story grammar. For example:

Characterization: a mouse, an 8-year-old girl, a horse, space invaders

Setting: movie theater, beach, ice cream store, forest

Setting: a party, a camping trip, a bad day, an accident

Once students have chosen their story parts, they can write short (no more than one-page) stories. Ms. Yarr encourages brevity. It is a fallacy that limiting students' writing limits their creativity. Instead, it can encourage creative thinking by focusing students' attention on saying what they want to say clearly and concisely. In addition, any writing problems that a student has will show up in the first 50 words and then tend simply to be repeated; therefore, teachers can evaluate students' writings that are one page in length as effectively as writings that are two to three pages.

Teaching Non-Narrative Forms of Writing

Unlike narrative forms, most students are not familiar with expository writing. In fact, most students are not introduced to non-narrative forms of writing until about the third grade. At that point, students begin seeing more writing whose purpose is to report, explain, and clarify. Most of these writings are in their content area textbooks. Ms. Yarr uses the following steps to help her students better understand expository writing:

1. Predict
2. Listen/read
3. Summarize
4. Share

Each student brings a wealth of prior knowledge and experience to the classroom. Given a particular content topic, such as dinosaurs, which might be studied in a science class, students can be asked to use their prior knowledge to predict the kinds of information they may encounter in the text. Students can do library research to gather important information to include in their expository writing. This strategy encourages students to become actively involved in their own learning. Their predictions can be illustrated on a semantic map similar to the one in Figure 10–10. This activity also sets a purpose and helps students focus on major points as they read or listen to the text.

Next, students either read or listen to the material. After the pre-reading work done in Step 1, a mind-set has been created to help students become critical readers/listeners, a skill they will use throughout their school careers.

Finally, students can make their own semantic maps using the information they have either read or listened to. During this activity, they can compare their predictions with the new information. Also, through discussion, teachers can help students differentiate main ideas from details and supporting evidence. Once this has been done, students can write their main idea statement and relevant details as a four- to six-sentence expository paragraph.

Then, by reading their paragraphs aloud, either in pairs, in small groups, or to the entire class, students can hear and discuss the various ways in which individuals have synthesized and organized the information. This sharing/discussion step is

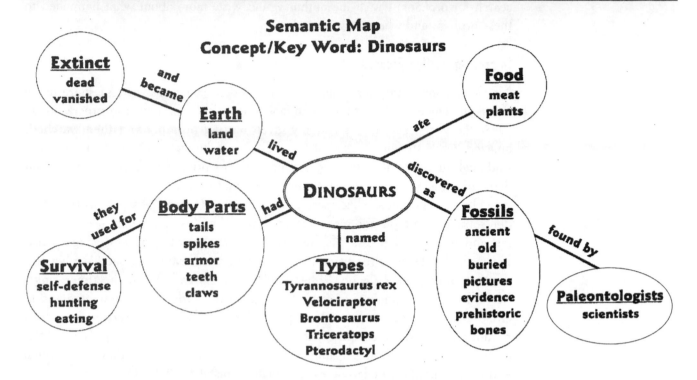

Figure 10–10 A semantic map. From Brassell, D., and Flood, J. (2004). *Vocabulary Strategies Every Teacher Needs to Know.* San Diego, CA: APD. Permission is granted to produce this graphic from Academic Professional Development.

extremely important, for through this process, Ms. Yarr can guide students' conceptions and eliminate misconceptions concerning expository text.

Reading Logs

Ms. Yarr uses reading logs to help students respond to and evaluate the content of their books. She knows that response to literature is one of the common assessments that comprise the state test and she wants her students to do well when presented with this type of writing task. Other highly assessed writing genres include summaries, reports of information, and biographical/autobiographical events.

Reading logs are journals, and the goal is for students to read, reflect on, and respond to what they have read in a personal way. The emphasis is on a quantity of thoughtful writing and not on polished products or formal essays. These writings can include the following:

1. responses to characters, the plot, the setting, or a particular passage
2. summaries
3. comments about how the work relates to the reader's life
4. predictions about what will follow
5. evaluations

Ms. Yarr uses reading logs to help students gain an appreciation for literature through careful analysis and reflection, with entries serving as records of students' thoughts or as reference points for discussions about literary pieces. An entry from

Anna's reading log in response to the non-narrative book *We Rode the Orphan Trains* (Warren, 2001) said, "There were so many orphans, and no one wanted them. I wonder what we do with orphans today. I think I'll look on the Internet and search for orphans. I wish the author would write more about what happened to these orphans and where they are today."

Improving Writing Fluency

Ms. Yarr knows that most young writers (and in fact most writers) share many things in common. One of these commonalities is the willingness to procrastinate. Over the years, she has mistakenly given writing prompts and then watched, amazed, while students looked at the ceiling and "thought" about their response. Although she knows that thinking is important for writing, Ms. Yarr also knows that there are many ways to improve students' writing fluency.

The strategy that she likes best is power writing (Fearn & Farnan, 2001). Students are given a topic and a specific amount of time (usually 1 minute) to write as fast and as well as they can. Ms. Yarr also uses power writing as a focusing activity. For example, during a recent unit on the American Revolution, she gave her students 1 minute to write on "The Boston Tea Party." When the timer rings, Ms. Yarr asks her students to count the number of words they have written and to circle any words they believe they spelled incorrectly. For the second and third round, she provides the topics "American militia" and "The Stamp Act." After each of these power writings, students count the number of words they have written and circle what they believe are their spelling mistakes. After these three rounds, students graph their highest number on a piece of graph paper stapled in the front of their writer's notebook.

In addition to increasing their writing fluency and focusing their attention on content information, Ms. Yarr knows that these entries can be used for essays. She provides her students time each week to select one of the power writing responses and develop it into an essay for her review. The students in her class know that they can combine several entries that they have written on a topic and get to work on editing.

Teaching Grammar Through Writing

In addition to procrastination, Ms. Yarr knows that writers do not always focus on the grammar rules that guide the English language. She uses given word sentences or generative sentences (Fearn & Farnan, 2001; Fisher & Frey, 2003) as a way to provide students instruction in grammar and sentence structure. For example, Ms. Yarr may ask students to write a sentence that begins with the word *because.* The various sentences can then be shared with the whole class, and Ms. Yarr can determine whether students understand that construct or she can provide instruction. She may also ask students to write sentence with a dependent clause, a sentence that has the word *have* in it, and a sentence with three commas.

These student-generated sentences vary by the student's interest and skill in writing, but contain common characteristics—those given by the teacher. As students share their sentences, Ms. Yarr determines which grammar rules her students know and can use and which rules they confuse or do not know. This information can also be used in the lessons with which she begins her reading or writing workshops.

Understanding Students' Thinking Through Writing to Learn

Learning Log

In all content areas, writing can be used effectively as a writing-to-learn strategy, a practice in which writing about what has been read supports the learning process. The learning log is one such strategy. A journal-like activity similar to the reading log, it differs in that students are prompted to focus not on personal responses but on summarizing, discussing main ideas, and applying information in different contexts. Writings in learning logs are valuable starting points for small-group or whole-class discussions. A typical activity might be structured as follows. Students can be asked to write three points from the previous day's work that they think are important. Then, in groups of three to five, they share their ideas, discussing why they chose similar and different points as important. Each group can be asked to reach a consensus on three to five points they feel are most important to share with the entire class. Group reports then generate further input for discussion. At the same time, teachers can guide the discussions as students' insights and misconceptions are brought to light.

RAFT

Another writing-to-learn activity that Ms. Yarr uses is called RAFT, which stands for *role*, *audience*, *format*, and *topic* (Santa, Havens, & Harrison, 1996). Students are taught each of these components of writing. When they understand the various components, they can be given writing prompts that are not explicitly written for the teacher. For example, during her unit of study on the American Revolution, Ms. Yarr used a RAFT prompt that read:

R = Paul Revere
A = Townspeople
F = Newspaper article
T = My Midnight Ride

Ms. Yarr uses these writing-to-learn prompts not only to determine whether her students understand the content, but also for information about their writing development. She can focus on spelling, grammar, punctuation, thesis development, supporting details, and organization (in addition to whether or not the students understood the content of the lesson).

READING AND WRITING: A STRONG CONNECTION

Over the past decade, nearly every professional publication related to language arts has contained at least one article on the relationship between reading and writing, and professional conferences have devoted a myriad of workshops and seminars to exploring this topic. Why? The answer lies in research that brought to light the striking similarities between these two language skills, skills that previously had been perceived and taught as two entirely separate content areas.

Obviously, reading and writing are not identical. One deals with the production of print, whereas the other deals with print that has already been produced. However, when we look beyond this highly visible difference, we see that both involve the construction of meaning.

The connections between reading and writing suggest that they are mutually supportive language skills. We know, for example, that when beginning reading programs incorporate extensive early writing, children show significant gains in early reading. In a classic study, Durkin (1966) observed that for many children who come to school knowing how to read, writing comes first. Similarly, evidence on student achievement in high-poverty schools suggests that among other things, a focus on writing instruction leads to success (Reeves, 2000).

WRITING INSTRUCTION AND TECHNOLOGY

Dahl and Farnan (1998) pointed out in their book *Children's Writing* that computers and technology have significantly altered the ways in which people experience the world. Researchers have attempted to document positive outcomes when students use computers as part of their writing process program. As Dahl and Farnan noted, the research results are complex. For example, Russell (1991), in her meta-analysis, found that the relationship between technology and writing was significantly influenced by the social interactions that students had in the computer lab although the writing was higher quality when students used word processing software and computers.

In a study of first graders' use of word processing software, Jones and Pellegrini (1996) found that the technology facilitated the students' writing of narratives. These researchers hypothesized that the use of the computer shifted the focus away from the mechanical aspects of writing to focus on words and ideas. Similarly, in a case study of a 5-year-old writer, Cochran-Smith, Kahn, and Paris (1990) noted that the computer provided a mechanism that supported the child's writing. More specifically, the computer allowed the child to focus more directly on his or her words and ideas than on handwriting, letter formation, and alignment of words.

Similar results have been documented for older students as well. In their study of middle school students, Owston, Murphy, and Wideman (1991) found that students wrote higher-quality essays using word processing software than they did when they wrote their essays in cursive. The students in their study were all experienced computer users. The researchers hypothesized that the reason for the high quality was related to the number of times students revised their work on the computer. Odenthal (1992) found similar results among second-language learners. Haas (1989) documented similar results; she found that easy-to-use software programs facilitated the revision process. The results of these studies indicate that technology:

1. helps children to focus on content rather than on mechanics;
2. encourages the production of more and better developed essays; and
3. reduces the drudgery of editing.

Chapter 12 on technology and media includes a number of ideas for using computers and the Internet in writing instruction.

CONCLUSION

Whereas writing develops in predictable ways, the teacher ensures that his or her students become strong writers. Writing instruction is a critical component of reading instruction, given the interconnectedness of literacy. As Anna Quindlen (1998), the author of several best-selling novels, aptly noted, "There are only two ways, really, to become a writer. One is to write. The other is to read" (p. 53). We have devoted this chapter to providing you, the teacher, with ideas for teaching writing. We also agree with Ms. Quindlen and have devoted the majority of this book to helping children read.

QUESTIONS

1. How would you explain the statement "reading and writing are similar language skills?" Discuss the instructional implications of this similarity.

2. At the primary level, what should be the emphasis on correct form in writing? Give specific examples to support your answer.

3. What is the structure of a writer's workshop? What is the role of the teacher in each component of the workshop?

4. Why is fluency important? What can a teacher do to improve writing fluency?

5. What role can technology and media play in writing instruction?

REFERENCES

Bear, D. R., Invernizzi, M., Templeton, S., & Johnston, F. (2003). *Words their way: Word study for phonics, vocabulary and spelling instruction* (3rd ed.). Upper Saddle River, NJ: Merrill Prentice Hall.

Brassell, D., & Flood, J. (2004). *Vocabulary strategies every teacher needs to know* (p. 62). San Diego, CA: APD Press, Academic Professional Development.

Calkins, L. M. (1994). *The art of teaching writing.* Portsmouth, NH: Heinemann.

Cochran-Smith, M., Kahn, J., & Paris, C. L. (1990). Writing with a felicitous tool. *Theory Into Practice, 29,* 235–247.

Dahl, K. L., & Farnan, N. (1998). *Children's writing: Perspectives from research.* Newark, DE: International Reading Association and National Reading Conference.

Durkin, D. (1966). *Children who read early: Two longitudinal studies.* New York: Teachers College Press.

Emig, J. (1971). *The composing processes of twelfth graders.* Urbana, IL: National Council of Teachers of English.

Fearn, L., & Farnan, N. (2001). *Interactions: Teaching writing and the language arts.* Boston: Houghton Mifflin.

Fisher, D., & Frey, N. (2003). Writing instruction for struggling adolescent readers: A gradual release model. *Journal of Adolescent & Adult Literacy, 46,* 396–405.

Flood, J., Lapp, D., & Fisher, D. (Eds.). (2004). *Teaching writing: Strategies for developing the 6+1 traits.* San Diego, CA: Academic Professional Development.

Frey, N., & Fisher, D. (2005). *Language arts workshop: Purposeful reading and writing instruction.* Upper Saddle River, NJ: Merrill Prentice Hall.

Graves, D. (1983). *Writing: Teachers and children at work.* Exeter, NH: Heinemann.

Haas, C. (1989). Does the medium make a difference?: Two studies of writing with computers. *Human Computer Interaction, 4,* 149–169.

Jones, I., & Pellegrini, A. D. (1996). The effects of social relationships, writing media, and microgenetic development of first-grade students' written narratives. *American Educational Research Journal, 33,* 691–718.

McCarrier, A., Pinnell, G. S., & Fountas, I. C. (2000). *Interactive writing: How language and literacy come together, K-2.* Portsmouth, NH: Heinemann.

Mellon, J. C. (1969). *Transformational sentence combining: A method for enhancing the development of syntactic fluency in English composition.* Urbana, IL: National Council of Teachers of English.

O'Hare, F. (1973). *Sentence combining: Improving student writing with formal grammar instruction.* Urbana, IL: National Council of Teachers of English.

Odenthal, J. M. (1992). *The effect of a computer-based writing program on the attitudes and perform-ance of students acquiring English as a second language*. Unpublished doctoral dissertation, San Diego State University & Claremont Graduate University, San Diego, CA.

Owston, P. D., Murphy, S., & Wideman, H. H. (1991). On and off computer writing of eighth grade students experienced in word processing. *Computers in the Schools, 8,* 67–87.

Quindlen, A. (1998). *How reading changed my life*. New York: Ballantine Publishing.

Reeves, D. (2000). *Accountability in action: A blueprint for learning organizations*. Denver, CO: Advanced Learning Centers.

Santa, C. M., Havens, L., & Harrison, S. (1996). Teaching secondary science through reading, writing, studying, and problem solving. In D. Lapp, J. Flood, & N. Farnan (Eds.), *Content area reading and learning: Instructional strategies* (2nd ed., pp. 165–179). Boston: Allyn & Bacon.

Spandel, V. (2001). *Creating writers through 6-trait writing assessment and instruction*. New York: Addison Wesley Longman.

Teale, W. H. (1987). Emergent literacy: Reading and writing development in early childhood. *National Reading Conference Yearbook, 36,* 45–74.

Viorst, J. (1972). *Alexander and the terrible, horrible, no good, very bad day*. New York: Aladdin.

Warren, A. (2001). *We rode the orphan trains*. Boston: Houghton Mifflin.

Writing

Assessment Scoring Guide

WOW!
Exceeds expectations

- IDEAS
- ORGANIZATION
- VOICE
- WORD CHOICE
- SENTENCE FLUENCY
- CONVENTIONS
- PRESENTATION

⑤ STRONG:
shows control and skill in this trait; many strengths present

④ EFFECTIVE:
on balance, the strengths outweigh the weaknesses; a small amount of revision is needed

③ DEVELOPING:
strengths and need for revision are about equal; about half-way home

② EMERGING:
need for revision outweighs strengths; isolated moments hint at what the writer has in mind

① NOT YET:
a bare beginning; writer not yet showing any control

©Northwest Regional Educational Laboratory

1

IDEAS AND CONTENT
(Development)

5 *This paper is clear and focused. It holds the reader's attention. Relevant anecdotes and details enrich the central theme.*
   A. The topic is **narrow** and **manageable**.
   B. **Relevant, telling, quality details** give the reader important information that goes **beyond the obvious** or predictable.
   C. Reasonably **accurate details** are present to support the main ideas.
   D. The writer seems to be writing from **knowledge** or **experience**; the ideas are **fresh** and **original**.
   E. The reader's questions are **anticipated and answered**.
   F. **Insight**—an understanding of life and a knack for picking out what is significant—is an indicator of high level performance, though not required.

3 *The writer is beginning to define the topic, even though development is still basic or general.*
   A. The **topic is fairly broad**; however, you can see where the writer is headed.
   B. **Support is attempted**, but doesn't go far enough yet in fleshing out the key issues or story line.
   C. **Ideas are reasonably clear**, though they may not be detailed, personalized, accurate, or expanded enough to show indepth understanding or a strong sense of purpose.
   D. The writer seems to be drawing on knowledge or experience, but **has difficulty going from general observations to specifics**.
   E. The reader is **left with questions**. More information is needed to "fill in the blanks."
   F. The **writer generally stays on the topic** but does not develop a clear theme. The writer has not yet focused the topic past the obvious.

1 *As yet, the paper has no clear sense of purpose or central theme. To extract meaning from the text, the reader must make inferences based on sketchy or missing details. The writing reflects more than one of these problems:*
   A. The writer is **still in search of a topic**, brainstorming, or has not yet decided what the main idea of the piece will be.
   B. Information is **limited** or **unclear** or the **length is not adequate** for development.
   C. The idea is a **simple restatement** of the topic or an **answer** to the question with little or no attention to detail.
   D. The writer has **not begun to define the topic** in a meaningful, personal way.
   E. **Everything seems as important as everything else**; the reader has a hard time sifting out what is important.
   F. The text may be **repetitious**, or may read like a collection of **disconnected, random thoughts** with no discernable point.

©Northwest Regional Educational Laboratory
2

Chapter Ten

ORGANIZATION

5 *The organization enhances and showcases the central idea or theme. The order, structure, or presentation of information is compelling and moves the reader through the text.*

    A. An **inviting introduction** draws the reader in; a **satisfying conclusion** leaves the reader with a sense of closure and resolution.

    B. **Thoughtful transitions** clearly show how ideas connect.

    C. Details seem to fit where they're placed; **sequencing is logical** and **effective**.

    D. **Pacing is well controlled**; the writer knows when to slow down and elaborate, and when to pick up the pace and move on.

    E. The **title**, if desired, is **original** and captures the central theme of the piece.

    F. Organization **flows so smoothly** the reader hardly thinks about it; the choice of structure matches the **purpose** and **audience**.

3 *The organizational structure is strong enough to move the reader through the text without too much confusion.*

    A. The paper has a **recognizable introduction and conclusion**. The introduction may not create a strong sense of anticipation; the conclusion may not tie-up all loose ends.

    B. **Transitions often work well**; at other times, connections between ideas are fuzzy.

    C. **Sequencing** shows **some logic**, but not under control enough that it consistently supports the ideas. In fact, sometimes it is so predictable and rehearsed that the **structure takes attention away from the content.**

    D. **Pacing is fairly well controlled,** though the writer sometimes lunges ahead too quickly or spends too much time on details that do not matter.

    E. A **title (if desired) is present,** although it may be uninspired or an obvious restatement of the prompt or topic.

    F. The **organization sometimes supports the main point or storyline;** at other times, the reader feels an urge to slip in a transition or move things around.

1 *The writing lacks a clear sense of direction. Ideas, details, or events seem strung together in a loose or random fashion; there is no identifiable internal structure. The writing reflects more than one of these problems:*

    A. There is **no real lead** to set-up what follows, **no real conclusion** to wrap things up.

    B. Connections between ideas are **confusing** or not even present.

    C. **Sequencing needs** lots and lots of **work.**

    D. **Pacing feels awkward;** the writer slows to a crawl when the reader wants to get on with it, and vice versa.

    E. **No title is present** (if requested) or, if present, **does not match** well with the content.

    F. Problems with organization make it **hard for the reader to get a grip** on the main point or story line.

©Northwest Regional Educational Laboratory
3

VOICE

5   *The writer speaks directly to the reader in a way that is individual, compelling and engaging. The writer crafts the writing with an awareness and respect for the audience and the purpose for writing.*

     A. The tone of the writing **adds interest** to the message and is **appropriate for the purpose and audience.**

     B. The reader feels a **strong interaction** with the writer, sensing the **person behind the words.**

     C. The writer **takes a risk** by revealing who he or she is consistently throughout the piece.

     D. **Expository or persuasive** writing reflects a **strong commitment** to the topic by showing **why** the **reader needs to know this** and why he or she should care.

     E. **Narrative** writing is **honest, personal, and engaging** and makes you **think about, and react to,** the author's ideas and point of view.

3   *The writer seems sincere but not fully engaged or involved. The result is pleasant or even personable, but not compelling.*

     A. The writer seems aware of an audience but discards personal insights in favor of **obvious generalities.**

     B. The writing communicates in an **earnest, pleasing, yet safe** manner.

     C. Only **one or two moments here or there** intrigue, delight, or move the reader. These places may **emerge strongly for a line or two, but quickly fade away.**

     D. **Expository or persuasive** writing **lacks consistent engagement** with the topic to build credibility.

     E. **Narrative** writing is **reasonably sincere,** but doesn't reflect unique or individual perspective on the topic.

1   *The writer seems indifferent, uninvolved, or distanced from the topic and/or the audience. As a result, the paper reflects more than one of the following problems:*

     A. The writer is **not concerned with the audience.** The writer's style is a **complete mismatch** for the intended reader or the writing is **so short** that little is accomplished beyond introducing the topic.

     B. The writer speaks in a kind of **monotone** that flattens all potential highs or lows of the message.

     C. The writing is **humdrum and "risk-free."**

     D. The writing is **lifeless or mechanical**; depending on the topic, it may be overly technical or jargonistic.

     E. The development of the topic is **so limited** that **no point of view is present**—zip, zero, zilch, nada.

©Northwest Regional Educational Laboratory
4

WORD CHOICE

5 *Words convey the intended message in a precise, interesting, and natural way. The words are powerful and engaging.*

A. Words are **specific** and **accurate**. It is easy to understand just what the writer means.
B. **Striking words and phrases** often catch the reader's eye and linger in the reader's mind.
C. Language and phrasing is **natural**, **effective**, and **appropriate** for the audience.
D. **Lively verbs** add energy while **specific nouns** and **modifiers** add depth.
E. Choices in language **enhance** the **meaning** and **clarify** understanding.
F. **Precision** is obvious. The writer has taken care to put just the right word or phrase in just the right spot.

3 *The language is functional, even if it lacks much energy. It is easy to figure out the writer's meaning on a general level.*

A. Words are **adequate and correct in a general sense**, and they support the meaning by not getting in the way.
B. Familiar **words and phrases communicate** but rarely capture the reader's imagination.
C. **Attempts at colorful language** show a willingness to stretch and grow but sometimes reach beyond the audience (thesaurus overload!).
D. Despite a **few successes**, the writing is marked by **passive verbs**, **everyday nouns**, and **mundane modifiers**.
E. The words and phrases are **functional** with only **one or two fine moments**.
F. The words may be **refined in a couple of places**, but the language looks more like **the first thing that popped into the writer's mind**.

1 *The writer demonstrates a limited vocabulary or has not searched for words to convey specific meaning.*

A. Words are so **nonspecific and distracting** that only a **very limited meaning** comes through.
B. Problems with language **leave** the **reader wondering**. Many of the **words** just **don't work** in this piece.
C. Audience has not been considered. **Language is used incorrectly** making the message secondary to the misfires with the words.
D. **Limited vocabulary** and/or **misused parts of speech** seriously impair understanding.
E. Words and phrases are so **unimaginative** and **lifeless** that they detract from the meaning.
F. **Jargon or clichés** distract or mislead. **Redundancy** may distract the reader.

©Northwest Regional Educational Laboratory
5

© **Northwest Regional Educational Laboratory. Reprinted with permission.**

SENTENCE FLUENCY

5 *The writing has an easy flow, rhythm, and cadence. Sentences are well built, with strong and varied structure that invites expressive oral reading.*

   A. Sentences are constructed in a way that underscores and enhances the **meaning**.

   B. Sentences **vary in length as well as structure**. Fragments, if used, add style. Dialogue, if present, sounds natural.

   C. **Purposeful** and **varied sentence beginnings** add variety and energy.

   D. The use of **creative and appropriate connectives** between sentences and thoughts shows how each relates to, and builds upon, the one before it.

   E. The writing has **cadence**; the writer has thought about the sound of the words as well as the meaning. The first time you read it aloud is a breeze.

3 *The text hums along with a steady beat, but tends to be more pleasant or businesslike than musical, more mechanical than fluid.*

   A. Although sentences may not seem artfully crafted or musical, **they get the job done in a routine fashion.**

   B. Sentences are **usually constructed correctly;** they **hang together;** they are **sound.**

   C. **Sentence beginnings** are not ALL alike; **some variety is attempted.**

   D. The reader sometimes has to **hunt for clues** (e.g., connecting words and phrases like *however, therefore, naturally, after a while, on the other hand, to be specific, for example, next, first of all, later, but as it turned out, although,* etc.) that show how sentences interrelate.

   E. **Parts** of the text **invite expressive oral reading**; others may be stiff, awkward, choppy, or gangly.

1 *The reader has to practice quite a bit in order to give this paper a fair interpretive reading. The writing reflects more than one of the following problems:*

   A. Sentences are **choppy, incomplete, rambling or awkward**; they need work. **Phrasing does not sound natural.** The patterns may create a sing-song rhythm, or a chop-chop cadence that lulls the reader to sleep.

   B. There is little to **no "sentence sense"** present. Even if this piece was flawlessly edited, the sentences would not hang together.

   C. Many **sentences begin the same way**—and may follow the same patterns (e.g., *subject-verb-object*) in a monotonous pattern.

   D. **Endless connectives** (*and, and so, but then, because, and then,* etc.) or a **complete lack of connectives** create a massive jumble of language.

   E. The text **does not invite expressive oral reading.**

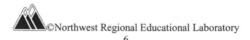

©Northwest Regional Educational Laboratory
6

© **Northwest Regional Educational Laboratory. Reprinted with permission.**

CONVENTIONS

5 *The writer demonstrates a good grasp of standard writing conventions (e.g., spelling, punctuation, capitalization, grammar, usage, paragraphing) and uses conventions effectively to enhance readability. Errors tend to be so few that just minor touch-ups would get this piece ready to publish.*

A. **Spelling is generally correct**, even on more difficult words.
B. The **punctuation is accurate**, even creative, and guides the reader through the text.
C. A thorough understanding and consistent application of **capitalization** skills are present.
D. **Grammar and usage are correct** and contribute to clarity and style.
E. **Paragraphing tends to be sound** and reinforces the organizational structure.
F. The writer **may manipulate conventions** for stylistic effect—and it works! The piece is very close to being **ready to publish.**

GRADES 7 AND UP ONLY: The writing is sufficiently complex to allow the writer to show skill in using a wide range of conventions. For writers at younger ages, the writing shows control over those conventions that are grade/age appropriate.

---

3 *The writer shows reasonable control over a limited range of standard writing conventions. Conventions are sometimes handled well and enhance readability; at other times, errors are distracting and impair readability.*

A. **Spelling** is usually **correct or reasonably phonetic on common words,** but more difficult words are problematic.
B. **End punctuation is usually correct**; internal punctuation *(commas, apostrophes, semicolons, dashes, colons, parentheses)* is sometimes missing/wrong.
C. **Most words are capitalized correctly**; control over more sophisticated capitalization skills may be spotty.
D. **Problems with grammar or usage are not serious** enough to distort meaning but may not be correct or accurately applied all of the time.
E. **Paragraphing is attempted** but may run together or begin in the wrong places.
F. **Moderate editing** (a little of this, a little of that) would be required to polish the text for publication.

1 *Errors in spelling, punctuation, capitalization, usage, and grammar and/or paragraphing repeatedly distract the reader and make the text difficult to read. The writing reflects more than one of these problems:*

A. **Spelling errors are frequent**, even on common words.
B. **Punctuation** (including terminal punctuation) is often **missing or incorrect**.
C. **Capitalization is random** and only the easiest rules show awareness of correct use.
D. **Errors in grammar or usage are very noticeable**, frequent, and affect meaning.
E. **Paragraphing is missing, irregular, or so frequent** (every sentence) that it has no relationship to the organizational structure of the text.
F. The reader must **read once to decode**, then again for meaning. **Extensive editing** (virtually every line) would be required to polish the text for publication.

©Northwest Regional Educational Laboratory
7

© **Northwest Regional Educational Laboratory. Reprinted with permission.**

PRESENTATION
(optional)

5 *The form and presentation of the text enhances the ability for the reader to understand and connect with the message. It is pleasing to the eye.*

A. If handwritten (either cursive or printed), the **slant is consistent**, letters are clearly formed, **spacing is uniform** between words, and the text is easy to read.

B. If word-processed, there is **appropriate use of fonts and font sizes** which invites the reader into the text.

C. The use of **white space** on the page (spacing, margins, etc.) allows the intended audience to easily focus on the text and message without distractions. There is just the right amount of balance of white space and text on the page. The formatting suits the purpose for writing.

D. The use of a **title, side heads, page numbering, bullets,** and evidence of correct use of a style sheet (when appropriate) makes it easy for the reader to access the desired information and text. These markers allow the hierarchy of information to be clear to the reader.

E. When appropriate to the purpose and audience, there is **effective integration of text and illustrations, charts, graphs, maps, tables, etc.** There is clear alignment between the text and visuals. The visuals support and clarify important information or key points made in the text.

3 *The writer's message is understandable in this format.*

A. **Handwriting is readable,** although there may be **discrepancies in letter shape and form, slant, and spacing** that may make some words or passages easier to read than others.

B. **Experimentation with fonts and font sizes** is successful in some places, but begins to get fussy and cluttered in others. The **effect is not consistent** throughout the text.

C. While margins may be present, **some text may crowd the edges.** Consistent spacing is applied, although a different choice may make text more accessible (e.g., single, double, or triple spacing).

D. Although some markers are present (titles, numbering, bullets, side heads, etc.), they are not used to their fullest potential as a guide for the reader to access the greatest meaning from the text.

E. An **attempt is made to integrate visuals** and the text although the connections may be limited.

1 *The reader receives a garbled message due to problems relating to the presentation of the text.*

A. Because the letters are irregularly slanted, formed inconsistently, or incorrectly, and the spacing is unbalanced or not even present, it is **very difficult to read and understand the text.**

B. The writer has gone **wild with multiple fonts and font sizes.** It is a major distraction to the reader.

C. The **spacing is random and confusing** to the reader. There may be little or no white space on the page.

D. **Lack of markers** (title, page numbering, bullets, side heads, etc.) leave the reader wondering how one section connects to another and why the text is organized in this manner on the page.

E. The visuals do not support or further illustrate key ideas presented in the text. They may be **misleading, indecipherable, or too complex** to be understood.

 ©Northwest Regional Educational Laboratory
8

© **Northwest Regional Educational Laboratory. Reprinted with permission.**

11

Discovering the World
Through Literature

─────────── CHAPTER GOALS ───────────

To help the reader

- understand the importance of teaching literature in the elementary school.
- understand ways to select and present appropriate literature for all students.
- understand how literature can be taught.
- understand the relationship of literature to other dimensions of the classroom reading program.

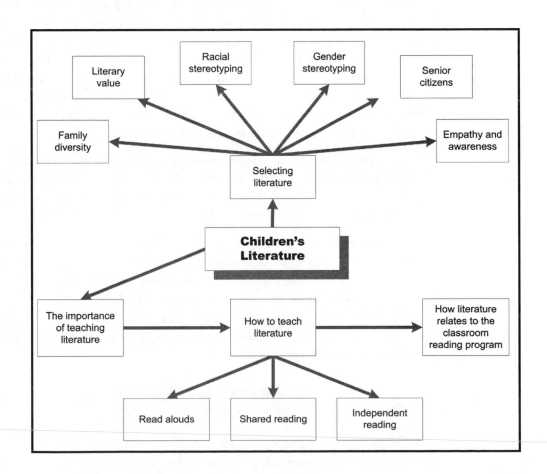

Your Turn

What was your favorite book as a child? Why? Try to find that book today in the library or at your family home. If you can, read that book again and consider the characters and plot. Regardless of whether or not you find the book again, write down the things you liked about this book. Why did it speak to you as a reader?

"Mr. Richardson's classroom is like visiting the library," says fifth grader Sophiny Jackson. She continues, "It's a library for *us*." Visitors notice that Mr. Richardson has books everywhere, books on the walls, books in boxes, books on his desk, and books all over the tables. In some areas of the classroom, Mr. Richardson has organized books around genres. Students can easily find realistic fiction, biographies, poems, and the like. In his classroom "library" area, books are leveled by reading difficulty so that students can quickly find a book that is just right for them. In other areas of the classroom, books are organized by topics. For example, during the introduction to the American Revolution, Mr. Richardson had more than 25 books on the topic spread around the social studies work area. These books comprised a wide range of reading difficulty levels.

During the study of this topic children were encouraged to reading texts independently or in partners as they gained and shared information through both oral and written publication. During the study of this topic Mr. Richardson began each day with a related shared reading or a read aloud. He typically selects texts to read aloud that are more difficult than his students can read themselves. He does so to expand the topical knowledge of his students while modeling the fluency and processes used by a proficient reader. He believes that through listening to and talking about texts he and his students will "grow into a community of learners and view themselves as readers and writers" (Wepner & Feeley, 1993, p. 28). He also provides his students with time each day to read books independently. He knows that these two activities are critical for student motivation and achievement. When asked about the importance of reading and children's literature, Mr. Richardson shared the following quote from Katherine Paterson, a noted children's author:

> I am called to listen to the sound of my own heart—to write the story within myself that demands to be told at that particular point in my life. And if I do this faithfully, clothing that idea in the flesh of human experience and setting in a true place, the sound from my heart will resound in the reader's heart. (Paterson, 1978)

As Katherine Paterson and Mr. Richardson remind us, books allow us a glimpse inside author's minds and inside ourselves. Literature allows us to learn about people we may never meet and to see places we may never visit. Literature is both a window to the world and a mirror of it (Cullinan, 1989; Yopp & Yopp, 2002). This chapter focuses on how to teach literature in elementary school, the need for children to read literature, and the ways in which literature can be integrated through the classrooms.

WHY TEACH LITERATURE IN THE ELEMENTARY SCHOOL?

What is your answer? Pause for a second. Think about yourself, your friends. Why do you or they like to read a good novel? Why do we often see travelers, and people relaxing at beaches enjoying a good book? One reason is that the reading of literature allows us to embark on a personal journey of exploration; it causes us to make connections between our lives and literary figures. The reading of literature ensures thinking and enjoyment.

Aesthetics and Enjoyment

Avid readers know what it is to be "lost" in a book: The realities of the reader's life, whether age 5 or 50, are no longer apparent as the reader is drawn into the lives and experiences of the story's characters. Students who have these experiences will develop a strong desire to read, which is the ultimate goal of a school reading program (Rosenblatt, 1976).

Teachers hope that their literature instruction will enable all students to develop insights that will lead to a better understanding and appreciation of themselves and others. Literature is a mirror that allows us to look at ourselves through the lives of others. Each of us needs to feel connected to our culture, to our world. Although we need to know that we are unique, we also need to know that we are similar to others in many ways and dissimilar to others in many ways. Literature provides the vehicle for taking a journey that will help us to develop this knowledge.

Cultural Literacy

To be "culturally literate" is to know about and to have read the books of one's own cultural heritage. Knowledge of the classics in children's literature enables students to acquire information that can be used to understand and interpret the language of their world. It enables them to learn the ideas and the words of their language. It also forms the basis for understanding and interpreting adult literature. For example, knowledge of fables provides the background for understanding when a student encounters the following expressions in everyday situations:

- Don't cry over spilled milk.
- She's just crying wolf.
- He's a wolf in sheep's clothing.

Make a list of other examples of expressions found in literature. Can you find the origin of the expressions? What information would a child need to make sense of this expression when found in literature.

Although *children's literature* is relatively new when it is viewed in the context of all literature, modern classics written for children do exist. This list continues to grow as we add selections from many cultures. Today children can choose from thousands of books published annually in the United States and from approximately 90,000 children's books that are currently in print (Huck, Hepler, Hickman, & Kiefer, 2000).

Because children's literature is often one's first literary experience, it is the place where expectations about literature are formed. Students who hear or read the classics of children's literature will be prepared to understand and appreciate cultures and classics through books such as *Charlotte's Web* by E. B. White, *The Hob-*

bit by Tolkien, *David Copperfield* by Charles Dickens, or *Roll of Thunder, Hear My Cry* by Mildred Taylor.

Language Enrichment

Research shows that children make language that they hear their own (Gray, 1995). Students adopt and use language patterns that are rich in vocabulary and imagery when they read and hear the classics. "Stories told or read to children give them opportunities to hear words in use and, in the process, to support, expand, and stimulate their own experiments with language" (Cullinan, 1989, p. 15). Language is acquired as children are engaged in conversations, discussions, and hearing and telling stories; "the ability to think for one's self depends upon one's mastery of language" (Didion, 1968, p. 14). Literature often provides a richer language model than what is shared in a conversation. In *Caddie Woodlawn*, Carol Ryrie Brink (1935) provides a descriptive language base as she describes the complexity of Caddie through her actions.

> She had just unfastened the many troublesome little buttons on the back of her tight-waisted dress, and before taking it off, she paused a moment to see if she could balance a fresh-water clam shell on her big toe. (p. 2)

Models of language used by Katherine Paterson in *The Great Gilly Hopkins* (1978) such as "trailing clouds of glory" and "flower child gone to seed" expand children's spoken and written language. Language expansion, which is generally context bound (Wilson, Malmgren, Ramage, & Schutz, 1993), occurs when children explore texts throughout the curriculum.

DID YOU NOTICE . . .
Did you notice that students know when they are reading well-written literature and when they are reading poorly-written text? Think about books you love to read and which ones you put down after a few pages. Is it the language the keeps you glued to the book? The engaging plot? Young students need good books just as much as adults, if not more!

In addition, students can tell the difference between literature that is well written and that which is not; they are intrigued by the language and held spellbound by an action-filled plot. A poorly written story or poem often leaves students restless. Reading good literature in the classroom will provide students with opportunities to see, hear, and imitate language patterns and to develop their sense of story and an appreciation for different types of literature. When Mr. Richardson selects literature, he uses the criteria found in Table 11–1 as a checklist because each of the criteria addressed help him to introduce his students to literature that is powerful in its ability to satisfy, explain, invite, explore, and compel (Hillman, 2003). Literature enables children to develop a sharper and critical mind (Langer, 1992; Strickland, 1987).

> Very young children who are just beginning to learn to read need many experiences with real books. Reading one book teaches us how to read another. It's one of the "prior knowledge" factors in reading. So, along with knowledge of the world, and language, and print, children need to develop knowledge of how books work. (Fox, 1987, p. 23)

As important as hearing the language of literature and having ample opportunities to apply reading skills is the content of good literature. Students develop feelings about and an understanding of concepts such as good and evil, love, vengeance, justice, loyalty, and death (Farnan & Romero, 1996). When reading stories that deal with these concepts, students experience events vicariously, often before they have the opportunity to experience them in their own lives. Such

TABLE 11–1
Literature Selection Criteria

Criteria	Check if YES	Check if NO
Will this text be a pleasurable read?	☐	☐
Does the topic reflect a typical childhood experience or interest?	☐	☐
Is the text written from a child's perspective?	☐	☐
Are the characters children or do they exhibit childlike characteristics?	☐	☐
Is the plot simple, direct, and easily understood?	☐	☐
Is the language appropriate to the targeted age?	☐	☐
Does the text value the innocence of children?	☐	☐
Is the feeling of optimism implied by the text and characters?	☐	☐
Does the text combine fantasy and reality?	☐	☐
Is the text culturally sensitive?	☐	☐
Will the theme of the selection withstand the test of time?	☐	☐

experiences allow students to understand themselves better and to empathize with others.

Literacy Development

Wide reading of good literature also improves one's reading and writing skills. Comprehension is enhanced when the text is interesting and well written because "children struggling to learn to read find out that reading is worth the effort" (Cullinan, 1989, p. 137), and students' vocabularies increase as a result of reading a wide variety of books and stories. Young children who hear good literature read aloud develop a sense of story; they know what to expect from stories and can predict what will happen next. This information enables them to better understand the stories they read and forms the basis for telling or writing original stories. Students who are avid readers see books as sources—they learn to write by reading the writings of others.

Imagination and Motivation

Finally, good literature used in the classroom will develop students' imaginations and increase their desire to read. Well-written texts encourage the reader to form mental images, respond emotionally, and think critically. Readers who find themselves facing the story's antagonist or helping characters find a solution to their problems become involved in creative thinking and problem solving. Students come to know literary characters as good friends and search for additional books in which they appear. They develop passions for books about particular subjects and read everything in the library on those subjects. Certain authors or illustrators become favorites. Students fortunate enough to enjoy good literature in the elementary classroom are likely to become readers for life.

WHAT ISSUES SHOULD BE CONSIDERED WHEN SELECTING CHILDREN'S LITERATURE?

As children's poet Lillian Morrison reminded us, children select books for many reasons. Some want to find out about themselves or their family; others want to know how planes work. Regardless of the reason for book selections, teachers can help students by filling their classrooms with quality books that present all people in a fair and respectful way. Morrison said it this way in her poem:

Get Into Books

Would you like
stories that surprise you
and/or hypnotize you,
a mystery, a history,
a volume to advise you,
how to fix a motor,
build your own computer,
use a tape recorder,
get along with mother?
How about a voyage
into outer space,
romance with an Alien
of a future race?
Then dip in, dig in
grapple in with books,
dive in, delve in

GET INTO BOOKS.
—Lillian Morrison (*Book Poems*, 1998)

Literary Value

Books chosen for the elementary school classroom should cover a wide variety of genres, such as folktales, tall tales, fables, myths, legends, biography, poems, fantasy, realistic and historical fiction, nonfiction, and science fiction (see Figure 11–1). Beginning readers enjoy cumulative stories (i.e., *The Gingerbread Boy* [1987]), sequential books (i.e., *Joseph Had an Little Overcoat* by Simms Taback [1999]), and repetitive books (i.e., *Brown Bear, Brown Bear, What Do You See?* by Bill Martin, Jr. and Eric Carle [1967]).

Teachers must know children's literature very well because wide reading of children's literature that is appropriate for the particular age levels of students will enable better book selection. Books selected for use in the classroom should be well written and include well-developed characters, interesting language, and captivating plots. In addition to developing an awareness of the stereotypes and issues discussed in the following, teachers who know their students well are better able to select books to match the students' interests and abilities. In general, we suggest that teachers choose texts with "(1) literary quality that has been demonstrated by reviews, awards, and trusted word of mouth recommendations; (2) aesthetic qualities that cover a wide array of

Figure 11–1   Genre wheel.

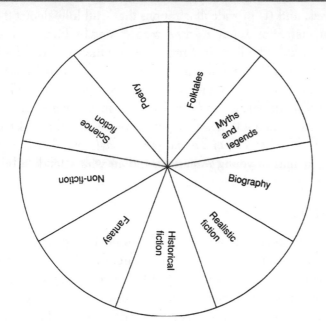

genre that will elicit thoughtful responses from children; (3) concepts and ideas that children can grasp with guidance; and (4) opportunities to lead children to unique discoveries" (Fisher, Flood, & Lapp, 1999, p. 124).

In addition, teachers often used literature to address and counter stereotypes. Literature influences how children perceive themselves, others, and the world in which they live. Teachers must be aware of how authors portray characters of various races, men and women, individuals with disabilities, various family structures, and senior citizens to avoid choosing books that could perpetuate stereotypes.

Racial Stereotyping

Literature is a medium through which our values are conveyed (Kiefer, 1988). Children either see their life experiences reflected in the literature and receive affirmation of them, or they observe that their life experiences are omitted or degraded and are therefore not valued. Racial stereotypes presented in children's literature not only affect the members of the group misrepresented but also influence the way people are viewed by students from other ethnic backgrounds. Teachers must select literature that promotes understanding for all people as individuals.

The way to gain understanding is to become informed. Inaccurate information about members of various cultures has been found in children's books (e.g., Schon, 1996). Such inaccuracies can result in the formation of stereotypes. Books that are selected for use in the classroom should contain accurate information and portray all people as individuals in nonstereotypical roles. We suggest that teachers select books that (a) accurately portray the history and geographic locations of the group; (b) acknowledge the contributions that people from the cultural/ethnic group have made; (c) reflect the differences in lifestyle, socioeconomic level, interests, and abilities of different groups; (d) contain characters that represent roles in society apart

DID YOU NOTICE , , ,
Did you notice that children s literature should portray accurate information and portray all people as individuals in nonstereotypical roles? Teachers must engage students in lively discussions about the text they are reading, clarifying misconceptions, myths, and stereotypes.

from and uninfluenced by their racial/ethnic heritage; (e) use language that reflects the linguistic richness of the culture portrayed while respective of the authentic cultural perspectives; and (f) provide illustrations that truthfully depict the ethnic qualities of the characters. For example, *Esperanza Rising* by Pam Munoz Ryan introduces readers to a girl who lived in Mexico among the wealthy. Her family had to emigrate to the United States and rebuild their lives. This young adult novel challenges the idea that every immigrant is poor and has no history. The picture book *Grandpa, Is Everything Black Bad?* by Holman introduces students to questions about colors and why many things that people perceive to be bad have "black" in their name. In *The Ledgerbook of Thomas Blue Eagle* by Matthaei and Grutman, students meet Thomas, a young American Indian who attends a boarding school and does not yet understand the rules.

Gender Stereotyping

Students' images of themselves and their roles in life may be strongly influenced by the portrayal of male and female roles in literature. Gender role stereotypes in literature can influence a child's values, attitudes, goals, purposes, and patterns of response, and messages influencing self-concept can be conveyed simply by the number of male and female characters presented in books. There is evidence that recent publications include more equality in gender representation (e.g., Trepanier-Street & Romatowski, 1999) than books in the past; however, books in which the greater number of main characters are male are still available to the young reader. Texts that misrepresent gender roles through stereotypes or omission convey some of the following messages:

- Girls don't do interesting or exciting things.
- It's all right for girls to read what boys like, but boys don't read stories that girls like.
- Boys are active and aggressive, not passive and reflective.

Books that include stereotypes generally portray males as more physically and mentally competent than females. Male heroes are strong, daring, courageous, and intellectual, whereas female heroines are frequently caring and nurturing, and when they do something courageous and daring, it is not expected by the other characters. Teachers need to be aware of gender role stereotypes and search for books that portray males as having nurturing, caring traits as well as other abilities, and in which females are portrayed as decisive, intelligent leaders as well as caring, nurturing people. Well-developed characters that go beyond the stereotypical roles provide the best models for children.

Teachers also need to be aware of the existence of differences in how the act of reading is perceived. Reading is often perceived as a feminine activity by both boys and girls (Millard, 1997). The content of the reading material, however, can influence the ways in which reading activities are perceived; reading TV guides, comic books, and science books is often viewed as a masculine activity whereas reading dictionaries or poetry books is perceived as a feminine activity (Kelly, 1983). It is possible that the achievement differences in reading between boys and girls result in part from this perception of reading as a feminine activity. To counter the effects of this attitude, boys should be provided with and encouraged to read materials, even if they are materials that they perceive as more feminine. A number of books provide students an opportunity to consider different perspectives of gender. For example, *Oliver Button Is a Sissy* by T. de Paola introduces readers to a young boy who wants to tap dance. Readers are delighted to learn that Oliver's peers gain respect for him when he enters a talent contest and comes in second place. The book *In the Year of the Boar and Jackie Robinson* by B. Lord introduces readers to an immigrant girl who is very interested in baseball and the new African-American player who is the first to play on an integrated team. *Sam Johnson and the Blue Ribbon Quilt* by L. Ernst introduces readers to an older man who likes to sew quilts and wins the local contest. *Am I Blue? Coming Out from the Silence* by M. D. Bauer provides readers with a number of short stories about the gay and lesbian experience. Finally, *Riding Freedom* by P. Ryan retells the true story of a young woman who pretended to be a man so that she could drive a stagecoach legally.

Senior Citizens

The elderly are frequently stereotyped by children (Kupetz, 1993); they are seen as passive, unproductive, tired, helpless, and ready to die. Many children do not spend time with elderly people, and as a result, their perceptions are formed from the books they read. Therefore, it is essential that literature to which they are exposed portrays the elderly in a positive and realistic manner. For example, *The Giver* by L. Lowry is a young adult novel about a utopian society in which one older person holds all the pain for the community. *Wilfrid Gordon McDonald Partridge* by Mem Fox is an excellent story in which a young child and an elderly woman form a warm and understanding relationship. Similarly, *Mrs. Katz and Tush* by P. Palacco shares the wisdom of a senior citizen.

Empathy and Awareness

Children's literature can be used to develop children's understanding of themselves and others and their relationships with others, and it can develop an awareness of the world around them. For example, bibliotherapy is a way for adolescents to develop problem-solving skills to deal better with stress and anger in their own lives (Shechtman, 2000). Alternatively, young children can understand and work through their apprehensions about starting school or changing schools by reading and discussing books that deal with those situations. In addition, children's literature can be used to promote understanding about and respect for students with disabilities

Different Just Like Me by Lori Mitchell. Used with permission by Charlesbridge Publishing, Inc.

(Blaska & Lynch, 1998). *Different Just Like Me* by L. Mitchell introduces students to people who experience the world in all kinds of ways—from a person who uses a wheelchair to someone who is blind and reads Braille. In *Tru Confessions* by J. Tashjian, readers meet a young woman named Tru who wants to be a TV anchor. She can't find anything to report until she realizes that she has a lot of footage of her brother who has a development disability. As she develops her video project, she begins to see her brother in a whole new way. *Stuck in Neutral* by T. Trueman is a shocking young adult novel told from the perspective of a young man who has a significant disability and cannot speak. This young man cannot tell his father that he is happy, and the father wants to put his "disabled son out of misery."

Character education is receiving attention in many schools. Look in your school libraries and in bookstores and begin collecting titles of books that would be positive examples for young children. Which character traits could the books support?

DID YOU NOTICE . . .
Did you notice that some of the most appropriate and well-loved books are not always the most current? Look at your collection of books when you were young. What books can you find at a garage sale, used book sale, or library? Students will often gravitate to the books their teachers love even if the pages are a little torn and tattered.

All Kinds of Families

A final area in which teachers can use books to encourage students to understand differences focuses on family structures. Books on this topic are often difficult for teachers and community members to agree upon—you may want to check with your administrator before using some of these books. However, the topic is important. Students must understand that their neighbors have family structures different from their own. Children who do not live in "nuclear family" structures will appreciate your attention to this area. For example, *Adoption Is for Always* by L. Girard explains the adoption process and informs students that adopted children are loved. *All Kinds of Families* by N. Simon portrays the variety of families that are found in the community, including single families, children raised by extended families, foster families, and families with gay or lesbian parents. Finally, *At Daddy's on Saturdays* by L. Girard matter-of-factly shares the experience of a child whose parents are divorced. The author points out that this child is still loved by both parents.

Francie **by K. English** © **2002 by NY: Farrar, Straus & Groux.**

SOURCES OF CHILDREN'S LITERATURE

It is impossible for even the most dedicated teachers to read all of the children's books published each year. Fortunately, there are many excellent resources available to aid teachers in selecting books that are most appropriate for their students. Appropriate books may not always be the most current releases. Realizing this, you may want to begin a class library and add to it throughout your career.

Several book awards are presented annually to newly published books worthy of distinction. The Newbery Medal Award is given to the most distinguished contribution to American literature for children in the year of its publication. The award was begun in 1922; therefore, the list of award winners and honor selections is substantial. A listing of recent Newbery Medal winners is presented in Table 11–2. The Caldecott Medal and Honor Award have been presented annually since 1938 to the best-illustrated children's books. A partial listing of Caldecott Medal winners is presented in Table 11–3.

The Coretta Scott King award is given annually to a black author and a black illustrator to commemorate the life and work of the late Dr. Martin Luther King, Jr., and to honor Mrs. Coretta Scott King for her courage and determination in continuing to work for peace and world brotherhood. Recent award winners include the following:

1990: Text—P. and F. McKissack, *A Long Hard Journey: The Story of the Pullman Porter.*
Illustration—J. S. Gilchrist, *Nathaniel Talking*

1991: Text—M. D. Taylor, *The Road to Memphis*
Illustration—L. and D. Dillon, *Aida*

1992: Text—W. D. Myers, *Now Is Your Time! The African-American Struggle for Freedom*
Illustration—F. Ringgold, *Tar Beach*

1993: Text—P. McKissack, *The Dark-Thirty: Southern Tales of the Supernatural*
Illustration—K. A. Wilson, *The Origin of Life on Earth: An African Creation Myth*

1994: Text—A. Johnson, *Toning the Sweep*
Illustration—T. Feelings, *Soul Looks Back in Wonder*

1995: Text—P. and F. McKissack, *Christmas in the Big House, Christmas in the Quarters*
Illustration—J. Ransome, *The Creation*

1996: Text—V. Hamilton, *Her Stories*
Illustration—T. Feelings, *The Middle Passage: White Ships/Black Cargo*

1997: Text—W. D. Myers, *Slam!*
Illustration—J. Pinkney, *Minty: A Story of Young Harriet Tubman*

1998: Text—S. M. Draper, *Forged by Fire*
Illustration—J. Steptoe, *In Daddy's Arms I Am Tall: African Americans Celebrating Fathers*

1999: Text—A. Johnson, *Heaven*
       Illustration—M. Wood, *I See the Rhythm*

2000: Text—C. P. Curtis, *Bud, Not Buddy*
       Illustration—B. Pinkney, *In the Time of the Drums*

2001: Text—J. Woodson, *Miracle's Boys*
       Illustration—B. Collier, *Uptown*

2002: Text—M. D. Taylor, *The Land*
       Illustration—J. Pinkney, *Goin' Someplace Special*

2003: Text—N. Grimes, *Bronx Masquerade*
       Illustration—E. B. Lewis, *Talkin' About Bessie: The Story of Aviator Elizabeth Coleman*

2004: Text—A. Johnson, *The First Part Last*
       Illustration—A. Bryan, *Beautiful Blackbird*

2005: Text—T. Morrison, *The Journey to School Integration*
       Illustration—K. Nelson, *Ellington Was Not a Street*

The Orbis Pictus Award for Outstanding Nonfiction for Children is awarded annually to promote and recognize excellence in nonfiction writing. The award is named in commemoration of the book *Orbis Pictus* (The World in Pictures) by Johann Comenius. It was originally published in 1657 and is considered to be the first informational book written specifically for children. Recent award winners include the following:

1990: J. Fritz, *The Great Little Madison*

1991: R. Freedman, *Franklin Delano Roosevelt*

1992: R. Burleigh, *Flight: The Journey of Charles Lindbergh*

1993: J. Stanley, *Children of the Dust Bowl: The True Story of the School at Weedpatch Camp*

1994: J. Murphy, *Across America on an Emigrant Train*

1995: D. Swanson, *Safari Beneath the Sea: The Wonder World of the North Pacific Coast*

1996: J. Murphy, *The Great Fire*

1997: D. Stanley, *Leonardo da Vinci*

1998: L. Pringle, *An Extraordinary Life: The Story of a Monarch Butterfly*

1999: J. Armstrong, *Shipwreck at the Bottom of the World: The Extraordinary True Story of Schackleton and the Endurance*

2000: R. Bridges, *Through My Eyes*

2001: J. Stanley, *Hurry Freedom: African Americans in Gold Rush California*

2002: S. Bartoletti, *Black Potatoes: The Story of the Great Irish Famine, 1845–1850*

2003: P. Ryan, *When Marian Sang: The True Recital of Marian Anderson: The Voice of a Century*

2004: J. Murphy, *An American Plague: The True and Terrifying Story of the Yellow Fever Epidemic of 1793*

2005: R. Blumberg, *York's Adventures With Lewis and Clark: An African-American's Part in the Great Expedition*

The International Reading Association provides teachers with many opportunities to find new books. The Children's Choices and Teachers' Choices are two awards given by children and teachers, respectively. Each year in the October or November issue of *The Reading Teacher*, the choices are listed. This is an outstanding way for teachers to keep current with good examples of children's literature. In addition, the International Reading Association gives the Children's Book Award to a book whose author "shows unusual promise in the children's book field." This award is specifically awarded to authors for their first or second book written for children.

The teacher may select books based on his or her familiarity with an author or illustrator who has achieved recognition. The following awards are presented to writers and illustrators to acknowledge and honor the contribution their collective works have made to the field of children's literature.

The National Council of Teachers of English Award for Excellence in Poetry for Children is presented to a living American poet in recognition of his or her work. Beginning in 1985, the award has been made every 3 years. Some current recipients include the following:

1980: Myra Cohn Livingston

1981: Eve Merriam

1982: John Ciardi

1985: Lilian Moore

1988: Arnold Adoff

1991: Valerie Worth

1994: Barbara Juster Esbensen

1997: Eloise Greenfield

2000: X. J. Kennedy

2003: Mary Ann Hoberman

The Laura Ingalls Wilder Award is given every 3 years to an author or illustrator whose books, published in the United States, have made a significant and enduring contribution to children's literature. Recent recipients include the following:

1980: Theodor Geisel (Dr. Seuss)

1983: Maurice Sendak

1986: Jeanne Fritz

1989: Elizabeth George Speare

1992: Marcia Brown

1995: Virginia Hamilton

1998: Russell Freedman

2001: Milton Meltzer

2003: Eric Carle

2005: Laurence Yep

The Hans Christian Andersen Award is given every 2 years to one living author and one living illustrator whose works have made a significant international contribution to children's literature. Recent award recipients are as follows:

1982: Author—Lygia Bojunga Nunes (Brazil)
Illustration—Zbigniew Rychlicki (Poland)

1984: Author—Christine Nostlinger (Austria)
Illustration—Mitsumasa Anno (Japan)

1986: Author—Patricia Wrightson (Australia)
Illustration—Robert Ingpen (Australia)

1988: Author—Annie M. G. Schmidt (The Netherlands)
Illustration—Dusan Kallay (Yugoslavia)

1990: Author—Tormod Haugen (Norway)
Illustration—Lisbeth Zwerger (Austria)

1992: Author—Virginia Hamilton (United States)
Illustration—Kveta Pacovska (Czechoslovakia)

1994: Author—Michio Mado (Japan)
Illustration—Jörg Müller (Switzerland)

1996: Author—Uri Orlev (Israel)
Illustration—Klaus Ensikat (Germany)

1998: Author—Katherine Paterson (United States)
Illustration—Tomi Ungerer (France)

2000: Author—Ana Maria Machado (Brazil)
Illustration—Anthony Browne (United Kingdom)

2002: Author—Aidan Chambers (United Kingdom)
Illustration—Quentin Blake (United Kingdom)

2004: Author—Martin Waddell (Ireland)
Illustration—Max Velthuijs (The Netherlands)

Classics in children's literature prepare the reader for adult literary classics. An excellent resource for identifying classics in children's literature is *Children's Literature in the Elementary School* by Charlotte Huck, Susan Hepler, Janet Hickman, and Barbara Kiefer (2000).

The following professional journals include regular book review sections to aid the teacher in keeping abreast of the great number of newly published children's books: *The Reading Teacher, Language Arts, The Horn Book Magazine, Dragon Lode, Book Bag Magazine, Book Links,* and *The Journal of Children's Literature.* In addition, several Web sites provide lists of children's literature and sample lesson plans, including the following:

The Children's Literature Web Guide: http://www.acs.ucalgary.ca/,dkbrown/

Children's Literature (with a comprehensive datebase): http://www.childrens lit.com/home.htm

Kidlit: http://mgfx.com/kidlit/

Bookhive: http://www.bookhive.org/

Children's Literature Assembly: http://www.uta.edu/soe/CLA/

TABLE 11–2
Recent Newbery Award Books

Year	Gold Medal Winner (and Author)	Honor Books
2005	*Kira-Kira* by C. Kadohata	*Al Capone Does My Shirts* by G. Choldenko *The Voice That Challenged a Nation: Marian Anderson and the Struggle for Equal Rights* by R. Freedman *Lizzie Bright and the Buckminster Boy* by G. D. Schmidt
2004	*The Tale of Despereaux: Being the Story of a Mouse, a Princess, Some Soup, and a Spool of Thread* by K. DiCamillo	*Olive's Ocean* by K. Henkes *An American Plague: The True and Terrifying Story of the Yellow Fever Epidemic of 1793* by J. Murphy
2003	*Crispin: The Cross of Lead* by Avi	*The House of the Scorpion* by N. Farmer *Pictures of Hollis Woods* by P. R. Giff *Hoot* by C. Hiaasen *A Corner of the Universe* by A. Martin *Surviving the Applewhites* by S. Tolan
2002	*A Single Shard* by L. S. Park	*Everything on a Waffle* by P. Horvath *Carver: A Life in Poems* by M. Nelson
2001	*A Year Down Yonder* by R. Peck	*Because of Winn-Dixie* by K. DiCamillo *Hope Was Here* by J. Bauer *Joey Pigza Loses Control* by J. Gantos *The Wanderer* by S. Creech
2000	*Bud, Not Buddy* by C. P. Curtis	*Getting Near to Baby* by A. Couloumbis *26 Fairmount Avenue* by T. dePaola *Our Only May Amelia* by J. L. Holm
1999	*Holes* by L. Sachar	*A Long Way From Chicago* by R. Peck
1998	*Out of the Dust* by K. Hesse	*Ella Enchanted* by G. C. Levine *Lily's Crossing* by P. R. Giff *Wringer* by J. Spinelli
1997	*The View From Saturday* by E. L. Konigsburg	*A Girl Named Disaster* by N. Farmer *The Moorchild* by E. McGraw *The Thief* by M. W. Turner *Belle Prater's Boy* by R. White
1996	*The Midwife's Apprentice* by K. Cushman	*What Jamie Saw* by C. Coman *The Watsons Go to Birmingham: 1963* by C. P. Curtis *Yolonda's Genius* by C. Fenner *The Great Fire* by J. Murphy
1995	*Walk Two Moons* by S. Creech	*Catherine, Called Birdy* by K. Cushman *The Ear, the Eye and the Arm* by N. Farmer
1994	*The Giver* by L. Lowry	*Crazy Lady* by J. L. Conly *Dragon's Gate* by L. Yep *Eleanor Roosevelt: A Life of Discovery* by R. Freedman
1993	*Missing May* by C. Rylant	*What Hearts* by B. Brooks *The Dark-Thirty: Southern Tales of the Supernatural* by P. McKissack *Somewhere in the Darkness* by W. Dean Myers
1992	*Shiloh* by P. R. Naylor	*Nothing but the Truth: A Documentary Novel* by Avi *The Wright Brothers: How They Invented the Airplane* by R. Freedman
1991	*Maniac Magee* by J. Spinelli	*The True Confessions of Charlotte Doyle* by Avi

Holes © 1999 by Louis Sachar. Jacket art © 1998 by Vladimir Radunsky. Used with the permission of Farrar, Straus & Giroux.

Belle Prater's Boy © 1997 by Ruth White. Jacket art © 1996 by Elizabeth Sayles. Used with the permission of Farrar, Straus & Giroux.

(continued)

TABLE 11–2   (Continued)

Year	Gold Medal Winner (and Author)	Honor Books
1990	*Number the Stars* by L. Lowry	*Afternoon of the Elves* by J. T. Lisle *Shabanu, Daughter of the Wind* by S. F. Staples *The Winter Room* by G. Paulsen

1989	*Joyful Noise: Poems of Two Voices*
	  by P. Fleischman
		In the Beginning: Creation Stories From
		  Around the World by V. Hamilton
		Scorpions by W. D. Myers

1988	*Lincoln: A Photobiography* by R. Freedman	*After the Rain* by N. F. Mazer *Hatchet* by G. Paulsen

1987	*The Whipping Boy* by
	  S. Fleischman
		A Fine White Dust by C. Rylant
		On my Honor by M. D. Bauer
		Volcano: The Eruption and Healing of
		  Mount St. Helens by P. Lauber

1986	*Sarah, Plain and Tall* by
	  P. MacLachlan
		Commodore Perry in the Land of the
		  Shogun by R. Blumberg
		Dogsong by G. Paulsen

1985	*The Hero and the Crown* by R. McKinley	*Like Jake and Me* by M. Jukes *The Moves Make the Man* by B. Brooks *One-Eyed Cat* by P. Fox

An excellent way for you to continue to be informed about children's literature and ways of using it in the classroom is to become active in the professional organizations of the field. Membership in the local and state chapters (as well as on the national level) of the International Reading Association and the National Council of Teachers of English will allow the teacher access to the newest and best information available. Membership costs include subscriptions to the organizations' journals. Members are provided information about conferences and new publications.

HOW SHOULD LITERATURE BE TAUGHT?

All children should be exposed to the joys of literature. Less able readers are frequently subjected to lessons devoted entirely to skills instruction, the focus of which is often word attack skills. Although these skills are important, they should not constitute the entire reading program. Literature should not be reserved for those students who have mastered the skills and who comprehend reading material with ease. Developing readers also need good literature as much as proficient readers. As we described in chapter 10 when we presented a readers' workshop model, we believe a comprehensive literacy program for every students needs to provide experiences with literature through the following:

1. Read alouds
2. Independent reading
3. Discussion and reflection
4. Responses shared through writing, conversation, drama, art, and music
5. Integrated units of study

TABLE 11–3
Recent Caldecott Award Books

Year	Gold Medal Winner	Honor Books
2005	*Kitten's First Full Moon* by K. Henkes	*The Red Book* by B. Lehman *Coming on Home Soon* by J. Woodson *Knuffle Bunny*: A cautionary tale illustrated and written by M. Willems
2004	*The Man Who Walked Between the Towers* by M. Gerstein	*Ella Sarah Gets Dressed* by M. Chodos-Irvine *What Do You Do With a Tail Like This?* illustrated and written by S. Jenkins and R. Page *Don't Let the Pigeon Drive the Bus* by Mo Willems
2003	*My Friend Rabbit* by E. Rohmann	*The Spider and the Fly* illustrated by T. DiTerlizzi, written by M. Howitt *Hondo & Fabian* by P. McCarty *Noah's Ark* by J. Pinkney
2002	*The Three Pigs* by D. Wiesner	*The Dinosaurs of Waterhouse Hawkins* by B. Kerley *Martin's Big Words: The Life of Dr. Martin Luther King, Jr.* by D. Rappaport *The Stray Dog* by M. Simont
2001	*So You Want to Be President?* by D. Small	*Casey at the Bat* by C. Bing *Click, Clack, Moo: Cows That Type* by B. Lewin *Olivia* by I. Falconer
2000	*Joseph Had a Little Overcoat* by S. Taback	*Sector 7* by D. Wiesner *The Ugly Duckling* by J. Pinkney *A Child's Calendar* by T. S. Hyman *When Sophie Gets Angry—Really, really angry ...* by M. G. Bang
1999	*Snowflake Bentley* by M. Azarian	*No, David!* by D. Shannon *Snow* by U. Shulevitz *Tibet: Through the Red Box* by P. Sís *Duke Ellington: The Piano Prince and His Orchestra* by B. Pinkney
1998	*Rapunzel* by P. O. Zelinsky	*The Gardener* by S. Stewart *There Was an Old Lady Who Swallowed a Fly* by S. Taback *Harlem: A Poem* by W. D. Myers
1997	*Golem* by D. Wisniewski	*The Graphic Alphabet* by D. Pelletier *Hush! A Thai Lullaby* by M. Ho *The Paperboy* by D. Pilkey *Starry Messenger* by P. Sís
1996	*Officer Buckle and Gloria* by P. Rathmann	*Tops and Bottoms* by J. Stevens *Zin! Zin! Zin! A Violin* by L. Moss *Alphabet City* by S. T. Johnson *The Faithful Friend* by R. San Souci
1995	*Smoky Night* by D. Diaz	*Swamp Angel* by A. Isaacs *Time Flies* by E. Rohmann *John Henry* by J. Lester and J. Pinkney
1994	*Grandfather's Journey* by A. Say	*Peppe the Lamplighter* by E. Bartone and T. Lewin *In the Small, Small Pond* by D. Fleming *Owen* by K. Henkes

Snow © 1999 by Uri Shulevitz. Used with the permission of Farrar, Straus & Giroux.

Tibet: Through the Red Box © 1999 by Peter Sís. Used with the permission of Farrar, Straus & Giroux.

(continued)

TABLE 11–3   (Continued)

Year	Gold Medal Winner	Honor Books
		Raven by G. McDermott
		Yo! Yes? by C. Raschka
1993	*Mirette on the High Wire* by E. McCully	*Working Cotton* by S. A. Williams and C. Byard
		Seven Blind Mice by E. Young
		Stinky Cheese Man and Other Fairly Stupid Tales by J. Scieszka and L. Smith
1992	*Tuesday* by D. Wiesner	*Tar Beach* by F. Ringgold
1991	*Black & White* by D. Macaulay	*More More More Said the Baby: 3 Love Stories* by V. B. Williams
		Puss in Boots by C. Perrault, M. Arthur, and F. Marcellino
1990	*Lon Po Po* by E. Young	*Bill Peet: An Autobiography* by B. Peet
		Color Zoo by L. Ehlert
		Hershel and the Hanukkah Goblins by E. Kimmel and T. S. Hyman
		The Talking Eggs by R. D. San Souci and J. Pinkney
1989	*Song & Dance Man* by S. Gammell	*The Boy of the Three-Year Nap* by D. Snyder and A. Say
		Free Fall by D. Wiesner
		Goldilocks and the Three Bears by J. Marshall
		Mirandy and Brother Wind by P. C. McKissack and J. Pinkney
1988	*Owl Moon* by J. Schoenherr	*Mufaro's Beautiful Daughters: An African Tale* by J. Steptoe
1987	*Hey, Al* by R. Egielski	*Alphabatics* by S. MacDonald
		Rumpelstiltskin by P. O. Zelinsky
		The Village of Round and Square Houses by A. Grifalconi
1986	*Polar Express* by C. Van Allsburg	*King Bidgood's in the Bathtub* by A. Wood and D. Wood
		The Relatives Came by C. Rylant and S. Gammell
1985	*Saint George and the Dragon* by M. Hodges and T. S. Hyman	*Hansel and Gretel* by R. Lesser and P. O. Zelinsky
		Have You Seen My Duckling? by N. Tafuri
		The Story of Jumping Mouse by J. Steptoe

Read Alouds

Many very young children beg their parents and the other important adults in their lives to read stories to them. It is enjoyable to both the adult and the child, and through this warm and pleasant activity, many children develop a love of books. Reading stories aloud to children in the classroom is one way teachers can attempt to replicate the treasured activity of lap reading experienced by many children at home (Fisher, Flood, Lapp, & Frey, 2004; Frey, Fisher, Lapp, & Flood, 1999).

Those children unfortunate enough not to have had numerous lap-reading experiences have a desperate need for the teacher to welcome them to the world of literature and to experience reading in this manner. By reading aloud, the teacher models reading behavior; students see that reading is a pleasurable experience, a way of learning, and something to be shared with others. Listening to books being read aloud is also a way for students to experience those books that are too difficult for them to read themselves or that are of a genre they themselves may not have chosen. Teachers of every grade should read aloud to their students every day of the school year.

In primary grade classrooms, read-aloud time is frequently scheduled during the morning literacy block or immediately following lunch. If a regular time is reserved for reading aloud, students expect and anticipate the activity.

Teachers should select books appropriate for the interests and needs of their students. Young children enjoy picture books with predictable story lines and repetitious texts. Students quickly learn repeated phrases and join in with the teacher as they are read. Intermediate grade teachers may allow students to select books to be read aloud. However, it is important, particularly in the primary grades, that all books read be examples of well-written literature. Books read by the teacher are perceived by students as those worthy of the teacher's time and attention; therefore, they set the standard for the types of books the students will choose for independent reading.

The teacher of young children can follow a few simple guidelines to make the most of the experience. Children should be seated comfortably on the floor or on small chairs in a semicircle around the teacher, who is also seated on the floor or on a low chair. The book should be held so that the illustrations are visible to all children. By pausing after each page is read, the teacher provides the students with time to view the illustrations in detail and to offer relevant comments or ask questions about the story. The teacher may also pause periodically at appropriate times to ask students to make predictions about the story. The sensitive teacher allows students to determine the pace of the read-aloud session and responds to their need to stop and discuss the story in an unhurried manner. Time may also be allotted for discussion following a reading. Activities related to the story (e.g., singing a song or pantomiming a scene) are often done at the end of the read aloud. Response activities are wonderful but should not be used to excess; sometimes it's desirable just to hear a good story. When reading books that take several days to complete, the teacher should read ahead and identify appropriate stopping places. It is important, particularly in the primary grades, for books that are read aloud by the teacher to be placed in the classroom library. Martinez and Teale (1988) found that kindergarten students chose familiar books from the classroom library more frequently than unfamiliar books, and they displayed more emergent reading behaviors when looking at books that were familiar to them. This study also confirmed the importance of selecting books with predictable structures; emergent reading behaviors were more evident with books that had predictable story structures.

It cannot be overemphasized that reading aloud should not be an activity exclusive to the primary grades. All students enjoy and benefit from the experience.

Shared Reading

Shared reading is a variation of read alouds—the book is read aloud. Many of the same recommendations found in the read aloud section apply to shared reading. The difference between read alouds and shared reading is that shared reading requires that the students all see the text as the teacher reads. Many primary grade teachers do this with big books. Upper grade teachers sometimes photocopy their reading material and place it on the overhead. As with read alouds, in shared reading lessons the selection of texts is critical. For shared reading, we suggest that the teacher purposefully select a text and identify a specific teaching point. For example, *Wings* by James Marshall is a tale of two chickens. One enjoys reading, and the other does not. The one who doesn't like reading is captured by a fox. Anyway, this text could be used for shared reading with any one of the following lessons in mind:

- Focus on how the author uses punctuation—., ! ? " are all used
- Focus on dialogue and how authors indicate that characters are talking— "..."
- Focus on specific spelling patterns

Shared reading lessons often last between 15 and 20 minutes. Intermediate level teachers usually do not read the entire text as a shared reading—they select the part of the text that contains the information for the lesson that day and then finish the text as a read aloud or invite students to read the remainder of the text independently or in partners. Remember, shared reading should allow students to see a clear connection between the text that is read to them and some aspect of text structure that you teach.

Independent Reading

Independent reading is a sacred time each day in which students can select books to read on their own. These books should not be too difficult for students to read independently. Thus, teachers must teach students how to select books that they can read independently. Some teachers teach students to select books based on their interest, but to put the book back if they come across five words on the first page or two that they do not know. Other teachers label their books with colored stickers based on difficulty. Students in these classes are taught to look for interesting books with specific colors of stickers that relate to their independent reading level. Regardless of the selection method students are taught to use, the classroom library must be well stocked to meet the instructional needs of a diverse group of students.

The teacher who takes the time to establish a classroom literature library provides an invaluable service for students. Although the school library may house a large collection of the finest children's literature, students who are provided immediate access to books via a well-designed classroom library spend more time doing independent reading (Lowe, 1998). In one study, students in classrooms with literature libraries were found to read up to 50% more than those in classrooms without such resources (Bissett, 1970).

Classroom Library

The physical arrangement of the classroom library is an important factor in determining how frequently and in what way students will use it. The library area should be both physically and visually accessible from the other areas of the classroom and should comfortably accommodate five to seven students. Open-faced shelves from which book covers may be seen encourage students to pick up books and read them. Comfortable chairs, pillows, and cushions provide inviting spaces in which students may read. Attractive bulletin boards in the library area allow the teacher to display posters, school or classroom reading motivation charts, literature about books, and provide a place for the students to display their written and visual responses to books. A small table with a tape recorder and headphones allows students to read along with taped recordings of books or to listen to music while they read. A special area should be set aside for books that the teacher has read aloud to the class or has introduced in some way, for such attention promotes selection of the books by the students (Morrow, Tracey, Woo, & Pressley, 1999).

Students who use the classroom literature library independently are free to select and check out books for their recreational reading and return them when they are finished. A simple and efficient check out and return system will enable accurate records to be kept and will allow the library to function without the daily attention of the teacher. For example, a clipboard with an attached pen or pencil and forms such as the following can be maintained by students:

The arrangement of the books on the shelves depends on the amount of time the students and teacher wish to invest in the project. The books may simply be arranged in a neat and orderly fashion, in no particular sequence and under no particular classification, or they may be separated into fiction and nonfiction sections, alphabetized by author, or ordered by text difficulty. Whatever system is adopted, it should be maintained by the students as they select and return books. Remember that younger children enjoy seeing the covers of books so displays that allow the fronts to show will probably increase their use.

The teacher generally supplies the classroom library with books from the school and/or public library. The book collection in the classroom should be as large as possible, representing a wide range of reading levels and including books of several genres and subjects, some of which can be rotated frequently. Children's magazines such as *Weekly Reader, Highlights*, and *Music Express* should also be included if possible.

Students may wish to keep a record of their recreational reading and share their responses to the books with their classmates. One way to accomplish this is to keep in the library a file box of 4 × 6 inch note cards. The title of each book in the library is written at the top of one of the cards. After students have read the book, they write their names on the card and one or two sentences telling what they thought about the book. Students selecting books can flip through the file box and locate the books recommended by their classmates.

Name	Title/Author	Date Out	Date In

The classroom literature library can also be designed to support the basal reading program. Books from which basal reader selections were chosen should be included in the classroom collection, as well as works by authors and illustrators featured in the basal readers. Also included should be books with themes, contents, and styles complementary to those of basal reader selections. The classroom library then functions as an extension of the basal reading program and can be used by the students to complete required or optional reading activities.

To enhance fully the reading/language arts program, an area near the classroom library area should be supplied with bins of lined and unlined paper, pencils, crayons or markers, scissors, tape or glue, and a flat table at which the students can work. Students will use these materials as they create their responses to the literature. A bulletin board area for displaying students' projects is also desirable. Many materials contained in a small area tend to make the area cluttered and messy. It is important that the teacher design the area with the age level of the students in mind, thereby allowing them to maintain order and keep the area tidy. A library area that allows students to choose books, materials, and activities freely will be used by the students.

Maintaining a classroom literature library requires effort on the part of the teacher and students; however, this effort may be one of the most significant investments a teacher can make in the students' education. Immediate access to books and the resultant shared experiences inspire and motivate students and form the foundation for an attitude that will support students' movement toward lifelong reading.

Reader's Theater

In addition to read alouds, shared reading, guided reading, and independent reading, another way to engage students with books is through a reader's theater activity. Reader's theater is a form of oral interpretation in which the students fully participate as readers and, for that reason alone, its inclusion in the language arts curriculum is validated. Beyond that, reader's theater builds fluency and increases reading comprehension (Martinez, Roser, & Strecker, 1998–1999). The activity is nonthreatening; students read from a script, so fear of forgetting lines is nonexistent. Readers' parts vary in length and difficulty so that students of differing reading abilities can participate in the same activity.

Although prepared scripts are available commercially, many children's literature selections can be easily arranged or rewritten into a script format by the teacher or by students. Stories consisting mainly of dialogue are most easily adapted; however, a good story with a moderate amount of narration should not be overlooked. Lengthy sections of narration may be divided between two or more narrators. Poetry may also be adapted for reader's theater. A poem consisting entirely of narration may be scripted using solo and small-group voices, thus resembling a verse choir. The only stage directions included in the script are indications to the reader to enter (face the audience) and exit (turn one's back on the audience). Students enjoy deciding where each reader is to stand during the activity, and this may be indicated by a diagram on the title page of the script. Scripts should be typed, copied (one copy per reader), and mounted on construction paper or placed in manila file folders. Students indicate their parts on the script with a highlighting marker.

The story or poem should be read in its original form to students prior to the reader's theater activity. After hearing the story, the students interpret story characters by imagining how they look and by dramatizing individually or as a group how they walk, gesture, and speak. Students portray their characters through their facial expressions and voices as they read the scripts. At times, minimal props or costumes may be appropriate as an indication of a character's identity. For example, a student portraying a dog might draw whiskers on his face with an eyebrow pencil, and a father character might wear a paper necktie. Students enjoy making these props out of construction paper. Teacher and students must remember, however, that the purpose of the props is to indicate the identity of the character; they must not be a distraction to either the reader or the audience.

A reader's theater script may be performed once or several times, with or without an audience; the participation in the activity itself is of value. Table 11–4 is an example of literature arranged in a reader's theater script fashion.

Literature Charts

The development of literature charts is an excellent way to introduce students to many different types of literature. Students can visually process the texts they read. Literature charts also

1. provide an impetus for conversation.
2. preserve students' thinking and language development.
3. make links between books, ideas, and concepts.
4. encourage organized, creative thinking.
5. ensure the development of reading/language arts strategies across curriculum areas.

TABLE 11–4
Reader's Theater Script for Adaptation of Miss Nelson Is Back

Characters:

Miss Nelson/Viola Swamp	Mr. Blandsworth (Mr. B)
Child 1	Narrator 1
Child 2	Narrator 2
Child 3	Big Kid
Child 4	

Characters facing the audience: Miss Nelson, Children 1–4, Narrators 1 and 2
Characters with backs toward audience: Big Kid, Mr. Blandsworth

Narrator 1:	One Friday Miss Nelson told her class that she was going to have her tonsils out.
Miss Nelson:	I'll be away next week,
Narrator 1:	she said.
Miss Nelson:	And I expect you to behave.
Children 1–4:	Yes, Miss Nelson,
Narrator 2:	said the kids in 207. But at recess it was another story. (Miss Nelson: back toward audience, Big Kid: face audience)
Children 1–4:	Wow!
Narrator 1:	said the kids.
Child 1:	While Miss Nelson is away, we can really act up!
Big Kid:	Not so fast!
Narrator 2:	said a big kid from 309.
Big Kid:	Haven't you ever heard of Viola Swamp?
Child 2:	Who?
Narrator 1:	said one of Miss Nelson's kids.
Big Kid:	Miss Swamp is the meanest substitute in the whole world,
Narrator 2:	said the big kid.
Big Kid:	Nobody acts up when she's around.
Children 1–4:	Oooh!
Narrator 1:	said Miss Nelson's kids.
Big Kid:	She's a real witch,
Narrator 2:	said the big kid.
Children 1–4:	Oooh!
Narrator 1:	said Miss Nelson's kids.
Big Kid:	I'll just bet you get the Swamp!
Narrator 2:	said the big kid.

Source: Adapted from *Miss Nelson Is Back* (p. 20) by H. Allard and J. Marshall, 1982. Boston: Houghton Mifflin. Copyright 1982 by Houghton Mifflin.

Chapter Eleven

Roser (1990) elaborates on these ideas when she provides the following reasons for using language/literature charts. She encourages the use of literature charts:

1. *As a testimony to the importance of the sharing and study of literature in your classroom.* A language chart is a message. It signals that children in your classroom read and talk about books. Because language charts are the products of a creative effort, they represent both individuals' thoughts, feelings, responses, as well as group-constructed meanings. Language charts stimulate interest and interaction about books. They are noticeable to all who enter your room, becoming a topic of discussion and explanation.

2. *As an historical account of your work with literature in your classroom.* Language charts that are revisited again and again throughout the year allow children to recall favorites and to make connections. Therefore, language charts should not be discarded when work with the unit is completed. For the teacher, there is important information here that is related to growth over time.

3. *As a demonstration of oral to written language connections.* Children benefit from the opportunity to see their own words recorded. They benefit from the experience of hearing others read their words and returning to read for themselves their own comments. Children learn to recognize and use "book talk," the language of stories, as they reflect and respond.

4. *As a stimulus for the expression of personal responses to literature.* Good literature provides multiple levels of response. The nature and quality of an individual's response to literature are in large part a function of that individual's experience, beliefs, and values. Through the language chart, you and your children are encouraged to explore similarities and differences in responses.

5. *As an occasion for connecting the individual books to the element that undergirds the unit study.* The sharing of a good piece of literature is a valuable experience for the student in and of itself. Beyond this, you are encouraging students through the use of language charts to make connections between and among books. The fostering of these connections is important for developing higher order concepts and values that are critical to becoming fully literate.

6. *As an opportunity for teaching literary elements.* Through the sharing of literature, children are led to use the language of literate people as they discuss author techniques such as characterization, theme, point of view, style, mood, tone, and format. Children come to understand the notions and their labels through discussions focused by the language chart.

7. *As an opportunity for teaching the characteristics of literary genre.* Through the matrix format of the language chart, you can lead children to recognize characteristics that stories share, (e.g., characters, settings, problems, solutions, and outcomes), characteristics of particular genres (e.g., tall tales, fables, myths, and historical fiction), and motifs that are unique to a particular genre (e.g., trickery, magical objects, or the number three).

8. *As a bridge between tradebooks and content area study.* Language charts permit the collection and organization of information from tradebooks in a purposeful way, framing content area studies (e.g., social studies, science, and health). This integration of curriculum can promote transfer of learning from text. Questions that guide children's reading help to frame the format of the language chart. Answers (and additional questions) are recorded as children learn from expository text.

Literature charts can be organized by

- favorite authors/illustrators (Keats, de Paola, Scieszka).
- common themes or topics (friendships, prejudice, art and artists, traveling, immigration).
- common genres (folktales, poems, historical adventures, science activities).

Students can compile copies of their own literature charts in a 9 × 12 inch manila tagboard booklet held together with three brass fasteners. Through their personal collections, students can be praised and encouraged by the variety of reading they are experiencing.

In Mr. Richardson's class, students used language charts to analyze various characters from the books they were reading (see Figure 11–2). In addition, Mr. Richardson used a language chart to analyze a series of folktales that the students were reading as part of one of their genre studies units (see Table 11–5).

Story Structure/Mapping

Story structure is a focus for literary discussion with intermediate grade students, and visual diagrams are appropriate at this level as well as at the primary grade level. Students in the intermediate grades will probably have heard their teachers use terms traditionally used to identify elements of story structure (i.e., *setting, initiating event, problem, goal, conflict, event, climax, resolution,* and *denouement*). If not, it would be appropriate to introduce the terms at this time. A step diagram incorporating the terms enables the students to visualize the structure. *James and the Giant Peach* by Roald Dahl is used in Figure 11–3.

Literature Circles

Another way that teachers use literature in their classrooms is through literature circles or book clubs (Daniels, 1994; Roser & Martinez, 1995). This involves small groups of students reading and discussing pieces of literature. Typically, students are seated in circles of four to six students, and they read, write, speak, and listen based on a process that is established during the first week of school (see Table 11–6). Often the class members will agree on several general guidelines for operating book clubs or literature circles (see Table 11–7 for an example).

Again, text selection is important. Some teachers identify several books, discuss the books with the whole class, and then allow students to choose the book they would like to read. Other teachers assign books to groups based on interest, reading fluency, and time. Literature circles and book clubs allow teachers to differentiate their instruction. All students in the class can be reading books about the topic

Figure 11–2 Character analysis language chart.

Friends are Wonderful

	Author	Title	Type of text	Who were friends?	How did they act like friends?	Would you like these friends for your own? Why?
Book 1	Janice Lee Smith	The Kid Next Door and Other Head-Aches	Fiction	Adam, Joshua and Nelson	Even though they were opposite in almost every aspect of their behavior + habits. Adam, Joshua and Nelson shared everything from a treehouse to their troubles.	I'm not sure. These two seem to find themselves in trouble a lot. But they have a true friendship and that's important.
Book 2	Betsy Byars	The Pinballs	Fiction	3 Foster Children Harvey, Thomas J., Carlie	They learned to care about themselves and others.	Yes, because they never gave up on one another. It's reassuring to have loyal friends who are there for you.
Book 3	Walt Morey	Gentle Ben	Fiction	Mark Anderson and a bear named Ben	Mark and Ben protected each other from harm in the outside world. Their actions show their dedication to each other.	Yes, because I like the special bond that grows between a "wild" animal* and a human. *Not normal pet.

TABLE 11–5
Language Chart for Folktales Unit

Text	Characters	Setting	Problem	Solution
The Rabbit and the Dragon King (San Souci, 2002)	Dragon King, turtle, rabbit	In the sea On the land	A sickly king needs a heart	Rabbit tricks him by send a persimmon

Figure 11–3 Reading attitude inventory.

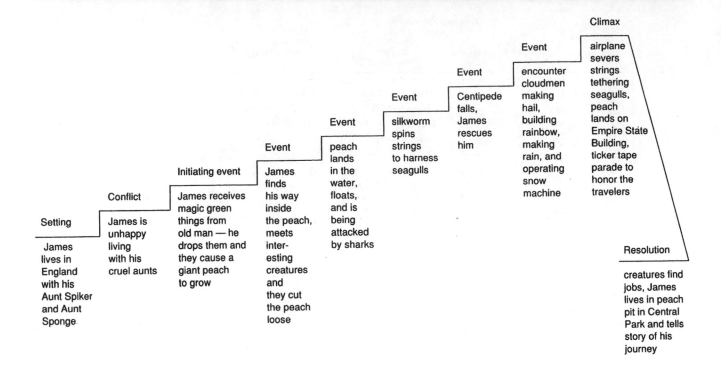

under study, but different groups could be reading books written at different difficulty levels.

In more formal literature circles, each student in the group is assigned a role or roles. Daniels (1994) suggests the following roles:

- *Discussion director*—the person who develops questions to ask about the reading to keep the conversation moving.

- *Literary luminary*—the person who captures words and phrases that are especially interesting to share and discuss during group conversations.

- *Illustrator*—the person who draws (either free-hand or with a computer) pictures related to the reading and who can invite discussion about the illustrations during group conversations.

- *Connector*—the person who finds connections between the book the group is reading and other books that have been studied, personal experiences, or things happening in the world.

- *Investigator*—the person who researches background information on the author, geography, time period, or setting of the book.

- *Summarizer*—the person responsible keeping time and summarizing the group's discussion at the end of the meeting.

Teachers often want some accountability during literature circles. Table 11–8 provides an example of a journal entry that students can complete independently as they participate in literature circles or book clubs as a means of assessment.

DID YOU NOTICE. . .
Did you notice that each literature circle can include six students with varying roles? If your literature circles are smaller than six students you will eliminate some of the roles. You also may have two students assume one role (i.e. two discussion leaders) depending on the needs of your students.

TABLE 11–6
Literature Circle Guidelines (Teachers or Students)

1. Have students write a journal response to the text being read (2–4 minutes; individually)
2. Share responses with a partner (2–4 minutes; pairs)
3. Lead discussion with the group (1–15 minutes; group)
   Begin by asking students to share thoughts based upon their reading/writing and discussion of text with their partner
   Have content specific questions ready to focus the discussion if it strays too far afield or becomes bogged down on a point that seems to be unresolvable
4. Postdiscussion writing (4 minutes; individually)
5. Share responses with a partner (4 minutes; pairs)
6. Return to discussion with whole group (10 minutes; group)
   Invite responses based on the previous writing
7. Write a journal entry (2–4 minutes; individually)
   Ask students to write about their response to the text as a result of reading, writing, and discussing with their peers

HOW DOES LITERATURE AFFECT PERSONAL GROWTH?

Teaching literature in the elementary classroom, rather than merely making it available, improves students' chances of becoming readers for life. Literature provides an opportunity for students to learn more about themselves and their own culture as well as about the lives and cultures of others. Literature in the elementary classroom provides language models for students and guides them as they develop a sense of story. When given the opportunity to read literature in the classroom, students can practice the skills they are learning using well-written and inspiring texts. The contents of such texts allow them to experience many events and situations vicariously. Finally, literature taught in the elementary classroom sparks students' imaginations and helps them appreciate reading as fun and worthwhile.

Students of all ages and reading abilities have the right to study quality literature in the classroom. Books with repetitive texts can be used to enhance the reading program in the primary grades by encouraging students to make predictions and providing them with models for original stories. Intermediate grade students benefit from activities that focus on more complex aspects of the story, such as character development and story structures. Students can become aware of the characteristics of various genres and of the common elements of literature, including setting, plot, climax, and so on. Several activities are appropriate for students in both primary

TABLE 11–7
Classroom Guidelines for Literature Discussion

- Be prepared to discuss your thoughts about the text by completing your reading and writing before the literature discussion begins.
- Be courteous by listening to everyone's comments.
- Be sensitive to people's feelings as you make contributions to the discussion.
- Wait until the speaker is finished before beginning your comments.
- Make your comments positive and constructive.
- Feel free to question and agree/disagree by clearly and calmly stating your opinion.
- Assume responsibility for your own growth.

TABLE 11–8
Journal Entry From a Literature Circle

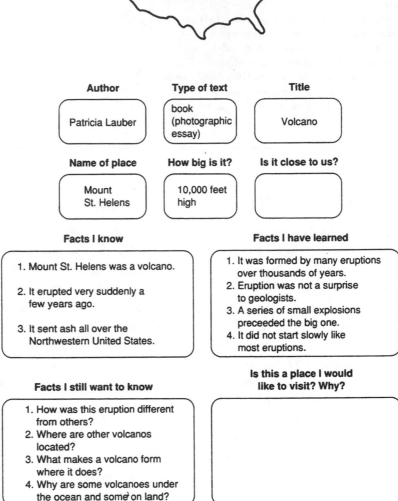

and intermediate grades. Reader's theater is one form of oral interpretation appropriate for and enjoyed by students in both primary and intermediate grades. Students of all reading abilities may participate in this nonthreatening form of interpretation and response.

Several of the techniques discussed in this chapter apply to poetry. For example, effective discussions enable students to understand and appreciate what is significant and meaningful in a work. However, because poetry can elicit students' responses differently from those for other genres, some additional consideration is warranted. To appreciate fully the sounds and rhythms of our language as they are used in poetry, poetry should be heard. Discussions of poetic language enable students to see the word pictures that poems create. Music, art, and creative dramatics are ways in which students can respond to the poems they study.

Teachers of all grades must not underestimate the value of reading aloud to their students. This activity encourages emergent reading behaviors in young students, allows students to experience books that are too difficult to be read by themselves, and creates shared experiences among teacher and students that cannot be replicated in other ways.

The use of classroom literature libraries has been found to increase the amount of students' independent reading. The physical arrangement of the library and the selection of books are critical to its effectiveness. When carefully supplied and maintained, classroom libraries can enhance the reading/language arts programs.

Teachers and students who invest their time in the reading and study of quality literature reap benefits that last a lifetime. In the words of Lawrence Clark Powell (the librarian who raised the status of the role from clerical to professional), "Reading books is good, rereading good books is better." We hope that you will teach your students to love books by reading with them every day.

QUESTIONS

1. During a parent conference you are asked why you think it is important to have students read and listen to literature being read aloud in school. As you respond be sure to support your position by discussing the power of literature to promote language expansion, personal response, social justice, and student engagement.

2. Describe the criteria you will use to select literature for your classroom library. Be sure to also describe how the selections will be displayed and organized for student use.

3. During a discussion with some of your colleagues you're asked how you teach literature. As you consider a response think about the importance of read alouds, literature circle discussions, independent reading, and multiple types of texts as a motivating factor.

4. Your principal asks why you invite your students to share their responses to a favorite author or piece of literature in a personal way. As you respond you decide to share students' drawings, letters to a character, book jackets, poems, etc. Please explain the importance of encouraging students to compose creative responses that illustrate their novel understandings and engagement.

5. Please describe how literature is related to the other dimensions of your classroom literacy program. Be sure to make connections to the other curriculum areas as well as to reading, writing, and oral language development.

REFERENCES

Bissett, D. (1970). The usefulness of children's books in the reading program. In J. Catterson (Ed.), *Children and literature* (pp. 65–78). Newark, DE: International Reading Association.

Blaska, J. K., & Lynch, E. C. (1998). Is everyone included? Using children's literature to facilitate the understanding of disabilities. *Young Children, 53*(2), 36–38.

Brink, C. R. (1935). *Caddie Woodlawn*. Macmillan: New York.

Cullinan, B. E. (1989). *Literature and the child* (2nd ed.). San Diego, CA: Harcourt Brace Jovanovich.

Daniels, H. (1994). *Literature circles: Voice and choice in the student-centered classroom*. York, ME: Stenhouse.

Didion, J. (1968). *Slouching toward Bethlehem*. New York: Ballantine.

Farnan, N., & Romero, A. (1996). Understanding literature: Reading in the English or language arts classroom. In D. Lapp, J. Flood, & N. Farnan (Eds.), *Content area reading and learning: Instructional strategies* (2nd ed.) (pp. 209–225). Boston: Allyn & Bacon.

Fisher, D., Flood, J., & Lapp, D. (1999). The role of literature in literacy development. In L. B. Gambrell, L. M. Morrow, S. B. Neuman, & M. Pressley (Eds.), *Best practices in literacy instruction* (pp. 119–135). New York: Guilford.

Fisher, D., Flood, J., & Lapp, D., & Frey, N. (2004). Interactive read alouds: Is there a common set of implementation practices? *The Reading Teacher, 58*, 8–17.

Fox, M. (1987). The teacher disguised as writer, in hot pursuit of literacy. *Language Arts, 64*, 18–32.

Frey, N., Fisher, D., Lapp, D., Flood, J. (1999). Literacy: Opening books for learning. In B. E. Buswell, C. B. Schaffner, & A. B. Seyler (Eds.), *Opening doors: Connecting students to curriculum, classmates, and learning* (2nd ed.). Colorado Springs, CO: Peak Parent Center.

Gray, L. S. (1995). Taking from books by asking questions. *Journal of Research in Childhood Education, 10*, 23–28.

Hillman, J. (2003). *Discovering children's literature* (3rd ed.). Upper Saddle River, NJ: Merrill/Prentice Hall.

Huck, C. S., Hepler, S., Hickman, J., & Kiefer, B. Z. (2000). *Children's literature in the elementary school* (7th ed.). New York: Macmillan.

Kelly, P. (1983). *Sex stereotypes of reading materials*. Unpublished master's thesis, San Diego State University.

Kiefer, B. (1988). Picture books as contexts for literary, aesthetic, and real world understandings. *Language Arts, 65*, 260–271.

Kupetz, B. N. (1993). Bridging the gap between young and old. *Children Today, 22*(2), 10–13.

Langer, J. A. (1992). *A new look at literature instruction*. ERIC Digest: Bloomington, IN: Indiana University Clearinghouse on Reading and Communication Skills.

Lowe, J. (1998). Creating an A+++ classroom library. *Instructor, 108*(1), 61–63.

Martinez, M., Roser, N. L., & Strecker, S. (1998–1999). "I never thought I could be a star": A reader's theatre ticket to fluency. *The Reading Teacher, 52*, 326–334.

Martinez, M., & Teale, W. H. (1988). Reading in a kindergarten classroom library. *The Reading Teacher, 41*, 568–572.

Millard, E. (1997). Differently literate: Gender identity and the construction of the developing reader. *Gender and Education, 9*, 31–48.

Morrow, L. M. Tracey, D. H., Woo, D. G., & Pressley, M. (1999). Characteristics of exemplary first-grade literacy instruction. *The Reading Teacher, 52*, 462–476.

Paterson, K. (1978) *The Great Gilly Hopkins*. New York: Crowell.

Rosenblatt, L. M. (1976). *Literature as exploration* (3rd ed.). New York: Noble and Noble.

Roser, N. (1990). *The importance of using literature charts for language and reading development*. Paper presented at the International Reading Association Conference, Atlanta, GA.

Roser, N., & Martinez, M. (Eds.). (1995). *Book talk and beyond: Children and teachers respond to literature*. Newark, DE: International Reading Association.

Schon, I. (1996). Good and questionable books about Latinos. *MultiCultural Review, 5*, 39–42, 49.

Shechtman, Z. (2000). An innovative intervention for treatment of child and adolescent aggression: An outcome study. *Psychology in the Schools, 37*, 157–167.

Strickland, D. (1987). Literature: Key element in the language and reading program. In B. E. Cullinan (Ed.), *Children's literature in the reading program* (pp. 68–76). Newark, DE: International Reading Association.

Trepanier-Street, M. L., & Romatowski, J. A. (1999). The influence of children's literature on gender role perceptions: A reexamination. *Early Childhood Education Journal, 26*, 155–159.

Wepner, S. B., & Feeley, J. T. (1993). *Moving forward with literature: Basals, books and beyond*. Upper Saddle River, NJ: Merrill/Prentice Hall.

Wilson, L., Malmgren, D., Ramage, S., & Schuttz, L. (1993). *An integrated approach to learning*. Portsmouth, NH: Heinemann.

Yopp, R. H., & Yopp, H. K. (2000). *Literature-based reading activities* (3rd ed.). Boston: Allyn & Bacon.

12

Technology and Media in the Literacy Classroom

─────────────── CHAPTER GOALS ───────────────

To help the reader

- understand how to use CDs, videos, TV, and newspapers in the classroom.
- understand how to integrate computers and the Internet into the classroom.
- understand what forms of print and nonprint media are available for use in the classroom.
- understand the critical thinking skills students should know to comprehend multiple media.

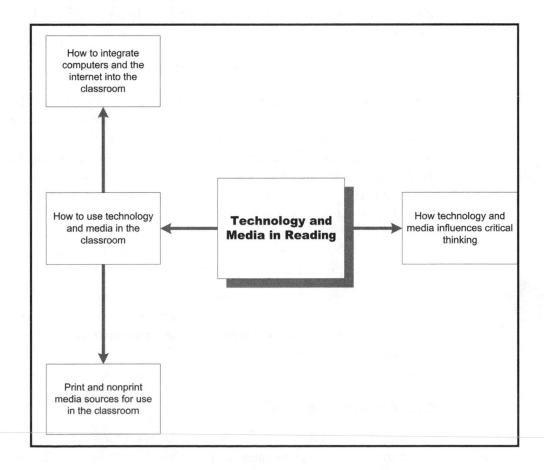

Your Turn

How many forms of technology have you used in the past 24 hours? Think about that for a moment. Write down a few of the pieces of technology that make your life (and your learning) easier.

Maribeth Smith, a student teacher, told us that during her 24 hour time block she used a cell phone to talk with a member of her study group (and sent a picture of the book she was planning to use in her lesson plan over the phone line). Later that afternoon, she took her laptop computer to a local coffee store and used the wireless services in the store to visit Web sites on which her class homework was posted. While she was doing this, she received an e-mail with an attachment of the group's paper and a request to meet to discuss the paper. Consulting her handheld personal data assistant (PDA), she reviewed her calendar and responded to the e-mail with dates and times that were good for her.

She laughed at the e-mail from her mom requesting that she fax her grades thinking, "Oh Mom, fax machines are so outdated." Of course, she was happy to share her grades with her mom who was so proud of her new career in teaching. Later that night, she listened to a CD in her car, previewed a DVD on volcanoes that she was thinking of using for her science lesson, and downloaded some songs and lesson plans from a Web site to share with her cooperating teacher.

How many of these technology aids have you used in the last 24 hours? How many have your students used? Of course, there are many more technological conveniences that we take for granted—microwaves, home security systems, air traffic control guidance systems, and satellite TV, to name a few.

TECHNOLOGY IN THE CLASSROOM

DID YOU NOTICE . . .
Did you notice that her belief is similar to that of many teachers who view technology as a baby-sitting rather than instructional device?

Teachers also use various forms of technology in their classrooms. Ms. Peterson uses a great deal of technology in her fourth grade classroom, but she is not the most technologically advanced teacher at the school. She believes that technology can assist students in learning and that there are good and bad uses of technology and media in the classroom. Her classroom looks like any other in the school: she has an ethnically diverse group of students. She has desks, chairs, dry erase boards, and books in her classroom. She also has a number of computers, listening stations, PDAs, CD players, a TV/VCR/DVD, and other forms of technology that we will come to discover. Let's visit her classroom and learn more about the ways in which she incorporates technology and media into her instructional activities.

Your Turn

Before we visit Ms. Peterson's classroom, select one kind of technology located in her room. How would you use that technology to facilitate student learning? How has that type of technology helped you in your learning?

Using Audiotape Recordings

In Ms. Peterson's classroom, CD and cassette recordings are forms of technology that provide many opportunities for enhancing her students' language arts skills.

Literary recordings are excellent tools for improving listening skills and imagery. Students enjoy hearing authors read their own work and are often captivated by a skilled and professional narrator. Recordings often include background music and sound effects that enhance the work. The students in Ms. Peterson's class enjoy the listening center that is one of the rotations used during center time. (See chapters 2 and 11 for more information on guided reading and ceer activities.) At this center, six students can use headphones to listen to a book being read aloud. Some days Ms. Peterson uses commercially available cassette tapes. A favorite is the *Shiloh* series by Phyllis Naylor. This series tells the story of a dog that has been mistreated by its former owner. Ms. Peterson also records her own read alouds, and these are also available in the listening center. For example, Ms. Peterson read *The Incredible Journey* (Burnford, 1960) into a cassette recorder so that her students could read along at the listening center. When Ms. Peterson records the text herself, she likes to comment to her students and not just read the story. When she comes to a difficult word, she might ask them to write it down in their journal and then pause to give them time to write. She might also pause periodically and "think aloud" and model some of the comprehension strategies that she is using. After her "teacher version" in which she provides instruction during the recording, she will read the book straight through so that students can listen to the text a second time.

Read-along recordings, in which the oral reading is paced more slowly with voice inflections and expression and an aural signal to indicate page turns, are very useful for beginning and developing readers. Ms. Peterson's students also enjoy making read-along tapes themselves for younger readers. For example, Justin recorded the book *Click, Clack, Moo: Cows that Type* (Cronin, 2000) and gave it to a first grade class. This also gives the children who act as producers an additional opportunity to practice oral reading fluency. Recordings can also enhance a story or a particular area of study in the content areas. Musical recordings of songs popular during a particular period of history can bring a study of that era to life. A recording of Appalachian folk songs or western folklore can enliven the experience of reading a book set in that area of the country. Students may also produce their own recordings when reading passages from a favorite book, reciting poetry, or participating in reader's theater. Using Ms. Peterson's model, students can record their favorite books for other students to hear. Attention to the mood created by a poem or story can be attained by asking students to select recordings that might serve as appropriate background music.

Using Videotape Recordings, DVDs, and Digital Cameras

Teachers use videotapes and DVDs in the classroom for many reasons. They are excellent motivational devices to use in the literature class and can be shown before or after students read a story or book. They encourage discussion of the work itself as well as of the artist's interpretation of it. They provide an electronic field trip right in the classroom with minimal expense and time. Art films are a good stimulus for oral or dramatic interpretation, and they can inspire creative writing and oral discussion. Movies can also provide background information for a book or unit of study in the content areas.

We also need to mention that "movie time" can end up being wasted time without advance planning. Teachers and students need to have shared goals about what is to

DID YOU NOTICE . . .
Did you notice that she believes this is another way to increase their reading fluency?

TABLE 12–1
Collaborative Listening-Viewing Guide

Class: _____   Date: _____   Topic: _____

Student's Name: _____   Partner: _____

Group Members: _____

We know that:

My Notes	Our Group's Notes

We learned that:

We will find out:

Source: From Flood, J., Lapp. D., & Wood, K. (1998). Viewing: The neglected communication process or "When what you see isn't what you get." *The Reading Teacher, 52,* 300–304.

be accomplished through the movie viewing. Ms. Peterson has taught her students to use the collaborative listening-viewing guide when they watch a movie (see Table 12–1). Notice that this tool requires students to take notes during the movie and to have small group discussions about the movie when they have finished watching. This process not only increases engagement with the movie but also increases student comprehension of the content.

Ms. Peterson also uses videotaping in the classroom as part of her instruction. She likes to videotape students during their oral presentations. This allows them to complete a self-evaluation of their performance. (See chapter 4 on oral language for a speaking checklist that can be used.) Students can gauge their progress by viewing themselves over a period of time. Students in Ms. Peterson's class may also choose videotaping as a means of preserving their creative drama, pantomime, reports, and role-playing. These tapes are often shared with other classrooms. Two of her students, Donna and Jerimiah, produced a videotape of *Stellaluna* (Cannon, 1993) when they learned that the whole kindergarten was studying bats.

In addition to videotaping, students can use digital cameras to capture their learning experiences. Digital cameras are especially useful because students can immediately view the image for content and clarity. They can also transfer the image to a computer or import into a word processing document or a slide show presentation or manipulate the image with one of the various software programs available. Ms. Peterson periodically gives her students digital cameras to add visual information to their written work. One of her favorite units used a photoessay. Each student selected a theme for study (e.g., football, homelessness, cars, zoos, or environment). Based on this theme, students took 15 pictures and imported them into a word processing program. Under each image, the student provided text in the form of a poem, explanation, or story. Danny's theme was graffiti. Under one of the pictures he wrote, "the beauty of the word should not be wasted on the wall." On another page with a picture of a city worker painting over the graffiti, he wrote, "Time and money. Where do they come from and where do they go? The person with the most time and money wins the war against paint."

Using the Newspaper in the Classroom

Although often overlooked in discussions of technology and classroom materials, the newspaper is a valuable tool for teaching language arts skills in the classroom. Its content is current and relevant to students' lives. It can be used across grade levels and provides students with many opportunities to practice language arts skills throughout the curriculum. The newspaper has many different sections, contains a variety of information, and often has reviews or articles directed toward children. This variety will enable every student to find something of interest. The vocabulary words found in the newspaper are practical; they are often words that the students will hear and use many times in their lives. Teachers can help students develop a habit of reading the paper daily, a habit that will stay with them later in life.

Students in Ms. Peterson's class benefit from studying various writing styles and applying critical reading skills to newspaper articles and editorials. Ms. Peterson provides instruction in the differences in the form and content of editorials, news stories, and news features that improve their reading and writing skills. This study of the newspaper is then used as an introduction to a class-written newspaper. Students learn the organization of the newspaper, which helps them understand the purpose for each of its sections. Publishing their own paper gives Ms. Peterson's students multiple opportunities to practice their writing and editing skills and word processing and keyboarding skills.

The newspaper can also be used with very young students. Pictures provide opportunities for story telling and language experience stories. Students can use the comics to predict story outcomes. The newspaper can also be used for locating pictures or words beginning with a specific sound or letter or locating capital letters and punctuation marks. Many newspapers include a children's page with articles written at younger children's reading and interest levels. For example, a recent edition of the "Kid's Page" in our local newspaper focused on a baby koala at the local zoo. The pictures, activities, and vocabulary encouraged students to be actively involved in self-motivated learning.

Most major newspapers also post their articles online. This helps teachers find specific articles and print them for classroom discussions. Ms. Peterson reads her newspaper every morning and often finds a current events article that she likes. She goes on-line to print the article on an overhead transparency so that she can use this information text during her shared reading time. Of course, students can also find interesting newspaper articles to read online. Students in Ms. Peterson's class like to print their favorite newspaper articles from the computer and keep them in binders for reading during silent reading times.

Using a copy of a recent newspaper, identify five things that you could teach your students. Make sure that you are teaching academic content (e.g., science or social studies) as well as language skills.

Television at Home and at School

Television has been frequently criticized as being one of the major barriers to developing a love for reading. It is estimated that by the time the average American child finishes high school, he or she will have spent 10,000 to 15,000 hours watching television, more time than is spent in the classroom. Thus, children must be taught to understand the power of the medium of television to develop the skills required to view it critically. We believe that a person's initial spontaneous response to a film or television movie is emotional, not intellectual. An intellectual response is made after the film is over, and only when it is discussed and analyzed. Through discussion children can be asked to interpret and analyze what they have seen. Teachers who use television in the classroom can follow-up the viewing with discussion to ensure that students progress from an emotional to an intellectual response. However, students must learn some critical viewing techniques that they can apply when watching television at home. Young children often perceive what they see on television as reality. Some television characters find easy solutions to problems or choose violence as a solution to their problems, and children need to be made aware that this is not the best way to live their lives. Television commercials stress attractive looks, and advertisers create needs and desires for their products. Children must be taught how to protect themselves from being manipulated by these behaviors and values.

It is not uncommon for students in Ms. Peterson's class to write about television shows in their journals. Ms. Peterson encourages her students to think critically about the TV shows that they watch and to analyze the messages that may be hidden in the shows. A recent entry from Jamal's journal read, "I think that there should be more Black people on *ER*. We tape that show and I like it, but I want to see more Black doctors because there's only one Black doctor who is on every show."

It is important to note that the television and cable industries have attempted to develop new educational programs for children. For example, *Between the Lions* on the Public Broadcasting Service focuses on early language learning and reading. Of course, there is also the old favorite *Sesame Street* that engages children in critical thinking and language learning.

HOW CAN THE USE OF MEDIA HELP TEACH CHILDREN CRITICAL THINKING SKILLS AND STRATEGIES?

Whether the media format is a movie, television show, popular song, newspaper, or the Internet, critical thinking skills that will enable children to make rational judgments about what they have seen or heard must be taught. Students need practice making judgments, distinguishing fact from opinion, determining the validity of information presented as fact, and judging the adequacy of various information sources. They need to be able to make inferences about implied information and to draw thoughtful conclusions. Ms. Peterson uses an evaluation tool such as the one found in Table 12–2 when her students read a newspaper article. The tool applies to other media forms as well.

Advertising and Propaganda Concerns

Radio, television, newspapers, and many Web sites use advertising. Good advertising is necessary to promote competition, which ensures that good-quality products

TABLE 12–2
Evaluation Tool for Information Sources

Topic	Yes or No	Example
The Writer's Competency and Integrity: Is the writer an authority?		
Does the writer make sense?		
The Writer's Use of Sources and Evidence: Is evidence presented to document the assertions?		
Is this fact or opinion?		
Is anything missing?		
What is the writer's purpose?		
The Reader's Ability to Form, Revise, and Test Opinions: Are the premises valid?		
Are these facts important to me? If yes, Why?		
Do the conclusions necessarily follow?		
Have others commented on this topic? What have they said?		
Does my lack of knowledge keep me from accepting this?		
Does my background make me intolerant of this point of view?		
Is the information as true today as when it was written?		
What more do I need to know before come to my own conclusions?		

will be developed. Newspapers receive 70% of their revenue from advertising, and advertising permits the widespread availability of this valuable medium at a very low cost to the consumer. However, many advertisers use propaganda techniques to influence the public. Although these techniques often distort reality, young children often view this distortion as reality. Consequently, the values and desires they acquire may reflect those promoted by advertisements. With an awareness of these propaganda techniques, students will be able to view advertisements more objectively. The following techniques may be found in oral, electronic, and written form. The following examples were found by Ms. Peterson's class after they studied propaganda.

Name Calling: Creating a negative association with a person or product by identifying it with something undesirable (e.g., Only the Loch Ness Monster eats Bierkirk garlic potato chips).

Glittering Generalities: Using words that are vague but that appeal to people's emotions and to what they think is good, such as the phrase "the American way" (e.g., Bierkirk garlic potato chips are the apple pie of the potato chip world).

Plain Folks: Associating the person or product with ordinary people; often used by politicians (e.g., Bierkirk garlic potato chips remind me of dinner at my mom's house).

Snob Appeal: Creating an association with the elite if you use this product or vote for this person (e.g., Bierkirk garlic potato chips are served as appetizers at all of Tom Hanks' parties).

Transfer: Associating a person or product with a symbol that already creates a negative or positive impression. The feeling for the symbol transfers to the person or product (e.g., Bierkirk garlic potato chips—just do it!).

Testimonial: Giving of an endorsement by a celebrity (e.g., Michael Jordan loves Bierkirk garlic potato chips).

Bandwagon: Suggesting that one should follow the crowd and buy a product or endorse a person because everyone else does (e.g., Bierkirk garlic potato chips—they're everywhere you want to be!).

Repetition: Using words or phrases so often that they become accepted as true (e.g., Bierkirk garlic potato chips taste good. Bierkirk garlic potato chips are fun on a picnic. Bierkirk garlic potato chips will make you new friends).

Card Stacking: Presenting only one side of an issue, hiding or omitting some facts, or mixing facts and opinion (e.g., Bierkirk garlic potato chips are lower in fat and taste great).

Technology provides you with multiple opportunities to teach students about propaganda. Review several Web sites and determine whether they use any of these propaganda tools. Do the same thing with billboards around campus and newspapers.

USING THE COMPUTER EFFECTIVELY IN THE LANGUAGE ARTS CLASSROOM

The computer has had a profound impact on our schools and the manner in which students receive instruction. The field of educational computing continues to change, making it difficult to predict and stay current with all innovations in hardware and software.

When computers were first introduced into elementary classrooms, the primary focus was to teach the students general computer literacy and programming in various computer languages such as Basic and Pascal. By necessity their primary application was in the fields of mathematics and science. To accommodate this thrust, college courses were designed to provide instruction in *programming* in the various computer languages.

During the past decade the number of computers used in classrooms has significantly increased. In 2001, schools averaged one computer for every six students nationwide (*Education Week*, 2003); 10 years ago there was approximately one computer for 30 students. The annual budget for school computers topped $5 billion in 2000.

Healy (1998) maintained that we need to assess the impact of computers and technology on student literacy as schools attempt to expand the numbers of computers per classroom. Healy explained that we need to understand a complex set of issues that include the questions: When should computers be introduced into our classrooms and what computer activities are most beneficial for students? The significance of the computer as an instructional tool has been noted by Reinking (1998) who stated "questions about whether students using word processing write as well or better than those using conventional materials have given way to questions about how students might adapt to and employ effective electronic forms of reading and writing" (p. xxiv). Language arts educators have been able to capitalize on computer applications for their instruction.

Computer Applications in the Language Arts

Although the most prevalent uses of the computer in the language arts classroom today are computer-assisted instruction (CAI), word processing, graphic organizers, and teacher utility programs, computers are also used to access the Internet. We will explore common classroom uses of the computer followed by a discussion of Internet applications.

Computer-Assisted Instruction

There is a wide variety of commercially produced software designed to instruct students in various aspects of language arts and reading. Common uses of computer software include tutorials, instructional games, drill and practice, and simulations. Although these categories appear to be clear-cut at first glance, educators have found that many programs overlap several categories and others fail to fit into any category.

1. *Tutorial*: These programs present self-paced lessons that teach new information in a step-by-step manner by using explanations, examples, questions, and branching. For example, a student may be tutored on spelling through word families. The program may present the word *hop* orally while the student is asked to spell it on the keyboard. The next word might be *pop* followed by *stop* and then *flop*.

2. *Instructional games*: Through these programs students develop reasoning and problem-solving skills through inductive and deductive thinking processes. In these programs students apply information to a new setting and learn how to think logically and follow directions. For example, an instructional game may require a student to read through a word problem that shows a picture of five people. The instructions require that each person is named. Students can move the graphic with the person's name until the correct configuration is obtained. The information available indicates that "James never stands next to Jessica. Susan is in the middle. Erica has no one on her left and Jesse has no one on his right." Thus, the correct configuration is shown in Diagram 12–1.

JESSE   JESSICA   SUSAN   JAMES   ERICA

3. *Drill and practice*: These programs are designed to be used after the student has gained an initial proficiency or understanding of the material to be learned. They provide the student with additional practice for mastery of the new skills or information. Many of these drill and practice programs are designed so that the teacher can customize the program to address skills being taught in that particular classroom. In this way the same piece of software can be used in several different grade levels.

4. *Simulations*: These programs imitate a real or imaginary system based on the theory of the way that system operates. The students apply principles, discover relationships, and test assumptions in a realistic context. For example, a computer program allows students to take care of their virtual pet. The program tracks how often the pet is fed, walked, played with, cleaned up after, and so on, and provides students with a simulation of the responsibilities of pet ownership.

There is a wide range of CAI software available from a wide range of software companies. Their capabilities and prices vary dramatically from tens to thousands of dollars. Some have periodic assessments, student instruction, prescriptive learning, and many other features. You should always assess your own student/school needs to determine the program with the best fit. Some programs are on disk or CDs; others reside on the Internet and may be accessed through a special password once you have purchased the rights.

Your Turn

Search the Internet for "computer assisted instruction." You'll probably find this type of instruction in multiple disciplines from veterinary medicine to flight control. Read a few different web pages and share the similarities among the web pages with your peers.

Word Processing

Word processing software transforms the computer into a sophisticated electronic typewriter and, thereby enhances the writing program. Some of the extensions of word processing into the classroom might include student stories, class newspapers, recipes, letters and messages, lists, diaries, reports, journals, and keyboarding skills.

Some word processing programs have added an interactive dimension to the software program in which students are led by various clues or writing aids on the

computer screen as they compose texts. This alleviates the frustration of looking at a blank computer screen and wondering how to begin and what to say.

As students learn how to write different types of letters, they can be introduced to the use of templates on the computer. Software programs such as Microsoft® Word or Appleworks™ include a variety of these, which can be found when opening a new file document (Click on File, New, then choose from Letters & Faxes, Memos, Other Documents, and Web Pages.) Templates can also be customized to create personal letterhead, class stationery, certificates, newspapers, or similar documents. Students can access these templates and just fill in required information. Letters can then be printed and mailed by traditional "snail mail" (stamps or interdistrict mail) or they could be attached to an e-mail message and sent electronically. Writing letters to relatives, friends, classmates, or teachers via the computer offers students a different way to communicate and also to become familiar with a variety of letter formats and their uses. Students can take advantage of spell-check and grammar-check before completing the letter.

Ms. Peterson knows that her students are going to pass notes in class because she did it when she was a student and she has watched countless students pass notes under their tables. She decided to encourage letter writing among her students. One area of the bulletin board has envelope "mailboxes" for each student. The students in her class know that they can deposit mail for their friends in these mailboxes or send the mail electronically via e-mail when they have computer time. Ms. Peterson realizes that this "authentic writing" experience is good for her students because they practice their writing skills, and they learn to write for people other than her.

Since there is a high demand for using the computer as a word processing tool, companies such as AlphaSmart™ are developing less costly portable keyboards dedicated to word processing and keyboarding skills. That frees up the classroom computers so they can be used for other purposes such as the Internet and/or instructional software.

DID YOU NOTICE
Did you notice that this is an authentic means of language expression?

Graphic Organizers

In addition to word processing, computer software programs can be used by students to create graphic representations of their thinking, book reviews, or notes. Probably the most common software program used for this today is Inspiration™ or its kid version, Kidspiration™ (http://www.inspiration.com). This software provides students with templates that help them organize their thinking on a topic (e.g., a Venn diagram about Abe Lincoln or Johnny Appleseed). There are also templates that follow common text structures such as temporal/sequential, cause/effect, and problem/solution.

Ms. Peterson also uses Inspiration™ in her presentations and lectures. For example, during the reading of *Shiloh* (Naylor, 1991), Ms. Peterson updated her graphic display of Marty (the main character) after each chapter. This class-generated graphic was then used by students in the class as they wrote their character analysis essay. In addition, Ms. Peterson provides students time to work with Inspiration™ when they are beginning a new piece of writing. She has found that this software program helps many of her students organize their thinking and that the graphic organizers they produce result in higher quality writing. Students can brainstorm ideas fully and comment and group similar ones. Students can also move from graphic display to outline form with the touch of a key. This is a feature that many teachers find useful when teaching note taking and outlining.

Teacher Utility Programs

Teachers can use the computer in a great variety of ways to enhance instruction. Graphics software enables them to produce professional looking charts, graphs, and posters. Authoring programs make it possible for teachers to produce computer-assisted instruction without learning a programming language. Teachers are then able to customize computer materials to the particular levels and abilities of their students. They can also produce a variety of worksheets that are tailor-made for the students.

The computer can also assist the teacher in managing classroom instruction. This can be done through various programs: readability analysis, record keeping, grade book, calculator, and so on. In many cases the program can help teachers sort through the information they have collected about students, then analyze it, draw conclusions, and write reports based on the information. Some programs can also diagnose student problems or needs on the basis of a test and then direct individual students to certain assignments and lessons.

Ms. Peterson uses her PDA to record student grades and participation on a daily basis. At least once per week, she synchronizes her hand-held device with her desktop computer for long-term storage. Ms. Peterson has tried several different electronic gradebooks including the following:

Gradebook 2: http://www.gradebook.com

Teachers P.E.T.: http://www.coffeepotsoftware.com

Making the Grade: http://www.gradebusters.com

Classroom Wizard: http://www.classroomwizard.com

Select one of the above gradebook Web sites or one of your choosing to review. What grading features are provided? How is the software different from a paper version of a gradebook? Do you think the program seems easy to use? Would you recommend this software to your peers? Are you familiar with other grading programs that you would recommend?

Suggestions for Maximum Computer Usage

We suggest the following guidelines to aid you in achieving maximum use of the computer in your classroom even if you have a limited number of computers available to you.

1. Use the computer only for those activities that would best be served by the computer rather than by nonelectronic teaching methods.

2. Use the computer in conjunction with more traditional teaching methods and materials.

3. Make use of the computer for whole-group or small-group instruction when appropriate. Introducing a new piece of software to an entire group may alleviate the necessity to repeat the directions to each new student at the computer.

4. Prepare your students before they go to the computer, because each piece of software may have a different set of instructions.

5. Arrange a user schedule for the computer to provide equity. Students should be told what they are to do at the computer and at what time.

6. Use computer activities for peer-tutoring experiences. Student-to-student instruction on the computer is very successful in many instances.

7. Make a commitment to use the computer. Teachers must be careful not to restrict groups, time, and individuals.

8. If possible use a projection system connected to your computer for student projects or whole-group presentations. There is also a cost-effective way to connect a computer to a TV display for whole-group viewing.

9. Check your school's Student Internet Use Policy. It may be necessary to acquire parent signatures before students are allowed to access the Internet. Internet safety and suitability should be addressed before its use. This is addressed later in this chapter.

There are many advantages to using the computer in the classroom. Some of these are taking the drudgery out of routine activities, freeing the teacher for more time for teaching and reteaching, giving students immediate feedback, providing a very patient tutor, making learning interesting electronically, and allowing students to study at their own pace. There is no reason for educators to be concerned about computers replacing the teacher. The computer is merely a tool that challenges educators to tap its full potential.

Using Hand-Held Computers (Personal Data Assistants)

As computers have changed the classroom, so will hand-held versions or PDAs. Although most classrooms have fewer than four computers, every student could have a PDA. They are portable, low-cost, and versatile. Using PDAs, students can write, draw, present, create concept maps and diagrams, surf the web, send messages, perform scientific experiments, and get organized.

Ms. Peterson invites her students to draft their papers on PDAs and then synchronizes them to one of the desktop computers for editing. By operating her writers' workshop this way, every student can be working electronically. Ms. Peterson has also purchased two collapsible keyboards students can use for word processing with their PDAs. Her students especially like to "beam" their papers to her for editing and feedback. In addition to using the PDAs as writing tools, Ms. Peterson posts homework assignments and due dates on the computer. As students sync their PDAs, their calendars are updated with this type of information. You can also purchase special attachments and probes for the PDAs for use with science projects.

The PDAs in her classroom can also access the World Wide Web in her "wireless" classroom. Students can access Web sites and e-mail from their PDAs when she has the network turned on (she has a master control switch that allows her to monitor on-line access within her classroom). Now let's turn to the opportunities and challenges that the Internet provides teachers.

What is your philosophy on the use of the Internet in the classroom? Some researchers suggest that reading web pages with hyperlinked texts changes the way that students read. Do you read web pages differently from printed texts? How do you think this will affect your students?

USING THE INTERNET EFFECTIVELY
IN THE LANGUAGE ARTS CLASSROOM

The ever-expanding nature of the Internet, with all the World Wide Web sites and e-mail opportunities, has provided teachers with a vast array of new approaches to teaching reading. We will review a few of the more common uses of the Internet for language arts.

Electronic Book Club Discussions

As you know, book clubs offer a wealth of opportunities for students to read, write, interpret, react, predict, and share ideas with their peers about literature (Flood, Lapp, & Fisher, 1999). Book club activities can be enhanced by including an online discussion that enables students to post late-breaking thoughts, new insights, or ideas. Electronic submission might alleviate fears that the shy child may have about sharing thoughts and ideas in front of peers. A simple discussion board format can be created on a class Web site for students to access on an individual basis. All discussions are asynchronous, that is, posted at any time (versus setting up a specific time to participate in a "real-time" chat). The responses remain on the board, so that anyone logging on to post a message can read the previous messages. This is particularly beneficial for students who may need more time to compose their ideas before sharing with their classmates. If necessary, students have the opportunity to write their responses in a word processing program and edit their writing before copying and pasting it into the discussion board. Ms. Peterson provides discussion boards for each of her literature groups. At any given time, there may be six different groups of students reading books together in their literature circles. Ms. Peterson provides this web space to ensure that each student has the opportunity to contribute to the conversation and react to others comments about the book. One group of five students was reading *Love That Dog* (Creech, 2001). AnaMaria wrote on the discussion board: "I agree with Jack, poetry is boring. Who wants to figure all that out? But I wonder what happened. Why does Jack write about a blue car speeding? I am worried that the dog is going to get hurt." One of the responses was from Jamie who wrote, "Poetry isn't boring if you let it get in you. I like this kind of poetry, all the words don't have to rhyme. I think that the car is speeding away, has Jack in it, and that he went to a new city and found a new friend and his new friend is the dog from the title. I don't think that that dog is going to get hurt."

WebQuests

A WebQuest is an inquiry-oriented activity in which some or all of the information that learners interact with comes from resources on the Internet, optionally supplemented with videoconferencing (Dodge, 1995). WebQuests are deliberately designed to make the best use of a learner's time by directing the students to specific Web sites to complete creative tasks. As educators, we often question the educational value of inviting students to "surf the net" without a clear task in mind. A WebQuest typically is organized into several categories. WebQuests are a structured way to facilitate learning via the World Wide Web and should contain at least the following parts (Dodge, 1995):

- An *introduction* that sets the stage and provides some background information.
- A *task* that is interesting and can be completed.
- A set of *information sources* needed to complete the task. Many (though not necessarily all) of the resources are embedded in the WebQuest document itself as anchors pointing to information on the World Wide Web. Information sources might include web documents, experts available via e-mail or real-time conferencing, searchable databases on the Internet, and books and other documents physically available in the learner's setting. Because pointers to resources are included, the learner is not left to wander through Web space completely adrift.
- A *description of the process* the learners should go through in accomplishing the task. The process should be broken out into clearly described steps.
- Some guidance on *how to organize the information* acquired. This can take the form of guiding questions or directions to complete organizational frameworks such as timelines, concept maps, or cause-and-effect diagrams.
- A *conclusion* that brings closure to the quest; it reminds the learners about what they've learned and encourages them to extend the experience into other domains.

These are often found on a Web site that the teacher has created with an accompanying Teacher Page, thus making links to additional resources more accessible. There are a number of WebQuests already available at the Web site http://webquest .sdsu.edu/webquest.html. This site encourages new submissions of WebQuests and has been growing exponentially since 1995.

E-mail Correspondence

Comparing and contrasting the format for letters and memos with the format of the e-mail message helps students clarify the appropriateness of each. Just as spoken language inside the classroom is different from the language that students use at lunch or in their neighborhoods, written language must also be adapted to the environment. Setting up a class listserv for students to send e-mail messages to one another or so the whole class can be integrated as part of many curricular activities (i.e., to share predictions, reactions, or other comments on a particular lesson). Ms. Peterson uses the listserv to provide her students with newsletter items and asks that they write to the listserv at least three times per week. Some weeks she asks them to predict what will happen next in the book she is reading aloud. Other times she asks students to share some of their writing. Still other times, she invites students to plan recess events or vote on an important class issue, such as adopting a turtle. As noted earlier, e-mail can also be used to replace the traditional "passing notes in class" communication.

Students may want to build a glossary of *emoticons* and their meanings so that everyone understands this new cyber-language. For example, a sideways smile, =), is often used to signify a joke or sarcasm, and a frown, :(, is used to express displeasure, acknowledgment of something sad, or an apology. Many abbreviations are also used in e-mail such as IMHO (in my humble opinion), LOL (laughing out loud), and TIA (thanks in advance).

Students can also find an E-Pal (electronic pen pal) in another country so that they can report on "first-person" stories from around the world. The KeyPals Web site (http://www.teaching.com/keypals/) helps teachers locate appropriate matches for their students.

Multimedia Presentations

When doing reports or other classroom presentations, students can use software such as Appleworks™ (presentation), PowerPoint™, or Illustrator™ to present their ideas and projects. These programs can include pictures, graphs, tables, and more and can be shown in a slide show format from a very simple slideshow presentation or with more complex audio, video clips, and transitions. Most programs provide a way to easily rearrange the sequence as necessary. Using this same feature, Ms. Peterson prepares slides to give previews of a story as an anticipatory set, provide pieces of a story that the students could sequence correctly, or offer different endings to a story that the students would complete. For example, when she introduced the book *Only Passing Through: The Story of Sojourner Truth* (Rockwell, 2000), Ms. Peterson used PowerPoint™ to provide students with background information about slavery and the historical era in which this book is set. Ms. Peterson used the Internet to find photos about slavery and journal entries from slaves and inserted these into her PowerPoint™ presentation.

Technology and software advances have made multimedia presentations and projects so easy to construct that many classrooms, from elementary to college, have started using software programs such as iMovie or MovieWorks for student projects. Using slides or digital movies, students can add music, voice, and on screen writing to produce valuable literature and poetry presentations. Although a digital camcorder with a soundproof room for audiotape recording would greatly enhance such projects, still slides with on-screen writing can be just as effective.

Using a digital camera, students at any grade level can take pictures of the photos in a favorite book, wordless picture book or graphic novel. Once the pictures are inserted in iMovie (www.Apple.com) or other movie making software they can record their voice reading each page, or they can write and then record a matching text for the wordless books and novels. When doing so students are developing their literacy and technology skills. The following URLs provide additional informational resources that will help you incorporate technology into your instruction. www.kitzu.org; http://halldavidson.net; http://www.digitalstories.org; http://www.discoveryeducatornetwork.com.

Webliography

This activity provides students with an opportunity to describe and critique the Web sites that they find on a specific topic. The webliography is similar to an annotated bibliography. There is freedom in "searching," which is similar to looking for books or magazine articles. However, the search is limited to a specific topic. The product is a list of web resources that can be shared with members of the class. Typically students report the following features: (a) ease of navigation through the site; (b) appropriateness to the subject area; (c) links to related sites; and (d) the use of graphics, pictures,

TABLE 12–3
Sample Webliography Format

URL: _____

_____

1. Title of Web site _____

2. What's the main purpose of the site? _____
    - Is it selling something?
    - Does it describe a service?
    - Is it an educational site?

3. Who created the site? _____
    - Is there a contact name?
    - Is it a private company?
    - Is it a school?
    - Is it a government agency?

4. How current is the site? (When was it last updated?) _____
    (This should be listed at the bottom of the home page.)

5. Are links available to other sites? Do they really link? (try at least some of them) ____

    _____

    (These are often listed as: Links, Resources, Other Web Sites)

6. Accessibility
    - Is the site user-friendly? (easy to figure out, follow, find information)
    - Is site available in graphics and text only options? (This is helpful to know if you have students who are blind and use a screen-reading software.)

7. What did you learn from this site? _____

    _____

    _____

sounds, or alternative formats. Table 12–3 provides a format that students can use to collect and evaluate Web sites for their webliography. Ms. Peterson often uses this assignment as a way for students to learn to navigate the Internet. For example, during a unit on Westward Expansion, groups of students produced webliographies for use by other students in the class.

Internet Research

Once students understand how to obtain information from Web sites, they can use the Internet for research. Just about anything can be found on the Internet, which is both good and bad in the classroom. Most schools have protection software on their school computers to block students' access to inappropriate sites (e.g., sexually explicit or extremely violent sites). However, there is little protection at the present time from inaccurate and biased information contained in various Web sites.

Ms. Peterson uses the information in Table 12–4 to teach students about evaluating information they receive from the Internet. She also models Internet research for her students so that they understand different search engines (e.g., Google, AltaVista, and others) and search protocols (e.g., Boolean). She also teaches students how to reference Web sites they use in their reports and projects just as they would any written resources.

TABLE 12–4
Evaluation of Web-Based Information

Evaluation of Web Documents	*How to Interpret the Basics*
1. Accuracy of Web Documents • Who wrote the page and can you contact him or her? • What is the purpose of the document and why was it produced? • Is this person qualified to write this document?	Accuracy • Make sure author provides e-mail or a contact address/phone number. • Know the distinction between author and web master.
2. Authority of Web Documents • Who published the document and is it someone separate from the web master? • Check the domain of the document; what institution publishes this document?	Authority • What credentials are listed for the author(s)? • Where is the document published? Check URL domain.
3. Objectivity of Web Documents • What goals/objectives does this page meet? • How detailed is the information? • What opinions (if any) are expressed by the author?	Objectivity • Determine whether the page is a mask for advertising; if so, information might be biased. • View any web page as you would an infomercial on television. Ask yourself why was this written and for whom?
4. Currency of Web Documents • When was it produced? • When was it updated? • How up-to-date are the links (if any)?	Currency • How many dead links are on the page? • Are the links current or updated regularly? • Is the information on the page outdated?
5. Coverage of the Web Documents • Are the links (if any) evaluated, and do they complement the document's theme? • Is the page all images or a balance of text and images? • Is the information presented cited correctly?	Coverage • If the page requires special software to view the information, how much are you missing if you don't have the software? • Is it free, or is there a fee, to obtain the information? • Is there an option for text only, or frames, or a suggested browser for better viewing?

Source: Jim Kapoun, reference and instruction librarian at Southwest State University, *College and Research Libraries News* (July/August, 1998): 522–523. Used with permission of author.

Podcasting

Podcasting is a technology that is growing tremendously and becoming easier to use and produce. Podcasting is a combination of iPod and broadcasting and is a way for people should be able to select, subscribe and have audio and video delivered so you can listen whenever you want on a computer, an MP3 player, or an iPod. A Google search in September 28, 2004 on the word "Podcast" reported 28 hits. The same search done in November 11, 2005 reported 101,000,000 hits. (Computer Using Educators conference, Palm Springs, California, March 11, 2006). Educators are finding more and more ways to include this in the curriculum. One second grade classroom has used podcast as a way to share what is happening in their classroom. Each week they work with their teacher to produce a radio show which includes reporting classroom news, jokes by the students, and upcoming events. This is a wonderful way for the community to learn more about the school and for parents and grandparents in any location to keep up with their child's activities. It is a chance for students to work on oral presentations, summaries of class activities, interview techniques and script writing.

Secondary and college teachers are also using podcasting as a way to provide additional information about their courses, provide access to guest lectures, and post lectures that students may have missed.

CONCLUSION

Technology and media have always provided teachers with novel ways of engaging students. Ranging from CD players to PDAs to computers to Internet access with wireless high-speed cable modems, teachers can use technology in ways that facilitate learning. Technology and media have also added a tremendous creativity element in the classroom as students learn *with* technology, create *through* technology, revise, and present *using* a wide range of technology tools. However, don't be fooled by glitz and glimmer as the content is still paramount. It should also be noted and emphasized that technology and the Internet can help teachers find and organize information. For example, there are hundreds of Web sites that provide free lesson plans for teachers. There are also chat rooms and listservs that teachers can use to communicate, pose questions, and provide information for colleagues with similar interests.

QUESTIONS

1. Identify three types of technology that could be useful in teaching a unit about the rain forest.
2. In what ways can CDs and audiotape recordings be useful in the language arts classroom?
3. What types of critical thinking skills can be taught to students as they are exposed to increasing amounts of propaganda?
4. How can computers and the Internet be incorporated into your teaching?
5. What safeguards need to be in place for students to use the Internet in the classroom?

REFERENCES

Burnford, S. (1960). *The incredible journey*. New York: Bantam.

Cannon, J. (1993). *Stellaluna*. San Diego: Harcourt Brace.

Creech, S. (2001). *Love that dog*. New York: HarperCollins.

Cronin, D. (2000). *Click, clack, moo: Cows that type*. New York: Simon & Schuster.

Dodge, B. (1995). WebQuests: A technique for internet-based learning. *Distance Educator, 1*(2), 10–13.

Education Week. (2003). *Technology counts: Putting school technology to the test*. Bethesda, MD: Author.

Flood, J., Lapp, D., & Fisher, D. (1999). Book clubs that encourage students to examine their cultural assumptions. In S. Totten, C. Johnson, L. R. Morrow, & T. Sills-Briegel (Eds.), *Practicing what we preach: Preparing middle level educators* (pp. 261–263). New York: Falmer.

Healy, J. M. (1998, October 7). The 'meme' that ate childhood. *Education Week, 18*(6), 56, 37.

Naylor, P. (1991). *Shiloh*. New York: Maxwell Macmillan.

Reinking, D. (1998). Introduction: Synthesizing technological transformations of literacy in a post-typographic world. In D. Reinking, M. C. McKenna, L. D. Labbo, & R. D. Kieffer (Eds.), *Handbook of literacy and technology* (pp. xi–xxx). Mahwah, NJ: Lawrence Erlbaum Associates.

Rockwell, A. (2000). *Only passing through: The story of Sojourner Truth*. New York: Knopf.

13

Teaching Reading to Students Who Are Learning English

―――――――――――――― CHAPTER GOALS ――――――――――――――

To help the reader

- understand background information about English language learners in U.S. schools.
- identify the needs of students who are learning English.
- understand linguistic differences between English and other languages.
- understand important issues that impact effective instruction for English language learners.
- evaluate the effectiveness of materials and instructional programs designed for English language learners.

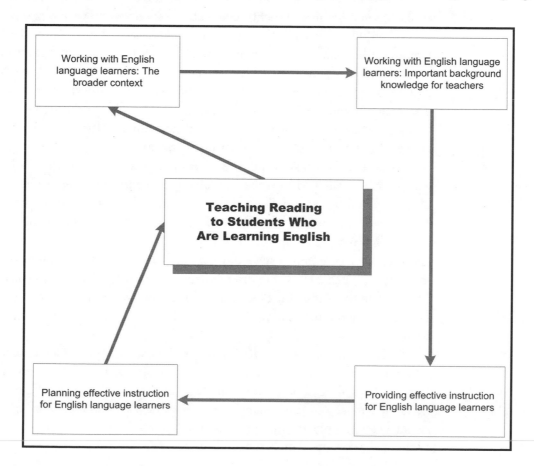

Students come to school with a wide variety of skills, abilities, and interests as well as varying proficiency in English and other languages. The wider the variation of the student population in each classroom, the more complex becomes the teacher's role in organizing high-quality curriculum and instruction in the language arts and ensuring that each student has access according to the student's current level of achievement (California State Department of Education, 1999, p. 225).

We begin this chapter with a vignette about an English language learner named Deng. We use this vignette—and others throughout the chapter—to contextualize the key ideas we present throughout the chapter.

VIGNETTE: DENG—AN AMERICAN FIFTH GRADER

Mrs. Weber looked at her fifth grade class list for the upcoming year. She would begin the year with 29 students. Because there was a fairly high student transient rate at her school, she knew that student enrollment would vary considerably across the year. In fact, because it was several weeks before the beginning of school, she knew that it was highly likely that her class enrollment would change even before the first day of school.

As she perused the names on the list, she noticed that a child named Deng Xiong was going to be in her class. Mrs. Weber had taught children from a wide variety of cultural and linguistic backgrounds over the years and had learned a great deal about many different cultures. However, the surname, Xiong, was unfamiliar to her. She made a mental note to pay careful attention to Deng's cumulative folder as she studied her new students' cumulative folders.

When Mrs. Weber looked at Deng's folder several days later, she found that Deng and his family were Hmong and that they had emigrated from Laos to the United States a year earlier. Deng had attended fourth grade at her school. Even though Deng's folder provided Mrs. Weber with some information about him, the documentation in the folder was fairly sketchy. Mrs. Weber decided to pay a visit to Deng's fourth grade teacher to see what additional information she could learn about him that she could use for her instructional planning.

After looking at his cumulative record folder and talking with his fourth grade teacher, here's what Mrs. Weber was able to piece together about Deng. Deng and his family had fled their village in the highlands of Laos 5 years earlier. Deng had not received any formal schooling while in Laos. His family had spent 4 years living in Thai refugee camps before coming to the United States a little over 1 year ago. He received minimal schooling (in Thai) in Thai refugee camps prior to coming to the United States. He did not begin to learn English until he arrived in the United States. Although Deng's first language was Hmong, he spoke Hmong, but did not write in Hmong. He also spoke some Lao, and he spoke and wrote some Thai.

There were only about 30 Hmong speakers in Deng's elementary school of approximately 540 students. Like Deng, many of the Hmong speakers in the school also spoke a little Thai. However, the children's level of proficiency in Thai depended mostly on how many years they and their families had spent in Thai refugee camps prior to coming to the United States. Overall, there were very few Hmong speakers in Deng's school district.

In the fourth grade, Deng had been in an English as a Second Language (ESL) pull-out program daily for about 1 hour each day. During Deng's pull-out lesson, his ESL teacher worked with him and three to four other children who were learning English. ESL instruction focused on basic conversational English (e.g., greetings and asking permission to use the restroom). He also received Title I reading assistance in fourth grade daily for about 45 minutes. According to the notes made by Deng's fourth grade teachers, he was a quiet conscientious student and a very hard worker. He had made considerable progress learning conversational English; however, he experienced a great deal of difficulty in most academic subjects because he did not understand the lessons that were conducted in English. Deng was quite proficient at sounding out words in English at about the mid-third grade level. However, he experienced a great deal of difficulty with English comprehension. Additionally, while he showed progress in English writing, he experienced considerable difficulty with English spelling and grammar.

Let's explore your thoughts about what Mrs. Weber should do to accommodate Deng's literacy learning in her classroom. When you finish, you may want to compare your ideas with those of your peers. Also, you can compare your initial ideas with the ideas that we will share with you throughout this chapter about literacy instruction for Deng, as well as other English language learners whose backgrounds and grade levels differ from his.

1. What tentative assumptions about Deng's academic needs might Mrs. Weber make as a result of the background information that she collected about him? For example, what should Mrs. Weber expect about Deng's level of English proficiency? How could she find out more about his level of English proficiency?

2. How should Mrs. Weber determine what kinds of classroom literacy instruction might benefit Deng most?

3. What additional information should Mrs. Weber plan to collect about Deng at the beginning of the year to plan quality literacy instruction for him?

WHAT PERCENTAGE OF CHILDREN IN U.S. SCHOOLS ARE ENGLISH LANGUAGE LEARNERS?

The number of children like Deng, who do not speak English as their first language, has increased dramatically in the United States in the last few decades (August & Hakuta, 1997; Genesee, 1994). For example, yearly since 1975 approximately one million immigrants have entered the United States. Immigration of this proportion has not been seen since the great 1900 to 1910 wave of immigration (Garcia, 1984). Children from many different cultural and linguistic backgrounds (e.g., Cuban, Puerto Rican, Mexican, Chinese, Vietnamese, Laotian, Cambodian, Haitian, Russian, Arab, and ethnic Bosnian) will comprise from three fourths to almost all of the student enrollment in the nation's 15 largest school systems within the next decade; however, children from diverse backgrounds are also increasingly enrolling in suburban and rural schools (Cummins, 1994; Faltis, 2001; Fitzgerald, 1995).

Given these statistics, it is not hard to understand why more English language learners enter schools every year in the United States. American schools have historically been designed to accommodate mainstream, middle-class European American children. Moreover, 85% to 90% of the teachers in U.S. schools are middle- to lower-middle-class European American women (Florio-Ruane, Raphael, Glazier, McVee, & Wallace, 1997; Gold, 1997). Clearly, U.S. schools, and the educators and administrators working within them must engage in the important task of changing schools and classrooms to provide effective instruction for large and growing numbers of children from diverse backgrounds (Samway & McKeon, 1999).

The nature and quality of instruction that English language learners receive in U.S. schools can vary dramatically across schools, school districts, and states. For example, some states and districts provide for a wide variety of different instructional services and programs. Others do not. In the section that follows, we provide a brief overview of some important terms pertaining to English language learners as well as an overview of some programs that may be available in your school or district. The focus of this chapter, however, is on what you can do as a classroom teacher to understand more about the English language learners in your classroom and to provide them with effective literacy instruction. You will, of course, want to check with your school and district to find out about specific instructional programs and services that are provided for English language learners.

Although it may seem obvious to you, we wish to underscore the fact that English language learners are not disadvantaged. On the contrary, like Deng, they have the privilege of knowing some portion of two or more languages. You will have an opportunity to experience this language abundance when you are teaching students who are learning English. Unfortunately, many well-intentioned teachers have taken inappropriate steps with English language learners and, inadvertently, have frustrated them to the point of total withdrawal. However, it is not our intention to dwell on the failings of teachers or programs. Rather, our intention is to present a concise body of information about English language learners that will help you to provide quality instruction for these students in your classroom.

Background Information About Terms and Programs Pertinent to English Language Learners

The following subsections may help you to understand some of the different programs and practices associated with instruction for English language learners like Deng.

Terms and Programs Associated With Bilingual Education

Bilingualism is the ability to function in a second language in addition to one's home language. *Bilingual education* is a process by which learning experiences provided in the home and in other educational institutions enable a person to function in a second language and culture in addition to the home language and culture. There are many kinds of bilingual education programs; two include *transitional bilingual programs* and *dual-language programs* (Faltis, 2001). The goal of transitional bilingual programs is to assist the child in adapting to school and progressing on par with his or her peers in all subject areas while learning English. The goal of dual-language programs is to help children develop competency in the native language as well as in the second language in every subject area.

Teachers who have received *bilingual education training* are prepared to teach in a bilingual setting in which students are often taught in two languages during the school day. Bilingual teachers are fluent in two languages and provide instruction in both languages to their children throughout each day. In school districts with comprehensive bilingual programs, parents can often choose to have their children enroll in bilingual classrooms for many or most of their elementary school years. Bilingual education was not an option for Deng because there were no bilingual teachers certified to teach in Hmong or Thai in Deng's school district.

Terms and Programs Associated With English as a Second Language Education

English immersion means that English language learners are immersed solely in English contexts with no support in their home languages. Although the goal of English immersion is to develop English language and literacy skills, the reality is that it is very difficult to learn a new language as well as to learn literacy in a new language with no support in one's home language (August & Hakuta, 1997).

TESOL stands for *teaching English to speakers of other languages. ESL* refers to *English as a second language.* In many states, it is possible for teachers to earn TESOL or ESL certification to work with children who are learning English. Recall that Deng participated in an ESL pull-out program during fourth grade. Each day he left his fourth grade classroom to receive small-group instruction in an ESL pull-out program by a teacher who was specially certified to work with children who are learning English as a second or additional language. ESL programs can vary widely depending on the nature of ESL training received by teachers as well as philosophies of specific school districts, schools, and teachers. Typically, ESL teachers speak only English and work short-term (1 year or less) with children who are learning English. ESL instruction frequently—but not always—focuses on teaching children the basic English that they will need to survive in school and in the community.

Terms Associated With English Language Learners

You'll undoubtedly encounter a host of terms used to refer to English language learners. These could include, but are not limited to, non-English proficient (NEP), limited English proficient (LEP), fully English proficient (FEP), and second language learners (Faltis, 2001). Throughout this book, we use the term English language learners to refer to children who are learning English as an additional language. Here's why. Scholars (e.g., Cummins, 2001; Faltis, 2001) argue that terms such as NEP and LEP have negative connotations. That is, they focus on what children cannot do rather than on what they can do and what they are learning. A potential problem with the term *second language learner* is that many times children are learning English as their third or fourth language. This was the case with Deng. When Deng arrived to the U.S. with his family, he already spoke Hmong, Thai, and Lao. Consequently, English was his fourth language. We urge you to exercise caution as you make decisions about the labels that you use with your children learning English because labels can sometimes stigmatize children in negative ways.

WHAT SPECIAL ISSUES SHOULD WE CONSIDER IN OUR WORK WITH ENGLISH LANGUAGE LEARNERS?

Learning to teach English language learners involves knowledge about three important and interrelated sets of issues. These include (a) knowing about the second language acquisition process, (b) understanding how interactions can vary from culture to culture and how they can significantly impact children's classroom literacy learning, and (c) maintaining high academic expectations for English language learners while valuing the linguistic, cultural, and family backgrounds that English language learners bring to our classrooms. Let's begin our discussion of these areas by finding out if you have any experiences acquiring a second language that you can draw upon as you read about the second language acquisition process. We believe that insider knowledge of the complexities of second language acquisition can help teachers to empathize with the children in their classrooms who are experiencing this complex process.

After jotting down your responses to these questions, compare them with a classmate to see if he or she has had similar experiences.

- Have you ever tried to learn a language other than your home language? Please note that we're talking about trying to achieve native-like proficiency in a different language so that you can engage in complex academic tasks (e.g., studying literature, physics, and social sciences) in the new language. If you haven't ever tried to learn a new language, find someone who has, and interview her or him about the process.
- Describe the context(s) and describe how you (or your interviewee) felt as a foreign language learner. How proficient did you become in the other language(s)? Explain. What factors affected your ability to become proficient in the other language(s)? Explain in detail.

How Is a Second Language Acquired?

Let's see how your experiences or the experiences of the person you interviewed relate to the research about second language acquisition. If you have ever tried to really learn a second language to the point of attaining native-like proficiency, you undoubtedly have some idea about the arduous process involved in second language acquisition (Collier, 1989, 1995). However, consider this. Many English language

My Name is Yoon. ©2003 Helen Recorvits. Illustrations ©2003 by Gabi Swiatowska. Used with the permission of Farrar Straus Giroux.

learners in U.S. schools, like Deng, were uprooted from familiar home and cultural surroundings and placed into American school contexts where they not only did not understand the culture, but also couldn't speak, read, or write in the language of instruction. The process of entering U.S. public schools for non-English speakers can be traumatic (Igoa, 1996).

Notwithstanding the trauma that many English language learners experience when entering U.S. public schools, the process of learning a new language and culture is a long and complex one. It takes from 5 to 7 years for most children to become proficient in a second language (Collier, 1995). Many factors contribute to the length of time that it takes to become proficient in a second language as well as the complexity of the second language acquisition process (Cummins, 2001; Krashen, 1985, 1992). For example, the literacy proficiencies and academic competence a child has acquired in his or her first language will transfer to the second language (Cummins, 1996). Consequently, the more a child knows and understands about reading and writing processes and purposes in her first language, the less she will have to learn about the purposes and processes of reading and writing in English. Hence, the less time it will take for the child to learn to read and write in English. As an example, consider the situation with Deng. Recall that Deng had attained oral proficiency in his home language of Hmong, and he had attained some oral proficiency in Lao and Thai prior to coming to the United States. However, he had very little knowledge about reading and writing in any language. Thus, Deng had little background knowledge about the process and purposes of reading and writing to draw on while he was in the process of learning to read and write in English.

Other factors besides reading and writing proficiency in a child's home language impact the second language acquisition process. For example, a child's desire and motivation to learn the second language, the nature of interactions in classrooms in which English language learners are assigned, the relationship between the language learner and the classroom teacher, and teacher attitude and expectations all contribute to the time and complexity of acquiring a second language (Angelil-Carter, 1997; Cummins, 1994; Krashen, 1998; Toohey, 1998).

We mentioned earlier that teachers sometimes inadvertently sabotage the learning of English language learners. One way that this can happen is when teachers misjudge English language learners' proficiency levels. Cummins (1994) makes an important and useful distinction between *conversational competence* and *academic competence* in second language acquisition. Conversational competence involves the ability to use the new language to engage in informal conversations, such as greeting others and talking about the weather. Cummins refers to this level of language competence as *basic interpersonal communication skills* (BICS). Children often acquire conversational competence (or BICS) in their second language within 1 year of learning the new language. The ability to converse informally, however, is very different from the kind of academic language competence required to understand science, social studies, and mathematics concepts in a new language. Cummins refers to this kind of academic language competence as *cognitive academic language proficiency* (CALP). Acquiring academic competence (or CALP) in a new language takes many years. If teachers mistake conversational competence for academic competence, they may not provide English language learners with the necessary support to understand complex ideas in different academic subjects. Without sustained and adequate support, English language learners can fall behind in subject matter learn-

DID YOU NOTICE...
Did you notice that understanding a child s level of language competence (BICS and CALP) will help you plan appropriate instruction? Spending time with English language learners on the playground and during lunchtime will surely give you insight about the kinds of competencies a child is and is not acquiring. We want our students to acquire the academic language of the classroom and also the interpersonal skills to be successful communicators in the larger context.

ing while they are in the long process of acquiring academic competence in their new language. Again returning to the case of Deng, it is clear why his fourth grade teacher said that he was experiencing difficulty in the different academic subjects. Deng needs additional support from his teacher and peers for many years so that he can learn social studies, science, and mathematics concepts while he is in the process of learning English.

When teachers misjudge the milestones that language learners make in the process of acquiring an additional language, they may also inadvertently sabotage the learning of English language learners. *Interlanguage* is the term linguists apply to the intermediate language that learners speak while they are in the process of acquiring a more formal version of a target language (Freeman & Freeman, 2001). Language learners draw upon four different types of knowledge in constructing interlanguage including "knowledge about the second language, competence in their native language, ability to use the functions of language, and their general world knowledge" (Diaz-Rico & Weed, 2002, p. 18). Teachers must be aware that interlanguage is different in form from the English spoken by native speakers of English. For example, an English language learner may say, "He asked me that should he go." In this case the language learner has "overgeneralized the question-word-order rule" (Diaz-Rico & Weed, 2002). Thus, although the sentence is syntactically incorrect, the language learner has demonstrated the ability to apply a complex cognitive strategy while he or she is in the process of trying to learn English.

What should or can we do as teachers to help our English language learners while they are in this interlanguage phase? According to Diaz-Rico and Weed (2002), the first thing that teachers should not do is to see their English language learners as "bumblers whose every mistake needs 'fixing'" (p. 36). Instead, teachers should view their English language learners "as intelligent, hypothesis-forming individuals who use the knowledge of their first language and a growing awareness of the second to progress toward native-like second language fluency" (p. 36). Some of the most effective ways to help children progress on the continuum toward more native-like proficiency include modeling appropriate use of English in interactions with English language learners and providing lots of opportunities for English language learners to interact with native speakers both in and out of the classroom. Additionally, teachers can work with their English language learners to target one or two skills or strategies at a time to work on in their speaking and writing. As children appropriate these skills and strategies, the student and the teacher can move on to new skills and strategies (Cary, 2000; Diaz-Rico & Weed, 2002; Freeman & Freeman, 2001). Throughout the remainder of this chapter, we provide specific examples of teachers working with English language learners in meaningful ways to assist them in the process of acquiring more native-like proficiency in English as well as to develop academic competence across subjects.

Understanding Different Patterns of Interactions Across Cultures

Have you ever experienced a context that was very unfamiliar to you? For example, have you ever spent time living and traveling in a different country? (Spending time in five-star hotels that cater to Americans in other countries doesn't count!) Or, maybe you have moved from a rural farming community in North Dakota to New York City. Essentially, we're asking if you have ever had a significantly different cultural or social experience. Jot your ideas in the following "Your Turn" and be ready to discuss these in class.

Your Turn

If you have ever experienced a significantly different culture or context, describe what you noticed and how you felt in the different context. If you have not experienced this situation, find someone who has and ask that person to describe, in detail, the experience to you.

If you have ever spent time in a context that is very different for you or if you just interviewed someone who has, then you know that different cultural groups have different norms, values, beliefs, behaviors, and ways of acting and interacting (Gee, 1996). Because we know our own cultures so well, our cultural norms are often tacit and taken for granted. Many of us are not aware of the norms that constitute our cultural ways of being because we are all steeped in our own cultures. Often the experience of entering into an unfamiliar culture can make us acutely aware that we don't fit in because we don't know the "rules" or norms for how to behave in that new culture.

Just being aware that American classrooms and schools function according to mainstream, middle-class European American cultural values can help us to understand that there can be a cultural mismatch between schools and the children they serve (Deschenes, Cuban, & Tyack, 2001). We briefly introduced the work of

Shirley Brice Heath in Chapter 1. Let's think about her work again to illustrate the significance of potential mismatches between home and school cultures.

Shirley Brice Heath spent 10 years studying the communities, families, and schools in the Piedmont Carolinas (Heath, 1983). Roadville and Trackton were two communities that she studied extensively. Here's what she learned about the families in those communities. Both Trackton and Roadville were working-class communities, but the families in Trackton were primarily African American, and the families in Roadville were primarily European American. The families in both communities engaged in literacy-related traditions; however, those traditions varied from community to community. Reading materials in the homes of Trackton families included newspapers, advertisements, church materials, school notices, and so forth; however, there were few books besides family bibles, school books, and church-oriented books. Newspaper articles and various sections of the newspaper, for example, were discussed socially, and much writing (e.g., writing church bulletins) was done socially. Thus, the families engaged in literate traditions that were primarily social and group oriented.

Homes in Roadville tended to have considerably more reading materials than Trackton homes. These materials included children's books, magazines, newspapers, church brochures, and so on. Reading and writing practices in Roadville homes varied from practices in Trackton, however. Parents often read to their children before bedtime, but reading involved little questioning or interpretation on the children's part. In general, children were taught to listen passively when adults read to them. Moreover, aside from reading newspapers and magazines, adults did not engage in many sustained reading practices. Families in Roadville did little writing that was not functional writing such as writing letters to family members, writing checks to pay bills, and so forth.

Whereas families in both Roadville and Trackton used literacy in various different ways in their homes and communities, the uses of literacy did not match closely with the ways literacy was used in middle-class homes or the local schools. For example, middle-class families in the community had considerably more reading materials available in their homes and engaged in a much wider variety of reading and writing activities on a daily basis. One of these practices included reading bedtime stories daily to their children and discussing and critiquing the stories with them in the ways that teachers typically discussed stories with school children (Heath, 1983). This particular literacy practice, as well as others engaged in by middle-class families, matched closely with literacy practices in the local schools. Consequently, when children from middle-class families entered schools, they typically experienced more school success because their literacy-related backgrounds and prior experiences were more closely aligned with school-based literacy practices. A key point here is that families from Roadville or Trackton were not deficit; rather, their literacy and language-related practices at home varied from the language and literacy-related practices in the middle-class community and the local schools. When teachers understand that children may come to their classrooms from community contexts wherein literacy and language are used differently as compared to the ways they may be used in schools, teachers can work with children, building on the strengths they bring to school, and helping them with appropriate school-based literacy practices.

Maintaining High Expectations and Valuing the Languages and Cultures of English Language Learners

We have discussed the lengthy process of learning a new language as well as potential mismatches between the cultures of home and school. It is crucial for teachers to understand that differences in language and culture do not mean lack of intellectual ability or potential (Au, 1993). It is important that, as teachers, we maintain high expectations for English language learners and provide the necessary academic support to help children achieve those expectations (Delpit, 1995). Additionally, teachers should help all children—including English language learners—to set high academic expectations for themselves (Allington & Walmsley, 1995).

Perhaps the most important characteristic of any good teacher is his or her ability to accept each child without prejudice or preconception. This unconditional acceptance sets a positive tone in the classroom that significantly affects the learning that occurs there (McDermott, 1977). Students quickly and thoroughly sense rejection by their teachers. In a multicultural/multilingual setting, the teacher must be quick to accept children's language because it is the language of their homes and their parents. Language and self-concept are so closely intertwined that students can be made to feel foolish and worthless when their accents or dialects are ridiculed by their teachers or peers. Trust and confidence between teachers and students must precede linguistic corrections. Linguistic differences should not be viewed as a hindrance to literacy development.

One way to capitalize on the diversity in any classroom is to get to know the children in your classroom and the families and communities from which they come. In an effort to bridge school and neighborhood communities to be more successful in school, Moll, Amanti, Neff, and Gonzalez (1992) shifted the focus of the "typical" home–school relationship in their powerful and groundbreaking work in the Southwest. Working with many Latino families, Moll and his teacher colleagues have become learners who respect learning about children, their families, and the communities served by the local schools. They learned that the families had powerful "funds of knowledge" about topics such as working on automobiles and natural herbal medicines to share in the school context. These "funds of knowledge" became the foundation on which the teachers built as they helped the children in their classrooms learn to engage in school literacy learning. In this context, the "typical" focus of requiring or expecting the children and their families to learn about and adapt to the school norms shifted. Rather than expecting that a one-way bridge be built by parents to the schools, the teachers in Moll's project saw the value of building a two-way bridge between school and home. That is, the teachers valued learning about the cultures and experiences of the children and their families, while helping them learn about the school culture.

HOW CAN WE PROVIDE EFFECTIVE INSTRUCTION FOR ENGLISH LANGUAGE LEARNERS?

We share another story with you about an English language learner named Adriana to explore examples of ways that you can provide effective instruction for English language learners in your classroom. We know that one vignette will not cover the scope

DID YOU NOTICE . . .
Did you notice how the Moll teachers built a bridge between the students homes and school? If you do not live in the same community in which you work, it is important to spend time getting to know the stores, community centers, restaurants, and people. Scheduling home visits will also give you insight into the possible disconnect between home and school. This can benefit you and your students as you bring their backgrounds and experiences into the classroom.

of different situations that you'll experience as a classroom teacher. However, these examples can serve as a framework to help you to think about how to serve the English language learners that you will have in your classroom.

Vignette: Adriana—An American Second Grader

Adriana entered Mrs. Pitner's second grade classroom in a semirural community in the Northwest at the end of the first week of school. Adriana and her family had just arrived in the United States from Colombia. She spoke only a few words in English. If you were Mrs. Pitner, what would you do to create an effective instructional program for Adriana?

Think about Adriana. List your tentative plans and instructional ideas. Also, share your ideas with a peer. Next, read on and compare your instructional plan for Adriana with Mrs. Pitner's plan.

Mrs. Pitner was beginning her third year of teaching. This was her first opportunity to work with an English language learner in her classroom. She had spent 1 year studying abroad in Asia during college, so she knew first hand what it felt like to enter into a totally new context where she didn't know the language or culture. Mrs. Pitner had been a young adult when she studied abroad. She could only imagine how frightening it must be to a second grader like Adriana moving to a totally new cultural context.

Mrs. Pitner's first concern was to make Adriana feel comfortable and welcomed in her classroom. Here are some of the things that Mrs. Pitner did. First, she *gathered information that could inform her instruction* by contacting Mrs. Duchek, an ESL teacher at the same school who spoke Spanish at a moderately fluent level. She asked Mrs. Duchek for suggestions about how to help Adriana feel comfortable in the classroom as well as how to begin to develop an instructional plan for her. Mrs. Pitner asked Mrs. Duchek how to greet Adriana and welcome her to the classroom in Spanish. The two teachers also agreed that Mrs. Duchek would be in the classroom on Adriana's first morning of school so that Adriana would know that there was an adult close by who spoke Spanish and would always be there if Adriana needed to communicate something to an adult. Also, Mrs. Pitner wanted Adriana to know that Mrs. Duchek would be her ESL teacher.

Next, Mrs. Pitner *created a comfortable learning environment* for Adriana by having her sit next to a Spanish-speaking peer partner, Gabriela, in her classroom. Gabriela was an exceptional student, and Mrs. Pitner suspected that she would be an excellent peer partner for Adriana. In a sense, Mrs. Pitner saw Gabriela as serving in the capacity of a language broker (Tse, 2001). That is, Gabriela would do much more than merely translate words for Adriana. She would help to translate cultural practices in and outside of school for Adriana.

For example, from her own international travel, Mrs. Pitner was aware that schooling practices vary significantly across cultures. She suspected that many of the schooling practices that Adriana would soon encounter in her classroom would vary significantly from the schooling practices Adriana was used to in Colombia. One of many such practices includes Mrs. Pitner's use of book club (see Raphael & McMahon with Goatley & Pardo, 1997) in her classroom whereby children talked about authentic literature in small peer-led discussion groups.

Mrs. Pitner also did several additional things to prepare for Adriana's arrival. She had labeled most of the items in the classroom in English (e.g., door, window, and blackboard). Mrs. Duchek suggested that she place the Spanish names of all of the labels of the items in the room next to the English names. Also, Mrs. Pitner went to the library resource center and checked out a stack of first, second, and third grade level books in Spanish to place in the classroom library for Adriana and others to check out. Mrs. Pitner's school district did not have a bilingual education program, so bilingual education was not an option for Adriana. ESL instruction was the only service provided for English language learners in Mrs. Pitner's district. Mrs. Pitner made arrangements for Adriana to start working with Mrs. Duchek, the ESL teacher. The two teachers decided to work closely together as they developed and implemented an instructional plan for Adriana. Mrs. Pitner spoke with her principal about other possible resources for Adriana and her principal agreed to arrange to have a Spanish-speaking assistant who normally worked in the upper elementary grades work in Mrs. Pitner's classroom for 45 minutes to 1 hour each day. Mrs. Pitner had to sort out many different issues in planning her work with Adriana. We discuss some of the key issues that she worked through in the following.

Mrs. Pitner's Underlying Beliefs About Effective Instruction for English Language Learners

In her teacher preparation program Mrs. Pitner had learned that historically, English language learners were taught English by imitating what they hear. Incorrect usage and punctuation were corrected when speakers failed to communicate effectively. Teachers began teaching oral language by having children mimic and memorize. They emphasized proper sounds and the acquisition of native-like accents by language learners. The assumption of this transmission approach was that in memorizing enough samples of natural speech, the learner would be able to make proper use of these structures in the appropriate context.

However, Mrs. Pitner knew that more recent constructivist approaches to language learning emphasize the ability of all children to generate sentences that have been neither imitated nor memorized in their native language. Instead of emphasizing either reading or speaking exclusively, teachers now explore the many interconnected dimensions of reading, writing, speaking, and listening with English language learners. The teacher's goal is to create meaningful contexts that stimulate communication in the new language (Au, 1993).

Mrs. Pitner knew that she would avoid pronunciation drills with Adriana. Instead, she would structure classes for meaningful social and academic interaction. Conversation and informal sharing would provide Adriana opportunities to practice English and learn from and with her peers. Mrs. Pitner planned to help Adriana understand content area vocabulary, and she planned to facilitate Adriana's comprehension by the use of visuals as well as giving her ample opportunities to talk about the content of the material before and after reading.

DID YOU NOTICE . . .
Did you notice that because Mrs. Pitner believes that structuring a classroom around meaningful social and academic interactions is necessary to literacy development she has seated Adriana next to another Spanish speaking student? Undoubtedly, Mrs. Pitner will be allowing all students many opportunities throughout the day to share their thoughts with partners (or small groups of students) first and then to the whole class. This pair-share technique will give students a chance to clarify and rehearse their thoughts in a comfortable, low-anxiety setting before speaking out in front of the larger group.

How Mrs. Pitner Began to Assess
Adriana's Literacy Learning Needs

Mrs. Pitner went to Mrs. Duchek and asked the following question, "Okay, where do I begin with Adriana?" Mrs Duchek suggested that to plan effective instruction for Adriana, she would first have to assess what Adriana knew about English and about literacy. Here is what Mrs. Duchek said to Mrs. Pitner:

> The first question you should ask when working in English with an English language learner is "How much English does the child know?" The first issue is to assess Adriana's proficiency in English. In most cases it will be advantageous for you, as the teacher, to conduct a structured, but informal, nonthreatening interview with your student to determine her ease in speaking English. You should be aware that most tests designed to assess language dominance have ignored the fact that children have many variations in their language abilities. Sometimes their native language is their dominant, preferred language for a particular task, but sometimes it is not. This seems eminently logical because many adults experience the same phenomenon; for example, a Spanish-speaking adult who studies advanced statistics in the United States may prefer to use English when discussing statistics. Therefore, before assessing a student's language dominance globally, you should ask "What is the specific task that the student is being asked to perform?" and "What is the language of the person to whom the student will speak during the instructional period?" These questions will provide useful information that will enable you to begin to develop your instructional program.

Mrs. Duchek further suggested that she would be doing some formal assessments of Adriana after Adriana's first week or two at school—as soon as Adriana became comfortable with her. Because Mrs. Duchek is an experienced and sensitive ESL teacher, she knows that testing children too soon when they first arrive at a school is problematic. They are often frightened and uncertain of the new context. These conditions militate against children being able to show the test examiner what they really know in English. Formal assessments, such as the Language Assessment Scale (LAS) and the California English Language Development Test (CELDT) used in conjunction with informal assessments conducted by Mrs. Pitner and Mrs. Duchek would help to give an indication of Adriana's English competency as well as her understanding of reading and writing in English and Spanish.

Additional information can be found about the CELDT on the Web site (http://www.cde.ca.gov/ta/tg/el). Briefly, according to the "Facts about the CELDT for 2004–05" (California State Department of Education, 2004):

- Federal guidelines for No Child Left Behind, Title III, require that state educational agencies receiving Title III funds establish English language proficiency standards, identify or develop and implement English language proficiency assessments, and define annual measurable achievement objectives for monitoring the progress.
- The CELTD has three purposes: (1) to identify new students who are English learners in kindergarten through grade twelve; (2) to determine their level of English proficiency; and (3) to annually assess their progress in acquiring listening, speaking, reading, and writing skills in English.

Figure 13–1 Matrix for identifying the instructional needs of English language learners.

	Student 1	Student 2	Student 3	Student 4	Student 5
Speaks	Spanish _____	Spanish English	Spanish _____	Spanish English	Spanish English
Reads	_____ _____	_____ _____	Spanish _____	_____ English	Spanish English

After discussing some initial ideas about assessing Adriana, Mrs. Pitner asked Mrs. Duchek to begin to discuss specifics about instruction for Adriana. Mrs. Duchek said that there is not one route, one reading methodology, for all English language learners. To illustrate her point, she shared the following chart with Mrs. Pitner so that she could begin to understand some of the differences among English language learners with regard to their ability to read and write. Five different combinations are represented in the matrix in Figure 13–1.

Although the example provided to Mrs. Pitner by Mrs. Duchek is a comparison between English and Spanish, the same combinations could occur between any primary language and English. You should note that reading and writing instruction for students 3, 4, and 5 will be less difficult because each of them speaks and reads at least one language, and, as we discuss further later in the chapter, many literacy and language practices transfer from one language to another. Teaching student 3 to read in English or student 4 to read in Spanish depends upon several factors: age, the child's progress in English at the present time, the need for reading in a second language, and the availability of a bilingual reading program in the child's district. Teaching students 1 and 2 will be the most difficult because they do not know how to read in any language.

Figure 13–2 presents one possible approach to teaching each of these students. When planning reading instruction, teachers should ask themselves questions like the following.

1. What is the home language?
2. How fluent is the child in his or her native language?
3. What is the child's reading level in the native language?
4. What is the child's past school history (e.g., achievement and attendance)?
5. What are the child's language skills in English (reading and listening comprehension, speaking, and writing)?
6. What knowledge and experiences does the child have in subject areas offered in English?

After Mrs. Pitner and Mrs. Duchek finished formal and informal assessments for Adriana, they noted that her situation was similar to the scenario for student 3 in Figure 13–2. Adriana was reading Spanish at the beginning second grade level. Also, she only spoke in Spanish. They decided to begin oral instruction in English

Student 1	Focus on teaching oral English before heavily focusing on reading instruction in either language. If possible, begin reading instruction in Spanish. (This depends on students' and parents' wishes as well as availability of bilingual instruction in the child's school/district.)
Student 2	Begin reading instruction in one of the two languages, depending on the following factors: (a) student's preference, (b) local expertise, (c) age, (d) cultural factors, and (e) family preference.
Student 3	Begin oral instruction in English. Begin reading instruction in English. (Bilingual instruction is an option if available in the child's district and the child and his or her family wish for continued development of Spanish literacy.)
Student 4	Begin reading instruction in Spanish and continue reading instruction in English (if Spanish instruction is available in district and desired by the child and his or her family).
Student 5	Continue reading instruction in English and Spanish (if Spanish instruction is available in district and desired by the child and his or her family).

and reading instruction in English. Unfortunately, bilingual instruction in Spanish was not an option for Adriana because, as noted earlier, it was not offered in her school district.

Important Instructional Considerations for English Language Learners

Mrs. Duchek reminded Mrs. Pinter that to achieve second-language fluency takes time and practice; as noted earlier, such fluency in academic undertakings may take as long as 5 to 7 years or more before proficiency is achieved (Collier, 1989; Cummins, 1984). Further, the development of oral language fluency helps provide a base for reading/writing fluency, which may be more difficult than oral language fluency for some students to accomplish (Chamot & O'Malley, 1986). The fact that English language learners need to speak some English before they learn to read English may seem obvious, but adult learners, who already read their native language, frequently learn to read English before speaking it. However, for a child who does not read at all or who is learning to read, it is helpful to learn to speak some of the language before learning to read it. Please note, however, that teachers should not wait too long to begin teaching a child to read in English. Waiting too long to begin instruction in reading can set the child too far behind in his or her learning to read and write (Samway & McKeon, 1999). Finally, there are four general categories in which English language learners require reading instruction:

1. *Experimental/information/conceptual background.* Students (and anyone for that matter) frequently find it difficult to read about things that are totally outside their experience. Thus, teachers need to make certain that they get a sense of their English language learners' experiential backgrounds and make sure that they gear lessons toward experiences their children can draw upon to make sense of the lessons. Or, teachers can be

certain that they spend considerable time helping their English language learners acquire the background knowledge necessary to understand lessons that may focus on topics outside their experiential backgrounds.

2. *Auditory discrimination.* The phonological structures of different languages (i.e., the sound systems of different languages) differ. Sometimes the letters in one language may be pronounced differently in another language. For example, in some Spanish dialects, the *th* heard by English speakers in *thanks* may be pronounced as a *t*, making *thanks* sound like *tanks*. Also, sometimes sounds in one language do not exist in other languages. It is important for teachers to know that when sound variations do not exist in a speaker's native language, it is very difficult for the student to produce them in the early stages of second language acquisition. Consider the following examples of sounds that exist in English but not in Spanish:

- Spanish-speaking children learning English may have difficulty pronouncing the following vowels because these vowel sounds are not used in Spanish:

    /i/ *sit*   /ae/ *cat*   /u/ *pull*

- The following is a list of some sounds in English that are not present in Spanish:

/p/ *point*	/z/ *pleasure*	/h/ *hear*
/t/ *take*	/v/ *vine, vote*	/y/ *yet*
/k/ *car*	/r/ *rode*	/w/ *what*
/j/ *judge*	/tt/ *cotton*	/s/ *shoe*

We want to point out that differences in sounds across languages or differences in pronunciations of sounds by language speakers are NOT deficiencies; rather, they reflect differences in the linguistic and phonological structures of languages and the ways that languages are spoken. If you are not already fluent in another language and have tried to learn it, you, too, would experience patterns of pronunciation differences when compared with native speakers.

3. *Vocabulary.* When working with Latino students one must beware of *false cognates*, that is, words that look or sound similar but have quite different meanings, for example:

libreria	bookstore, not library
embarazada	pregnant, not embarrassed
chanza	joke, not chance

4. *Syntax (especially word order).* Many languages (e.g., French and Spanish) permit or prefer placement of adjectives after nouns.

La casa blanca	(the house white)	the white house
Les livres jaunes	(the books yellow)	the yellow books

Most speakers of Asian or African languages will have difficulty with *a* and *the* because most languages on those continents do not use articles. Other languages

(e.g., Russian) do not use the copula verb (i.e., the *to be* verb) in the present tense, as English does. Consequently, speakers of other languages may be confused about the use of *to be* in English, resulting in such forms as the following:

What the English language learner may say:	*English equivalent:*
1. Lamp here	1. The lamp is here.
2. Today he work in store.	2. He was working in the store today.
3. Freddy in school.	3. Freddy is in school.

Plurals, comparatives, and possessives are other forms that tend to give language learners trouble:

What the English language learner may say:	*English equivalent:*
1. My tooths hurt.	1. My teeth hurt.
2. This book is more heavy.	2. This book is heavier.
3. Is this the pen of Rose?	3. Is this Rose's pen?

DESIGNING EFFECTIVE INSTRUCTION FOR TEACHING ENGLISH LANGUAGE LEARNERS

Given the differences among students . . . there can be no single plan of reading instruction designed to meet the needs of all of them. There are, however, modifications in instruction which can make the knowledge and skills of English more accessible to English language learners. These adaptations of the curriculum should be *developmental* in nature, not *remedial*. Students who do not possess sufficient fluency and literacy in English should be considered as students with the need to acquire new skills rather than as students who need compensatory efforts for their deficiencies and defects. (Thonis, 1989, p. 26)

One of the best ways to teach very young children English, if their first language is not English, is to let them play and learn with children whose first language is English. Young children are less encumbered by introspection and are less self-conscious than older children and adults. They are willing to create new words and to decipher the complex and often unintelligible speech of their peers. However, not all children learn a second language spontaneously. It is foolish to think that every English language learner will learn English merely because he or she is young. Children need formal instruction in English.

Integrated Language-Experience Method

An effective method of teaching reading to English language learners is the integrated language-experience method because it elicits language from the child. The teacher or the child, when able, transcribes the oral language, and the child reads what he or she has spoken.

Scholars have long advocated for the use of dialogue journals to help students develop their English skills in a meaningful context (Au, 1993; Flores & Hernandez, 1988; Garcia, 2000). As an example of how to use dialogue journals, each day the child writes about a self-selected topic and reads the entry to the teacher. The teacher then writes a response and reads it to the student. Such journals present an authentic vehicle for communication for all students.

In this section, we describe sample lessons for English language learners in two different classrooms—Mrs. Wood's first grade classroom and Ms. Jackson's third grade classroom.

Vignette: Proko and His First Grade Classmates Learn About Zoos

The following lesson description provides one example of a way to adapt an integrated language-experience method of instruction for English language learners at the primary level. We focus on an English language learner named Proko from Bosnia-Herzegovina for this lesson description. Proko and his family moved to Detroit when Proko was 5 years. He started kindergarten in Detroit and is currently in first grade. There are a total of 23 children in Proko's mainstream classroom. Proko's teacher, Mrs. Wood, typically uses simple stories and poems for listening exercises and as language models with her children. Mrs. Wood also uses stories that repeat patterns of words as well as folktales and stories that include familiar experiences, characters, food, clothing, shelter, transportation, and recreation because these stories can help to provide an appropriate experiential base for reading for English language learners.

Mrs. Wood decided to engage her children in a series of reading, writing, and listening activities as well as experiences pertaining to zoos. One of the books Mrs. Wood read several times to her class was Mem Fox's book *Zoo Looking*. She also showed pictures of zoos to her children and placed labeled pictures of various zoo animals around her classroom. After reading *Zoo Looking* to her class multiple times, Mrs. Wood placed the book at the listening center where children could read the book along with a tape-recorded version of Mem Fox reading the book. Additionally, Mrs. Wood read several different expository texts about zoos—including information in the local newspaper about renovations at the Detroit Zoo. Throughout her lessons, Mrs. Wood is careful to introduce her children to the format/language of many types of reading materials, including magazines, calendars, tele-

DID YOU NOTICE , , ,
Did you notice what Mrs. Wood did to build background knowledge for Proko? Instead of only reading a story about the zoo, Mrs. Wood immersed Proko in literacy-related activities. The looking at pictures in the classroom, listening about zoo animals at the listening center, interacting with narrative and expository text, and visiting a zoo first hand all played a part in giving Proko the initial background knowledge he will need to learn more about zoo animals now and in the future.

phone books, story books, and fact books. She also models how to use chapter headings, boldface and italic cues, charts, maps, illustrations, glossaries, summaries, and so on.

Next, Mrs. Wood's children made phrase books by drawing a picture of a zoo animal and writing a short caption beneath it. Mrs. Wood, or parent volunteers in her classroom, helped some children write their captions by asking the children to dictate their captions to them. The contributions of all of the children became a class book about animals found at a zoo.

Mrs. Wood knows that it is important for all of her children—but especially her English language learners—to have opportunities for first-hand experiences pertaining to the various subjects and ideas they study. Mrs. Wood typically takes her children for outings to the country, to various locations in the city, on bus or train rides, for birthday celebrations, and to sporting events. In this case, Mrs. Wood arranged to take her class on an excursion to the Detroit Zoo. Mrs. Wood suspected that Proko had never visited a zoo, so the excursion provided a common base of experience for language and literacy development.

After visiting the zoo, Mrs. Wood provided model sentence starters on a large chart in the front of her room. These included the following:

Today we visited _____

We saw _____

My favorite animal was _____

We traveled by _____

Proko and his classmates completed the sentences in their personal journals. These model sentence starters provided Proko and other English language learners in Mrs. Wood's classroom with initial English sentence structures for their writing. Additionally, Proko and other English language learners in his class were invited by Mrs. Wood and parent volunteers to dictate additional sentences for their journals. After dictating their sentences, the children read them back to the adults.

Ariana and Her Third Grade Classmates Study Halloween

Ms. Jackson is a third grade teacher in Los Angeles. This year she has a large number of English language learners who are new arrivals to the United States and who have a wide array of different oral and written language skills. She developed the following language-experience lessons to introduce her English language learners to the theme of Halloween as well as new vocabulary words about Halloween. After being introduced to the vocabulary associated with Halloween, Ms. Jackson wanted her English language learners to be able to read at least two words related to Halloween that would be added to their word bank, and she wanted her English language learners to correctly identify in context the word *Halloween* and any other word(s) of their choice.

First, Ms. Jackson placed pictures about Halloween around the room to stimulate discussions about Halloween. She also placed books about Halloween in the class library and the listening center. Then she introduced the concept of Halloween to the children by reading a picture book to the entire class. The class then developed an experience chart about Halloween. The teacher elicited responses from the children by asking questions such as the following:

1. What do children do on Halloween?
2. What will you dress up as for Halloween?
3. What will you wear?
4. What do you say when someone answers the door?
5. What are some things we have to be careful of on Halloween?

Ms. Jackson sought to get as many of her English language learners as possible to dictate a word or a phrase for the chart. The chart resembled the following:

Things That Remind Us of Halloween

Ariana:	trick-or-treat
Jaime:	scary
Wolfgang:	monsters
Cullen:	costumes
Tran:	candy
Soo-Lin:	parties
Nicole:	pumpkins
Elisabeth:	excited

Each child was then given a word card with Halloween written on it. The children were also given a piece of drawing paper to illustrate whatever they liked best about Halloween. While the children were drawing, the teacher helped each child write another word card of his or her choice for the word bank. The more advanced readers wrote several word cards.

When the children finished their drawings, they labeled or were helped to label them by dictating to the teacher a descriptive word, phrase, sentence, or several sentences. Several children in class did additional research about Halloween and wrote about what they learned. Ms. Jackson then compiled the children's labeled drawings as well as the additional information about Halloween into a book. The children in class created a tape-recorded version of the book—each reading their own pages on tape. Then Ms. Jackson placed the tape and the book in the listening center for the children to enjoy.

Although the preceding examples from Mrs. Wood's and Ms. Jackson's classrooms provide some specific language-experience examples, teachers of English language learners will also want to provide a wide array of experiences in a variety of different participation structures for their children. English language learners need lots of opportunities to engage in hands-on activities that involve visual, auditory, and kinesthetic components. For example, in social studies children can create charts, displays, talking murals, and bulletin boards. In science children can develop collections and label displays of various items being studied such as leaves or rocks

(O'Brien, 1983). In literacy children can develop classroom newspapers, engage in whole- and small-group storytelling, recite poetry, record recitations of poetry and stories for others to listen to at a listening center, engage in choral and echo reading, listen to books on tape in a listening center, develop puppet shows, engage in creative dramatics, participate in a reader's theater, and participate in show and tell (Diaz-Rico & Weed, 2002; O'Brien, 1983).

Children need opportunities to engage in hands-on activities such as the ones just mentioned while engaging in a variety of different participation structures. That is, children should have opportunities to work in whole-class activities, small-group activities, and individually. Please be aware, however, that it is especially important for English language learners to have lots of opportunities to work with others (including the teacher and peers) in pairs and small groups. If English language learners work with helpful partners or in supportive small groups, then they have a safe context to seek help when they need language support (Freeman & Freeman, 2001).

Deciding What to Teach and Evaluating Student Progress

Selection of Materials

In planning a program for English language learners, you will need to purchase a variety of materials. If you are in a position to purchase materials for use in your own classroom or your school, you will probably want to establish criteria for their selection. The checklist in Figure 13–3 will help you with this task.

Student Progress

Most educators agree that literacy is measurable, but they do not always agree on the most appropriate instruments for measuring student progress. We cannot protect our students or ourselves from accountability. The argument about standardized tests is not whether to use them, but which ones to use; that is, which instruments adequately assess the abilities of English language learners at their present stage of development in English? If a student of age 5 or 15 is just beginning English instruction, let us be absolutely certain that our tests take into consideration this level of limited exposure to English. For example, we present the following fictional test item:

Instructions: Read this brief passage and answer the two questions that follow.

"There he is up around the bend; come on down over here," Ian said.

"We will box him in and ambush him like Butch Cassidy used to do with the Sundance Kid."

Answer the following:
1. To whom is Ian talking?
2. What is Ian's suggested plan of action?

There are very few polysyllabic words in the passage; most of the words are monosyllabic. The only word to be counted as a difficult word would be ambush. Almost any young native English speaker would be able to comprehend this pas-

Figure 13–3   Criteria to be used when selecting materials for English language learners.

Criteria	Yes	No
1. Teacher Competency		
a. Must you be a content specialist to use the materials?	☐	☐
b. Must you be bilingual to use the materials?	☐	☐
c. Are the materials usable by inexperienced teachers?	☐	☐
d. Does the publishing company or the school system provide consultants to instruct you in the use of the materials?	☐	☐
2. Learners		
a. Do the materials provide for student differences in intelligence, experience, and language fluency?	☐	☐
b. Do the materials contain stories of equal interest to both boys and girls?	☐	☐
c. Do the materials contain high-interest, low-vocabulary selections?	☐	☐
d. Do the materials pose questions that go beyond the literal informational level to levels of analysis and evaluation?	☐	☐
3. Program Sequence		
a. Does the developmental sequence of the program closely parallel the development of language learning?	☐	☐
b. Does the program build on the language strengths of the student?	☐	☐
c. Does the program make provisions for the development of all the language arts?	☐	☐
d. Does the program provide for content area skill development?	☐	☐
e. Do the materials provide for individualizing instruction?	☐	☐
f. Are the materials free from cultural stereotyping?	☐	☐
g. Can the materials be integrated within an existing program?	☐	☐
4. Program Packaging		
a. Do the materials contain charts, CDs, tapes, flash cards, and other supplementary materials?	☐	☐
b. Are the supplementary aids easily used by children?	☐	☐
c. Are materials provided for reinforcement, review, and evaluation?	☐	☐
d. Are the costs consistent with available program funds?	☐	☐
e. Are program time constraints consistent with time allowances for classroom implementation?	☐	☐

sage, but it would be extremely difficult for someone just learning English for the following reasons:

- *Syntax:* The syntax is complex: "used to" is a sophisticated structure.
- *Idioms:* This brief selection uses three idioms that the English language learner may not be able to understand: "up around the bend," "Come on down over here," and "box him in."
- *Cultural/experiential background:* The child needs to have some knowledge of Butch Cassidy to appreciate the passage fully.

As we have illustrated, there are many items in this short passage that would be impossible for an English language learner to interpret. Consequently, we urge extreme caution when using any standardized test to measure the reading growth of English language learners. Further, we urge you to analyze the test thoroughly and to interpret it in light of the student's present level of functioning in English. If test items are based on complex syntactic structure, English idioms, and English lexical items demanding a specific cultural experience, make a note of the items and interpret your students' scores according to your knowledge of his or her level of English proficiency.

Students' progress is best measured by using a variety of measures. These include the following:

- Teacher observations
- Personal interviews with students to see how they think they are doing
- Teacher-made tests
- Standardized tests (used with caution).

QUESTIONS

1. Why is it important for all teachers in mainstream classrooms to understand about English language learners?

2. Identify important background knowledge for teachers who work with English language learners. Explain why teachers should have this background knowledge that you identify.

3. Describe an effective lesson for English language learners. Explain why the lesson you described is effective.

4. Identify important issues that a teacher must consider when planning effective instruction for English language learners.

5. Describe the kinds of teacher attitudes and dispositions that set the tone for effective learning environments for English language learners.

CLASSROOM PROJECTS

1. Plan a unit on nutrition. Ask students in the class to report on the food staples from their various cultures. Discuss how each culture meets the five food group requirements with different foods.

2. Plan a unit on holidays. Have each student do a brief oral report on a favorite holiday from his or her cultural background.

3. Plan a unit on literature (fables, myths, legends) from various cultures. Ask students to think of their favorite childhood story. They can take turns telling their stories to small groups or to the whole class. They can also illustrate their stories, which can be displayed in the classroom.

4. Create a classroom map that targets the ancestral heritage of each student. Display this map of the world, with each student's ancestral name marked. Each student's picture can be placed on the map beside the place(s) from which his or her family originated. (Students may have more than one place of ancestry, of course!)

5. Collect newspapers and magazines for classroom use. During the school year, students can make thematic collages and alphabet books using cutouts from classroom materials. For example, students can begin with a blank sheet of paper and add pictures to create a "family collage." They can take turns sharing their collages orally with classmates, explaining the pictures and what they mean.

6. Have fun with choral readings. Begin by reading a poem to the class. Create markings to indicate the pace and tone of readings. Discuss these markings with students. Then give them copies of a poem similar to the one in Figure 13–4. Divide the class into groups, perhaps a separate group for each marking, and allow them to practice. When they are ready, they can read and act out parts.

7. Design a game that encourages oral language practice. For example, "What's Missing" is a whole-class game in which a set of items are placed in full view of the class. Each item is identified with the class. Ask students to close their eyes and remove one item. Then ask them to open their eyes. The first student to identify the hidden item becomes the leader and gets to hide the next item.

8. Put up a permanent bulletin board. Ask each student to find (or draw) a picture to display. The name of each picture should be written by the child. Each child can share his or her picture with a small group or with the whole class. These bulletin boards can be changed every week or at whatever interval best fits the class schedule.

Figure 13–4   Poem suitable for a choral reading.

```
—  Poor old lady, / she swallowed a fly.
?  I don't know why she swallowed a fly.
—  Poor old lady, / I think she'll die.

—  Poor old lady, / she swallowed a spider
•  It squirmed and wriggled and turned inside her.
✓✓ She swallowed the spider to catch the fly.
?  I don't know why she swallowed a fly.
—  Poor old lady, / I think she'll die.

—  Poor old lady, / she swallowed a bird.
/  How absurd! She swallowed a bird.
✓✓ She swallowed the bird to catch the spider.
✓✓ She swallowed the spider to catch the fly.
?  I don't know why she swallowed a fly.
—  Poor old lady, / I think she'll die.

—  Poor old lady, / She swallowed a cat.
/  Think of that! She swallowed a cat.
✓✓ She swallowed the cat to catch the bird.
✓✓ She swallowed the bird to catch the spider.
✓✓ She swallowed the spider to catch the fly.
?  I don't know why she swallowed a fly.
—  Poor old lady, / I think she'll die.

—  Poor old lady, / She swallowed a horse.
/  She died, of course!
```

Markings:

— Read slowly
/ Slight pause
? Sounding like a question
• Make movement
✓✓ Read faster
/ With excitement

9. Create a lesson in which students dramatize a story that the teacher has read. Then ask students in small groups to read the story once. Discuss and write down what they remember from the reading. The teacher can answer questions and may want to read the story again. Finally, students will write and put on a play about the story.

10. Create a system in which students read a story to their parents over a certain period of time. Ask students to be ready to share with the class (or small groups) their parents' reactions to the story. Also, students can plan to ask their parents specific questions, such as "Which part of the story did you like best?" Students can discuss with the class the varied answers to the questions. Students can receive points or prizes for reading a specific number of pages.

TEACHER DEVELOPMENT ACTIVITIES

Ask several teachers at your school to join you to form a professional book club. Choose from a variety of different books to read and discuss. These may include books about crossing cultural and linguistic boundaries such as Eva Hoffman's *Lost in Translation* or books about current issues pertaining to educating children from diverse cultural and linguistic backgrounds such as *Working with Second Language Learners: Answers to Teachers' Top Ten Questions* (Cary, 2000), *Between Worlds: Access to Second Language Acquisition* (Freemen & Freeman, 2001), *Accommodating Differences Among English Language Learners: 75 Literacy Lessons* (Jacobson, Lapp, & Mendez, 2004).

REFERENCES

Allington, R. L., & Walmsley, S. A. (1995). *No quick fix: Rethinking literacy programs in America's elementary schools*. Newark, DE: International Reading Association.

Angelil-Carter, S. (1997). Second language acquisition of spoken and written English: Acquiring the skeptron. *TESOL Quarterly, 31*, 263–288.

Au, K. (1993). *Literacy instruction in multicultural settings*. Fort Worth, TX: Holt, Rinehart & Winston.

August, A., & Hakuta, K. (1997). *Improving schooling for language-minority children: A research agenda*. Washington, DC: National Academy Press.

California State Department of Education. (1999). *Reading-language arts framework for California public schools: Kindergarten through grade twelve*. Sacramento: California State Department of Education.

California State Department of Education. (2004) Legal requirements and purpose (ii–1), Facts about the CELDT for 2004–2005. Retrieved September 2004, from http://www.cde.ca.gov/ta/tg/el.

Cary, S. (2000). *Working with second language learners: Answers to teachers' top ten questions*. Portsmouth, NH: Heinemann.

Chamot, A. U., & O'Malley, J. M. (1986). *A cognitive academic language learning approach: An ESL content-based curriculum*. New York: National Clearinghouse for Bilingual Education.

Collier, V. (1989). How long? A synthesis of research on academic achievement in a second language. *TESOL Quarterly, 23*, 509–531.

Collier, V. (1995). Acquiring a second language for school. *Directions in Language and Education, 1*(4), 1–14.

Cummins, J. (1984). *Bilingualism and special education: Issues in assessment and pedagogy*. Clevedon, England: Multicultural Matters.

Cummins, J. (1994). Knowledge, power, and identity in teaching English as a second language. In F. Genesee (Ed.), *Educating second language learners: The whole child, the whole curriculum, the whole community* (pp. 33–58). New York: Cambridge University Press.

Cummins, J. (1996). *Negotiating identities: Education for empowerment in a diverse society.* Ontario, CA: California Association for Bilingual Education.

Cummins, J. (2001). *Language, power and pedagogy: Bilingual children in the crossfire.* Clevedon, England: Multicultural Matters.

Diaz-Rico, L. T., & Weed, K. Z. (2002). *The crosscultural, language, and academic development handbook: A complete K-12 reference guide* (2nd ed.). Boston, MA: Allyn & Bacon.

Delpit, L. (1995). *Other people's children: Cultural conflict in the classroom.* New York: The New Press.

Deschenes, S., Cuban, L., & Tyack, D. (2001). Mismatch: Historical perspectives on schools and students who don't fit them. *Teachers College Record, 103*(4), 525–547.

Faltis, C. J. (2001). *Joinfostering: Teaching and learning in multilingual classrooms* (3rd ed.). Columbus, OH: Merrill/Prentice Hall.

Fitzgerald, J. (1995). English-as-a-second language reading instruction in the United States: A research review. *Journal of Reading Behavior, 27,* 115–152.

Flores, B., & Hernandez. E. (1988, December). A bilingual kindergartner's sociopsychogenesis of literacy and biliteracy. *Dialogue, 3,* 43–49.

Florio-Ruane, S., Raphael, T., Glazier, J., McVee, M., & Wallace, S. (1997). Discovering culture in discussion of autobiographical literature: Transforming the education of literacy teachers. In C. Kinzer, K. Hinchman, & D. Leu (Eds.), *Inquiries in literacy theory and practice* (pp. 452–464). Chicago, IL: International Reading Conference Yearbook.

Freeman, D. E., & Freeman, Y. S. (2001). *Between worlds: Access to second language acquisition* (2nd ed.). Portsmouth, NH: Heinemann.

Garcia, E. F. (1984). Education in the 1990's: A demographic view. In A. M. Ochoa & J. Hurtado (Eds.), *Educational and societal futures: Meeting the technological demands of the 1990's* (pp. 62–71). Proceedings of a conference held at the Anaheim Convention Center. San Diego, CA: National Origin Desegregation Law Center.

Garcia, E. E. (2000). *Student cultural diversity: Understanding and meeting the challenge.* New York: Houghton Mifflin.

Gee, J. (1996). *Social linguistics and literacies: Ideology in discourse* (2nd ed.). Bristol, PA: Taylor and Francis.

Genesee, F. (1994). Introduction. In F. Genesee (Ed.), *Educating second language children: The whole child, the whole curriculum, the whole community* (pp. 1–12). New York: Cambridge University Press.

Gold, S. (1997). Teachers of LEP students: Demand, supply and shortage. Sacramento: California State Department of Education.

Heath, S. B. (1983). *Ways with words: Language, life, and work in communities and classrooms.* Cambridge, England: Cambridge University Press.

Hoffman, E. (1989). *Lost in translation: A life in a new language.* New York: Penguin Books.

Igoa, C. (1996). *The inner world of the immigrant child.* New York: St. Martin's Press.

Jacobson, J., Lapp, D., & Mendez, M. (2004). *Accommodating differences among English language learners: 75 literacy lessons.* San Diego, CA: APD Press.

Krashen, S. D. (1985). *The input hypothesis: Issues and implications.* New York: Longman.

Krashen, S. D. (1992). *Fundamentals of language education.* Torrance, CA: Laredo Publishing.

Krashen, S. D. (1998). *Bilingual education and the dropout argument.* Washington, DC: National Clearinghouse for Bilingual Education.

McDermott, R. P. (1977). *The ethnography of speaking and reading* (p. 8). In R. Shuy (Ed.), *Linguistic theory: What can it say about reading?* Newark, DE: International Reading Association.

McMahon, S. I., & Raphael, T. E., with Goatley, V. G. & Pardo, L. M. (Eds.). *The book club connection: Literacy learning and classroom talk.* Language and Literacy Series. New York: Teachers College Press.

Moll, L. C., Amanti, C., Neff, D., & Gonzalez, N. (1992). Funds of knowledge for teaching: Using a qualitative approach to connect homes and classrooms. *Theory into Practice, 31,* 132–141.

O'Brien, C. (1983). *Teaching the language different child to read.* Columbus, OH: Merrill.

Samway, K., & McKeon, D. (1999). *Myths and Realities: Best Practices for Language Minority Students.* Portsmouth, NH: Heinemann.

Thonis, E. W. (1989). Bilingual students: Reading and learning. In D. Lapp, J. Flood, and N. Farnan (Eds.), *Content area reading/learning: Effective instructional strategies* (pp. 53–72). Englewood Cliffs, NJ: Prentice-Hall.

Toohey, K. (1998). "Breaking them up, taking them away": ESL students in grade 1. *TESOL Quarterly, 32,* 61–84.

Tse, L. (2001). *"Why don't they learn English?": Separating fact fallacy in the U.S. language debate.* New York: Teacher College Press.

14

All Students Are Special: Some Need Supplemental Supports and Services to Be Successful

CHAPTER GOALS

To help the reader

- gain an understanding of the rationale behind inclusive education and the implementation of PL 94-142 (and its amendments).

- appreciate the need for close cooperation between classroom teachers and special education teachers with regard to the individualized education plan (IEP).

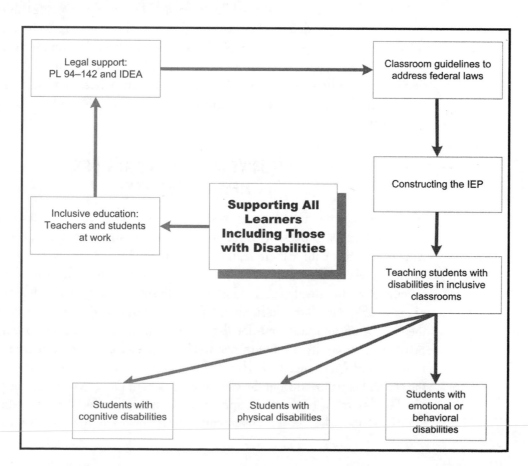

- explore educational considerations for students with disabilities in the regular classroom in relation to both general socialization and literacy development.
- recognize the characteristics of students with learning disabilities.
- develop a personal teaching philosophy to fully meet the needs of all students in the classroom including those with disabilities.

Describe your thoughts about students with disabilities. What was your experience with peers who had disabilities when you were in school? Do you think that education has changed such that students with disabilities are welcomed in classrooms today?

With the implementation of PL 94-142, the Education for All Handicapped Children Act, in 1975 (and the amendments to this law, The Individuals with Disabilities Education Act [IDEA]), children with an array of disabilities have been *included* or educated in regular classroom settings. The teaching of reading must encompass a wide variety of strategies to adequately support students with the many reading levels within one classroom (Lapp, Flood, Fisher, Sax, & Pumpian, 1996). Not only do we now have the usual range of students reading at or near grade level (either above or below) whose skills need to be developed and advanced, but appropriate techniques must also be employed to help those students with physical, cognitive, or behavioral disabilities learn. This chapter provides an overview of the guidelines provided in IDEA, as well as specific teaching techniques for considerations in inclusive classrooms. Because students with reading disabilities can present a challenge to the classroom teacher, particular attention will be given to students with reading disabilities. But first, let's meet Ms. James, a fourth grade teacher and Ms. Noyes, a special educator who works with all of the fourth and fifth grade teachers.

INCLUSIVE CLASSROOMS AT WORK: MEET THE TEACHERS

Ms. Noyes is a special education resource teacher assigned to grades four and five. In this role, Ms. Noyes provides supplemental instructional support to students with disabilities within their regular classrooms. Ms. Noyes is not in Ms. James' classroom every day, all day. Rather, she is scheduled into Ms. James' classroom at specific times to provide specific instruction based on the individualized educational plans (IEPs) (see later discussion) of Tyler, Maria, and Kristen. In other words, the IEP team allocates time for the special educator to support specific students. Kristen may require 11 hours per week of special educator time, whereas Tyler needs 4 and Maria needs 3. Remember that this time does not have to mean that the student is removed from the classroom. Instead, the special educator can join the regular classroom to provide supplemental instruction for students who have disabilities. Similarly, the IEP team can allocate instructional time from speech and language specialists, physical therapists, occupational therapists, psychologists, nurses, and other professionals.

Ms. James and Ms. Noyes meet regularly and plan the instruction needed for the students in this class. They discuss student needs, identify materials that are appropriate for the range of student skills, and plan their small group reading instruction.

Meet a special educator at your school site. Interview this professional about his or her duties. How does this special educator spend his or her day? How are students with disabilities supported in your school?

INCLUSIVE CLASSROOMS AT WORK: MEET THE CLASS

Of the 32 students in Ms. James' fourth grade classroom, 3 of the students are identified as having a disability. Two of the students, Tyler and Maria, have learning disabilities and one student, Kristen, has a more significant cognitive disability. This pattern is consistent with current thinking on inclusive education and is called *natural proportions*; i.e., all classrooms should be representative of the diversity found within the larger community. Because approximately 10% of the school-age population has been identified as having a disability, each classroom should contain approximately 10% students with disabilities.

Figure 14–1 contains a profile of Kristen prepared by her IEP team members (the IEP process will be explained in greater detail later in this chapter). This profile (and ones like it) is helpful for teachers as they consider the unique learning needs of their students with disabilities. The specific components of the student profile, which is based on the IEP, are as follows (adapted from Fisher, Frey, & Sax, 2000).

Skills to Be Addressed

These skills are often taken from the "goals and objectives" section of the IEP and written in accessible language for teachers. This section of the profile often changes year to year to address the specific requirements in a grade. General education teachers should keep the student's IEP goals and objectives clearly in mind when creating accommodations and modifications to assignments. In Kristen's case, the IEP team, which consists of at least her general education teacher, special education teacher, parents, and an administrator, is asking the teacher to focus her literacy instruction on sight vocabulary words, conversations, and questions. In addition, the team would like Kristen to manage her belongings (school supplies, backpack, etc.) and complete classroom jobs such as paper-passer/collector, supply monitor, or time-keeper.

Areas of Strength and Interest

This is important information for tailoring successful learning activities for students. Effective classroom teachers build on student strengths to address needs and do not dwell on things that the student cannot do. Effective teachers often use the informa-

Figure 14–1 Student profile for Kristen.

School Name: *Martin Luther King Elementary*

Student Name: *Kristen Green*

Age: *10*   Grade: *4*

Parent/Guardian: *Ms. Yolanda Green*   Phone #: *555-5432*

Classroom Teacher: *Ms. James*

Special Education Teacher: *Ms. Noyes*

Skills to be addressed: Complete class jobs, increase sight word vocabulary, participate in conversations, answer "wh" questions, request assistance as needed, and manage belongings (school supplies, backpack, etc.).

Areas of strengths/interests: Kristen is very helpful and develops a good rapport with her teachers and classmates. She often involves herself in social situations. Kristen enjoys music, animals, free time with peers, and being read aloud to. In third grade, her sight vocabulary increased from 18 words to 53 words.

Successful learning strategies/modifications/adaptations needed: Kristen needs the targeted vocabulary to be highlighted in assigned reading materials and taped recordings of more difficult readings. Her IEP allows for extended time on assignments and tests. Kristen works well with peer supports in cooperative learning groups when each group member has clearly defined roles. The use of pictures (photos, magazine clippings, etc.) support her writing.

Communication strategies: Kristen utilizes picture schedules to manage her time and anticipate transitions. She needs complicated tasks explained in 1–2 step directions. Kristen understands the directions better when verbal and visual cues are paired. When frustrated, Kristen may begin repeating words and phrases or hitting her hand on the desk. This is usually an indicator that too many directions have been given at one time.

Positive behavior support strategies: Kristen uses a visual schedule for her daily activities. She needs advance notice when changes in the environment or schedule occur. She experiences frustration when there is a prolonged wait in line, when the area is overcrowded, and/or when she falls behind in classwork. Kristen needs peer supports when entering new environments and activities.

Grading and assessment accommodations: Kristen maintains a 4th grade literacy portfolio. Grading rubrics for projects may need to be modified to reflect her learning goals. She often requires extra time to complete some assignments and tests.

Important health/family information: Kristen is hypersensitive to noise, smell, and sometimes to touch. She responds well to light pressure on her shoulders, fingers, and elbows. She has a cognitive disability that impacts communication and socialization.

tion in this section of the IEP to make decisions about cooperative groups, partner activities, and peer support. In Kristen's case, this form identifies a number of areas that the teacher can use to engage her in activities. For example, knowing that Kristen likes animals allows the teacher to draw her into the class conversations about the book *Shiloh* (Naylor, 1991) that the class is reading.

Successful Learning Strategies, Accommodations, and Modifications

Again, focusing on successful strategies from the past increases the likelihood that the student will be successful in the future. This section describes successful curriculum accommodations and modifications that have been implemented thus far in the student's educational experience. This information can become a roadmap for teachers to follow in designing individual class assignments as well as group activities. In Kristen's case, the IEP team has identified a number of procedures that can be used to keep Kristen focused on the task at hand as well as strategies that increase her participation in and understanding of the lesson.

Communication Strategies

This section describes any type of augmentative or alternative communication supports that have been developed. In addition to specific modes or methods of communication, such as Picture Communication Symbols (see Figure 14–2) or sign language, this section can include information about ways to engage the student in conversation and how the student initiates interactions. In Kristen's case, the team identifies the type of directions that work well for her and note that a picture schedule reduces her frustration during transitions. In addition, this section notes events that cause Kristen frustration, which may lead to problematic behaviors.

Positive Behavior Support Strategies

Behavioral issues can pose challenges for all students. For some students with disabilities, positive behavioral support techniques are an important consideration. Teachers need to know what causes the behavior and what to do when the problem behavior occurs. In effect, this section should provide answers to two questions: "What does the student need to be successful at school?" and "How can supports

Figure 14–1   A Picture Communication Symbol (PCS) communication board. (*Source:* BOARDMAKER by Mayer-Johnson, Inc., Solana Beach, CA; http://www.mayer-johnson.com). Used with permission.

be provided to the student to prevent challenging behaviors from happening?" In Kristen's case, a visual schedule reduces her frustration. In addition, she gets frustrated with environmental changes and the team recommends advance notice for these events.

Grading and Assessment Accommodations

To be successful, students may require additional time on tests, large print, oral versions of tests, preferential seating, and so forth. These strategies, agreed upon during an IEP meeting, should be recorded, and classroom teachers should be informed of these decisions. For example, a student may need additional time on the required state assessment. In Kristen's case, she maintains a fourth grade portfolio of her work, and teachers are recommended to modify grading rubrics to consider her unique learning needs.

Important Health or Family Information

Health histories or other information from the family that is important for teachers to know can be recorded here. Especially important is information about seizures, allergies, sound or light sensitivity, assistance required for eating or using the restroom, and positioning for comfort and increased access to the environment. In Kristen's case, the team notes information that has been shared or discovered over the years. Importantly, information about her hypersensitivity is provided.

Using the student profile information presented for Kristen, talk with a partner about the teaching implications you see. How would your reading language arts instruction change if Kristen were in your class?

The student profile is a useful tool to assist teachers in deciding how assignments and activities can be tailored for a particular student and how that student can build upon personal experiences to learn new material. Given this information, general and special education teachers can provide meaningful instruction to students with disabilities that is challenging, but not frustrating.

INCLUSIVE CLASSROOMS AT WORK: PROVIDING INSTRUCTION TO A DIVERSE GROUP OF LEARNERS

As Ms. James finishes her shared reading lesson on main ideas and students move into small groups for their center rotation activities, Ms. Noyes enters the classroom. Ms. James invites four students with similar reading needs, including Tyler, to a guided reading table. She has selected a newspaper article and provides small group instruction to these students as they identify the main ideas in the lead article.

Ms. Noyes also provides small group, homogeneous instruction. Her group consists of Maria and two other students. Although the text Ms. Noyes uses is easier to read than the text being used by Ms. James because of the assessed student needs, she still focuses her instruction on main ideas. During the group work, Maria observes that the main idea is often in the first sentence. Justin, another student in this small group, asks, "Is it always this way? I mean do you want us to find the first sentence?" Because Ms. Noyes knows that the texts these students will read will become increasingly difficult and the main idea will not necessarily be in the first sentence, she realizes that before she continues, she needs to review the concept of main idea and its placement in the text.

The other students who are not in one of these two groups are working at centers. Because Kristen is not receiving direct teacher instruction, she is with a heterogeneous group of students at a listening station listening to a recorded text and reading along (recall the Center Activity Rotation System [CARS] from chapter 2). Ms. James and Ms. Noyes know that this fluency and vocabulary-building activity, which was identified in her IEP, will strengthen her literacy skills and independence.

Talk with a partner about the rationale for using CARS with students with disabilities. What are the benefits? Are there any potential problems or concerns?

During the next rotation, Ms. James invites Kristen over to the table and asks her to practice her sight words. Ms. Noyes has another small group, this time with Tyler and two other students, and they are working on words and spelling. Maria has moved to the computer center and is working independently.

Following these two rotations, Ms. Noyes moves on to another classroom and Ms. James finishes the center activities. When the center activities are completed, the students move into a writer's workshop. Today, Ms. James has provided students with a sentence starter and has asked that they use this starter as the main idea sentence of a paragraph that they write. Kristen dictates her sentence to a peer who writes it in her journal and then Kristen illustrates her idea. Tyler uses a computer with word prediction software to complete his assignment. Maria prefers to write out her paragraph and then ask for assistance with spelling and punctuation from Ms. James.

As you can see, inclusive classrooms bustle with activity. Students are grouped and regrouped throughout the day. Although peers often provide assistance, they do not complete the work for a student. General and special education teachers work together to create learning opportunities for all of the students in the classroom. You have probably noticed that the special educator does not simply focus on the students who have been identified as having a disability. The two educators, together, differentiate instruction for all of the students in the class. In this way, students are provided a free and appropriate public education—the goal of the legislation that created "special education."

WHAT ARE PL 94-142 AND IDEA?

Public Law (PL) 94-142 was passed by Congress in 1975 in response to a growing awareness that students with disabilities in our society were receiving second-class educational treatment. Historically, students with disabilities were victims of an "out of sight, out of mind" philosophy that typified the residential school approach of the mid-nineteenth century. Although this system, established largely through the efforts of social activists and educators such as Horace Mann, Samuel

Gridley Howe, Dorothea Dix, and the Reverend Thomas Gallaudet, was a vast improvement over the complete social ostracism prevalent up to that time, the residential schools kept children who were blind, deaf, or mentally retarded out of the mainstream of society (Winzer, 1993). After World Wars I and II, attitudes toward people with physical and mental disabilities began to change because of the influence of returning veterans who had become disabled as a result of combat. At about the same time, the prime moving force in changing public opinion that finally resulted in PL 94-142 was activated. This force was the parents who wanted their children to benefit from the public school experience. For more information on disability and disability rights groups, see Table 14–1.

Visit one of the Web sites from the list in Table 14–1. Meet with a group of peers who have all examined different Web sites from this list and learn more about advocacy and education groups that are focused on disability issues.

Classroom Guidelines

PL 94-142 was implemented in 1977. Interestingly, the impact of that law is still felt in classrooms across the country. The law's intention is to provide a "free appropriate public school education" to all students with disabilities between the ages of 3 and 21 years. The key word here with regard to teachers is *appropriate* because it is in seeking to provide the most suitable instruction that PL 94-142,

TABLE 14–1
Disability Information and Disability Rights Groups

Group	Description	Web Site
PEAK Parent Center	A nonprofit organization that provides current information for families and teachers	www.peakparent.org
TASH-Worldwide Advocacy	An international advocacy group for the full rights of people with disabilities	www.tash.org
Disabilityinfo.gov	Federal Web site of disability-related government resources	www.disabilityinfo.gov
National Council on Disability	An independent federal agency making recommendations to the President and Congress on issues affecting 54 million people with disabilities	www.ncd.gov
World Institute on Disability	A nonprofit research, training and public policy center promoting the civil rights and the full societal inclusion of people with disabilities	www.wid.org

and its amendment IDEA, delineate four essential guidelines for what occurs in the classroom as well as outside of it:

1. *Unbiased test procedures:* Students with disabilities will be protected against discrimination in the evaluation process by assuring that the testing materials utilized for identification will be free from racial and cultural bias and when possible will be administered in the child's native language. Tests will have established validity, be administered by trained personnel, and test specific areas of educational need rather than IQ alone. Students with sensory or physical disabilities will be tested in a manner consistent with their support needs. Further protection comes from the guarantee that no single test will be used as the sole evaluation instrument but, rather, other factors, including socialization and physical and emotional development, will be considered.

2. *The least restrictive environment:* According to the law, students with disabilities must be placed, "to the maximum extent possible," in regular classrooms alongside their peers without disabilities. To accomplish this, the law requires school districts to provide supplemental supports and services to ensure that students' individual needs are addressed. In the sections that follow, we discuss the ways in which general and special education teachers can work together to ensure that supports and services are in place.

3. *Individualized education program:* The IEP includes a written statement of the child's present educational level, annual goals, instructional objectives, and any special education or related services provided for the child. The plan must be developed jointly by parents, educators, and, when appropriate, the child, and it must be reviewed regularly. The IEP should not only guide the provision of supplemental supports and services but should also provide guidance in terms of curriculum goals and objectives.

4. *Procedural safeguards:* Parents have access to all the student's records and have the right to obtain an outside evaluation if desired. They are to be given prior notice for approval of any change in the placement of their child, and they have the right to challenge anything done by the teacher or the school, including the right to court action. The parents and the schools have the right to appeal any decision made regarding the placement of a handicapped student, During any hearing, the child in question will be allowed to remain in school or be admitted to school until the final decision has been reached.

Constructing an IEP

According to Seyler and Buswell (2001), an IEP is arrived at through a series of steps, which include the following:

1. *Referral:* The student is referred for evaluation, and a multidisciplinary evaluation team is chosen to complete these evaluations. Parent consent must be obtained to conduct the evaluation. In most school districts, it is policy to involve the parent when the classroom teacher suspects that a student may have a disability. In Kristen's case, her preschool teacher discussed her development with the family and together they made a referral to a learning specialist.

2. *Multidisciplinary evaluation:* The team members assess the student on abilities and disabilities from the viewpoint of their own area of expertise. These assessments often include reading and other skills such as social, speech, or motor. In Kristen's case, she has regular evaluations from a speech and language specialist and a physical therapist.

Once the preliminary evaluations have been accomplished, a meeting is scheduled to formulate a formal plan called the *individualized educational plan* (IEP). The IEP team must include the family and a general education teacher, in addition to special educators and professionals as indicated by the assessments, such as a speech therapist or psychologist. In addition, the students should attend their own IEP meetings whenever possible.

Once the team is assembled, the information gathered during the assessments is analyzed, and educational decisions are suggested. The IEP itself includes the following information and provisions, which are then incorporated into the student profile:

1. A written statement of the child's present educational level. This may include not only academic achievement scores but functional levels of achievement also.

2. A written statement of annual goals, accompanied by specific instructional objectives that are more easily realized and measured on a progressive and short-term basis.

3. A written statement of the special education and related services required by the student and to be provided by the school. This includes a designation of the amount of time to be spent in the regular classroom, as well as any other specific programs to meet special needs (i.e., speech therapy, physical therapy, visual training, and so on).

4. The commencement date for the special services and a projected time frame for the duration of the program are written down to facilitate a timely start to the process.

5. Objective criteria, evaluation procedures, and schedules for achievement of instructional objectives are determined and written to ensure that annual progress reports will be accomplished.

After a successful drafting of the IEP, the implementation of the program must begin through placement and instruction. The plan has a built-in monitoring component that guarantees that the program will be reevaluated at least once a year. The IEP provides a detailed framework with fairly specific guidelines for teachers to follow. As suggested by Archer and Gleason (1990), the real work is then done by the teacher in composing actual lesson plans to put the IEP plan into action, and by the student in realizing the benefits of the services provided.

Attend an IEP meeting if at all possible. The information discussed during this meeting is very important to the success of the student. Learning about the process now will serve you well over your career. Share experiences with IEP meetings with your peers— no two meetings are alike!

HOW CAN WE BEST SERVE OUR
STUDENTS WITH DISABILITIES?

One of the terms currently being applied to disabled or handicapped individuals is *differently abled*, a term that focuses on the person's capabilities rather than on his or her deficits. It is this positive approach to students with disabilities that, as teachers, we must foster in ourselves as well as in our classrooms. Whereas it is nonproductive to ignore a student's needs and to pretend that the child is not disabled, it is equally nonproductive to single out the student for extraordinary attention based solely on these special needs. A constructive approach must be taken in relation to both behavior and academic tasks, specifically in regard to teaching reading. This approach is based on an understanding of the student's abilities and disabilities and on a cooperative effort on the part of the classroom teacher and the specialist handling the other portions of the student's curriculum.

Coherent reading instruction is fundamental to the academic success of any student, and even more so with students receiving special education as well as classroom instruction. With the inclusion of children with disabilities in the regular classroom has come an urgent need for educators to talk to one another about the needs of their students. Although this has always been true, it is even more true now as studies show that children who experience unsatisfactory progress in regular classrooms are usually those who are participating in remedial instruction or in special education programs (Fisher & Frey, 2001). When teachers fail to work together, students fail to achieve because they are receiving a fragmented curriculum consisting of two different and distinct tracks.

On the basis of these studies and of other concerns that have emerged, Madeline Will proposed the *regular education initiative* (REI) (Will, 1986). This proposal was among the first attempts to unify regular and special education and focus more attention on cooperative efforts to educate students with disabilities in the regular classroom exclusively without the use of pull-out programs. Advocates of this proposal believe that many students who have been labeled as learning or emotionally disabled are in fact slow learners, underachievers, behavioral problems, and children with English as a second language whose English is minimal.

Because these students are often considered disruptive to the regular classroom, teachers often seek placement in segregated special education programs as a means of alleviating a disruption. As funding has been reduced for compensatory education programs that might better benefit these children (e.g., reading labs), special education is often the only pull-out program available. To minimize the number of students who are pulled out of class and to provide the cohesive education these children especially need, current research and best practices recommend that children with disabilities be instructed in the regular classroom (Roach, 1999). In fact, the International Reading Association in 2003 took the position that students with disabilities need access to high-quality teachers in the regular classroom.

Has your thinking about students with disabilities in regular classrooms changed at all as you have read this chapter? If so, how? What is your role in ensuring that all students have access to quality literacy instruction?

Changes in the relationship between the regular and special education programs will no doubt come as the system continues to be refined. Until policy changes are made, however, it is up to the teachers to make their instructional decisions in the best interests of all their students. Buswell (1999) suggested that teachers initiate the sharing of knowledge between general and special educators to build a consistent program for students with disabilities. This can be accomplished by following these guidelines (e.g., Allington & Broikou, 1988):

1. Seek out the specialist who is working with the student. If there is no specialist on site, look for the specialist at the district level. In most school systems, there is a special education resource teacher available to coordinate the IEPs for students with disabilities who are educated in regular classrooms.

2. Meet to review materials available in each of the classroom settings. It is important to collaborate to make the most of the materials at hand.

3. The core curriculum should serve as the starting point from which to develop instructional strategies that will serve the student in the regular classroom and be augmented by the specialist.

4. Regularly scheduled meetings between the regular classroom teacher and the specialists to review progress and monitor instruction should be implemented.

By using the resources that are available to you within your school and your district and by familiarizing yourself with the needs of students you may encounter, you will be better prepared to successfully teach the students with disabilities in your class.

WHAT SUPPORTS DO STUDENTS WITH DISABILITIES TYPICALLY REQUIRE?

In terms of numbers, 80% of all students with disabilities are identified as *learning disabled*. Of those, 50% have a primary disability in the area of reading. Thus, a great number of students in your class who have disabilities will need assistance with reading. In addition to the students identified as learning disabled, there are a number of other disabilities identified in federal legislation that students in you classroom may have. These include physical disabilities such as cerebral palsy, deafness, and blindness, and cognitive disabilities such as mental retardation. In addition, there are a number of students with specific conditions such as Down syndrome or autism who will qualify for special education supports and services.

The following sections of this chapter deal with defining the characteristics, considerations for classroom conditions, instructional methods, and specific teaching techniques to facilitate the teaching of reading to children with disabilities who are included in general education classrooms. Given that specific medical conditions do not provide instructional guidance for teachers, we have focused this section on specific types of support that students often require. In other words, knowing that a student has Down syndrome (an extra chromosome that results in specific physical features) does not provide you, the teacher, with any information about what a student needs to learn. Instead, we have organized our discussion around instructional plans for students with cognitive disabilities, physical disabilities, and emotional or behavioral disabilities.

Students With Cognitive Disabilities

Students with learning disabilities are by far the largest group of children with disabilities today. They run the gamut from mild emotional difficulty to severe dyslexia. There is an excellent chance that you will have one or more students identified as learning disabled in your classroom. In addition, there are a number of students with mental retardation who attend general education classes full-time. Remember that there is no one profile for students with cognitive disabilities. Some students have difficulty paying attention whereas others process auditory and/or visual information slowly. Still others have dyslexia and transpose letters as they read and write.

The focus in elementary education for these youngsters, as for all other young children, is on literacy (i.e., learning to read and to develop other basic academic skills). As students get older, they need increased attention on content area learning. For too many students with learning disabilities, school personnel often continue to cycle through "learning to read" activities in the upper grades, and they neglect the important content areas of science, social studies, and math.

Because many of the students with disabilities in your classroom will be below grade level in their reading skills due to the nature of their disability, standard reading techniques, modified to suit specific special needs, will be useful. As with all instruction, it is important to keep up a good pace with regard to reading instruction. Although repetition and drill have their place, the importance of access to connected text in longer pieces can't be stressed enough. Many researchers have noted that because students with reading disabilities are poor readers, they have significantly less access to books than their peers who are reading well (Stanovich, 1986).

Interview a student who has a reading disability about his or her reading habits and interests. What kinds of books capture this student's interests? What books can you recommend for this student?

Classroom Considerations for Students with Cognitive Disabilities

Because of the complex nature and the vast differences in types of cognitive disabilities, the classroom teacher must keep in mind a wide variety of teaching strategies while trying to meet the needs of all children in the regular classroom. Ranging from the hyperactive child who creates general chaos to the quiet student who cannot seem to follow directions, students with cognitive disabilities should have individualized programs to meet their specific educational requirements, and they should be allowed to participate with the rest of the class whenever possible to further develop their social skills and literacy skills. The methods described in the following sections may be adapted for use either individually or in a whole-class situation.

Before we discuss these approaches, some additional suggestions should be kept in mind:

1. Never assume that students have understood directions even if the instructions are perfectly clear to everyone else. Go to the children and ask if the directions were indeed comprehended.

2. When a child with a cognitive disability is working with the class, try to make the exercises short and success oriented. Team games are especially useful when there is no direct individual pressure on the members (e.g., word knowledge or Jeopardy).

3. Alternative teaching and response methods may be useful with some children, such as the use of a computer or tape recorder for completing assignments.

4. Divide the time into small segments with varying activities: quiet independent work, work with a tutor or aide, classroom work, and physical work (filing, board games, and so on).

5. Provide "previews" of the topics to come by listing the main points and new words, so that students may prepare in advance and be more familiar with the material when the class discusses it.

The classroom teacher is a crucial person in the life of a student with a cognitive disability, and the relationship between teacher and student must be as close as possible. Rappaport (1966) calls for a *relationship structure*, which he defines as the "ability of the adult (parent or teacher or therapist or otherwise) to understand the child sufficiently well at any given moment, through his verbal and nonverbal communications, to relate in a way which aids the child's development of impulse control and other ego functions" (p. 26).

Instructional Methods Useful for Students with Cognitive Disabilities

As has been stressed repeatedly throughout this chapter, students with disabilities are a composite of many gifts and challenges that are unique to each individual; consequently, no one method of teaching will satisfactorily meet the needs of all students with cognitive disabilities

Many theories or methods of teaching students with cognitive disabilities exist, and it is necessary to compose a comprehensive instructional framework (CIF) for each child, which consists of selecting those methods (or aspects of them) that best remedy the deficiencies exhibited by a particular individual. Once the theoretical methods of instruction are chosen, an IEP, pinpointing specific goals, techniques, and exercises, can be developed. If an educational outline based on the major instructional approaches is established first, the actual teaching techniques and the rest of the classroom program will easily and naturally build up around this theoretical framework.

As in teaching children with other types of disabilities, the method of reading instruction with which the teacher is competent and comfortable is probably the most acceptable. However, certain modifications of the method may be necessary for certain types of disabilities. Therefore, suggested techniques for adapting existing academic material are presented here. In general, teachers should exaggerate the item being taught, thus causing the student to focus all of his or her attention on the task. For example, when teaching new vocabulary words in context, highlight the words with larger print or color or to aid comprehension skills, highlight the main ideas of a text in one color and the supporting details in another. Then have the student read the color-coded copy first; then present a plain copy and ask him or her to use the colored pencils to mark the main ideas and details. The student can compare the two copies for immediate feedback.

Teachers such as Ms. Noyes have found that using a tape recorder is beneficial. For example, you could have a student read the material to be learned (vocabulary, spelling words, sequence of a story, or facts of a history lesson) into the tape recorder and then listen to the tape. The student could then repeat the material, saying it into the tape recorder using no notes.

Similarly, old-fashioned drill and repetition may be useful in learning new concepts. Use similar exercises or study skills books to reemphasize an idea (such as parts of speech, sentence construction, or vocabulary). Having said that, remember that many students with cognitive disabilities never get to the book. We know that the goal of reading is to read for information and for pleasure. Although drill and repetition are important, remember that all students, including those with cognitive disabilities will want to read books on their own.

In addition, students with cognitive disabilities may require accommodations and modifications to the curriculum. In general, *accommodations* are changes to the access students have to the curriculum. For example, some students need large print to read whereas others need books on tape and still others read in Braille. Specific accommodations will be identified on the students' IEP and teachers must, according to federal law, implement the approved accommodations. Importantly, the accommodations that students use in class are often the same ones that they use for standardized testing. Teachers should be sure to note which accommodations have been approved for state assessments and which are not.

Modifications are changes to the curriculum. These are also listed on the students' IEP but are typically the responsibility of the special educator. For example, Kristen (the student in Ms. James' class) requires that teacher-created tests be modified. Instead of five responses to a multiple choice question, Kristen's test has two. Similarly, Kristen completes a modified essay. Her version includes pictures that have been cut from magazines, and she dictates her words to a peer or special educator instead of writing herself. Remember that these modifications do not change the core content that is being taught. When the class studied Ancient Egypt, so did Kristen. Her assignments, however, were created to challenge but not frustrate her. Figure 14–3 contains a list of sample modifications and accommodations.

Think for a minute about accommodations and modifications that you may use in your own schooling experience. Do you use a Palm Pilot™ or other PDA to remember phone numbers and date? Do you use a tape recorder to record lectures? Do you rely on your peers for feedback on homework before turning it in?

Students with Physical Disabilities

Just as the constructed category of *cognitive disability* is very diverse, so too is the category of *physical disability*. This includes students who are deaf or hard-of-hearing. It also includes students who are blind, have physical motor coordination difficulties, or have injuries that limit their movement.

Figure 14—3   Sample accommodations and modifications.

Ideas for Use with Instructional Materials
- Provide a calculator.
- Supply graph paper to assist in organizing and lining up math problems.
- Tape lectures.
- Allow film or video and supplements in place of text.
- Provide practice opportunities using games, computers, language master, oral drills, and board work.
- Offer a personal dry erase board
- Allow student to record thoughts and write while listening to an audiotape or watching a videotape of the lecture or class assignment.
- Provide visual aids to stimulate ideas.
- Allow the use of computers for writing.
- Provide student with ink stamps for numbers, letters, date, and signature.
- Tape the assignment to the desk or provide a clipboard that can be clamped to the desk or wheelchair tray to secure papers.
- Use print enlarger or light box to illuminate text.
- Use tactile materials.
- Find accompanying enrichment materials on the student's reading level.
- Use adapted computer hardware or software.

Ideas for Use with Class Activities
- Break down new skills into small steps.
- Simplify instruction by demonstrating and guiding learning one step at a time.
- Role play historical events.
- Underline or highlight important words and phrases.
- Group students into pairs, threes, fours, etc., for different assignments and activities.
- Pair students with different and complementary skills.
- Pick key words from book to read on each page.
- Turn pages in book while others read.
- Rewrite text or use easy to read versions.
- Have student complete sentences supplied by the teacher orally or in writing.
- Supply incomplete sentences for student to fill in appropriate words or phrases.
- Engage students in read, write, pair, and share activities.
- Use hands-on activities.
- Color code important words or phrases.

Ideas for Use With Projects or Homework
- Assign smaller quantities of work.
- Relate problems to real-life situations.
- Highlight problems to be completed.
- Read problems and equations aloud.
- Allow more time for completion.
- Provide study questions in advance of an assignment.
- Encourage oral contributions.
- Assign concept maps.
- Provide sample sentences for students to use as a model.
- Dictate report to a partner who writes it out or types it on the computer.
- Assign homework partners.
- Assign group projects to illustrate a story setting (collages and dioramas).
- Substitute projects for written assignments and reports.
- Use complementary software or adapted computer hardware.
- Organize pictures instead of words into categories.
- Have student survey other students using targeted questions on the topic.

Ideas for Use With Assessments
- Underline or highlight text directions.
- Read word problems aloud.
- Re-word problems using simpler language.
- Underline key words.
- Space problems further apart on the page.

(continued)

Figure 14—3 *(Continued).*

- Reduce the number of questions by selecting representative items.
- Permit oral responses.
- Put choices for answers on index cards.
- Use the sentence or paragraph as a unit of composition rather than an essay.
- Allow oral responses to tests using a tape recorder.
- Use photographs in oral presentations to the class.
- Re-word test questions in easier terms.
- Assign final group projects with each student responsible for specific roles.
- Encourage the use of other media for final products (film, videotape, audiotape, photos, drawings, performances, etc.).

Source: Adapted from Fisher, D., Frey, N., & Sax, C. (1999). *Inclusive elementary schools: Recipes for success.* Colorado Springs, CO: PEAK Parent Center. Used with permission.

Because federal law (especially the Americans With Disabilities Act) requires architectural access and adequate facilities that provide access for individuals with disabilities, the classroom teacher's environmental concern should be for proper placement of the student in the classroom. Where the student sits should depend on any sensory-related disabilities and accessibility (i.e., maneuvering space) to various parts of the classroom (the student's desk, free reading center, individual study carrels, media center, and games) so that the student is as free to participate in the same learning options as are the other students with as little help as possible.

Because reading involves connecting speech and print, students who are deaf or blind may require additional instruction to learn to read. Remember that deafness and blindness are not cognitive disabilities, but rather, they are physical disabilities that impact a student's ability to access text or information. For example, students with vision-related disabilities may encounter difficulties with learning to read, including left-to-right orientation or clarity of the word image itself. Students who are deaf or hard-of-hearing may not have the auditory discrimination skills to rhyme words and thus may need alternatives to this type of instruction.

Classroom Considerations for Students with Physical Disabilities

Students with physical disabilities, whether partially sighted or blind, students who use wheelchairs, or students who have limited hearing are easily accommodated within the regular classroom when certain considerations and adaptations are made.

First and foremost, putting a child at ease in the school environment is essential to successful instruction. Two key words to remember when working with students with physical disabilities are *orientation*, which refers to a person's spatial placement in relation to objects in the environment, and *mobility*, which refers to the ability to move about in the environment. Orientation and mobility instruction are special skills, and most children will receive this training from a specialist. The classroom teacher must, however, assist in orienting the student to the classroom and the school environment. Suggestions for accomplishing this are as follows:

1. Spend time with the student in the classroom before the school year begins or, if this is not possible, make time available before or after school. Make

sure that the student is comfortable with the surroundings and knows how to find the appropriate desk, books, and materials. Similarly, acquaint the student with the layout of the entire school, including the cafeteria, library, and restrooms. When appropriate, ask peers to assist with this orientation to ensure that the child will be acquainted with some of his or her classmates.

2. Discuss and practice the fire drill procedures and evacuation route before drills or emergencies.

3. Encourage all students, especially those with physical disabilities, to ask for help when they need it and ask peers to assist when called upon.

4. Provide ample work space for extra equipment such as Braille books, magnifying devices, speech output devices, positioning equipment, or tape recorders.

5. Present new vocabulary words by writing them down, pronouncing them, and using them in several sentences. New words may be written on a list for the child to take home for study with parents or tutors.

6. Institute a "buddy" or "note taker" system to aid students with physical disabilities with any details missed during class. Note takers are especially useful because it may be difficult for a child to watch the speaker intently and write at the same time or writing may be an extremely labor-intensive process. Naturally, note takers also benefit by taking more complete notes.

7. Many children with physical or mobility-related disabilities tire easily, so classroom work should be varied to include rest or quiet periods when the student can read, draw, or nap as indicated. Do not expect all students with physical disabilities to keep up with the pace of the rest of the class but always include the child, providing the option to rest if he or she is tired.

Your Turn

How have school buildings changed? Walk through your school and identify barriers that a student who uses a wheelchair would encounter. Make a list of these physical barriers and share them with your peers. Schools are more accommodating today than ever before, but there are improvements to be made.

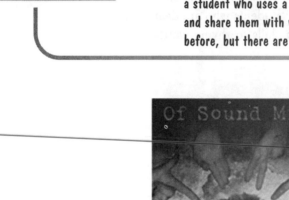

Of Sound Mind © 2001 by Jean Ferris. Jacket art © 2001 by Gret Spalenka. Used with the permission of Farrar Straus Giroux.

Instructional Methods for Students with Physical Disabilities

The method of teaching reading that the teacher normally uses will no doubt agree with the child who has a physical disability as long as the teacher uses a multisensory approach and presents concepts in as concrete a manner as possible. Classroom activities should be explained or narrated to provide a vivid picture of what is going on. Whenever possible, tactile experiences should be provided to illustrate elements or characteristics of the concept being discussed. For example, instead of saying that a mouse is a small, furry animal, say that a mouse can be held in the palm of your hand and provide a piece of fur for the student to touch. Better still, of course, would be to present a real mouse.

As Ms. James and Ms. Noyes have found, pre-reading activities are especially useful to students with physical disabilities. These pre-reading activities should include discussions of new vocabulary words and concepts using a concrete multisensory approach. For students who have low vision, large, clear pictures are useful for explaining ideas as well as for promoting creative language-experience stories. To illustrate concepts such as *rough, smooth, soft, hard, sticky, slick, lumpy, fluffy,* and so on, cards can be covered with various types of fabric, cotton balls, plastic, sandpaper, or any number of substances that will provide the desired tactile response.

In the primary grades, it is common for teachers to label different objects around the room such as walls, doors, windows, the fish tank, desks, books, and so on. For students with physical disabilities, these labels should be printed in a size large enough to be read by all students in the class. In addition, these labels could include the word in Braille, the word in American Sign Language, or the word in a standard line drawing such as Picture Communication Symbols (PCS). These PCS symbols are widely used across the country for students who have difficulty with print but who want to convey their thinking on a topic (see Figure 14–3).

For many students with physical disabilities, writing is a significant challenge. Alternatives to handwriting assignments may include the use of a computer (sometimes it is necessary to use a head wand when hand coordination is not sufficient to type with the fingers) or a tape recorder for oral responses. Tape recorders are essential and may be used to record student's thinking and responses to writing prompts, to record a teacher lecture for studying, or for the development of listening skills as students record and then critique their own speech.

Ms. James especially likes reader's theater as an instructional strategy for her students who have physical disabilities. She knows that it is very beneficial to students with vision disabilities because it gives them a chance to participate in oral expressive reading with their classmates. Although their reading rate may be slower at first than that of the sighted children, with practice an accomplished production can be performed.

In her role as a special education teacher, Ms. Noyes provides classroom teachers with photographs and illustrations from magazines related to the content the class is studying. She knows that this is excellent stimuli for vocabulary development. Scrapbooks and photograph albums compiled by the student (using pictures he or she has taken or cut from magazines), with captions offering information about concrete items in the pictures or abstract feelings about them, are also an excellent way to improve language skills. Ms. Noyes makes this an ongoing journal of day-to-day experiences. Some of these journal entries are later expanded into essays in which the students practice more refined writing skills by making rough, intermediate, and final drafts.

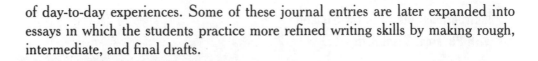

Try keeping a journal of your experiences as a teacher. When you look back on your journal, you'll realize how much you have learned and how much you think about your teaching. This is referred to as reflective practice and is one of the characteristics of highly effective teachers.

Unfortunately, absenteeism is often a significant concern for students with physical disabilities. Many students with physical disabilities need to visit their physicians and therapists on a regular basis. In addition, some students with physical disabilities have associated health-related disabilities that impact their attendance. When practical and appropriate, send work home with classmates who live nearby, allowing the child contact with peers and providing tutoring that benefits both children. If the absence is prolonged or if hospitalization is required, special tutors may be needed to help the child keep up with the classwork. Encourage the child to keep a journal of his or her thoughts during the time away from school and periodically have the class write letters, make objects, or visit the child when possible.

Students with Emotional or Behavioral Disabilities

Whereas some students have cognitive or physical disabilities, others have emotional or behavioral disabilities. Unfortunately, for some of these students their behavioral support needs are extensive, and they require significant amounts of support from special educators. However, it is important to note that these situations are relatively rare. However, a large number of students who exhibit attention, hyperactivity, and impulsivity disabilities. Students with these types of disabilities may have difficulty determining which elements in the environment require attention and which do not. The result may include a short attention span; perseveration, which is the repetition of an idea in speech or writing; and distractibility, which occurs when the child is unable to focus attention on the task at hand because of external or internal distractions. Hyperactivity, perhaps one of the best-known characteristics of this group of children, is shown in the child who is constantly in motion, whose motor activity is too high for the age group.

In terms of teaching reading to students with emotional or behavioral disabilities, the most important thing that teachers can remember is *attention*. Students have all kinds of ways of paying attention—you'll have to identify the ways in which your students can best attend to their learning. This may sound strange, but we have had students who can focus the most while pacing in the back of the room. One student could focus best with her head down on the table, thus removing all visual stimuli.

Beyond attention, students with emotional or behavioral disabilities may need specific, individualized behavioral management plans. Although good classroom organization and interesting lessons will go a long way in providing the structure that students with emotional or behavioral disabilities need, some students need more. Working with a special education resource teacher to develop a behavior support plan will be time well spent. After all, you can't teach a student to read if he or she is being sent to the principal's office on a regular basis.

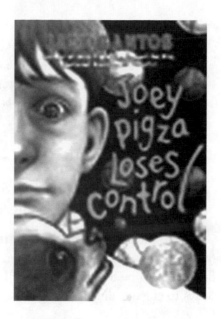

Joey Pigza Loses Control
© 2000 by Jack Gantos. Jacket
art © 2000 by Beata Szpura.
Used with the permission of
Farrar Straus Giroux.

Classroom Considerations for Students With Emotional or Behavioral Disabilities

Like other groups of students with disabilities, the range of support needs for this group of students is extensive. In general, students with emotional or behavioral disabilities do better when the teacher establishes and follows a predictable routine. In other words, the classroom schedule should be fairly predictable for students. Additionally, when schedule changes occur, the teacher should make a specific point of informing the class. This will prevent a number of behavioral problems and lost instructional time.

Interestingly, the most common time for students with emotional or behavioral disabilities to get into trouble is during transitions. Moving from one instructional activity to another is often an antecedent event that triggers problem behavior. When this is the case, the teacher should give serious attention to the "between activities" time and attempt to provide students with emotional or behavioral disabilities with additional support. For example, it may be helpful to give a student a 2-minute warning so that he or she can prepare for the transition and not be caught in the middle of something and become angry. Alternatively, it may be helpful to assign a specific responsibility, such as collecting the papers, to a student with an emotional or behavioral disability so that the transition time is even more structured.

Another important classroom consideration for students with emotional or behavioral disabilities is seating. It is important to plan your seating chart and identify appropriate places for specific students to sit before seating the rest of the class. For example, one student may need to sit near the teachers' desk whereas another student may focus more on classwork when far removed from the windows and doors. Still other students may perform best when seated next to a specific peer who can provide behavioral reminders and redirection. Regardless of the seating arrangements, teacher proximity is still an important way to maintain classroom order. Teachers can walk around the room and stand near a student who is having difficulty focusing on the lesson. Sometimes a simple hand on the shoulder will do the trick and allow the student to return to the task at hand.

Your Turn

What drives one teacher nuts may not bother another teacher at all. We all have different tolerance levels for different problematic behaviors. What student behaviors really push your buttons? How will you respond to such students? Are there behaviors that you'll need to learn to accept as you become a teacher? Talk with your peers about behaviors they can and cannot accept. Also ask how they respond when problematic behaviors occur.

Instructional Methods Useful for Students with Emotional or Behavioral Disabilities

Again, the method for teaching reading to students with emotional or behavioral disabilities is similar to that of teaching all other groups of students. The main difference may be the distractibility of the learner. Frey (2004) provides a number of ways to engage all learners. Teachers may want to try some of the following:

1. Ensure that the student with an emotional or behavioral disability receives individual reading instruction regularly. This could be from the classroom teacher or from a special educator. Either way, this individual time with an adult may be the only time the student really focuses on reading.

2. Given that many students need quiet places to work, create "offices" from carrels, partitions, or appliance crates that are free from distracting stimuli. Children may be assigned "office hours" when the space is for their own private use.

3. Provide students with emotional or behavioral disabilities frequent breaks. Because long assignments often cause frustration for students, provide instruction on only one or two steps at a time and provide multiple opportunities for students to re-engage in the activity.

CONCLUSION

This chapter has focused on the types of support necessary for students with disabilities to be successful in the classroom. We should also note that students with disabilities will bring a richness to your classroom. Teacher after teacher has reported that providing instruction for a student with a disability has helped them grow as professionals. In addition, students with disabilities can be a catalyst for learning on the part of students who do not have disabilities. Understanding the full range of human experience and the different ways we all learn is an important lesson that students can learn from inclusive classrooms.

QUESTIONS

1. Considering the educational climate for students with disabilities before the passage of PL 94-142 and the controversy that still surrounds inclusive education, discuss the success and failures of the law.

2. What are the long-term consequences of the IEP as it relates to both the student and the teacher? Analyze the IEP process, discuss the rationale for this process, and identify the role of the classroom teacher in this process.

3. What should be the relationship between the special and general educator?

4. What is your personal philosophy regarding teaching students with disabilities?

5. Identify three children's books that have children with disabilities as main characters. Describe how you will use these books in your classroom.

CLASSROOM PROJECTS

1. Based on a real student of your acquaintance or on a case history of your invention, describe the steps you would take to design an IEP for this child.

2. Design a floor plan for a classroom that accommodates the needs of the three students with disabilities identified in this chapter (Tyler, Maria, and Kristen). Describe the seating arrangements and why you made your decisions.

3. Prepare a reading comprehension lesson to illustrate one of the techniques identified in this chapter. Include the text to be studied and a modeling script to illustrate the technique.

4. Using the blank student profile form found in Figure 14–4, compile information about a student with a disability.

Figure 14–4   Student profile form.

Student Profile for _____   Age: _____

School Name: _____

Student Name: _____   Grade: _____

Parent/Guardian: _____   Phone #: _____

Classroom Teacher: _____

Special Education Teacher: _____

Skills to be addressed:

Areas of strengths/interests:

Successful learning strategies/modifications/adaptations needed:

Communication strategies:

Positive behavior support strategies:

Grading and assessment accommodations:

Important health/family information:

Source: Adapted from Fisher, D., Frey, N., & Sax, C. (1999). *Inclusive elementary schools: Recipes for success.* Colorado Springs, CO: PEAK Parent Center. Used with permission.

REFERENCES

Allington, R. L., & Broikou, K. A. (1988). Development of shared knowledge: A new role for classroom and specialist teachers. *The Reading Teacher, 41*, 806–811.

Archer, A., & Gleason, M. (1990). Direct instruction in content area reading. In D. Carnine, J. Silbert, & E. Kameenui (Eds.), *Direct instruction reading* (2nd ed., pp. 339–393). Columbus, OH: Merrill.

Buswell, B. (1999). Families: The key to continuity. In D. Fisher, C. Sax, & I. Pumpian (Eds.), *Inclusive high schools: Learning from contemporary classrooms* (pp. 171–182). Baltimore: Brookes.

Fisher, D., & Frey, N. (2001). Access to the core curriculum: Critical ingredients for student success. *Remedial and Special Education, 22*, 148–157.

Fisher, D., Frey, N., & Sax, C. (2000). *Inclusive elementary schools: Recipes for success*. Colorado Springs, CO: PEAK Parent Center.

Frey, N. (2004). *The effective teacher's guide: 50 ways for engaging students in learning*. San Diego, CA: Academic Professional Development.

Lapp, D., Flood, J., Fisher, D., Sax, C., & Pumpian, I. (1996). From intrusion to inclusion: Myths and realities in our schools. *The Reading Teacher, 49*, 580–584.

Naylor, P. R. (1991). *Shiloh*. New York: Bantam Doubleday.

Rappaport, S. R. (1966). *Proceedings of the 1965 Pathway School Institute*. Narbeth, PA: Livingstone.

Roach, V. (1999). Reflecting on the least restrictive environment policy: Curriculum, instruction, placement: Three legs of the achievement stool. In D. Fisher, C. Sax, & I. Pumpian (Eds.), *Inclusive high schools: Learning from contemporary classrooms* (pp. 145–156). Baltimore: Brookes.

Seyler, A. B., & Buswell, B. E. (2001). *Individual educational plans: Involved effective parents*. Colorado Springs, CO: PEAK Parent Center.

Stanovich, K. E. (1986). Cognitive processes and the reading problems of learning-disabled children: Evaluating the assumptions of specificity. In J. Torgensen & B. Wong (Eds.), *Psychology and educational perspectives on learning disabilities* (pp. 122–134). New York: Academic Press.

Will, M. (1986). *Educating students with learning problems: A shared responsibility*. Washington, DC: U.S. Department of Education.

Winzer, M. A. (1993). *The history of special education: From isolation to integration*. Washington, DC: Gallaudet University.

15

Historical Perspectives on Reading and Reading Instruction

CHAPTER GOALS

To help the reader

- examine a brief history of reading and reading instruction in the United States.
- explore various methods of reading instruction past to present.
- discern strengths and limitations of each method presented.
- explore definitions of reading.
- understand the importance of developing a personal definition of reading on which to base instructional decisions.

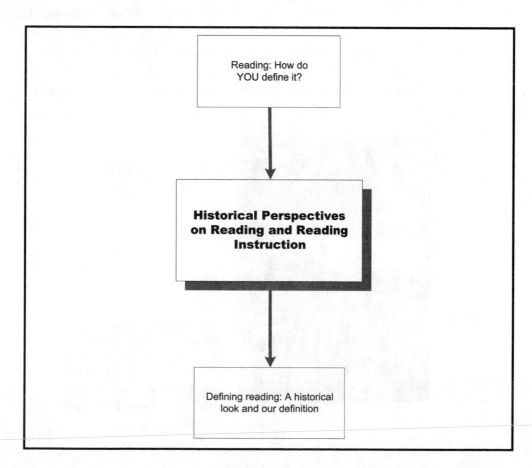

Reading: How do YOU define it?

Historical Perspectives on Reading and Reading Instruction

Defining reading: A historical look and our definition

At the outset, let us state that there is no one miracle method that will teach all children to read. Children are individuals and will learn individually, using the approach or approaches most meaningful to them. Thus, the teacher must be familiar with all approaches and materials (Matthes, 1977, p. 9).

There is no one "perfect method" for teaching reading to all children. Teachers, policy makers, researchers, and teacher educators need to recognize that the answer is not in the method but in the teacher (Duffy & Hoffman, 1999, p. 10).

The two introductory quotes to this chapter were written more than 20 years apart. What was true in the past is true today: there is no simple answer or single program for efficiently and effectively teaching all children to read (Allington & Walmsley, 1995). If there were a simple answer to the question "How do I teach a child to read?" there would not be the great controversy and diversity evident in American society and classrooms today. We maintain that the classroom teacher lies at the heart of effective literacy instruction for each child. The answer to effective literacy instruction is found in the ways that knowledgeable, thoughtful, and caring teachers use methods, materials, and programs with their students rather than in the methods, materials, and programs themselves.

As a teacher, you will have an almost overwhelming number of decisions to make, decisions about issues such as effectiveness of materials, evaluation of students' progress, selection of optional materials, and approaches to instruction based on students' needs. The purpose of this chapter, as well as the rest of the book, is to facilitate these decision-making processes.

An important component in knowing how to teach reading effectively is thinking carefully about what it is that you're teaching when you are teaching reading. So, we'll begin this chapter with you and your beliefs, understanding, and background with reading and reading instruction. Then, we'll talk about how reading has been conceptualized and taught from the past to the present.

When you're reading about the history of reading and reading instruction, check to see whether any of your current beliefs relate to any beliefs in the field that

Old People, Frogs, and Albert © 1999 by Nancy Hope Wilson. Illustrations © 1999 by Marcy D. Ramsey. Used with the permission of Farrar Straus Giroux.

have evolved historically. Next, drawing on our own work and the work of others, we'll share some core beliefs about reading and reading instruction. Finally, coming full circle, we'll ask you to reexamine the initial thoughts and ideas you listed at the beginning of this chapter about reading and reading instruction.

We believe that this chapter will give you important background information about reading and reading instruction that you can use as a foundation to think about current conceptions of reading. Knowledge about the history of reading and reading instruction as well as current information can help you make daily instructional decisions with your own students in your current and/or future classrooms.

READING: HOW DO YOU DEFINE IT?

In this chapter, we will examine major approaches to the teaching of reading and the various methods that have evolved over time from these philosophical points of view. The reading program that you decide to implement in your classroom will depend largely on your personal definition of reading. As a teacher, you must ask yourself these questions: "What do I think reading is?" and "How will I teach a child to read?"

Let's start with your current ideas about reading and teaching reading. Your current ideas will serve as an important starting place for your evolving definition of reading and best practices for reading instruction. First, describe the reading practices in your home as a child. What do you remember about reading and writing at home with your family? You may want to think about this both prior to entering school and after you started school.

Now, think back to elementary school. What do you recall about reading practices in your elementary school classrooms? List your recollections. After listing your recollections, share them with several classmates. How were your early reading/writing experiences at home and school similar to and/or different from those of your peers?

Finally, let's see what your current ideas are about reading and reading instruction. How do you currently define reading? What, in your opinion, constitutes best practices in reading instruction? Why? (Please note, we'll ask you to reconsider these important questions at the end of this chapter to see how your thinking may have evolved as you read the information presented here.)

We asked you to identify your past experiences with reading and to formulate your current conceptions of reading because we know that our experiences and beliefs as teachers shape our daily instructional decisions. Also, we think that you may find it particularly interesting to contextualize your own elementary reading instruction as you read about various approaches and practices. To continually grow as professionals, we need to identify our beliefs and then engage in the continual process of examining, critiquing, and refining them.

To help you revise and refine your personal views about reading, we offer a historical perspective on reading based on the work of reading educators. We begin by presenting a brief overview of the ways reading instruction has occurred in the United States to understand how educators in the past answered the question,

DID YOU NOTICE . . .
Did you notice that what you believe about how a child learns to read and reads to learn will influence your daily classroom instruction?

"What is reading, and how do I teach a child to read?" We hope this will provide you with insights concerning advances that have been made in reading instruction, as well as the progress that has been made in understanding effective teaching. Additionally, this historical look provides conceptual background for current approaches and methods that we discuss in this book. As you read the historical information we present, we will ask you to consider what underlying beliefs about the nature of reading and the reading process that proponents of each approach may have held.

As we mentioned earlier, we think you will find it interesting to try to contextualize your own reading instruction experiences as you read about different historical approaches to reading instruction. We also think that you may find it interesting to contextualize the information about the history of reading by interviewing an older family member or friend. So, here's what we'd like you to do. As you are looking at Table 15–1 and reading the information about the history of reading, think about someone you can interview about her or his recollections of reading and reading instruction. For example, you could interview a parent, a grandparent, or older aunt or uncle. (The older the person you interview, the better.) When you have finished reading the sections on the history of reading and reading methods, plan to conduct your interview. Plan to use the information you read in the following two sections to help guide your interview. Be sure to ask your informant about the materials she or he used, how she or he was taught to read, and how her or his teacher grouped his or her class for reading instruction.

HISTORICAL PERSPECTIVES ON READING APPROACHES AND MATERIALS

The brief historical overview of reading instruction practices in the United States that we present in this section may shed some light on important factors that you will have to examine before selecting the methods of instruction for your students. Although we present major trends in reading instruction across time, we wish to make it clear that there was variability in the nature of reading instruction during each of the different time periods identified and discussed in the following. For example, Horace Mann had some forward-thinking ideas about silent reading and comprehension that were not actually implemented widely until over a century or more after they were proposed. In this section of the chapter, we share general trends across time. Please note that we drew heavily on an early seminal work presenting a comprehensive history of American reading instruction that was developed by Smith (1965). The eras of reading instruction in Table 15–1 up to 1965 come from Smith's work. Table 15–1 provides a concise overview of historical perspectives in reading that will be discussed in more detail after we present the table. Also, we include examples of pages from actual early materials throughout our discussion.

As you read Table 15–1, see if you recognize any of the approaches we mention. Circle, or place a checkmark next to the approaches that are familiar to you. Be prepared to discuss in class how and why these different approaches are familiar to you.

TABLE 15–1
Summary of the Changing Focus of Reading Instruction

Approximate Date	Eras of Reading Instruction	Learning Approach/Philosophy	Materials and Methods
1600s to late 1700s	*Religious Emphasis* • Primary purpose of reading instruction was teaching children to read religious materials (such as the Bible)	• Alphabet spelling system • Sequential skills	• Hornbook *New England Primer* • Oral reading • Memorization • Recitation
Late 1700s to mid-1800s	*Nationalistic–Moralistic* • Politics (especially after the American Revolution) now replaced theology as the center of intellectual interest	• Whole-word method • Sequential skills	• Silent reading • Oral reading • Reading for comprehension
Mid to late 1800s	*Education for Intelligent Citizenship* • Realization that a successful democracy requires an educated citizenry.	• Artificial phonics system • Sequential skills	• McGuffey *Eclectic Readers* • Silent reading • Controlled repetition of words
Late 1800s to early 1900s	*Reading as a Cultural Asset* • Tranquil time in American history, and education reflected this serenity.	• Look-and-say method • Sequential skills • Silent reading method	• Sight-word emphasis • Testing initiated • Elaborate testing and measurement • Silent reading emphasis
Early 1900s to mid-1900s	*Scientific Investigation and Intensive Research and Application* • Development of scientific instruments of measurement made it possible to assess the effectiveness of reading methods and materials. • Many new research studies were undertaken, and research was applied in classrooms.	Basal reader approaches • Sequential skills	• Student and teacher workbooks; Dick & Jane, Alice & Jerry • Controlled vocabulary • Oral & silent reading; • Phonics influence
Mid-1900s	*International Conflict* • This era was marked by national and international unrest.	Phonics strongly emphasized • Words in color • Programmed instruction • Language experience method • Sequential skills and constructive approaches	• SRA materials • Individualization • Individual language patterns • Personalization
1950s to 1960s	*Expanding Knowledge and Technological Revolution* • Reading instruction became a national concern and was emphasized heavily in U.S. education.	• Linguistic influence	• Let's Read • Patterned word units
Mid 1960s–1980s	*Humanistic/Behavioristic Influences on Reading & Reading as Information Processing* • Emphasis on instruction meeting individual needs, thus instruction is personalized. • Focus on the process of reading and the computer became the metaphor for the process.	• Managed language/reading • Sequential skills	• Use of a variety of methods and materials (e.g., Ginn 720, Macmillan R) • Personalization • Individualization • Sequential organization
1980s to mid-1990s	*Whole-Language Perspectives* • Evolving from humanistic philosophies, reading was seen as a process of meaning construction. • Language learning viewed as a naturally occurring event, and literacy development promoted through meaningful reading and writing.	• Whole-language basal/trade books (integration of language arts) • Constructive approaches	• Use of narrative and expository tradebooks • Basal texts • Integration of all language arts (reading, writing, speaking, and listening) • Use of language in meaningful functional contexts; reading in all content areas emphasized

(continued)

TABLE 15–1 (Continued)

Approximate Date	Eras of Reading Instruction	Learning Approach/Philosophy	Materials and Methods
Mid-1990s to 1999	*Word Study Emphasis* • Renewed emphasis on the role of the teacher in teaching the skills and strategies associated with reading and writing. • Renewed emphasis on skills development —phonics —decoding —word study —fluency —comprehension • Emphasis on the role of social, cultural, and historical aspects of literacy and learning in research literature and studies.	• Sequential skills development • Constructive approaches to literacy and language arts	• Use of narrative and expository tradebooks • Basal texts become anthologies • Various phonics and spelling programs (e.g., Open Court and Word Study) • Reading in all content areas emphasized • Skills instruction—usually taught in a meaningful context • The role of phonics in learning to read debated. • Teacher's role in helping children to learn literacy emphasized through a reader's and writer's workshop model • Literature-based instruction emphasized
2000 to present	*Government Intrusion* • National political emphasis on literacy focusing on scientifically based reading research. • List of acceptable research methodologies and findings. • Medical model—quantitative research • No Child Left Behind legislation • Reading First grants • Vouchers • Faith-based school support • Continued emphasis on skills and strategies associated with reading in the areas of phonemic awareness, phonics, vocabulary, fluency, and comprehension. • National Reading Panel • State and federal mandates	• Bottom-up model • Sequential skills development • English only • List of acceptable consultants for instruction • Less emphasis on literature • Less focus on an integrated curriculum	• Increased testing • Use of narrative and expository trade books • Basal texts • Various phonics and spelling programs (e.g., Open Court and Word Study)

In the colonial period (which roughly parallels Smith's religious emphasis and nationalistic–moralistic eras), an *alphabet spelling system* was the methodology used to teach reading. The four sample pages shown in Figure 15–1 are from Noah Webster's *The Elementary Spelling Book*, which was published in 1800. Instruction was given in single-letter recognition; then combined letter–sound correspondences, such as *ab* and *ac*; then parts of words, such as *tab*; and finally, the whole word, *table*. Reading was almost a totally oral process in these early years because it included intensive instruction in pitch, stress, enunciation, gesticulation, memorization, and recitation.

Because of the religious emphasis of the era, instruction was directed to a single purpose: the reading of prayer books and religious and moral books. Robinson (1977) told us that "content was considered more important than any methodology directed toward developing independent readers. Oral reading was promoted as *the* reading procedure for social and religious needs" (p. 46). Because the goal of reading instruction was solely to enable people to read religious materials, it was an

Figure 15–1 Noah Webster's The Elementary Spelling Book.

---

8   THE ELEMENTARY

ANALYSIS OF SOUNDS
IN THE ENGLISH LANGUAGE.

The Elementary Sounds of the English language are divided into two classes, *vowels* and *consonants.*

A *vowel* is a clear sound made through an open position of the mouth-channel, which molds or shapes the voice without obstructing its utterance; as *a* (in *far,* in *fate,* etc.), *e, o.*

A *consonant* is a sound formed by a closer position of the articulating organs than any position by which a vowel is formed, as *b, d, t, g, sh.* In forming a consonant the voice is compressed or stopped.

A *diphthong* is the union of two simple vowel sounds, as *ou* (ăŏ) in *out, oi* (aī) in *noise.*

The English Alphabet consists of twenty-six letters, or single characters, which represent vowel, consonant, and diphthongal sounds—a, b, c, d, e, f, g, h, i, j, k, l, m, n, o, p, q, r, s, t, u, v, w, x, y, z. The combinations *ch, sh, th,* and *ng* are also used to represent elementary sounds; and another sound is expressed by *s,* or *z;* as, in *measure, azure,* pronounced *mĕzh'yoor, ăzh'ur.*

Of the foregoing letters, *a, e, o,* are always simple vowels; *i* and *u* are vowels (as in *in, us*), or diphthongs (as in *time, tune*); and *y* is either a vowel (as in *any*), a diphthong (as in *my*), or a consonant (as in *ye*).

Each of the vowels has its regular long and short sounds which are most used; and also certain *occasional* sounds, as that of *a* in *last, far, care, fall, what; e* in *term, there, prey; i* in *firm, marine; o* in *dove, for, wolf, prove;* and *u* in *fur, rude,* and *pull.* These will now be considered separately.

A. The regular long sound of *a* is denoted by a horizontal mark over it; as, ān'cient, pro-fāne'; and the regular short sound by a curve over it; as, căt, păr'ry.

Occasional sounds.—The Italian sound is indicated by two dots over it; as, bär, fä'ther;—the short sound of the Italian *a,* by a single dot over it; as, fȧst, lȧst;—the broad sound, by two dots below it; as, b̤all, st̤all;—the short sound of broad *a,* by a single dot under it; as, whạt, quạd'rȧnt;—the sound of *a* before *r* in certain words like *care, fair,* etc., is represented by a sharp or pointed circumflex over the *a,* as, câre, hâir, fâir, etc.

E. The regular long sound of *e* is indicated by a horizontal mark over it; as, mēte, se-rēne'; the regular short sound, by a curve over it; as, mĕt, re-bĕl'.

Occasional sounds.—The sound of *e* like *a* in *care* is indicated by a pointed circumflex over the *e,* as in thêir, whêre; and of short *e* before *r* in cases where it verges toward short *u,* by a rounded circumflex, or wavy line, over it; as, hẽr, pre-fẽr'.

I, O, U. The regular long and short sounds of *i, o,* and *u* are indicated like those of *a* and *e* by a horizontal mark and by a curve; as, bīnd, bĭn; dōle, dŏll; tūne, tŭn.

Occasional sounds.—When *i* has the sound of long *e* it is marked by two dots over it; as, fa-tïgue', ma-rïne';—when *o* has the sound of short *u,* it is marked by a single dot over it; as, dȯve, sȯn;—when it has the sound of ŏŏ, it is marked with two dots under it; as, mọve, prọve;—when it has the sound of ŏŏ, it is marked with a single dot under it; as, wọlf, wọ'man;—when it has the sound of broad *a,* this is indicated by a pointed circumflex over the vowel; as, nôrth, sôrt;—the two letters *oo,* with a horizontal mark over them, have the sound heard in the words bōōm, lōōm;—with a curve mark, they have a shorter form of the same sound; as, bŏŏk, gŏŏd;—when *u* is sounded like short *oo,* it has a single dot under it; as, fụll, pụll; while its lengthened sound, as when preceded by *r,* is indicated by two dots; as in rüde, rü'ral, rü'by.

NOTE.—The long *u* in unaccented syllables has, to a great extent, the sound of *oo,* preceded by *y,* as in *educate,* pronounced ĕd'yoo-kāte: *nature,* pronounced năt'yoor.

---

24   THE ELEMENTARY

BÄR, LȦST, CÂRE, FẠLL, WHẠT; HẼR, PRẸV, THÊRE; ĜET; BĪRD, MARÏNE; LINK;

ăpt	eärt	stärt	hûrt	pást	jĕst
chapt	dart	pẽrt	shirt	vast	lest
kĕpt	hart	vert	flirt	dĭdst	blest
slept	chart	wert	eäst	midst	nest
erept	mart	shôrt	fast	bĕst	pest

No. 25.—X X V.

rĕst	quĕst	mĭst	eŏst	thïrst	lŭst
erest	west	grist	first	bŭst	must
drest	zest	wrist	bûrst	dust	rust
test	fĭst	wist	eurst	gust	erust
vest	list	lŏst	durst	just	trust

Fire will burn wood and coal.
Coal and wood will make a fire.
The world turns round in a day.
Will you help me pin my frock?
Do not sit on the damp ground.
We burn oil in tin and glass lamps.
The lame man limps on his lame leg.
We make ropes of hemp and flax.
A rude girl will romp in the street.
The good girl may jump the rope.
A duck is a plump fowl.
The horse drinks at the pump.
A pin has a sharp point.
We take up a brand of fire with the tongs.
Good boys and girls will act well.
How can you test the speed of your horse?
He came in haste, and left his book.
Men grind corn and sift the meal.
We love just and wise men.
The wind will drive the dust in our eyes.
Bad boys love to rob the nests of birds.
Let us rest on the bed, and sleep, if we can.
Tin and brass will rust when the air is damp.

SPELLING BOOK.   25

MỌVE, SȮN, WỌLF, FỌOT, MŌON, ÔR; RỤLE, PỤLL; EXIST; Ç=K; Ĝ=J; Ş=Z; ÇH=SH.

No. 26.—X X V I.
WORDS OF TWO SYLLABLES, ACCENTED ON THE FIRST.

bā'ker	trō ver	sō lar	wō fụl	pā pal
sha dy	elo ver	po lar	po em	eō pal
la dy	do nor	lū nar	fo rum	vī al
tī dy	vä por	sō ber	Sā tan	pē nal
hō ly	fa vor	pā çer	fū el	ve nal
lī my	fla vor	ra çer	du el	fī nal
sli my	sa vor	grō çer	erụ el	ō ral
bō ny	ha lo	çī der	grụ el	ho ral
po ny	sō lo	spi der	pū pil	mū ral
po ker	hē ro	wä fer	lä bel	nä ṣal
tī ler	ne gro	ea per	lī bel	fa tal
eä per	tỹ ro	tī ĝer	lō eal	na tal
pa per	out go	mä ker	fo eal	rụ ral
ta per	sä go	ta ker	vo eal	vī tal
vī per	tū lip	ra ker	lĕ gal	tō tal
bi ter	çĕ dar	sē ton	re gal	o val
fĕ ver	brī er	rụ in	dī al	plī ant
ō ver	fri ar	hỹ men	tri al	ĝi ant

Bakers bake bread and cakes.
I like to play in the shady grove.
Some fishes are very bony.
I love the young lady that shows me how to read.
A pony is a very little horse.
We poke the fire with the poker.
The best paper is made of linen rags.
Vipers are bad snakes, and they bite men.
An ox loves to eat clover.
The tulip is very pretty, growing in the garden.
A dial shows the hour of the day.
Cedar trees grow in the woods.
The blackberry grows on a brier.

extremely simplified process. In addition, because of the scarcity and expense of books, only a limited number of people were actually taught to read. Most children learned letters of the alphabet from Hornbooks (first used in the mid-1500s) and the *New England Primer*, which were among the earliest readers in the United States. "These instructional materials were aimed at combining the learning of skills with religious salvation—the ultimate goal" (Cullinan, 1989, p. 17).

Horace Mann, an educational pioneer who worked in the mid to late 1800s, was instrumental in introducing the *whole-word method* of reading instruction in American schools. He advocated memorizing entire words before analyzing letters and letter patterns. His approach stressed silent reading and reading for comprehension; however, neither of these forward-thinking ideas took hold in the overall field of reading until the 1920s and 1980s, respectively. During the time of Horace Mann's work, the McGuffey *Eclectic Reader*, which emphasized controlled repetition of words, was introduced. Children were beginning to be taught to read through the use of stories, parables, moral lessons, and patriotic selections in an attempt to develop good citizens. Note that overall societal goals had shifted from religious training to good citizenship training. Although the McGuffey *Readers* did not have the most interesting narrative stories (see Figure 15–2), they were an improvement over the existing texts of the time because of their organizational scheme. Sentence length and vocabulary were controlled to match students' perceived developmental levels.

Figure 15–3 includes sample selections from the primer and the sixth reader of the McGuffey *Eclectic Readers* (1881, 1879). They are included to demonstrate the differences between the early and more advanced readers. Note the differences in print size, vocabulary, syntactic control, and content. Smith (1965) suggested that "McGuffey must be given the credit of being the first author to produce a clearly defined and carefully graded series consisting of one reader for each grade in the elementary school" (pp. 105–106).

DID YOU NOTICE . . .
Did you notice that graded basal readers have been around for more than 100 years? We still see grade level anthologies in classrooms in addition to the many leveled readers that support our students varying reading proficiencies.

The next important innovation in reading instruction occurred during the second half of the nineteenth century. It was a *phonetics method using a synthetic phonics system*. Horace Mann is often credited with having introduced phonics as a learning-to-read strategy. The goal of phonics is to give children strategies that will enable them to unlock unfamiliar words independently (Adams, 1990). Phonics has been used widely since the late 1800s, when educators recognized the value of letter–sound relationships as an aid to identifying unfamiliar words. Although the importance of this process is quite obvious, it is equally important to realize that phonics can be only a partial word analysis process because the English language does not have an exact one-to-one sound–symbol correspondence. Even given this limitation, however, phonics instruction is important and has for decades been an important part of most reading series.

It is important to note that phonics has fallen in and out of favor with educators across time. For example, in the early 1900s many teachers became dissatisfied with phonics because proponents of this method placed too much attention on word analysis and too little on comprehension. This method was temporarily abandoned, being replaced sometime around 1910 with the new *look-and-say method*. This method involved learning entire words as sight words. The look-and-say method

Figure 15—2 McGuffey Readers.

20   *ECLECTIC SERIES.*

LESSON XIV.

hōldṣ	tǫ
blind	Mā′rў
hănd	kīnd
ā	ǫ	k	ў

This old man can not see. He is blind.

Mary holds him by the hand. She is kind to the old blind man.

LESSON XV.—REVIEW.

I see ducks on the pond; Tom will feed them.

McGUFFEY'S PRIMER.   21

Tom is blind; he holds a box in his hand.

Nell is kind to him.

This old hen has a nest.

Mary will run and get the eggs.

LESSON XVI.

Sūe	dŏll	drĕss	new	hĕr
				lĕt
				ĕ
				ū
				ew

Sue has a doll.

It has a new dress.

42   *ECLECTIC SERIES.*

LESSON XXXVI.

Mĭss	wạnts	wọuld	tĕllṣ
			rụle
			kēep
			ḡŏŏd
			thăt
			ēach

ụ

The girls and boys all love Miss May; she is so kind to them.

Miss May tells them there is a rule that she wants them to keep. It is, "Do to each one as you would like each one to do to you."

McGUFFEY'S PRIMER.   43

This is a good rule, and all boys and girls should keep it.

LESSON XXXVII.

sehōol	child
chûrch	whĕn
bŏŏks	
slātes	

What kind of house is this? Do you think it is a schoolhouse, or a church?

It looks like a church, but I think it is a schoolhouse.

Figure 15–3   McGuffey Eclectic Readers.

V. THE VOICE.

PITCH AND COMPASS.

The **natural pitch** of the voice is its keynote, or governing note. It is that on which the voice usually dwells, and to which it most frequently returns when wearied. It is also the pitch used in conversation, and the one which a reader or speaker naturally adopts—when he reads or speaks—most easily and agreeably.

The **compass** of the voice is its range above and below this pitch. To avoid monotony in reading or speaking, the voice should rise above or fall below this keynote, but always with reference to the sense or character of that which is read or spoken. The proper natural pitch is that above and below which there is most room for variation.

To strengthen the voice and increase its compass, select a short sentence, repeat it several times in succession in as low a key as the voice can sound naturally; then rise one note higher, and practice on that key, then another, and so on, until the highest pitch of the voice has been reached. Next, reverse the process, until the lowest pitch has been reached.

EXAMPLES IN PITCH.

High Pitch.

NOTE.—Be careful to distinguish *pitch* from *power* in the following exercises. Speaking in the open air, at the very top of the voice, is an exercise admirably adapted to strengthen the voice and give it compass, and should be frequently practiced.

1. Charge`! Chester`, charge`! On`! Stanley, on`!

2. A horse`! a horse`! my kingdom` for a horse`!

3. Jump far out`, boy`, into the wave`!
   Jump`, or I fire`!

4. Run`! run`! run for your lives!

5. Fire`! fire`! fire`! Ring the bell`!

6. Gentlemen may cry peace´! peace´! but there is no peace!

7. Rouse`, ye Romans! rouse`, ye slaves`!
   Have ye brave sons´? Look in the next fierce brawl
   To see them die`. Have ye fair daughters´? Look
   To see them live, torn from your arms`, distained`,
   Dishonored`, and if ye dare call for justice´,
   Be answered by the lash`!

Medium Pitch.

NOTE.—This is the pitch in which we converse. To strengthen it, we should read or speak in it as loud as possible, without rising to a higher key. To do this requires long-continued practice.

1. Under a spreading chestnut tree,
   The village smithy stands`;
   The smith, a mighty man is he,
   With large and sinewy hands`;
   And the muscles of his brawny arms
   Are strong as iron bands.

2. There is something in the thunder's voice that makes me tremble like a child. I have tried to conquer` this unmanly weakness`. I have called pride` to my aid`; I have sought for moral courage in the lessons of philosophy`, but it avails me nothing`. At the first moaning of the distant cloud, my heart shrinks and dies within me.

3. He taught the scholars the Rule of Three´,
   Reading, and writing, and history`, too`;
   He took the little ones on his knee´,
   For a kind old heart in his breast had he´,
   And the wants of the littlest child he knew`.
   "Learn while you're young`," he often said´,
   "There is much to enjoy down here below`;
   Life for the living´, and rest for the dead´,"
   Said the jolly old pedagogue`, long ago`.

CXV. THE LAST DAYS OF HERCULANEUM.

Edwin Atherstone, 1788–1872, was born at Nottingham, England, and became known to the literary world chiefly through two poems, "The Last Days of Herculaneum" and "The Fall of Nineveh." Both poems are written in blank verse, and are remarkable for their splendor of diction and their great descriptive power. Atherstone is compared to Thomson, whom he resembles somewhat in style.

THERE was a man,
A Roman soldier, for some daring deed
That trespassed on the laws, in dungeon low
Chained down. His was a noble spirit, rough,
But generous, and brave, and kind.
He had a son; it was a rosy boy,
A little faithful copy of his sire,
In face and gesture. From infancy, the child
Had been his father's solace and his care.

     Every sport
The father shared and heightened. But at length,
The rigorous law had grasped him, and condemned
To fetters and to darkness.

    The captive's lot,
He felt in all its bitterness: the walls
Of his deep dungeon answered many a sigh
And heart-heaved groan. His tale was known, and touched
His jailer with compassion; and the boy,
Thenceforth a frequent visitor, beguiled
His father's lingering hours, and brought a balm
With his loved presence, that in every wound
Dropped healing. But, in this terrific hour,
He was a poisoned arrow in the breast
Where he had been a cure.

6.—26.

eventually lost favor with many teachers because the child had to learn every word as a sight word, and many children made little progress in learning to read.

The rise of *silent reading* began around 1920, when scientific research was dominant in education. This method was much like the earlier program Horace Mann had advocated. Teachers were now urged to abandon all oral methods of instruction and testing. Robinson (1977) stated that "there were increasing demands placed on reading for meaning, instead of on oral exercise, in order to meet the varied needs of society" (p. 50). In addition, the scientific era marked the advent of intelligence testing and educational measurement, and "research reports began to show the superiority of silent reading over oral reading for both fluency and comprehension" (Robinson, 1977, p. 50). A great deal of reading research was widely conducted (Good, 1923–1953; Gray, 1925–1932), the results of which gave rise to the extremely popular method that followed, the basal reading method, launched throughout the United States in the early 1930s.

From the 1930s on, due largely to the earlier emphasis on research and scientific investigation, the basal readers were at the core of most reading instruction. *Basal reading programs* included a student text and a teacher's manual. Each basal reader presented a controlled vocabulary, introduced levels of syntactic complexity that paralleled children's perceived development, and provided a program of word recognition, including phonics instruction. The basal method dominated other methods until the 1950s and 1960s, when alternatives to phonics-based basal programs emerged. For example, in the 1960s, with the period of humanistic and behavioristic influences, educational efforts were focused on meeting the needs of individual children. Although intraclass grouping had occurred earlier, techniques for *individualizing reading instruction* were emphasized nationwide, and *programmed materials* were developed for use in classrooms.

Programmed instruction, an example of the sequential skills approach to reading instruction, was very popular in the 1960s and 1970s. It is a systematic effort to take a specific block of information and divide it into small units that are organized for logical, sequential learning. One of the most significant aspects of programmed instruction was its immediate feedback, positive reinforcement of correct responses, and instant correction of errors. With programmed instruction, learners usually completed one frame, or small block, of the program and checked to determine the correctness of their response before moving to the next frame. If the response was erroneous, learners were corrected at once, so that they did not continue thinking and using incorrect data.

Very few educators would argue against the theory of an individualized or personalized reading program for each child; however, the major problem with this approach was perceived to be a time constraint. Creating an efficient, well-organized system to manage 25 or 30 different personalized programs daily seemed an overwhelming task, even for excellent teachers. This difficult situation occurred because most teachers were not prepared to implement flexible grouping techniques, personalized contracts, and classroom management processes.

Throughout the 1970s and beyond, basal readers again gained prominence. They strengthened their phonics emphasis. In addition, from the late 1960s to the present, *linguistic points of view* influenced the structure of many basal readers. Extending the teaching of *word families* from earlier basal readers, linguists pro-

DID YOU NOTICE . . .
Did you notice that many teachers were not efficient at grouping students flexibly, designing personal instructional contracts, and managing classroom behavior 30 years ago?

moted the teaching of reading through patterned word units, a practice that, in the extreme, became a somewhat inane presentation of language. (For example, *Nan ran to the man.*) Basal readers continue to be used in schools and classrooms today.

Historically, basal readers have been used as a primary reading material in the majority of schools in the United States. Most American readers learned to read via a basal reader. Did you find this to be true with your own early reading experiences and the early reading experiences of the person you interviewed? In recent years, basal series have been the focus of much of the criticism directed to reading programs. It is not unusual to hear people speak critically of reading instruction and hurl disparaging remarks at Dick and Jane, those characters in the basal series that, at its peak, probably had been purchased and used more widely than any series ever produced. Poor Dick and Jane became the symbols of the boy and girl found in all beginning materials and, therefore, had to suffer the insult aimed at many similar basal series. Current basal readers have almost no similarity to the early Dick and Jane readers. However, many criticisms have been leveled at basal reading series. The most prominent of them include the following:

- The vocabulary and sentence patterns do not match the spoken language of the children.
- The content is not interesting to children.
- Basal readers do not contain appropriate literary selections.
- The books are developed for graded levels and perceived developmental levels, and the child is forced to read in the book for his or her grade level. In actual classrooms, many children often read above or below their grade level.
- The teacher's manual is considered the last word in instructional guidance and must be followed to the letter. As a result, the program is not adjusted to individual needs, and instruction often becomes sterile and uncreative.
- Use of a basal reader leads to a uniform three-achievement-level grouping plan.
- Children are asked to do workbook exercises that contain previously mastered strategies.
- The basal reader often provides the sole source of material used in teaching reading skills to children.
- Basal series do not provide explicit instructional procedures; rather, they often focus on directions for completing reading-related tasks.
- The content often furthers sexual, racial, and socioeconomic stereotypes.

Undoubtedly, in many early basal series there was justification for some of these criticisms. However, even though basal series are very different, we urge you to reexamine these criticisms in the context of these questions:

1. How many are actual criticisms of basal series of the 2000s?
2. How many are critical of the manner in which the basal series was used?

Many beginning readers possess an extensive oral vocabulary; it is true, however, that the content of beginning levels of basal series frequently does not reflect children's language and language patterns. This is an especially important issue to consider with growing numbers of children in U.S. classrooms from wide varieties of different cultural and linguistic backgrounds. Smith (1978) said that since the mid-1970s some basal series "have undergone a noticeable shift in content," part of which is "a more natural language, the kind of language people speak" (pp. 41–42). This certainly is true of current basal readers. The types of writing included in basal readers have changed throughout the history of the United States. Basal readers have evolved from religious treatises to a more eclectic collection of writing types. As Venezky (1987) noted, the types of writing in children's readers have varied depending on the historical, political, and economic constraints of the era in which they were published.

As a teacher, you must be ready to personalize reading instruction to facilitate the language development of your specific students. No publisher can produce a series that will reflect the oral vocabulary and experience of every child in the United States. As a teacher, you will need to supplement the basal series with additional readings, both fiction and nonfiction, and with the experiences of the children you are teaching. Remember, basal series are designed to be only the *base* of your program, not the entire program.

In an attempt to counter the criticism that basal readers tend to present the values and mores of European American middle-class families, current basal series often strive to reflect the ethnic diversity of American public schools. However, as a teacher, you should be aware of the fact that whenever people from various cultures are represented in writing—whether in basal readers of children's literature, issues such as stereotyping and misrepresentation of cultural norms and practices can occur. When considering the ways in which people from different cultures are represented in basal readers, it is a good idea to use criteria similar to those used for evaluating children's literature for authentic representations of people from different cultures. As you may recall, this issue was discussed in chapter 11, the chapter that focused on children's literature.

It is likely that basal series will always have their critics; however, remember that basal readers can be an asset to you as a classroom teacher when used properly. In recent years, publishers have made serious efforts to include relevant, high-quality literature and to encourage teachers to see the basal reader as one of many materials in a language-rich reading program. More holistic approaches to reading instruction and using basal readers need not be diametrically opposing methods of teaching reading. We urge you to examine a basal series and then decide whether is useful for your purposes. In doing so, you may find that basal readers, when used properly, can aid you in the process of developing a quality literacy program in your classroom.

Although basal series have been a mainstay in American reading instruction, views of reading began to shift in the second half of the 1980s. These shifting views impacted the content of basal readers as well as the use of authentic reading materials (i.e., real books) in the classroom. Instead of being defined as a set of skills to be mastered, notions of reading, although still seen as the functioning of highly complex processes, were summed up in one statement: *Reading is comprehension.* Recognizing the role of prior knowledge in reading comprehension, emphasis began to shift from discrete skills to students' active involvement in comprehension processes (National Assessment of Educational Progress, 1985). In other words, reading

began to be seen as the dynamic interactive process of constructing meaning by combining the reader's existing knowledge with the text information within the context of the reading situation. Holistic approaches to reading instruction moved to center stage. Holistic reading approaches were organized around levels of students' cognitive and language development; however, they were also highly dependent on the affective domain. By developing a curriculum that is of interest to children, the teacher would be able to foster children's literacy learning more effectively. The language experience approach and the whole language philosophy exemplify holistic approaches to reading.

The language experience approach is one of the most common methods through which teachers have attempted to personalize reading instruction. Please note that we talked about this approach in chapter 10, the chapter on writing. Philosophical parameters of this method rely heavily on the validity of premises such as Dewey's (1916) famous statement that "to learn from experience is to make a backward and forward connection between what we do to things and what we enjoy or suffer from things in consequence" (p. 125) and Jenkins' (1955) conclusion:

> Children work hard and long when they choose their own jobs. They move ahead when they have the opportunity to set their own goals. They read with greater enjoyment when they choose the material. In self-selection the teacher works with

the individuals and knows their interests and needs more adequately than when a group works on a single book chosen by the teacher (p. 125).

Goodman (1989) asserted that the *whole language* approach resulted from a "grass-roots movement" (p. xi), which deals with language learning as a whole, a totality greater than the sum of its parts. From this viewpoint, reading is not a process that can be broken down into myriad subskills that, if mastered, will then add up to proficiency in reading (or writing). Instead, this approach drew on knowledge about language development as an authentic process with function and communication at its core. In addition, it represented an evolution of child-centered approaches to reading instruction of the mid-twentieth century.

The whole language movement began to lose favor with some policy makers and educators in the mid-1990s, and greater emphasis was placed on the skills and strategies associated with reading and reading instruction. Although reasons for the shift in focus for literacy instruction abound, one explanation was that some educators were believed to not be providing enough guided and explicit instruction for students who did not know how to read and write. This shift in focus also represented a conceptual shift from an emphasis on holistic approaches to a renewed emphasis on skills development specifically in the area of word recognition, Increasing emphasis is being placed on phonics for decoding and word study.

BASAL READERS OF TODAY

Since 2000, there has been an even greater emphasis on literacy in national and state politics. Federal dollars have funded various reading initiatives including the "Reading Excellence Act" and "Reading First." Although there has been interest in reading research on the part of policy makers, the only research considered meritorious is scientifically based reading research (SBRR). This quantitative, positivist research is often conducted in laboratory settings removed from the rigors of classroom practice. The emphasis in this era is on sequential skills development. The following areas are highlighted in federal funding documents: phonemic awareness, phonics, vocabulary, fluency, and comprehension.

Basal readers in this decade reflect an emphasis on sequential skill development but not exclusively. As illustrated in the following examples of excerpts from Houghton Mifflin's (2001) "Traditions" series (see Figures 15–4 to 15–6) the basal readers of today also emphasize connections between reading and writing as well as children's personal connections with texts and issues of diversity.

Before reading on, think back to your own reading experiences in elementary school. Did you see any connections between your own reading experiences and the overview of approaches we have mentioned so far? If so, what were they?

Do you see any underlying similarities or differences between the approaches and techniques that we have previewed so far? Please jot your ideas below. You might want to refer back to Table 15–1 as you think about some key underlying similarities and differences across these historical approaches.

Figure 15—4 Student writing model. From *Traditions in Houghton Mifflin Reading: A Legacy of Literacy* by J. David Cooper and John J. Pikulski, et al. © 2001, Level 4. Used with permission.

Student Writing Model

A Personal Narrative

A personal narrative is a true story about something that happened to the writer. Use this student's writing as a model when you write a personal narrative of your own.

> A good **title** shows the reader what the narrative is about.

> A good **beginning** catches the reader's interest.

A Special Day at the Beach

"Whoopee!" I cried. We were going to the beach near our hotel. I couldn't sit still for a moment. But when my grandmother told me to simmer down, I definitely did. After I quickly ate my homemade pancakes, I questioned Grandma, "Can we go out on the beach now?" She said we could. So I got my flip flop sandals on and quickly ran to the beach.

I couldn't wait. I was squirting out the suntan lotion very quickly. After I finally blobbed it on, I did cartwheels on the sand. Then I had a great idea. My brother and I could cover me up with sand. We hurriedly got to work. Before you could say, "Let's play in the sand," we were finished. My mom wanted to take my picture, so I had to wait forever for her to get the camera ready. Finally, click went the camera. Then I got myself unburied, and off I ran to the water scattering sand all around me. After my swim, I grabbed a kite and off it swirled into the light blue sky.

Writing
Write narratives (W2.1)
Relate event or experience (W2.1.a)

58

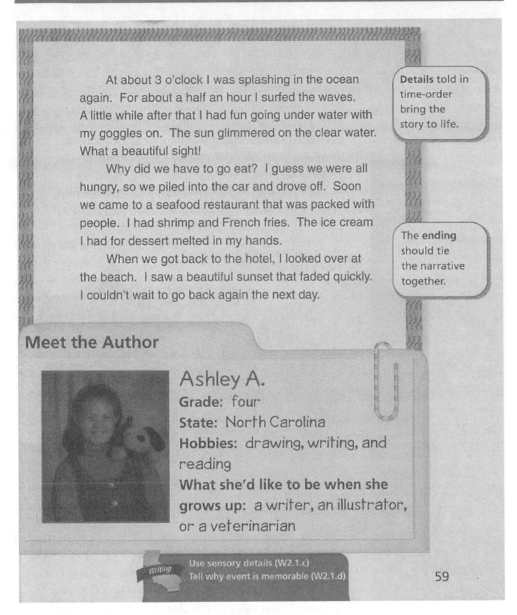

Figure 15–5 Student writing model. From *Traditions in Houghton Mifflin Reading: A Legacy of Literacy* by J. David Cooper and John J. Pikulski, et al. © 2001, Level 4. Used with permission.

At about 3 o'clock I was splashing in the ocean again. For about a half an hour I surfed the waves. A little while after that I had fun going under water with my goggles on. The sun glimmered on the clear water. What a beautiful sight!

Why did we have to go eat? I guess we were all hungry, so we piled into the car and drove off. Soon we came to a seafood restaurant that was packed with people. I had shrimp and French fries. The ice cream I had for dessert melted in my hands.

When we got back to the hotel, I looked over at the beach. I saw a beautiful sunset that faded quickly. I couldn't wait to go back again the next day.

Details told in time-order bring the story to life.

The **ending** should tie the narrative together.

Meet the Author

Ashley A.
Grade: four
State: North Carolina
Hobbies: drawing, writing, and reading
What she'd like to be when she grows up: a writer, an illustrator, or a veterinarian

Writing Use sensory details (W2.1.c)
Tell why event is memorable (W2.1.d)

59

As you continue to read this chapter, ask yourself if you can connect your interviewee's experiences with any of the historical approaches you encounter in this chapter. For example, you may find Table 15–1 to be a particularly helpful resource as you develop your interview questions. Additionally, because we present examples of pages from various early readers, you may even show your informant some of the sample pages in this text to see if any of them appear familiar to her or him.

PHILOSOPHY OF APPROACHES

We think that the approaches we have just discussed fall into two distinct categories. If you examine the historical trends in conjunction with the social trends reflected in each era, it becomes apparent that two different philosophies of reading instruction have existed throughout the history of teaching reading. We refer to the first of these philosophies as a *sequential skills reading approach*, which encourages the use of materials that are systematically designed according to the perceived developmental stages of children. The sequential skills reading approach is exemplified *in phonics and linguistic basal readers, programmed instruction, and leveled readers.* As these methods clearly demonstrate, the sequential development approaches emphasize decoding followed by comprehension.

The second philosophy is referred to as the *holistic reading approach*, which encourages the development of materials related to the organic interests of the child. The holistic reading approach is characterized by *language experience* and a *whole-language approach.* Reading for meaning from the initial stages of reading instruction is the major emphasis of this approach.

The goal of any approach, method, or philosophy has always been to teach children to read. In this respect, the primary goals of the sequential skills and constructive reading approaches are not entirely opposed to one another. However, the process of implementing each approach in its purest sense is quite different. It may be that most skilled teachers and scholars of reading understand that a combination of both of these philosophies is called for. That is, good readers must be skilled at decoding and identifying words. However, good readers must also see reading as a holistic and meaningful act whereby they comprehend the texts they read.

One of the reasons we have asked you to think about your own beliefs and experiences about reading instruction is that our own experiences shape our beliefs and understandings. Moreover, as teachers, we draw on our underlying beliefs about reading and instruction to decide which activities, materials, and methods we will use with our children on a daily basis. Unexamined beliefs may lead to ineffective literacy instructional practices.

Now that you have read about some important movements, materials, and approaches in the history of reading instruction, we would like to invite you to conduct an interview with an older friend or relative so that she or he can tell you her or his perspective on some of the reading methods, materials, and approaches she or he may have experienced in school. You may want to take this text with you as you engage in the interview. Perhaps some of the pictures of text pages in this chapter will be familiar to your interviewee.

What does your interviewee recall about her or his reading experiences prior to entering school? Did someone read to her or him prior to entering school? What books does she or he recall? Did someone continue to read to her or him in elementary school? How often and how long? Was she or he encouraged to read to an adult or other family member as she or he began to learn to read?

What does your informant recall about reading and writing in school—especially elementary school? What reading approaches and methods does she or he remember engaging in during elementary school?

How did your informant feel about reading as a child? Why? How does your informant feel about reading now? Why?

DEFINING READING: WHAT HAVE SOME EXPERTS SAID HISTORICALLY?

In the previous subsection, we discussed various materials and approaches to the teaching of reading. All of these approaches are based on people's beliefs about the nature of reading. In this section, we provide an overview of the various ways that different literacy scholars have defined reading. This is important because programs, methods, materials, and the uses to which they are put by teachers in classrooms reflect beliefs about what reading is and how it should best be taught.

Here's what we'd like you to do. Read carefully through this subsection on different experts' definitions of reading. Then, go back into the chapter and choose one program or approach we have explained. Determine the definition pertaining to reading that undergirds the approach or method. Make sure that you can provide justification for your ideas. When you go to class, you will discuss your ideas with others.

Smith and Dechant (1961) called attention to the fact that the *vantage point* from which one attempts to define reading strongly affects its definition:

> The *psychologist* is interested in reading as a thought process. The *semanticist* is concerned with meaning and considers the printed page to be the graphic representation of speech. The *linguist* concerns himself with the relationships between the sounds of language and its written form. The *sociologist* studies the interaction of reading and culture, and the *litterateur* reacts to the artistic nature of the production before him. (p. 21)

They point out that reading includes more than recognition of graphic symbols:

> Effective reading includes experiencing, learning, and thinking. It frequently requires reflection, judgment, analysis, synthesis, selection, and critical evaluation of what is being read. The reader is stimulated by the author's printed words, but in turn he vests the author's words with his own meaning. And frequently the reader must select one specific meaning from numerous meanings that he has acquired. (p. 22)

Gray and Leary's (1935) definition examines *the importance of reading in life*. They maintain that reading is an aid to meeting everyday needs, a tool for vocation, a pursuit for leisure time, an aid to enrichment of experience, a tool of citizenship, and a source of spiritual refreshment.

Robinson (1966), completing a refinement of a definition of reading that William S. Gray had begun prior to his death, identified five major components of reading: word perception, comprehension, reaction, assimilation, and rate, a dimension that Gray had not previously included in his analysis of major components of reading. According to the Gray-Robinson definition or model of reading, *word perception* includes word recognition and the association of meanings with words. The second dimension, *comprehension*, involves two levels of meaning, literal and implied. The third dimension, *reaction*, involves intellectual judgments and emotional responses. *Assimilation*, the fourth dimension, involves fusion of old ideas with new ideas that have been obtained through reading. *Rate*, the fifth dimension, is recognized as varying speed depending on the load of new words, the length of the lesson, or the time one is expected to read, and the concept load of material to be read.

Tinker and McCullough (1968) believed that

reading involves the identification and recognition of printed or written symbols, which serve as stimuli for the recall of meanings built up through past experiences, and, further, the construction of new meanings through the reader's manipulation of relevant concepts already in his possession. The resulting meanings are organized into thought processes according to the purposes that are operating in the reader. Such an organization results in modifications of thought, and perhaps behavior, or it may even lead to radically new behavior which takes its place in the personal or social development of the individual. (p. 8)

J. Smith (1973) emphasized the *creative aspect of reading* in his definition:

Reading is the ability to recognize and understand the printed symbols of the child's spoken vocabulary. Printed words, as well as spoken ones, are meaningful to the young child only insofar as his field of experience overlaps that of the author of the printed text. The old cliche, "You can take from a book only what you bring to it is, in essence, true. The reader learns from a book only if he is able to understand the printed symbols and rearrange them into vicarious experiences in his mind. His ability to think, to reason, and to conceptualize makes it possible for him to receive new ideas from a printed page without actually experiencing the new idea, *but he must have experienced each symbol that helps him make up the new idea.* (pp. 31–32)

Like many other reading scholars in the 1970s, Spache and Spache (1973), focus on *the process* rather than the use of reading. They define reading as skill development, a visual act, a perceptual act, a reflection of cultural background, a thinking process, an information process, and an associational learning process.

Rumelhart (1976) stresses the interactive nature of *the reading process:*

Reading is the process of understanding written language. It begins with a flutter of patterns on the retina and ends (when successful) with a definite idea about the author's intended message. Thus, reading is at once a "perceptual" and a "cognitive" process. It is a process which bridges and blurs these two traditional distinctions. Moreover, a skilled reader must be able to make use of sensory, syntactic, semantic and pragmatic information to accomplish his task. These various sources of information appear to interact in many complex ways during the process of reading. A theorist faced with the task of accounting for reading must devise a formalism rich enough to represent all of these different kinds of information and their interactions. (p. 1)

Frank Smith's model (1978) of reading describes *the process* from the printed words to comprehension (see Figure 15–7).

F. Smith (1978) also views reading as an interactive process, that is, as an interaction between reader and author:

Reading then can be defined as an interaction, a communication in which the author and the reader each brings his background language, and a common desire to reach the other person. No matter how else one defines reading, it must involve ideas, backgrounds, common language, common interest, and a mutual point of departure. (p. 28)

Figure 15–7   Frank Smith's model of reading.

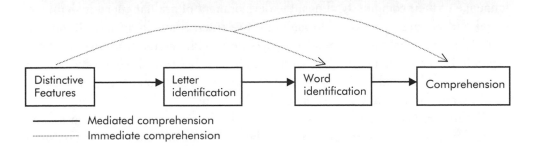

——————— Mediated comprehension
··················· Immediate comprehension

Harris and Sipay (1978) discuss the nature of reading, pointing out that reading is an extension of oral communication that must have listening and speaking skills as its foundation. He says that reading may be defined "as the act of responding with appropriate meaning to printed and written verbal symbols" and that "the reasoning side of reading becomes increasingly important as recognition is mastered" (pp. 3, 10).

Flood (1984) supports a view of reading that is both interactive and constructive:

> Comprehension is a constructive process in the full sense of the term. A text can be thought of as a set of building blocks: letters, words, sentences, paragraphs, chapters . . . .. Good writers are not completely explicit; like skilled block-builders they bridge many spaces for both economy and aesthetics. Moreover, competent readers do not examine all of the individual blocks. Some blocks are recognized as configurations and handled as chunks; others are superfluous and can be ignored altogether . . . .. Comprehension is also interactive; it entails both the analysis of text structure and the examination of preexisting memory structure. (p. vii)

Like Flood (1984), Pressley (2000) argues that reading is a complex developmental process:

> The development of comprehension skills is a long-term developmental process, which depends on rich world, language, and text experiences from early in life; learning how to decode; becoming fluent in decoding, in part, through the development of an extensive repertoire of sight words; learning the meanings of vocabulary words commonly encountered in texts; and learning how to abstract meaning from text using the comprehension processes used by skilled readers. The frequent admonition for children to "Read, read, read," makes sense in that extensive reading promotes fluency, vocabulary, and background knowledge (i.e., it promotes a number of competencies simultaneously). Immersion in reading alone, however, is unlikely to lead to maximally skilled comprehension. At the primary level, there is no compelling evidence that such immersion produces the skilled decoding that is important in permitting word-level recognition and comprehension, nor is there evidence that such immersion in the later elementary years results in the development of the many consciously articulated comprehension processes used by good readers. (p. 556)

OUR CURRENT WORKING DEFINITION OF READING

We believe that reading is a language-based literacy process that develops from birth as children begin to "make sense" of the oral language occurring in the environment in which they live. A child listens and babbles during the first years of life while being spoken to, played with, and reinforced for attempting to develop the spoken language of their community. Thus, the development of oral language is shaped by social and cultural contexts. Through effective interactions in social/cultural contexts, children's babbles become recognizable utterances that are answered and expanded as children share conversation, songs, and books and other forms of *communication*. The child begins to develop an awareness that language is *communication* in many forms. Language is the basis for reading.

We further believe that successful readers also learn to read in a similar manner as their exposures to and interactions with language become more focused on print. As a child is read to he or she develops an appreciation for written language and the realization that the language they hear spoken by the parents is the same language they are hearing in the "shared" book experiences. This occurs gradually over time through conversing and questioning about texts being shared. For example, after many readings of *Sylvester and the Magic Pebble*, a child may ask, "Is this where it says Max?" while pointing to some segment of print. By the time this occurs, the child may even have memorized the story and is comfortable enough to take a turn at reading. Although some children may appear to have learned to read without any help, the vast majority of children need help with learning to read just as they did with learning to talk. That is, literacy is a learned behavior shaped by social and cultural contexts.

To be able to read a language the reader must have an understanding of the concepts that are represented by his or her spoken language and the vocabulary to express the concepts. If one has a concept of *dog* before encountering the word in a text comprehension will more quickly occur. Additionally, a reader needs to have an understanding of the sound system of the language and how these sounds are represented by combinations of letters of the alphabet appearing in written text. This is often referred to as being phonemically aware. An individual with a strong language base will be able to learn to map the sounds of the spoken language to the graphs (letters) which represent these sounds in print.

As the child wonders about print, informal instruction at home and school continues as letters and words are identified and eventually recognized. All the while the child is learning how to hold the book and realizing that reading happens from left to right and top to bottom. Simultaneously a few letter consonants and a vowel should be introduced and the child should be taught to make words. Sight words should also be introduced to enable the child to create sentences and to read appropriate predictable texts. Children need to be taught sound–letter (phonics) correspondences for words that can be sounded out and taught, through use, how to pronounce and recognize those irregular ones that must be recognized as sight words (e.g., *come, where, soon, the, them, chamois, opossum*).

Children can be further guided to understand print concepts by being encouraged to write. As they write and view print they begin to wonder about spacing, spelling, and the content of their messages. They develop an awareness that their spoken language is shared orally, as well as through messages they write and books they read. So to answer the question, What is reading?, we believe reading is a language-based process situated in one's social and cultural context that begins through shared language and oral reading experiences coupled with instruction that illustrates that the message represented by print can be figured out through phonics or recognized as sight words. Through much exposure to books that are appropriate for early readers, children are provided opportunities to practice the reading process, thus developing automaticity as they become fluent readers. Effective reading instruction models the integration of all of the language processes.

SUMMARY

In this chapter, we have presented an overview of important components of the history of reading approaches and materials. The history of reading is vast, and many entire volumes have been devoted to it. We chose some aspects of the history of reading to share with you that, we thought, would be particularly salient to you as an educator. These included historical trends with respect to beliefs, instructional approaches, and materials. Two overarching philosophical approaches prevalent in the history of reading include sequential skills approaches and holistic approaches. The sequential skills approaches we discussed were programmed instruction and basal readers. The three approaches to holistic reading that we presented were basal anthologies, whole language, and the language experience approach. We also presented different scholars' historical definitions of reading. In addition, we present our current definition of reading. Additionally, we asked you to consider your own personal definition of reading. We argued that definitions of reading matter because our beliefs about what reading is drive our instructional decisions. Finally, throughout the chapter, we emphasized that the teacher, not materials or methods, is the heart of effective literacy instruction.

QUESTIONS

1. Why is it important to understand historical trends in reading instruction in the United States?
2. What are the various methods of reading instruction that have been used?
3. Identify three to four instructional approaches discussed in this chapter. What were the strengths of those approaches? Why? What were the limitations of those approaches? Why?
4. What trends in reading instruction do you anticipate becoming important in the future? Why?
5. Why is it important to develop a personal definition of reading?

CLASSROOM PROJECTS AND QUESTIONS

1. Examine a reading text currently in use in schools today. Which of the various methods is emphasized? If more than one instructional method is used, describe each. Provide examples to support your analysis.
2. Write a sketch of your own reading instruction as it occurred during your years in school. Describe it and any memories of its impact on you at the time.
3. In a professional publication, find at least one article discussing historical perspectives on reading instruction. Choose a perspective presented and discussed. Compare that perspective with the ones presented in this chapter.

How are they alike? How are they different? What issues were emphasized in the different perspectives, and what do you think are the reasons for the accompanying differences?

4. Choose a basal series and evaluate it according to current views of reading instruction. Be prepared to present your analysis and the criteria used to evaluate the materials.

5. Develop your own definition of reading. Write it in your own words and describe the types of materials that would complement it.

6. Interview practicing teachers. Ask them to give their definition of reading. Then inquire to what philosophical extent they feel that their classroom materials are a match or a mismatch for this definition.

7. Choose an older basal series and analyze its structure and contents. What philosophy of reading was prominent when this series was developed? Explain your conclusion.

REFERENCES

Adams, M. J. (1990). *Beginning to read: Thinking and learning about print.* Urbana-Champaign: University of Illinois at Urbana–Champaign, Center for the Study of Reading.

Allen, R. (1961). *Report of the reading study project*, Monograph No. 1. San Diego, CA: Department of Education, San Diego County.

Allen, R. (1976). *Language experiences in communication.* Boston, MA: Houghton Mifflin.

Allen, V., Smith, C., Flood, J., & Lapp, D. (1989). *Macmillan connections series.* New York: Macmillan.

Allington, R. L., & Walmsley, S. A. (Eds.) (1995). *No quick fix: Rethinking literacy programs in America's elementary schools.* New York: Teachers College Press.

Aukerman, R. (1971). *Approaches to beginning reading.* New York: Wiley.

Black, 1. (1966). *The Bank Street readers.* New York: Macmillan.

Bloomfield, L., & Barnhart, C. (1961). *Let's read: A linguistic approach.* Detroit, MI: Wayne State University Press.

Brink, C. R. (1935, 1963, 1973). *Caddie Woodlawn.* New York: Macmillan.

Bruner, J. (1960). *The process of education.* Cambridge, MA: Harvard University Press.

Buchanan, C., & Sullivan Associates. (1966). *Programmed reading.* St. Louis, MO: Webster Division, McGraw-Hill.

Burmeister, L. (1971). Content of a phonics program. In N. Smith (Ed.), *Reading methods and teacher improvement* (pp. 27–33). Newark, DE: International Reading Association.

Calvin, A. (1967, February). How to teach with programmed textbooks. *Grade Teacher, 84,* 81.

Carillo, L., & Bissett, D. (1967–1968). *The Chandler language experience readers.* San Francisco: Chandler.

Cheek, M., & Cheek, E. (1980). *Diagnostic-prescriptive reading instruction.* Dubuque, IA: William C. Brown.

Clymer, T. (1963, January). The utility of phonic generalizations in the primary grades. *The Reading Teacher, 16,* 252–258.

Clymer, T., Christenson, B., & Brown R. (1976). *Reading 720.* Lexington, MA: Xerox Corporation.

Costa, A. (1989). Re-assessing assessment. *Educational Leadership, 46,* 2.

Cullinan, B. E. (1989). *Literature and the child* (2nd ed.). San Diego, CA: Harcourt Brace Jovanovich.

Dale, E., & Chall, J. (1948, January). A formula for predicting readability. *Educational Research Bulletin, 27,* 11–20.

Dallman, M., Rouch, L., Chang, L., & DeBoer, J. (1974). *The teaching of reading* (4th ed.). New York: Holt, Rinehart and Winston.

Dewey, J. (1916). *Democracy and education.* New York: Macmillan.

Duffy, G. G., & Hoffman, J. V. (1999). In pursuit of a flawed illusion: The flawed search for a perfect method. *The Reading Teacher, 53*(1), 10–16.

Durkin, D. (1974). *Teaching them to read* (2nd ed.). Boston: Allyn & Bacon.

Durkin, D. (1976). *Teaching young children to read* (2nd ed.). Boston: Allyn & Bacon.

Durr, W. K. (1989). *Houghton Mifflin literary readers.* Boston: Houghton Mifflin.

Durrell, D. (1958, February). Success in first grade reading. *Boston University Journal of Education, 140,* 2–47.

Eller, W., Farr, R., McClenathan, D., & Roser, N. L. (1980). *Laidlaw reading program.* River Forest, IL: Laidlaw.

Fisher, J. (1974, August). Dialect, bilingualism and reading. In R. Karlin (Ed.), *Reading for all.* Proceedings of the World Congress of the International Reading Association, Buenos Aires, Argentina.

Flesch, R. (1943). *Marks of readable style: A study of adult education.* New York: Bureau of Publications, Teachers College Press, Columbia University.

Flood, J. (Ed.). (1984). *Understanding reading comprehension.* Newark, DE: International Reading Association.

Flood, J., & Lapp, D. (1989a). *Are basal reading programs changing? A comparison of types of writing included in basal reading programs—1983 and 1989.* Paper presented at The National Reading Conference, Austin, TX.

Flood, J., & Lapp, D. (1989b). Reporting reading process: A comparison portfolio for parents. *The Reading Teacher, 42,* 508–515.

Fries, C. (1962). *Linguistics and reading.* New York: Holt, Rinehart and Winston.

Fries, C. (1964). *Reading in the elementary school.* Boston: Allyn & Bacon.

Fries, C. (1966). *Merrill linguistic readers.* Columbus, OH: Merrill.

Fry, E. (1969). Programmed instruction and automation in beginning reading. In A. Beery, T. Barnett, & W. Powell (Eds.), *Elementary reading instruction* (pp. 400–413). Boston: Allyn & Bacon.

Gattegno, C. (1962). *Words in color.* Chicago: Learning Materials.

Glim, T. E. (1968). *Palo Alto reading program. Sequential steps in reading,* Books 1 and 20 (pp. 10, 11). New York: Harcourt Brace Jovanovich.

Good, C. (1953). Doctoral studies completed or underway. *Phi Delta Kappa.* Special issue.

Goodman, K. S. (1965, December). Dialect barriers to reading comprehension. *Elementary English, 42,* 852–860.

Goodman, K. S. (Ed.). (1968). *The psycholinguistic nature of the reading process.* Detroit, MI: Wayne State University Press.

Goodman, K. S. (1986). *What's whole in whole language?* Portsmouth, NH: Heinemann.

Goodman, K. S. (1989). Whole language is whole: A response to Heymsfeld. *Educational Leadership, 46,* 69–71.

Goodman, K. S., Bird, L. B., & Goodman, Y. M. (1991). *The whole language catalog.* New York: Macmillan/McGraw Hill.

Goodman, K. S., Goodman, Y. M., & Hood, W. J. (Eds.). (1989). *The whole language evaluation book.* Portsmouth, NH: Heinemann.

Goodman, Y. (1970, February). Using children's reading miscues for new teaching strategies. *The Reading Teacher, 23,* 455–459.

Gray, L. (1963). *Teaching children to read* (3rd ed.). New York: Ronald Press.

Gray, W. (1932). Summary of investigations relating to reading. *Elementary School Journal.* Special issue.

Gray, W., & Leary, B. (1935). *What makes a book readable.* Chicago: University of Chicago Press.

Hafner, L., & Jolly, H. (1972). *Patterns of teaching reading in the elementary school.* New York: Macmillan.

Hall, M. (1975). *Reading as a language experience.* Columbus, OH: Merrill.

Hall, M. (1981). *Teaching reading as a language experience* (3rd ed.). Columbus, OH: Merrill.

Harris, A. J., & Sipay, E. R. (1978). *How to increase reading ability.* (6th ed.) New York: Longman.

Heyrnsfeld, C. R. (1989, March). Filling the hole in whole language. *Educational Leadership, 46,* 65–68.

Hoffman, J. V., & Roser, N. (Eds.). (1987, January). The basal reader in American reading instruction. *The Elementary School Journal, 87,* 3.

Houghton Mifflin. (2001). *Traditions.* Boston: Houghton Mifflin Company.

Jenkins, M. (Ed.). (1955, November). Here's to success in reading self selection helps. *Childhood Education, 32,* 124–131.

Karlin, R. (1971). *Teaching elementary reading: Principles and strategies.* New York: Harcourt Brace Jovanovich.

Lapp, D., Bender, H., Ellenwood, S., & John M. (1975). *Teaching and learning: Philosophical, psychological, curricular applications*. New York: Macmillan.

Lorge, I. (1944, March). Predicting readability. *Teachers College Record, 45*, 404–419.

MacLachlan, P. (1985). *Sarah, plain and tall*. New York: Harper & Row.

Matthes, C. (1977). *How children are taught to read* (2nd ed., p. 9). Lincoln, NE: Professional Educators Publications.

Mazurkiewicz, A., & Tanzer, H. (1965–1966). *I.T.A. handbook for writing and spelling*. New York: Initial Teaching Alphabet Publications.

McKim, M., & Caskey, H. (1963). *Guiding growth in reading* (2nd ed.). New York: Macmillan.

Model curriculum standards: Grades nine through twelve. (1985). Sacramento: California State Department of Education.

National Assessment of Educational Progress (1985). *The reading report card* (Report No. 15R-01). Princeton, NJ: Educational Testing Service.

New directions in reading instruction. (1988). Urbana, IL: International Reading Association.

Pitman, Sir J., Mazurkiewicz, A., & Tanzer, H. (1964). *The handbook on writing and spelling in iltla*. New York: i/t/a Publications.

Pressley, M. (2000). *What should comprehension instruction be instruction of?* In Kamil, M., Mosenthal, P., Pearson, D. & Barr, R. Handbook of Reading Research. Volume I. Lawrence Erlbaum Associates, Publishers, NJ, (545–563).

Recommended readings in literature: Kindergarten through grade eight (1986). Sacramento: California State Department of Education.

Robinson, H. (Ed.). (1966). *Reading: Seventy-five years of progress*. Supplementary Educational Monographs, No. 96. Chicago: University of Chicago Press.

Robinson, H. (Ed.). (1977). *Reading and writing instruction in the United States: Historical trends*. Newark, DE: International Reading Association.

Rumelhart, D. (1976). *Toward an interactive model of reading*. Center for Human Information Processing, Technical Report No. 56. La Jolla: University of California, San Diego.

Samuels, S. (1972). The effect of letter-name knowledge on learning to read. *American Educational Research Journal, 9*, 65–74.

Sartain, H. (1972). The place of individualized reading in a well planned program. In A. Harris & E. Sipay (Eds.), *Readings on reading instruction* (2nd ed., pp. 193–199). New York: David McKay.

Savage, J. (1973). *Linguistics for teachers*. Chicago: Science Research Associates.

Schulwitz, B. (Ed.). (1975). *Teachers, tangibles, techniques. Comprehension of content in reading*. Newark, DE: International Reading Association.

Searfoss, L. (1989, May–June). Integrated language arts: Is it whole language? *The California Reader, 22*, 1.

Serwer, B. (1969). Linguistic support for a method of teaching beginning reading to black children. *Reading Research Quarterly, 4*, 449–467.

Shuy, R, (1969, Spring). Some considerations for developing beginning reading materials for ghetto children. *Journal of Reading Behavior, 1*, 33–44.

Silvaroli, N. (1965). Factors in predicting children's success in first grade reading. In *Reading and inquiry, proceedings of the international reading association* (pp. 296–298). Newark, DE: International Reading Association.

Smith, C. (1975). *The Macmillan R*. New York: Macmillan.

Smith, C. (1979). *Reading activities for middle and secondary schools—A handbook for teachers*. New York: Holt, Rinehart and Winston.

Smith, C., & Wardhaugh, R. (1980). *Macmillan reading, series R*. New York: Macmillan.

Smith, F. (1978). *Understanding reading* (2nd ed.). New York: Holt, Rinehart and Winston.

Smith, H., & Dechant, E. (1961). *Psychology in teaching reading*. Englewood Cliffs, NJ: Prentice-Hall.

Smith, J. (1973). *Creative teaching of reading in the elementary school* (2nd ed.). Boston: Allyn & Bacon.

Smith, N. (1965). *American reading instruction*. Newark, DE: International Reading Association.

Spache, G. (1973). Psychological and cultural factors in learning to read. In R. Karlin (Ed.), *Reading for all. Proceedings of the Fourth IRA World Congress on Reading* (pp. 43–50). Newark, DE: International Reading Association.

Spache, G., & Spache, E. (1973). *Reading in the elementary school* (3rd ed.). Boston: Allyn & Bacon.

Stahl, S. A., & Miller, P. D. (1989, Spring). Whole language and language experience approaches for beginning reading: A quantitative research synthesis. *Review of Educational Research, 59,* 87–116.

Stauffer, R. (1965). The language experience approach. In J. Kerfort (Ed.), *First grade reading programs. Perspectives in reading,* (No. 5, pp. 86–116). Newark, DE: International Reading Association.

Stauffer, R. (1970). *The language-experience approach to the teaching of reading.* New York: Harper & Row.

Stauffer, R. (1975). *Directing the reading-thinking process.* New York: Harper & Row.

Strang, R. (1964). *Diagnostic teaching of reading.* New York: McGraw-Hill.

Strickland, R. (1962, July). The language of elementary school children: Its relationship to the language of reading textbooks and the quality of reading in selected children. *Bulletin of the School of Education, 38,* 4.

Teale, W. H., Heibert, E. H., & Chittenden, E. A. (1987). Assessing young children's literacy development. *The Reading Teacher, 40*(8), 772–777.

Tinker, M., & McCullough, C. (1968). *Teaching elementary school* (3rd ed.). New York: Appleton-Century-Crofts.

Veatch, J. (1985). *Reading in the elementary school* (2nd ed.). New York: Richard C. Owen.

Veatch, J., Sawicki, F., Elliott, G., Flake, E., & Blakey, J. (1979). *Key words to reading: The language experience approach begins* (2nd ed.). Columbus, OH: Merrill.

Venezky, R. (1987, January). A history of the American reading textbook. *The Elementary School Journal, 87,* 247–265.

Wardhaugh, R. (1969). Is the linguistic approach an improvement in reading instruction? In N. Smith (Ed.), *Current issues in reading* (pp. 254–267). Newark, DE: International Reading Association.

Wilder, L. I. (1953). *Little house in the big woods.* New York: Harper & Row.

Author Index

Subject Index